Lecture Notes in Computer Science 12575

More information about this subseries at http://www.springer.com/series/7407

Sriram Chellappan · Kim-Kwang Raymond Choo ·
NhatHai Phan (Eds.)

Computational Data and Social Networks

9th International Conference, CSoNet 2020
Dallas, TX, USA, December 11–13, 2020
Proceedings

Editors
Sriram Chellappan
University of South Florida
Tampa, FL, USA

Kim-Kwang Raymond Choo
The University of Texas at San Antonio
San Antonio, TX, USA

NhatHai Phan
New Jersey Institute of Technology
Newark, NJ, USA

ISSN 0302-9743 ISSN 1611-3349 (electronic)
Lecture Notes in Computer Science
ISBN 978-3-030-66045-1 ISBN 978-3-030-66046-8 (eBook)
https://doi.org/10.1007/978-3-030-66046-8

LNCS Sublibrary: SL1 – Theoretical Computer Science and General Issues

This Springer imprint is published by the registered company Springer Nature Switzerland AG
The registered company address is: Gewerbestrasse 11, 6330 Cham, Switzerland

Preface

The 9th International Conference on Computational Data and Social Networks (CSoNet 2020), held online, is a forum intended to bring high quality researchers, practitioners, and students from a variety of fields encompassing interests in massive scale complex data networks and big-data emanating from such networks.

Core topics of interest included theories of network organization, network scaling, big-data management, human-centered aspects, data provenance, security, trust, and privacy. The conference welcomed presentation of original research results, while also facilitating open exchange and discussions of truly innovative theoretical advancements and outcomes of practical deployments in the broad area of complex data networks. A total of 83 papers were submitted, from which 22 were accepted as regular papers, and 3 were accepted as two-page extended abstracts. Similar to past years, a number of special tracks with specific themes were organized. A total of 21 papers were accepted for inclusion in the Blockchain, Fact-Checking, Fake News and Malware Detection in Online Social Networks, and Information spread in social and data networks special tracks.

This conference would not have been possible without the support of a large number of individuals. First, we sincerely thank all authors for submitting their high-quality work to the conference. We also thank all Technical Program Committee members and sub-reviewers for their willingness to provide timely and detailed reviews of all submissions. Working during the COVID-19 pandemic was especially challenging, and the importance of team work was all the more visible as we worked towards the success of the conference. We also offer our special thanks to the publicity and publication chairs for their dedication in disseminating the call, and encouraging participation in such challenging times, and the preparation of these proceedings. Special thanks are also due to the special tracks chair, finance chair, and the web chair. Lastly, the support and patience of Springer staff members throughout the process are also acknowledged.

November 2020

Valery Kalyagin
My T. Thai
Sriram Chellappan
Kim-Kwang Raymond Choo

Preface

Organization

Organizing Committee

General Chairs

Valery Kalyagin	National Research University Higher School of Economics, Russia
My T. Thai	University of Florida, USA

Technical Program Committee (TPC) Chairs

Sriram Chellappan	University of South Florida, USA
Kim-Kwang Raymond Choo	The University of Texas at San Antonio, USA

Special Track Chairs

Blockchain

Erwu Liu	Tongji University, China
Pan Hui	University of Helsinki, Finland
Zhengqing Zhang	Tongji University, China

Fact-Checking, Fake News and Malware Detection in Online Social Networks

Arcangelo Castiglione	University of Salerno, Italy
B. B. Gupta	National Institute of Technology, India

Information spread in social and data networks

Alexander Semenov	University of Florida, USA

TPC Members (CSoNet 2020)

Esraa Al Alumary	Universiti Sains Malaysia, Malaysia
Mohammed Ali	The University of Manchester, UK
Aris Anagnostopoulos	Sapienza University of Rome, Italy
Martin Atzmueller	Osnabrück University, Germany
Nikita Basov	Saint Petersburg State University, Russia
Pratool Bharti	Northern Illinois University, USA
Livio Bioglio	University of Turin, Italy
Vladimir Boginski	University of Central Florida, USA

Zhipeng Cai	Georgia State University, USA
K. Selcuk Candan	Arizona State University, USA
Hocine Cherifi	University of Burgundy, France
Gianni D'Angelo	University of Salerno, Italy
Vachik Dave	Indiana University Purdue University Indianapolis, USA
Hasan Davulcu	Arizona State University, USA
Neelanjana Dutta	Teradata Labs R&D, USA
Christian Esposito	University of Salerno, Italy
Francesco Fontanella	Dipartimento di Ingegneria Elettrica e dell'Informazione, Italy
Bharti Goel	University of South Florida, USA
Jinyoung Han	Sungkyunkwan University, South Korea
Henri Heinonen	Jyväskylä University, Finland
Ting Hua	Virginia Tech, USA
Alberto Huertas	University of Murcia, Spain
Patrick Hung	Ontario Tech University, Canada
Roberto Interdonato	CIRAD–UMR TETIS, France
Andrzej Jarynowski	Jagiellonian University, Poland
Taekyoung Kwon	Seoul National University, South Korea
Gang Li	Deakin University, Australia
Octavio Loyola-González	Tecnologico de Monterrey, Mexico
Miguel Angel Medina Pérez	Instituto Nacional de Astrofísica, Óptica y Electrónica (INAOE), Mexico
Weizhi Meng	Technical University of Denmark, Denmark
Alessio Merlo	University of Genoa, Italy
Franco Maria Nardini	ISTI-CNR, Italy
Mona Minakshi	University of South Florida, USA
Mario Molinara	Dipartimento di Ingegneria Elettrica e dell'Informazione, Italy
Raul Monroy	Tecnologico de Monterrey, Mexico
Vincenzo Moscato	Dipartimento di Ingegneria elettrica e delle Tecnologie dell'Informazione, Italy
Tathagata Mukherjee	The University of Alabama in Huntsville, USA
Alexander Nikolaev	University at Buffalo, USA
Marek Ogiela	AGH University of Science and Technology, Poland
Lidia Ogiela	Pedagogical University of Krakow, Poland
George Pallis	University of Cyprus, Cyprus
Francesco Palmieri	University of Salerno, Italy
Jia-Yu Pan	Google, USA
Ioannis Panagis	Copenhagen University, Denmark
Vamsi Paruchuri	University of Central Arkansas, USA
Raffaele Pizzolante	University of Salerno, Italy
Lara Quijano-Sanchez	Universidad Autónoma de Madrid, Spain
Marjan Kuchaki Rafsanjani	Shahid Bahonar University of Kerman, Iran
Balwinder Raj	NITTR, India

Huawei Shen	Chinese Academy of Sciences, China
Anurag Singh	NIT Delhi, India
Dimitris Spiliotopoulos	University of Houston, USA
Mukundan Sridharan	ST Engineering IDirect, USA
Vijayan Sugumaran	Oakland University, USA
Andrea Tagarelli	University of Calabria, Italy
Lu-An Tang	NEC Labs America, USA
Srinivas Chakravarthi Thandu	Amazon, USA
Gabriele Tolomei	Sapienza University of Rome, Italy
Sho Tsugawa	University of Tsukuba, Japan
Alexander Veremyev	University of Central Florida, USA
Ingmar Weber	Qatar Computing Research Institute, Qatar
Bin Wu	Beijing University of Posts and Telecommunications, China
Yuan-Chih Yu	National Taipei University of Technology, Taiwan
Qipeng Zheng	University of Central Florida, USA
Hongyi Zhu	The University of Texas at San Antonio, USA

Publication Chair

Hai Phan	New Jersey Institute of Technology, USA

Publicity Chairs

Luca Chiaraviglio	Tor Vergata University of Rome, Italy
Wei Jiang	University of Missouri, USA
Kaitai Liang	University of Surrey, UK
William Liu	Auckland University of Technology, New Zealand
Saed Saleh Al Rabaee	United Arab Emirates University, UAE

Finance Chair

Thang N. Dinh	Virginia Commonwealth University, USA

Web Chair

Lan N. Nguyen	University of Florida, USA

List of Subreviewers

Amin Azmoodeh
Alla Kammerdiner
Ana Mestrovic
Andrea Mastropietro
Antonio Caliò
Artem Prokhorov
Carolina Del Valle Soto
Changxin Yang

Cheng-Lung Chen
Danilo Valdes-Ramirez
Diana Laura Aguilar
Dicle Berfin Köse
Dimosthenis Stefanidis
Dmitry Grigoryev
Eeti Jain
Erol Kazan
Fang-Yu Lin
Gabriel Lopez Zenarosa
Geng Yuanzhe
Giorgos Argyriou
Himangshu Kumar Paul
Ioannis Savvidis
Ismay Pérez Sánchez
Jiaheng Xie
Leonardo Cañete
Marwen Elkamel
Md Arquam
Miryam Elizabeth Villa-Pérez
Paras Bhatt
Roberto Alonso
Shuo Yu
Truc Nguyen
Wu Wei
Xintong Ling
Xinyu Qu
Yidong Chai
Zhecheng Qiang

Extended Abstracts

A Bicriteria Streaming Algorithm to Balance Coverage and Cost with Cardinality Constraint

Yijing Wang[1], Dachuan Xu[1], Donglei Du[2], and Yanjun Jiang[3,(✉)]

[1] Department of Operations Research and Information Engineering, Beijing University of Technology, Beijing 100124, P.R. China
yjwang@emails.bjut.edu.cn, xudc@bjut.edu.cn

[2] Faculty of Management, University of New Brunswick, Fredericton E3B 5A3, Canada
ddu@unb.ca

[3] School of Mathematics and Statistics Science, Ludong University, Yantai 264025, P.R. China
jyjmath@163.com

Abstract. In this work, we investigate a streaming algorithm with the aim to balance the coverage and cost in team formation. This problem can be formulated as maximizing the difference of two set functions $f - \ell$ subject to a cardinality constraint, where function f is non-negative monotone approximately submodular, and function ℓ is non-negative linear. We provide a bicriteria algorithm by exploiting the embeded structure.

Keywords: Streaming algorithm · Approximately submodular · Linear function · Balance · Bicriteria

In this paper, we study a bicriteria algorithm to balance the coverage and cost in team formation with cardinality constraint under the streaming setting [1]. This model can be summarized as maximizing the profit gained and minimizing the cost incurred simultaneously, which can be characterized by maximizing the difference between two set functions subject to a cardinality constraint:

$$\max_{S \subseteq V} f(S) - \ell(S) \text{ s.t. } |S| \leq k,$$

where f is non-negative normalized monotone submodular function, and ℓ is non-negative linear function.

Here we give some notations. For a ground set $V = \{e_1, e_2, \ldots, e_n\}$, we call a set function $f : 2^V \to \mathbb{R}$ is monotone if $f(X) \leq f(Y)$, for any subsets $X \subseteq Y \subseteq V$; non-negative if $f(X) \geq 0$, for any subset $X \subseteq V$ and normalized if $f(\emptyset) = 0$. Function f is submodular if it satisfies $f(X) + f(Y) \geq f(X \cap Y) + f(X \cup Y)$, for any subsets X, Y in V. An equivalent definition is $\sum_{e \in Y \setminus X} f(e|X) \geq f(X \cup Y) - f(X)$ for any subset $X, Y \subseteq V$, where $f(e|X) := f(X \cup \{e\}) - f(X)$ characterizes the marginal gain of f with respect to X and e. Harshaw et al. [4] modify this definition and generalize submodular functions to γ-weakly submodular if it satisfies $\sum_{e \in Y \setminus X} f(e|X) \geq \gamma(f(X \cup Y) - f(X))$, for all subsets $X, Y \subseteq V$ and $\gamma \in (0, 1]$. Actually it is submodular if and only if $\gamma = 1$. A function ℓ is non-negative linear function if it satisfies $\ell(X) = \sum_{e_i \in X} \ell(e_i)$ and $\ell(Y \setminus X) = \ell(X \cup Y) - \ell(X)$.

From the above definitions and the model we know the objective function $g(S) = f(S) - \ell(S)$ is submodular but potentially negative and non-monotone. Furthermore it is *NP*-hard to determine whether the optimum value of $g(S)$ is positive or not. In fact, it is inapproximable to maximize a potentially negative submodular function and there may not exist constant multiplicative factor approximation. By exploiting the structure of this model, we focus on bifactor approximation: an algorithm is (α, β)-bifactor if it outputs a solution S such that $f(S) - \ell(S) \geq \alpha \cdot f(OPT) - \beta \cdot \ell(OPT)$, where OPT is an optimal solution and $0 \leq \alpha \leq 1$.

Based on the definition of bifactor approximation, Ene [3] obtains a $\left(\frac{1}{2}(3 - \sqrt{5}), 1\right)$-approximation algorithm for the submodular minus linear model. However, there are many non-submodular functions arising in real-life applications. Inspired by this new trend, we propose a flexible bicriteria [2] streaming algorithm when function f is γ-weakly submodular. The main idea is to construct a surrogate function $\hat{g}(S) = f(S) - (1 + \gamma)\ell(S)$ in our algorithm. For each arriving element e in the streaming, we add it into the solution set S if it satisfies $f(e|S) - (1 + \gamma)\ell(e) \geq \tau$ and $|S| < k$. The parameter τ will be determined in the analysis. For the computational complexity, we assume there are given oracles to evaluate the functions f and ℓ, and the number of oracle calls represents the algorithm's computational complexity. The main conclusion is shown in Theorem 1.

Theorem 1. *The bifactor ratio of the streaming algorithm is* $\left(\frac{\gamma}{2+\gamma}, \frac{\gamma(1+\gamma)}{2+\gamma}\right)$, where $\gamma \in (0, 1]$.

Acknowledgements. The first and second authors are supported by Beijing Natural Science Foundation Project (No. Z200002) and National Natural Science Foundation of China (No. 11871081). The third author is supported by National Natural Sciences and Engineering Research Council of Canada (NSERC) grant 06446, and National Natural Science Foundation of China (Nos. 11771386, 11728104). The fourth author is supported by National Natural Science Foundation of China (No. 11801251).

References

1. Badanidiyuru, A., Mirzasoleiman, B., Karbasi, A., Krause, A.: Streaming submodular maximization: massive data summarization on the fly. In: Proceedings of SIGKDD, pp. 671–680 (2014)
2. Du, D., Li, Y., Xiu, N., Xu, D.: Simultaneous approximation of multi-criteria submodular functions maximization. J. Oper. Res. Soc. China, **2**(3), 271–290 (2014)
3. Ene, A.: A note on maximizing the difference between a monotone submodular function and a linear function. arXiv preprint arXiv: 2002.07782 (2020)
4. Harshaw, C., Feldman, M., Ward, J., Karbasi, A.: Submodular maximization beyond non-negativity: guarantees, fast algorithms, and applications. In: Proceedings of ICML, pp. 2634–2643 (2019)

Perturbing Internal Opinions to Achieve Lower Polarization

Inzamam Rahaman and Patrick Hosein

The University of the West Indies, St. Augustine, Trinidad and Tobago

Abstract. An increase in the use of Online Social Networks (OSNs) has led to an attendant increase in polarization. This polarization is undesirable and can have negative social consequences. Consequently, it has become desirable to design interventions that reduce polarization by exploiting theoretical models of opinion spread.

In this extended abstract, we present a convex programming formulation for intervening into opinion spread, assuming a Freidkin-Johnson opinion formation model.

Keywords: Social Networks · Polarization · Opinion Formation · Optimization

1 Model

Let $\mathcal{G}$ be a weighed undirected graph, where $\mathcal{V}$ is the set of nodes. The graph contains $|\mathcal{V}| = N$ nodes, and is equipped with a non-negative weight matrix $W \in \mathbb{R}^{N \times N}$ where $W_{ij} > 0$ if and only if the nodes i and j are connected by an edge. Furthermore, W_{ij} represents the relative strength of the relationship between nodes i and j. Let D be a diagonal matrix where $D_{ii} = \sum_{j=1}^{N} W_{ij}$. The graph laplacian, $\mathcal{L}$ is defined as $\mathcal{L} = D - W$.

Opinions can be mapped onto the closed interval $[-1, 1]$ with 0 indicating neutrality [5]. Per Friedkin and Johnson [2], opinion expression and spread occurs in discrete steps. Each node i has an internal opinion $y_i \in [-1, 1]$; $y \in [-1, 1]^N$ is the vector of internal opinions. The opinion expressed by nodes at time t is captured by the vector $z(t)$, where $z_i(t)$ is the opinion of node i. With $z(0) = y$, $z_i(t+1)$ is computed by $z_i(t+1) = \frac{y_i + \sum_{j=1}^{N} W_{ij} z_j(t)}{1 + \sum_{j=1}^{N} W_{ij}}$.

According to Bindel et al. [1], the vector of opinions expressed at equilibrium, i.e. $\lim_{t \to \infty} z(t) = z^*$, is given by Qy where $Q = (I + \mathcal{L})^{-1}$.

2 Problem Definition

We can compute the polarization [5] of a network by $\frac{1}{N}||z^*||_2^2 = \frac{1}{N}||Qy||_2^2$. Suppose that prior to information spread we can intervene into the internal opinion of a node i, in other words we can perturb their internal opinion y_i by δ_i such that $y_i + \delta_i \in [-1, 1]$. Suppose that every perturbation incurs some cost, and we have a limited budget $B \in \mathbb{R}^+$; hence we limited in terms of the perturbations we can apply to the network. If we want to reduce polarization, this can be expressed as the following optimization problem:

$$\begin{aligned} \min_{\delta \in \mathbb{R}^N} \quad & ||Z^* + Q\delta||_2^2 \\ s.t. \quad & -1 \le y_i + \delta_i \le 1 \;\; \forall i \in [1, N] \\ & \sum_{i=1}^{N} \delta_i^2 \le B \end{aligned} \tag{1}$$

3 Experimental Result and Conclusion

The above problem can be treated as a second-order cone programme under disciplined convex programming [3] and solved using the Splitting Cone Solver [6].

To evaluate the effect of optimization, we used the aggregated Facebook ego-net dataset from the SNAP repository [4], and randomly generated internal opinions in the range [−1, 1]. To randomly generated these opinions, we considered two truncated normal distributions - one centered on -0.5, and the other on 0.5 - and then randomly selected a draw from these distributions for each node.

We ran our experiments five times with a budget of 2, and achieved a mean reduction in polarization of 18.5% with a standard deviation of 0.7%. In addition, we considered the Spearman's correlations between the degree centrality, Pagerank, betweeness centrality, and closeness centrality against the computed perturbations and found only weak correlations.

Hence, we have shown that it is possible to use convex programming to reduce polarization under a Friedkin-Johnson opinion formation model. In future work, we plan to present an alternative approach that involves leveraging a sparse approximation for Q.

References

1. Bindel, D., Kleinberg, J., Oren, S.: How bad is forming your own opinion? Games Econ. Behav. **92**, 248–265 (2015)
2. Friedkin, N.E., Johnsen, E.C.: Social influence and opinions. J. Math. Sociol. **15**(3-4), 193–206 (1990)

3. Grant, M., Boyd, S., Ye, Y.: Disciplined convex programming. In: Global optimization, pp. 155–210. Springer (2006)
4. Leskovec, J., Krevl, A.: SNAP Datasets: Stanford large network dataset collection, June 2014. http://snap.stanford.edu/data
5. Matakos, A., Terzi, E., Tsaparas, P.: Measuring and moderating opinion polarization in social networks. Data Min. Knowl. Discov. **31**(5), 1480–1505 (2017)
6. O'donoghue, B., Chu, E., Parikh, N., Boyd, S.: Conic optimization via operator splitting and homogeneous self-dual embedding. J. Optim. Theory Appl. **169**(3), 1042–1068 (2016)

Differentially Private k-center Problems

Fan Yuan[1], Dachuan Xu[1], Donglei Du[2], and Min Li[3,(✉)]

[1] Department of Operations Research and Information Engineering, Beijing University of Technology, Beijing 100124, P.R. China
yuanfan@emails.bjut.edu.cn, xudc@bjut.edu.cn
[2] Faculty of Management, University of New Brunswick, Fredericton E3B 5A3, Canada
ddu@unb.ca
[3] School of Mathematics and Statistics, Shandong Normal University, Jinan 250014, P.R. China.
liminemily@sdnu.edu.cn

Abstract. In this paper, we study several k-center problems under the framework of differential privacy, which formalizes the idea of protecting the privacy of individual input elements. We show these problems have good approximation algorithms that preserve differential privacy.

Keywords: Differentially privacy · Approximation algorithm · k-center · Outlier

1 Introduction

Clustering is an important class of machine learning problems with extensive applications. In clustering problems, we aim to find a best set of centers (w.r.t. some cost function), and then partition the data points into clusters by assigning each data point to its nearest center. With over 60 years of research, center-based clustering is an intensively-studied key-problem in unsupervised learning.

If the locations of the clients are sensitive information that we would like to keep private. One client may be concerned that other clients may collude and exchange their information to obtain certain information about his location. We must design some good algorithms for this problem that preserve the privacy of the clients. Recent years have been a significant amount of work aimed at constructing good clustering algorithms that work under the framework of differential privacy [1, 4].

One of the most fundamental clustering problems is the k-center problem. In this paper, we study three problems: the k-center problem, the distributed k-center problem, and the distributed k-center with Outliers under the framework of differential privacy.In the k-center problem problem, we are given a n-point discrete metric (V, d), and an integer k. For a point $i \in V$ and a set $S \subseteq V$, we define $d(i, S) = \min_{j \in S} d(i, j)$. In this problem our goal is to find a set $S \subseteq V$ of size k to minimize $\max_{i \in V} d(i, S)$. Let $\Delta = \max_{i,j \in V} d(i, j)$ be the diameter of the space, and OPT is the cost of the optimal solution.

In the distributed k-center problem, the data points of V are stored on m machines. The goal is to find a set $S \subseteq V$ of size k to minimize $\max_{i \in V} d(i, S)$. In the distributed

k-center problem with outliers, the data points of V are stored on m machines and the goal is to choose a set S of k points and a set Z of z points such that $\max_{i \in V \setminus Z} d(i, S)$ is minimized. There have been several previous work on the k-center problem with outliers such as [2, 3].

Definition 1. *[5](Differential Privacy) We say a randomized computation M has ε-differential privacy iffor any two input sets A and B with symmetric difference one, and for any set of outcomes $F \subseteq Range(M)$,*

$$\boldsymbol{Pr}[M(A) \in F] \leq \exp(\varepsilon) \times \boldsymbol{Pr}[M(B) \in F]$$

2 Main result

Our main results are summarized in the following two theorems.

Theorem 1. *There is an Algorithm that preserves $(2\varepsilon \Delta k)$ differential privacy and outputs a solution with cost at most $2OPT + 3\ln n/\varepsilon$ with probability $O(1 - k/n^2)$ for the differential privacy k-center problem.*

Theorem 2. *There is an Algorithm that preserves $((m+1)2\varepsilon \Delta k)$ differential privacy and outputs a solution with cost at most $4OPT + 6\ln n/\varepsilon$ with probability $O(1 - m^3 k/n^2 - 1/(km^2))$ for the differential privacy distributed k-center problem.*

3 Acknowledgements

The first and second authors are supported by Beijing Natural Science Foundation Project No. Z200002 and National Natural Science Foundation of China (No. 11871081). The third author is supported by National Natural Sciences and Engineering Research Council of Canada (NSERC) grant 06446, and National Natural Science Foundation of China (Nos. 11771386, 11728104). The fourth author is supported by Higher Educational Science and Technology Program of Shandong Province (No. J17KA171) and Natural Science Foundation of Shandong Province (No. ZR2019MA032) of China.

References

1. Gupta A, Ligett K, McSherry F, Roth A, Talwar K. Differentially private combinatorial optimization. In: Proceedings of SODA, pp 1106–1125 (2010)
2. Malkomes G, Kusner M J, Chen W, Weinberger K Q, Moseley B. Fast distributed k-center clustering with outliers on massive data. In: Proceedings of NIPS, pp 1063–1071 (2015)

3. Li S, Guo X. Distributed k-clustering for data with heavy noise. In: Proceedings of NIPS, pp 7838–7846 (2018)
4. Balcan M, Dick T, Liang Y, Mou W, Zhang H. Differentially private clustering in high-dimensional euclidean spaces. In: Proceedings of ICML, pp 322–331 (2017)
5. Mcsherry F, Talwar K. Mechanism design via differential privacy. In: Proceedings of FOCS, pp 94–103 (2007)

Contents

Combinatorial Optimization and Learning

Computational Methods for Social Good Applications

NLP and Affective Computing

Privacy and Security

Combinatorial Optimization and Learning

An Adaptive Algorithm for Maximization of Non-submodular Function with a Matroid Constraint

Xin Sun[1], Dachuan Xu[1], Dongmei Zhang[2], and Yang Zhou[3](✉)

[1] Department of Operations Research and Information Engineering, Beijing University of Technology, Beijing 100124, People's Republic of China
athossun@emails.bjut.edu.cn, xudc@bjut.edu.cn

[2] School of Computer Science and Technology, Shandong Jianzhu University, Jinan 250101, People's Republic of China
zhangdongmei@sdjzu.edu.cn

[3] School of Mathematics and Statistics, Shandong Normal University, Jinan 250014, People's Republic of China
zhyg1212@163.com

Abstract. In this paper, we consider the problem of maximizing a non-submodular set function subject to a matroid constraint with the continuous generic submodularity ratio γ. It quantifies how close a monotone function is to being submodular. As our main contribution, we propose a $(1 - e^{-\gamma^2} - O(\varepsilon))$-approximation algorithm when the submodularity ratio is sufficiently large. Our work also can be seen as the first extension of the adaptive sequencing technique in non-submodular case.

Keywords: Non-submodular optimization · Matroid constraint · Submodularity ratio · Adaptive sequencing

1 Introduction

As a classical problem in submodular optimization, maximization of a monotone submodular function subject to a single matroid constraint has been intensively studied in recent years. It is well-known that the standard greedy algorithm [15] gave a 1/2-approximation ratio for this problem. In previous works, Feige [13] showed that there exists no polynomial-time algorithm with an approximation ratio better than $(1 - e^{-1})$. Also, Nemhauser and Wolsely [20] showed that any improvement over $(1 - e^{-1})$ has to make sacrifice for an exponential number of queries to the value oracle. In recent years, Calinescu et al. [6, 22] presented a randomized continuous greedy technique based $(1 - e^{-1})$-approximation algorithm for the above problem. This is a breakthrough result that perfectly matches the conjecture given by Feige [13] and it also lays a solid foundation for the technique used in this paper. This approach resembles a common paradigm for designing approximation algorithms and is composed of two steps. In the first step, a fractional solution is found for a relaxation of the problem. In the second step, the

S. Chellappan et al. (Eds.): CSoNet 2020, LNCS 12575, pp. 3–13, 2020.
https://doi.org/10.1007/978-3-030-66046-8_1

fractional solution is rounded to obtain an integral one while incurring only a small loss in the objective. This approach has been used to obtain improved approximations to this problem with various cases, including monotone [6], non-monotone [14] and recently in differencial privacy [21]. Another excellent work of this problem is done by Filmus and Ward [16]. It gave a non-oblivious local search algorithm with an approximation ratio of $(1 - e^{-1})$ utilizing the combinatorial structure of this problem. Lately, Buchbinder et al. [5] made a step forward from deterministic perspective. They gave an 0.5008-approximation algorithm based on greedy-like technique.

However, for many applications in practice, including subset selection [1], experimental design and sparse Gaussian processes [19], the corresponding set function is close to submodular, but not strictly submodular [18]. Naturally the results in submodular function setting do not hold any more. To depict the difference between submodular and non-submodular, a crucial parameter should be introduced to describe the characteristics of the non-submodular functions. Das and Kempe [11] proposed the submodularity ratio, $\hat{\gamma} = \min_{\Omega, S \subseteq N} \frac{\sum_{j \in \Omega \setminus S} f_S(j)}{f_S(\Omega)}$. It is a quantity characterizing how close a set function is to being submodular.

In this context, Bian et al. [4] showed that, under a cardinality constraint, the standard greedy algorithm enjoys an approximation factor of $(1-e^{-\hat{\gamma}})$, where $\hat{\gamma}$ is the submodularity ratio [11] of the set function. Very recently, Harshaw et al. [17] have also shown that there is no polynomial algorithm with better guarantees. Moreover, for the same problem subject to a general matroid constraint, it has only been studied very recently by Chen et al. [10], who offered a randomized version of the standard greedy algorithm with approximation guarantee of $(1 + 1/\hat{\gamma})^{-2}$.

1.1 Our Contribution

In this paper, we propose an approximation algorithm with low adaptive rounds for the problem of maximization of a monotone closely submodular function over matroid constraints. Our technique is based on the *adaptive sequencing* algorithm [3]. It is a powerful method and can be applied to several cases like cardinality constraint, non-monotone set functions, partition matroids and intersection of P matroids. Here, we first generalize this algorithm to the weakly submodular case.

Besides, we also reach the approximation guarantee with the help of *generic submodularity ratio* γ' and its continuous version. It is a quantity characterizing how close a nonnegative nondecreasing set function is to be submodular. Compared with $\hat{\gamma}$, it is derived from a different equivalent definition of submodular functions and has more flexible properties. Our main theorem is stated as following.

Theorem 1.1. *For any* $\varepsilon > 0$, *there is an* $O\left(\frac{\log n \log \frac{k}{\varepsilon}}{\frac{1}{\varepsilon^2} \log n \log \frac{1}{\gamma} - \frac{1}{\varepsilon} \log(1-\varepsilon)}\right)$ *adaptive algorithm that, with probability* $1-o(1)$, *obtains* $(1-e^{-\gamma^2}-O(\varepsilon))$ *approximation for maximizing a* γ*-weakly submodular function under matroid constraints when*

γ is near to 1, where n and k are the ground set size and the matroid rank respectively.

1.2 Technical Overview

The result is inspired by the brilliant work of Balkanski et al. [3] and it can naturally reduce to their primal conclusions when the set function is strictly submodular. They obtained a $(1 - e^{-1} - O(\varepsilon))$-approximation with only requiring $O(\log n \log k)$ adaptive rounds for maximization of a monotone submodular set function over a matroid constraint. When designing a new algorithm for the γ-weakly submodular case, we extend the adaptive sequencing technique. The crucial challenge is making carefully adjustment thanks to the continuous generic submodularity ratio γ such that all selected elements in every step in the algorithm own nearly optimal marginal contribution and satisfy the feasibility constraints.

1.3 Organization

The remainder of the paper is organized as below: Sect. 2 gives preliminary definitions of the paper; Sect. 3 presents the new adaptive algorithm for non-submodular model; Sect. 4 shows the analysis of the algorithms; Sect. 5 finally concludes the paper. In addition, the formal proofs are omitted due to the length limitation but are nevertheless given in the appendix.

2 Preliminaries

This section gives the formal definition of the terms and notations used in the paper. We define the set function $f : 2^N \to \mathbb{R}$ on a *ground set* $N = [n]$, which is *non-decreasing*. Moreover, we say f is *monotone* if $f(S) \leq f(T)$ whenever $S \subseteq T \subseteq N$. Given such a function, the *marginal profit* of adding an element $j \in N$ to S is defined by $f_S(\{j\}) \doteq f(S \cup \{j\}) - f(S)$. For simplicity, we abbreviate $f_S(\{j\})$ and $f(S \cup \{j\})$ as $f_S(j)$ and $f(S \cup j)$, respectively.

Informally, the adaptivity of an algorithm is the number of sequential rounds of queries it makes, where every round allows for polynomially-many parallel queries. We present the formal definition here.

Definition 2.1. *Given a value oracle f, an algorithm is **r-adaptive** if every query $f(S)$ for the value of a set S occurs at a round $i \in [r]$ s.t. S is independent of the values $f(S')$ of all other queries at round i.*

Also, we consider f is *weakly submodular* characterized by *generic submodularity ratio* γ'. The generic submodularity ratio of f is the largest scalar γ' such that for any subset $S \subseteq T \subseteq N$ and any element $j \in N \backslash T$, $f_S(j) \geq \gamma' \cdot f_T(j)$. It measures how close a non-negative increasing set function is to be submodular. For generic submodularity ratio γ' we have the following properties.

Proposition 2.1. *For an increasing set function $f : 2^N \rightarrow \mathbb{R}_{\geq 0}$ with generic submodularity ratio γ', it holds that*

(a) $\gamma' \in (0, 1]$;
(b) $f(\cdot)$ *is submodular* $\iff \gamma' = 1$;
(c) $\sum_{j \in T \setminus S} f_S(j) \geq \gamma' \cdot f_S(T)$, *for any set* $S, T \subseteq N$.

A pair $\mathcal{M} = (N, \mathcal{I})$ is called a *matroid* w.r.t. a ground set N, if and only if the independence system $\mathcal{I}$ is a non-empty collection of subsets of N satisfying the following properties:

(i) If $S \subseteq T \subseteq N$ and $T \in \mathcal{I}$, then $S \in \mathcal{I}$;
(ii) If $S, T \in \mathcal{I}$ and $|S| < |T|$, then there is an element $j \in T \setminus S$ such that $S + j \in \mathcal{I}$.

For a matroid $\mathcal{M} = (N, \mathcal{I})$ [12], a subset S of N is called *independent* if and only if S belongs to $\mathcal{I}$. The common size of all maximal independent subset is called the *rank* of $\mathcal{M}$ and denoted by $r(\mathcal{M})$. Also, we assume that the algorithms have access to matroids only through an independence oracle that for a given set $S \subseteq N$ answers whether S is independent or not. The matroid polytope $\mathcal{P}(\mathcal{M})$ [12] is the collection of points $\mathbf{x} = (x_1, \ldots, x_n) \in [0, 1]^n$ in the convex hull of the independent sets of $\mathcal{M}$, or equivalently the points $\mathbf{x}$ such that $\sum_{i \in A} x_i \leq r(\mathcal{M})$ for all $S \in N$.

The multilinear extension of a set function f is defined as $F : [0, 1]^n \rightarrow \mathbb{R}_{\geq 0}$, which maps a point $\mathbf{x} \in [0, 1]^n$ to the expected value of a random set $R \sim \mathbf{x}$ containing each element $j \in [n]$ with probability x_j independently, i.e. $F(\mathbf{x}) = \mathbb{E}_{R \sim \mathbf{x}}[f(R)]$. We note that given an oracle for f, one can estimate $F(\mathbf{x})$ arbitrarily well in one round by querying in parallel a sufficiently large number of samples $R_1, \ldots, R_m$ draw i.i.d from $\mathbf{x}$ and taking the average value of $f(R_i)$ over $i \in [m]$ [7,8]. For ease of presentation, we assume throughout the paper that we are given access to an exact value oracle for F in addition to f. The results which rely on F then extend to the case where the algorithm is only given an oracle for f with an arbitrarily small loss in the approximation, no loss in the adaptivity, and additional $O(n \log n)$ factor in the query complexity With $O(2n \log n)$ samples, $F(\mathbf{x})$ is estimated within a $(1 \pm \epsilon)$ multiplicative factor with high probability [8].

Besides, we also define *continuous generic submodularity ratio*, which is an extended version of generic submodularity ratio. It is more flexible in the analysis of the multilinear extension.

Definition 2.2 (Continuous generic submodularity ratio). *Given any normalized set function f, the continuous generic submodular ratio is defined as the largest scalar $\gamma \in [0, 1]$ subject to*

$$F_{\mathbf{x} \setminus i}(i) \geq \gamma F_{\mathbf{y} \setminus i}(i), \ \mathbf{x} \leq \mathbf{y}.$$

It is obvious that $\gamma \leq \gamma'$ by comparing their definitions.

In this paper, we are interested in the problem of maximizing a weakly submodular function $f : 2^N \to \mathbb{R}_{\geq 0}$ subject to a matroid $\mathcal{M} = (N, \mathcal{I})$ constraint in an adaptive model. The value of the optimal solution O for this problem is denoted by $\mathtt{OPT}$, i.e. $O := \arg\max_{A \in \mathcal{M}} f(A)$ and $\mathtt{OPT} := f(O)$.

Definition 2.3 (Chernoff bound [2]**).** *Let X_i, $i = 1, \ldots, k$, be mutually independent random variables such that $\mathbb{E}[X_i] = 0$ and $|X_i| \leq 1$ for any i. Set $S = X_1 + \ldots + X_k$ and denote by a positive real number. Then*

$$\Pr[|S| > a] \leq 2e^{-a^2/2k}.$$

3 The Adaptive Algorithm for Non-submodular Set Function

In this section we show the new adaptive algorithm in the case of weakly-submodular set function maximization problem over a matroid constraint. This algorithm is used as a subroutine in the main algorithm which achieves an approximation arbitrarily close to $1 - e^{\gamma^2}$ with $O(\log(n)\log(k))$ adaptivity when the continuous generic submodularity ratio γ is sufficiently large. It points out an update direction $\mathbf{1}_S$ for the current continuous solution. Comparing with [3], the procedure of locating this direction S is more complicated. The cause is how to make sure that all chosen elements in every rounds preserve nearly optimal marginal contribution and fulfill the matroid constraints.

For the convenience of readers, we restate an important definition which defined a random generalized feasible elements set for matroid $\mathcal{M}$.

Definition 3.1 (Random Feasible Sequence [3]**).** *Given a matroid $\mathcal{M}$ we say $(a_1, \ldots, a_{r(\mathcal{M})})$ is a* ***random feasible sequence*** *if for all $i \in [r(\mathcal{M})]$, a_i is an element chosen u.a.r. from $\{a : \{a_1, \ldots, a_{i-1}, a\} \in \mathcal{M}\}$.*

And, we put the technical algorithm in [3] below for producing a random sequence of elements defined above without any adaptive cost.

Algorithm 1. Random Sequence

Input: matroid $\mathcal{M}$
Output: $a_1, \ldots, a_{r(\mathcal{M})}$

```
for i = 1 to r(M) do
    X ← {a : {a_1, ..., a_{i-1}, a} ∈ M}
    a_i ∼ a uniformly random element from X
end for
```

Algorithm 1 selects an element in each iteration uniformly at random on the condition that the output set constructed by all elements is feasible. Also, it is noticeable that the adaptivity of this algorithm is zero since the generated elements set is irrelevant with set function f.

Algorithm 2. Adaptive Sequencing for Non-submodular Function

Input: function f, feasibility constraint $\mathcal{M}$
Output: S

$S \leftarrow \emptyset$, $t \leftarrow \max_{a \in N} f(a)$
for Δ iterations **do**
  $X \leftarrow N$
  while $X \neq \emptyset$ **do**
    $a_1, \ldots, a_{r(\mathcal{M}(S,X))} \leftarrow$ Random Sequence($\mathcal{M}(S,X)$)
    $X_i \leftarrow \{a \in X : S \cup \{a_1, \ldots, a_i, a\} \in \mathcal{M}$ and $f_{S \cup \{a_1, \ldots, a_i\}} \geq t\}$
    $i^\star \leftarrow \min\{i : |X_i| \leq (1-\varepsilon)|X|\}$
    $S \leftarrow S \cup \{a_i, \ldots, a_{i^\star}\}$
    $X \leftarrow X_{i^\star}$
    if $X \neq \emptyset$ **then**
      $t \rightarrow t/\gamma'$
    end if
  end while
  $t \leftarrow (1-\varepsilon)t$
end for

The fact that the sequence is randomly generated is very important. It ensures that the final conclusion of this paper is established with a high probability.

Similar with the adaptive sequencing algorithm, the new adaptive algorithm for non-submodular model utilizes the random feasible sequence produced by Algorithm 1 in each adaptive loop. It verifies which fragment of the sequence ought to be inserted to the solution and abandons the rest part of the output automatically. The algorithm starts from a empty set and selects part of random sequence so as to allocate the chosen elements into the current solution. All sequence components are invented from a specific set, which is conveyed from last iteration. We describe an element is *good* if the following two critical conditions can be satisfied. One is appending an element a to the current solution and a portion of the sequence w.r.t. an index i meets the matroid constraint, i.e. $S \cup \{a_1, \ldots, a_i\} \cup a \in \mathcal{M}$; the other is the marginal contribution of the fresh set above is beyond the threshold. After constructing all good set regarding to entire index i from 0 to n, we need to find a suitable location $i^\star$ which ensure the number of the remaining good elements set X in the next round is over $1-\varepsilon$ and the rest elements are thrown away certainly. This discarding guarantees that there are at most logarithmically many iterations until X is empty. As a result, the algorithm adds $\{a_1, \ldots, a_{i^\star}\}$ to S when we finish this iteration. In fact, the reason that adding those elements to the current solution S is the marginal profit of anyone in the set is nearly optimal in expectation. We will characterize this result in the analysis.

A conspicuous thing in weakly-submodular setting is that the threshold t is sluggish growth instead of maintaining unchanged in the inner loop. This means that the threshold no longer drops monotonically throughout the execution of the algorithm. The reason is the threshold value needs to arbitrarily close to the optional marginal contribution all the time and it can not be without submodularity. Therefore we need to give a modification to the algorithm by the aid of submodularity ratio γ' after elements appending. This trick makes adaptive sequencing algorithm possible in the problem of weakly submodular.

Additionally, the term $\mathcal{M}(S, X) := \{T \subseteq X : S \cup T \in \mathcal{M}\}$ in Algorithm 2 also denotes a matroid related to sets S and X. A subset of X is feasible in the new matroid if its union with S is feasible in $\mathcal{M}$.

Now the main algorithm can be unveiled on the stage naturally. Similar with the standard continuous greedy algorithm [22], the accelerated continuous greedy algorithm follows a guidance of an output update direction $\mathbf{1}_S \in \mathcal{M}$ too. What makes this algorithm "accelerated" is the manner of how to choose and use the direction. The solution $\mathbf{x} \in [0, 1]^n$ moves along $\mathbf{1}_S$ given by Algorithm 2 in a measurement of the surrogate function g. The function g can be seen as the marginal profit value of the multilinear extension when the solution $\mathbf{x}$ marches a step size λ in the direction $\mathbf{1}_S$. That is, $g(S) := F_{\mathbf{x}}(\lambda \mathbf{1}_S) = F(\mathbf{x} + \lambda \mathbf{1}_S) - F(\mathbf{x})$, where S actually means $\mathbf{1}_S$. In this way, the continuous solution can be improved in a constant step size and returned also in a constant rounds. In our setting of non-submodular set function, the adaptivity of each round is the same comparing with [3], i.e. $O(\log(n)\log(k))$, which is much faster than the linear-time required by the standard continuous greedy algorithm. Algorithm 3 finally yields a continuous solution whose approximate ratio is with high probability arbitrarily close to $1 - e^{\gamma^2}$. Then, the technique of dependent rounding [9] or contention resolution schemes [23] can help it reduce to a feasible discrete solution almost without any loss in approximation guarantee and any additional burden in adaptivity.

Algorithm 3. Accelerated Continuous Greedy

Input: matroid $\mathcal{M}$, step size λ
Output: $\mathbf{x}$

```
for 1/λ iterations do
    define g : 2^N → ℝ to be g(T) = F_x(λT)
    S ← Adaptive Sequencing For Non-submodular (g, M)
    x ← x + λS
end for
```

4 Analysis

Using the above denotations, we can now give the formal analysis for Algorithm 2 and Algorithm 3. The following lemma proves that at any time the threshold t in Adaptive Sequencing For Non-submodular is a good imitator to the optimal marginal profit of the current solution S.

Lemma 4.1. *Assume that f is weakly submodular with submodularity ratio γ'. Then, at any iteration of the algorithm, the lower bound of the threshold value is close to the near-optimal marginal profit of the current solution, i.e. $t \geq (1 - \varepsilon)\max_{a: S \cup a \in \mathcal{M}} f_S(a)$.*

Now we prove the conclusion that for any element in the returned solution $S = \{a_1, \ldots, a_l\}$, the marginal profit of inserting a_i for $i \le l$ to $\{a_1, \ldots, a_{i-1}\}$ is close to optimal in expectation comparing with all possible element a such that $\{a_1, \ldots, a_{i-1}, a\} \in \mathcal{M}$. Before given the next lemma, we denote that $X_i^{\mathcal{M}} := \{a \in X : S \cup \{a_1, \ldots, a_i\} \cup a \in \mathcal{M}\}$.

Lemma 4.2. *Assume that $a_1, \ldots, a_{r(\mathcal{M}(S,X))}$ is a generated random feasible sequence, then for all $i \le i^*$, the expectation value of the marginal profits for each element is nearly optimal*

$$\mathbb{E}_{a_i}[f_{S\cup\{a_1,\ldots,a_{i-1}\}}(a_i)] \ge (1-\varepsilon)^2 \max_{a:S\cup\{a_1,\ldots,a_{i-1}\}\cup a\in\mathcal{M}} f_{S\cup\{a_1,\ldots,a_{i-1}\}}(a_i).$$

Then we give the analysis of the approximate ratio of Algorithm 2.

Lemma 4.3. *Assume that the output $S = \{a_1, \ldots, a_k\}$ of Algorithm 2 gives the result $\mathbb{E}_{a_i}[f_{S_i}(a_i)] \ge (1-\varepsilon)\max_{a:S_{i-1}\cup a\in\mathcal{M}} f_{S_{i-1}}(a)$ where $S_i = \{a_1, \ldots, a_i\}$. Then, for the expectation value of S, we have $\mathbb{E}[f(S)] \ge \left(1 - \frac{1}{1+(1-\varepsilon)\gamma'^2}\right)\mathtt{OPT}$.*

At the end, we give the analysis of the adaptivity of this algorithm.

Theorem 4.1. *With $\Delta = O\left(\frac{\log\frac{k}{\varepsilon}}{\frac{1}{\varepsilon}\log n\log\frac{1}{\gamma}-\log(1-\varepsilon)}\right)$,* Adaptive Sequencing for Non-submodular *has adaptivity $O\left(\frac{\log n\log\frac{k}{\varepsilon}}{\frac{1}{\varepsilon^2}\log n\log\frac{1}{\gamma}-\frac{1}{\varepsilon}\log(1-\varepsilon)}\right)$.*

Therefore, we have the following similar result of Adaptive Sequencing for Non-submodular and the proof can be adopted the same approach in [3]

Theorem 4.2. *For any $\varepsilon > 0$, Algorithm 2 is an $O\left(\frac{\log n\log\frac{k}{\varepsilon}}{\frac{1}{\varepsilon^2}\log n\log\frac{1}{\gamma}-\frac{1}{\varepsilon}\log(1-\varepsilon)}\right)$ adaptive algorithm that has $1 - \frac{1}{1+(1-\varepsilon)\gamma'^2}$ approximation guarantee with probability $1 - o(1)$ for maximizing a monotone weakly submodular function under a matroid constraint.*

In [3], they discussed the relationship between the value $g(S)$ and the residual value $\mathtt{OPT} - F(\mathbf{x})$ on the premise $F(\mathbf{x}) < (1-e^{-1})\mathtt{OPT}$. This bound is the tight approximation ratio for the problem of maximizing submodular function over matroid constraints. Then, they derived that $\mathtt{OPT} \le e(\mathtt{OPT} - F(\mathbf{x})))$. Therefore, in Lemma 7 of [3] they can have such assumption of the direction value on the surrogate function and the residual value. However, for the problem of maximizing a weakly submodular set function subject to a matroid constraint, there is no such bound found yet. Instead, we assume $F(\mathbf{x}) \le (1-1/\zeta)\cdot\mathtt{OPT}$ for weakly submodular case. Then

$$\mathtt{OPT} \le \zeta \cdot (\mathtt{OPT} - F(\mathbf{x})).$$

So we could make assumption like [3] and have the following functional lemma, which concludes the sum of the whole marginal profits on g of the optimal elements to S is arbitrarily close to $\gamma\lambda(1-\lambda)\cdot(\mathtt{OPT} - \mathtt{F}(\mathbf{x}))$.

Lemma 4.4. *Assume that* $g(S) \leq \lambda(\mathtt{OPT} - F(\mathbf{x}))$*, then*

$$\sum_i g_{S \setminus O_{i:k}}(o_i) \geq \gamma\lambda(1-\lambda) \cdot (\mathtt{OPT} - \mathrm{F}(\mathbf{x})).$$

Combining Lemma 4.2, that all elements picked into the direction S have near-optimal marginal profits, with Lemma 4.4, we can obtain the following result. It characterizes the relationship between the expectation value of $g(S)$ and the residual value $\mathtt{OPT} - F(\mathbf{x})$ in every iteration.

Lemma 4.5. *Let* $\Delta = O\left(\frac{\log \frac{k}{\varepsilon}}{\frac{1}{\varepsilon}\log n \log \frac{1}{\gamma} - \log(1-\varepsilon)}\right)$ *and* $\lambda = O(\varepsilon)$*. For any* $\mathbf{x}$ *s.t.* $\mathtt{OPT} \leq \zeta(\mathtt{OPT} - F(\mathbf{x}))$*, the set* S *returned by* Adaptive Sequencing$(g, \mathcal{M})$ *has the following result when* γ *is near to* 1*:*

$$\mathbb{E}[F_{\mathbf{x}}(\lambda S)] \geq \left(\gamma^2 - O(\varepsilon)\zeta\right) \cdot \lambda(\mathtt{OPT} - \mathrm{F}(\mathbf{x})).$$

So far, we get the lower bound in expectation of the marginal contribution for current solution $\mathbf{x}$ of the main algorithm in the update direction S. The lower bound is portrayed by the residual value $\mathtt{OPT} - F(\mathbf{x})$. Therefore, we can use inductive method in greedy-like algorithms to obtain the approximate ratio in expectation.

Lemma 4.6. *Assume that* Adaptive Sequencing For Non-submodular *outputs* $S \in \mathcal{M}$ *s.t.*

$$\mathbb{E}[F_{\mathbf{x}}(\lambda S)] \geq \Phi \cdot \lambda(\mathtt{OPT} - F(\mathbf{x})),$$

where $\Phi = \gamma^2 - O(\varepsilon)\zeta$ *at every iteration of* Accelerated Continuous Greedy*. Then* Accelerated Continuous Greedy *outputs* $\mathbf{x} \in P(\mathcal{M})$ *s.t.*

$$\mathbb{E}[F(\mathbf{x})] \geq \left(1 - e^{-\Phi}\right)\mathtt{OPT}.$$

At last we also need a technical lemma which exists for proving that the guarantee of Accelerated Continuous Greedy holds with high probability in the very end. The statement is below and it can be easily followed with the same idea in [3].

Lemma 4.7. *Assume that* Adaptive Sequencing For Non-submodular *outputs* $S \in \mathcal{M}$ *s.t.* $F_{\mathbf{x}}(\lambda S) \geq \alpha_i \lambda(\mathtt{OPT} - F(\mathbf{x}))$ *at every iteration* i *of* Accelerated Continuous Greedy *and that* $\lambda \sum_{i=1}^{\lambda^{-1}} \alpha_i \geq \Phi$*, where* $\Phi = \gamma^2 - O(\varepsilon)\zeta$*. Then* Accelerated Continuous Greedy *outputs* $\mathbf{x} \in P(\mathcal{M})$ *s.t.* $F(\mathbf{x}) \geq \left(1 - e^{-\Phi}\right)\mathtt{OPT}$.

Finally we can present the proof of Theorem 1.1.

Proof *(Proof of Theorem* 1.1*).* The adaptivity can be easily obtained due to Theorem 4.1. For the approximation result, from Lemma 4.5 we have $F_{\mathbf{x}}(\delta S) \geq$

$\alpha_i\lambda(\mathtt{OPT} - F(\mathbf{x}))$ at every iteration i with $\mathbb{E}[\alpha_i] \geq \Phi$. By a Chernoff bound with $\mathbb{E}[\lambda\sum_{i\in[\lambda^{-1}]}\alpha_i] \geq \Phi$,

$$\Pr\left[\lambda\sum_{i\in[\lambda^{-1}]}\alpha_i < (1-\varepsilon)\Phi\right] \leq e^{-\varepsilon^2\Phi\lambda^{-1}/2}.$$

Thus, with probability $p = 1-e^{-\varepsilon^2\Phi\lambda^{-1}/2}$, $\lambda^{-1}\alpha_i \geq \Phi - \varepsilon$. By Lemma 4.7, we conclude that w.p. p, $F(\mathbf{x} \geq (1-e^{-\Phi}))\mathtt{OPT}$. With step size $\lambda = O(\varepsilon^2/\log(1/\delta))$, we get that with probability $1-\delta$,

$$F(\mathbf{x}) \geq \left(1-e^{-\Phi}\right)\mathtt{OPT} \geq \left((1-e^{\gamma^2}) - O(\varepsilon)\right)\mathtt{OPT},$$

where $\Phi = \gamma^2 - O(\varepsilon)\zeta$. □

5 Conclusions

In this paper, we first generalize the adaptive sequencing algorithm in the problem of maximizing a weakly submodular set function subject to a matroid constraint. This technique provides a continuous solution with $1-e^{\gamma^2}-O(\varepsilon)$ approximation guarantee when the continuous generic submodularity ratio is sufficiently large. This result can be easily rounded to a feasible discrete solution almost without any loss by using either dependent rounding [9] or contention resolution schemes [23]. Besides, the generalized algorithm maintains few set function evaluations like [3] and the adaptivity is $O\left(\frac{\log n \log\frac{k}{\varepsilon}}{\frac{1}{\varepsilon^2}\log n\log\frac{1}{\gamma} - \frac{1}{\varepsilon}\log(1-\varepsilon)}\right)$.

Acknowledgements. The first and second authors are supported by Beijing Natural Science Foundation Project (No. Z200002) and National Natural Science Foundation of China (No. 11871081). The third author is supported by National Natural Science Foundation of China (No. 11871081). The fourth author is supported by Natural Science Foundation of Shandong Province of China (No. ZR2019PA004) and National Natural Science Foundation of China (No. 12001335).

References

1. Altschuler, J., Bhaskara, A., Fu, G., Mirrokni, V., Rostamizadeh, A., Zadimoghaddam, M.: Greedy column subset selection: new bounds and distributed algorithms. In: Proceedings of ICML, pp. 2539–2548 (2016)
2. Alon, N., Spencer, J.H.: The Probabilistic Method, vol. 3, pp. 307–314. Wiley, New York (2008)
3. Balkanski, E., Rubinstein, A., Singer, Y.: An optimal approximation for submodular maximization under a matroid constraint in the adaptive complexity model. In: Proceedings of STOC, pp. 66–77 (2019)
4. Bian, A.A., Buhmann, J.M., Krause, A., Tschiatschek, S.: Guarantees for greedy maximization of non-submodular functions with applications. In: Proceedings of ICML, pp. 498–507 (2017)

5. Buchbinder, N., Feldman, M., Garg, M.: Deterministic ($1/2+\varepsilon$)-approximation for submodular maximization over a matroid. In: Proceedings of SODA, pp. 241–254 (2019)
6. Călinescu, G., Chekuri, C., Pál, M., Vondrák, J.: Maximizing a monotone submodular function subject to a matroid constraint. SIAM J. Comput. **40**, 1740–1766 (2011)
7. Chekuri, C., Jayram, T.S., Vondrák, J.: On multiplicative weight updates for concave and submodular function maximization. In: Proceedings of ITCS, pp. 201–210 (2015)
8. Chekuri, C., Quanrud, K.: Submodular function maximization in parallel via the multilinear relaxation. In: Proceedings of SODA, pp. 303–322 (2019)
9. Chekuri, C., Vondrák, J., Zenklusen, R.: Dependent randomized rounding for matroid polytopes and applications. In: Proceedings of FOCS, pp. 575–584 (2010)
10. Chen, L., Feldman, M., Karbasi, A.: Weakly submodular maximization beyond cardinality constraints: does randomization help greedy? In: Proceedings of ICML, pp. 804–813 (2018)
11. Das, A., Kempe, D.: Submodular meets spectral: greedy algorithms for subset selection, sparse approximation and dictionary selection. In: Proceedings of ICML, pp. 1057–1064 (2011)
12. Edmonds, J.: Submodular functions, matroids, and certain polyhedra. Comb. Optim. **2570**, 11–26 (2003)
13. Feige, U.: A threshold of $\ln n$ for approximating set cover. J. ACM **45**, 634–652 (1998)
14. Feldman, M., Naor, J., Schwartz, R.: A unified continuous greedy algorithm for submodular maximization. In: Proceedings of FOCS, pp. 570–579 (2011)
15. Fisher, M.L., Nemhauser, G.L., Wolsey, L.A.: An analysis of approximations for maximizing submodular set functions-II. Math. Program. Stud. **8**, 73–87 (1978)
16. Filmus, Y., Ward, J.: Monotone submodular maximization over a matroid via non-oblivious local search. SIAM J. Comput. **43**, 514–542 (2014)
17. Harshaw, C., Feldman, M., Ward, J., Karbasi, A.: Submodular maximization beyond non-negativity: guarantees, fast algorithms, and applications. In: Proceedings of ICML, pp. 2634–2643 (2019)
18. Krause, A., Singh, A., Guestrin, C.: Nearoptimal sensor placements in Gaussian processes: theory, efficient algorithms and empirical studies. J. Mach. Learn. Res. **9**, 235–284 (2008)
19. Lawrence, N., Seeger, M., Herbrich, R.: Fast sparse Gaussian process methods: the informative vector machine. Adv. Neural Inf. Process. Syst. **1**, 625–632 (2003)
20. Nemhauser, G.L., Wolsey, L.A.: Best algorithms for approximating the maximum of a submodular set function. Math. Oper. Res. **3**, 177–188 (1978)
21. Rafiey, A., Yoshida, Y.: Fast and private submodular and k-submodular functions maximization with matroid constraints. arXiv:2006.15744 (2020)
22. Vondrák, J.: Optimal approximation for the submodular welfare problem in the value oracle model. In: Proceedings of STOC, pp. 67–74 (2008)
23. Vondrák, J., Chekuri, C., Zenklusen, R.: Submodular function maximization via the multilinear relaxation and contention resolution schemes. In: Proceedings of STOC, pp. 783–792 (2011)

A Fast Class Noise Detector with Multi-factor-based Learning

Wanwan Zheng(✉) and Mingzhe Jin

Doshisha University, Kyoto, Japan
cyac1004@mail4.doshisha.ac.jp

Abstract. Noise detection algorithms commonly face the problems of over-cleansing, large computational complexity and long response time. Preserving the original structure of data is critical for any classifier, whereas over-cleansing will adversely affect the quality of data. Besides, the high time complexity remains one of the main defects for most noise detectors, especially those exhibiting an ensemble structure. Moreover, numerous studies reported that ensemble-based techniques outperform other techniques in the accuracy of noisy instances identification. In the present study, a fast class noise detector called FMF (fast class noise detector with multi-factor-based learning) was proposed. FMF, three existing ensemble-based noise detectors and the case with original data were compared on 10 classification tasks. C5.0 acted as the classifiers to access the efficiency of these algorithms. As revealed from the results, the FMF shortened the processing time at least twelve times by three baselines, and it achieved the highest accuracy in most cases.

Keywords: Noise detection · Over-cleansing · High time complexity · Multi-factor-based learning · Fast execution

1 Introduction

Noise detection [1] is a preprocessing technique that can be employed in any given dataset to identify potentially noisy instances. In practice, uncertain or contaminated training sets are commonly conducted. Besides, some studies estimated that even in controlled environments at least 5% of errors exist in a dataset [2,3].

It is suggested that some objects can be impacted by feature or class noise, which offer misleading information and then hinder the learning process of classifiers. Moreover, class noise is potentially more harmful than feature noise, and the reasons are presented below. First, there are numerous features, whereas there is only one label. Second, each feature for learning has different importance, whereas labels always significantly impact learning [4]. Third, the consequences of class noise detection will impact many feature noise detection techniques (e.g. feature selection) directly. Thus, detecting class noise prior to the analysis of

S. Chellappan et al. (Eds.): CSoNet 2020, LNCS 12575, pp. 14–25, 2020.
https://doi.org/10.1007/978-3-030-66046-8_2

polluted data appears to be necessary. In this study, instances that should be misclassified are defined as class noise.

In noise detection field, over-cleansing and the high time complexity are primarily difficult to solve. Preserving the original structure of data is uttermost important for any classifier. Obviously, over-reduction causes information loss, even the original structural failure may occur and then the quality of data would be affected adversely. Moreover, large training data size is crucial for supervised learning tasks. Therefore, though removing noisy instances is considered to be capable of enhancing the accuracy of learning model, the fact is that applying noise detectors reduces the accuracy with great potential, especially for the powerful classifiers. [5] proposed the MCIS (multi-class instance selection) and in the six datasets they used, the accuracies of MCIS are higher than using the entire training data only two times; the enhancements of both are 0.01. [6] proposed MOCHC (multi-objective CHC algorithm for instance selection), which achieves about 50% reduction rates, whereas the accuracies decrease for seven datasets in the applied eight datasets. ElkMSI (evolutionary local k with multi-selection of instance) is superior, as proposed by [7]. In their experiments, a total of 150 datasets were used, and ElkMSI achieves the identical averaged accuracy with the original data.

As described above, in the field of noise detection, one of recurrent problems is the trade-off between the reduction rate and the classification quality. To address this problem, INFFC (an iterative class noise filter based on the fusion of classifiers with noise sensitivity control) was proposed in [8]. INFFC focuses more on the removal of those instances that must be deleted (class noise) instead of the reduction rate. The experiment was based on 25 datasets. ENN (edited nearest neighbor), All k-NN (all k-nearest neighbors), ME (multiedit), CF (classifier filter), EF (ensemble filter), NCNE (nearest centroid neighbor edition), IPF (iterative partitioning filter) seven well-known noise detectors acted as the comparisons. Furthermore, 1-NN and robust classifiers C4.5 and SVM were employed to compute the accuracies. As indicated from the experimental results, INFFC enhances the performance of the other methods as well as the case with the entire training data.

The high time complexity remains one of the main defects for most noise detectors; such problem is scaling up [9]. It is a common way to get better performance at the cost of higher computational complexity. Two representative examples are ensembles and deep neural networks. In machine learning studies, the more powerful algorithms should be capable of learning complex nonlinear relationships. By definition, they are robust to noise, show good balance between high variance and low bias, and meaning predictions vary with the specific data used to train them. This added flexibility and power usually come at the cost of large-scale training data and algorithm which is robust enough to handle the large-scale training data.

Especially in the era of big data, data are increasing in scale and exhibiting critical roles in various fields (e.g., text classification, handwritten recognition and face detection). Furthermore, the quality and size of training data are crucial for supervised learning tasks. Accordingly, how to build a noise detection algorithm that exhibits high detection performance and fast execution is of notable significance.

This study proposed a fast class noise detector with multi-factor-based learning, which is capable of alleviating the possibility of over-cleansing and performing favorably to three existing ensemble-based techniques and the original data in terms of classification accuracy. Moreover, the fast execution makes it possible to deal with large-scale datasets.

The rest of this article is organized as follows: In Sect. 2, the algorithm is presented to build FMF. In Sect. 3, the characteristics of this method are discussed. In Sect. 4, this method is empirically compared with three existing noise detectors and the original data. Lastly, in Sect. 5, conclusions and future research directions are drawn.

2 Algorithm of FMF

FMF is a three-stage process. Because no method will be efficient for all of data, the first stage determines the proper similarity index for the applied data. The second stage exploits the determined similarity index to make a multi-factor-based learning to yield a noise score for respective instance. In the third stage, a threshold is given to remove the noisy instances. The workflow of FMF is illustrated in Fig. 1.

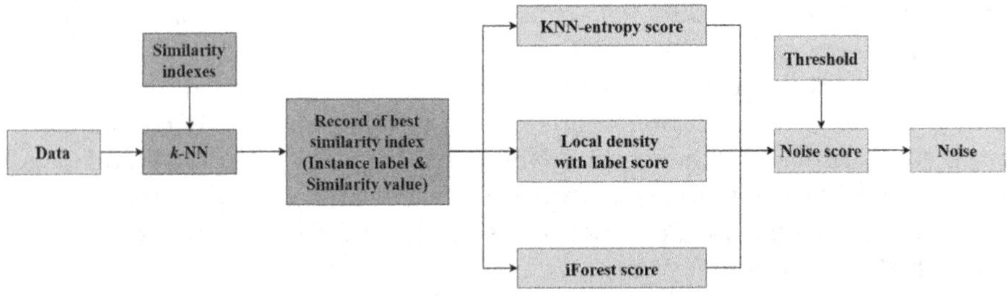

Fig. 1. The workflow of FMF.

2.1 The Determination of the Proper Similarity Index

In this study, KNN was adopted to determine the proper similarity index for its efficiency and fast execution. It learns very quickly because it reads in the training data without much further processing. The computational complexity of KNN is $O(n^2)$, which is significantly smaller than most of the recent methods.

For the similarity indexes, Euclidean distance (Euclidean), Canberra distance (Canberra), Probabilistic symmetric chi-squared measure (Schi), Mahalanobis distance (MD) and Pearson correlation coefficient (Pearson) were selected. To make the selection more accurate, the numeric label was adopted to obtain the

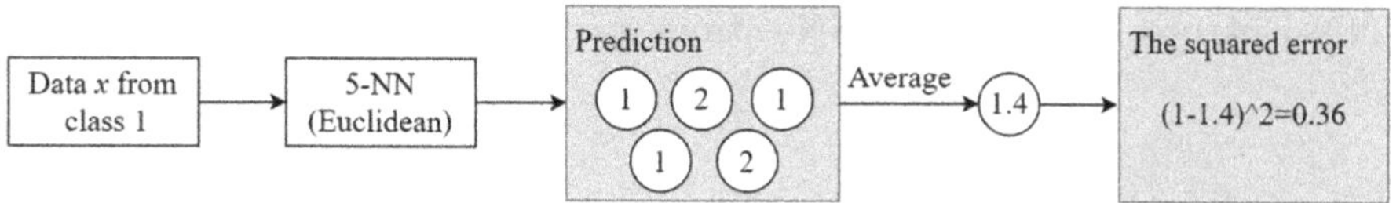

Fig. 2. An example of the squared error computation.

minimum squared error in the case of binary classification. On the other hand, the characteristic label was adopted for multi-class classification. An example of the squared error computation is illustrated in Fig. 2 with Euclidean. The nearest five neighbors of data x with label 1 are 1, 2, 1, 1, 2; thus, the label of data x is predicted as 1.4, and the squared error will be 0.36. Using this method to obtain the prediction squared errors of the rest instances, finally the sum is taken as the squared error of Euclidean. The similarity index that achieves the minimum squared error will be taken as the proper one; its results (for data x_i ($i = 1, 2, 3, \ldots, n$): the labels of the nearest k neighbors, l_j ($j = 1, 2, \ldots, k$) and their similarity values with data x_i, s_j ($j = 1, 2, \ldots, k$)) are transferred to the next stage to process multi-factor-based learning. In this study, k is set to 5.

2.2 Multi-factor-based Learning

For a noise detector, the output can be one of two types, i.e., noise scores and binary labels. This study processed a multi-factor-based learning to output a noise score for respective instance. The output of noise score was taken because noise score retains all of information provided by our algorithm and the possibility of conversion into binary label, besides, it also helps assess the performance of FMF with visualization methods. Furthermore, though classifier is frequently employed in noise detectors, several classifiers are even employed to build an ensemble model, FMF criterion is independent of the classifier(s) in determining the noise score. Thus, the quality of obtained clean data will not be impacted by any classifier.

The noise score s of an instance x is defined as:

$$s(x,k) = weight_k \times ke(x,k) + weight_l \times ldl(x,k) + weight_f \times iForest(x) \quad (1)$$

$$weight_k + weight_l + weight_f = 1 \quad (2)$$

Where k is the number of nearest neighbors. The $ke(x,k)$, $ldl(x,k)$ and $iForest(x)$ represent KNN-entropy score, local density with label score and iForest score, respectively. In this study, $weight_k$, $weight_l$ and $weight_f$ are set to 1/3.

KNN-Entropy Score. The KNN-entropy score (ke) is defined as:

$$ke(x,k) = \begin{cases} 0 & p(x,k) = 0 \\ 1 & p(x,k) = 1 \\ p(x,k) \times (1 - entropy(x,k)) & 0 < p(x,k) < 1 \end{cases} \tag{3}$$

Where $p(x, k)$ is the proportion of the enemies of instance x in the nearest k neighbors. The enemy of x refers to the instance from the other classes. Therefore, the higher $p(x, k)$, the more likely it is noise. The problem is how to determine the value of k. Considering the possibility of data imbalance (in fact, most of real-world data in many domains are reported to be imbalanced), in this study, k is defined as:

$$k = min(I_1, I_2, \ldots, I_n) \tag{4}$$

Where I_n is the number of instances in class n and $n >= 2$. The $entropy(x, k)$ measures the complexity of the k nearest neighbors of x, which takes the same value with:

$$H(X) \triangleq -\sum_{k=1}^{K} p(X = k) \log_e p(X = k) \tag{5}$$

Where X is a random instance label, K is the number of classes, $p(X = k)$ is the proportion of instances from class k.

Therefore, the instances which enter another class completely will get the largest KNN-entropy score, followed by the instances around the decision boundary and normal instances.

A drawback of KNN-entropy score is that it ignores the order of k-nearest neighbors. The local density with label score is designed to alleviate this problem.

Local Density with Label Score. The local density presents the local deviation of density of a given instance with respect to its neighbors. For a given data point x, let $L_k(x)$ be the set of points within the k-nearest neighbor distance of x. Note that $L_k(x)$ will typically contain k points, but may sometimes contains more than k points because of ties in the k-nearest neighbor distance. Then the local density of x is defined as:

$$ld(x,k) = \left(\frac{\sum_{y \in L_k(x)} dist(x,y)}{k} \right)^{-1} \tag{6}$$

Based on the consideration that an outlier should have a substantially lower density than their neighbors, the smaller the local density, the more likely it is outlier. Inspired by the idea of local density, the local density with label score (ldl) is defined as:

$$ldl(x,k) = \begin{cases} 0 & p(x,k) = 0 \\ 1 & p(x,k) = 1 \\ 1 - sigmoid(\frac{ddif(x,h)}{dhit(x,f)}) & 0 < p(x,k) < 1, h + f = k \end{cases} \tag{7}$$

$$dhit(x,h) = \frac{\sum_{y \in H_h(x)} dist(x,y)}{h}, h < k \tag{8}$$

$$ddif(x,f) = \frac{\sum_{y \in F_f(x)} dist(x,y)}{f}, f < k \tag{9}$$

Within the k-nearest neighbor distance of x, $H_h(x)$ is the set of points from the same class with x and the number is h; $F_f(x)$ is the set of points from different class(es) and the number is f. in Eq. (7):

$$\begin{cases} when \;\; h = 0 & \rightarrow & f = k & \rightarrow & p(x,k) = 1 & \rightarrow & ldl(x,k) = 1 \\ when \;\; h = k & \rightarrow & f = 0 & \rightarrow & p(x,k) = 0 & \rightarrow & ldl(x,k) = 0 \\ when \;\; 0 < h < k & \rightarrow & \frac{ddif(x,k)}{dhit(x,k)} > 0 & \rightarrow & 0 < ldl(x,k) < 1 \end{cases} \tag{10}$$

iForest Score. iForest utilizes the isolation trees rather than distance or density measures to detect outliers. In an isolation tree, the data is recursively partitioned with axis-parallel cuts at randomly chosen partition points in randomly selected attributes, so as to isolate the instances into nodes with fewer and fewer instances until the points are isolated into singleton nodes containing one instance. In such cases, the tree branches containing outliers are noticeably less deep, because these data points are located in sparse regions. Therefore, the distance of the leaf to the root is used as the outlier score. An iForest is an ensemble combination of a set of isolation trees and the final combination step is performed by averaging the path lengths of the data points in the different trees of the iForest.

Because the iForest is an unsupervised outlier detector, the iForest score is calculated in class unit in this study. The iForest score ranges from 0 to 1, and the higher the score, the higher the potential of being noise.

2.3 Removal of Noisy Instances

As the definition, the final noise score is the average of KNN-entropy score, local density with label score and iForest score, ranging from 0 to 1. However, because iForest score has relatively higher value and lower standard deviation, the $min - max\ normalization$ was taken for three types of score to avoid any one leading the average result.

To detect univariate extreme values, the box-plot (or box and whisker diagram) was used, which is reported to be a particularly useful approach in the context of visualizing noise score. In a box-plot, the statistics of a univariate distribution are summarized in terms of five quantities, which are the "minimum/maximum" (whisker), the 25th empirical quartile and 75th empirical quartile (box), and the median (line in the middle of box). The distance between the 25th and 75th quartiles is referred to as the $inter - quartile\ range\ (IQR)$. The "minimum" and "maximum" are enclosed quotations because they are defined in a non-standard way:

$$\text{``}minimum\text{''} = 25th\ empirical\ quartile \quad - \quad range \times IQR \tag{11}$$

$$\text{``}maximum\text{''} = 75th\ empirical\ quartile \quad + \quad range \times IQR \tag{12}$$

In this study, range is set to 1 and the threshold is equal to "maximum". Values more than "maximum" are considered as the extreme cases, which will be removed as noisy instances.

3 Noise Detection with FMF

This section presents a detail discussion about the noise score of FMF with iris dataset. Fig. 3 presents the distribution of noise scores and the noise score of each instance. The minimum and maximum of noise scores were 0 and 0.94, respectively. The reduction rate was about 5.33% ($\approx 100 \times 8/150$) referring to threshold 0.63. According to Fig. 3, the detected noisy instances distributed at the right with higher values and had a distribution different (in location and distributional form) from the other instances.

Figure 4 presents the result of Principal component analysis (PCA) of iris to visualize the relationship between the position and noise score. For each class, a color gradient from blue to red specifics the data points positioned in the center zone, middle zone and border zone. Three points must be remarked:

1. The instances that completely enter another class (e.g., data points with ID 107 and 120) and the outliers (data point with ID 42) got the maximum scores, showing the maximum possibility to be the noise.
2. The data points around the decision boundary (e.g., data points with ID 71, 84, 135) got median scores, showing median possibility to be the noise.
3. The central data points of each class get the minimum scores, showing the maximum possibility to be the normal instances (or representative instances).

4 Comparison Between FMF and the Baselines

In the second experiment, FMF was compared with the case of using the original data, All k-NN, dynamicCF and INFFC, which showed higher accuracy and faster processing in the preliminary experiment. To access the accuracy achieved by the mentioned algorithms, C5.0 was applied. Table 1 lists the datasets. All

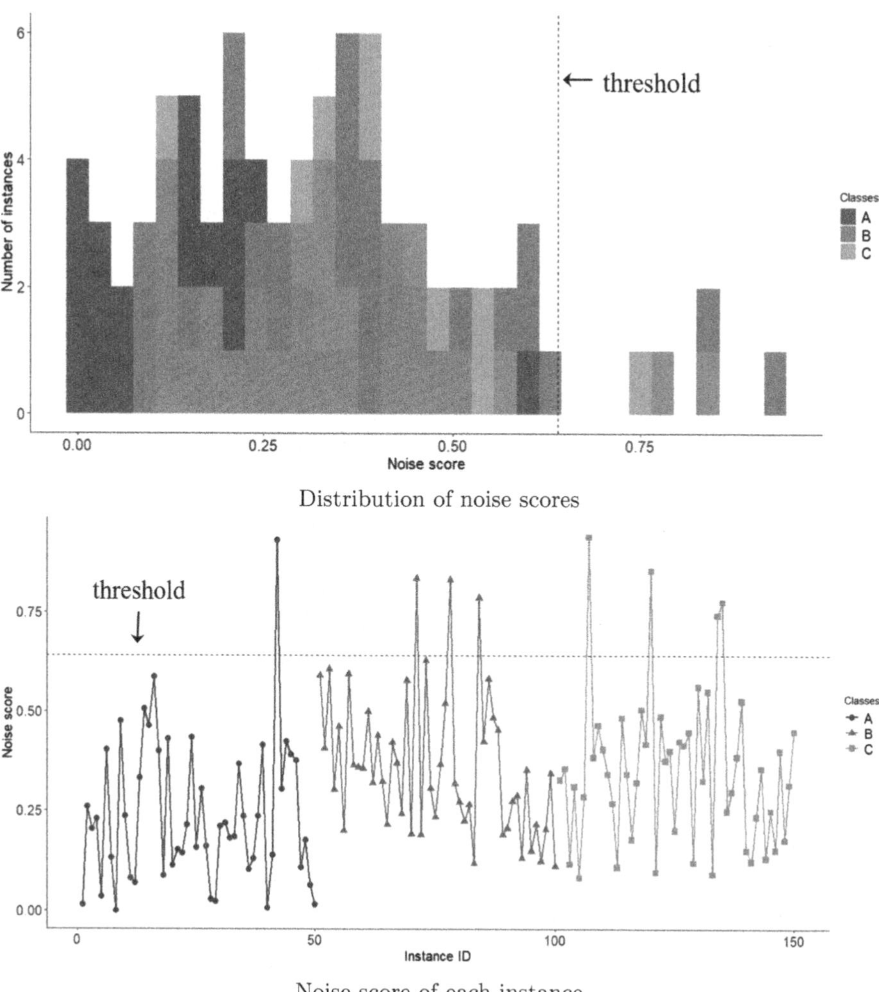

Distribution of noise scores

Noise score of each instance

Fig. 3. The distribution of noise scores and the noise score of each instance (iris, the best similarity index: Euclidean).

the datasets were collected from the existing studies of noise detection, including climate data, biological data, physical data, image data as well as text data.

Because noise detection is a multi-objective optimization problem, the classification accuracy of C5.0 (Table 2), the reduction rate (Table 3) and the processing time (Table 4) are shown to verify the hypothesis of the enhanced performance of FMF statistically.

In Table 2, on average, the increases in accuracy were about 3.0%; The largest percentage improvement (PI) was 10% and there were no percentage deteriora-

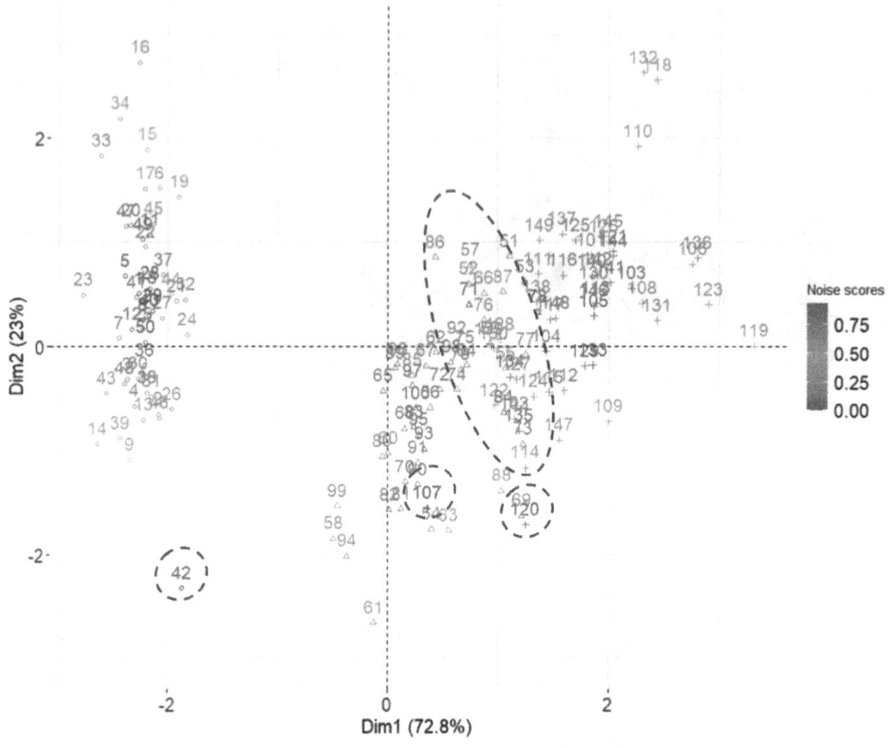

Fig. 4. Principal component analysis (PCA) of iris data.

Table 1. Details of the 10 datasets used in the experiment, including the total number of instances (#instance), the number of attributes (#attribute) and the number of classes (#class).

ID	Dataset	#instance(per class)	#attribute	#class
1	automobile	192(22/23/31/52/64)	14	5
2	heart	267(55/212)	44	2
3	haberman	306(81/225)	3	2
4	SAheart	462(192/270)	9	2
5	fir_c4_500	500(216/284)	25	2
6	climate	540(46/494)	17	2
7	isolet	600(300/300)	546	2
8	halloffame	1340(57/68/1215)	14	3
9	segment	2310(330 $\times$ 7)	19	7
10	ozone	2534(160/2374)	72	2

Table 2. Average macro-Fs and ranks for each algorithm in the case of C5.0 works as the classifier. These results are averaged over 10-fold cross-validation. The PI column correspond to the percentage improvement (positive) or percentage deterioration (negative) score, calculated as: $(FMF - All) \times 100$. The highest macro-F of each data is shown in bold.

	All	All k-NN	DynamicCF	INFFC	FMF	PI (%)
automobile	0.75	0.57	0.65	0.70	**0.76**	+1
heart	0.61	0.57	0.57	0.63	**0.67**	+6
haberman	0.52	0.59	0.58	0.52	**0.62**	+10
SAheart	0.55	0.54	**0.57**	0.52	0.55	
fir_c4_500	0.85	0.82	0.82	0.80	**0.87**	+2
climate	0.89	**0.91**	**0.91**	**0.91**	**0.91**	+2
isolet	0.96	0.96	NA	**0.97**	**0.97**	+1
halloffame	0.57	0.60	0.59	0.59	**0.63**	+6
segment	0.96	0.96	0.96	0.96	0.96	
ozone	0.60	0.57	0.52	0.59	**0.64**	+4
Average	0.73	0.71	0.69	0.72	**0.76**	

Table 3. Average reduction rates of all algorithms. These results were averaged over 10-fold cross-validation. The highest reduction rate of each data is shown in bold.

	All k-NN	dynamicCF	INFFC	FMF
automobile	**0.32**	0.25	0.18	0.05
heart	**0.29**	0.20	0.07	0.07
haberman	**0.37**	0.27	0.21	0.04
SAheart	**0.49**	0.41	0.35	0.04
fir_c4_500	**0.37**	0.14	0.17	0.05
climate	0.13	0.09	0.07	**0.20**
isolet	0.01	0.00	0.00	**0.03**
halloffame	**0.09**	0.07	0.05	0.01
segment	**0.04**	0.02	0.01	0.01
ozone	0.07	0.06	0.04	**0.25**
Average	**0.22**	0.15	0.12	0.08

tion (PD) cases; Additionally, among the 10 datasets applied, the win, tie and loss of FMF were 8, 2, 0, respectively.

In Table 3, All k-NN achieved a performance in terms of reduction rate that is better comparable to the performances of the other methods considered in the assessment, which is 22% on average. Followed by dynamicCF (15%), INFFC (12%) and FMF (8%). FMF removed the fewest instances.

Table 4. Average processing time(s) of all algorithms. These results were averaged over 10-fold cross-validation. The fastest processing of each data is shown in bold.

	All k-NN	dynamicCF	INFFC	FMF
automobile	2.92	5.07	29.03	**0.09**
heart	6.68	8.25	29.67	**0.55**
haberman	1.40	2.13	30.55	**0.53**
Saheart	4.02	6.43	297.53	**0.30**
fir_c4_500	10.22	13.03	242.70	**0.48**
climate	10.88	12.07	45.39	**0.42**
isolet	286.56	NA	346.12	**8.97**
halloffame	28.54	25.52	160.37	**1.92**
segment	98.01	80.41	210.36	**5.15**
ozone	227.87	188.08	1293.67	**8.94**
Average	67.71	37.89	268.54	**2.73**

In Table 4, FMF processed significantly faster than the other methods. On average, the processing time was 2.73 s per run, which was about 1/25, 1/12 and 1/90 of the averaged processing times of All k-NN, dynamicCF and INFFC, respectively. Note that one important reason for taking All k-NN, dynamicCF and INFFC as the baselines is because of their faster processing; however, according to the results obtained, FMF was the fastest one.

5 Conclusions

Most of the existing noise detectors are very expensive when the size of the training dataset is large, which was also demonstrated in our preliminary experiment. This study proposed a fast noise detector with fundamentally different structure that makes a multi-factor-based learning rather than the normal simple learning (e.g., density-based learning) or ensemble-based learning with classifiers. Removing the noisy instances which completely enter other classes first and then smoothing the decision boundary allows FMF to achieve a promising result.

According to the results, (1) removing instances identified by FMF for training achieved the highest overall classification accuracy compared with the classifiers trained on the entire training data as well as with noise removed by the other methods. The classification accuracy was improved up to 10%; (2) FMF efficiently speeded up the computation. Compared with the second fast dynamicCF and the slowest INFFC, its speed was about 12 times and 90 times faster, respectively; (3) FMF reached the lowest reduction rate. Compared with All k-NN which achieved the maximum reduction rate, the value of FMF was about its 1/3. However, the low reduction rate also demonstrates the low possibility of over-cleansing.

In the subsequent study, we are interested in detecting the redundant data points with the noise scores.

References

1. Garcia, L., de Carvalho, A., Lorena, A.C.: Effect of label noise in the complexity of classification problems. Neurocomputing **160**, 108–119 (2015)
2. Hu, Z., Li, B., Hu, Y.: Fast sign recognition with weighted hybrid k-nearest neighbors based on holistic features from local feature descriptors. J. Comput. Civ. Eng. **31**(5) (2017). https://doi.org/10.1061/(ASCE)CP.1943-5487.0000673
3. Liu, F.T., Ting, K.M., Zhou, Z.H.: Isolation forest. In: Proceeding of 2008 Eighth IEEE International Conference on Data Mining, pp. 413–422 (2008) Location (1999). https://doi.org/10.1109/ICDM.2008.17
4. Sáez, J., Galar, M., Luengo, J., Herrera, F.: Analyzing the presence of noise in multi-class problems: alleviating its influence with the one vs one decomposition. Knowl. Inf. Syst. **38**, 1–28 (2014)
5. Chen, J., Zhang, C., Xue, X., Liu, C.L.: Fast instance selection for speeding up support vector machines. Knowl. Based Syst. **45**, 1–7 (2013)
6. Rathee, S., Ratnoo, S., Ahuja, J.: Instance selection using multi-objective chc evolutionary algorithm. In: Fong, S., Akashe, S., Mahalle, P.N. (eds.) Information and Communication Technology for Competitive Strategies. LNNS, vol. 40, pp. 475–484. Springer, Singapore (2019). https://doi.org/10.1007/978-981-13-0586-3_48
7. de Haro-García, A., Pérez-Rodríguez, J., García-Pedrajas, N.: Combining three strategies for evolutionary instance selection for instance-based learning. Swarm Evol. Comput. **42**, 160–172 (2018)
8. Sáez, J.A., Galar, M., Luengo, J., Herrera, F.: INFFC: an iterative class noise filter based on the fusion of classifiers with noise sensitivity control. Inf. Fusion **27**, 19–32 (2016)
9. Garcia, L., Lehmann, J., Carvalho, A., Lorena, A.: New label noise injection methods for the evaluation of noise filters. Knowl. Based Syst. **163**, 693–704 (2019)

Efficient SDN-Based Traffic Monitoring in IoT Networks with Double Deep Q-Network

Tri Gia Nguyen[1(✉)], Trung V. Phan[2], Dinh Thai Hoang[3], Tu N. Nguyen[4], and Chakchai So-In[5]

[1] Faculty of Information Technology, Duy Tan University, Danang 50206, Vietnam
nguyengiatri@duytan.edu.vn
[2] Chair of Communication Networks, Technische Universität Chemnitz, 09126 Chemnitz, Germany
[3] School of Electrical and Data Engineering, University of Technology Sydney, Sydney, NSW 2007, Australia
[4] Department of Computer Science, Purdue University Fort Wayne, Fort Wayne, IN 46805, USA
[5] Department of Computer Science, Faculty of Science, Khon Kaen University, Khon Kaen 40002, Thailand

Abstract. In an Internet of Things (IoT) environment, network traffic monitoring tasks are intractable to achieve due to various IoT traffic types. Recently, the development of Software-Defined Networking (SDN) enables outstanding flexibility and scalability abilities in network control and management, thereby providing a potential approach to mitigate challenges in monitoring the IoT traffic. In this paper, we propose an IoT traffic monitoring approach that implements deep reinforcement learning technique to maximize the fine-grained monitoring capability, i.e., level of traffic statistics details, for several IoT traffic groups. Specifically, we first study a flow-rule matching control system constrained by different expected levels of statistics details and by the flow-table limit of the SDN-based gateway device. We then formulate our control optimization problem by employing the Markov decision process (MDP). Afterwards, we develop Double Deep Q-Network (DDQN) algorithm to quickly obtain the optimal flow-rule matching control policy. Through the extensive experiments, the obtained results verify that the proposed approach yields outstanding improvements in terms of the ability to simultaneously provide different required degrees of statistics details while protecting the gateway devices from being overflowed in comparisons with those of the conventional Q-learning method and the typical SDN flow rule setting.

This work was supported in part by Vietnam National Foundation for Science and Technology Development (NAFOSTED) under Grant 102.01-2019.322, and the Thailand Science Research and Innovation (TSRI) and National Research Council of Thailand (NRCT) via the International Research Network Program (IRN61W0006).

S. Chellappan et al. (Eds.): CSoNet 2020, LNCS 12575, pp. 26–38, 2020.
https://doi.org/10.1007/978-3-030-66046-8_3

Keywords: Traffic monitoring · Internet of Things · Software-defined networking · Double Deep Q-Network · Deep reinforcement learning

1 Introduction

Internet of Things (IoT) culminates the interconnection of ubiquitous end-devices with unique digital identity, e.g., smart devices and industrial systems [11]. Nevertheless, it exhibits several challenges in the network control and management tasks, particularly for network traffic monitoring that can provide beneficial information to other crucial applications, e.g., traffic engineering and anomaly detection. Consequently, it is essential to acquire a solution that can dynamically afford a fine-grained traffic monitoring capability to aid applications with high demands about detailed traffic information in the IoT networks. This primary requirement is challenging to be realized due to the diversity of IoT traffic types in a ubiquitous context [11].

Recently, Software-Defined Networking (SDN) technology [8] has been drawing a notable breakthrough in Telco industries due to significant improvements concerning dynamics and flexibility in traffic control and management tasks. In particular, SDN defines a new design and management strategy for networking. The key innovation of this design is the separation of the control and data planes. The SDN controller (e.g., ONOS [9]) makes the control decision and the SDN data plane manages the data forwarding. The communication between two planes is performed through southbound APIs, e.g., OpenFlow [3]. Henceforward, with SDN's unique features, they enable the IoT networks with the ability to mitigate network control and management challenges [2]. Ultimately, it has become a new IoT research area that has been recently attracting the concentration of researchers [2,7].

1.1 Related Work

In order to avoid overflow problems in flow-tables of the SDN forwarding devices, Avant-Guard [12] framework is proposed, in which the control plane distributes intelligence, i.e., a connection migration module, into switches to identify hosts that unlikely finish TCP connections. Thereby, diminishing abnormal flow rules that may flood flow-tables in the case of saturation, e.g., TCP SYN flood attack. A reinforcement learning algorithm [6] is proposed with the primary purpose of obtaining the long-term intention of diminishing the monitoring overhead and of being aware of the overflow problem in the forwarding devices. Likewise, SDN-Mon framework [10] is proposed to improve the traffic monitoring granularity that promotes many networking applications, in which the monitoring logic is separated from the forwarding logic by modifying OpenvSwitch and the Lagopus software switch. Afterwards, additional monitoring/functional tables are appended to the end of the forwarding pipeline. Nevertheless, one of the main weaknesses of these proposals is that a comprehensive customisation effort is required in the data plane devices, which violates the origin of SDN design.

Distinctly, in this study, we investigate a win-win equilibrium[1] between different IoT traffic groups concerning their granularity degree demands as one of the crucial evaluation criteria. Because the monitoring operation should fairly observe the sufficient statistics details of all IoT traffic groups. Therefore, we are strongly motivated to develop an innovative approach in the SDN-based IoT networks to efficiently provide a traffic monitoring capability while protecting the SDN switches from being overflowed.

1.2 Our Proposal

In this paper, we propose a traffic monitoring approach that employs deep reinforcement learning technique to maximize the degree of traffic statistics details and to provide a win-win equilibrium of the monitoring capability for several traffic groups in the SDN-based IoT environment, as shown in Fig. 1. Specifically, we study an SDN-based flow matching control system constrained by the required granularity levels of traffic groups and the capacity of the SDN-based gateway. We then formulate the control optimization problem by applying the Markov decision process (MDP), and develop an advanced reinforcement learning technique, i.e., Double Deep Q-Network (DDQN) algorithm, to quickly obtain the optimal policy for large-scale systems. The experiment results confirm the effectiveness of our proposed approach in terms of providing a sustainable degree of IoT traffic granularity while avoiding the gateway overflow issue in comparison with other traditional methods.

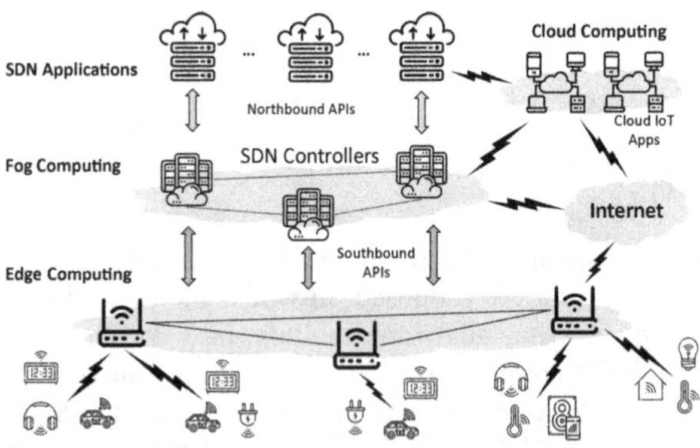

Fig. 1. SDN-based IoT networks.

[1] Different IoT traffic groups can meet their traffic granularity requirements at the same time.

2 System Model

2.1 Basic SDN Packet Forwarding Strategy

As presented in Fig. 2, the basic SDN packet forwarding in a gateway can be described as follows. Firstly, an incoming packet arrives at the gateway, i.e., step (1). Next, the searching process of a matched flow rule is performed by checking the packet header information to *match fields* in every flow rule, i.e., step (2). If the header information is suited to all *match fields* of a flow rule, this means that a matched flow is determined[2] and *Instructions* supervise the incoming packet in the matched flow rule, e.g., *forward* the packet to a particular gateway port (step (5)) or *drop* the packet. Contrarily, a *table-miss* event occurs for the entered packet, and the gateway creates a packet_in message and sends to its corresponding SDN controller for further guidance, i.e., step (3). Later, the SDN controller depends on its traffic forwarding plans and installs a new flow rule into the gateway with a selection of match fields and instructions, i.e., step (4). Then, a packet_out message is delivered out of the gateway, i.e., step (5), and the sent packet is the first packet of the new flow rule.

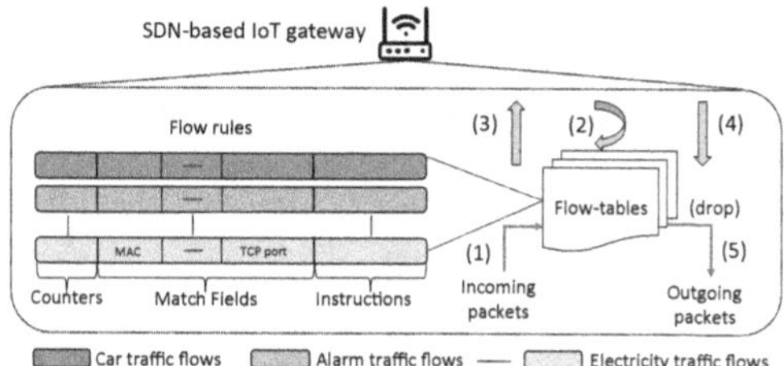

Fig. 2. Typical SDN packet forwarding logic.

To sum up, the determination of *match fields* in a flow rule represents a critical position in the SDN packet forwarding and flow matching in the gateway devices. In addition, the traffic statistics details collected by the control plane [8] are mainly defined by the number of match fields at the gateway. Accordingly, to adjust the traffic granularity degree, a flow matching control system controlling the match fields determination should be examined to obtain an efficient traffic monitoring capability in the SDN-based networks.

2.2 System Model

As aforementioned, it is essential to correctly and dynamically determine the right collection of match fields in traffic flows of various IoT devices. Therefore, we examine a flow matching control system operating as an SDN application

[2] For ease of comprehension, we study this simple matching strategy in this paper, more complex matching designs can be found in [3], e.g., multiple flow-tables searching.

that consists of a statistics collector, a control agent, a database, and a flow matching policy-maker. In which, the control agent controls the process of flow matching in flow-tables at an SDN-based IoT gateway i.

As stated in [1], from a macro scale, IoT traffic is realized as heterogeneous but group-specific from the representation of each local network. Accurately, IoT devices serving different applications can be attached in separate virtual local area networks (VLANs), which can be directed at the IoT networks' edge, i.e., the SDN-based IoT gateway. Hence, we consider $\mathscr{N}$ IoT traffic types traversing the gateway. For each traffic group, the required granularity for monitoring goals, i.e., the number of match fields in a flow rule, is denoted as Θ_n ($n \in \mathscr{N}$), where $0 < \Theta_n \leq \mathscr{M}_{max}$ and $\mathscr{M}_{max}$ is the maximum value of match fields in a flow rule. Originally, the control agent implements a policy to change the flow matching strategy of particular traffic groups into the gateway. Then, by relying on the collected statistics data, the control agent evaluates the effectiveness of the performed policy, i.e., the traffic granularity level of all traffic groups in the gateway, in comparison with the Θ_n value (*first* constraint) and the capacity of flow-tables of the gateway device (*second* constraint) indicated as $\mathscr{G}_{max}$. These processes are repeated to travel new policies and observations. Therefore, we can express the objective function of the control system as follows:

$$\max_t \sum_{n=1}^{\mathscr{N}} \theta_n, \quad \text{s.t.} \begin{cases} 0 < \Theta_n \leq \theta_n \leq \mathscr{M}_{max}, & \forall n \in \mathscr{N}, \\ 0 \leq \mathscr{F}_t < \mathscr{G}_{max}, \end{cases} \tag{1}$$

where θ_n is the actual granularity of the traffic group n and $\mathscr{F}_t$ is the total number of flow rules in the gateway at time step t.

3 Problem Formulation

To maximize the granularity degree of traffic while providing a win-win equilibrium for $\mathscr{N}$ traffic groups at the gateway, we adopt the Markov decision process (MDP) model [13] to present the control system operation as illustrated in Fig. 3. This framework allows the control system dynamically to perform optimal

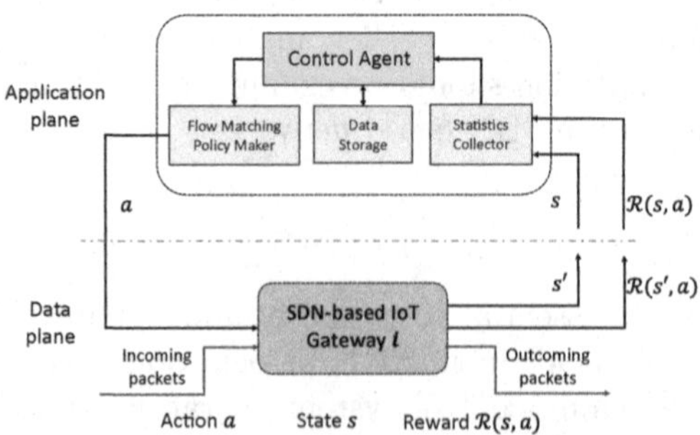

Fig. 3. Reinforcement learning based model.

actions based on its observations to maximize its average long-term reward. The MDP is defined by a tuple $< \mathscr{S}, \mathscr{A}, \mathscr{R} >$ where $\mathscr{S}$ represents the state space, $\mathscr{A}$ expresses the action space, and $\mathscr{R}$ signifies the immediate reward function.

3.1 State Space

As discussed previously, from the perspective of each local network, there are $\mathscr{N}$ traffic groups carrying traffic through the gateway [1]. Here, we aim to maximize the total traffic granularity degrees of all groups. Therefore, the state space of the gateway can be determined as follows:

$$\mathscr{S} \triangleq \{((\theta_1, f_1), ..., (\theta_n, f_n), ..., (\theta_{\mathscr{N}}, f_{\mathscr{N}}))\}, \tag{2}$$

where θ_n ($\theta_n \leq \mathscr{M}_{max}$) and f_n ($f_n \leq \mathscr{G}_{max}$) show the actual current granularity levels and the total number of flow rules of the traffic group n, respectively. The reason for choosing f_n is that the higher number of flow rules intimates the more match fields in a flow rule of the traffic group. Hence, a state of the system can be defined by $s = ((\theta_1, f_1), ..., (\theta_n, f_n), ..., (\theta_{\mathscr{N}}, f_{\mathscr{N}}))$.

3.2 Action Space

Recall the objective function in Eq. (1), one of the essentials is to always hold all θ_n values greater or equal to their corresponding Θ_n ones. Thus, the control agent should quickly construct actions whenever θ_n does not meet the requirement. However, the principal goal is to maximize the total of actual traffic granularity; hence, the control agent should implement actions even in the case when all θ_n values meet the requirement. Furthermore, the strategy is to execute actions for only the traffic group holding the lowest θ_n value at a time step. If the flow matching strategy of all traffic groups changes at the same time, this could lead to a significant variation in the gateway's flow-tables and more latency due to table-miss events and packet_in messages.

$\mathscr{C} = \{c_1, c_2, ..., c_k\}$ expresses a list of all feasible match field combinations, e.g., c_k =<*matchTcpUdpPorts, matchIpv4Address,...*> defined in *Reactive Forwarding* application of the ONOS SDN controller [9]. Therefore, the action space for changing the flow matching tactic in the gateway is determined by

$$\mathscr{A} \triangleq \{a : a \in \mathscr{C}\}. \tag{3}$$

It is noted that if the executed action is the same in comparison with the current one of the chosen traffic group, this indicates that the control agent goes to the sleep mode and waits for the next state observation.

3.3 Immediate Reward Function

Whenever, by executing an action, the total number of current flow entries $\mathscr{F}_t$ in the gateway reaches the limit $\mathscr{G}_{max}$, which may lead to either a degradation of the gateway forwarding performance or a packet_in flooding attack to the SDN controller, the control agent should be immensely punished for this taken action. Otherwise, the more match fields in a flow rule of a group, the higher the granularity level the group presents. Moreover, in case there exists a group getting $\theta_n < \Theta_n$, a little punishment[3] is applied for the immediate reward of the control agent. Consequently, we formulate the immediate reward function of the control agent as the total achieved granularity values abstracting the total punishments for groups not satisfying their requirements, which is described as follows:

$$\mathscr{R}(s,a) = \begin{cases} \sum_{n=1}^{\mathscr{N}} \theta_n, \text{ if } \theta_n \geq \Theta_n, \ \forall n \in \mathscr{N} \text{ and } \mathscr{F}_t < \mathscr{G}_{max}, \\ \sum_{n=1}^{\mathscr{N}} \theta_n - \sum_{n=1}^{\mathscr{N}} \Delta_{\mathscr{R}_n}, \text{ if } \theta_n < \Theta_n \text{ and } \mathscr{F}_t < \mathscr{G}_{max}, \\ -\mathscr{M}_{max}, \text{ if } \mathscr{F}_t = \mathscr{G}_{max}, \end{cases} \tag{4}$$

where $\mathscr{F}_t$ is the current total number of flow entries in the gateway, and $\mathscr{M}_{max}$ exhibits the maximum number of match fields in a flow rule.

3.4 Optimization Formulation

We formulate an optimization problem to obtain the optimal policy, denoted as $\pi^*(s)$, that maximizes the control system's average long-term reward, i.e., the traffic granularity level of all groups at the gateway. Hence, the optimization problem is described as follows:

$$\begin{aligned} \max_{\pi} \quad & \mathfrak{R}(\pi) = \sum_{t=1}^{\infty} \mathbb{E}(\mathscr{R}(s_t, \pi(s_t))) \\ \text{s.t.} \quad & \begin{cases} \mathscr{R} \in \mathbb{R}, \quad s_t \in \mathscr{S}, \quad \pi(s_t) \in \mathscr{A}, \\ 0 < \Theta_n \leq \theta_n \leq \mathscr{M}_{max}, \quad \forall n \in \mathscr{N}, \\ \mathscr{F}_t < \mathscr{G}_{max}, \end{cases} \end{aligned} \tag{5}$$

where $\mathfrak{R}(\pi)$ is the average reward of the control agent under the policy π and $\mathscr{R}(s_t, \pi(s_t))$ is the immediate reward function under the policy π at time step t.

[3] Difference between the gained θ_n and required Θ_n values is calculated by $\Delta_{\mathscr{R}_n} = \Theta_n - \theta_n$, which is the punishment of the group n.

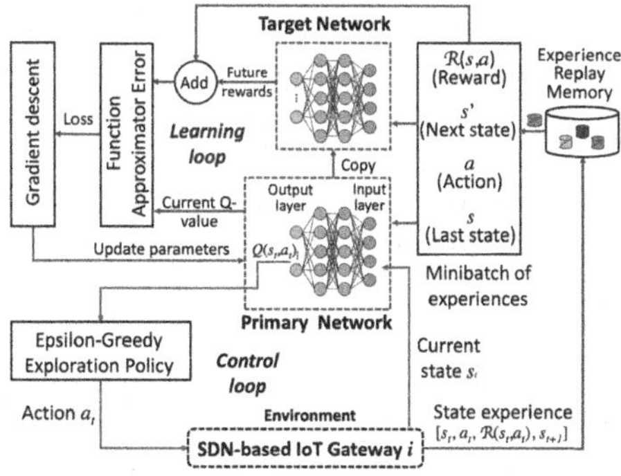

Fig. 4. Double Deep Q-Network based model.

4 Efficient SDN-Based IoT Traffic Monitoring with Double Deep Q-Network

The considering MDP model is with a large number of states due to the combinations between $\mathscr{N}$ traffic groups, as represented in Eq. (2). In this section, we develop the DDQN algorithm [14] to quickly obtain the optimal policy for the control agent. Specifically, the DDQN algorithm is developed to improve the performance of the Deep Q-Network (DQN) algorithm [5] that employs a deep neural network as a nonlinear function approximator to find the approximated values of $Q^*(b, a)$. The original intention of the DDQN is to determine an action according to an online or primary neural network Q_{net} (primary Q-network), and it uses a target neural network $\hat{Q}_{net}$ (target Q-network) to estimate the target Q-value of the executed action, as shown in Fig. 4. In our approach, an experience replay mechanism and a target Q-network are implemented as follows:

Experience Replay Mechanism: We deploy a replay memory pool, $\mathscr{E}$, to store the control agent's experience at each time step, $e_t = [s_t, a_t, \mathscr{R}(s_t, a_t), s_{t+1}]$, over many episodes, and $\mathscr{E} = \{e_1, ..., e_t\}$. The collected samples of experiences from $\mathscr{E}$ are picked up at random to execute the neural network updates. This approach allows achieving a high data usage efficiency since each experience is trained many times by the neural networks. Additionally, the randomizing technique reduces the correlations between the observed samples and therefore lessening the variance of the neural network updates.

Target Q-Network: During the learning period, the Q-values will be corrected resulting in changes of the value calculations if the shifting set of values is applied for refurbishing the primary Q-network Q_{net}, and this destabilizes the learning algorithm. Hence, to improve the stability of the algorithm with neural networks, we employ a separate network $\hat{Q}_{net}$, called target Q-network, for generating the target Q-values in the update process of the primary Q-network Q_{net}. More precisely, after every C time steps, we clone the Q_{net} and replace the $\hat{Q}_{net}$ by the cloned Q_{net}, then the renewed $\hat{Q}_{net}$ is used for the following C steps to the Q_{net}. This modification addresses divergence or oscillations, thereby stabilising the learning algorithm.

The details of the DDQN algorithm for the control system are explained in Algorithm 1. Specifically, the learning process contains many episodes, and in each episode, the control agent conducts an action according to the ϵ-greedy policy, and it then observes a new state and determines an immediate reward. Next, an experience is stored in the experience replay memory $\mathscr{E}$ for the training process at the next episodes. During the learning process, the control agent acquires a random minibatch of experience to update the primary Q-networks by minimising the following lost function [14].

$$\begin{aligned} L_{\phi}(\theta_{\phi}) = \mathbb{E}_{(s,a,\mathscr{R}(s,a),s')\sim U(\mathscr{M})}[&\mathscr{R}(s,a) \\ &+ \gamma\hat{Q}_{net}(s', \arg\max_{a'} Q_{net}(s', a'; \theta); \theta^{-}) - Q_{net}(s,a;\theta_{\phi})]^2, \end{aligned} \tag{6}$$

where γ indicates the discount factor, θ_{ϕ} are parameters of the primary network Q_{net} at episode ϕ, and θ^{-} are the parameters of the target network $\hat{Q}_{net}$.

A fundamental innovation in [5] was to freeze the parameters of the $\hat{Q}_{net}$ for a fixed number of time steps C while updating the Q_{net} by gradient descent, which strengthens the stability of the algorithm. Furthermore, we hence differentiate the loss function in Eq. (6) concerning the weight parameters of Q_{net} and $\hat{Q}_{net}$, and then we can obtain the gradient update as follows:

$$\begin{aligned} \nabla_{\theta_{\phi}} L_{\phi}(\theta_{\phi}) = \mathbb{E}_{(s,a,\mathscr{R}(s,a),s')}[(&\mathscr{R}(s,a) + \gamma\hat{Q}_{net}(s', \arg\max_{a'} Q_{net}(s', a'; \theta); \theta^{-}) \\ &- Q_{net}(s,a;\theta_{\phi}))\nabla_{\theta_{\phi}} Q_{net}(s,a;\theta_{\phi})]. \end{aligned} \tag{7}$$

Rather than calculating the full expectations in the gradient in Eq. (7), the loss function in Eq. (6) can be minimized by the gradient descent algorithm, which is the essential engine of most deep learning algorithms.

It is noted that the target network parameters θ^{-} are used by the primary network parameters θ_{ϕ} for every C time steps and are settled fixed between different updates. In addition, the learning process of the DDQN algorithm is conducted by updating the neural network parameters utilizing prior experiences in an online manner.

Algorithm 1. Efficient IoT traffic granularity acquisition with Double Deep Q-Network

```
Initialize replay memory 𝓔 with a buffer size ℕ.
Initialize the primary Q-network Q_net with arbitrary weights θ.
Initialize the target Q-network Q̂_net with arbitrary weights θ⁻ = θ, C (the target network
  replacement frequency), and T (terminal step in an episode).
for episode ϕ ∈ {1, 2, ..., ϕ_max} do
    for t ∈ {1, 2, ..., T} do
        Select a random action a_t with probability ϵ, otherwise select a_t =
          arg max_{a∈𝓐} Q*(s_t, a_t; θ).
        Perform action a_t at the gateway and observe a new state s_{t+1} and calculate an
          immediate reward 𝓡(s_t, a_t).
        Store experience e_t = (s_t, a_t, 𝓡(s_t, a_t), s_{t+1}) in 𝓔 and replace s_t by s_{t+1}.
        Sample random minibatch of experience (s_j, a_j, 𝓡(s_j, a_j), s_{j+1}) from 𝓔 as
          y_j = 𝓡(s_j, a_j) + γQ̂_net(s_{j+1}, arg max_{a_{j+1}∈𝓐} Q_net(s_{j+1}, a_{j+1}; θ); θ⁻).
        Execute a gradient descent step on ||y_j − Q_net(s_j, a_j; θ)||² with respect to the θ.
        Replace Q̂_net ← Q_net every C time steps.
        Go to next episode if t = T.
    end for
end for
```

5 Performance Evaluation

5.1 Experiment Setup

To evaluate the proposed approach, we emulate an SDN-based IoT network following the architecture shown in Fig. 1, which consists of 6 OvS (Open vSwitch) running as SDN-based IoT gateway devices and several contained-based hosts (24 hosts/OvS), and it is under control by an ONOS controller (v.1.3) [9]. The emulation operates on the machine with Intel(R) Core(TM) i7-7700 computer with clock speed 3.60 GHz, 64 GB RAM, and NVIDIA GeForce GTX 1080 Ti. Initially, two out of six OvS gateways OvS1 and OvS2 are chosen for the supervision of associated control Agent1 and Agent2, respectively, residing in another machine. To show the improvements of the deep reinforcement learning algorithm, we implement the same setup but apply the Q-learning algorithm [13] to solve our optimization problem.

5.2 Parameter Setting

For Q-learning algorithm, the learning rate α and the discount factor γ are empirically set at 0.6. For the DDQN algorithm, we apply parameters based on the common settings for designing neural networks [5], i.e., two-fully connected hidden layers are used together with input and output layers (as shown in Fig. 4), the size of the hidden layers is 128, the size of the output layer is 10 (which indicates 10 flow matching strategies), the mini-batch size is 32, the replay memory $\mathscr{E}$ holds a size $\mathbb{N}$ of 10,000, the target network replacement frequency C is 100 iterations, and the discount factor γ is 0.6. In the learning process of two algorithms, ϵ-greedy algorithm is employed with the initial value of 1.0 and its final value of 0.1 [5], the duration of an iteration is 5 s, and the maximum iterations in an episode T is 100. We let the capacity of flow-tables of the gateway device $\mathscr{G}_{max} = 3000$. Note that we perform 10 different flow matching tactics and 11 primary match fields provided by the ONOS controller [9], that indicates $|\mathscr{C}| = 10$, and $\mathscr{M}_{max} = 11$.

As discussed previously in Sect. 2, we can generalize three common traffic groups, i.e., sensor traffic, monitor traffic, and alarm traffic. *Sensor traffic*: IoT sensor devices generate traffic in a particular period with a low number of packets per flow. *Monitor traffic*: identify by a small number of flows but a significant number of packets per flow. *Alarm traffic*: we assume this traffic group contains a moderate amount regarding both the number of flows and packets per flow. Besides, Hping3 tool [4] is utilized to randomly generate TCP/UDP traffic flows between hosts.

From the above classification, it indicates that $\mathscr{N} = \{sensor, monitor, alarm\}$, and experiments are performed with two settings of required granularity levels as follows: *Diverse*: $\Theta_{sensor} = 3$, $\Theta_{monitor} = 6$, $\Theta_{alarm} = 9$; and *High*: $\Theta_{sensor} = \Theta_{monitor} = \Theta_{alarm} = 9$.

5.3 Results

Convergence Rate of Reinforcement Learning Algorithms. As illustrated in Fig. 5, the average reward value is acquired after every 1,000 iterations during the training period of the Agent1 that controls the gateway OvS1. The convergence rate of the DDQN algorithm is considerably higher than that of the Q-learning algorithm. In particular, the DDQN algorithm requires around 40,000 iterations to achieve the significant average value, i.e., approximately 25.0, for the total actual granularity in both the *Diverse* and *High* settings. This is because the higher required degree of granularity regularly demands actions that give a higher number of match fields in a flow rule, resulting in the higher probability of overflowing the gateway (i.e., more flow rules installed) and in the more critical penalty to the control agent.

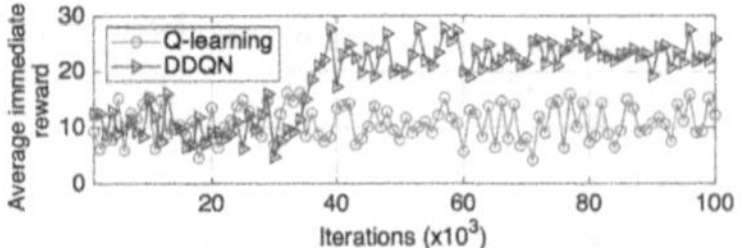

(a) Diverse required granularity level

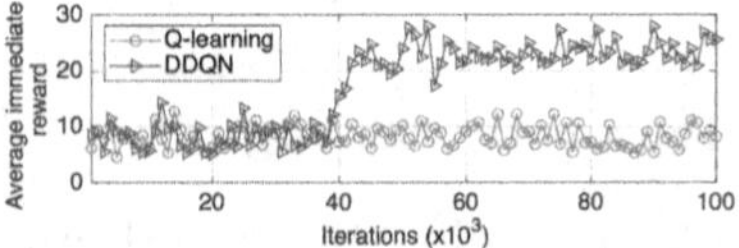

(b) High required granularity level

Fig. 5. Average reward derived from Agent1 during the training.

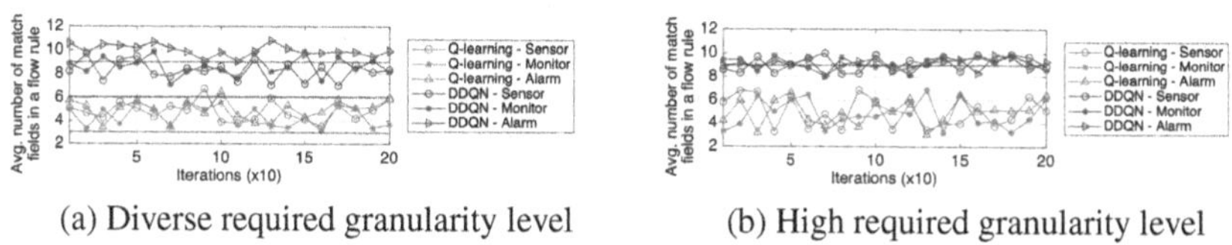

(a) Diverse required granularity level

(b) High required granularity level

Fig. 6. Average number of match fields in a flow rule derived from OvS1 during the testing.

Reliable and Win-Win Equilibrium Traffic Granularity. As demonstrated in Fig. 6), one can see that all traffic groups applying the DDQN based solution outperform those utilizing the Q-learning algorithm in terms of the average number of match fields in a flow rule during the testing phase. Accurately, in the case of *Diverse* scenario (Fig. 6 (a)), the traffic groups under the supervision of the DDQN algorithm usually account for a substantial number of match fields in a flow rule that varies from 7.0 to 11.0 ($\mathscr{M}_{max}$), and these degrees all satisfy the prerequisites. For the *High* setting (Fig. 6 (b)), due to a very high precondition of granularity ($\Theta = 9.0$) and a highly dynamic traffic behaviour, the DDQN based control agent cannot satisfy that the requirements all the time. However, in overall, it keeps a significant total degree of the gained granularity.

Data Plane Overflow Avoidance. Next, we measure the overflow frequency caused by different mechanisms during the testing phase with the *High* setting at gateways including OvS1 and OvS2, and reinforcement learning based solutions are compared with the typical ONOS flow setting that uses the MAC address, IP address, and port number. Results presented in Fig. 7 show that no overflow events are observed at two gateways in the DDQN based solution. Accordingly, the DDQN outperforms the regular ONOS flow matching and the Q-learning based mechanism in terms of the ability of data overflow avoidance.

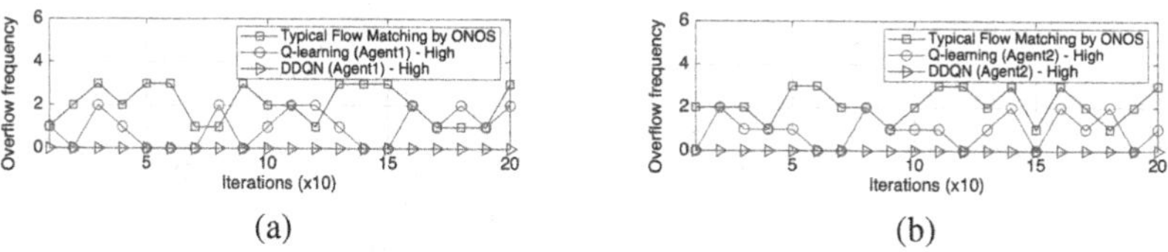

(a)

(b)

Fig. 7. Overflow frequency derived from (a) OvS1, (b) OvS2.

6 Conclusion

In this paper, we have developed the efficient IoT traffic monitoring solution employing the advances of SDN and deep reinforcement learning technique. Specifically, we first have introduced the MDP-based flow matching control system supervising a particular SDN-based IoT gateway. Next, the DDQN algorithm has been developed to maximize the average long-term traffic granularity level of all traffic groups while avoiding the overflow problem. Results obtained from extensive experiments have confirmed that the proposed monitoring approach using the DDQN algorithm can not only provide a reliable and win-win equilibrium traffic granularity level for all groups, but also completely avoid the data plane overflow issue. To the best of our knowledge, this is the first monitoring system in IoT networks, which can efficiently provide a network traffic monitoring capability in an equilibratory manner for different IoT traffic types, and the proposed approach can be applied to various IoT networks with the SDN integration.

References

1. Alam, F., Mehmood, R., Katib, I., Albogami, N.N., Albeshri, A.: Data fusion and IoT for smart ubiquitous environments: a survey. IEEE Access **5**, 9533–9554 (2017). https://doi.org/10.1109/ACCESS.2017.2697839
2. Bera, S., Misra, S., Vasilakos, A.V.: Software-defined networking for internet of things: a survey. IEEE Internet Things J. **4**(6), 1994–2008 (2017). https://doi.org/10.1109/JIOT.2017.2746186
3. Open Networking Foundation: Openflow switch specification version 1.5.1 (2020)
4. Hping3: Description of the hping3 tool, October 2020. www.hping.org
5. Mnih, V., et al.: Human-level control through deep reinforcement learning. Nature **518**, 529–533 (2015)
6. Mu, T.Y., Al-Fuqaha, A., Shuaib, K., Sallabi, F.M., Qadir, J.: SDN flow entry management using reinforcement learning. ACM Trans. Auton. Adapt. Syst. **13**(2), 11:1–11:23 (2018). https://doi.org/10.1145/3281032
7. Nguyen, T.G., Phan, T.V., Nguyen, B.T., So-In, C., Baig, Z.A., Sanguanpong, S.: SeArch: a collaborative and intelligent NIDS architecture for SDN-based cloud IoT networks. IEEE Access **7**, 107678–107694 (2019). https://doi.org/10.1109/ACCESS.2019.2932438
8. Nunes, B.A.A., Mendonca, M., Nguyen, X., Obraczka, K., Turletti, T.: A survey of software-defined networking: Past, present, and future of programmable networks. IEEE Commun. Surv. Tutor. **16**(3), 1617–1634 (Third Quarter 2014). https://doi.org/10.1109/SURV.2014.012214.00180
9. ONOS: Description of the ONOS controller, October 2020
10. Phan, X.T., Fukuda, K.: SDN-Mon: fine-grained traffic monitoring framework in software-defined networks. J. Inf. Process. **25**, 182–190 (2017). https://doi.org/10.2197/ipsjjip.25.182
11. Qiu, T., Chen, N., Li, K., Atiquzzaman, M., Zhao, W.: How can heterogeneous internet of things build our future: a survey. IEEE Commun. Surv. Tutor. **20**(3), 2011–2027 (2018). https://doi.org/10.1109/COMST.2018.2803740
12. Shin, S., Yegneswaran, V., Porras, P., Gu, G.: Avant-guard: scalable and vigilant switch flow management in software-defined networks. In: Proceedings of the 2013 ACM SIGSAC Conference on Computer & Communications Security, pp. 413–424. ACM, NY, USA (2013). https://doi.org/10.1145/2508859.2516684
13. Sutton, R.S., Barto, A.G.: Introduction to Reinforcement Learning, 1st edn. MIT Press, Cambridge (1998)
14. Van Hasselt, H., Guez, A., Silver, D.: Deep reinforcement learning with double q-learning. In: Thirtieth AAAI Conference on Artificial Intelligence (2016)

Large Scale Graph Analytics for Communities Using Graph Neural Networks

Asif Ali Banka[1,2](✉) and Roohie Naaz[1]

[1] National Institute of Technology, Srinagar, India
asifbanka@nitsri.net
[2] IUST Awantipora, Awantipora, India

Abstract. One of the challenging research areas in modern day computing is to understand, analyze and model massively connected complex graphs resulting due to highly connected networks because of newly accepted paradigm of Internet of Things. Patterns of interaction between nodes reflect a lot of information about nature of underlying network graph. The connectedness of nodes has been studied by several researchers to provide near optimal solution about topological structure of the graphs. This is more commonly known as community detection, which in mathematical and algorithmic terms is often referred to as graph partitioning. The study is broadly based on clustering of nodes, which share similar properties. Lower order connection patterns that detect communities at node and edge level are extensively studied. A wide range of algorithms has been studied to identify communities in large-scale networks. Spectral clustering, hierarchical clustering, Markov models, modularity maximization methods, etc have shown promising results in context to application domains under consideration. In this paper, the authors propose a neural network based method to identify the communities in large-scale networks. The study is broadly based on clustering of nodes, which share similar properties. This work is devoted to identify the efficacy of neural networks in community detection for large and complex networks in comparison to existing methods. The approach is motivated by neural network pipeline for data embedding into lower dimensional space, which is expected to simplify the task of clustering data into communities with inherent ability to learn between mapping and predicted communities.

Keywords: Community detection · Graph neural networks · Deep leaning · Hyper-parameter optimization

1 Introduction

Identifying group of nodes sharing similar properties is active research area in many disciplines like social science, telecommunication, computer networks, semantic web, protein networks, social networks etc. [2,4]. Community detection

S. Chellappan et al. (Eds.): CSoNet 2020, LNCS 12575, pp. 39–47, 2020.
https://doi.org/10.1007/978-3-030-66046-8_4

algorithms accept the graph as input dataset and outputs the community label for each node. Nodes in same community share similar properties with each other than with nodes outside the community. The community detection term is best fit for social networks rather than other domains where community is referred to as clusters or modules.

On the other hand, computer researchers are working day in and day out to incorporate deep learning into every field of study due to its efficient and accurate results. Deep learning has shown successful results in domains like image processing, computer vision and natural language processing etc. Relating deep learning to graphs seems challenging as graphs are sparse in nature and while deep learning shows outstanding results with dense matrices. Graphs depicting complicated relationships among objects have seeked attention from machine learning researchers to fit deep learning models over graphs that inherently are not natural fit for such models.

Dynamic nature of graphs with undefined structure and complex interconnections are challenging factors for deep learning engineers. Various supervised and unsupervised architectures have been proposed and adopted. Graph Neural Networks (GNN), Graph Convolutional Networks (GCN), Graph Auto-Encoders (GAE), Graph Recurrent Neural Networks (GRNN) and Graph Reinforcement Learning are architectures that have evolved in past few years to address graph related problems. Figure 1 presents a broad classification of deep learning methods implemented on graphs that have evolved over time. A detailed survey of these architectures is presented by Ziwei Zhang et al. in their work Deep Learning on Graphs: A Survey [14].

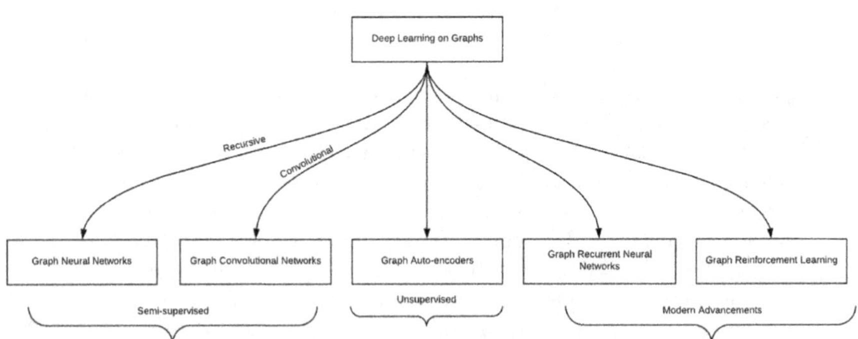

Fig. 1. GNN Classification

GNN and GCN adopt semi supervised model of machine learning where as GAE are unsupervised and GRNN and Graph Reinforcement Learning are more recent advancements in neural networks towards graph based problems. Graphs are usually studied from graph centric or node centric point of view and this distinction is emphasized more rigorously by different deep learning models. Node classification, link prediction and node recommendation are examples of node centric classification while as graph centric tasks are associated with the whole graph. Examples include graph classification, estimating certain properties of the graph and community detection [12].

2 Graph Neural Networks and Graph Convolutional Networks

Graphs are high dimensional in nature and a simple underlying principle of Graph Neural Networks (GNNs) is to represent each node as a lower dimensional state vector s_i. The state of a node may be represented to assign label to each node as $s : V \rightarrow \{1, k\}$ where k is number of labels.

Recursively the states can be represented as

$$\mathbf{s}_i = \sum_{j \in \mathcal{N}(i)} \mathcal{F}\left(\mathbf{s}_i, \mathbf{s}_j, \mathbf{F}_i^V, \mathbf{F}_j^V, \mathbf{F}_{i,j}^E\right)$$

To obtain the objective function which is to minimize loss and improve accuracy between ground-truth and predicted values, an iterative algorithm like the Jacobi method [9] followed by gradient descend is performed [1,8] until convergence. GNN unifies the recursive nature neural networks and markov chains to take advantage of states in learning parameters. GNN formalizes the basis for GCN wherein each layer reaches a stable state. Since many iterations are required for gradient descent step and all previous states are maintained, GNN becomes computationally expensive. GCN replaces the recursive nature of neural network by convolution operation. GCN is an advancement of GNN focusing on training based on learning parameter. Underlying principle of GCN is convolution, which cannot be directly used in graph due to lack of dense matrix representing graphs [11]. Convolution on graphs Laplacian $\mathcal{L}$ for first time was introduced by Bruna et al. [3,10]. Typical convolution over a graph can be defined as

$$\mathbf{u}_1 *_G \mathbf{u}_2 = \mathbf{Q}\left(\left(\mathbf{Q}^T \mathbf{u}_1\right) \odot \left(\mathbf{Q}^T \mathbf{u}_2\right)\right) \tag{1}$$

where Q are eigen vectors of $\mathcal{L}$ and u_1 and u_2 are signals defined on nodes. Filter operation $\mathbf{u}'$ on signal can therefore be defined as $\mathbf{u}' = \mathbf{Q}\Theta\mathbf{Q}^T\mathbf{u}$ where $\mathbf{u}'$ is output signal and Θ is diagonal matrix of learnable filters. Convolution can thus be defined by applying different filters on different input and output signals. Passing the input through filters that can learn and aggregate the information after transformation is underlying idea of convolution. By using node features as the input layer and stacking multiple convolutional layers, the overall architecture becomes similar to CNNs.

3 Methodology

In this study, the authors are interested in employing graph convolutional networks to detect communities using neural networks, compare the overlap with ground truth (or true community structures) and improve the accuracy. Since the neural networks are data driven and provide flexibility of learning by gradient descent and hyper-parameter optimization which make model efficient and robust against wrong heuristics. More formally, a GCN model is a neural network that operates on graphs. Given a graph $G = (V, E)$, a GCN takes as input, an input feature matrix X and an adjacency matrix A. X is a $N \times \mathbf{F}_i^V$ feature matrix, where N is the number of nodes and $\mathbf{F}^V$ represents the features for each node. Adjacency matrix A is an $N \times N$ matrix representation of the graph structure of graph G. At each layer input β is transformed via convolution applied to the array of operators[15]. The hidden layer of a neural network is represented as function of previous layer and adjacency matrix governed by a propagation rule. $H_i = f(H_{i-1}, A)$ [6].

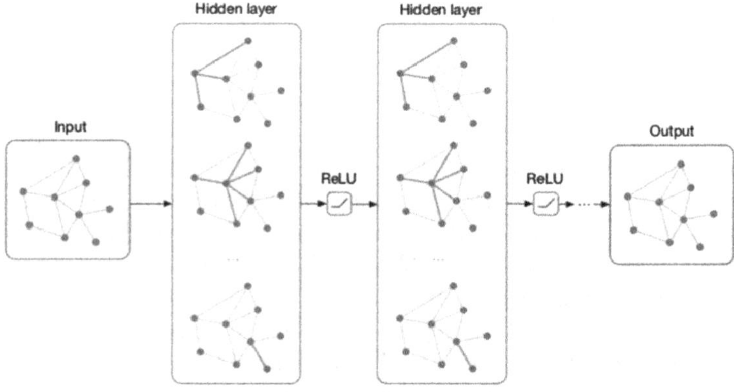

Fig. 2. GNN architecture [6]

Figure 2 is a pictorial representation of algorithm proposed in [6] for graph neural networks. Input to the first layer of model is a feature matrix X and adjacency matrix A. Features are aggregated using propagation rule f which enhances the abstraction in consecutive layers. The propagation rule may vary and one of simplest is one where weighted matrix and activation function is considered. This can be written as $f(H_i, A) = \rho(AH_iW_j)$ where W_i is the weight matrix for layer i and ρ is an activation function. This is similar to filtering operation as these weights are shared across nodes in the network. Nodes with higher degree will have larger values for their feature representation. This will explode the gradient which is typically used to train networks as they are sensitive to scale of input features. Similarly, nodes with smaller degree have diminishing effects on gradient descent which is typically used to train networks. Each node in network is represented as aggregate of features of neighbouring nodes, however, its own features are not considered if there is not any self loop. Identity matrix I is used to address self loops, as the features of node get summed to its own features before applying propagation rule. Since the feature space gets exploded, multiplying adjacency matrix with inverse degree matrix can be used to normalize the features as the weights in each row are divided by degree of each node [5]. The propagation rule is modified as $f(X, A) = D^{-1}AX$.

Algorithm 1. Graph Neural Network for Community Detection

Input: Graph $G = (V, E)$

Output: A clustering of the vertices v into k clusters. This can be encoded as a function $F : V \rightarrow \{1, 2, ..., k\}$.

procedure GNN

Input feature matrix X and an adjacency matrix A. X is a $N \times \mathbf{F}_i^V$ feature matrix, where N is the number of nodes and $\mathbf{F}^V$ represents the features for each node. Adjacency matrix A is an $N \times N$ matrix representation of the graph structure of graph G

Hidden layer is $H_i = f\,(H_{i-1}, A)$

$f\,(H_i, A) = \rho\,(AH_iW_j)$ where W_i is the weight matrix for layer i and ρ is an activation function.

Identity matrix I is used address self loops

The propagation rule is modified as $f(X, A) = D^{-1}AX$

If $\beta \in \mathbb{R}^{v \times k}$ is input where V is the number of vertices and k is the number of communities we want to detect. $\mathbb{R}^{n \times k}$ is a one-hot encoding of the clustering. The output of final layer is one hot encoding of the community labels. Finally, we divide the train and test sets by enforcing test examples to contain disjoint communities from those in the training set. Input at each layer can be represented as

$$\beta^{V+1} = \beta_1^{V+1} + \beta_2^{V+2}$$

where

$$\beta_1^{V+1} = \mu(I \cdot \beta^V, A \cdot \beta^V, D^{-1} \cdot \beta^V)$$

and

$$\beta_2^{V+1} = \rho \circ \mu(I \cdot \beta^V, A \cdot \beta^V, D^{-1} \cdot \beta^V)$$

4 Experimentation and Results

Our performance measure is the overlap between predicted and true labels, which quantifies how much better than random guessing, a predicted labelling is. The GNNs were all trained with 10, 20, 30 and 40 layers, 10 feature maps and J = 3 in the middle layers. We varied the optimization parameter and evaluated the performance for Adamax and rmsprop [5]. The learning rate was changed from 0.001 to 0.00001 with varying decay between 0 and 0.01. The effect of variation of epoches was also measured. The experimentation was performed on intel i7 processor with 32 GB RAM and 1070 GPU. All the trainings were performed on GPU.

Diverse datasets from SNAP were used to train the GNN with community labels provided. These datasets used vary from social networks to hierarchical co-purchasing networks [7]. Different dataset with known community structures enable us to understand how well the model behaves. Top 5000 quality communities provided in dataset were used. These were used to identify those edges (i, j) that cross at least two different communities. For each of such edges, we consider the two largest communities C1,C2 such that i $\notin$ C2 and j $\notin$ C1, i $\in$ C1,j $\in$ C2, and extract the subgraph determined by C1 $\cup$ C2, which is connected since all the communities are connected. Finally, we divide the train and test sets by enforcing test examples to contain disjoint communities from those in the training set. Table 1 lists the datasets used for experimentation.

Table 1. Datasets used for Graph Neural Networks.

Dataset	Number of vertices	Number of edges	Diameter	Average Degree
Amazon	334,863	925,872	44	3.4576
DBLP	317,080	1,049,866	21	6.6221
Youtube	1,134,890	2,987,624	20	5.8167

Multiple experiments were performed to realize the performance of model and performance achieved was compared with the Community-Affiliation Graph Model (AGM). The AGM is a generative model defined in [13] that allows for overlapping communities where over-lapping area have higher density. This is a statistical property observed in many real datasets with ground truth communities. The hyper-parameters like learning rate, number of layers, number of ephocs were studied. Effect of changing optimizer and batch size was also explored. Table 2 list the results for AGM experiment carried over datasets. Among the three datasets Amazon dataset showed the best results with 73.32% overlap.

Table 2. Accuracy of Community-Affiliation Graph Model

Dataset	Training size	Test size	AGMFIT overlap
Amazon	359	34	72.32
DBLP	7751	1274	64.01
Youtube	211678	33290	57.01

Figure 3(a) depicts the results for ten layer hundred ephocs and ten layer two hundred ephocs carried over datasets. DBLP dataset showed best results with 83.0724% overlap compared to Amazon and YouTube dataset on 10 layer hundred ephoc configuration, however, the accuracy of Amazon and YouTube

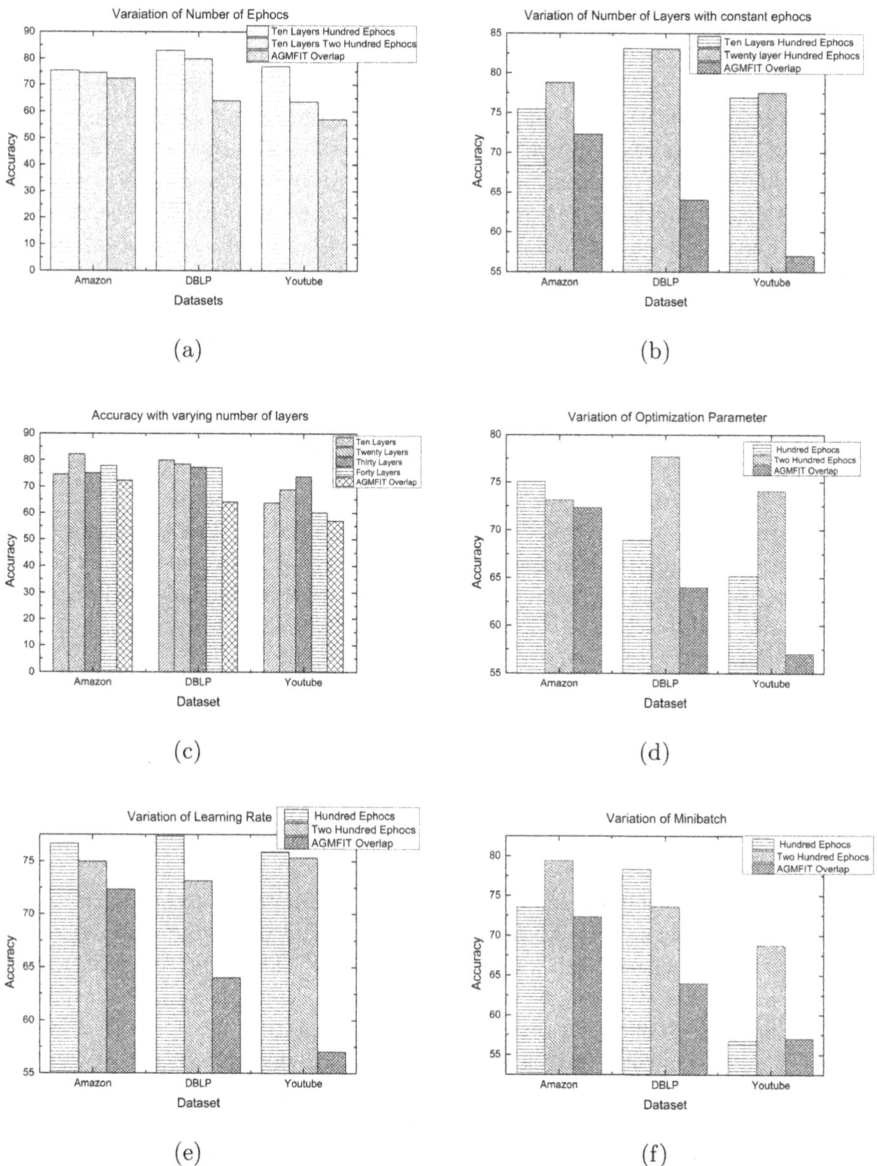

Fig. 3. Effect of variation of hyper-parameters on Community Detection.

dataset decreased on ten layer hundred ephoc configuration. DBLP dataset showed best results for twenty layers hundred configuration with 79.9042% overlap. The effect of variation of number of layers with constant ephocs was also studied. The results of variation of ten layers and twenty layers with hundred ephocs is depicted in Fig. 3(b). The overlap for ten layer configuration showed best results for DBLP dataset whereas, for twenty layer configuration Amazon dataset showed better results compared to DBLP and Youtube datasets.

Again, the experimentation was carried to study the effect of variation of number of layers on accuracy. It was observed Amazon dataset showed accuracy of 82.1791% for twenty layer whereas, it showed accuracy of 75.0693 and 77.7470% for thirty layer and forty layer neural networks respectively. For twenty layer configuration best results were obtained for DBLP dataset with 79.9042%. For thirty and forty layer configuration best results were obtained for DBLP (877.1397) and Amazon (77.7470) datasets respectively. Best accuracy for Youtube dataset was achieved with thirty layer neural network configuration. The reults are shown in Fig. 3(c).

Results for variation is change of gradient optimization technique were also studied. Among the datasets rmsprop with two hundred ephocs showed best results with 77.6961% accuracy for DBLP. Amazon dataset showed better results with rmsprop among datasets when trained with hundred ephocs only. Figure 3(d) list the results for variation in optimization technique.

The learning rate was modified and its effect was studied. The effect was studied with hundred and two hundred ephocs configurations. In general modifying learning rate with hundred ephocs showed better results that modified learning rate over two hundred ephocs. Figure 3(e) depicts the results for varying learning rate hyper-parameter.

Figure 3(f) shows the results for variarion in minibatch size hyper-parameter. The results were best obtained for Amazon dataset with an accuracy of 79.4090% in two hundred ephocs configuration.

5 Discussion

A significant contribution of this work is the study of multiple hyper-parameters and their effect on accuracy. We began the experimentation with 10 layers and model was studied with 20, 30 and 40 layers as well. The effect of variation of number of layers was also studied along with the effect of selection of optimizer. The combined effect of variation of ephocs and variation in number of layers was also studied. Learning rate and batch size were also changed to study the corresponding effect. The complexity of running time varied exponentially with respect to depth of neural network which is a function of addition and multiplication operations in neural network. The DBLP dataset showed promising results for 10 layered 100 ephoc configuration with 83.0724 overlap percentage, however it decreased as we increased the number of ephocs to 200. The decrease in accuracy is result of over-fitting of data. Amazon dataset showed 82.1791% overlap for 20 layer 200 ephoc configuration and Youtube dataset showed 77.5156% overlap with 20 layer 200 ephoc configuration. Among 10, 20, 30 and 40 layers with 200 ephocs our model showed 82.1791 % over lap for Amazon dataset for 20 layer 200 ephocs, DBLP showed 79.9042 % overlap for 10 layers and Youtube showed 73.7482% overlap for 30 layers. When the choice of optimizer was varied to rmsprop with 100 and 200 ephocs the Amazon dataset showed overlap of 75.0693 on 100 ephocs and DBLP and Youtube showed overlap of 77.6951 and 74.0590% respectively. Change of learning rate performed better with 100 ephocs only with overlap of 76.6390, 77.3466 and 75.8534 for Amazon, DBLP and Youtube datasets respectively. Only DBLP showed overlap of 78.3441 on 100 ephocs when batch size was varied. Amazon and Youtube showed overlap of 79.4090 and 68.7747 respectively on 200 ephocs settings. The results obtained with the proposed model in all configurations outperformed the accuracy achieved by AGM model.

References

1. Almeida, L.B.: A learning rule for asynchronous perceptrons with feedback in a combinatorial environment. In: Proceedings, 1st First International Conference on Neural Network, Vol. 2, pp. 609–618. IEEE (1987)
2. Aridhi, S., Nguifo, E.M.: Big graph mining: frameworks and techniques. Big Data Res. **6**, 1–10 (2016)
3. Bruna, J., Zaremba, W., Szlam, A., LeCun, Y.: Spectral networks and locally connected networks on graphs (2013). arXiv preprint: arXiv:1312.6203
4. Han, M., Daudjee, K., Ammar, K., Özsu, M.T., Wang, X., Jin, T.: An experimental comparison of pregel-like graph processing systems. Proc. VLDB Endow. **7**(12), 1047–1058 (2014)
5. Kingma, D.P., Ba, J.: Adam: a method for stochastic optimization (2014). arXiv preprint: arXiv:1412.6980
6. Kipf, T.N., Welling, M.: Semi-supervised classification with graph convolutional networks (2016). arXiv preprint: arXiv:1609.02907
7. Leskovec, J., Krevl, A.: SNAP Datasets: Stanford large network dataset collection. http://snap.stanford.edu/data (Jun 2014)
8. Pineda, F.J.: Generalization of back-propagation to recurrent neural networks. Phys. Rev. Lett. **59**(19), 2229 (1987)
9. Powell, M.J.: An efficient method for finding the minimum of a function of several variables without calculating derivatives. Comput. J. **7**(2), 155–162 (1964)
10. Scarselli, F., Gori, M., Tsoi, A.C., Hagenbuchner, M., Monfardini, G.: The graph neural network model. IEEE Trans. Neural Netw. **20**(1), 61–80 (2009)
11. Shuman, D.I., Narang, S.K., Frossard, P., Ortega, A., Vandergheynst, P.: The emerging field of signal processing on graphs: Extending high-dimensional data analysis to networks and other irregular domains (2012). arXiv preprint: arXiv:1211.0053
12. Wang, X., Cui, P., Wang, J., Pei, J., Zhu, W., Yang, S.: Community preserving network embedding. In: Thirty-First AAAI Conference on Artificial Intelligence (2017)
13. Yang, J., Leskovec, J.: Community-affiliation graph model for overlapping network community detection. In: 2012 IEEE 12th International Conference on Data Mining, pp. 1170–1175. IEEE (2012)
14. Zhang, Z., Cui, P., Zhu, W.: Deep learning on graphs: a survey (2018). CoRR abs/1812.04202: http://arxiv.org/abs/1812.04202
15. Zhou, Z., Li, X.: Graph convolution: a high-order and adaptive approach (2017). arXiv preprint: arXiv:1706.09916

Flexible Interval Intermittent Jamming Against Eavesdropping in WAVE Based Vehicular Networks

Hao Li[1] and Xiaoshuang Xing[2(✉)]

[1] The George Washington Univeristy, Washington, DC 20052, USA
haoli@gwu.edu

[2] Department of Computer Science and Engineering,
Changshu Institute of Technology, Changshu, Jiangsu, China
xing@cslg.edu.cn

Abstract. In this paper, we are focusing on the eavesdropping issue in Wireless Access in Vehicular Environments (WAVE) based vehicular networks. We proposed a flexible interval intermittent jamming (IJ) approach against the eavesdropper. This approach makes further improvement in reducing the energy cost of the existing IJ scheme while preventing eavesdropper sniffing acute information. We conducted a numerical analysis to explore and performed a simulation to compare the performance of our flexible interval IJ with the existing IJ scheme. The results show that our strategy is nearly saving 10% energy and guarantees the same security level as IJ can provide.

Keywords: WAVE · Friendly jamming · Vehicular networks · Physical layer security

1 Introduction

WAVE (Wireless Access in Vehicular Environments) based vehicular network has been considered as a promising way to improve the driving experience and safety with vehicular level information exchange playing the most critical role. Due to the broadcasting nature of wireless communication, the exchanged information, including vehicle identities, locations, speeds, and so on, are vulnerable to eavesdropping threats. To protect this private information from leakage, reliable eavesdropping defense mechanisms must be designed for WAVE based vehicular networks.

Friendly jamming is an effective approach to defense against eavesdropping [10,13,15,17,20]. Concurrent works are mainly focusing on continuous jamming (CJ) where the friendly jammer continuously sends jamming signals during the whole transmission of the legitimate transmitter. The eavesdropper is disabled while much energy is consumed by the jammer. Xing et al. argued in their recent work [24] that it is unnecessary to jam the whole transmission. A data packet can be protected from eavesdropping even if only part of the packet is jammed.

S. Chellappan et al. (Eds.): CSoNet 2020, LNCS 12575, pp. 48–58, 2020.
https://doi.org/10.1007/978-3-030-66046-8_5

Therefore, they proposed an intermittent jamming (IJ) scheme where the friendly jammer sends the jamming signal only in the jamming interval (JI) and keeps silent in the jamming-free interval (JF). This IJ scheme can keep the safety of the communication information while having a low energy cost. However, the length of JI and JF was fixed in their design (as shown in Fig. 1) without considering the length of the packet transmitted by the legitimate transmitter. The drawback of this fixed design comes from the following aspects. When the length of the transmitted packet is short, unnecessary energy will be consumed during a long JI. On the other hand, a combination of JI and JF will occur repeatedly for a long packet. The jammer should change between JI and JF frequently and energy will be wasted due to the switching loss. Therefore, the length of the transmitted packet should be considered when designing the length of JI and JF to achieve better energy efficiency.

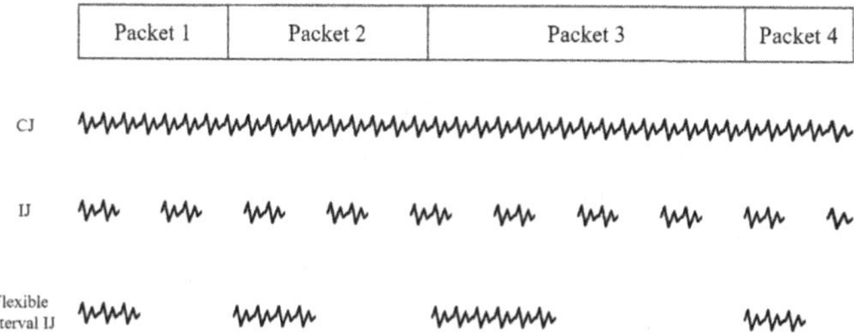

Fig. 1. Continuous jamming, intermittent jamming and flex interval intermittent jamming

In this paper, we aim at further reducing the energy cost of the IJ scheme by enabling the flexible length of JI and JF (as illustrated in Fig. 1). The following contributions are made in this paper.

- The physical packet structure in WAVE based vehicular networks is analyzed and the time length of the "Application Data", which contains the core information to be transmitted, is obtained.
- A flexible interval IJ scheme is designed where the length of JI varies with the length of the transmitted packet such that the friendly jammer disables the eavesdropper with less energy cost.
- The performance of our design is investigated through numerical study and an enhanced flexible interval IJ scheme is simulated to further reduce the energy cost.

The paper is organized as follows. The related works are discussed in Sect. 2. We illustrate the system model and formulate the problem in Sect. 3. The flexible interval IJ scheme is designed in Sect. 4. We display and analyze the numerical results in Sect. 5, and make a conclusion in Sect. 6.

2 Related Works

From the application layer to the link layer, the security threat has long been under concern [12,16,18,19]. The multimedia streaming scheme proposed in [3] aimed the security in the application layer. An authentication scheme [4,22,23] is frequently considered to ensure the confidentiality of communication in the transport layer security. The secured routing protocol proposed in [8] and [5] provide a safe transmission in the network layer. A new approach [9] is proposed to detect possible denial of service ahead of confirmation time in the link layer. A cooperative detection mechanism [7] was proposed and tested for reactive jamming.

According to the IEEE 802.11p standard, driving information is transmitted between vehicles and between vehicles and infrastructure. Sensitive information such as identity, location, speed, and direction is transmitted on the air. Due to the natural characteristics of wireless communication, despite numerous studies on a higher layer, eavesdropping attack in the physical layer is still a threat in securing sensitive information transmission. By eavesdropping this information, a malicious user may keep the track of driving information which could be used to possess and analyze driving route of legitimate user.

Friendly jamming is widely considered in defending eavesdropping attacks which is a threat to privacy and confidentiality. It can help to improve the security of vehicle localization [6], location verification [21] and secure communication [14]. In most existing friendly jamming schemes, friendly jammers keep sending signals. These schemes are known as CJ which are power consuming. In order to reduce power consumption, [2] proposes temporary jamming to provide information security when encryption is limited. A later research [24] advances an IJ scheme where the friendly jammer sends the jamming signal only in the jamming interval (JI) and keeps silent in the jamming-free interval (JF). The IJ scheme greatly decreases the power consumption while providing information security by ensuring the eavesdropper is always having a high package error rate (PER). However, this scheme fixes the length of JI and JF without considering the length of the packet transmitted by the legitimate transmitter. For a short physical packet, unnecessary energy will be consumed during a long JI. On the other hand, a combination of JI and JF will occur repeatedly for a long packet. Energy will be wasted during the frequent change between JI and JF. In order to further reduce the energy cost of the IJ scheme, this paper proposes to design flexible JI and JF depending on the length of the transmitted packet.

3 Problem Formulation

We are under a general vehicle communication scenario in vehicular network under WAVE protocol. As shown in Fig. 2, the legitimate user U_A is sending its driving information to U_B. Meanwhile, there is an eavesdropper U_E trying to overhear the packets being send. A cooperative jammer U_J located near U_A is sending jamming signals with power P_J to degrade the packets received by eavesdropper U_E.

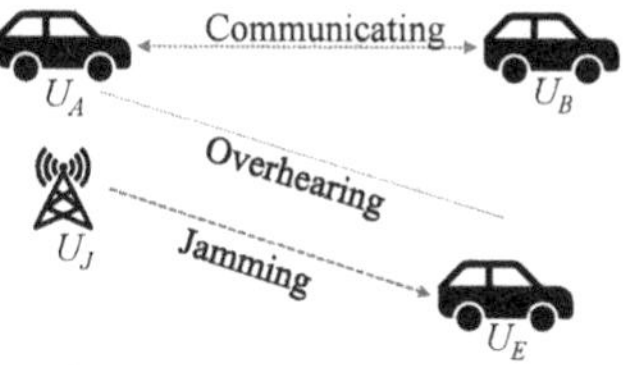

Fig. 2. General communication scenario

For a physical packet with time length T, U_J sends jamming signals in the JI with length T_J and keeps silence in the JF with length T_F. Here, $T_J \leq T$, $T_F \leq T$, and $T_J + T_F = T$. Let W_J indicate the energy cost of the cooperative jammer, B_J indicates the bit error rate (BER) of U_E during JI, B_F indicates the BER of U_E during JF, and B_E indicate U_E's average BER within T. It can be derived that

$$W_J = T_J \cdot P_J \tag{1}$$

$$B_E = \frac{T_J}{T} \cdot B_J + \frac{T_F}{T} \cdot B_F \tag{2}$$

The closed-form expressions of the BERs for different modulation schemes have been given in [11]. It can be found that BER is always an increasing function of the signal to noise plus interference ratio (SNIR), denoted by γ_b. During JF, no jamming signal is transmitted by the jammer. Therefore $\gamma_b^{JF} = \frac{E_b}{N_0}$ when calculating B_F with N_0 being the power spectral density of the noise. On the other hand, the receiving performance of U_E is degraged by the jammer during JI. Therefore, $\gamma_b^{JI} = \frac{E_b}{N_0+\phi_J}$ when calculating B_J. Here, $\phi_J = \frac{P_J|h_{JE}|^2}{B}$ is the received jamming signal power spectral density with $|h_{JE}|^2$ indicating the channel gain from U_J to U_E and B being the channel bandwidth. Obviously, $\gamma_b^{JI} \geq \gamma_b^{JF}$ and $B_J \geq B_F$. Therefore, B_E is an increasing function of T_J. According to (1), it can be found that W_J is also an increasing function of T_J. Recall that we want to disable the eavesdropping of U_E with low energy cost, we need to decide a proper T_J that can ensure a high enough BER at U_E while achieving a W_J as low as possible.

4 Design of Flexible Interval IJ Scheme

In order to obtain a high enough B_E while maintaining a low W_J, the jammer should transmit jamming signals only during the transmission time of the most significant part of the physical packet. Figure 3 shows the component of a physical packet. Intuitively, the "Application Data" contains the core information to be transmitted by U_A to U_B. Therefore, "Application Data" is the most significant part of the physical packet. If the jammer can identify the time duration within which the "Application Data" is transmitted and send jamming signals only during this time, U_E's eavesdropping will be disabled and U_J's energy cost

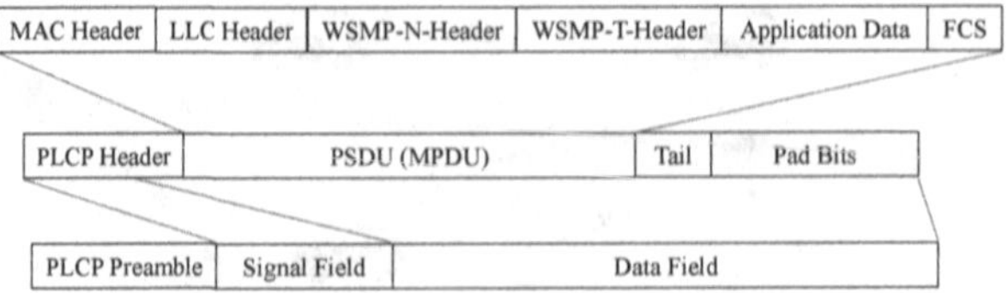

Fig. 3. Physical packet structure

will be reduced. Therefore, the main challenge to be solved in our design is to identify the time duration within which the "Application Data" is transmitted.

According to [1], a physical packet is consisting of a 16 µs PLCP preamble, a 4 µs Signal Field, and a variable-length Data Field. The Data Field is constructed by 16 bits of the PLCP Header, the WSMP-T-Header, the WSMP-N-Header, the LLC Header, the MAC Header, 32 bits FCS, 6 bits Tail, and variable-length Application Data. Moreover, n bits pad bits are also added in the Data Field to make the length of the Data Field divisible by N_{DBPS}. Therefore, n takes value between 0 to $N_{DBPS} - 1$. The value of N_{DBPS} depends on the modulation schemes and the coding rates. Typical values of N_{DBPS} in WAVE based vehicular networks are listed in Table 1.

Table 1. Values of N_{DBPS} for different modulation schemes and coding rates

Modulation	Coding Rate	N_{DBPS} (bits)	Modulation	Coding Rate	N_{DBPS} (bits)
BPSK	1/2	24	16-QAM	1/2	96
BPSK	3/4	36	16-QAM	3/4	144
QPSK	1/2	48	64-QAM	2/3	192
QPSK	3/4	72	64-QAM	3/4	216

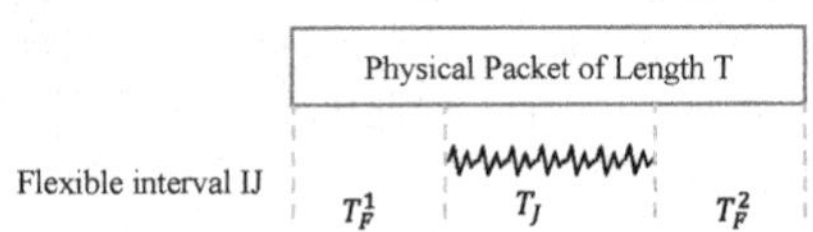

Fig. 4. Flexible interval IJ scheme for a physical packet of length T

When the Data Field is constructed, it will be divided into symbols. Each symbol consists of N_{DBPS} bits and is 4 µs long in time. According to [24], the minimum length of the WSMP-T-Header, the WSMP-N-Header, the LLC Header, and the MAC Header are 2 bytes, 2 bytes, 2 bytes, and 24 bytes respectively. There are a total of 30 bytes, which are 240 bits, in the physical packet before the Application Data in the Data Field. In time domain, the time length of these 240 bits will be $t_1 = \frac{240}{N_{DBPS}} \times 4\,\mu s$. As mentioned before, there are 6 bits tail bits, 32 bits FCS, and 0 to $N_{DBPS} - 1$ bits pad bits after the Application Data. These are total 38 to $37 + N_{DBPS}$ bits and the time length of these bits is denoted by t_2. t_2 takes value from $\frac{38}{N_{DBPS}} \times 4\,\mu s$ to $\frac{37+N_{DBPS}}{N_{DBPS}} \times 4\,\mu s$. Since the PLCP preamble, the Signal Field, and the headers are transmitted before the Application Data. The time length before transmitting the Application Data in the physical packet, which is denoted by T_F^1, can be calculated as $T_F^1 = 16\,\mu s + 4\,\mu s + t_1$. On the other hand, the FCS, the tail bits, and the pad bits are transmitted after the Application Data. Therefore, the time length after transmitting the Application Data in the physical packet, which is denoted by T_F^2, can be calculated as $T_F^2 = t_2$. Then, for a physical packet of length T, the flexible interval IJ scheme will be designed as shown in Fig. 4. According to the value of N_{DBPS} given Table 1, the value of T_F^1, T_F^2 can be easily obtained. For example, $T_F^1 = 60\,\mu s$ and $6.3\,\mu s \leq T_F^2 \leq 10.17\,\mu s$ when the physical packet is BPSK modulated with coding rate being $\frac{1}{2}$. Then, we have $T_J = T - T_F = T - T_F^1 - T_F^2$. Theoretically, the best anti-eavesdropping performance can be achieved when T_F^2 takes the lower bound value, which is $T_F^2 = 6.3\,\mu s$ in the aforementioned example. While most energy can be saved when T_F^2 takes the upper bound value, that is $T_F^2 = 10.17\,\mu s$ in the example.

5 Numerical Results

In this section, we validate the performance of our design for securing the transmission of the physical packets with varying lengths. The length of the physical packet is indicated by the length of the PSDU part shown in Fig. 3. The performance of the proposed flexible interval IJ scheme is compared with the IJ scheme proposed in [24]. Besides, the performance of our design when T_F^2 takes the lower bound value (referred to as FIJ-shortest TF in the following) and the upper bound value (referred to as FIJ-longest TF in the following) is also investigated. The simulation is performed in MATLAB 2018b and using the WLAN toolbox. We use function ‘wlanNonHTConfig’ to generate non-HT packets transmitted in WAVE based vehicular network. The channel bandwidth is set to 10 MHz and we are using the default sampling rate for 10 MHz. We set the delay profile as ‘Urban NLOS’ because most of the V2V communication happens in an urban area and do not have a line of sight. BPSK modulation is used and the coding rate r is set to be $\frac{1}{2}$ and $\frac{3}{4}$.

The performance comparison is conducted from two aspects. To validate the anti-eavesdropping performance of our design, the packet error rate (PER) of U_E, which is the ratio of the number of physical packets not successfully decoded by U_E to the number of the physical packets sent by the transmitter U_A, is adopted. The function ‘V2VPERSimulator’ from MATLAB is utilized to simulate the PER. The energy cost for sending jamming signals referred to as the jamming energy cost in the following is used to investigate the energy efficiency of our design.

According to [24], the optimal transmission power of U_J is set to be $P_J = 760\,\mathrm{mW}$ for BPSK modulation with coding rate r being $\frac{1}{2}$. The corresponding T_J and T_F are 47.12 us, and 28.88 us respectively in the IJ scheme. While for BPSK modulation with $r = \frac{3}{4}$, the IJ scheme is set as $P_J = 760\,\mathrm{mW}$, $T_J = 37.2\,\mathrm{us}$, and $T_F = 22.8\,\mathrm{us}$. The setting of the IJ scheme is fixed regardless of the length of the transmitted physical packet. On the other hand, the length of T_J and $T_F = T_F^1 + T_F^2$ in our design are flexible which can be calculated as given in Sect. 4. U_J's transmission power in our flexible interval IJ scheme is set to be the same as that in the IJ scheme, which is $P_J = 760\,\mathrm{mW}$.

We change the length of the PSDU from 38 Octets to 438 Octets and the PER of U_E is shown in Fig. 5. It can be found that U_E's PER increases with the increasing of the PSDU length for schemes other than FIJ-shortest TF. With the increase of the PSDU length, more information bits are enclosed in a physical packet. The probability of information bits within a physical packet being incorrectly decoded will increase resulting in an increased PER. For the FIJ-shortest TF scheme, U_E's SNR keeps low since U_J sends jamming signals during the whole transmission time of the "Application Data". Therefore, U_E's PER is always close to 100% regardless of the PSDU length. Small performance fluctuations occur for the FIJ-longest TF scheme. In the FIJ-longest TF scheme, the length of TF_2 is fixed to be $\frac{37+N_{DBPS}}{N_{DBPS}} \times 4\,\mu\mathrm{s}$ by assuming that there are always $N_{DBPS} - 1$ pad bits in the physical packet. However, the length of the pad bits varies with the PSDU length leading to insufficient jamming of the "Application Data" for some PSDU length and thus performance fluctuations on U_E's PER. Moreover, one can see that a higher coding rate r causes a higher PER. A higher r implies more information bits and less redundant bits are enclosed in a physical packet, which means that more information is transmitted in a physical packet and the transmission efficiency is improved. However, the redundant bits play an important role in error correction, and less redundant bits can decrease U_E's error correction capability and lead to a higher PER.

The results regarding the jamming energy cost are given in Fig. 6. We found that our flexible interval IJ scheme consumes less energy when the physical packet is short (for example when the PSDU is 100 bytes long). While for long physical packets, the IJ scheme performs better in terms of energy cost. This is because the length of T_J and T_F is fixed in IJ. In other words, $\frac{T_J}{T}$ is fixed for any PSDU length (i,e, any physical packet length). In the flexible interval IJ scheme, the length of $T_F = T_F^1 + T_F^2$ is fixed, while the length of $T_J = T - T_F$ increases with the length of the physical packet. Therefore, $\frac{T_J}{T}$ increases with the increasing of the PSDU length leading to more jamming energy cost compared with the IJ scheme propose in [24].

In order to further improve the jamming energy cost of the flexible interval IJ scheme. We conduct enhanced-FIJ in our simulation study. The enhanced-FIJ is designed by taking the same TF_1 and TF_2 as that of the FIJ scheme. While for the "Application Data" transmitted within T_J, the IJ scheme proposed in [24] is applied. That is, T_J is further divided into sub-jamming intervals and sub-jamming-free intervals according to the IJ scheme proposed in [24]. The

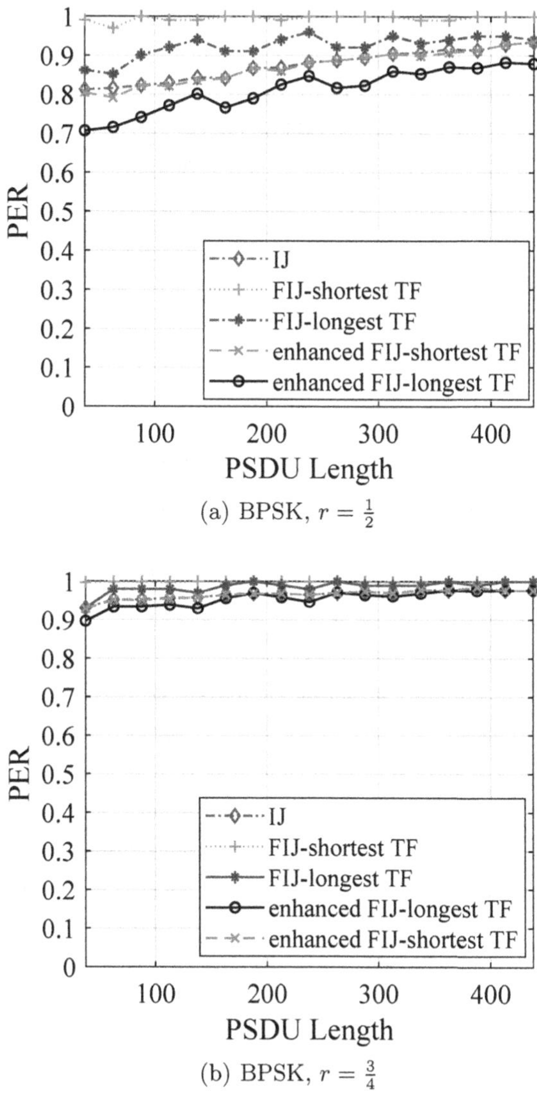

(a) BPSK, $r = \frac{1}{2}$

(b) BPSK, $r = \frac{3}{4}$

Fig. 5. Packet Error Rate comparison with different PSDU length

performance of enhanced FIJ-shortest TF and enhanced FIJ-longest TF are shown by green dashed lines and black solid lines in Fig. 5 and Fig. 6. We found that enhanced FIJ-shortest TF can achieve PER performance almost the same as the IJ scheme while saving 10% energy.

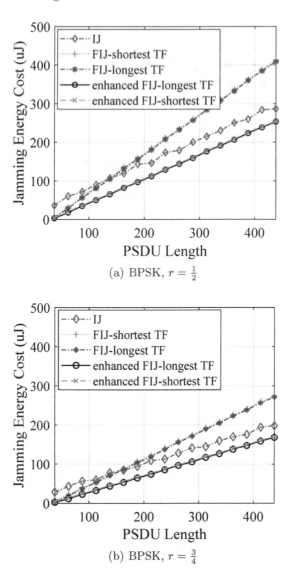

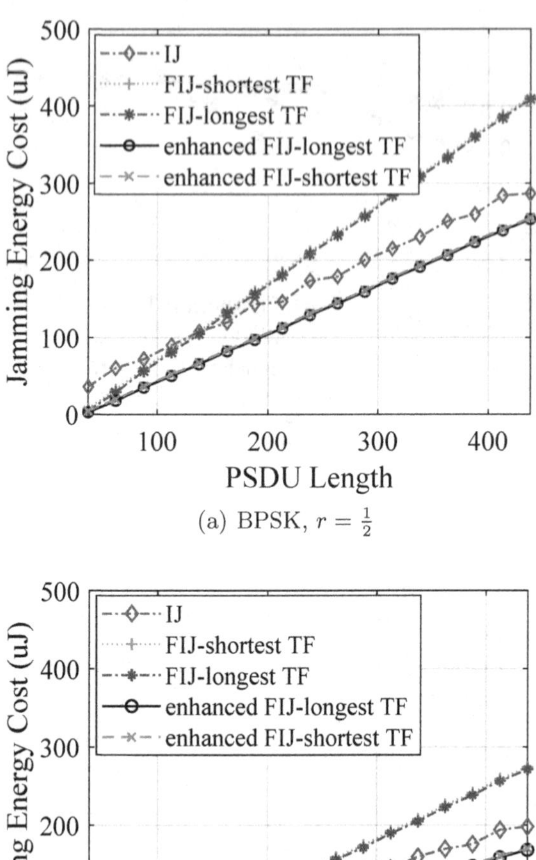

(a) BPSK, $r = \frac{1}{2}$

(b) BPSK, $r = \frac{3}{4}$

Fig. 6. Jamming energy cost comparison with different PSDU length

6 Conclusion

In conclusion, our contribution is providing a method to save more energy when dealing with eavesdropping attacks in WAVE based vehicular networks. The proposed flexible interval IJ approach can further save more energy than the existing IJ approach. Simulation results confirm our design is capable of defense against the eavesdropping attacks while enhancing the performance in energy saving.

References

1. IEEE standard for information technology-telecommunications and information exchange between systems local and metropolitan area networks-specific requirements part 11: Wireless LAN medium access control (MAC) and physical layer (PHY) specifications. IEEE Std 802.11-2012 (Revision of IEEE Std 802.11-2007), pp. 1–2793 (2012)
2. Allouche, Y., Arkin, E.M., Cassuto, Y., Efrat, A., Grebla, G., Mitchell, J.S., Sankararaman, S., Segal, M.: Secure communication through jammers jointly optimized in geography and time. Perv. Mob. Comput. **41**, 83–105 (2017)
3. Challita, U., Ferdowsi, A., Chen, M., Saad, W.: Machine learning for wireless connectivity and security of cellular-connected UAVs. IEEE Wirel. Commun. **26**(1), 28–35 (2019)
4. Cui, J., Zhang, J., Zhong, H., Xu, Y.: SPACF: a secure privacy-preserving authentication scheme for VANET with cuckoo filter. IEEE Trans. Veh. Technol. **66**(11), 10283–10295 (2017)
5. DasGupta, S., Chaki, R., Choudhury, S.: SBRPV: Security based routing protocol for vehicular ad hoc networks. In: 2019 4th International Conference on Computer Science and Engineering (UBMK), pp. 745–750. IEEE (2019)
6. Deka, B., Gerdes, R.M., Li, M., Heaslip, K.: Friendly jamming for secure localization in vehicular transportation. In: Tian, J., Jing, J., Srivatsa, M. (eds.) SecureComm 2014. LNICST, vol. 152, pp. 212–221. Springer, Cham (2015). https://doi.org/10.1007/978-3-319-23829-6_16
7. Del-Valle-Soto, C., Mex-Perera, C., Aldaya, I., Lezama, F., Nolazco-Flores, J.A., Monroy, R.: New detection paradigms to improve wireless sensor network performance under jamming attacks. Sensors **19**(11), 2489 (2019)
8. Feng, L., Xiu-Ping, Y., Jie, W.: Security transmission routing protocol for MIMO-VANET. In: Proceedings of 2014 International Conference on Cloud Computing and Internet of Things, pp. 152–156. IEEE (2014)
9. Fotohi, R., Ebazadeh, Y., Geshlag, M.S.: A new approach for improvement security against DOS attacks in vehicular ad-hoc network (2020). arXiv preprint: arXiv:2002.10333
10. Gao, Q., Huo, Y., Ma, L., Xing, X., Cheng, X., Jing, T., Liu, H.: Joint design of jammer selection and beamforming for securing MIMO cooperative cognitive radio networks. IET Commun. **11**(8), 1264–1274 (2017)
11. Goldsmith, A.: Wireless Communications. Stanford University, California (2004)
12. Hasrouny, H., Samhat, A.E., Bassil, C., Laouiti, A.: VANET security challenges and solutions: a survey. Veh. Commun. **7**, 7–20 (2017)
13. Huo, Y., Fan, X., Ma, L., Cheng, X., Tian, Z., Chen, D.: Secure communications in tiered 5G wireless networks with cooperative jamming. IEEE Trans. Wirel. Commun. **18**(6), 3265–3280 (2019)
14. Lee, H., Eom, S., Park, J., Lee, I.: UAV-aided secure communications with cooperative jamming. IEEE Trans. Veh. Technol. **67**(10), 9385–9392 (2018)
15. Li, Y., Zhang, R., Zhang, J., Gao, S., Yang, L.: Cooperative jamming for secure UAV communications with partial eavesdropper information. IEEE Access **7**, 94593–94603 (2019)
16. Mejri, M.N., Ben-Othman, J., Hamdi, M.: Survey on VANET security challenges and possible cryptographic solutions. Veh. Commun. **1**(2), 53–66 (2014)
17. Mobini, Z., Mohammadi, M., Tellambura, C.: Wireless-powered full-duplex relay and friendly jamming for secure cooperative communications. IEEE Trans. Inform. Forens. Secur. **14**(3), 621–634 (2018)

18. Mokhtar, B., Azab, M.: Survey on security issues in vehicular ad hoc networks. Alex. Eng. J. **54**(4), 1115–1126 (2015)
19. Raya, M., Hubaux, J.P.: Securing vehicular ad hoc networks. J. Comput. Secur. **15**(1), 39–68 (2007)
20. Siyari, P., Krunz, M., Nguyen, D.N.: Distributed power control in single-stream MIMO wiretap interference networks with full-duplex jamming receivers. IEEE Trans. Signal Process. **67**(3), 594–608 (2018)
21. Tithi, T., Deka, B., Gerdes, R.M., Winstead, C., Li, M., Heaslip, K.: Analysis of friendly jamming for secure location verification of vehicles for intelligent highways. IEEE Trans. Veh. Technol. **67**(8), 7437–7449 (2018)
22. Wang, X., Li, S., Zhao, S., Xia, Z.: A VANET privacy protection scheme based on fair blind signature and secret sharing algorithm. Automatika **58**(3), 287–294 (2017)
23. Wei, Z., Li, J., Wang, X., Gao, C.Z.: A lightweight privacy-preserving protocol for VANETS based on secure outsourcing computing. IEEE Access **7**, 62785–62793 (2019)
24. Xing, X., Sun, G., Qian, J.: Intermittent Jamming for Eavesdropping Defence in WAVE based Vehicular Networks, pp. 1–10 (2019)

Graph Neural Network Combined Knowledge Graph for Recommendation System

Dong Nguyen Tien and Hai Pham Van(✉)

Hanoi University of Science and Technology, Hanoi, Vietnam
dongnguyentien1996@gmail.com, haipv@soict.hust.edu.vn

Abstract. With a view to increase recommendation systems accuracy and practical applicability, using traditional methods which are namely interaction model between users and items, collaborative filtering and matrix factorization cannot achieve the supposed results. In fact, the properties between users or items always remains as social and knowledge relations. In this paper, we have proposed a new graph deep learning model associated with knowledge graph with the aim of modeling the latent feature of user and item. We exploit the relations of items based on knowledge graph as well as the relationships between users in social. Our model supplies the principle of organizing interactions as a graph, combines information from social network and all kind of relations in the heterogeneous knowledge graph. The model is evaluated on real world datasets to demonstrate this method's effectiveness.

Keywords: Recommendation system · Graph neural network · Knowledge graph · Social recommendation

1 Introduction

The traditional method of the RS is collaborative filtering [1], based on the behavior of users and modeling their interactions by analyzing matrix factorization [2] or neural networks. In the recent years, neural network technology for graph data have made lots of remarkable developments [3] which are called Graph Neural Networks (GNN) [4]. In terms of creating features, recent studies like [6, 7] not only use individual features but also link them together to form knowledge graph (KG). KG is a directional heterogeneous graph where the nodes correspond to the items and the edges correspond to the relationships. Combining KG benefits the results in three ways: (1) The rich semantic relatedness among items in a KG can help explore their latent connections and improve the precision of results; (2) Different types of relation in a KG are useful to logically extend user interests and increase the variety of proposed items; (3) KG connects a user's historically-liked and recommended items. In Fig. 1, the graph includes social relations, interaction graph between users and items, and knowledge graph of items. As a result, with its advantages, incorporating GNNs with the KG provides an unprecedented opportunity to enhance the results.

S. Chellappan et al. (Eds.): CSoNet 2020, LNCS 12575, pp. 59–70, 2020.
https://doi.org/10.1007/978-3-030-66046-8_6

This paper has presented a new model to assemble multiple aspects of data which is shown in Fig. 1, simultaneously addressing the mentioned challenges. Contributions include: Propose a model combining a KG called **KconvGraphRec**; provide an approach to building model from three base graphs and combine them to make predictions, experiment and demonstrate the effectiveness on real world datasets.

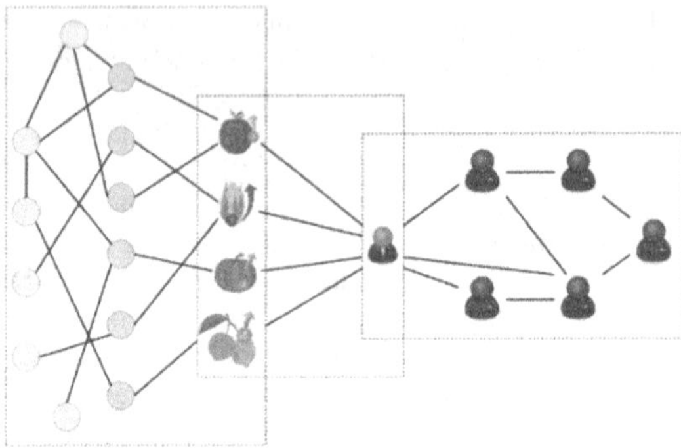

Fig. 1. Graph data in recommendation system. Includes interaction graph between user - item (middle), user social relationship graph (right corner) and items knowledge graph (left corner)

2 Related Work

Recently, the application of graph neural networks in recommendation systems, using data from social relations and knowledge graph to make representation vector for users and items. The exploitation of data related to the user's social relationship is great interest recently [8, 9]. One common assumption about these models is that a user's preference is like or influenced by the people around him/her (nearest neighbours), which can be proven by social correlation theories [10]. TrustMF [11] modeled mutual influence between users, and mapped into two low-dimensional spaces: truster space and trustee space, by factorizing social trust networks. SoDimRec [12] applies community detection algorithms to divide users into clusters, then exploits the social relationships and weakly dependent connections. A comprehensive overview of the social relations recommendation system can be found in the survey [13].

Although neural network had flourished but the use in social recommendation systems was unusual by far. NeuMF [1] presented a neural collaborative filtering model to learn non-linear interactions between users and items. For graph data, there have been currently studies of applying neural networks to graph data and have proven their effectiveness compared to conventional data types [14]. GraphRec [15] - state of the art model for applying social relations data of users and the interaction between users and items.

Knowledge graph is being abundantly studied lately [8, 16]. However, the fact that KG is directly applied to the RS is still insignificant. KGAT [8] proposes the attention mechanism for the KG, the end-to-end framework in order to model high-order structural connections in graph neural networks. KGCN [17] uses the idea of convolution graph network to predict binary subclass. This method works directly on the original graph and determines convolutional for group of nodes. In order to process different sized neighborhoods and maintain the sharing information, the researchers proposed sample a fixed-sized neighborhood group in KGCN. DKN [18] focused on solving by embedding the KG, capturing the ratings from the users to the item with their implicit relationships. DKEN explores the relationship between users and entities that interact with items in the KG. Lately, HAGERec [19], which is further improved from KGCN, can aggregate more hops and change the model to evaluate the impact of users in KG.

3 The Proposed Model

3.1 Definitions and Notations

Let $U = \{u_1, u_2, \ldots, u_n\}$ and $V = \{v_1, v_2, \ldots, v_m\}$ are the set of users and items respectively, where n is number of users and m is number of items. We assume $R \in R^{n \times m}$ is interaction matrix users-items. If u_i rate item v_j, r_{ij} is a rating score, otherwise $r_{ij} = 0$. Let $N(i)$ is set of users have relations with user u_i in social graph, C(i) is set of items which rated by user u_i and B(j) is set of users who have interacted item v_j. Social graph $T \in R^{n \times n}$ with $T_{ij} = 1$ if u_i has a relation to user u_j and 0 otherwise. Knowledge graph $\mathfrak{G}$, form with triple entity – relation – entity (h_g, r_g, t_g) where $h_g \in \mathcal{E}, t_g \in \mathcal{E}, r_g \in \mathfrak{R}$ are head, tail and relation respectively. ε, $\mathfrak{R}$ are the number of entities và relations in this knowledge graph. Then users-items **R**, social relations graph **T** và knowledge graph $\mathfrak{G}$, we aim to predict the missing rating value r of set user-item in **R.** We use user embedding vector u_i is $p_i \in R^d$, item embedding vector v_j is $q_j \in R^d$ where d is number dimension of embedding vector.

3.2 The Proposed Model

In this paper, the data input included: rating data users to items, social data and knowledge graph for items (entity). These datasets will be modeled concurrently and processed with the output set as the result of predictive rating of user – item.

The proposed model includes 3 parts as follows: user modeling, item modeling and rating modeling. Firstly, user modeling which to learn user latent vector. Because the data includes two different of graph: social graph and interaction graph, two aggregations are introduced to respectively process these two different graphs. The second component is item modeling, which learn item latent vector.

3.3 User Modeling

User modeling aims to learn user latent vector, denoted as $h_i \in R^d$ for user u_i. First is aggregator from item space $h_i^I \in R^d$ of interaction graph. The second aggregate from social space $h_i^S \in R^d$. After that, they are combined to the final user latent vector h_i

Item Aggregation

Interactions between user and item contain rating score from 1 to 5. The purpose of item aggregation is to learn item-space latent vector, which has a function as (Fig. 2):

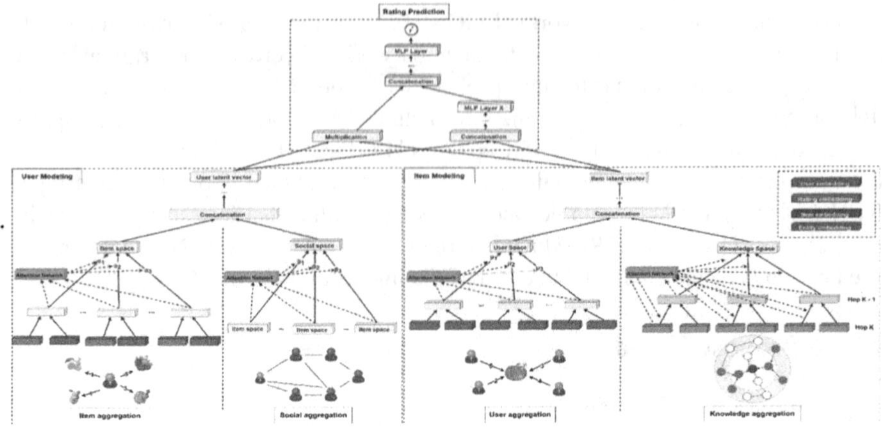

Fig. 2. Detailed architecture of the proposed model KconvGraphRec

$$h_i^I = \sigma(W.Aggre_{items}(\{x_{ia}, \forall a \in C(i)\}) + b) \tag{1}$$

With C(i) set of items which are interacted by *user* u_i, x_{ia} is representation vector to denote opinion-aware interaction from *user* u_i to *item* v_a and $Aggre_{items}$ is aggregation function. W, b, σ are hyper parameter of neural network. To modeling opinions, we have opinion embedding vector $e_r \in R^d$ of rating $r \in \{1, 2, 3, 4, 5\}$ respectively. For each rating, x_{ia} combined vector item embedding q_a vector opinion embedding e_r via Multi-Layer Perceptron (MLP), denoted as g_v:

$$x_{ia} = g_v([q_a \oplus e_r]) \tag{2}$$

where $\oplus$ is concatenation operation. Next, we will introduce of $Aggre_{items}$:

$$h_i^I = \sigma\left(W.\left\{\sum\nolimits_{\alpha \in C(i)} \alpha_{ia} x_{ia}\right\} + b\right) \tag{3}$$

Where α_{ia} is coefficient attention, output of 2 layers neural network and obtained by normalizing using softmax function:

$$\alpha_{ia}^* = W_2^T.\sigma(W_1.[x_{ia} \oplus p_i] + b_1) + b_2 \tag{4}$$

$$\alpha_{ia} = \frac{\exp(\alpha_{ia}^*)}{\sum_{\alpha \in C(i)} \exp(\alpha_{ia}^*)} \tag{5}$$

Social Aggregation

The social correlation theories [14] have demonstrated the impact of the relationship between people on the interests of each individual. The relationship depends on how much of general interaction according users. In other words, constructing the user vector from social space needs to consider heterogeneous relationships in society. Then, the social space user latent vector as the follow:

$$h_i^S = \sigma(W.Aggre_{neighbors}(\{h_i^o, o \in N(i)\}) + b) \tag{6}$$

$$h_i^S = \sigma\left(W.\left\{\sum\nolimits_{o\in N(i)} \beta_i h_i^o\right\} + b\right) \tag{7}$$

With β_i is the attention score, built via 2 layers neural network from item-space vector with user embedding vector p_i.

$$h_i^S = \sigma\left(W.\left\{\sum\nolimits_{o\in N(i)} \beta_{io} h_i^o\right\} + b\right) \tag{8}$$

$$\beta_{io}^* = W_2^T.\sigma\left(W_1.\left[h_i^o \oplus p_i\right] + b_1\right) + b_2 \tag{9}$$

$$\beta_{io} = \frac{\exp\left(\beta_{io}^*\right)}{\sum_{o\in N(i)} \exp\left(\beta_{io}^*\right)} \tag{10}$$

Learning User Latent Vector

In order to learn better user latent vector, social space and item space need to be considered together, since the social graph and interaction graph supply 2 aspect of user. We combine these two latent factors via standard MLP. Formally, with l is the number of hidden layers, the user latent vector is defined as:

$$c_1 = \left[h_i^I \oplus h_i^S\right] \tag{11}$$

$$c_2 = \sigma(W_2.c_1 + b_2) \tag{12}$$

$$h_i = \sigma(W_l.c_{l-1} + b_l) \tag{13}$$

3.4 Item Modeling

Item latent vector, denoted as z_j, is the combination of two components: user aggregation and knowledge aggregation. We are not only construct from the interactions of all users for item v_j, but also utilizing the information from KG of items.

User Aggregation

Similar with User modeling, each *item* v_j, we synthesis all interaction of *users* who rated with *item* v_j, denoted as B(j). Even on the same item, users might express different opinions. These opinions from different users can capture the characteristics of the same item in different ways, which help to learn better item latent. For an interaction user u_t to *item* v_j with rating r, the function f_{jt} which is obtained from the user embedding p_t and opinion embedding e_r via a MLP, denoted as g by following:

$$f_{jt} = g_u\left(\left[p_t \oplus e_r\right]\right) \tag{14}$$

Then, attention mechanism to differentiate the importance weight μ_{jt}, represent the influence of different user for different item, it depends on rating score:

$$z_j^U = \sigma\left(W.\left\{\sum\nolimits_{t\in B(j)} \mu_{jt}.f_{jt}\right\} + b\right) \tag{15}$$

$$\mu_{jt}^{*} = W_2^T.\sigma\left(W_1.\left[f_{jt} \oplus q_j\right] + b_1\right) + b_2 \tag{16}$$

$$\mu_{jt} = \frac{\exp\left(\mu_{jt}^{*}\right)}{\sum_{t \in B(j)} \exp\left(\mu_{jt}^{*}\right)} \tag{17}$$

Knowledge Aggregation

In KG, item (entity) has many relations in triple (head, relation, tail). The key idea is to aggregate and incorporate neighborhood information when calculating the representation of a given entity. This design has advantages: (1) Through the neighborhood, the local proximity structure is captured and stored in each entity. (2) Neighbors are weighted dependent on the relation and specific user, which characterizes both the semantic information and users 'personalized interests. (3) Attention mechanism leveraging weight have well-established node classification. To resolve the size of an entity's neighbors varies and maybe large, we sample a fixed-size neighborhood.

For each pair user u_i and item (entity) v_j. Having $N_g(v)$ is set of entities which have relationship with item v_j and so we denote r_{e_i,e_j} is the relation score of entity e_i and e_j. We have a function to calculate score between user and relation in KG:

$$\pi_r^u = g(u \oplus v) \tag{18}$$

Where $u \in R^d$ và $r \in R^d$ are the representations of user and item v and d is the dimension vector. Weight π_r^u represents the importance of relation r to user u. To alleviate the limitation of mean-based aggregator, we utilize MLP to build attention weigh to express the specificity of each user for specific relation in knowledge graph:

$$\pi_r^u = W_2^T.\sigma(W_1.[u \oplus v] + b_1) + b_2 \tag{19}$$

To characterize the topological proximity structure of item v, we compute the linear combination of v's neighborhood.

$$v_{N_g(v)}^u = \sum_{e \in N_g(n)} \tilde{\pi}_{r_{v,e}}^u \boldsymbol{e} \tag{20}$$

$$\tilde{\pi}_{r_{v,e}}^u = \frac{\exp\left(\pi_{r_{v,e}}^u\right)}{\sum_{e \in N_g(n)} \exp\left(\pi_{r_{v,e}}^u\right)} \tag{21}$$

Where $\tilde{\pi}_{r_{v,e}}^u$ is the normalized user-relation score, $\boldsymbol{e}$ is entity embedding vector and $\tilde{\pi}_{r_{v,e}}^u$ is the attention score. We uniformly sample a fixed size set of neighbors. The neighborhood area of entity v and $v_{S_g(v)}^u$, where $S(v) = \left\{e|e \in N_g(v) \,\&\, \left|S_g(v)\right| = K\right\}$, K is constant. Finally, we aggregate the entity representation v and its neighborhood $v_{S_g(v)}^u$ into single vector: $R^d \times R^d \rightarrow R^d$ (Fig. 3).

$$z_j^K = \sigma\left(W.\left(v + v_{S_g(v)}^u\right) + b\right) \tag{22}$$

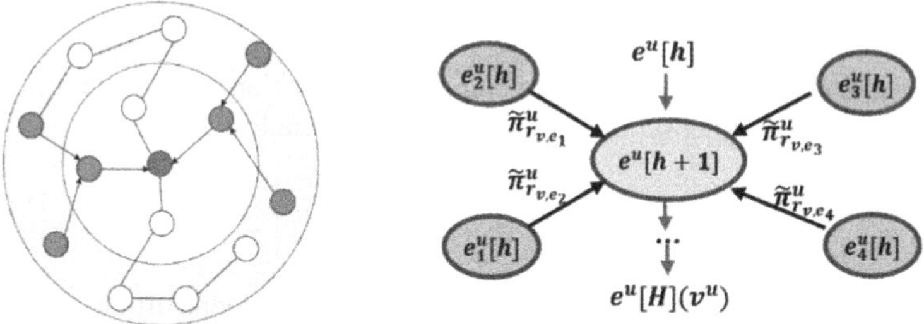

Fig. 3. The neighborhood (green entities) in 2 hops of item (blue entity) in KG (left corner). The formation to aggregate the information set of neighboring nodes about item (right corner) (Color figure online)

Learning Item Latent Vector

To learning item latent vector, user-space and knowledge-space item latent vector are needed to be combined. We combine these by two latent factors via a standard MLP. With l is number of hidden layers, item latent vector is denoted as:

$$c_1 = \left[z_j^U \oplus z_j^K\right] \tag{23}$$

$$z_j = \sigma(W_l.c_{l-1} + b_l) \tag{24}$$

3.5 Rating Prediction

In this section, we combine item latent vector and user latent vector for rating prediction. In this work, we apply method which is proposed in NeuMF [1]. We utilize Generalized Matrix Factorization (GMF) and Multi-layer perceptron (MLP). Then, we combine these models together to superimpose their desirable characteristics before feeding into neural network standard to calculate final rating prediction. GMF use the operator element wise of user latent vector and item latent vector while MLP concatenate latent vector of user and item as input and feed into neural network.

Finally, concatenation g_{gmf} and g_{mlp} to feed into NeuMF to predict final score:

$$g_1 = \left[g_{gmf} \oplus g_{mlp}\right] \tag{25}$$

$$g_{k-1} = \sigma(W_{k-1}.g_{k-1} + b_{k-1})$$

$$r'_{ij} = W^T.g_{k-1} \tag{26}$$

Where k is the number of hidden layers and r'_{ij} is prediction score of user u_i to item v_j.

3.6 Training Model

To building model hyper parameters, we construct the loss function to optimize. Since the target is to predict rating score from user to item, so the loss function is:

$$Loss = \frac{1}{2|\mathcal{O}|}\sum\nolimits_{i,j\in\mathcal{O}}\left(r_{ij}^{'} - r_{ij}\right) \tag{27}$$

Where, $|\mathcal{O}|$ is the number of observed ratings, r_{ij} is the ground truth of user u_i to item v_j. To optimize the objective function, we adopt the RMSprop [20]. There are 4 vectors embedding in model, included item (entity) embedding q_j, user embedding p_i, opinion embedding e_r and relation embedding r. They are randomly initialized and jointly learned during the training state. By embedding high-dimensional sparse features into low-dimensional latent space, the model can be easy to train and reduce time for training.

4 Experiment

4.1 Experimental Settings

Dataset
In our experiments, we use the datasets which are downloaded from public. There are Ciao, Epinions, MovieLens 1M[1], LastFM[2]

- Dataset Ciao, Epinions can take from popular social networking website Ciao (http://www.ciao.co.uk) and Epinions (www.epinions.com). Both has the data of rating users to items and social networking relations data.
- MovieLens 1M consists of approximately more than 1 million explicit ratings (ranging from 1 to 5) on the MovieLens website.
- Last.FM contains musician listening information from a set of 2 thousand users from Last.fm online music system.

All 4 datasets do not have enough data as expected, including: interactions data between users and items, social network relations among users and KG of items. Under that challenge, we propose to build a dataset for the following cases:

- For Ciao and Epinions, we will construct KG for items by the way that KB4Rec [22] proposed. Specifically, we consider the triple (head, relation, tail) have directly related to the entities associated with the items regardless of head or tail.
- For MovieLen 1M and Last.FM, since there are no data on social relationships, we use the social connections of Epinions dataset, and normalize user ID in Epinions to match in MovieLen 1M and Last.FM datasets (Table 1).

[1] https://grouplens.org/datasets/movielens.
[2] https://grouplens.org/datasets/hetree-2011.

Table 1. Statistics of the datasets

Dataset	Ciao 1hop	Ciao 2hop	Epi 1hop	Epi 2hop	Movie 2hop
#Users	7,375	7,375	49,289	49,289	138,159
#Items	106,797	106,797	261,649	261,649	16,954
#Rating	283,319	283,319	764,352	764,352	1,501,622
#Social connection	111,781	111,781	487,184	487,184	487,184
#Entities	128,572	190,961	205,868	315,548	102,569

Evaluation Metric

In order to evaluate the quality of the algorithms, two popular metrics are adopted namely Mean Absolute Error (MAE) and Root Mean Square Error (RMSE) [23]. Smaller values of MAE and RMSE indicate better predictive accuracy. Note that small improvement in RMSE or MAE terms can have a significant impact on the quality of the top-few recommendations [24].

Baseline

To evaluate the performance, we compared our **KconvGraphRec** with four groups of methods including traditional RS, social recommender systems and deep neural network-based RS. For each group, we select representative baselines and below we will detail them:

- NeuMF [1]: This method is a state-of-the-art matrix factorization model with neural network architecture. The original implementation is for recommendation ranking task and we adjust its loss to the squared loss for rating prediction.
- GCMC+GN [22]: This model is a state-of-the-art recommender system with graph neural network architecture
- KGCN [17]: The model proposes KG convolutional network method to aggregate the neighborhood data of the entity. Thereby building the vector representation of the entity that carries the full information of the KG.
- GraphRec [15]: is model state of the art using graph deep learning for both rating information graphs and social graphs to predict rating between users and items.
- HAGERec [19]: utilizes a bi-directional information propagation strategy to fully exploit the semantic information and high-order connectivity. It can learn the central entity's embedding from its local proximity structure.
- Without attention: Proposed model without attention in knowledge aggregation.

4.2 Experiment Results

Table 2. Performance comparison of different recommender systems

Dataset	Metric	Algorithms					
		KGCN	NeuMF	GCMC+GN	GraphRec	Without attention	**KconvGraphRec**
Ciao 1hop	MAE	–	0.8062	0.7526	0.7504	0.7330	**0.7218**
	RMSE	–	1.0617	0.9931	1.0917	1.0216	**0.9914**
Ciao 2hop	MAE	0.8124	0.8062	0.7526	0.8015	0.7215	**0.7179**
	RMSE	1.1187	1.0617	0.9931	1.0928	0.9852	**0.9725**
Epi 1hop	MAE	–	0.9072	0.8590	0.8285	0.8202	**0.8092**
	RMSE	–	1.1476	1.0711	1.1298	1.1183	**1.0146**
Epi 2 hop	MAE	0.8554	0.9072	0.8590	0.8287	0.8137	**0.8057**
	RMSE	1.1398	1.1476	1.0711	1.1357	1.0949	**1.0104**
Movie 2 hop	MAE	0.7591	–	–	0.7280	0.7271	**0.7152**
	RMSE	1.0012	–	–	0.9856	0.9783	**0.9624**

As a result, in Table 2, we have a few evaluations as follows:

- The proposed model outperforms four state of the art methods NeuMF, GCMC+GN, GraphRec and KGCN. That shows the effectiveness of the proposed model for the problem of the recommendation system.
- The model has proven the correctness when combining social network, knowledge graph and interaction between the users and items to synthesize many aspects into the corresponding representation vector to improve the result.

Table 3. Performance comparison with KGCN and HAGERec in AUC, ACC metric

Algorithms	Movie Lens 1M		Last.FM	
	AUC	ACC	AUC	ACC
KGCN	0.907	0.833	0.796	0.724
HAGERec	**0.923**	0.847	**0.814**	0.743
KconvGraphRec	0.9102	**0.848**	0.798	**0.747**

In Table 3, we compare the proposed model with KGCN, HAGERec in MovieLens 1M and Last.FM. Because 2 above models use the metric AUC and ACC for binary classification, we add sigmoid function to the output. To avoid imbalance data, we random sampling to generate data to equalize class 0 and 1. The results show that the proposed model continues to outperform KGCN. For HAGERec, the number of epochs is 200 which is much greater than 30 of proposed model (Fig. 4).

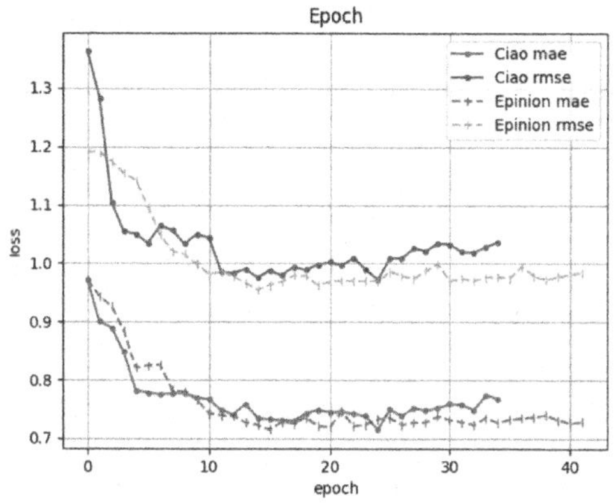

Fig. 4. Number of epochs in training model

5 Conclusion

The paper has proposed a neural network application model in graphs with a social relation data and knowledge graphs to solve the challenges in the recommendation system. Additionally, the paper proves that the theoretical basis and experimental results are much better than the recent state-of-the-art models. Experiments have demonstrated the interplay of implicit factors of users and items that contribute to boosting the predictive results of the recommender system and the model performance. We only incorporate social graphs into recommendations while many real scenarios are linked to a lot of other information. Thus, exploring graph neural networks to make proposals with those features will be considered as a suggestion in the future.

Acknowledgement. This research is funded by Vietnam National Foundation for Science and Technology Development (NAFOSTED) under grant number 102.05-2019.316.

References

1. He, X., Liao, L., Zhang, H., Nie, L., Hu, X., Chua, T.S.: Neural collaborative filtering. In: 26th International World Wide Web Conference, WWW 2017, pp. 173–182 (2017)
2. Jamali, M., Ester, M.: A matrix factorization technique with trust propagation for recommendation in social networks. In: Proceedings of 4th ACM Conference on Recommender Systems, RecSys 2010, pp. 135–142 (2010)

3. Kipf, T.N., Welling, M.: Semi-supervised classification with graph convolutional networks. In: 5th International Conference on Learning Representations, ICLR 2017 - Conference Track Proceedings, pp. 1–14 (2017)
4. Hamilton, W.L., Ying, R., Leskovec, J.: Inductive representation learning on large graphs. In: Advances in Neural Information Processing Systems, NIPS, pp. 1025–1035 (2017)
5. Defferrard, M., Bresson, X., Vandergheynst, P.: Convolutional neural networks on graphs with fast localized spectral filtering. In: Advances in Neural Information Processing Systems, NIPS, pp. 3844–3852 (2016)
6. Zhang, Z., Cui, P., Zhu, W.: Deep learning on graphs: a survey. http://arxiv.org/abs/1812.04202 (2018)
7. Goyal, P., Ferrara, E.: Graph embedding techniques, applications, and performance: a survey. Knowl.-Based Syst. **151**, 78–94 (2018)
8. Wang, X., He, X., Cao, Y., Liu, M., Chua, T.S.: KGAT: knowledge graph attention network for recommendation. In: Proceedings of the ACM SIGKDD International Conference on Knowledge Discovery & Data Mining, pp. 950–958 (2019)
9. Cao, Y., Hou, L., Li, J., Liu, Z.: Neural collective entity linking, no. Figure 1.http://arxiv.org/abs/1811.08603 (2018)
10. Yang, B., Lei, Y., Liu, J., Li, W.: Social collaborative filtering by trust. IEEE Trans. Pattern Anal. Mach. Intell. **39**(8), 1633–1647 (2017). https://doi.org/10.1109/TPAMI.2016.2605085
11. Wang, H., et al.: RippleNet: propagating user preferences on the knowledge graph for recommender systems. In: International Conference on Information and Knowledge Management Proceedings, no. 1, pp. 417–426 (2018). https://doi.org/10.1145/3269206.3271739
12. Tang, J., et al.: Recommendation with social dimensions. In: 30th AAAI Conference on Artificial Intelligence, AAAI 2016, pp. 251–257 (2016)
13. Ji, S., Pan, S., Cambria, E., Marttinen, P., Yu, P.S.: A survey on knowledge graphs: representation, acquisition and applications, pp. 1–26. http://arxiv.org/abs/2002.00388 (2020)
14. Van Pham, H., Nguyen, V.T.: A novel approach using context matching algorithm and knowledge inference for user identification in social networks. In: Proceedings of the 4th International Conference on Machine Learning and Soft Computing, pp. 149–153 (2020)
15. Fan, W., et al.: Graph neural networks for social recommendation. In: Web Conference 2019 – Proceedings of World Wide Web Conference, WWW 2019, pp. 417–426 (2019). https://doi.org/10.1145/3308558.3313488
16. Zhen, F., Zhang, Z., Lu, H.: A review of social recommendation. In: Proceedings of 13th IEEE IEEE Conference on Industrial Electronics and Applications, ICIEA 2018, pp. 537–542 (2018). https://doi.org/10.1109/iciea.2018.8397775
17. Wang, H., Zhao, M., Xie, X., Li, W., Guo, M.: Knowledge graph convolutional networks for recommender systems. In: Web Conference 2019 – Proceedings of World Wide Web Conference, WWW 2019, pp. 3307–3313 (2019). https://doi.org/10.1145/3308558.3313417
18. Wang, H., Zhang, F., Xie, X., Guo, M.: DKN: deep knowledge-aware network for news recommendation. In: Web Conference 2018 – Proceedings of World Wide Web Conference, WWW 2018, pp. 1835–1844 (2018). https://doi.org/10.1145/3178876.3186175
19. Yang, Z., Dong, S.: HAGERec: hierarchical attention graph convolutional network incorporating knowledge graph for explainable recommendation. Knowl.-Based Syst. **204**, 106194 (2020). https://doi.org/10.1016/j.knosys.2020.106194
20. Wang, S., Tang, J., Wang, Y., Liu, H.: Exploring hierarchical structures for recommender systems. IEEE Trans. Knowl. Data Eng. **30**(6), 1022–1035 (2018)
21. Logani, M.K., Solanki, V., Slaga, T.J.: Factorization meets the neighborhood: a multifaceted collaborative filtering model. Carcinogenesis **3**(11), 1303–1306 (1982). https://doi.org/10.1093/carcin/3.11.1303
22. van den Berg, R., Kipf, T.N., Welling, M.: Graph convolutional matrix completion. http://arxiv.org/abs/1706.02263 (2017)

Computational Methods for Social Good Applications

An Analysis of Users Engagement on Twitter During the COVID-19 Pandemic: Topical Trends and Sentiments

Sultan Alshamrani[1(✉)], Ahmed Abusnaina[1], Mohammed Abuhamad[2], Anho Lee[3], DaeHun Nyang[4], and David Mohaisen[1]

[1] University of Central Florida, Orlando, FL 32816, USA
salshamrani@knights.ucf.edu
[2] Loyola University Chicago, Chicago, IL 60660, USA
[3] Korea University, Seoul, South Korea
[4] Ewha Womans University, Incheon, South Korea

Abstract. The outbreak of COVID-19 pandemic raised health and economic concerns. With social distancing along with other measures that are enforced in an attempt to limit the spread of the virus, our life has dramatically changed. During this period, the web and social media platforms have become the main medium for communication, expression, and entertainment. Such platforms are a rich source of information, enabling researchers to better understand how the pandemic affected the users' everyday life, including interaction with and perception of different topics. In this study, we focus on understanding the shift in the behavior of Twitter users, a major social media platform used by millions daily to share thoughts and discussions. In particular, we collected 26 million tweets for a period of seven months, three months before the pandemic outbreak, and four months after. Using topic modeling and state-of-the-art deep learning techniques, the trending topics within the tweets on monthly-bases, including their sentiment and user's perception, were analyzed. This study highlights the change of the public behavior and concerns during the pandemic. Users expressed their concerns on health services, with an increase of 59.24% in engagement, and economical effects of the pandemic (34.43% increase). Topics such as online shopping have had a remarkable increase in popularity, perhaps due to the social distancing, while crime and sports topics witnessed a decrease. Overall, various topics related to COVID-19 have witnessed an improved sentiment, alluding to users adoption to the pandemic and associated topics of the public discourse.

Keywords: Coronavirus · COVID-19 · Sentiment analysis · NLP · Topic modeling.

1 Introduction

The coronavirus disease 2019 (COVID-19) is the largest pandemic in the information age. Caused by SARS-CoV-2, a highly transmissible respiratory virus,

S. Chellappan et al. (Eds.): CSoNet 2020, LNCS 12575, pp. 73–86, 2020.
https://doi.org/10.1007/978-3-030-66046-8_7

COVID-19 is the biggest public health concern of this century, declared as a global pandemic by the World Health Organization on March 11, 2020 [19]. As of August 2020, there are close to 21 million confirmed COVID-19 cases, with close to 6.4 million active cases, 750 thousand deaths, and 14 million recovered cases [20]. The outbreak of COVID-19 has changed people's life and behavior, including their interaction and communication. Social distancing and other measures are taken in an attempt to limit the spread of COVID-19, making the Web, and social media, in particular, the main medium for communication, expression, and entertainment.

In such a period, data science and mining play a central role in understanding the effect of the pandemic on users, and their behavior and perception. Several studies focused on the users' behavior on social media, including Twitter as a major platform [1,2,8,16]. Understanding the trends, and people's perception, using sentiment analysis allows a better understanding of users' behavior, and their reaction toward a particular topic. In this work, we study the effect of COVID-19 on the behavior of users on Twitter, and how the trends and topics have shifted, including the user sentiment and perceptions. In particular, we collected 26 million tweets from four English-speaking countries for the period of October 2019 to April 2020, three months before the COVID-19 outbreak, and four months after. We investigate the change of the users' behaviors through the duration, in both topics discussed, and their sentiments and thoughts toward each topic. Our findings highlight increased concerns about the economic effects of the pandemic, the quality of the provided health services. In addition, several topics gained popularity during the pandemic, such as online shopping and social media-related tweets, with an increase of more than 30% in popularity.

Contributions. This work studies the shift in the Twitter user's behavior coinciding with COVID-19 pandemic. In particular, we make the following contributions:

- We collected a large dataset of 26 million tweets from four English-speaking countries, namely, the United States, Canada, England, and Australia, and provided an in-depth analysis of the collected tweets, including their sentiments and the topics they discuss.
- We used state-of-the-art deep learning and natural language processing techniques to extract and track topics discussed in the social media platform along with the trends of user behavior towards these topics. For topic modeling, we used Latent Dirichlet Allocation, and for per-topic sentiment analysis, we used BERT to track behavioral changes within topics during the studied period. Revealing 23 distinct topics, and the increase of popularity in certain topics during the pandemic, such as health services, economy, and online shopping. Highlighting the public concerns and general trend during the lock-down.

Organization. This remaining of the paper is organized as follows. In Sect. 2, we review the related work in the field of users' perceptions and behavior analysis during the COVID-19 pandemic. Section 3 provides a description of the data collection approach and measurements. In Sect. 4, we perform topic modeling to uncover a variety of topics and their trends during the pandemic from our data. Section 5 provides deep learning-based analysis on users' perceptions and emotions towards different topics raised on the social media platform. Finally, we conclude our work in Sect. 6.

2 Related Work

The huge impact of COVID-19, potential and actual, has led many researchers to study and investigate users' perceptions and behavior coping with and conducting activities during the pandemic. This interest of studying users' perception is motivated by the need for providing well-informed measures to address the spread of misinformation about the pandemic. Several studies have examined the spread of COVID-19 misinformation on Twitter, as it is considered one of the most utilized social media platforms.

Ordun *et al.* [13] conducted an exploratory analysis using different topics, terms, and features on Twitter, to investigate the speed at which the information about COVID-19 spreads in comparison to Chinese social media. The study also examined the network behavior during the COVID-19 pandemic using various techniques, such as machine learning, topic modeling, uniform manifold approximation and projection, and statistical analysis. The findings of this study showed that the median retweeting time of COVID-19-related posts is roughly 50 min faster than the re-postings on Chinese social media about the Avian influenza A H7 (H7N9) outbreak in March 2013. Another study focusing on the spread of COVID-19 misinformation on Twitter was presented by Kouzy *et al.* [9]. The authors studied the amount of COVID-19 misinformation on Twitter by collecting and analyzing tweets from 14 different hashtags and words related to COVID-19. The study employed statistical analysis, by comparing terms and hashtags, to identify certain tweets and account characteristics. Using a dataset of 673 tweets, the authors reported 153 tweets to have some degree of misinformation, and 107 to be posted from unverifiable sources.

Schild *et al.* [14] analyzed data from Twitter and 4Chan for a period of five months to investigate the presence of Sinophobia, an issue that was raised at the beginning of the pandemic outbreak, across these two platforms. The study showed a strong correlation between the spread of Sinophobia-related content and COVID-19, and such a correlation was less obvious on mainstream platforms such as Twitter than other platforms such as 4Chan. In addition to analyzing users' behavior during the pandemic and the spread of misinformation regarding COVID-19, recent studies focused on providing techniques to help researchers and scholars mitigating the risk of spreading the virus. For example, Latif *et al.* [11] surveyed several papers, repositories, and datasets related to the pandemic with the intent of making them available to the public to help to track and mitigate the spread of the virus. Their work contributes to highlighting challenges and strategies, as well as creating a live repository for the latest data in this space.

In this study, we provide insights into how the pandemic has impacted people's behavior towards topics discussed on Twitter. Moreover, we analyze trends and shifts of emotions and feelings observed when discussing these topics before and after the pandemic. We utilize state-of-the-art techniques to detect, model, and track different topics from tweets collected in time-frame covering periods before and after the COVID-19 outbreak. After observing the major topics discussed during the data collection period, we adopted a deep learning-based sentiment analysis to study the people's perceptions of these topics before and after the pandemic.

3 Data Collection and Measurements

3.1 Dataset

In this study, we aim to understand the change in the users' behavior and trends before and after COVID-19 outbreak towards certain topics. As such, we collected 26 million tweets from four English-speaking countries, namely, the United States, England, Canada, and Australia. In particular, we collected tweets from 14 major cities with the highest number of daily tweets from a seven-month period, starting from the beginning of October 2019 until the end of April 2020. The data collection period consists of three months before the outbreak and four months after. We used the GetOldTweets3 API [12] to collect tweets from the social media platform, Twitter. In addition to our collected tweets, we obtained Sentiment140 dataset [7], a collection of 1.6 million tweets, including 800,000 tweets labeled as positive, and 800,000 tweets labeled as negative. The latter dataset is used as a ground-truth benchmark for the sentiment analysis task.

Data Collection: Statistics and Measurements. The collected tweets are distributed over a span of seven months across four countries, as shown in Fig. 1. Since the United States has by far the largest number of users on Twitter (62.55 million users), this is reflected in the dataset, where 67% of the tweets are from the United States [6]. Since both Australia and Canada have fewer users, we limited the number of cities from these countries to one city from each country, with the highest number of tweets originated from Toronto (Canada) and Sydney (Australia) as shown in Fig. 2. The 26 million tweets are distributed over seven months, as shown in (Fig. 3), with an average of 3.5 million tweets per month, with a peak of 4 million tweets in March 2020, which represents the duration of the peak of the first wave of the outbreak [17].

3.2 Data Preprocessing

In order to understand users' behavior on twitter before and after COVID-19 outbreak, two tasks are required: topic modeling and sentiment analysis. The topic modeling task aims to detect topics that were discussed during the collection period and while keeping track of the evolution of trends related to these topics. The sentiment analysis task aims to explore people's perceptions

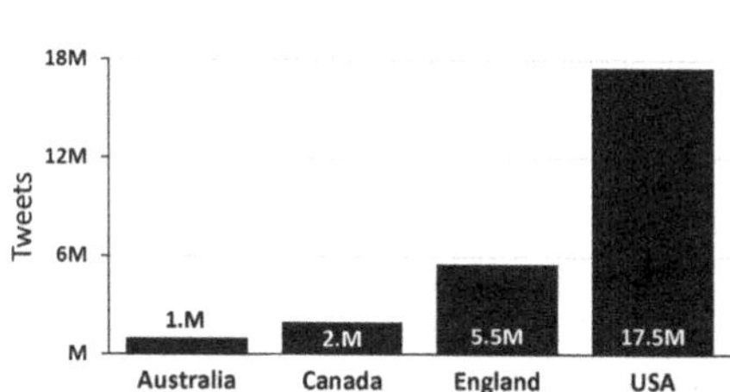

Fig. 1. The distribution of collected tweets over countries. 67% of the tweets are collected from the United States.

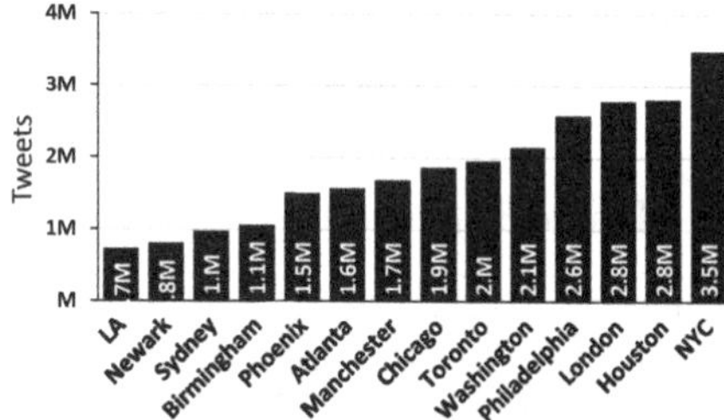

Fig. 2. The distribution of collected tweets over different cities. Eight cities (57%) are within the United States.

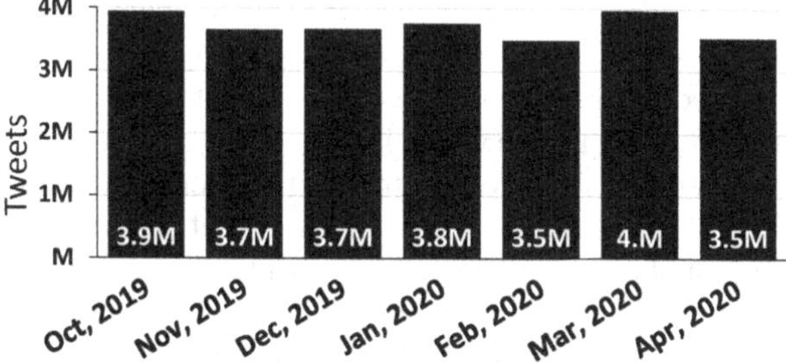

Fig. 3. The number of collected tweets per month within the studied duration. Note that the number of tweets is evenly distributed over the months, with an average of 3.7 million tweets per month.

on topics and whether the behaviors towards these topics are impacted by the pandemic (in a correlation-based analysis).

Each task requires different data preprocessing steps. For topic modeling, we cleaned the collected tweets by removing any special characters, hashtags, URLs, as well as non-English characters. Then, we removed the stopwords and short phrases with less than three characters. This preprocessing step is important considering the targeted task, *i.e.*, topic modeling, since topics are informed by keywords that occur across a large number of documents. Cleaning the collected tweets from unrelated and/or infrequent words can positively impact the outcome of the topic modeling task.

To handle data for sentiment analysis, we kept the original tweets and applied WordPiece tokenization [15] on the collected tweets. Skipping the other preprocessing steps, such as the eliminations of stopwords and non-English characters representing emojis, improves the performance without impacting the accuracy of the analysis as we employ Bidirectional Encoder Representations from Transformers (BERT), which utilizes WordPiece tokenization anyway. WordPiece tokenization is a word segmentation algorithm that forms a new subword of a token using a pre-trained likelihood probability model, *e.g.*, the word "working" is divided into two subwords "work" and "ing". Such an approach is beneficial when handling the out-of-vocabulary problem. We describe our use of WordPiece in the following section.

3.3 Data Representation

Each of the two tasks we conducted (topic modeling, and sentiment) requires certain numerical representation. For that, we used bag-of-words representation for topic modeling, and WordPiece tokenizer for sentiment analysis.

Bag-of-Words Representations. For the topic modeling task, we represent tweets with bag-of-words. Representing the tweets as clusters of different topics, based on the similarity score of their context, goal, or interest, requires considering frequent keywords from the content of tweets.

In order to utilize different state-of-the-art topic modeling techniques, tweets are first represented using a bag-of-words method during the data representation phase, in which a tweet is transformed into a vector of values that represent the presence or the weight of all unique words in the corpus in relation to the tweet. In the bag-of-words scheme, a tweet is commonly represented with a hot-encoding vector that highlights the existing words of the tweet against all terms in the corpus. The collection of all unique terms in a corpus is often referred to as a dictionary. Considering the fact that most of the employed datasets are large in size, the dictionary can be very large, producing sparse and high-dimensional bag-of-words representations. To optimize the bag-of-words representation of tweets, we adopted several steps, including: (1) removing frequent and rare words, and (2) feature selection. Common words that appear in more than, for example, 50% of all tweets are maybe general terms with less discriminative power than other less frequent words. Rare words, that appear less than 1,000 times in the entire corpus, for example, are also eliminated. We note that we created a pre-defined list of words related to COVID-19 in the final feature set, to have enough features to produce topics related to COVID-19 outbreak. This list of terms include terms such as: *coronavirus*, *virus*, *corona*, *covid19*, *covid-19*, and *covid*.

To reduce the dimensionality of the bag-of-words representation and after the preprocessing step, we selected the most frequent 10,000 words to be the features for representing the tweets. In a preliminary experiment, choosing the 10,000 words produced the best trade-off between performance and accuracy for the topic modeling task.

WordPiece-based Representations. Due to the difference in the two tasks, we utilized different methods in the data representation. For the sentiment analysis task, we use a WordPiece-based representation method to represent tweets to the BERT model [5]. The WordPiece technique creates a vocabulary of a fixed number of words, sub-words and characters, and solves the out-of-vocabulary problem by splitting unrecognized words into sub-words, if no sub-word match in the pre-defined dictionary, it is then split further into characters, and then mapped to the corresponding embedding. This technique has been proven efficient as opposed to other embedding mechanisms that map all of the out-of-vocabulary words to one token such as 'UNK' [15,21].

Tweets are represented as a matrix with rows fixed as the number of words in the representation and columns as the embedding of each word. For our implementation, we used 70 words as the length of tweets, and 768 as the length of the word embedding vector, *i.e.*, each tweet is represented as 70×768 matrix representation. We use 70 words to represent a tweet because the majority of tweets (99.8%) in our dataset were within this length, and the 768 is the pre-defined size of the word embeddings of BERT.

Fig. 4. The general flow of the sentiment analysis pipeline. Sentiment140 dataset is used to fine-tune BERT-based model for sentiment classification task.

4 LDA-Based Topic Modeling and Tracking

This study aims to explore the user's perceptions and behavior in response to a variety of topics and subjects during the data collection period. Moreover, we aim to investigate the trends of these topics and the impact of the pandemic on users' reactions to these topics (in a correlation analysis), requiring powerful tools and techniques such as topic modeling. Topic modeling is an unsupervised machine learning technique, that is typically used to extract a set of topics in a group of documents. Topic modeling processes a set of documents and detects the repeated patterns of word and phrase across documents, to cluster the documents based on their similarities [3,10]. This study utilizes the MALLET's Latent Dirichlet Allocation (LDA)-based topic modeling technique, a state-of-the-art topic modeling approach that maps each document in the corpus to a set of topics. Each document, *i.e.*, each tweet, is assigned to a topic with a probability score, allowing the tweet to be recognized in different topics. However, we assign the tweet to the topic with the highest score. Using the topic modeling, topics are represented with a cluster of similar and related words [4]. This enables the detection and tracking of topics through the data collection period. Accurate detection of topics allows real-time analysis and observation of trends, *e.g.*, users' reactions and behavior towards topics.

4.1 LDA-Based Topic Modeling: Configuration

After the collection and processing of data, tweets are represented with vector representations of a bag-of-words. Extracting the bag-of-words representation is described in Sect. 3. Receiving input vectors of 10,000 bag-of-word representation, the LDA model assigns topics for each tweet. The abstract pipeline of the

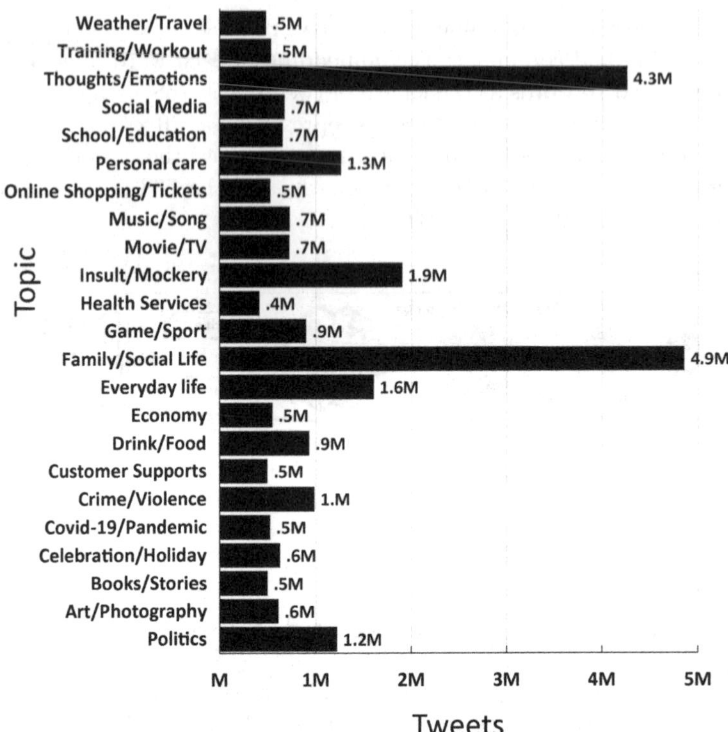

Fig. 5. The distribution of tweets over LDA generated topics. Most tweets are associated with "Thoughts/Emotions" and "Family/Social Life" related topics.

process is presented in Fig. 7. Establishing the topic model requires a training phase in which a number of topics are investigated in terms of the coherence score of topics. The coherence score is a score calculated for each topic, by measuring the semantic similarity between words that have the highest score within the given topic, the word score is calculated based on the frequency of the word within the topic, and its inverse frequency with other topics. This method provides distinguishable measurements between topics that are semantically similar. The higher the coherence value the better the quality of the clustering, indicating better topic modeling and assignment. We examined the effect of changing the number of the extracted topics on the modeling task. We explored extracting 15 to 50 topics with an increase of 5 topics, each iteration, while observing the coherence score achieved in each iteration. The LDA-model achieves the best performance when the number of extracted topics is 40 with a coherence score of 0.55.

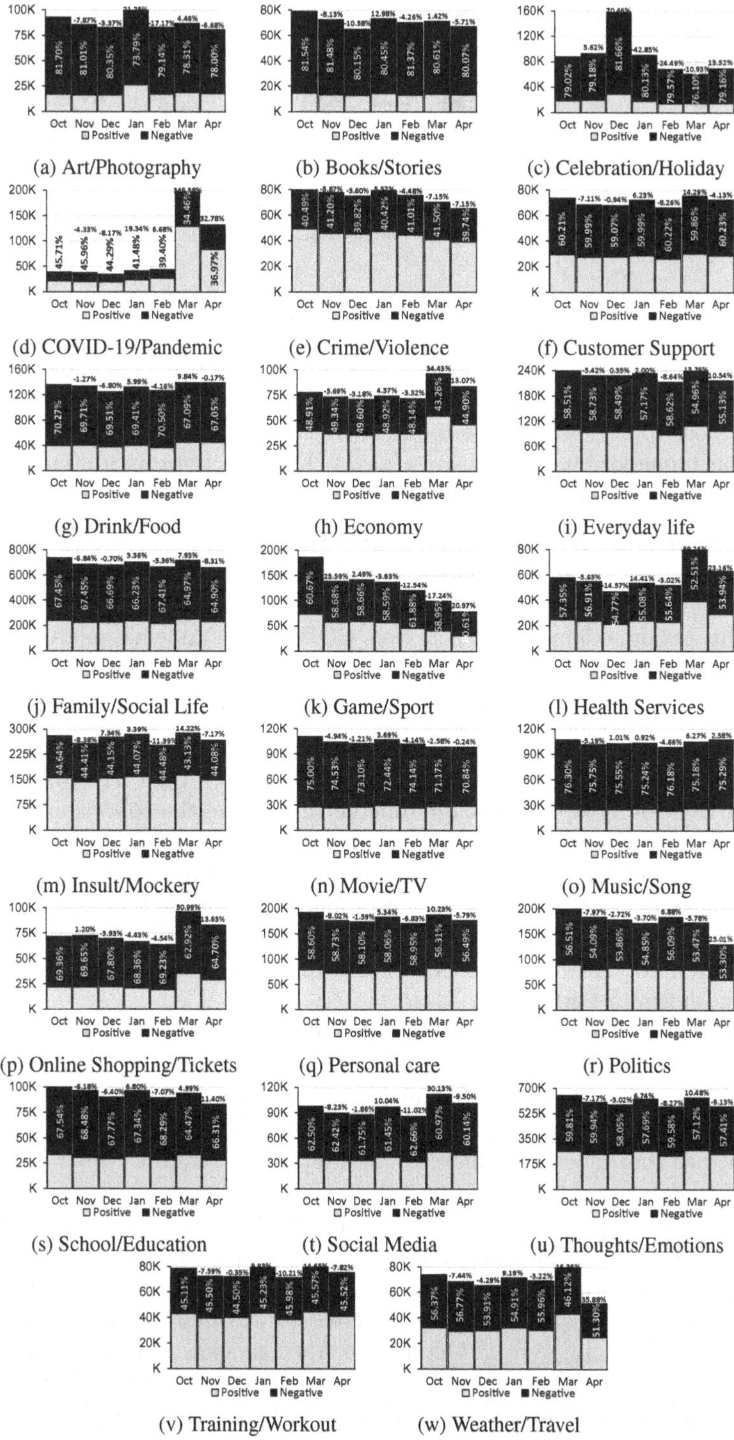

(a) Art/Photography (b) Books/Stories (c) Celebration/Holiday (d) COVID-19/Pandemic (e) Crime/Violence (f) Customer Support (g) Drink/Food (h) Economy (i) Everyday life (j) Family/Social Life (k) Game/Sport (l) Health Services (m) Insult/Mockery (n) Movie/TV (o) Music/Song (p) Online Shopping/Tickets (q) Personal care (r) Politics (s) School/Education (t) Social Media (u) Thoughts/Emotions (v) Training/Workout (w) Weather/Travel

Fig. 6. The over-time distribution of positive and negative tweets per generated topic.

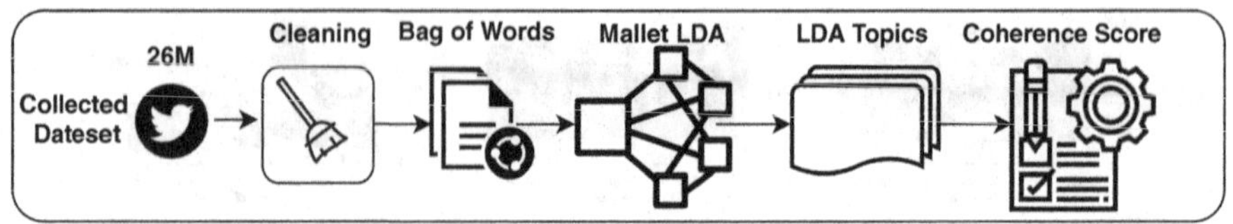

Fig. 7. The general flow of the topic modeling task. Each tweet is represented as bag-of-words generated vector for LDA topic modeling training.

4.2 LDA-Based Topic Modeling: Outcome

Using the best-performing LDA model, we manually inspected the topics through the frequent keywords generated for each topic, and assigned names and descriptions to those topics. Since some topics share similar keywords, we assigned the same topic name for multiple clusters (*i.e.,* LDA-extracted topics). This manual inspection of topics produced 23 unique topics.

Topic-Tweet Distribution. Fig. 5 shows the distribution of topics across the collected tweets in the seven months. The topics related to "Family/Social Life" and "Thoughts/Emotions" represent 35.38% of the collected tweets. Moreover, during this period, 0.5 million tweets were COVID-19/Pandemic-related. In general, except for the aforementioned topics, the tweets are distributed in the range of 0.4–2 million tweets per topic.

Topic Temporal Tracking. Using the best-performing model, we tracked topics through time to observe trends and topic evolution. Figure 6 shows the temporal distribution of tweets through different months of the collection period.

An obvious increase in the tweets related to "COVID-19/Pandemic" is observed in March as the World Health Organization declared COVID-19 as a global pandemic. This increase is shown in Fig. 6d with a 472.15% rise in the volume of the tweets from December to March. A similar trend is observed for topics related to "Health Services" with a 76.7% increase from December to March, as shown in Fig. 6l.

This pandemic has also affected the trends of topics related to "Economy", as governments and organizations started enforcing lock-downs and social distancing. Topics related to the economy have enjoyed a 35.64% increase in tweets between December and March, as shown in Fig. 6h. The "Online Shopping/Tickets" topic has shown a similar increase, of around 34%, from October to March, as shown in Fig. 6p.

The negative impact of the pandemic on the volume of tweets is observed on topics related to entertainments, *e.g.,* "Game/Sport" with a decrease of 57.95% from October to April as most sports events were suspended around the world. We also observed a decrease of tweets related to "Crime/Violence" with more than 21% drop in volume from October to April as shown in Fig. 6e, although unclear if that is due to a decrease in crime rates or the engagement of users with crime-related contents. The full illustrations of the trends of the topics are shown in Fig. 6.

5 Topic-Derived Sentiment Analysis

The second part is to investigate the trends and shift of perceptions of certain topics discussed on Twitter during the data collection period. This part is done by examining the sentiments observed on different topics before and after the pandemic. To establish a baseline sentiment analysis model, we used a ground-truth benchmark dataset of 1.6 million annotated tweets for sentiment analysis task [7]. At the beginning of our research, we conducted several preliminary experiments to define the best model architecture to perform the task, including deep learning-based techniques such as Deep Neural Networks (DNN), Convolutional Neural Networks (CNN), Long Short Term Memory (LSTM), and BERT. Using the ground-truth dataset, the achieved F-1 scores were 80.53%, 82.03%, 81.65%, and 87.06% for DNN, CNN, LSTM, and BERT, respectively. Table 1 shows the achieved results of different models performing the sentiment analysis in terms of true positive rate, true negative rate, precision, and the F-1 score. Note that BERT outperforms all others, achieving a precision accuracy of 87.35%. Therefore, we selected the BERT model to perform the sentiment analysis in our study. An illustration of the pipeline of the workflow to conduct the sentiment analysis using BERT is shown in Fig. 4, including the preprocessing and data representation stages.

5.1 BERT-Based Sentiment Analysis

In essence, Bidirectional Encoder Representations from Transformers (BERT) [5] is a language model that benefits from the attention mechanism used in the transformer architecture [18]. This attention mechanism has two six-layers of encoders that have the ability to learn contextual relation between words in a given text, as well as six layers of decoders that generate the needed output for a given task. As opposed to traditional NLP models that read textual data sequentially from right-to-left or left-to-right, the transformer encoder is considered bidirectional since it reads the entire given text at once, allowing the model to capture the context of each word based on its surroundings. Since BERT is a language model, it uses only the encoder part of the transformer. By adding a new layer to the core model. BERT fits a wide variety of NLP language tasks, such as classification, question answering, as well as named entity recognition. In our implementation of BERT, we used the same structure and model configuration of the original work. For more details, we refer the reader to the original research paper in [5]. In this study, tweets are separated per sentence, with two special tokens indicating the start of the tweet and end of each sentence. Then, each tweet is fed into the trained BERT model, providing the embedding of each word in the tweet considering its surroundings. The output of the BERT model is a one-neuron output layer with a sigmoid activation function for binary classification signaling the polarity of the tweet, *i.e.*, either positive or negative sentiment.

Table 1. The evaluation of deep learning models on sentiment analysis task. BERT-based model outperform its counterparts, therefore, used as the baseline in our analysis.

Model	True Positive Rate	True Negative Rate	Precision	F-1 score
DNN	80.15%	80.97%	80.91%	80.53%
CNN	81.51%	82.67%	82.55%	82.03%
LSTM	81.60%	81.62%	81.71%	81.65%
BERT	86.77%	87.45%	87.35%	87.06%

Topics-Derived Sentiment. Fig. 6 shows the observed positive and negative tweets for different topics. Generally, the percentage of reported sentiments are approximately similar throughout the collection period for all topics. However, the tweets related to "COVID-19/Pandmeic" have shown a significant decrease in negative tweets from 41.48% in January to 34.46% in March. Such negativity drop is also observed on tweets related to "Weather/Travel" with 56.37% of negative tweets in October to 46.12% in March. For the tweets related to "Health Services", the results show an increase of the positivity in the tweets, as the percentage of positive tweets increased from 42.65% in October, to 47.49% in March. Similar trends in the sentiment analysis of the topic related to "Online Shopping/Tickets" with an increase in the positive tweets from 30.64% in October to 37.08% in March. While it is impossible to accurately pinpoint the root cause of the "positivity", it seems as though that the overall pandemic and associated measures are accepted by some as a reality, reducing the negative reaction.

6 Conclusion

In this study, we aim to better understand the effect of the pandemic on users' interaction on social media, including their public perception. Using a large-scale dataset of 26 million English tweets from four countries, and 14 major cities, we conducted topic modeling across 23 topics, and performed a temporal and semantic analysis on monthly-bases. Our analysis highlights the increasing concern in the public discourse on the provided health services, shifting the public discussing from topics such as sports and politics, into online shopping and economical effects of the pandemic on the society. More interesting, over time, at the aggregate-level, users have become more positive in their expression, as measured by the sentiment in their tweets on various topics.

Acknowledgement. This work was supported by NRF grant 2016K1A1A2912757 (Global Research Lab) and a gift from NVIDIA. S. Alshamrani was supported by a scholarship from the Saudi Arabian Cultural Mission.

References

1. Alshamrani, S., Abuhamad, M., Abusnaina, A., Mohaisen, D.: Investigating online toxicity in users interactions with the mainstream media channels on YouTube. In: The 5th International Workshop on Mining Actionable Insights from Social Networks, pp. 1–6 (2020)
2. Alshamrani, S., Abusnaina, A., Mohaisen, D.: Hiding in plain sight: a measurement and analysis of kids' exposure to malicious URLs on YouTube. In: Third ACM/IEEE Workshop on Hot Topics on Web of Things, pp. 1–6 (2020)
3. Blei, D.M., Lafferty, J.D.: Topic models. In: Text Mining, pp. 101–124 (2009)
4. Blei, D.M., Ng, A.Y., Jordan, M.I.: Latent Dirichlet allocation. J. Mach. Learn. Res. **3**, 993–1022 (2003)
5. Devlin, J., Chang, M., Lee, K., Toutanova, K.: BERT: pre-training of deep bidirectional transformers for language understanding. In: Burstein, J., Doran, C., Solorio, T. (eds.) Proceedings of the 2019 Conference of the North American Chapter of the Association for Computational Linguistics: Human Language Technologies, NAACL-HLT 2019, Minneapolis, MN, USA, June 2–7, 2019, Volume 1 (Long and Short Papers). pp. 4171–4186 (2019)
6. Clement, J.: Leading countries based on number of twitter users as of July 2020 (2020). https://bit.ly/3gDVbrt
7. KazAnova: Sentiment140 dataset with 1.6 million tweets (2020). https://www.kaggle.com/kazanova/sentiment140
8. Kouloumpis, E., Wilson, T., Moore, J.: Twitter sentiment analysis: the good the bad and the OMG! In: Fifth International AAAI Conference on Weblogs and Social Media (2011)
9. Kouzy, R., et al.: Coronavirus goes viral: quantifying the COVID-19 misinformation epidemic on twitter. Cureus **12**(3), e7255 (2020)
10. Landauer, T.K., Foltz, P.W., Laham, D.: An introduction to latent semantic analysis. Discourse processes **25**(2–3), 259–284 (1998)
11. Latif, S., et al.: Leveraging data science to combat COVID-19: a comprehensive review (2020)
12. Mottl: GetOldTweets3 Twitter Scrapping API (2020). https://github.com/Mottl/GetOldTweets3
13. Ordun, C., Purushotham, S., Raff, E.: Exploratory analysis of covid-19 tweets using topic modeling, umap, and digraphs (2020). CoRR abs/2005.03082
14. Schild, L., Ling, C., Blackburn, J., Stringhini, G., Zhang, Y., Zannettou, S.: Go eat a bat, Chang!: an early look on the emergence of Sinophobic Behavior on Web Communities in the Face of COVID-19 (2020). CoRR abs/2004.04046
15. Schuster, M., Nakajima, K.: Japanese and Korean voice search. In: 2012 IEEE International Conference on Acoustics, Speech and Signal Processing, ICASSP 2012, Kyoto, Japan, March 25–30, 2012, pp. 5149–5152. IEEE (2012)
16. Severyn, A., Moschitti, A.: Twitter sentiment analysis with deep convolutional neural networks. In: Proceedings of the 38th International ACM SIGIR Conference on Research and Development in Information Retrieval, pp. 959–962 (2015)
17. The Atlantic: The public deserves the most complete data available about COVID-19 in the us. No Official Source is Providing it, so we are (2020). https://covidtracking.com/
18. Vaswani, A., et al.: Attention is all you need. In: Guyon, I., et al. (eds.) NeuRIPS (2017)

19. World Health Organization: WHO Director-General's opening remarks at the media briefing on COVID-19 - 11 March 2020 (2020). https://tinyurl.com/vyvm6ob
20. WorldOMeter: COVID-19 Coronavirus Pandemic (2020). https://www.worldometers.info/coronavirus/
21. Wu, Y., et al.: Google's neural machine translation system: bridging the gap between human and machine translation (2016). CoRR abs/1609.08144

A Data Conversion Approach Between GAMA and DIGIPLANT Simulating Rice Plant Growth Under Brown Planthopper Infestation

Hiep Xuan Huynh[1(✉)], Man Ba Huynh[1], Hoa Thi Tran[2], and Hai Thanh Nguyen[1]

[1] Can Tho University, Can Tho, Vietnam
hxhiep@ctu.edu.vn
[2] Thai Binh University, Thai Binh, Vietnam

Abstract. Rice plays an important role in the lives of the people of Vietnam and the world. It is not only a major food source but also contributes greatly to the export activities. Brown planthopper (BPH) is one of the harmful objects in the production of rice to make rice weakened, poorly developed. Besides, BPH is a disease brokerage yellow dwarf and twisted leaves. In this study, we propose a data model to convert between GAMA and DIGIPLANT to simulate the development of rice under the destructive BPH. The model is trained with the images of rice plants when they were attacked by BPH on the DIGIPLANT software. The scope of this work is to study BPH transmit yellow dwarf disease on rice. This study combines the methods of modelling and agent-based modeling to develop an approach for simulating the growth and propagation of BPH under the impact of various environmental on GAMA. Agriculturists have provided the level of influence the height of the rice yellow dwarf disease infection based on the output of modelling the growth and propagation of BPH. The proposed method can change the rate the parameters of DIGIPLANT to display images of the rice according to the level of influence.

Keywords: Brown planthopper · Rice · Digiplant · GAMA · Simulation

1 Introduction

Rice is an important food crop of agricultural countries and especially in the Mekong River Delta (Mekong Delta). Rice cultivation is a traditional profession of the Vietnamese people from a very ancient time. The advances of science and technology in rice production have strongly promoted countries' rice-growing industry to catch up with the world's advanced level with daily productivity and quality improved. However, in order to research, cross-breed and test a

S. Chellappan et al. (Eds.): CSoNet 2020, LNCS 12575, pp. 87–99, 2020.
https://doi.org/10.1007/978-3-030-66046-8_8

rice variety, a new technique or a certain effect (aphids, pests, etc.) on the rice plants according to traditional methods, we have to sow seeds, wait for the rice to increase. and checking the rice development status, this process takes a lot of time, effort and money.

BPH is a dangerous insect on rice that can spread on a large scale [1–6]. In addition, BPH is also a carrier to transmit the virus causing yellow dwarf and twisted leaves dwarf diseases, reducing rice yield. Since the summer-autumn crop 2006, aphids, yellow dwarf and twisted leaves dwarf diseases have arisen and caused serious damage in the southern provinces. According to the report of the Department of Crop Production in 2008, localities in the Mekong Delta had 223,255 ha of summer-autumn and autumn-winter rice infected with BPH, of which over 36,300 ha were seriously infected. The area infected with aphids concentrated in the provinces of Dong Thap, An Giang, Tra Vinh, Soc Trang, and so on. Especially, there are 2,866 ha infected by the yellow dwarf and twisted leaves dwarf diseases mainly in Dong Thap and Tra Vinh [7] in that year.

There are numerous studies which have been attempting simulation modeling methods to solve the BPH problem. One of them is a study which named "Building a simulation model of aphid spread in rice fields" by Vo Thanh Tung, a Master thesis in Information Technology (2010), Can Tho University [7]. In which, the author attempted the GAMA multi-agent simulation support tools combined with the geographic information system (GIS) to carry out his thesis. The author's research work had initially achieved very positive results. However, the above simulation model only simulated the spread of BPH and did not show the image of rice plants when they were attacked by BPH. The proposed study namely Digiplant program [8] was introduced by Paul Henry Cournede and his colleagues showing a model with "virtual tree planting" to reproduce the development image of rice plants on the computer through the computerized model and vivid visualization. The method can both save effort and money in the experiments. However, this program only reproduced the image of rice growing normally, it had not yet enabled us to simulate the images of rice plants when they were attacked by BPH.

Therefore, with the work namely "Model of data conversion between GAMA [10] and Digiplant [9], we aim to simulate the growth of rice plants under the destruction of BPH" to find a way to convert data between GAMA and Digiplant to display the image of rice plants attacked by BPH on Digiplant.

The rest of this study contains sections as follows. We present the importance of the work and introduce some state-of-the-arts related to the study in Sect. 2. The detailed information of the proposed method is presented in Sect. 3. Experimental results will be exhibited in Sect. 4. In Sect. 5, we conduct some closing remarks of this work.

2 Related Work

The rice area infected with BPH and yellow dwarf disease is increasing rapidly. Meanwhile, dwarfism does not currently have a cure. Therefore, the project focuses on researching rice plants when infected with the yellow dwarf disease, affecting the height growth of plants, to reproduce the image of rice when sick to warn people. Farmers as well as agronomists degree the influence of rice crops to dwarf diseases, thereby giving appropriate measures to handle the pest situation of BPH. Based on the topic "Building a simulation model of aphid spread on rice plants" by Vo Thanh Tung, Master Thesis of Information Technology (2010), Can Tho University [7]. We obtain aphid infected area, the number of aphids and the corresponding age of rice. Through the above data in combination with the aphid prevalence and the loss of height of rice plants provided by farmers, we will adjust the input values of the Digiplant program to Display rice plants when attacked by BPH.

The study in [11] proposed a model of overseas movement to shown the importance of large-scale systems' changes and coordination in overseas migration. Authors in [12] introduced different responses to abrupt and gradual CO2 increases. They calculated the performance of BPH (Nilaparvata lugens (Stål)) reared on rice for 15 successive generations under three CO2 levels. Authors in [13] presented a method of sequencing to the genomes of brown planthopper populations and illustrate that the Indochinese peninsula is the major source of migration into temperate China.

3 Data Conversion Model Between GAMA and DIGIPLANT

3.1 Modeling to Render Data on BPH Transmission in Rice Fields to Assist Experts in Determining the Rate of Reduction of Plant Height

The degree of decreasing the height of the plant depends on many factors: the number of aphids that carry the disease, the early or late disease of rice. Therefore, in order to assist experts in deciding the rate of reducing the height of the plant, it is necessary to have the number of aphids and rice age. Data were extracted during the implementation of BPH propagation simulation in GAMA (Fig. 1).

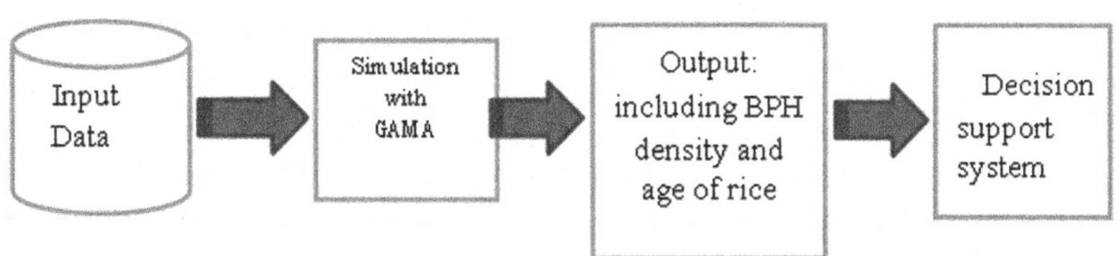

Fig. 1. Modeling for preprocessing data of BPH and rice age

Describe data on BPH and rice age in the text file: This is a text file containing information about areas in Dong Thap province, the number of aphids and the age of rice in the form as shown in Fig. 2. The file contains the number of lines corresponds to the simulation date. Data include name of region, density of BPH and age of rice tree.

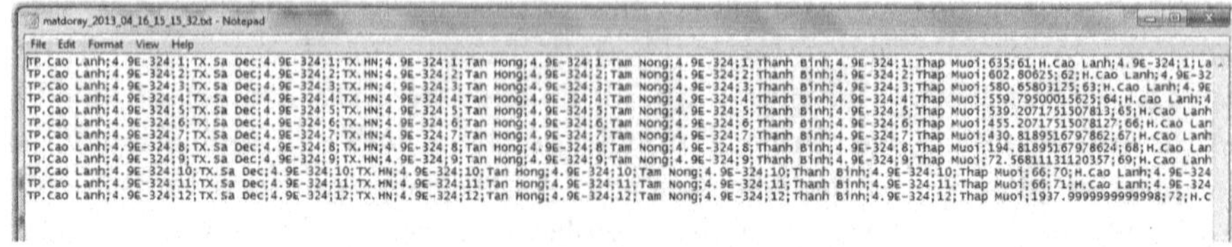

Fig. 2. File containing data after performing simulation in GAMA

3.2 Data Conversion Model Between GAMA and Digiplant

This section describes the data conversion system between GAMA and Digiplant. A general diagram of the data conversion system is shown in the figure. The system is divided into three parts revealed in Fig. 3.

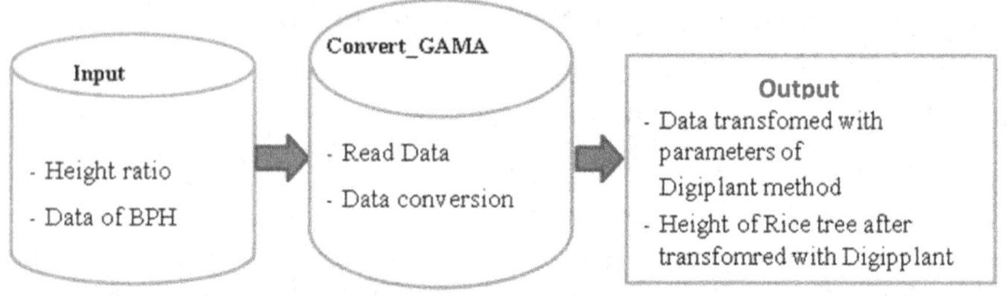

Fig. 3. Data conversion model between GAMA and Digiplant

Transition Input: Data on BPH is a file extracted from the simulation process in the GAMA above. Based on the data, the agronomist decides to enter an appropriate rate of tree height loss.

The System Performs Data Conversion Between GAMA and Digiplant: The process of creating data files containing a decrease in tree height in ascending order presented in Fig. 4. In order to perform data transformation, the data set must first be stored in the comparison table. This data is obtained by changing the slang lifetime values... under many scenarios, combined with checking the degree of change in tree height through biomass.data data file. Then, sort in descending order of tree height and save the above result in comparison-file.txt file. The table in Fig. 4 includes the first column showing tree height decrease rate arranged in ascending order and the other exhibiting the parameter corresponding to the decrease in tree height.

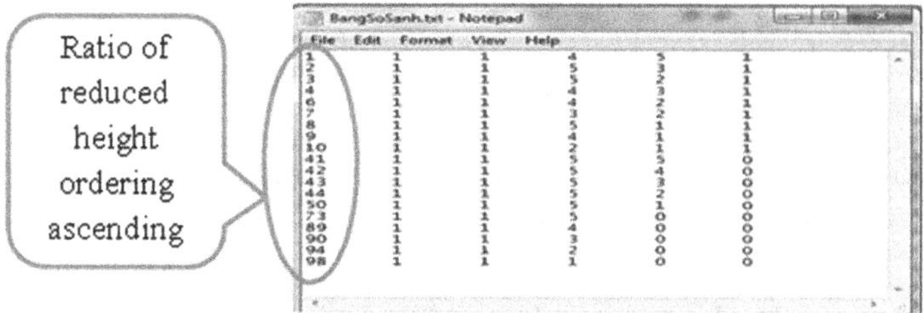

1	1	1	4	5	1
2	1	1	5	3	1
3	1	1	5	2	1
4	1	1	4	3	1
6	1	1	4	2	1
7	1	1	3	2	1
8	1	1	5	1	1
9	1	1	4	1	1
10	1	1	2	1	1
41	1	1	5	5	0
42	1	1	5	4	0
43	1	1	5	3	0
44	1	1	5	2	0
50	1	1	5	1	0
73	1	1	5	0	0
89	1	1	4	0	0
90	1	1	3	0	0
94	1	1	2	0	0
98	1	1	1	0	0

Fig. 4. Comparison table

Data Conversion Between GAMA and DIGIPLANT: The conversion process was performed by comparing the imported tree height reduction ratio value from an agricultural specialist with the values in the comparison table. If the input value is less than or equal to the value in the table, update the function file according to the parameters corresponding to the height in the comparison table.

Data Output of Data Transformation: After the data conversion process, the function file has updated its value. To display the image of the rice plant, the digiplant program is executed and references to the function file, performing operations that allow the program to perform calculations and display the image.

The Function of Converting Input Data of Digiplant Program According to the Reduction Ratio of Tree Height: This is the main function of the program, this function allows to change the values in the file (Fun-PA32_3D.txt) to display the cropped image as required.

Input includes text function data, shoot height reduction values, comparison data tables while Output consists of scaled-shift datasets are provided. Implementation steps include:

- Get shoot reduction rate value from a specialist
- Open the comparison table file.
- Open the functional file.
- Start the function that allows us to read each line of the comparison table.
- Repeat until it is false:
  - Perform the read at the beginning of the file to the end of the file.
  - Check if we are at the end of the file then the loop is terminated.
  - Check the rate of decrease in shoot height entered and height in the comparison table.
  - If the input value is less than or equal to the value in the table.
    - * Search for keyword "Internode_Expansion_Time"
    - * update values
  - Otherwise read the next line.

4 Experiments

4.1 Experiment on GAMA Model

Based on Scenario 1: This scenario is to find the parameter values for the area, the number of aphids and the age of rice.

4.2 Season and Hydrology of Dong Thap

Dong Thap (including one city and eleven districts and towns) is a province in the Mekong Delta region. Figure 5 shows the administrative map of Dong Thap Province processed using the OPENJUMP software with the original data being the main map of Dong Thap province. Communes within the same district are shaded similar to and different from the other districts.

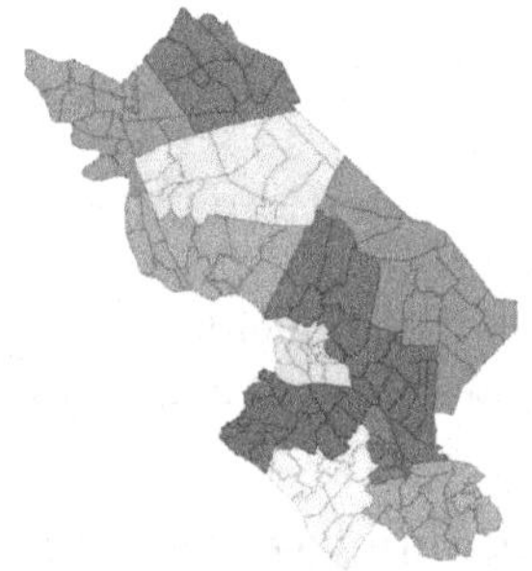

Fig. 5. A Map of Dong Thap province with districts shown in various colors.

In the year, Dong Thap has two main wind directions: southwest monsoon (from May to November) and northeast monsoon (from December to April next year). The rice-growing seasons of the year are distributed as shown in Table 1.

Experimental Data: Data used in this model are observed BPH observed data provided by Dong Thap Plant Protection Department and data on temperature, humidity, average rainfall in months of the year from Dong Thap Statistical Yearbook (2009) [7]. Scenario: risk of spreading BPH in the southwest direction Description: The time to start the simulation is July 1, 2009. According to the seasonal calendar, Dong Thap now starts the Summer-Autumn crop, most of the rice tea is 5–10 days after sowing. However, in Tan Hong, there is still some rice tea harvested well (Spring-Summer season) and according to the observed data, these rice teas are infested with high density and especially one and rice tea are in the seeding stage also infected. The wind direction in this season is southwest. Input data includes features such as the number of simulation days: 90 days, Wind direction: southwest, Wind speed: 12 km/h, Temperature: 25–28°C (read

Table 1. The rice crops in the year

Crops	Durations (months)
Winter–Spring	November–December to February–March
Springer–Summer	February–March to May–June
Summer–Autumn	May–June to August–September
Autumn–Winter	August–September to November–December

from the file temperature_data.csv) and Humidity: 84–86% (read from the file humidity_data.csv). The average rate of BPH: 3.5%. The data of aphids and rice age in some communes are as shown in Table 2.

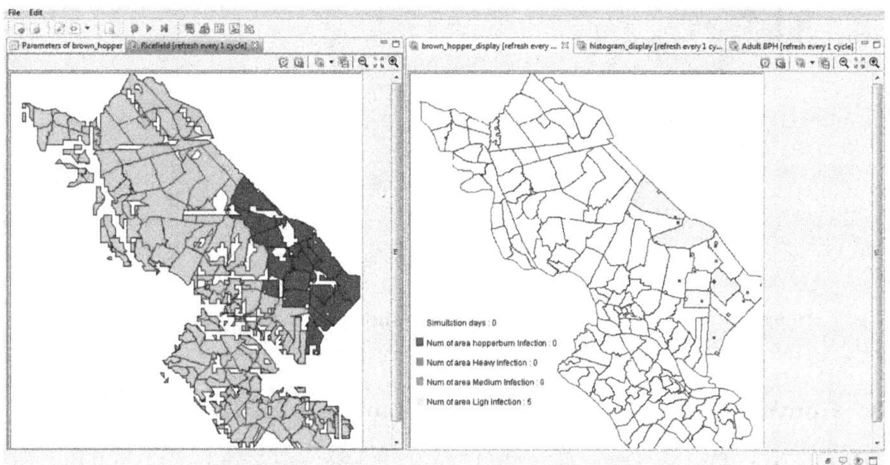

Fig. 6. BPH density in some communes in Dong Thap

Simulation Initialization: After initialization, the current status of aphids in the areas is shown in Fig. 6. After simulating 67 steps: BPH erupted in Tam Nong and Cao Lanh districts in the southwest wind direction, these areas were infected with very high density (red, purple) and some mild infections. (in blue) as shown in Fig. 7. After doing the simulation for 67 days, we obtained in the log directory matdoray_2013_04_07_16_09_49.txt file to store information of the infected area, number and age of rice.

Table 2. BPH density in some communes in Dong Thap province, Vietnam

Name of district	Commune	Rice agea	Adult aphid	baby aphid	Eggs
Tan Hong	Tan Thanh A	82	8.000	300	
	Tan Thanh B	5	700	300	100
Hong Ngu	Thuong Thoi Hau A	10	200	200	

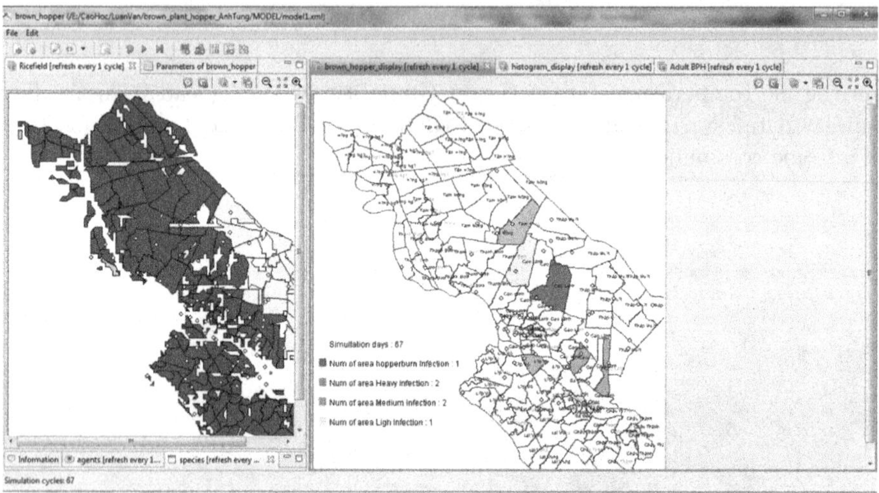

Fig. 7. Image of simulation results of the 67th simulation day (Color figure online)

4.3 Converting Data Between GAMA and DIGIPLANT

Initial Input Data: Data on aphids, age of rice and number of aphids are the basis to determine the prevalence of yellow dwarf disease and the effect on the reduction rate of shoot height of rice plants. This data is based on the output matdoray_2013_04_07_16_09_49.txt (output) of the experiment on GAMA 1.3 model in the above section. BPH is the vector that transmits bacteria virus diseases to rice such as rice grass disease, twisted leaves dwarf diseases, yellow dwarf diseases. In this work, only researching on brown planthopper that transmits dwarf disease In the function data file Fun-PA32_3D.txt, there is no parameter allowing to change the leaf color. Therefore, in this work, the color part of rice is not studied. The rate of BPH infected by yellow dwarf disease depends on many factors: disease, year, season, region and etc. so depending on the time that the agricultural experts will provide the corresponding prevalence of the yellow dwarf disease in the section. The rate of aphids carrying yellow dwarf diseases. In addition, the degree of decrease in bud height also depends on many factors: the number of aphids, early or late sick rice, etc. Therefore, the degree of decrease in the height of rice trees is chronologically determined by agricultural experts entered in the Tree height reduction function.

Experimental Scenarios

Scenario 1: The tree grows normally according to the default data values of the Digiplant program. The conversion process is done mainly to change the parameters of the extension time internode_expansion_time. To get the comparison results before and after changing the lifetime value of the log, we perform a check of the height of the tree according to the initial default values of the program. The default initial value for the lifetime of the slang is revealed in Fig. 8. After performing the calculation process to create the tree structure, the program creates biomass.data file containing information of the calculation process including the height (Hauteur - French) of the tree has the value 34.73 (cm) (Figs. 9 and 10).

Fig. 8. Image of rice plants with default data values

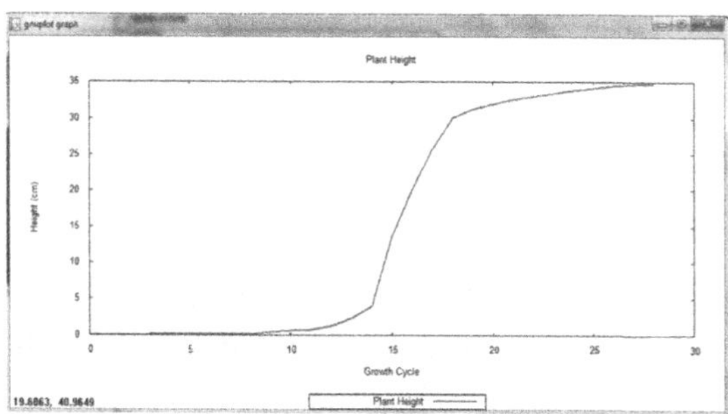

Fig. 9. Diagram showing the height of rice plants

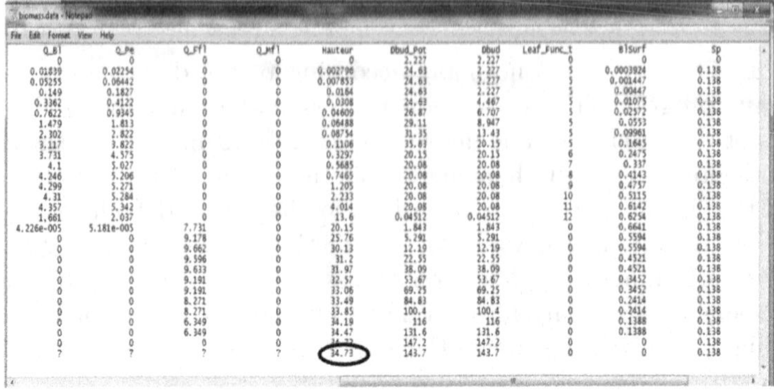

biomass.data - Notepad

File Edit Format View Help

Q_Bl	Q_Pe	Q_Ffl	Q_Mfl	Hauteur	Dbud_Pot	Dbud	Leaf_Func_t	BlSurf	Sp
0	0	0	0	0	2.227	2.227	0	0	0
0.01839	0.02254	0	0	0.002798	24.63	2.227	5	0.0003924	0.138
0.05255	0.06442	0	0	0.007853	24.63	2.227	5	0.001447	0.138
0.149	0.1827	0	0	0.0164	24.63	2.227	5	0.00447	0.138
0.3362	0.4122	0	0	0.0308	24.63	4.467	5	0.01075	0.138
0.7622	0.9345	0	0	0.04609	26.87	6.707	5	0.02572	0.138
1.479	1.813	0	0	0.06488	29.11	8.947	5	0.0553	0.138
2.302	2.822	0	0	0.08754	31.35	13.43	5	0.09961	0.138
3.117	3.822	0	0	0.1106	35.83	20.15	5	0.1645	0.138
3.731	4.575	0	0	0.3297	20.15	20.15	6	0.2475	0.138
4.1	5.027	0	0	0.5685	20.08	20.08	7	0.337	0.138
4.246	5.206	0	0	0.7465	20.08	20.08	8	0.4143	0.138
4.299	5.271	0	0	1.205	20.08	20.08	9	0.4757	0.138
4.31	5.284	0	0	2.233	20.08	20.08	10	0.5115	0.138
4.357	5.342	0	0	4.014	20.08	20.08	11	0.6142	0.138
1.661	2.037	0	0	13.6	0.04512	0.04512	12	0.6254	0.138
4.226e-005	5.181e-005	7.731	0	20.15	1.843	1.843	0	0.6641	0.138
0	0	9.178	0	25.76	5.291	5.291	0	0.5594	0.138
0	0	9.662	0	30.13	12.19	12.19	0	0.5594	0.138
0	0	9.596	0	31.2	22.55	22.55	0	0.4521	0.138
0	0	9.633	0	31.97	38.09	38.09	0	0.4521	0.138
0	0	9.191	0	32.57	53.67	53.67	0	0.3452	0.138
0	0	9.191	0	33.06	69.25	69.25	0	0.3452	0.138
0	0	8.271	0	33.49	84.83	84.83	0	0.2414	0.138
0	0	8.271	0	33.85	100.4	100.4	0	0.2414	0.138
0	0	6.349	0	34.19	116	116	0	0.1388	0.138
0	0	6.349	0	34.47	131.6	131.6	0	0.1388	0.138
0	0	0	0	[illegible]	147.2	147.2	0	0	0.138
?	?	?	?	34.73	143.7	143.7	0	0	0.138

Fig. 10. The file stores the height value of a tree after being calculated

Scenario 2: Tree height decrease value entered by experts is equal to the value in the comparison table. Assume the expert's height reduction value is 1% so change the lifetime value of the corresponding slang as shown in Fig. 11.

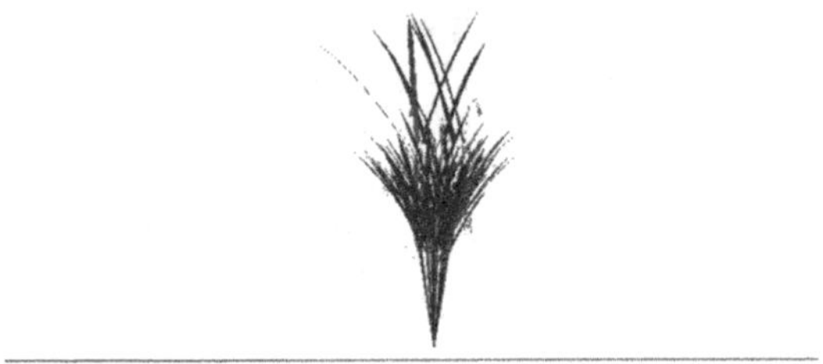

Fig. 11. Image of rice plants decreasing in height by 1%

The biomass.data file contains information about the calculation of the tree's structure which has the height of the tree is 34.4 (cm) as shown in the left chart in Fig. 12.

Scenario 3: The shoot height reduction value entered by experts of the value entered is not equal to the values stored in the comparison table. In this case, assume the expert's height reduction value is 30%. Compare the 30% value with the values in the comparison table, on the principle that the comparative value is less than or equal to the value in the table so that it is within 41% or less. Thus, the change in the lifetime value of the corresponding slang is:

The biomass.data file contains information about the calculation of the tree's structure which is exhibited in the right chart of Fig. 12 with the height of 20.63 (cm) (Figs. 13 and 14).

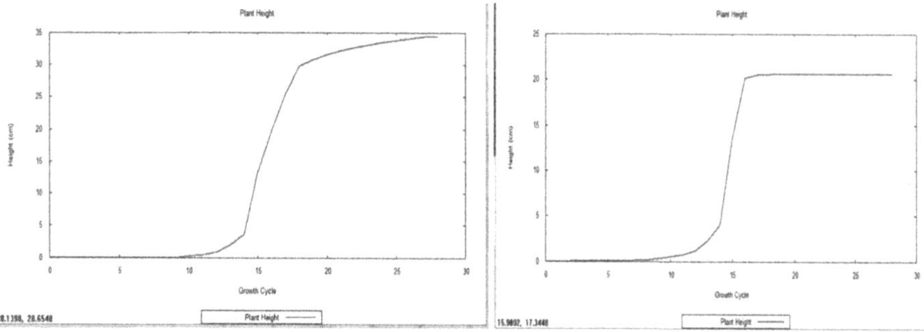

Fig. 12. Diagram of showing height when decreasing 1% (left) and 30% (right)

biomass.data - Notepad

File Edit Format View Help

Bl	Q_Pe	Q_Ffl	Q_Mfl	Hauteur	Dbud_Pot	Dbud	Leaf_Func_t	Blsurf	Sp	CI
0	0	0	0	0	2.226	2.226	0	0	0	0
84	0.02256	0	0	0	24.49	2.226	5	0.0003926	0.138	0.001421
62	0.06452	0	0	0	24.49	2.226	5	0.001449	0.138	0.005231
93	0.183	0	0	0	24.49	2.226	5	0.004476	0.138	0.01605
79	0.4142	0	0	0	24.49	4.452	5	0.01077	0.138	0.03802
68	0.9416	0	0	0	26.71	6.678	5	0.02582	0.138	0.08798
93	1.831	0	0	0	28.94	8.904	5	0.03562	0.138	0.177
26	2.852	0	0	0	31.16	13.36	5	0.1004	0.138	0.2895
49	3.861	0	0	0	35.62	20.03	5	0.166	0.138	0.4183
44	4.59	0	0	0	20.15	20.15	6	0.2498	0.138	0.538
08	5.036	0	0	0.2392	20.08	20.08	7	0.3396	0.138	0.6284
25	5.211	0	0	0.4173	20.08	20.08	8	0.417	0.138	0.6852
02	5.274	0	0	0.8759	20.08	20.08	9	0.478	0.138	0.7204
11	5.285	0	0	1.904	20.08	20.08	10	0.5131	0.138	0.7376
58	5.342	0	0	3.685	20.08	20.08	11	0.6158	0.138	0.7785
62	2.037	0	0	13.27	0.04512	0.04512	12	0.6262	0.138	0.782
05	5.181e-005	7.731	0	19.82	1.843	1.843	0	0.6649	0.138	0.7941
0	0	9.178	0	25.43	5.291	5.291	0	0.5598	0.138	0.7578
0	0	9.662	0	29.8	12.19	12.19	0	0.5598	0.138	0.7578
0	0	9.596	0	30.87	22.55	22.55	0	0.4523	0.138	0.7064
0	0	9.634	0	31.64	38.09	38.09	0	0.4523	0.138	0.7064
0	0	9.192	0	32.24	53.67	53.67	0	0.3453	0.138	0.6332
0	0	9.192	0	32.73	69.25	69.25	0	0.3453	0.138	0.6332
0	0	8.272	0	33.16	84.83	84.83	0	0.2415	0.138	0.5279
0	0	8.272	0	33.53	100.4	100.4	0	0.2415	0.138	0.5279
0	0	6.35	0	33.86	116	116	0	0.1388	0.138	0.3694
0	0	6.35	0	34.14	131.6	131.6	0	0.1388	0.138	0.3694
0	0	0	0	34.4	147.2	147.2	0	0	0.138	-1.#IO
?	?	?	?	34.4	143.7	143.7	0	0	0.138	-1.#IO

Fig. 13. File storing tree height value when reduced by 1%

biomass.data - Notepad

File Edit Format View Help

Root_mass	Qroot	Q_In	Q_Bl	Q_Pe	Q_Ffl	Q_Mfl	Hauteur	Dbud_Pot	Dbud	Leaf_Fun
0	0	0	0	0	0	0	0	2.227	2.227	
0	0	2.557e-005	0.01839	0.02254	0	0	0.002796	24.63	2.227	
0	0	7.309e-005	0.05255	0.06442	0	0	0.007853	24.63	2.227	
0	0	0.0002073	0.149	0.1827	0	0	0.0164	24.63	2.227	
0	0	0.002572	0.3362	0.4122	0	0	0.0308	24.63	4.467	
0	0	0.007414	0.7622	0.9345	0	0	0.04609	26.87	6.707	
0	0	0.01592	1.479	1.813	0	0	0.06488	29.11	8.947	
0	0	0.02715	2.302	2.822	0	0	0.08754	31.35	13.43	
0	0	0.03888	3.117	3.822	0	0	0.1106	35.83	20.15	
0	0	0.04618	3.731	4.575	0	0	0.3297	20.15	20.15	
0	0	0.0203	4.1	5.027	0	0	0.5685	20.08	20.08	
0	0	0.07007	4.246	5.206	0	0	0.7465	20.08	20.08	
0	0	0.1301	4.299	5.271	0	0	1.205	20.08	20.08	
0	0	0.1802	4.31	5.284	0	0	2.233	20.08	20.08	
0	0	0.2037	4.357	5.342	0	0	4.014	20.08	20.08	
0	0	6.213	1.661	2.037	0	0	13.6	0.04512	0.04512	
0	0	1.794	4.452e-005	5.458e-005	8.144	0	20.2	1.73	1.73	
0	0	0.4967	0	0	9.349	0	20.51	5.19	5.19	
0	0	0.1208	0	0	9.725	0	20.61	12.11	12.11	
0	0	0.0193	0	0	9.621	0	20.63	22.49	22.49	
0	0	0	0	0	9.641	0	20.63	38.06	38.06	
0	0	0	0	0	9.198	0	20.63	53.63	53.63	
0	0	0	0	0	9.198	0	20.63	69.19	69.19	
0	0	0	0	0	8.278	0	20.63	84.76	84.76	
0	0	0	0	0	8.278	0	20.63	100.3	100.3	
0	0	0	0	0	6.354	0	20.63	115.9	115.9	
0	0	0	0	0	6.354	0	20.63	131.5	131.5	
0	0	0	0	0	0	0	20.63	147	147	
0	0	?	?	?	?	?	20.63	143.6	143.6	

Fig. 14. The file stores tree height value showing a decrease in heights by 30%

4.4 Performance Evaluation

Through the experimental results, it is found that the closer the reduction rate of tree height by agricultural experts when imported to the rate of shoot reduction of the comparison table, the more similar the displayed image is. change the height of the tree, this difference ratio is not large. If the height reduction ratio of a tree is entered between 10 and 30 and between 70 and 90 then the ratio of height deviation is large.

5 Conclusion

In this study, we propose a model to understand how rice is affected by planthoppers migration, destroy and spread disease. Also, the study proposes an application in a combination of multi-agent modeling and simulation. The work also provides an understand tree growth and structure model. However, this work only focuses on researching about brown planthopper that transmits yellow dwarf disease makes rice plants dwarf.

The further research topic should pay attention to aphids that affect other parts of the plant.

References

1. Ministry of Agriculture and Rural Development (2006). Handbook on prevention and control of brown plant hopper that transmits yellow dwarf and twisted leaves dwarf diseases, National Agricultural Extension Center
2. Cuong, P.H.: The rice BPH pest, Master Thesis in Information Systems, Can Tho University (2009)
3. Nguyen, N.D.: Curriculum on Rice. Mekong Delta Development Research Institute, Can Tho University, Department of Crop Resources (2008)
4. Hien, N.C., Nguyen, P.T.A.: System and simulation professor, Science and Technology Publishing House, Hanoi (2006)
5. Van Kim, P.: Some important diseases in rice in the Mekong Delta. Can Tho University, Ministry of Plant Protection (2006)
6. Nguyen, N.T.: Geographical Information System, VNU University of Science, Hanoi National University
7. Tung, V.T.: Building a simulation model of aphid spread on rice fields, Master Thesis of information systems, Can Tho University (2010)
8. Cournede, P.H.: Digiplant. INRIA, Paris, France (2004)
9. Team Digiplant (2006). Modeling plants growth and plants architecture, INRIA
10. Platform GAMA. http://code.google.com/p/gama-platform/
11. Yang, S.J., Bao, Y.X., Chen, C., Lu, M.H., Liu, W.C., Hong, S.J.: Analysis of atmospheric circulation situation and source areas for brown planthopper immigration to Korea: a case study. Ecosphere J. (2020). https://doi.org/10.1002/ecs2.3079

12. Liu, J., et al.: Different adaptability of the brown planthopper, *Nilaparvata lugens* (Stål), to gradual and abrupt increases in atmospheric CO2. J. Pest Sci. **93**(3), 979–991 (2020). https://doi.org/10.1007/s10340-020-01221-x
13. Hereward, J., Cai, X., Matias, A., Walter, G., Xu, C., Wang, Y.: Migration dynamics of an important rice pest: the brown planthopper (Nilaparvata lugens) across Asia - insights from population genomics. Evol. Appl. (2020).https://doi.org/10.1111/eva.13047

Network Based Comparison of Indian Railways and Airways

Amit Kumar Dhar, Shivam Sharma, and Rishi Ranjan Singh(✉)

Department of Electrical Engineering and Computer Science,
Indian Institute of Technology, Bhilai, Chhattisgarh, India
{amitkdhar,shivamsh,rishi}@iitbhilai.ac.in

Abstract. We compare the Indian railways and domestic airways using network analysis approach. The analysis also compares different characteristics of the networks with a previous work and notes the change in the networks over a decade. In a populous country like India with an ever increasing GDP, more and more people are gaining the facility of choosing one mode of travel over the other. Here we have compared these two networks, by building a *merger* network. The need for such type of network arises as the order of both networks are different. This newly formed network can be used in identifying new routes and adding more flights on some of the popular routes in India.

Keywords: Transportation networks · Railway network · Airways network · Network analysis

1 Introduction

Transportation Systems are the backbone of the economy of a country. It drives the economy of the country as the foundation of tourism industry, aids in efficient mobility of goods and movement of people. Network analysis has been known as a widely applied tool to understand the structure and characteristics of public-transit systems across various countries. There exist some unique features in transportation networks like limited network sizes, slow rate of change in structures, bidirectional and weighted links with marginally varying frequency, which makes them different from other type of networks.

Transportation networks such as railways and airways network are very popular among public-transit systems. There are several general differences in the railways and airways network. For example, in the airways network, each airport is fairly independent. Whereas, In the railways network many smaller stations are present in between two main stations. Although being the two most popular mode for commuting, owing to this kind of differences in the structure of airways and railways networks, it becomes even more interesting to compare these two type of networks.

Over recent years, complex network analysis has been used to analyze many transport networks such as Airport Network of China, World-wide airport networks, US airport network etc [1,2,4,5,7,8]. There are some common features

S. Chellappan et al. (Eds.): CSoNet 2020, LNCS 12575, pp. 100–112, 2020.
https://doi.org/10.1007/978-3-030-66046-8_9

which has been observed in almost all transport networks. For example, almost all the transportation networks studied till now exhibit the small world properties [2,4–6,8]. Whereas some features show significant variations among different transportation networks. For example degree distribution of Indian railways network and Chinese railways network shows exponential behaviour [1,4]; degree distribution of Indian airport network and US airport network shows power law behaviour [2,5]. In terms of combining different types of transport network, there have been studies utilising the multi-modal nature of combined network for several purposes (e.g. [18,19]). In the present work, we compare two modes of transport network instead of combining and analysing them as one.

Indian railways network is one of the cheapest, largest as well as busiest rail networks. Every section of the country whether student, employees, household people or businessman etc. all use the railway service for different purposes. Railways is considered as the lifeline of India as it offers 24 * 7 services and countrywide connectivity. Railways Network of India is commonly depicted as the pillar of India's economy as it is the most durable, robust, efficient, economical and popular mode of long distance transportation. Indian civil aviation sector has also been expanding rapidly in recent times. Due to the recent active involvement of several low-cost private carriers, it is expanding at a faster pace and more people are choosing to travel by airways instead of railways.

Characteristics of railways as well as airways network have been studied individually but to the best of our knowledge, this is the first study which attempts to compare the two popular modes of transport (Airways and Railways) in Indian context. Due to a huge difference in the *order*, i.e., number of nodes in both type networks it becomes very difficult to effectively compare these two networks in Indian context. For example, an airport is not only used by the people of that particular city but also by the people of neighbouring cities. On the other hand, in the case of railway stations, almost every city has its own station. Here, we have done a thorough analysis of the two transport modes of India. To tackle the challenges in the comparison, we have proposed creation of a new type of network by merging the data of these two networks, which allows us to easily compare these networks.

The paper starts with a description of the creation of networks in Sect. 2. The data acquisition and representation chosen for different networks is explained in details in this section. Section 3 contains the result of analysis of different parameters of the networks obtained. We discuss in this section the interpretation of these results and their usefulness. Finally, Sect. 4 presents the discussion and conclusion of the present work.

2 Network Data

In this section, the creation of both the transport networks is discussed in detail. We have also detailed the network representation used in this paper. Finally, we also discuss the method of creation of the merger network.

2.1 Railways Network

There are two most common network representations of railways system. In the first one, railway stations are considered as the nodes and there exists an edge from an node i to another node j if there exists at least a single train which has scheduled halts on node i and at later point to node j. The obtained network is a directed and weighted network, where the weights on the edges represent the number of trains. As trains in India run with variety of frequency, we have aggregated the trains running in a week together. Thus, the weights on the edges represents the total number of trains in a week which have scheduled halts on node i and then on node j. Many previous studies on transportation network used this approach. Let us call this type of railways network as *S-Railways* Network. Checking some of the properties like resiliency is challenging in this type of representation which is tackled well by the another representation. This second representation of railways network also considers railway stations as nodes but here there exists an edge from an node i to another node j if there exists at least a single train which has scheduled halts on node i and next immediate halt to node j, i.e., node i and j are neighbours in the scheduled halts of at least a single train. The weight on the edge (i, j) represents the total number of trains presents in a week which have scheduled halts on node i and next immediate halt to node j. Let us say this type of railways network as *T-Railway* Network.

In this study, only express, mail and super-fast trains considered. Further only those stations are abstracted as nodes which are present as a halting station in the schedule of at least a train. The data was extracted from **etrain.info** in December 2019. From the collected trains data, we constructed the weighted S-Railway and T-Railway Networks.

The current Indian railways network comprises of 3441 stations(nodes) and 243368 links. The values of Average Shortest Path Length, Clustering Coefficient, Assortativity and Average Degree can be found in Table 1. The diameter of the S-Railways Network turns out to be 4, whereas the diameter of T-Railways Network turns out to 31. A reason for such change in diameter between two types of railway network is that S-Railways Network shows the connectivity of stations rather than the routes of the network. On comparing the current railways network with the network of a previous study of Indian Railways Network by Ghosh et al. [1] in 2011, we find that the railways network grew rapidly in this duration of time. There were only 3041 nodes and 181208 edges in that network which has reached to 3441 stations(nodes) and 243368 links in less than a decade. Most of the structural properties are coherent with the previous study, however, a few characteristics changed. Table 1 shows the changes in the various characteristics of the railways network from 2011 to 2020.

2.2 Airways Network

Airways Network, considered here, consists of domestic airports of India and airlines connecting them. The considered airways data in this paper includes flight schedule of all major domestic airlines in India along with few international airlines which gives services on domestic routes of India. The flight schedules are obtained from the official website of Directorate General of Civil Aviation in December 2019 (www.dgca.gov.in). A total of 12 airlines' schedules are taken into consideration namely Air Asia, Air India, Alliance Air, Deccan Air, Go Air, Heritage, Indigo, Pawan Hans, Spicejet, Star Air, Trujet, Vistara for forming this network. From the collected data, an Airways Network is formed in which nodes represent the airports and there is an edge from node i to node j if there exist at least one flight from node i to j in a week. The weights on the edges represent number of flights from node i to j in a week.

The current Indian Airways Network consist of 103 nodes and 908 links. The values of average shortest path length, average degree, clustering coefficient and assortativity can be found in Table 1. The diameter of the airways network turns out to be just 4 which is same as the diameter in the S-Railways network. On comparing the current airways network with the network of a previous study of Indian Airways Network by Bagler [2] in 2008, we realise that the airways network grew even more rapidly than the railways network in this duration of time. There were only 79 nodes and 442 edges in that network which has reached to 103 airports(nodes) and 908 links in approximately a decade. Most of the structural properties are coherent with the previous study, however, a few characteristics changed. Table 1 shows the changes in the various characteristics of the airways network from 2008 to 2020.

2.3 Merger Network

An effective comparison between the above two transportation networks was challenging due to a large variation in the order of the networks, i.e. the number of nodes in these networks. The creation of a network that can ease the comparison was essential. There are many ways to achieve this. In this paper we propose to compress the railways network to the order of the airways network. We do the following to get the *Merger* Network.

We collected the Latitude and Longitude coordinate of all the railway stations and all the airports from google map. Then we identified the nearest airport from each railway station. Afterwards, every railway station is mapped to the airport nearest to it. In this way, the railway stations for which the nearest airport is same, belong to the same set which corresponds to the airport. The nodes in the Merger Network represents a set of such railway stations and the nearest airport to all those railway stations. An edge exists between two nodes i and node j of the Merger Network, if there exists at least a single train connecting from at least one railway station in the set represented by node i to at least one railways station in the set represented by node j. The weights on the edges represent the total number of trains connecting two sets or nodes in a week. As train connectivity can be assumed as a notion of the quantity of commuters between regions, the edge-weights may be understood as commuting demand from one region to another region.

We got 103 nodes in the giant component of airways network but only 90 nodes in the giant connected component of the merger network. The rest of

Table 1. Network Characteristics table

		Nodes	**Links**	**ASPL**	**Clustering Coeff.**	**Assortativity**	**Ave. Degree**
Railways Network	Saptarshi Ghosh et al. (2011)	3041	181208	2.53	0.733	0.0813	119.177
	Current Network	3441	243368	2.45	0.6927	0.045	141.45
Airways Network	Bagler (2008)	79	442	2.26	0.6574	−0.4	5.77
	Current Network	103	908	2.188	0.6630439	−0.47647	8.815
Merger Network		90	5618	1.30	0.847	−0.077	62.4

13 nodes were isolated. This is because of the airports which are located on islands or in hilly areas without any train connectivity for e.g. Port Blair Airport or all the nearby stations are nearer to some other airport. While the current airways network had only 908 edges, the merger network contains 5618 edges over smaller number of nodes than the airways network. It shows that the airways network is very sparse than the demanded connectivity. Table 1 shows various characteristics of the merger network.

3 Network Analysis

In this section, we summarise various structural properties of the three networks (S-Railway Network, Airways Network and Merger Network) using popular network analysis tools. The analysis is similar to the one done by Ghosh et al. [1] and Bagler [2]. As the edges are bi-direction between nodes with almost similar weight, we consider the out going edges in most of the analysis.

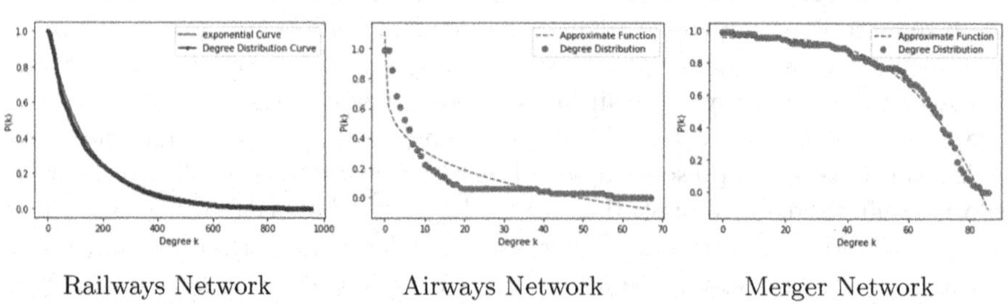

Fig. 1. Degree Distributions

3.1 Degree Distribution

Degree of a node i, is the total number of edges that are incident on the node i. In case of S-Railway Network, out degree of a node i represents the total number of stations which are reachable by a single train from node i. Cumulative Degree Distribution is defined as $D(k) = \sum_{i=k}^{\infty} d(i)$, Where d(i) $= n_k/N$, where n_k is the number of nodes having degree k and N is the total number of nodes in the network [14]. Cumulative degree distribution is used at place of simple degree distribution to avoid noise in the histogram [14]. Figure 1 shows the degree distribution of the three networks.

The cumulative degree distribution of Indian railways network still follows exponential decay as noted by Ghosh et al. [1]. The approximate fit for the curve of cumulative degree distribution turns out to be D(k) $\sim$ exp(-0.007k). The cumulative degree distribution of the Indian Airways Network still follows power law as noted by Bagler [2]. It is approximated by a power law curve with a scaling exponent y = 1.11 in $P(k) \sim k^{-y}$. The degree distribution of Merger Network is characterized by a power function with a scaling exponent 0.95.

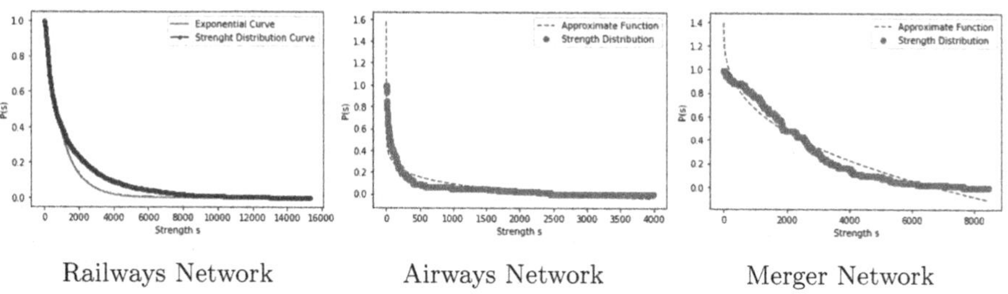

Railways Network Airways Network Merger Network

Fig. 2. Strength Distributions

3.2 Strength Distribution

The strength of a node i is defined as sum of the weights on the edges incident at i [1]. Strength at a node indicates the availability of transportation from that node. It can be understood as the weighted degree. The considered networks have weights on the edges, therefore, it is a good idea to study the strength distribution. It depicts the information about the traffic dynamics. The cumulative strength distribution [14] is defined as $S(k) = \sum_{i=k}^{\infty} s(i)$. Fig. 2 shows the cumulative strength distribution of the three networks. The cumulative strength distribution S(k) of the railways network is observed to be an exponentially decaying distribution with scaling $a = 0.001$ in the approximate fitting $S(k)\ exp(-ak)$. The Strength Distribution of the airways network and merger network follows power law with a scaling exponent y = 1.57 and 1.39 respectively.

3.3 Edge Weight Distribution

The weights on edges in networks represents the total number of trains/flights between two stations/airports in a week. Figure 3 shows the Edge Weight Distribution of the three Networks. The cumulative edge weight distribution of railways, airways and merger network follows exponential decay. The approximate fit for the curves of cumulative edge weight distribution turns out to be EW(e) $\sim$ exp(-0.09e), EW(e) $\sim$ exp(-0.04e) and EW(e) $\sim$ exp(-0.025e) respectively.

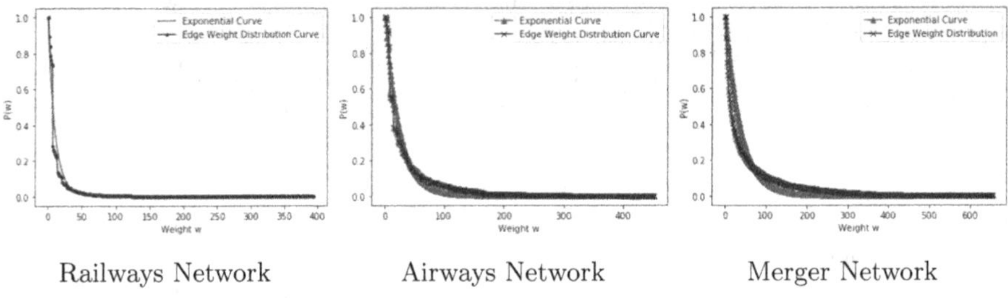

Fig. 3. Edge Weight Distributions

3.4 Strength Degree Correlations

The correlations between the degree and strength of a node may be used to understand the relationship between these two topological properties [1]. Figure 4 shows the strength degree correlations of the three networks. The plots for all the three networks follow power law. The approximate fit for the three curves of strength degree correlations turns out to be S(k) $\sim k^{1.39}$, S(k) $\sim k^2$ and S(k) $\sim k^2$ respectively.

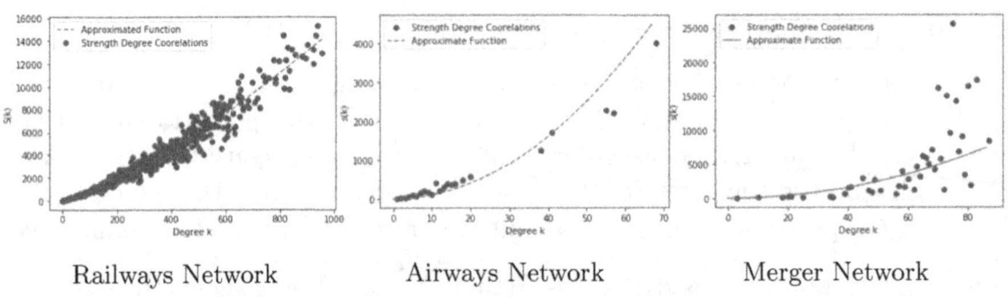

Fig. 4. Strength Degree Correlations

3.5 Average Clustering

Clustering coefficient of a node i is calculated using the following formula $cc_i = \frac{2t(i)}{d(i)(d(i)-1)}$ where $t(i)$ denotes the number of triangles on i [17]. In order to understand the distribution of clustering coefficient of nodes over the whole network, we plot the average clustering coefficient of nodes of degree k against k and summarize in Fig. 5. The plots for all the three networks seems to follow exponential decay. The approximate fit is cc(k) $\sim$ exp(-ak), where a = 0.002, 0.029 and 0.003 respectively for railways, airways and merger network.

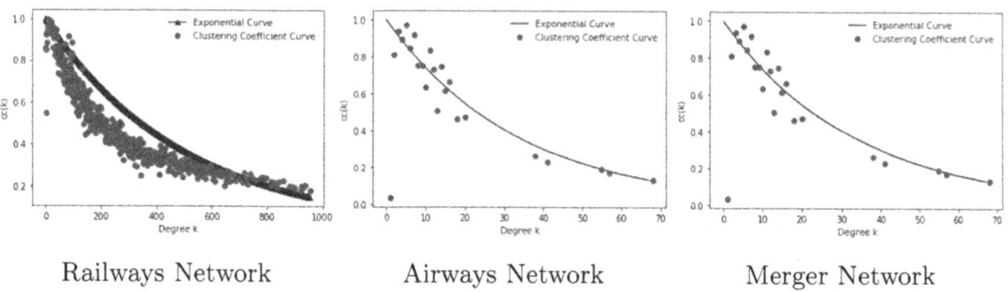

Fig. 5. Average Clustering of nodes having degree k

3.6 Assortativity

Assortativity is the phenomenon of nodes connecting with nodes of similar degree. The opposite phenomenon is called Disassortativity [15]. For checking this property we use similar formulations as used in [1]. Figure 6 shows the plot of average degree of nearest neighbors of degree k against k for the railways, airways and merger network.

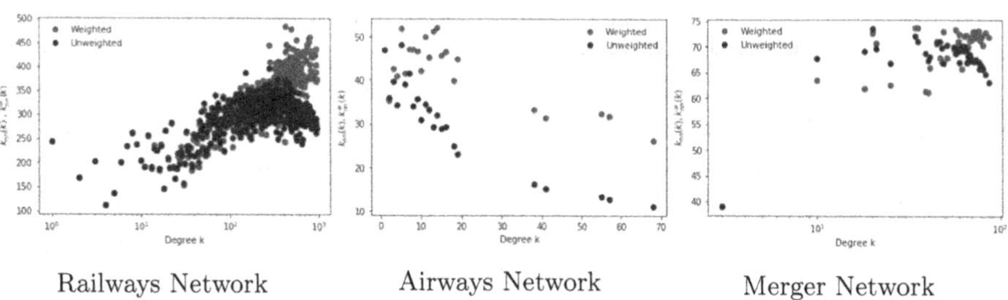

Fig. 6. Assortativity: average degree of nearest neighbors of nodes having degree k (both unweighted and weighted).

The plot for railway network exhibit that the relationship can not be predict as assortative or disassortative in case of unweighted version but if we look at the strength, the assortative behaviour of the network is seen. In case of airways network, it is observed that for small values of degree, airways network shows no specific assortative or disassortative nature but for large values of degree, it is clearly showing the disassortative nature. The disassortative nature of airways network can be explained by the fact that many large degree airports are connected to low degree airports. The plots for merger network in case of unweighted degree shows disassortative behaviour (as in case of Airways Network) and in case of strength, it shows assortative behaviour (as in case of Railways Network). Hence it is concluded that the topology of Merger Network is Disassortative, but if we consider the traffic dynamics then it is assortative.

3.7 Degree and Betweenness Centrality

Degree Centrality is a measure of the number of links a node has. In Railways Network HWH(Howrah Junction) has the highest degree centrality among all other railway stations. In Airways Network DEL(Delhi) has the highest degree centrality among all other airports. In Merger Network DEL(Delhi) has the highest degree centrality among all other nodes.

Betweenness centrality is a measure of the dominance of the node on the flow of information between each pair of nodes, assuming that information flows mainly along the shortest paths. In Railways Network HWH(Howrah Junction) has the highest Betweenness centrality. In Airways Network DEL(Delhi) has the highest betweenness centrality. In Merger Network, GAU(Guwahati) has the highest Betweenness centrality.

3.8 Resiliency

Resiliency of networks are studied in terms of how much the graph has to change in order to make some property of network vanish. Higher the amount of change, stronger the network posses that property. An important property of transport network is connectivity. In case of natural calamity, disruption in transportation network is normal. Using resiliency, we study how much disruption will make the transportation network disconnected. We consider connectivity property in all three types of networks. We find out the least number of nodes whose removal will make the network disconnected (both strongly and weakly). The approach for checking network resilience against connectivity is that we check for connectivity by removing every node one by one. If network doesn't get disconnected by this then remove pairs of every two nodes one by one and check for connectivity and so on until the network gets disconnected.

Railways Network is not strongly connected. It can be attributed to three trains Chhattisgarh Express(18237, CSMT DHI Express (11057) and KOAA PNBE Express (13131) which follows different routes on to and fro journey. On the other hand the railways network is weakly connected. Therefore, we discuss the resiliency of the railways network against weakly connected property. Using the above-mentioned approach, we get the following stations in the railways network which are dependent on a single railway station in the network.

Atari (ATT) is connected only with Delhi junction(DLI). Munabao (MBF) is connected only with Bhagat Ki Kothi (BGKT). Petrapol (PTPL) is connected only with Kolkata (KOAA).

It is found out that the airways network is strongly connected. Hence, we can analyse its resiliency for both properties i.e. strongly connected and weakly connected. For strongly connected property, Agatti Island (AGX) has incoming flights from only Cochin Airport (COK), Lilabari Airport (IXI) has outgoing flights only to Kolkata Airport (CCU), Pasighat Airport (IXT) has incoming flights only from Guwahati Airport (GAU), and Khajuraho Airport (HJR) has outgoing flights only to Varanasi Airport (VNS).

For weakly connected case, Adampur Airport(AIP), Bikaner Airport(BKB), Pathankot Airport(IXP) and Ludhiana Airport(LUH) are connected only with Delhi Airport (DEL), Dimapur Airport(DMU), Pakyong Airport(PYG) and Shillong Airport(SHL) are connected only with Kolkata Airport (CCU), Tezpur airport(TEZ) is connected only with Guwahati Airport(GAU), Mundra airport(MDA) is connected only with Ahemdabad airport(AMD), Bhuj Airport(BHJ) and Jamnagar airport(JGA) are connected only with Bombay airport(BOM), and Salem Airport(SXV) is connected only with Chennai Airport(MAA).

The merger network is also strongly connected. Hence, we analyse its resiliency for strongly connected as well as weakly connected property. The merger network lost its weakly connected property if at least 3 nodes are removed from the network. Those 3 nodes are GAU(Guwahati), TEZ(Tezpur), IXI(Lilabari). Removing these nodes makes the node IXT(Pasighat) disconnected from the network.

3.9 Edge-Based Comparison Between Airways Network and Merger Network

In this section we identify the major differences between the airways and merger network based on the edges and edge weights. If some edges are present in the airways network but not in the merger network, it is inferred that although two regions are directly connected by flights but there is no direct rail connectivity. It might be due to very long distance between two regions or due to geographical locations not suitable for railway lines. The top ten such pairs are mentioned in Table 2. If some edges are present in the merger network but not in the airways network, it is inferred that although two regions are directly connected by rail but there is no direct air-connectivity. Such pairs which have high weights on the edges in the merger network but are not adjacent in airways network are the best options for new flight routes. This is because yet no flights have been started on these routes and these regions have very good rail connectivity expressing the heavy demand of commuting. There are several such edges as the density of merger network is very high in comparison to the airways network. We have mentioned top 10 such pairs which are at least 118 Kms (the minimum distance between two airports with a direct connectivity) distance apart in Table 2.

Table 2. Regions between which direct flight connectivity is available but direct train connectivity is not available and vise-versa. The top 10 routes of each type are summarized below.

S.N.	Present in Airways but not in Merger Network		Present in Merge but not in Airways Network	
	Route	# Flights/Week	Route	# Trains/Week
1	Ahemdabad(AMD) ⟺ Nashik(ISK)	13	Kolkata(CCU) ⟺ Durgapur(RDP)	635
2	Amritsar(ATQ) ⟺ Bangalore(BLR)	7	Indore(IDR) ⟺ Varanasi(VNS)	624
3	Amritsar(ATQ) ⟺ Hyderabad(HYD)	7	Delhi(DEL) ⟺ Agra(AGR)	600
4	Bangalore(BLR) ⟺ Amritsar(ATQ)	7	Indore(IDR) ⟺ Bhopal(BHO)	595
5	Kolkata(CCU) ⟺ Lilabari(IXI)	6	Varanasi(VNS) ⟺ Allahabad(IXD)	506
6	Kannur(CNN) ⟺ Hubli(HBX)	7	Gwalior(GWL) ⟺ Agra(AGR)	448
7	Goa(GOI) ⟺ Lucknow(LKO)	7	Indore(IDR) ⟺ Allahabad(IXD)	426
8	Nagpur(NAG) ⟺ Goa(GOI)	14	Durgapur(RDP) ⟺ Patna(PAT)	419
9	Hyderabad(HYD) ⟺ Agartala(IXA)	4	Kadapa(CDP) ⟺ Vidyanagar(VDY)	412
10	Amritsar(ATQ) ⟺ Nanded(NDC)	2	Gaya(GAY) ⟺ Durgapur(RDP)	411

Next, we compare the edge weights between two airports in airways network denoting the current number of flights and the weights between the region covered by those two airports in the merger network representing the demand of connectivity and commuting fulfilled by the rail mode. It has been observed that between some regions, there are more flights than trains whereas between some regions there are more trains than flights. The top ten node pairs with high and low ratio has been summarized in the Table 3. Node pairs with very high trains to flight ratio helps identifying the airports and corresponding regions between which although there are air connectivity but it is relatively very low in comparison to the rail connectivity and demand of commuting. Adding more flights on these routes will turnout to be profitable than routes with lower trains to flights ratio. Node pairs with very low trains to flight connectivity are those which have large number of flights between them and yet due to distance or geography, relatively very small number of trains are operating between those node pairs.

Table 3. Regions between which the ratio of train connectivity and flight connectivity is very high and low. The pairs representing routes with top 10 high and low trains to flights ratio are summarized below.

S.N.	Very high ratio of trains to flight		Very low ratio of trains to flight	
	Route	Ratio	Route	Ratio
1	Delhi(DEL) ⟺ Gwalior(GWL)	140.33	Chennai(MAA) ⟺ Goa(GOI)	0.037
2	Delhi(DEL) ⟺ Ludhiana(LUH)	82.75	Guwahati(GAU) ⟺ Hyderabad(HYD)	0.042
3	Pantnagar(PGH) ⟺ Delhi(DEL)	80.25	Bangalore(BLR) ⟺ Jaipur(JAI)	0.05
4	Gwalior(GWL) ⟺ Indore(IDR)	73.33	Agartala(IXA) ⟺ Kolkata(CCU)	0.076
5	Varanasi(VNS) ⟺ Agra(AGR)	57	Goa(GOI) ⟺ Hyderabad(HYD)	0.082
6	Jalgoan(JLG) ⟺ Mumbai(BOM)	55.2	Bangalore(BLR) ⟺ Delhi(DEL)	0.093
7	Kolhapur(KLH) ⟺ Mumbai(BOM)	53.6	Guwahati(GAU) ⟺ Ahemdabad(AMD)	0.1
8	Dehradun(DED) ⟺ Pantnagar(PGH)	51.5	Bangalore(BLR) ⟺ Lucknow(LKO)	0.125
9	Kanpur(KNU) ⟺ Delhi(DEL)	51.14	Shirdi(SAG) ⟺ Chennai(MAA)	0.143
10	Agra(AGR) ⟺ Jaipur(JAI)	49.25	Jaisalmer(JSA) ⟺ Bangalore(BLR)	0.143

4 Discussion and Conclusion

In this paper, Indian railways and airways network have been studied as complex weighted network. It has been noted that both networks grew bigger in size, yet the basic topological properties remains almost unchanged over the last decade. Network Resilience against connectivity has been studied for both the network. In order to compare the railways traffic and airways connectivity between two regions of the country, we created a new network based on the two networks. After comparing the new merger network with the current airways network, It has been noticed that few regions have much better rail connectivity than the air connectivity and vice versa. This newly formed network can be very helpful in identifying new routes and adding more flights on some of the routes. Combination of merger and airways network forms a two-layer network and using network analysis tools for multi-layer networks may deliver better analysis. A different direction for further analysis could be considering multi-modal transport with better and complicated merger to closely reflect the real-world scenarios. A similar type of analysis for other countries is another open direction.

References

1. Ghosh, S., et al.: Statistical analysis of the Indian railway network: a complex network approach. Acta Phys. Pol. B Proc. Suppl. **4**(2), 123–138 (2011)

2. Bagler, G.: Analysis of the airport network of India as a complex weighted network. Phys. A: Stat. Mech. Appl. **387**(12), 2972–2980 (2008)
3. Barrat, A., Barthelemy, M., Pastor-Satorras, R., Vespignani, A.: The architecture of complex weighted networks. Proc. Nat. Acad. Sci. **101**(11), 3747–3752 (2004)
4. Li, W., Cai, X.: Statistical analysis of airport network of China. Phys. Rev. E **69**(4), 046106 (2004)
5. Li-Ping, C., et al.: Structural properties of US flight network. Chin. Phys. Lett. **20**(8), 1393 (2003)
6. Liu, C.M., Li, J.W.: Small-world and the growing properties of the Chinese railway network. Front. Phys. China **2**(3), 364–367 (2007). https://doi.org/10.1007/s11467-007-0039-y
7. Li, W., Cai, X.: Empirical analysis of a scale-free railway network in China. Phys. A: Stat. Mech. Appl. **382**(2), 693–703 (2007)
8. Sen, P., Dasgupta, S., Chatterjee, A., Sreeram, P.A., Mukherjee, G., Manna, S.S.: Small-world properties of the Indian railway network. Phys. Rev. E **67**(3), 036106 (2003)
9. Barabási, A.L., Albert, R.: Emergence of scaling in random networks. Science **286**(5439), 509–512 (1999)
10. Faloutsos, M., Faloutsos, P., Faloutsos, C.: On power-law relationships of the internet topology. ACM SIGCOMM Comput. Commun. Rev. **29**(4), 251–262 (1999)
11. Stam, C.J.: Modern network science of neurological disorders. Nat. Rev. Neurosci. **15**(10), 683–695 (2014)
12. Newman, M.E.: The structure of scientific collaboration networks. Proc. Nat. Acad. Sci. **98**(2), 404–409 (2001)
13. Seaton, K.A., Hackett, L.M.: Stations, trains and small-world networks. Phys. A: Stat. Mech. Appl. **339**(3–4), 635–644 (2004)
14. Newman, M.E.: The structure and function of complex networks. SIAM Rev. **45**(2), 167–256 (2003)
15. Newman, M.E.: Assortative mixing in networks. Phys. Rev. Lett. **89**(20), 208701 (2002)
16. Park, K., Yilmaz, A.: A social network analysis approach to analyze road networks. In: ASPRS Annual Conference, San Diego, CA, pp. 1–6, April 2010
17. Saramäki, J., Kivelä, M., Onnela, J.P., Kaski, K., Kertesz, J.: Generalizations of the clustering coefficient to weighted complex networks. Phys. Rev. E **75**(2), 027105 (2007)
18. Sankaranarayanan, H. B., Rukmangadha, P. V., Grosche, T.: A combinatorial approach for calculating rail-fly connectivity index in India based on fuzzy logic. In: 2016 Future Technologies Conference (FTC), pp. 150–155. IEEE, December 2016
19. Sankaranarayanan, H. B., Thind, R. S.: Multi-modal travel in India: a big data approach for policy analytics. In 2017 7th International Conference on Cloud Computing, Data Science and Engineering-Confluence, pp. 243–248. IEEE, January 2017

k-TruthScore: Fake News Mitigation in the Presence of Strong User Bias

Akrati Saxena[1(✉)], Harsh Saxena[2], and Ralucca Gera[3]

[1] Department of Mathematics and Computer Science, Eindhoven University of Technology, Eindhoven, Netherlands
a.saxena@tue.nl

[2] Department of CSE, KSVCEM Bijnor, Bijnor, India
harshraj.saxena.18@gmail.com

[3] Department of Mathematics, Naval Postgraduate School, Monterey, CA, USA
rgera@nps.edu

Abstract. Due to the extensive role of social networks in social media, it is easy for people to share the news, and it spreads faster than ever before. These platforms also have been exploited to share the rumor or fake information, which is a threat to society. One method to reduce the impact of fake information is making people aware of the correct information based on hard proof. In this work, first, we propose a propagation model called Competitive Independent Cascade Model with users' Bias (CICMB) that considers the presence of strong user bias towards different opinions, believes, or political parties. We further propose a method, called $k - TruthScore$, to identify an optimal set of truth campaigners from a given set of prospective truth campaigners to minimize the influence of rumor spreaders on the network. We compare $k - TruthScore$ with state of the art methods, and we measure their performances as the percentage of the saved nodes (nodes that would have believed in the fake news in the absence of the truth campaigners). We present these results on a few real-world networks, and the results show that $k - TruthScore$ method outperforms baseline methods.

Keywords: Fake News mitigation · Influence propagation · Competitive information propagation

1 Introduction

Since 1997, Online Social Networks (OSNs) have made it progressively easier for users to share the information with each other, and information reaches millions of people in just a few seconds. Over these years, people shared true as well as fake news or misinformation on OSNs, since no references or proofs are required while posting on an OSN. In 2017, The World Economic Forum announced that the fake news and misinformation is one of the top three threats to democracy worldwide [9]. Google Trend Analysis shows that the web search for the "Fake News" term began to gain relevance from the time of the U.S.

S. Chellappan et al. (Eds.): CSoNet 2020, LNCS 12575, pp. 113–126, 2020.
https://doi.org/10.1007/978-3-030-66046-8_10

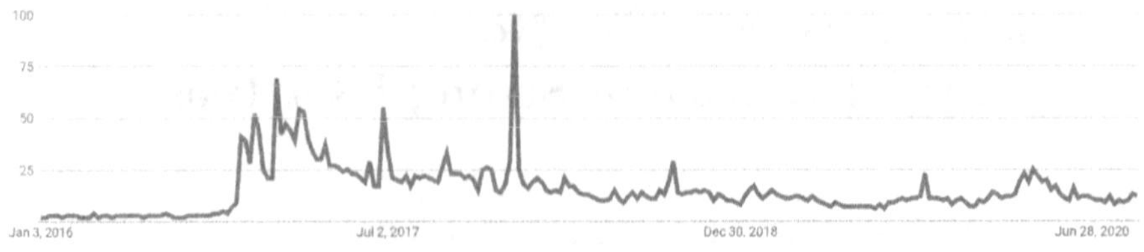

Fig. 1. Google Trend for "Fake News" web search since 2016.

presidential election in 2016 [1]; Fig. 1 shows the plot we generated using Google Trend data.

There are several reasons why people share fake news. Some of the threatening ones are changing the outcome of an event like an election, damaging the reputation of a person or company, creating panic or chaos among people, gaining profit by improving the public image of a product or company, etc. Less malicious reasons for sharing misinformation are due to the fame that users catch as a result of the news' catchiness or to start a new conversation while having no malicious intentions [5].

A study on the Twitter data shows that the false news spread faster, farther, and deeper [17,25], and these effects are even more prominent in the case of political news than financial, disaster, terrorism or science-related news [25]. A large volume of fake information is shared by a small number of accounts, and Andrews et al. [3] show that this could be combated by propagating the correct information in the time of crisis; the accounts propagating true information are referred to as "official" accounts.

In OSNs, users have high bias or polarity towards news topics, such as a bias for political parties [21,26]. Lee et al. [13] observe that the users who are actively involved in political discussions on OSNs tend to develop more extreme political attitudes over time than the people who do not use OSNs. Users tend to share the news confirming their beliefs. In this work, we propose a propagation model to model the spread of misinformation and its counter correct information in the presence of strong user bias; the proposed model is referred to as the Competitive Independent Cascade Model with users' Bias (CICMB). In the proposed model, the user's bias for a belief or opinion keeps getting stronger as they are exposed to more news confirming that opinion, and at the same time, their bias towards counter-opinion keeps getting weaken.

It is very challenging to mitigate the fake news in the presence of strong users' bias. Researchers have proposed various techniques to minimize the impact of fake news on a given social network. The proposed methods can be categorized as, (i) influence blocking (IB) techniques [2,18], and (ii) truth-campaigning techniques (TC) [4,22]. IB techniques aim to identify a set of nodes that can be blocked or immunized to minimize the spread of fake information in the network. However, in truth campaigning techniques, the aim is to identify an optimal set of users who will start spreading the correct information in the network so that the people are aware of true news and share it further. Psychological studies have shown that people believe in true news rather than fake news when they receive both, and this also reduces the sharing of fake information further [16,23].

Most of the existing methods identify truth campaigners in the network who can minimize the impact of fake information; however, they do not consider the factor that a chosen node might not be interested in starting a truth campaign if asked [4,15,22]. In this work, we consider a realistic approach where we have a given set of nodes which are willing to start a truth campaign; these nodes are referred to as *prospective truth campaigners.* We propose a method to identify k most influential truth campaigners from the given set of prospective truth campaigners to minimize the damage of fake news. We compare the proposed method, $k - TruthScore$, with state-of-the-art methods and the results show that the $k - TruthScore$ is effective in minimizing the impact of fake news in the presence of strong user bias.

The paper is structured as follows. In Sect. 2 we discuss the related literature. In Sect. 3, we discuss the proposed spreading model. Section 4 includes our methodology to choose truth-campaigners. Section 5 shows the comparison of methods on real-world networks. We conclude the paper with future directions in Sect. 6.

2 Related Work

The problem of fake news spreading needs public attention to control further spreading. In a news feed released by Facebook in April 2017 [14], Facebook outlined two main approaches for countering the spread of fake news: (i) a crowdsourcing approach leveraging on the community and third-party fact-checking organizations, and (ii) a machine learning approach to detect fraud and spam accounts. A study by Halimeh et al. supports the fact that Facebook's fake news combating techniques will have a positive impact on the information quality [10]. Besides Facebook, there are several other crowdsourced fact-checking websites including snopes.com, politifact.com, and factcheck.org.

Researchers have proposed various influence blocking and truth-campaigning techniques to mitigate fake news in different contexts. In influence blocking, the complexity of the brute force method to identify a set of nodes of size k to minimize the fake news spread is NP-hard [2]. Therefore, greedy or heuristic solutions are appreciated and feasible to apply in real-life applications. Amoruso et al. [2] proposed a two-step heuristic method that first identifies the set of most probable sources of the infection, and then places a few monitors in the network to block the spread of misinformation.

Pham et al. [18] worked on the Targeted Misinformation Blocking (TMB) problem, where the goal is to find the smallest set of nodes whose removal will reduce the misinformation influence at least by a given threshold γ. Authors showed that TMB is $\#P - hard$ problem under the linear threshold spreading model, and proposed a greedy algorithm that provides the solution set within the ratio of $1 + ln(\gamma/\epsilon)$ of the optimal set and the expected influence reduction is greater than $(\gamma - \epsilon)$, given that the influence reduction function is submodular and monotone. Yang et al. worked on two versions of the influence minimization problem called Loss Minimization with Disruption (LMD) and Diffusion Minimization with Guaranteed Target (DMGT) using Integer Linear Programming (ILP) [27]. Authors proposed heuristic solutions for the LMD problem where k nodes having the minimum degree or PageRank are chosen. They further proposed a greedy solution for the DMGT problem, where at each iteration, they choose a node that increases the maximal marginal gain.

In contrast to IB, truth campaigning techniques combat fake news by making the users aware of the true information. Budak et al. [4] showed that selecting a minimal group of users to disseminate "good" information in the network to minimize the influence of the "bad" information is an NP-hard problem. They provided an approximation guarantee for a greedy solution for different variations of this problem by proving them submodular. Nguyen et al. [15] worked on a problem called β_T^I where they target to select the smallest set S of influential nodes which start spreading the good information, so that the expected decontamination ratio in the whole network is β after t time steps, given that the misinformation was started from a given set of nodes I. They proposed a greedy solution called Greedy Viral Stopper (GVS) that iteratively selects a node to be decontaminated so that the total number of decontaminated nodes will be maximum if the selected node starts spreading the true information.

Farajtabar et al. [8] proposed a point process based mitigation technique using the reinforcement learning framework. The proposed method was implemented in real-time on Twitter to mitigate a synthetically started fake news campaign. Song et al. [22] proposed a method to identify truth campaigners in temporal influence propagation where the rumor has no impact after its deadline; the method is explained in Sect. 5.2. In [20], authors considered users' bias, though the bias remains constant over time. In our work, we consider a realistic spreading model where users' biases keep getting stronger or weaken based on the content they are exposed to and share further. Next, we propose $k-TruthScore$ method to choose top-k truth campaigners for minimizing the negative impact of fake news in the network.

3 The Proposed Propagation Model: CICMB

The Independent Cascade Model (ICM) [11] has been used to model the information propagation in social networks. In the existing ICM, each directed edge has an influence probability with which the source node influences the target node. The propagation is started from a source node or a group of source nodes. At each iteration, a newly influenced node tries to influence each of its neighbors with the given influence probability, and will not influence any of its neighbors in further iterations. Once there is no newly influenced node in an iteration, the propagation process is stopped. The total number of influenced nodes shows the influencing or spreading power of the seed nodes.

Kim and Bock [12] observed that peoples' beliefs construct their positive or negative emotions about a topic, which further affects their attitude and behavior

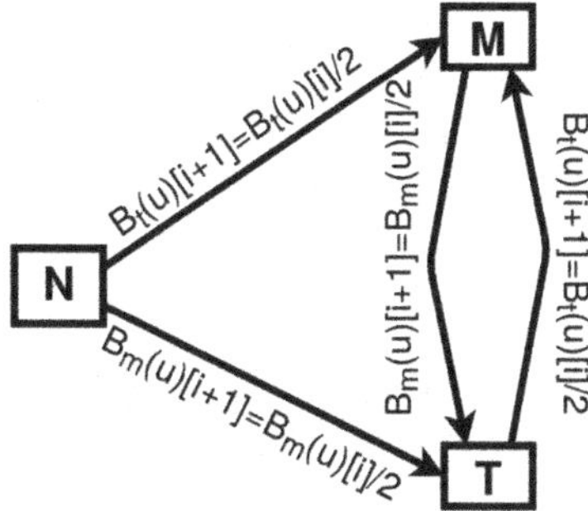

Fig. 2. CICMB Model used in the experiments, and the bias that is not displayed on the link stays constant between states.

towards the misinformation spreading. We believe that in real life, people have biases towards different opinions, and once they believe in one information, they are less willing to switch their opinion.

Competitive Independent Cascade Model with users' Bias (CICMB). In our work, we propose a Competitive Independent Cascade Model with users' Bias (CICMB) by incorporating the previous observation in the ICM model when two competitive misinformation and its counter true information propagates in the network. In this model, each user has a bias towards misinformation at timestamp i, namely $B_m(u)[i]$, and its counter true information, $B_t(u)[i]$. The influence probability of an edge (u, v) is denoted as, $P(u, v)$. Before the propagation starts, each node is in the neutral state, N. If the user believes in misinformation or true information, then it can change its state to M or T, respectively.

Once the propagation starts, all Misinformation starters will change their state to M, and truth campaigners will be in state T, and they will never change their state during the entire propagation being stubborn users. At each iteration, truth and misinformation campaigners will influence their neighbors as we explain next. A misinformation spreader u will change the state of its neighbor v at timestamp i with the probability $Prob = P(u, v) \cdot B_m(v)[i]$. If the node v change its state from N to M, its bias values are updated as $(B_m(v)[i+1], B_t(v)[i+1]) = f(B_m(v)[i], B_t(v)[i])$. Similarly, a truth campaigner u will influence its neighbor v with $P(u, v) \cdot B_t(v)[i]$ probability, and the bias values are updated as, $(B_m(v)[i+1], B_t(v)[i+1]) = f(B_m(v)[i], B_t(v)[i])$.

In our implementation, we consider that when a node u believes in one information, its bias towards accepting other information is reduced in half, using these functions:
(i). When u changes its state to M, $B_m(u)[i+1] = B_m(u)[i]$ & $B_t(u)[i+1] = B_t(u)[i]/2$.
(ii). When u changes its state to T, $B_m(u)[i+1] = B_m(u)[i]/2$ & $B_t(u)[i+1] = B_t(u)[i]$.

The model is explained in Fig. 2 for this linear function. As a second case for our research, we will present results for another stronger bias function, where the bias is reduced faster, using a quadratic function.

4 Methodology

We first introduce the problem formulation and then follow with our proposed solution.

4.1 Problem Formulation

In OSNs, when true or misinformation is propagated, users change their state between the elements of the set $\{N, M, T\}$. The state of a user u at timestamp i is denoted as $\boldsymbol{\pi}_u[i]$ with the following possible assignments: (i) $\boldsymbol{\pi}_u[i] = T$ if user believes in true information, (ii) $\boldsymbol{\pi}_u[i] = M$ if user believes in misinformation, and (iii) $\boldsymbol{\pi}_u[i] = N$ if user is in neutral state.

Given a set of rumor starters R who spreads misinformation, the deadline of misinformation spread α, and a set of prospective truth campaigners P, we aim to identify a set D of chosen truth-campaigners of size k from set P ($D \subset P$ and $|D| = k$) to start a truth-campaign such that the impact of misinformation is minimized.

Let u be a node such that $\boldsymbol{\pi}_u[\alpha] = M$ if only misinformation is propagated in the network and $\boldsymbol{\pi}_u[\alpha] = T$, when both misinformation and its counter true information is propagated in the network. The node u is considered a *saved node* at the deadline α as it believes in true information and would have believed in the misinformation in the absence of truth-campaign.

Problem Definition: Given a graph $G = (V, E)$, a rumor deadline α, a set of rumor starters R, and a set of prospective truth-campaigners P. Let S be the set of nodes whose state is M at time α when only nodes in the set R propagate misinformation using CICMB. Let I be the set of nodes whose state is T at time α when sets R and D propagate misinformation and true information, respectively, using CICMB. Our aim is to find a set $D \subset P$ of given size k, such that the number of saved nodes is maximized as follows:

$$f(D, M) = \sum_{v \in S \cap I} (1 | \boldsymbol{\pi}_v(\alpha) = T)$$

4.2 The Proposed Solution

In this section, we introduce our proposed algorithm, $k - TruthScore$, giving intuition for how it works, and we then summarize it at the end of the section. For a given set of misinformation starters R and prospective truth-campaigners P, our goal is to estimate which truth campaigner node will save the maximum number of nodes by the deadline α tracked by their TruthScore that we introduce below. We then choose top-k nodes having the highest TruthScore as truth-campaigners (D) to minimize the impact of misinformation.

To compute TruthScore, we assign to each node u, two arrays $mval$ and $tval$, each of length $(\alpha + 1)$, where $mval_u[i]$ and $tval_u[i]$ denote the estimated probability that node u will change its state to M and T at time i, respectively. To estimate these probability values, first, we create the Directed Acyclic Graph (DAG) $G'(V, E')$ of the given network G to remove the cycles from the network. Otherwise, if there would be a cycle in the network, then the nodes belonging to the cycle will keep updating the probabilities of each other in an infinite loop.

We now compute the probability of an arbitrary node u changing its state to M at some iteration i, namely $mval_u[i]$. For this to happen, we compute two probabilities:

1. the probability that the node u is not in state M at time $i - 1$ is computed as, $(1 - \sum_{j=1}^{i-1} mval_u[j])$, and
2. the probability that the node u will receive the misinformation at the ith step that considers all parents v of node u that have updated their $mval$ at $i - 1$ timestamp, $V_1 = \{v|(v, u) \in E' \;\&\; mval_v[i - 1] > 0\}$. Then we compute the value of $mval_u[i]$ by taking their product as shown in Eq. 1:

$$mval_u[i] = \sum_{v \in V_1} (mval_u[i] + (1 - mval_u[i]) \cdot (1 - \sum_{j=1}^{i-1} mval_u[j]) \cdot P(v, u) \cdot B_m(u) \cdot mval_v[i - 1]) \tag{1}$$

We use this formula to compute $mval_u[i]$ for all nodes from $i = 1$ to α. All the nodes whose $mval$ has been updated, are added to set A.

Next, we compute the TruthScore of each prospective truth-campaigner w. We estimate the probability that a node u will believe in true information at i_{th} timestamp when the true information is propagated from node w in the network. For this update $tval_w[0] = 1$, and compute for each node $u \in (V - R)$, $tval_u[i]$ from $i = 1$ to α.

The probability that node u will change its state to T at timestamp i is the probability that the node u has not changed its state to T at any previous timestamp multiplied by the probability of receiving the true information at i_{th} timestamp. It is computed using the same approach as defined in Eq. 1.

The estimated probability that a node u will change its state to T at time stamp i is computed as follows: Consider all parents v of node u who has updated $tval_v[i - 1]$ at $i - 1$ timestamp, $V_2 = \{v|(v, u) \in E' \;\&\; tval_v[i - 1] > 0\}$.

$$tval_u[i] = \sum_{v \in V_2} (tval_u[i] + (1 - tval_u[i]) \cdot (1 - \sum_{j=1}^{i-1} tval_u[j]) \cdot P(v, u) \cdot B_t(u) \cdot tval_v[i - 1]) \tag{2}$$

The $tval$ is computed for $i = 1$ to α. All the nodes whose $tval$ has been updated, are added to B. The truth score of truth-campaigner w is computed as:

$$TruthScore(w) = \sum_{v \in A \cap B} \sum_{i=1}^{\alpha} tval_v[i] \tag{3}$$

For the fast computation, a node v will update the $mval$ of its child node u at timestamp i, if $mval_v[i-1] > \theta$, where θ is a small threshold value. The same threshold value is used while computing $tval$ array of the nodes.

We now summarize the above described method, and we call it k-**TruthScore**:

1. Create $G'(V, E')$, the DAG of the given network G.
2. For all nodes in the set R of rumor starters, update $mval_u[0] = 1$. Compute $mval$ for the nodes reachable from R by the given deadline α using Eq. 1 and add these nodes to set A.
3. For each given prospective truth-campaigner w from set P,
   (a) Update $tval_w[0] = 1$
   (b) Compute $tval$ arrays for the nodes reachable by w by the given deadline α using Eq. 2, and add these nodes to set B.
   (c) Compute $TruthScore(w)$ by adding the values of $tval$ for the nodes in $A \cap B$ using Eq. 3.
4. Choose top-k truth-campaigners having the highest $TruthScore$.

5 Performance Study

We carry out experiments to validate the performance of the $k - TruthScore$ to identify top-k truth-campaigners.

5.1 Datasets

We perform the experiments on three real-world directed social networks, Digg, Facebook, and Twitter, as presented in Table 1. For each of them, the diameter is computed by taking the undirected version of the network.

Table 1. Datasets

Network	Nodes	Edges	Diameter	Ref
Digg	29652	85983	12	[7]
Facebook	43953	262631	18	[24]
Twitter	81306	1768135	7	[6]

We assign the influence probability of each edge (v, u) uniformly at random (u.a.r.) from the interval $(0, 1]$. Each node in the network has two bias values, one for the misinformation and another for the true information. For misinformation-starters, the bias for misinformation is randomly assigned a real value between $[0.7, 1]$ as the nodes spreading misinformation will be highly biased towards it. For these nodes, the bias for true information will be assigned as, $B_t[0] = 1 - B_m[0]$.

Similarly, the nodes chosen to be prospective truth campaigners will have a high bias towards true information, and it will be assigned u.a.r. from the interval $[0.7, 1]$. For prospective truth-campaigners, the bias for misinformation will be assigned as, $B_m[0] = 1 - B_t[0]$. For the rest of the nodes, the bias value for misinformation and their counter true-information will be assigned uniformly at random from the interval $(0, 1]$. Note that the size of the prospective truth-campaigners set is fixed as $|P| = 50$, and set P is chosen u.a.r. from set $(V - R)$. We fix $\theta = 0.000001$ for all the experiments.

5.2 Baseline Methods

We have compared our method to the following two state-of-the-art methods.

1. **Temporal Influence Blocking (TIB)** [22]. The TIB method runs into two phases. In the first phase, it identifies the set of nodes that can be reached by misinformation spreaders by the given deadline. Then, it identifies the potential nodes that can influence these nodes. In the second phase, it generates Weighted Reverse Reachable (WRR) trees to compute the influential power of identified potential mitigators by estimating the number of reachable nodes for each potential mitigator. In our experiments, we select the top-k nodes to be the prospective truth-campaigners having the highest influential power.
2. **Targeted Misinformation Blocking (TMB)** [19]. The TMB computes the influential power of a given node by computing the number of saved nodes if the given node is immunized in the network. Therefore, the influence reduction of a node v is computed as $h(v) = N(G) - N(G \setminus v)$, where $N(G)$ and $N(G \setminus v)$ denote the number of nodes influenced by misinformation starters in the G and $(G \setminus v)$, respectively. We then select top-k nodes having the highest influence reduction as truth-campaigners.
   After selecting top-k truth campaigners using TIB and TMB methods, the CICMB model is used to propagate misinformation and counter true information.

If set R starts propagating misinformation, then S is the set of nodes whose state is M at $t = \alpha$. If set R propagates misinformation, and set D propagates true information, then let I be the set of nodes whose state is T at $t = \alpha$. The performance of various methods is evaluated by computing the percentage of nodes saved, i.e., $\frac{|S|-|I|}{|S|} \cdot 100$.

We compute the results by choosing five different sets of misinformation starters and truth-campaigners. In several instances, each experiment is repeated 100 times, and we report their average value to show the percentage of saved nodes.

First, we study the performance of $k - TruthScore$ as a function of chosen truth-campaigners k, varying k from 2 to 10. We also set the deadline for the misinformation to be the network diameter, if not specified otherwise.

Figure 3 shows that the $k - TruthScore$ outperforms state-of-the-art methods for finding the top-k truth-campaigners. TIB and TMB methods are designed to choose truth-campaigners globally, and we restrict these methods to choose truth-campaigners from the given set of prospective truth-campaigners. Under this restriction, $k - TruthScore$ significantly outperforms both TIB and TMB methods.

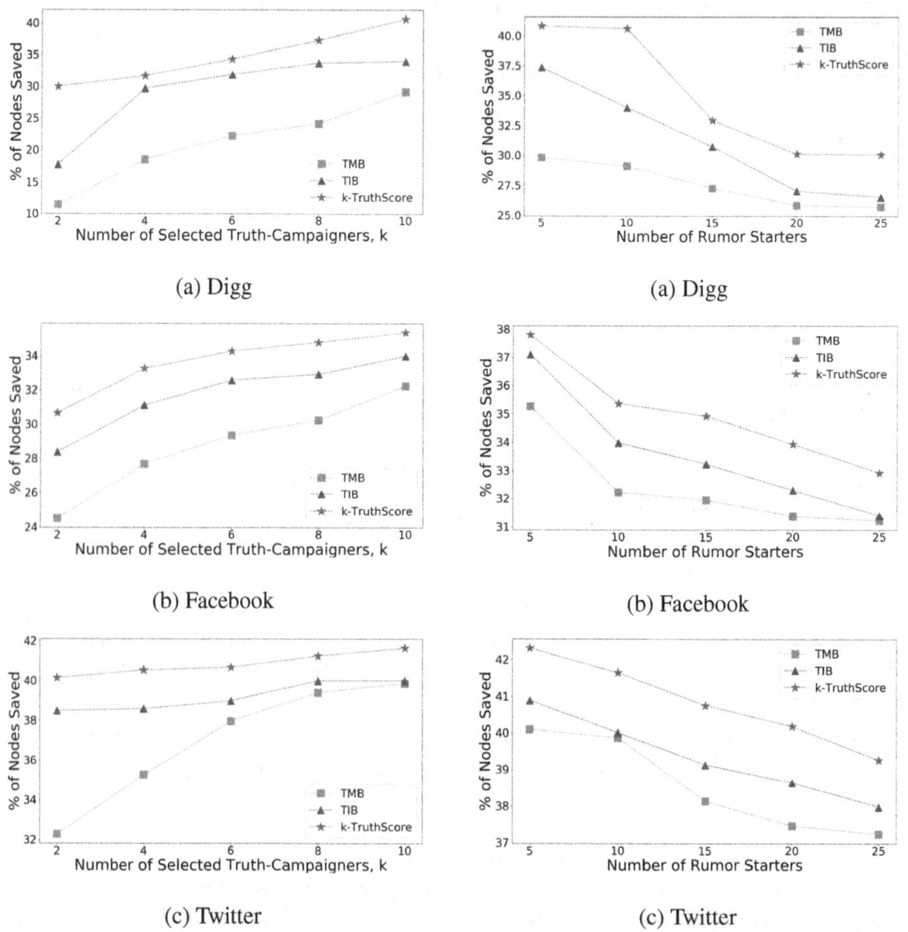

Fig. 3. Effect of varying k for node selection methods.

Fig. 4. Effect of varying $|M|$ when $k = 5$.

Next, we study the impact of varying the number of rumor starters. We fix $k = 5$, and allow M to vary from 5 to 25. Figure 4 shows that in this case, the percentage of nodes saved reduces as the number of rumor starters increases, while $k - TruthScore$ still outperforms TIB and TMB methods.

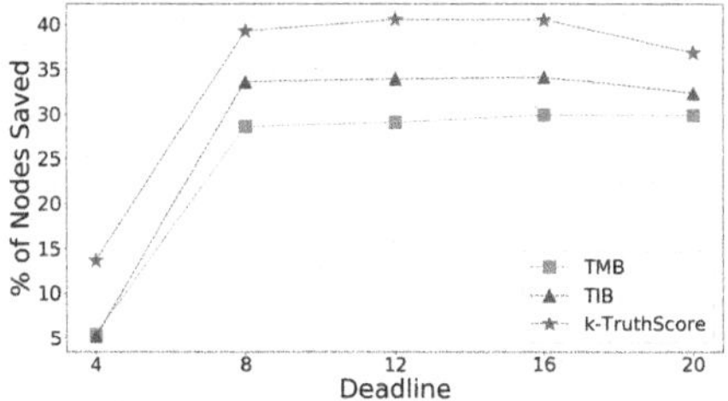

Fig. 5. Effect of varying deadline α on Digg Network.

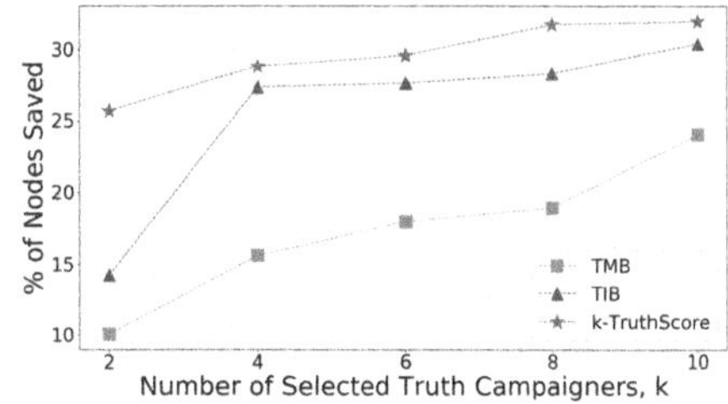

Fig. 6. Square-bias function on Digg Network.

We also study the impact of varying the deadline on the percentage of nodes saved when $|M| = 10$ and $k = 5$. The results are shown for the Digg network and α varying from 4 to 20. The results show that the percentage of the saved nodes is maximum around the iteration time $\alpha = diameter(G)$, and consistently $k - TruthScore$ outperforms at any other set deadline (Fig. 5).

The results discussed so far depend on linear degradation, as presented in Sect. 3. We now study the efficiency of $k - TruthScore$ for a quadratic bias function. We evaluate $k - TruthScore$ for the following bias function:
When u changes its state to M, $B_m(u)[i+1] = B_m(u)[i]$ & $B_t(u)[i+1] = (B_t(u)[i])^2$.
When u changes its state to T, $B_m(u)[i+1] = (B_m(u)[i])^2$ & $B_t(u)[i+1] = B_t(u)[i]$.

The results show that $k - TruthScore$ saves the maximum number of nodes for the quadratic bias function. However, the percentage of saved nodes is smaller than the ones observed in Fig. 6. This is due to the reason that the square function reduces the biases faster, and users are more stubborn to change their state once they have believed in one information.

6 Conclusion

The current research presents a solution to the problem of minimizing the impact of misinformation by propagating its counter true information in OSNs. In particular, we look to identify the top-k candidates as truth-campaigners from a given set of prospective truth-campaigners and given rumor starters. We first propose a propagation model called the Competitive Independent Cascade Model with users' Bias that considers the presence of strong user bias towards different opinions, believes, or political parties. For our experiments, we used two different functions to capture the bias dynamics towards true and misinformation, one linear and one quadratic.

Next, we introduce an algorithm, $k - TruthScore$, to identify top-k truth-campaigners, and compare the results against two state of the art algorithms, namely Temporal Influence Blocking and Targeted Misinformation Blocking. To compare the algorithms, we compute the percentage of saved nodes per network

G, by the deadline α. A node is tagged as saved if at the deadline α it believes in true information and would have believed in the misinformation in the absence of truth campaigners.

We compare the three algorithms under each of the two bias functions on three different networks, namely Digg, Facebook, and Twitter. Moreover, we compare the three algorithms by varying the number of originating rumor spreaders as well as varying the deadline at which we compute the TruthScore. Our results show that $k - TruthScore$ outperforms the state of the art methods in every case.

In the future, we would like to do an in-depth analysis of the CICMB model for different bias functions, such as constant increase/decrease (where the bias values are increased or decreased by a constant value, respectively), other linear functions (for example, if one bias value of a user increases then the other decreases), different quadratic functions, and so on. The proposed $k - TruthScore$ method outperforms for both the considered functions; however, one can propose a method, i.e., specific to a given bias function.

References

1. Google trends fake news. Accessed 11 September 2020
2. Amoruso, M., Anello, D., Auletta, V., Ferraioli, D.: Contrasting the spread of misinformation in online social networks. In: Proceedings of the 16th Conference on Autonomous Agents and MultiAgent Systems, pp. 1323–1331. International Foundation for Autonomous Agents and Multiagent Systems (2017)
3. Andrews, C., Fichet, E., Ding, Y., Spiro, E.S., Starbird, K.: Keeping up with the tweet-dashians: the impact of'official'accounts on online rumoring. In: Proceedings of the 19th ACM Conference on Computer-Supported Cooperative Work and Social Computing, pp. 452–465. ACM (2016)
4. Budak, C., Agrawal, D., El Abbadi, A.: Limiting the spread of misinformation in social networks. In: Proceedings of the 20th International Conference on World Wide Web, pp. 665–674. ACM (2011)
5. Chen, X., Sin, S.C.J., Theng, Y.L., Lee, C.S.: Why do social media users share misinformation? In: Proceedings of the 15th ACM/IEEE-CS Joint Conference on Digital Libraries, pp. 111–114. ACM (2015)
6. De Choudhury, M., Lin, Y.R., Sundaram, H., Candan, K.S., Xie, L., Kelliher, A.: How does the data sampling strategy impact the discovery of information diffusion in social media? In: Fourth International AAAI Conference on Weblogs and Social Media (2010)
7. De Choudhury, M., Sundaram, H., John, A., Seligmann, D.D.: Social synchrony: predicting mimicry of user actions in online social media. In: 2009 International Conference on Computational Science and Engineering, vol. 4, pp. 151–158. IEEE (2009)
8. Farajtabar, M., et al.: Fake news mitigation via point process based intervention. https://arxiv.org/abs/1703.07823 (2017)
9. Forum, W.E.: The global risks report 2017

10. Halimeh, A.A., Pourghomi, P., Safieddine, F.: The impact of Facebook's news fact-checking on information quality (IQ) shared on social media (2017)
11. Kempe, D., Kleinberg, J., Tardos, É.: Influential nodes in a diffusion model for social networks. In: Caires, L., Italiano, G.F., Monteiro, L., Palamidessi, C., Yung, M. (eds.) ICALP 2005. LNCS, vol. 3580, pp. 1127–1138. Springer, Heidelberg (2005). https://doi.org/10.1007/11523468_91
12. Kim, J.H., Bock, G.W.: A study on the factors affecting the behavior of spreading online rumors: focusing on the rumor recipient's emotions. In: PACIS, p. 98 (2011)
13. Lee, C., Shin, J., Hong, A.: Does social media use really make people politically polarized? Direct and indirect effects of social media use on political polarization in South Korea. Telemat. Inform. **35**(1), 245–254 (2018)
14. Mosseri, A.: Working to stop misinformation and false news (2017). https://newsroom.fb.com/news/2017/04/working-to-stop-misinformation-and-false-news/
15. Nguyen, N.P., Yan, G., Thai, M.T., Eidenbenz, S.: Containment of misinformation spread in online social networks. In: Proceedings of the 4th Annual ACM Web Science Conference, pp. 213–222. ACM (2012)
16. Ozturk, P., Li, H., Sakamoto, Y.: Combating rumor spread on social media: the effectiveness of refutation and warning. In: 2015 48th Hawaii International Conference on System Sciences (HICSS), pp. 2406–2414. IEEE (2015)
17. Park, J., Cha, M., Kim, H., Jeong, J.: Managing bad news in social media: a case study on domino's pizza crisis. In: ICWSM, vol. 12, pp. 282–289 (2012)
18. Pham, C.V., Phu, Q.V., Hoang, H.X.: Targeted misinformation blocking on online social networks. In: Nguyen, N.T., Hoang, D.H., Hong, T.-P., Pham, H., Trawiński, B. (eds.) ACIIDS 2018. LNCS (LNAI), vol. 10751, pp. 107–116. Springer, Cham (2018). https://doi.org/10.1007/978-3-319-75417-8_10
19. Pham, C.V., Phu, Q.V., Hoang, H.X., Pei, J., Thai, M.T.: Minimum budget for misinformation blocking in online social networks. J. Comb. Optim. **38**(4), 1101–1127 (2019). https://doi.org/10.1007/s10878-019-00439-5
20. Saxena, A., Hsu, W., Lee, M.L., Leong Chieu, H., Ng, L., Teow, L.N.: Mitigating misinformation in online social network with top-k debunkers and evolving user opinions. In: Companion Proceedings of the Web Conference, pp. 363–370 (2020)
21. Soares, F.B., Recuero, R., Zago, G.: Influencers in polarized political networks on twitter. In: Proceedings of the 9th International Conference on Social Media and Society, pp. 168–177 (2018)
22. Song, C., Hsu, W., Lee, M.: Temporal influence blocking: minimizing the effect of misinformation in social networks. In: 33rd IEEE International Conference on Data Engineering, ICDE 2017, San Diego, CA, USA, 19–22 April 2017, pp. 847–858 (2017). https://doi.org/10.1109/ICDE.2017.134
23. Tanaka, Y., Sakamoto, Y., Matsuka, T.: Toward a social-technological system that inactivates false rumors through the critical thinking of crowds. In: 2013 46th Hawaii International Conference on System Sciences (HICSS), pp. 649–658. IEEE (2013)
24. Viswanath, B., Mislove, A., Cha, M., Gummadi, K.P.: On the evolution of user interaction in Facebook. In: Proceedings of the 2nd ACM Workshop on Online Social Networks, pp. 37–42. ACM (2009)
25. Vosoughi, S., Roy, D., Aral, S.: The spread of true and false news online. Science **359**(6380), 1146–1151 (2018)

26. Wang, Yu., Feng, Y., Hong, Z., Berger, R., Luo, J.: How polarized have we become? A multimodal classification of Trump followers and Clinton followers. In: Ciampaglia, G.L., Mashhadi, A., Yasseri, T. (eds.) SocInfo 2017. LNCS, vol. 10539, pp. 440–456. Springer, Cham (2017). https://doi.org/10.1007/978-3-319-67217-5_27
27. Yang, L., Li, Z., Giua, A.: Influence minimization in linear threshold networks. Automatica **100**, 10–16 (2019)

Hierarchies in Inter-personal and Intergroup Communication in Social Media: Case 'Smart Voting'

Alexander A. Kharlamov[1,2,3] and Maria Pilgun[4](✉)

[1] Institute of Higher Nervous Activity and Neurophysiology, RAS, Moscow, Russia
kharlamov@analyst.ru
[2] Moscow State Linguistic University, Moscow, Russia
[3] Higher School of Economics, Moscow, Russia
[4] Institute of Linguistics, RAS, Moscow, Russia
mpilgun@iling-ran.ru
http://www.analyst.ru

Abstract. The research is devoted to the analysis of hierarchies in inter-personal and intergroup network communication an example of a strategy of the election campaign in the Moscow City Duma in 2019. The study involved a cross-disciplinary approach using neural network technologies, complex networks analysis. For the correct interpretation of the content, content analysis, semantic analysis and analysis of word association were performed. The dataset included social networks, microblogs, forums, blogs, videos, reviews. The expansion and enrichment of the users' world view in the network environment in the analyzed communicative situation occurs through spreading of a more developed and well-founded model of the world, the carrier of which is a social media influencer with the necessary set of knowledge, techniques, a high level of some assets, who is able to communicate current requirements. Also the study made it possible to identify a level of social stress.

Keywords: Social networks · Neural network technologies · Word associations · Political communication

1 Introduction

Network communications are an important component of modern media space. The specific features of inter-personal and intergroup communication are shown in numerous scientific studies. In particular, researchers note that social networks can filter actors, close groups, reduce the chance of unintentional communication, isolate themselves from other groups, which causes some dosage and reduction of intergroup interaction of communities with different goals, political goals, interests, etc. (Hayes et al. 2015; Carr et al. 2016; Yang et al. 2017). User clustering in political discussions has been investigated in (Bond et al., 2012; Mikolov 2013; Kramer 2014; Weaver 2018).

S. Chellappan et al. (Eds.): CSoNet 2020, LNCS 12575, pp. 127–138, 2020.
https://doi.org/10.1007/978-3-030-66046-8_11

On the other hand, the creation of filter bubbles, echo chambers in groups with specific interests leads to the isolation of intragroup communication, the strengthening of group relationships and norms, while at the same time it hinders communication between members of different virtual communities (Conover 2012; Colleoni 2014; Williams 2015).

Numerous and diverse studies are devoted to the analysis of social and political polarization that occurs in various communicative processes in the digital environment (McCright and Dunlap, 2011; Colleoni et al. 2014; Barberá et al. 2015; Rivero 2017; Evolvi, 2017; Duca and Saving 2017). On the other hand, the creation of filter bubbles, echo chambers in groups with specific interests leads to the isolation of intragroup communication, the strengthening of group relationships and norms, while at the same time it hinders communication between members of different virtual communities (Colleoni et al. 2014).

Meanwhile, some social and systemic features of social networks contribute to intergroup communication even more than offline or traditional communication channels. Scott A. Golder and Sarita Yardi show that two structural characteristics, transitivity and mutuality, are significant predictors of the desire to form new ties (Golder and Yardi 2010).

Thus, on the one hand, social media can unite communities and significantly facilitate intergroup contacts; on the other hand, network communications make it possible for different communities of actors to be isolated and limited only by intragroup communication, increasing intergroup distance. That is, the question remains, which methods and techniques are most effective for purposeful management of the virtual group behavior, both within the digital space and in real life.

It is worth recalling that Yu. M. Lotman introduced the concept of "semiotic universe", according to which the semiotic space was considered as a single mechanism, within which the "large system" called "semiosphere" turned out to be primary (Lotman 1992). It can be assumed that the modern information and communication universe as part of the noosphere is a society with a technological component that is subject to it, which provides for the collection, storage and exchange of information generated by individual members (and their groups) of the society. Since this society consists of separate individuals, the model for presenting information in the society is based on the model for presenting information about the world of an individual, i.e. the information and communication universe means models of the world of individual members (and their groups) within the society supplemented by their (individual members or their groups) intentional mechanisms complemented by natural and/or artificial means of communication.

Models of the world of individual members of the society are grouped and averaged as social groups of actors are formed, up to the formation of a single averaged model of the world of this society. In particular, the averaging process can be traced on the example of the analysis of texts in social groups during the transition from the individuals' texts to the texts of social groups of various sizes.

The objectives of this study are as follows:

1. Analysis of the hierarchy in inter-personal and intergroup communication in social networks.
2. Study of mechanisms of influence (Xu and Wu 2020) in social networks by means of expanding and enriching the users' world view by spreading a more developed and reasonable world model (segment of the world model).

Method: The study involved a cross-disciplinary approach (mixed method). For the correct interpretation of the content, content analysis, semantic analysis and analysis of word association were also used.

The neural network technology TextAnalyst was used as a toolkit to help form a semantic network common for the entire corpus of analyzed texts, from which the topic structure of the analyzed content was extracted; also, an associative search was performed.

Procedures:

1. Content selection and purification (filtering).
   1.1. Isolation and extraction of bots.
   1.2. Selection of posts.
      1.2.1. Selection and analysis of social media influencers' posts.
   1.3. Selection of comments.
2. Identification of the topic structure of the selected network content.
3. Identification of key topics.
4. Content ranking (messages, authors, loyalty, involvement, audience).
5. Extraction of the semantic core, which consists of nominations from the semantic network with a link weight of 98–100.
6. Text analysis of the semantic core.
7. Constructing a semantic network.
8. Performing an associative search, analysis of word association, constructing an associative network.
9. Detection of social stress (for the method of detecting social stress, see Kharlamov, Pilgun, 2020).

Tools: Brand Analytics (br-analytics.ru) social media monitoring and analysis system was used as a tool for data collection; TextAnalyst technology (http://www.analyst.ru), developed by one of the authors of the paper, A. Kharlamov, was used for neural network text analysis.

Data: The dataset included data from social networks, microblogs, forums, blogs, videos, reviews devoted of a strategy put forward by Alexey Navalny's team to deprive the pro-government party 'United Russia' of votes in regional and Federal elections in Russia. The goal of 'Smart voting' is to consolidate the votes of those who oppose 'United Russia'. Date of collection: 14.07.19–08.09.19. It should be noted that this time period was the period of the election campaign in the Moscow City Duma and was followed by active protests of civil society, online

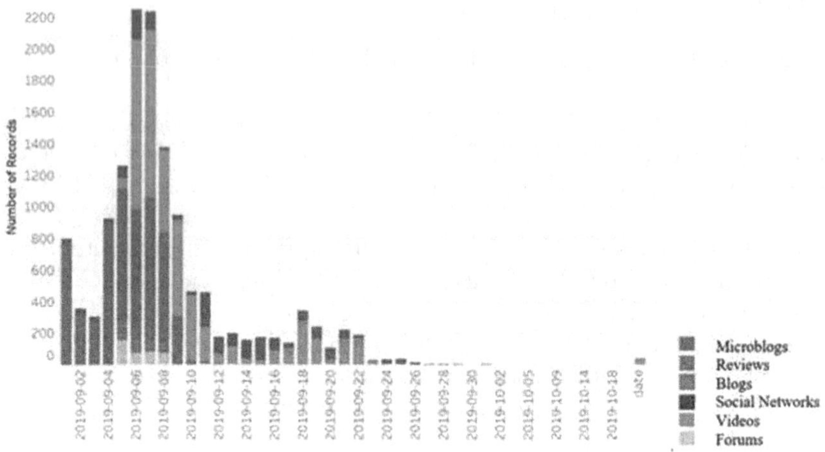

Fig. 1. Dynamics of publications comments.

activism, mass meeting, since, in the opinion of the public, the legitimacy of the procedures was violated (Fig. 1).

To achieve the objectives of the study, three verbal clusters were identified in the consolidated dataset: (1) posts (Fig. 2), (2) comments (Fig. 3), (3) social media influencer's posts (Fig. 4).

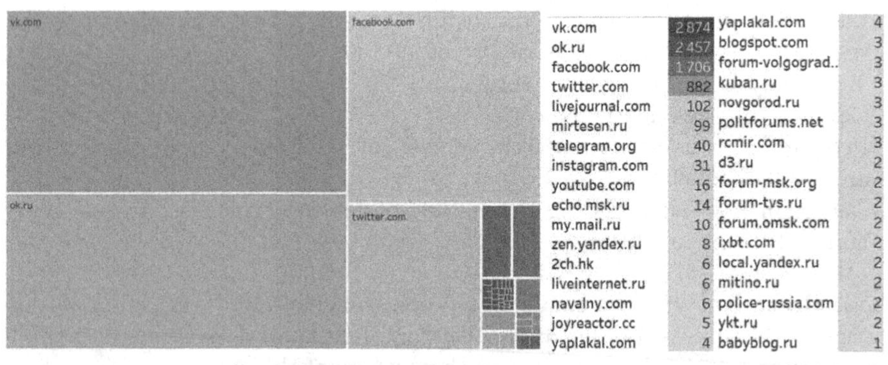

vk.com
facebook.com
ok.ru
twitter.com
vk.com 2 874
ok.ru 2 457
facebook.com 1 706
twitter.com 882
livejournal.com 102
mirtesen.ru 99
telegram.org 40
instagram.com 31
youtube.com 16
echo.msk.ru 14
my.mail.ru 10
zen.yandex.ru 8
2ch.hk 6
liveinternet.ru 6
navalny.com 6
joyreactor.cc 5
yaplakal.com 4
yaplakal.com 4
blogspot.com 3
forum-volgograd.. 3
kuban.ru 3
novgorod.ru 3
politforums.net 3
rcmir.com 3
d3.ru 2
forum-msk.org 2
forum-tvs.ru 2
forum.omsk.com 2
ixbt.com 2
local.yandex.ru 2
mitino.ru 2
police-russia.com 2
ykt.ru 2
babyblog.ru 1

Fig. 2. Posts on different resources.

As a result of the initial analysis of the consolidated database, 73 key topics were identified. Sentiment analysis of the data showed that only 4 of them are neutral, 4 are positive, and 65 are negative.

The analysis of the consolidated dataset for all topic blocks revealed the weights of the markers; the markers associated with "Smart Voting" (99) and "Investigation of the ACF – Vice Mayor" (82) topics received the greatest weights.

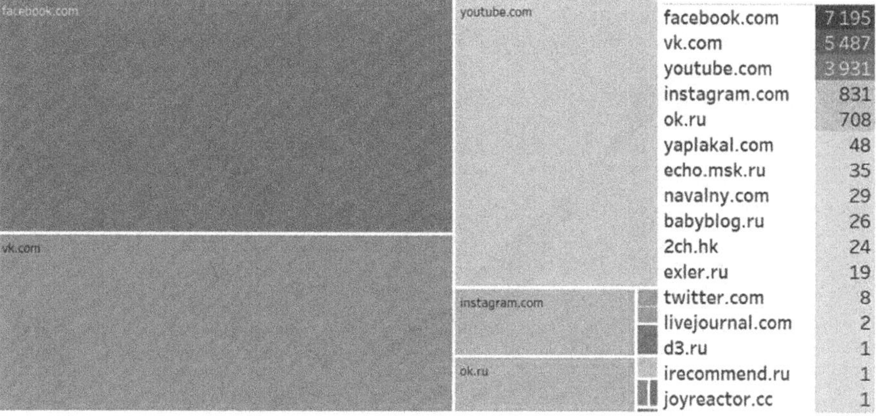

Fig. 3. Comments on various resources.

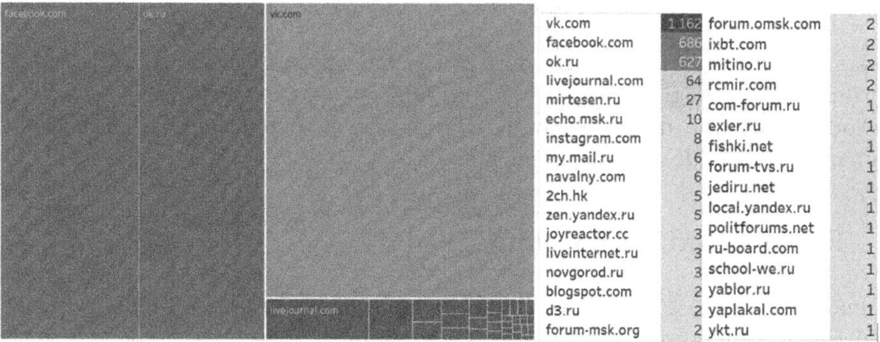

Fig. 4. Social media influencer's posts on various resources.

For the study, the "Smart Voting" topic block was selected as the one that received the greatest weights regarding relations, which reflects the maximum attention of users and the greatest significance in the network space over a given period.

In the course of the study, the verbal modus of the content was analyzed by relevant tags.

To analyze the hierarchy in inter-personal and intergroup political communication, datasets were used that contained users' posts and Alexey Navalny's posts as an social media influencer in this context. The "social media influencer" (Kharlamov and Pilgun 2020) status is confirmed by the analysis of digital footprints and speech behavior of the actor (Figs. 5 and 6).

In the study of the mechanisms of transition from lower permission levels to higher permission levels, a consolidated database was analyzed.

Intergroup communication was analyzed by the consolidated database, which made it possible to identify different types of actors (Figs. 7 and 8), and several

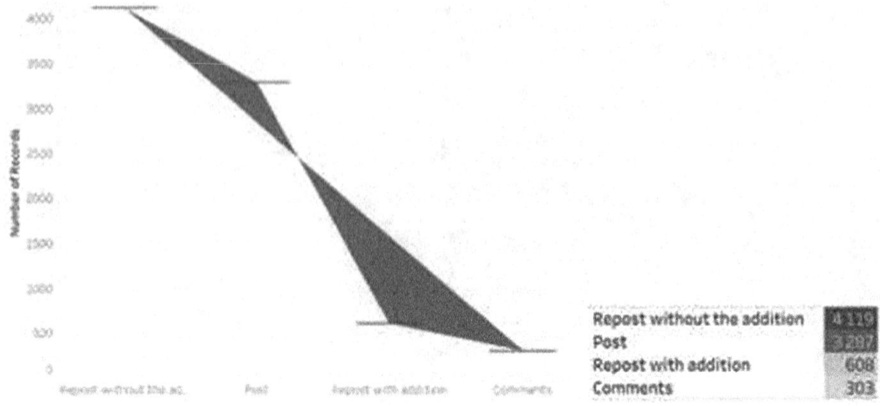

Fig. 5. Social media influencer's digital footprints (with his associates).

clusters with regards to the support of the influencer's views: committed supporters with a long history; new supporters who joined within the analyzed period; actors who do not share A. Navalny's views, but support the idea of "Smart Voting"; ideological opponents.

2 Results and Discussion

The analysis of the consolidated dataset for all topic blocks (see Fig. 1) revealed that the maximum weights of relations were those of lexical tags associated with "Smart Voting" (99) and "Investigation of the Anti-Corruption Fund (ACF) – vice-mayor" (82) (Biryukov, Sergunina). The above topics caused the maximum social tension of the actors in the network content during the pre-election period in the Moscow City Duma (September 8, 2019), which is explained by the general situation caused by the refusal to register and admit a number of opposition candidates to the Moscow City Duma. The incentives that define "Smart Voting" ensure the quantitative predominance of verbal content in the semantic core.

The rest of the topic blocks in calculating the level of social stress in the consolidated database are not represented at all.

Meanwhile, in the topic analysis of the consolidated database, the concepts that characterize the contrast between Moscow and the regions (the "Moscow feeds the regions" block) are prevailing, i.e. explicitly expressed information is mainly related to this topic.

Statements with markers with maximum relation weights:

(1) "... It's not Moscow that feeds Russia, but Russia that feeds Moscow..."

(2) "... 10 enterprises in Moscow and the Moscow region, and head offices of almost all largest Russian industrial holdings, as well as representative offices of the largest world companies that earn money in the regions and pay taxes in Moscow..."

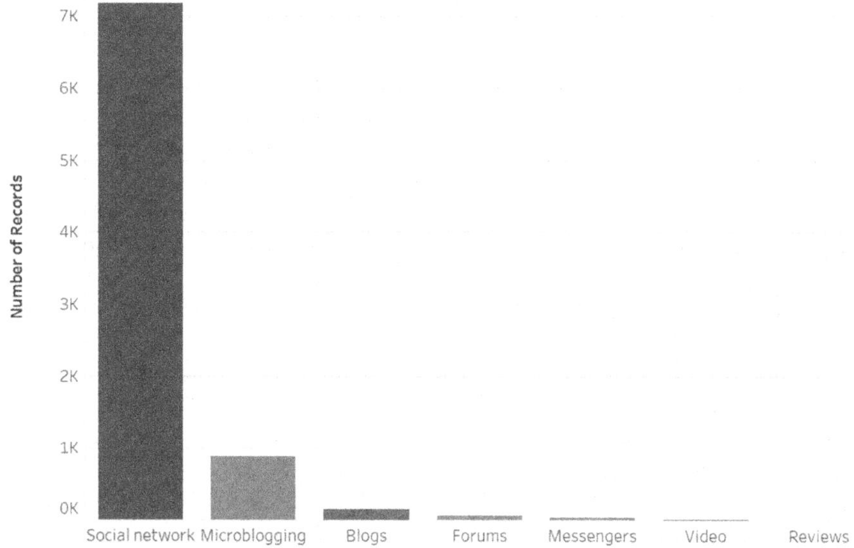

Fig. 6. Quantitative characteristics of user comments on social media influencer's posts on various resources.

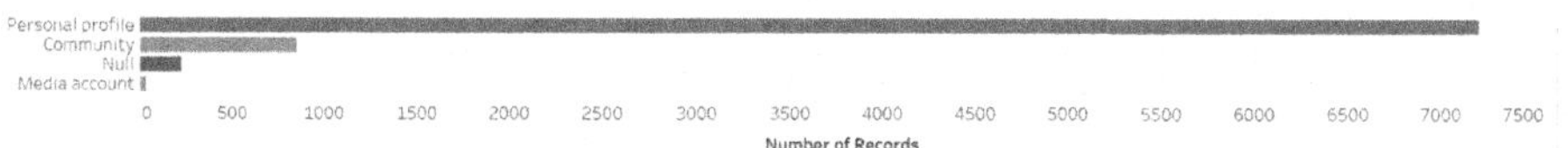

Fig. 7. Quantitative characteristics of messages of different types of users (personal profile, community, media account).

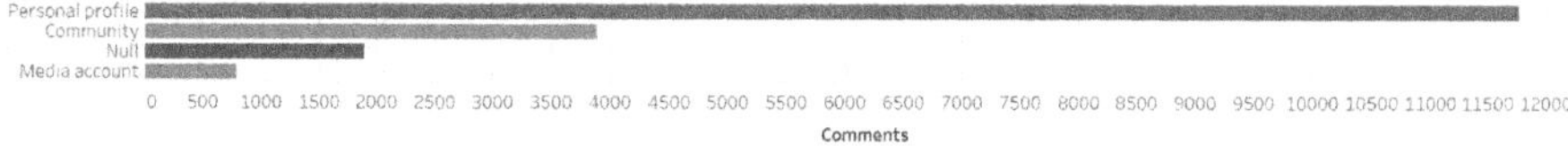

Fig. 8. Quantitative characteristics of comments of different types of users (personal profile, community, media account).

(3) "... the regions are not at the extreme of poverty, they merely survive... They are dying out)".

1.1. In the content devoted to the ACF investigations, the maximum relation weights are those of nominations with a negative connotation that characterize Deputy Mayor of Moscow Government for issues of housing maintenance and utilities and amenities Pyotr Biryukov (Biryukov (100), Master of Russia (Biryukov) (98), government official of the "experienced manager" type (89).

The users' attention was mostly attracted by the corruption element of P. Biryukov's activity, which is presented in the ACF investigation and is objectified as apartments and offices of the Biryukov family in Moscow (99):

(4) "Biryukov worked all his life as an official, but this did not prevent him from providing himself and his family with luxury real estate, luxury cars and a huge summer cottage-farm for a total of 5.5 billion rubles."

A set of concepts of the topic block defines a semantic field that describes the number and size of Biryukov and his family members' apartments and offices. The vice mayor's apartments and offices become, in the context of the discussion, a symbolic sign of corruption.

This topic block is characterized by the least number of denotations, but the maximum emotional intensity.

1.2. To analyze the hierarchy in inter-personal and intergroup communication due to the transition from lower permission levels of the world model to higher permission levels, datasets were selected containing users' posts and Alexei Navalny's posts as a social media influencer in this context. Alexey Navalny's posts from 01.09.2019, 03.09.2019, 04.09.2019, 06.09.2019, 07.09.2019 in VKontakte, Facebook and the blog were in the lead by user attention and received 1 770 comments (even without taking into account the content generated by the "Navalny Team").

Summarization of A. Navalny's posts enable identification of two main statements:

(5) "This day week, Putin, Medvedev, Sobyanin, Sergunin and that riot policeman who kicked a girl in the stomach with his fist will come to take their 90% of the seats in the Moscow parliament, St. Petersburg municipalities, city meetings of 22 regions of the country."

(6) "They need these 90% of the seats to claim continued unprecedented support."

1.3. Intergroup communication was analyzed on a consolidated database, which enabled identification of several clusters based on the support of the social media influencer's views:

- committed supporters with a long history;
- new supporters who joined during the analyzed period;
- actors who do not share A. Navalny's views, but support the idea of "Smart Voting";
- ideological opponents.

1.4. The topic structure of the actors' posts is a truncated form of the topic structure of A. Navalny's posts, reflects the secondary dependent nature of the content generated by users over the analyzed period.

Summarization of the actors' posts is a variation of the main topics proposed by the social media influencer:

(7) "Alexey Navalny posted on his blog a complete list of candidates to the Moscow City Duma recommended by the "Smart Voting"."

(8) "Alexey Navalny's strategy is the very same "smart voting"."

The analysis of the consolidated base of posts revealed that both inter-personal and intergroup communication (excluding the "ideological opponents" cluster) is a hierarchical system based on the pyramidal principle at the top of which stands the social media influencer, Alexey Navalny, who has the highest level of permission; he constructs and directs a communicative situation that allows transition of actors from lower permission levels of the world model to higher ones.

This position can also be confirmed by a semantic network of the actors' posts (Fig. 9).

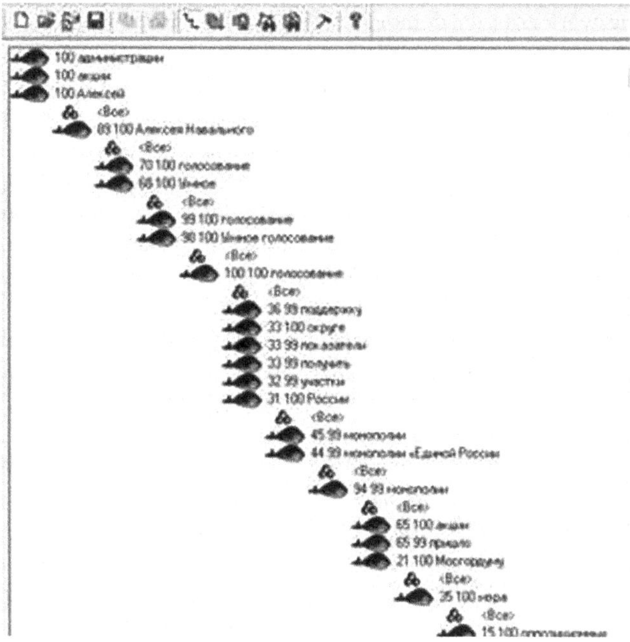

Fig. 9. Semantic network of ordinary actors' posts.

2.1. The analysis of the level of social stress regarding the "Smart Voting" topic block showed the highest relation weight among the markers characterizing the identification of the Moscow authorities and the country's authorities (negative connotation), as well as the markers characterizing the "Smart Voting" as an effective mechanism of struggle (positive connotation). About the method of calculating social stress (Kharlamov and Pilgun 2020):

(9) "Politician Aleksey Navalny is promoting the Smart Voting project, which aims to support average candidates from the parliamentary opposition in order to break the monopoly of United Russia in the Moscow City Duma."

2.2. The analysis of the semantic field associated with "Smart Voting", based on the users' comments showed an extremely negative attitude of the users to power in general: the Mayor's Office is identified with United Russia and causes the maximum indignation of the actors. The protest against the election campaign in Moscow City Duma is associated with the protest against United Russia, the Russian authorities, and Sobyanin and the Mayor's Office are perceived as part of it, and therefore are actively condemned.

(10) "The "Smart Voting" will make it possible for everyone to vote together for a candidate who has the maximum chance of defeating pro-government "self-nominees" from "United Russia"."

2.3. Violation of legitimate legal procedures during the course of the election campaign and voting:

(11) "Falsified votes already in 10 districts".

2.4. The network contact demonstrates that the actors were ready for active actions (legally) if they were sure of their result, which contributed to the success of the "Smart Voting" tactics and extreme dissatisfaction with the actions of law enforcement agencies that violated legal methods, according to the actors. The "Smart Voting", according to the actors, provided an effective legal mechanism for the struggle with power, and therefore received maximum support. Users considered the "Smart Voting" to be the most effective form of protest.

(12) "Sobyanin withdrew independent candidates from the elections, put innocent people in jail, drove state employees to polling stations, but preliminary estimates still speak of the possible victory of the "Smart Voting."

2.5. Violation of legitimate procedures during the election campaign and the disproportionate actions of the security apparatus during the protests caused a sharp negative reaction and was an incentive for the activation of previously passive actors:

(13) "It is the attempts to intimidate the protesters that explain the initiative to increase fines for unauthorized meetings and to detain protesters for 72 h."

2.6. Justification of the actions of those detained during the protests (emphasis on the legitimacy and peaceful nature of the actions), since they tried to resist the illegitimate actions of law enforcement agencies. On the contrary, condemnation of the actions of judicial structures that violate legitimate procedures and their lack of professionalism:

(14) "... and freedom just does not come easy. They fight and die for freedom. It can last for decades."

3 Conclusion

The analysis of the network content made it possible to analyze the hierarchy in inter-personal and intergroup network communication, as well as the mechanisms of influence in social networks, transition from lower permission levels to higher ones. The expansion and enrichment of the users' world view in the network environment in the analyzed communicative situation occurs through spreading of a more developed and well-founded model of the world (segment of the model of the world), the carrier of which is a social media influencer with the necessary set of knowledge, techniques, a high level of some assets, who is able to communicate current requirements.

Due to the transition from lower permission levels of the world model to higher permission levels in the digital media space, a significant number of actors begin to share the positions conveyed by an actor who is recognized in a particular communicative situation as an social media influencer.

In particular, analysis of the level of social stress indicates a growing misunderstanding, conflict between the leadership of Moscow and certain groups of the population.

The conflict is also reflected, in particular, in the opposition's "Smart Vote" protest campaign aimed at depriving the Pro-government United Russia party of votes in regional and Federal elections in Russia.

The degree of this misunderstanding is such that it will not be possible to solve the problem by simple means, such as organizing an additional information flow or expanding the dialogue between the authorities and the public after the protest actions in the summer of 2019. Before the protests during the election campaign in the Moscow City Duma in 2019, civil society had a clearly expressed expectation of a dialogue with the authorities, after which they expected particular political decisions and actions.

References

Barberá, P., Jost, J.T., Nagler, J., Tucker, J., Bonneau, R.: Tweeting from left to right: is online political communication more than an echo chamber? Psychol. Sci. **26**(10), 1531–1542 (2015)

Bond, R.M., et al.: Structural predictors of tie formation in Twitter: transitivity and mutuality. In: 2010 IEEE Second International Conference on Social Computing, pp. 88–95 (2010)

Carr, C.T., Hayes, R.A., Smock, A., Zube, P.: Facebook in presidential elections: status of effects. In: Richardson Jr., G. (ed.) Social Media and Politics: A New Way to Participate in the Political Process 2016. LNCS, vol. 9999, pp. 41–70. Praeger, Santa Barbara (2016)

Colleoni, E., Rozza, A., Arvidsso, A.: Echo chamber or public sphere? Predicting political orientation and measuring political homophily in Twitter using big data. J. Commun. **64**(2), 317–332 (2014)

Conover, M.D., Gonçalves, B., Flammini, A., Menczer, F.: Partisan asymmetries in online political activity. EPJ Data Sci. **1**(1), 1–19 (2012). https://doi.org/10.1140/epjds6

Hayes, R.A., Smock, A., Carr, C.T.: Face[book] management: self-presentation of political views on social media. Commun. Stud. **66**, 549–568 (2015)

Jo, T.: Text Mining - Concepts, Implementation, and Big Data Challenge. SBD, vol. 45. Springer, Cham (2019). https://doi.org/10.1007/978-3-319-91815-0

Kharlamov, A.A., Pilgun, M. (eds.): Neuroinformatics and Semantic Representations. Cambridge Scholars Publishing, Newcastle upon Tyne (2020)

Kramer, A.D.I., Guillory, J., Hancock, J.T.: Experimental evidence of massive-scale emotional contagion through social networks. Proc. Natl. Acad. Sci. **111**(24), 8788–8790 (2014)

Lotman, Y.M.: Culture and Explosion. Progress, Gnosis, Moscow (1992)
Settle, J., Fowler, J.H.: A 61-million-person experiment in social influence and political mobilization. Nature **489**(7415), 295–298 (2012)
Williams, H.T.P., McMurray, J.R., Kurz, T., Lambert, F.H.: Network analysis reveals open forums and echo chambers in social media discussions of climate change. Glob. Environ. Change **32**, 126–138 (2015)
Xu, W., Wu, W.: Optimal Social Influence. SO. Springer, Cham (2020). https://doi.org/10.1007/978-3-030-37775-5
Yang, J.H., Barnidge, M., Rojas, H.: The politics of "Unfriending": user filtration in response to political disagreement on social media. Comput. Hum. Behav. **70**, 22–29 (2017)

Design a Management System for the Influencer Marketing Campaign on Social Network

Hien D. Nguyen[1,2(✉)], Kha V. Nguyen[3], Suong N. Hoang[3], and Tai Huynh[3,4]

[1] University of Information Technology, Ho Chi Minh City, Vietnam
hiennd@uit.edu.vn
[2] Vietnam National University, Ho Chi Minh City, Vietnam
[3] Kyanon Digital, Ho Chi Minh City, Vietnam
{kha.nguyen,suong.hoang,tai.huynh}@kyanon.digital
[4] Ton Duc Thang University, Ho Chi Minh City, Vietnam

Abstract. Influencer marketing is an effective kind of digital marketing. It is useful to reach target audiences, and brands will be exposed to more valuable online consumers. The system for managing the influencer marketing campaign on a social network is very necessary to increase the effectiveness of an influencer marketing campaign. In this paper, a method for designing a management system for this marketing campaign is proposed. This system can collect data on the social network and extract information from data to detect emerging influencers for the brand to run the campaign. It works based on the measures of amplification factors, the passion point of a user with the brand, and the ability about content creation. This management system is also the foundation to establish commerce activities and build an advocate community of the brand. The built system shows the results of the campaign as a visual report in real time to support the brand giving the decision. The system has been tested in the real-world influencer marketing campaign and got positive feedback from the brands.

Keywords: Influencer marketing · Social network · Business intelligence · Information propagation · Passion point · Content creation score

1 Introduction

Digital marketing is the component of marketing which the brands use internet and digital technologies to advance their products and services [1]. Influencer marketing is a kind of digital marketing. Influencers are people with the ability to impact emerging customers of a product by recommending the items on social media [2, 3]. They play as endorsements for products. The influencer marketing focuses on using influencers to viral the information of a product/brand to the larger market [4]. It helps brands get campaign goals. Most influencer marketing campaigns are influencers expected to spread the word through their personal social channels [5].

An influencer marketing campaign is effective if it makes brands to build trust and expand reach to influencer followers, strengthen brand messaging through authentic

S. Chellappan et al. (Eds.): CSoNet 2020, LNCS 12575, pp. 139–151, 2020.
https://doi.org/10.1007/978-3-030-66046-8_12

endorsements, influence consumer buying decisions, reach more engaged and better-qualified audiences [6]. The influencer marketing really works if the brands can match the influencers to their target audience and their campaign goals. Thus, identifying the suitable influencers is necessary. There are three ways marketers find social media influencers are social search, influencer platforms, and having influencers reach out to them [5, 7].

The management system for an influencer marketing campaign on a social network is a system which manages the working of this campaign. Firstly, this system can collect data on social network based on the information of the determined brand, the consumer. Data is also organized to represent the relationships between objects of the social network. Secondly, though collected data, the system can detect emerging influencers for the brand who are able to be used to run an influencer marketing campaign. The measures, which computes the impact of a user to his/her audience, are studied and used to detect the potential influencers. Finally, in the influencer marketing campaign, the management system can trace the quality of customers and traffic from each influencer in the real time. It may show the visual report of the campaign results, such as the total of interactions, the rate of the conversation per click, the revenue. That report supports the brand to give the decision at the moment.

In this paper, a method for designing a management system for an influencer marketing campaign on a social network, called ADVO system, is proposed. Beside the working of a management system, this system is also the foundation supporting the businesses to deploy their commerce activities and build their advocate community. The system detects potential influencers for a brand based on the measures: amplification factors, the passion point of a user with the brand, and the ability about content creation. The architecture of the ADVO system includes three main functions: *AdvoSights* - use for social listening and analyze the users' behaviors on a social network, *AdvoBiz* – the foundation to establish commerce activities of the brand, and *AdvoFair* - help the brands building an advocate community of the brand. The ADVO system has been tested through real-world influencer marketing campaigns and got positive experimental results from the customer.

The next section presents some related works about the studying of detecting influencers on a social network. Section 3 presents the architecture of a management system for an influencer marketing campaign, called ADVO system, and its working. This architecture has advocates including three main functions: AdvoSights, AdvoBiz and AdvoFair. Section 4 presents some measures for detecting emerging influencers for a determined brand. Section 5 shows experimental results by testing in practice. The last section concludes the paper.

2 Related Work

There are many systems for supporting the influencer marketing, but those systems only search the influencers based on their set of users joining them, they have not supported the running of the campaign completely. Moreover, the methods for detecting influencers are only built based on some amplification factors about the number of relations between users and others, they have not mentioned to some characteristics of a user to the brand, such as the favorite of a user to a brand, the ability about creating content on the social network to attract audience.

Laroche et al. [7] studied the positive affect of brands to customers and their loyalty through social media. Based on the nomological network representing those relations, they proposed some measures for computing the impact of a brand to the community on a social network.

In [8], the authors proposed measures of influence for a user on Twitter. Those measures cover almost all impact values of a user to his/her audience on Twitter. Nonetheless, they have not yet mentioned the tweet propagation. Although the result in [9] presented an influential measure based on the speed of the post propagation in the duration time, this measure has not yet reflected the impact of users' information on a social network.

Tidke et al. used Heterogeneous Surface Learning Features to identify and rank influential nodes on social networks [16]. They proposed two methods Average Consensus Ranking Aggregation and Weighted Average Consensus Ranking Aggregation and tested them on real-world data collected from Twitter for topics about politics and economy. However, the results of those methods are not suitable for brands to use in their influencer marketing.

Beside that, some current systems for managing the influencer marketing campaign support the searching relationships between a brand and their sets of determined influencers [10–12]. The parameters measuring the influence of a user are the amplification factors, such as the number of friends, followers, reactions. In the real-world, the value of the loving of a user to a brand combing the user's amplification factors supports to compute the attraction of a post created by the user [13]. The evaluation of the post's impact on audience helps to recognize the users' reactions on that post [14]. Those are parameters need to measure the user's influence. However, those current methods have not yet mentioned the combination between the favorite of a user to a brand and the ability about creating post content for determining emerging influencers to run an influencer marketing campaign of a brand.

The SCWord in [15] is a system presenting the changes of users' sentiment on a social network in real time. This system gets a view of the relationship between dynamic topic clusters on social networks. Besides, the system also provides charts showing the changes in attitudes of users on the network. It reflects the aggregate polarization of social media posts. However, this system has not yet been used to identify influencers on social media.

The current management systems of the influencer marketing campaign only detect the influencers which are celebrities and key opinion leaders (KOL), they have not found the minor influencers, so the effectiveness of the marketing campaign is not optimal. Besides, those systems have not yet supported to manage real-time parameters in an influencer marketing campaign.

3 The Architecture of a Management System for an Influencer Marketing Campaign

The management system for an influencer marketing campaign, called ADVO system, has to be able to measure the impact of influencers to their audiences. It evaluates through the analyzing of the information on a social network. It also can trace the behaviors of users to recognize potential customers of the brand. This management system is the foundation for the brands to evaluate their influencer marketing campaigns and build an advocate community for those brands. In this section, the architecture of the ADVO system and its working are proposed.

3.1 The Architecture of the ADVO System

From the determined consumer of the brand, the ADVO system will be set up for automatically collecting data on a social network suitably. The data is crawled in the duration time. Based on the information of collected data, the system computes the measures to detect emerging influencers of that consumer for the brand. Those measures are studied in [9, 13], they consist of the amplification factors on a social network in a duration time, the passion point of a brand or a consumer, and the ability to create the post's content [14]. Besides, the ADVO system can manage all interactions with the emerging influencers in the influencer marketing campaign. It estimates the information propagation for each influencer, and determines the number of clicks on interactions, the conversion rate of clicks and orders, and the revenue. It also produces a final report for the campaign with the data visualization of results. The architecture of this management system is as Fig. 1. The advocates in this architecture include three main functions: AdvoSights, AdvoBiz and AdvoFair.

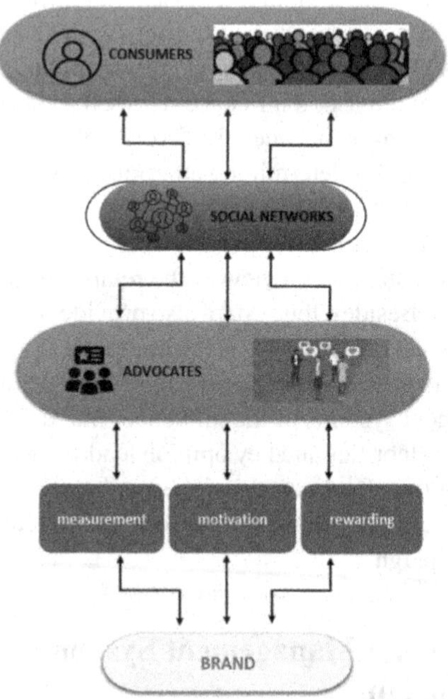

Fig. 1. The architecture of ADVO system.

AdvoSights: This is an important tool of ADVO system. It is used for social listening and analyzing the users' behaviors on a social network. It also measures the values to detect emerging influencers for a brand to run its influencer marketing campaign. Those measures for a user are the estimating the information propagation on a social network in a duration time, the passion point of a brand or a consumer, and the ability to create the post's content (content creation score). They are values to evaluate the affection of a user and the attraction to the audience to interact with the user's posts.

AdvoBiz: This is the foundation supporting the entrepreneurs to deploy their commerce activities. It is used to collect data on a social network. AdvoBiz is a tool to manage the influencer marketing campaigns. Using the AdvoBiz, the brand can create and observe a campaign. At a time, the system visualizes the report of the campaign about the total interactions, the rate of the conversation per click, etc. Through that, the brand can evaluate the effectiveness of the campaign and give a decision accordingly.

AdvoFair: This is a foundation to help the brands building their advocate community. It optimizes the value of the advocate community on social networks by oriented spreading the information of the brand quickly. The information will be given targeted customers naturally.

3.2 The Working of the ADVO System

The ADVO system has some working to establish its main functions. It needs to crawl data from the social network automatically. Those data are the resources to detect the emerging influencers for digital marketing. Besides that, the system has to have the ability to statistic the results of an influencer marketing campaign and visualize them on the campaign dashboard.

Data Crawling

The collected data is organized into three separate databases: Command and Mapping database, Raw crawled database, and Processed database. The data crawling system is shown in Fig. 2.

The data crawling system consists of 4 components:

- *Command receiver*: As the input of the system, the "command receiver" introduces a set of APIs for external systems to point out which should be crawled and when to start and end the crawling commands. The commands will be saved to the "command & mapping" database and parsed to messages which will be sent to the message queue for further processing.
- *Crawling worker*: It is the core of the system. It is responsible for collecting the requested data. Due to the fact that the variety of data sources are wide, several kinds of crawling workers are used. At the time of this material, there are two versions of crawling workers: API requesting and user emulating. The data collecting tasks are sent to crawling workers via message queue, the workers will decide how to get the desired data, and which part of information should be saved to the "raw" database. Besides, simple matching steps can be performed in order to narrow down the amount of data collected. When the desired data is saved, workers will notify the "data processor" using the message queue.

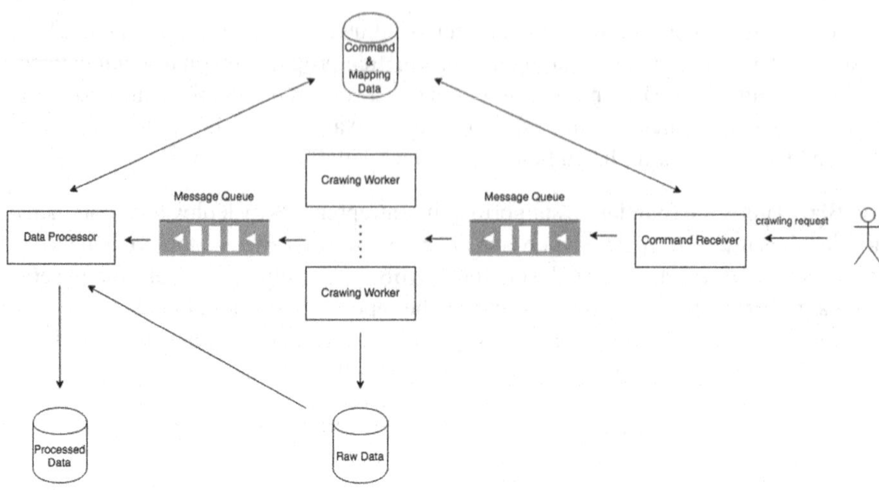

Fig. 2. Data crawling system.

- *Data processor*: This component is making the rough crawled data ready for external systems including removing html tags, adding missing information or connecting different pieces of data together. The final result is saved to the Processed database. At this level, the data is considered clean and ready to be processed by external systems. External systems can consume the processed data via API (provided by a sub component of the crawling system) or reading the database directly.
- *Message queue*: It distributes requests to different parts of the system, ensuring the stability by using asynchronous communication. Applying asynchronous communication style, a message queue system can be used to deliver crawling tasks to crawling workers, processing tasks to instances of data processors. This approach guarantees the stability and performance of the whole system. To be specific, popular message brokers such as RabbitMQ [17], ZeroMQ [18] or streaming platforms such as Kafka [19] can be utilized.

Detecting of the Emerging Influencers for the Brand

The influencers for a brand are determined based on the measures of users on the social network. Those measures are the estimating the amplification factors, such as information propagation, on a social network in a duration time, the passion point of a brand or a consumer, and the ability to create the post's content (content creation score). They evaluate the impact of a user to the audience, and the user's brand loving. The details of those measures are presented in Sect. 4.

With a brand, the system will collect information of a user which are related to this brand/product. Using the collected data, the measures of a user are computed. The system uses those values to detect the list of emerging influencers of the consumer for the determined brand.

Statistic of Parameters in the Campaign

As a matter of fact, for a business campaign, real-time tracking is often a required feature. A requirement such as "tracking this number on a daily basis" or "how this figure varies over time" might be demanded. Therefore, the simple approach of consuming processed data mentioned before would not be appropriate. In order to tackle the problem, an external system can provide a set of APIs to be called at run time ensuring the real-time feature. However, this method can lead to the coupling between our system and the external ones. On the other hand, whenever a new system occurs, some effort must be made to integrate it, and the crawling system will eventually do what is not its main responsibility. A better solution would be to create API hooks, which other systems can register on their interested data. This way, each change in the "processed" data can be considered as an event, and the burden of formatting the shape of data to be sent will be minimized. The crawling commands must now contain information at which rate a piece of data should be re-crawled.

Campaign Dashboard

After tracking and analyzing processes for the running of an influencer marketing campaign, the bunch of texture and numeric data is not easy for humans to quantify. For decision support based on those results that are tracked in the campaign, the data need to be shown in the visual form. With this insight, a dashboard to visualize the results is developed. To meet business requirements, the dash-plot is used to build the dashboard with an interactive interface. Viewers are allowed to define the benchmarks and sort it. The system allows viewers to identify concerned areas on the dashboard.

4 The Measures for Detecting Influencers on Social Network

AdvoSights is an important tool of the ADVO system. It can help the brands detect emerging influencers in their consumer to run their influencer marketing campaigns. For determining the influencers, there are measures to evaluate the impact of a user to their audience: amplification factors, the passion point of a user with the brand, and the ability about content creation. Those measures have been presented in [13, 14].

On a social network, we denote:

- **U** is the set of users on the social network,
- P_u is the set of posts of the user $u \in \mathbf{U}$,
- $word(p)$ is the number of words in a post p on the social network.

4.1 The Measure of Amplification Factors

For a user on a social network, besides the number of his/her friends and followers, the interactions on each post is an amplification factor to measure the influence on audience.

Moreover, an influencer marketing campaign is run in the duration time, so the parameter about the number of interactions for each post in the determined time is important to detect emerging influential users. In this section, the value of the average of interactions in the duration time is proposed.

Definition 4.1 [20]: (Social pulse) Given a post p, a user u on the social network, t_p is the timestamp of the post p, the time window δ.

(a) A set of users who are interested in post p in the time window δ.

$$I_p^u(\delta) = \{v \in \mathrm{U} | v \neq u,\ v \text{ interacted with } p \text{ in the time} \in [t_p, t_p + \delta]\} \quad (1)$$

where, "v interacted with p" means "v reacted, shared or commented with the post p"

(b) The social pulse for the post p in the time window δ is the value:

$$S_p(\delta) = \sum_{v \text{ shared post } p} card\,(I_p^v(\delta)) \quad (2)$$

Definition 4.2 [9]: (Average of Interactions) Let $u \in \mathbf{U}$ be a user; the average of interactions for each post of user u in the time window δ is computed by:

$$AI_u(\delta) = \frac{\sum_{p \in P_u} S_p(\delta)}{card\,(P_u)} \quad (3)$$

4.2 Passion Point

Passion point computes the loving of a user with a brand. If a user really likes the brand X, he/she will usually post information related to that brand. Besides, the user tends to have positive posts for the brand X. The sentiment of posts is determined based on the analyzing of their grammar structure and the improvement of self-attention network [21]. The formula of this point is computed based on the distribution of positive posts to the total of the user's posts. In this case, this distribution can be set as a binomial normal distribution [22]; hence, the Wilson score interval method may be used to determine the binomial proportion confidence interval [23].

Definition 4.3 [13]: (Passion point) Given a user u, the brand X.

(a) The ranking score for the user u with the brand X:

$$\text{ranking}_X(u) := \frac{\rho + \frac{z^2}{2.card\,(P_u)}}{1 + \frac{z^2}{card\,(P_u)}} - \frac{z}{1 + \frac{z^2}{card\,(P_u)}} \sqrt{\frac{\rho(1-\rho)}{card\,(P_u)} + \frac{z^2}{4(card\,(P_u))^2}} \quad (4)$$

where, $P_u^{positive}$ is the set of positive posts of the user u with the brand X.

$$\rho = card(P_u^{positive})/card(P_u): \text{ the binomial proportion}$$
$$z: \text{ the quantile of a standard normal distribution.}$$

(b) *The passion point of the user u with the brand X is computed by:*

$$PP_X(u) := \text{ranking}_X(u) + \log(card(P_u)) \tag{5}$$

4.3 Content Creation Score

In the real-world, although some posts do not have any meaning, they get lots of interactions from the audience because of the seeder's authority. In this study, a post is called meaningless if the number of words in that post is lower than the average number of words in each post. The quality of the user's content creation is only computed on the meaning posts.

Definition 4.4 [14]: (Quality of posts) Let $u \in \mathbf{U}$ be a user on social network.

(a) The average number of words in each post:

$$\phi := \frac{\sum_{p \in P_u} word(p)}{card(P_u)} \tag{6}$$

(b) The quality of u's posts, $Q(u)$, is computed by:

$$Q(u) := \frac{\sum_{\substack{p \in P_u \\ word(p) \geq \phi}} \frac{word_{positve}(p)}{w(p)}}{card(\{p \in P_u | word(p) \geq \phi\})} \tag{7}$$

where, $word_{positve}(p)$ is the number of positive words in the post p.

Definition 4.5: (Content creation score) Given a user $u \in \mathbf{U}$, and the brand X. The content creation score of the user u for the brand X, called $Content_X(u)$, is determined as follows:

$$Content_X(u) := PP_X(u) + \log(Q(u)) \tag{8}$$

where, $PP_X(u)$ and $Q(u)$ are computed by the formulas (5) and (7), resp.

The formula (8) combines the passion point and the quality of posts. If the user u likes the brand X, the value of $PP_X(u)$ will be increased; thus, the user will tend to have high quality posts for the brand X. Besides, *Quality*(u) is determined based on the number of positive words, its value in the formula (8) will compute the iterated positive words in posts.

5 Experimental Results

Fashion is the consumer attracting many people. There are many seasons for stimulating fashion shopping. In this section, the results of the ADVO system for a practical influencer marketing campaign are presented. The customer of the system is a fashionable brand. The marketing campaign is run in February 2020 and it only considers Vietnamese users on Facebook.

5.1 Phases of the Influencer Marketing Campaign

There are two phases when the brand runs its influencer marketing campaign in February 2020:

- Phase 1: From Feb. 12–17, 2020. The customer used 31 micro-influencers who were determined by our customer.
- Phase 2: From Feb. 18–23, 2020. The customer used 11 micro-influencers who were detected by AdvoSights of the ADVO system using the measures in Sect. 4.

The dataset for determining of this phase are crawled from Vietnamese users on Facebook who are working in fashion. The data are collected from June 2019–Dec. 2019. Using the collected data, the measures of users are computed and used for detecting emerging influencers of the brand.

After that, the customer uses AdvoBiz of the ADVO system to manage its campaign. The results of this campaign is shown in the next section.

5.2 Experimental Results

Our experiment performs on a list of influencers including 31 influencers in phase 1 and 11 influencers in phase 2. During the time of the experiment, a sales campaign was carried out; the profiles' social influence and sales outcome were recorded. Figure 3 shows the total of interactions on the brand of our customer in the campaign. In those

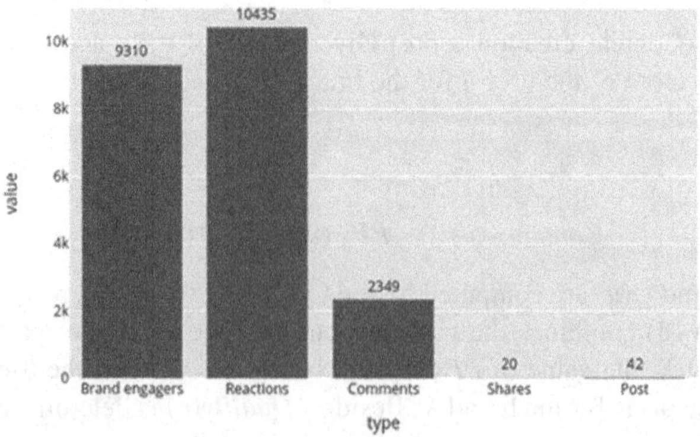

Fig. 3. Total of interactions of the influencer marketing campaign in Feb. 2020

results, the posts are only count for influencers. The details of interactions for each phase are shown in Table 1.

Table 1. Detail of interactions for each phase

Type of interactions	Posts	Reactions	Comments	Shares	Total of interactions
Phase 1	31	6,548	1,844	9	**8,410**
Phase 2	11	3,887	505	11	**4,403**
Total	**42**	**10,435**	**2,349**	**20**	**12,804**

When running a marketing campaign, the rate of click per interaction and the conversion rate for each click are important values to evaluate the effectiveness of a campaign. The values of those rates for the marketing campaign in Feb. 2020 are as Table 2.

Table 2. The values of effective rates for each interaction and click

	Phase 1	Phase 2
Interactions	8410	4403
Clicks	1511	636
Orders	**7**	17
Rate of click per interaction	**17.98%**	**14.44%**
Conversion rate per click	**0.46%**	**2.67%**

Through the results in Table 2, although phase 1 has the number of clicks more than phase 2, the effectiveness of phase 1 is lower than phase 2. The conversion rate of phase 2 performs that the revenue of this phase is better than another. Besides, Fig. 4 shows that the average influencer efficiency of phase 2 is also better than phase 1.

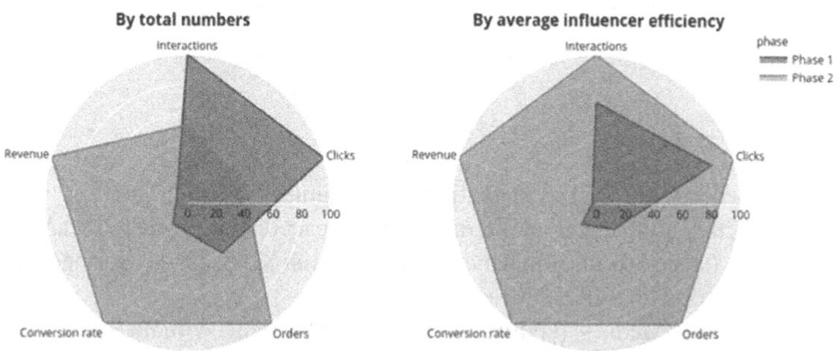

Fig. 4. The average influencer efficiency

The ADVO system can manage a small influencer marketing campaign which runs in a local market. The influencers detected by this system work effectively, they can approach more target customers and get the reality revenue. Besides, the ADVO system gives dash-boards of the campaign to report its status in real time. It can visualize the working of users on the posts of influencers, the revenue got by each influencer. The tracing of consumer behaviors when they interact with influencers helps the brand to construct its homophily which is the brand-lovers' community.

6 Conclusion and Future Work

In this paper, the architecture of ADVO system, which is a management system for influencer marketing on a social network, is proposed. This architecture includes three main functions: *AdvoSights* - social listening and analyzing the users' behaviors on a social network to detect emerging influencers, *AdvoBiz* – establishing commerce activities of the brand, and *AdvoFair* - building an advocate community of the brand. The ADVO system is a foundation supporting the businesses to manage their commerce activities through an influencer marketing campaign. The system can detect potential influencers for a brand based on the measures: amplification factors to measure the virality of information, the passion point of a user with the brand, and the ability about content creation. It also extracts the visual report for the campaign in real time. The ADVO system has been tested on real-world influencer marketing campaigns and got positive experimental results from the customers.

However, the current ADVO system only manages a small marketing campaign in a local market. In the next step, this system will be scaled up to manage the larger campaigns which have more users and higher frequency of interactions in the duration time of campaigns. In the future, some methods for increasing the attraction and influence of users will be researched. Those methods will escalate the effectiveness of influencers in the marketing campaign. Besides, the study of tracing the change of consumer behaviors supports the businesses to enlarge their market. Through the management system, our customers can track activities on the social network and build a useful plan of marketing campaigns.

Acknowledgment. This research is supported by Vingroup Innovation Foundation (VINIF) in project code DA132_15062019/year 2019.

References

1. Deiss, R., Henneberry, R.: Digital marketing for Dummies, Wiley (2016)
2. Tabellion, J., Esch, F.: Influencer marketing and its impact on the advertised brand. In: Bigne, E., Rosengren, S. (eds.) Advances in Advertising Research X, pp. 29–41. Springer, Wiesbaden (2019). https://doi.org/10.1007/978-3-658-24878-9_3
3. Vo, L.: Mining Social Media – Finding Stories in Internet data, William Pollock (2019)
4. Zimmerman, J., Ng, D.: Social Media Marketing All-in-One, 4th edn. Wiley, Dummies (2017)
5. Levin, A.: Influencer Marketing for Brands. Springer, NewYork (2019). https://doi.org/10.1007/978-1-4842-5503-2

6. Laroche, M., Habibi, M., Richard, M., Sankaranarayanan, R.: The effects of social media based brand communities on brand community markers, value creation practices, brand trust, and brand loyalty. Comput. Human Behav. **28**, 1755–1767 (2012)
7. Mediakix: Influencer marketing 2019 - Key statistics from our influencer marketing survey. https://mediakix.com/influencer-marketing-resources/influencer-marketing-industry-statistics-survey-benchmarks/. Accessed 11 Aug 2020
8. Riquelme, F., Gonzalez-Cantergiani, P.: Measuring user influence on Twitter: a survey. Int. J. Inf. Process. Manage. **52**(5), 949–975 (2016)
9. Huynh, T., Zelinka, I., Pham, X.H., Nguyen, H.D: Some influence measures to detect the influencer on social network based on Information Propagation. In: Proceedings of 9th International Conference on Web Intelligence, Mining and Semantics (WIMS 2019), Seoul, Korea (2019)
10. Hiips. https://hiip.asia/influencer/. Accessed 11 Aug 2020
11. 7Saturday. https://7saturday.com/en/index.html. Accessed 11 Aug 2020
12. Activate: https://try.activate.social. Accessed 11 Aug 2020
13. Huynh, T., Nguyen, H., Zelinka, I., Dinh, D., Pham, X.H.: Detecting the influencer on social networks using passion point and measures of information propagation. Sustainability **12**(7), 3064 (2020)
14. Nguyen, H.D., Huynh, T., Luu, S., Hoang, S., Pham, V., Zelinka, I.: Measure of the content creation score on social network using sentiment score and passion point. In: Proceedings of 19th International Conference on Intelligent Software Methodologies, Tools, and Techniques (SOMET 2020), Kitakyushu, Japan (2020)
15. Valdiviezo, O., Sánchez, J.A., Cervantes, O.: Visualizing sentiment change in social networks. In: Proceedings of the 8th Latin American Conference on Human-Computer Interaction (CLIHC 2017), Guatemala (2017)
16. Tidke, B., Mehta, R., Jenish Dhanani, J.: Consensus-based aggregation for identification and ranking of top-k influential nodes. Neural Comput. Appl. **32**, 10275–10301 (2020)
17. RabbitMQ. https://www.rabbitmq.com/. Accessed 11 Aug 2020
18. ZeroMQ. https://zeromq.org/. Accessed 11 Aug 2020
19. Kafka. https://kafka.apache.org/. Accessed 11 Aug 2020
20. Pham, X.H., Jung, J., Hwang, D.: Beating social pulse: understanding information propagation via online social tagging systems. J. Univers. Comput. Sci. **18**, 1022–1031 (2012)
21. Nguyen, H.D., Huynh, T., Hoang, S.N., Pham, V.T., Zelinka, I.: Language-oriented sentiment analysis based on the grammar structure and improved Self-attention network. In: Proceedings of 15th International Conference on Evaluation of Novel Approaches to Software Engineering (ENASE 2020), Prague, Czech Public (2020)
22. Kaas, R., Buhrman, J.M.: Mean, median and mode in binomial distributions. Stat. Neerl. **34**(1), 13–18 (1980)
23. Wilson, E.B.: Probable inference, the law of succession, and statistical inference. J. Am. Stat. Assoc. **22**, 209–212 (1927)

Group Influence Maximization in Social Networks

Yuting Zhong[1] and Longkun Guo[1,2](✉)

[1] College of Mathematics and Computer Science, Fuzhou University, Fuzhou, China
longkun.guo@gmail.com
[2] School of Computer Science, Qilu University of Technology, Jinan, China

Abstract. In emerging applications of social networks, groups play a vital role as most decisions are made by groups according to the opinion of the majority therein. This brings the problem of Group Influence Maximization (GIM) which aims to select k initial active nodes for maximizing the expected number of influenced groups. In the paper, we study GIM and focus on activating groups rather than individuals. Observing the known NP-hardness of GIM and the $\#P$-hardness of computing the objective function under Independent Cascade (IC) model, we devise an algorithm called Complementary Maximum Coverage (CMC) based on analyzing the influence of the nodes over the groups, ensuring the task of maximizing the number of activated groups. In addition, we also propose an algorithm called Improved Reverse Influence Sampling (IRIS) via adjusting the famous Reverse Influence Sampling (RIS) algorithm for GIM. Lastly, experiments are carried out to demonstrate that our CMC and IRIS both outperform the known baselines including Maximum Coverage and Maximum Out-degree algorithms in the average number of activated groups under IC model.

Keywords: Complementary Maximum Coverage (CMC) algorithm · Improved Reverse Influence Sampling (IRIS) algorithm · Group Influence Maximization (GIM) · Independent Cascade (IC) model

1 Introduction

With the development of the Internet and the continuous improvement of information technology, people are more and more inclined to conduct social activities on the Internet, and express their views or share their daily life on social software, thus giving rise to social networks mediated by social software. As a platform, social networks play an important role in the interaction between individuals and the dissemination of information and ideas. Among the commonly used social software, Facebook has 2.2 billion users, WeChat has 1 billion users, and Twitter has 340 million users [1]. People are not lonely in the real life as well as in social networks. They will form groups based on their common interests and hobbies or some kind of relationship. The group can be large or small: as

S. Chellappan et al. (Eds.): CSoNet 2020, LNCS 12575, pp. 152–163, 2020.
https://doi.org/10.1007/978-3-030-66046-8_13

small as two or three people, such as a family; or as large as a state or even a country. Because social networks have such important influence, they have great applications in information dissemination, advertising marketing, public opinion control and other aspects. We take viral marketing as an example, when advertising companies want to achieve a good marketing result with limited cost, they will use the "word-of-mouth" effect to select k users to maximize advertising audiences through their "mouths". In addition, individual decisions depend on group decisions. For example, a company needs to buy pens of a certain brand for all employees. When a majority of employees are promoted by a certain brand and decide to buy pens of that brand, the company will buy all pens of that brand. Another example is the US presidential election. If a presidential candidate wins a majority in a state election, he or she will have all the electoral votes of the state. This is also a practical example of maximizing group influence.

1.1 Related Work

To the best of our knowledge, Domingos and Richardson et al. [2] were the first to address the issue of Influence Maximization (IM). Kempe et al. [3] were the first to formulate IM as a discrete optimization problem. They showed the IM problem is NP-hard under either the Independent Cascade (IC) model or Linear Threshold (LT) model, while the objective function is submodular. They proposed a greedy algorithm using Monte Carlo method to simulate the process of influence propagation, which achieved $\left(1-\frac{1}{e}-\varepsilon\right)$ approximation solution for any $\varepsilon > 0$. However, the computation time of the greedy algorithm is expensive. Subsequently, more and more scholars have dedicated themselves to the study of IM problem and proposing approximation algorithms based on improved greedy approach and heuristic algorithms [4–8]. Heuristic algorithms are favored by scholars because of its fast computation speed, but its approximate quality is not as good as the approximation algorithms. In particular, the improved greedy algorithms are faster than the traditional greedy algorithms via making use of the submodularity of the objective function.

Due to the further study of many scholars, the algorithms for solving IM problem have also developed rapidly. Among them, Borgs et al. [9] proposed RIS algorithm, which greatly reduced the computational time of the simulation propagation process. Based on RIS algorithm, Tang et al. [10,11] proposed TIM, TIM^{+} and IMM algorithms, which guaranteed a $\left(1-\frac{1}{e}-\varepsilon\right)$ approximation ratio under IC model. Recently, Nguyen et al. [12] proposed the SSA and D-SSA algorithms, which were the first approximation algorithm which satisfies the strict theoretical threshold of IM with the minimum sample set.

A social network is divided into multiple communities by community discovery algorithms. The nodes within communities are closely connected while the nodes among communities are sparsely connected, so the influence within communities spreads quickly in a wide range. The two most commonly used community discovery algorithms are OASNET (Optimal Allocation in a Social NETwork) algorithm and CGA (Community-based Greedy Algorithm) algorithm.

The OASNET algorithm was proposed by Cao et al. [13] to solve the IM problem by using the optimal dynamic allocation of resources. CGA algorithm [14] combined the dynamic programming method and the greedy algorithm to allocate the optimal number of seed nodes for each community so as to maximize the influence. Ji et al. [15] proposed a new algorithm, which found out the hidden community structure in the network and then selected k nodes with the largest number of community coverage as seed nodes. Moreover, many researchers are committed to studying the property of community to solve IM aiming to maximize the number of eventually activated nodes, while the task of GIM is to activate maximum groups rather than individuals [16–22].

In terms of research on GIM, Zhu et al. [23] proposed a sandwich approximation framework based on D-SSA method to obtain seed nodes, which achieved an approximation guarantee of $\left(1 - \frac{1}{e} - \varepsilon\right)$. In addition, Zhu et al. [24] also proposed a sandwich approximation framework based on ED-SSA method, which approximated the upper and lower bounds of the objective function and compared them with the Group Coverage Maximization Algorithm (GCMA) to obtain the seed nodes. Although great breakthroughs have been made in GIM, many scholars are still working on more efficient algorithms.

1.2 Our Contribution

Our results can be summarized as in the following:

- We devise a heuristic algorithm called Complementary Maximum Coverage (CMC), which emphasizes the influence of the nodes over groups to solve GIM.
- We also propose the Improved Reverse Influence Sampling (IRIS) algorithm by adjusting the famous Reverse Influence Sampling (RIS) algorithm for GIM.
- Compared with Maximum Coverage (MC) algorithm and Maximum Outdegree (MO) algorithm by experiments, our proposed algorithms outperform both MC and MO regarding the average number of eventually activated groups under the IC model.

1.3 Organization

The remainder of the paper is organized as below: Sect. 2 gives the social network model, and formally introduces the GIM problem; Sect. 3 presents the CMC algorithm and IRIS algorithm; Sect. 4 evaluates the four algorithms under IC model through numerical experiments; Sect. 5 concludes the paper.

2 Problem Description

2.1 Network Model

We model the social network as $G = (V, E, P, U)$.

V represents the set of nodes which represent users in a social network. Assume that the social network has n users, then $V = \{v_1, v_2, \ldots, v_n\}$. The node can have influence on other nodes or be influenced by other nodes, which form edges. If there's an edge between two nodes, we could say that the two nodes are neighbors to each other.

E represents the set of edges which represent the influence between nodes. Assume that the social network has m edges, then $E = \{e_1, e_2, \ldots, e_m\}$. The edge can be directed or undirected. For example, in the directed graph, (u, v) means that node u has influence on node v, but node v has no influence on node u, u is the source node and v is the target node. The edge taking u as the source node is u's outgoing edge, and the edge taking u as the target node is u's entry edge. The sum of the number of u's outgoing edges is the out-degree of u, and the sum of the number of u's entry edges is the in-degree of u.

P represents the set of probabilities which are the weights of the edges, then $P = \{p_1, p_2, \ldots, p_m\}$, and $\forall p_i \in [0, 1], 1 \leq i \leq m$, i is a positive integer. The higher the probability is, the more likely the source node is to successfully activate the target node.

U represents the set of groups. Assume that the social network has l groups, then $U = \{u_1, u_2, ..., u_l\}$, and u_j is a subset of V, $1 \leq j \leq l$, j is a positive integer. In a social network, each node can be an individual or belong to one or more groups. When $\beta\%$ of the members in a group are affected, we assume that the group is successfully affected.

2.2 Group Influence Maximization

The IM problem is to study the maximum number of nodes that will be activated with k initial active nodes under the given information diffusion model. Figure 1a is a simple social network graph without groups. Each edge is directed, indicating that the influence flows from the source node to the target node, and each edge is probabilistic.

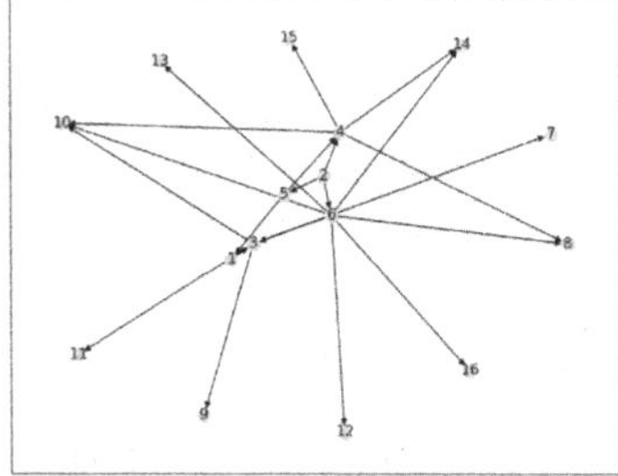

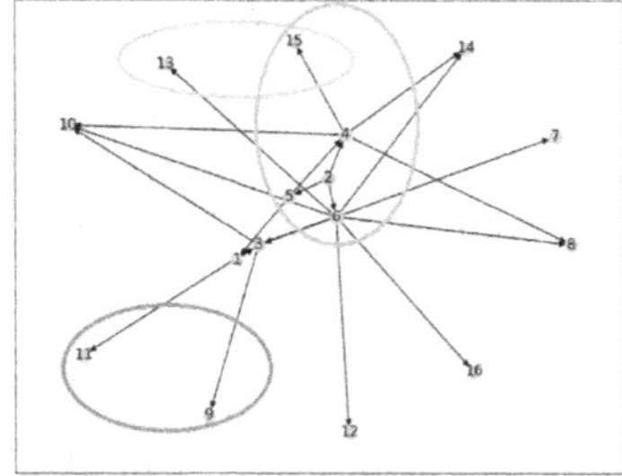

(a) A simple social network without groups (b) A simple social network with groups

Fig. 1. Examples of simple social networks with vs without groups (Color figure online)

The GIM aims to seek k nodes to maximize the expected number of eventually activated groups. Each node in GIM can be independent or belong to one or more groups, and a group will be activated only if the $\beta\%$ members of the group are activated. The larger the value of β is, the more difficult it is for the group to be activated.

The IM problem is a special example of the GIM problem. Each group in GIM represents each node in IM, and $\beta\% = 100\%$. The IM problem is NP-hard. Obviously, the GIM problem is also NP-hard. For a given graph $G = (V, E, P, U)$, the mathematical description of GIM is:

$$\begin{aligned} &\max\ \rho(S) \\ &s.t.\ |S| \leq k \end{aligned}$$

where S is the set of seed nodes, k is the number of initial seed nodes, and $\rho(S)$ is the expected number of groups activated by initial seed nodes under a given propagation model. It is difficult to calculate $\rho(S)$ because the activation is probabilistic and random. In the IM problem, computing $\rho(S)$ under IC model is #P-hard, likewise, in the GIM problem, computing $\rho(S)$ under IC model is also #P-hard [24].

Obviously, activating more nodes is not the same as activating more groups. As shown in Fig. 1b, there are three groups in the social network, that is $U = \{u_1, u_2, u_3\}$, u_1 is the yellow one, u_2 is the pink one, u_3 is the orange one. $u_1 = \{13, 15\}$, $u_2 = \{2, 4, 5, 6, 15\}$, $u_3 = \{9, 11\}$. The group activation threshold is assumed to be 50%, meaning that the group will be activated only when at least half of members of the group are active. For example, it is assumed that the seed node $\{2\}$ finally activates $\{2, 4, 15\}$, three nodes are activated, so u_1 and u_2 are activated, $\rho(S) = 2$. Another case is that seed node $\{2\}$ successfully influences $\{2, 4, 5, 6\}$, four nodes are activated, but only u_2 is activated, $\rho(S) = 1$. Therefore, activating more nodes is not the same as activating more groups. But the more nodes are activated, the more likely groups are to be activated.

3 The Algorithms for Solving GIM

In this section we discuss the algorithms to solve Group Influence Maximization (GIM) in the paper, including Complementary Maximum Coverage (CMC) algorithm and Improved Reverse Influence Sampling (IRIS) algorithm.

3.1 Complementary Maximum Coverage Algorithm

The CMC algorithm is the complementary of MC algorithm. MC algorithm aims to seek k seed nodes with maximum group coverage. However, MC algorithm does not take the contribution of nodes over groups into account. If a node covers maximum groups, but those groups require $\beta\%$ active members to be activated, and this node is only a member of the large groups. In case the node does not activate other members of the groups, then the node makes little contribution to

Algorithm 1. The Complementary Maximum Coverage algorithm

Input: An instance of GIM $G = (V, E, P, U)$, the number of seed nodes k, the activation threshold of groups β.
Output: the seed set S.
1: Set $S := \Phi$;
2: Calculate the f_c of each node following Equality 1.
3: Sort the nodes according to the computed f_c.
4: Add k nodes with maximum f_c into S.
5: **return** S.

the groups. The idea of CMC algorithm is to treat all the nodes as seed nodes, then remove $n - k$ seed nodes with the least influence over groups, and finally obtain k seed nodes. The influence of a node on a group is not only reflected in whether deleting the node has an impact on activating the group, but also in whether it can activate other members in the group. We use $f_c(v_i)$ to calculate the influence of v_i over groups which it covers. If a node does not belong to any group, its $f_c = 0$. If a node covers more than one group, then f_c equals the sum of its influence on groups. If the node has maximum group coverage, the f_c of the node may be larger. We have $f_c(v_i)$

$$f_c(v_i) = \sum_j \frac{a_{v_i}}{|u_j| - H_{u_j} + 1} \tag{1}$$

where j is the group number, u_j is the group covered by v_i, a_{v_i} is the number of members that v_i activates successfully in u_j, including v_i itself. All the nodes activated by v_i are obtained by breadth first search (BFS) method, then calculate the number of these nodes in u_j, the result is a_{v_i}. a_{v_i} measures the active degree of v_i in the group. The larger a_{v_i} is, the more members of the group can be activated, which also increases the possibility of activating the group. $|u_j|$ is the total number of members of u_j, H_{u_j} is the activation threshold of u_j, and $H_{u_j} = \beta\% \times |u_j|$. $|u_j| - H_{u_j}$ means that u_j allows $|u_j| - H_{u_j}$ nodes to be deleted, and the larger $|u_j| - H_{u_j}$ is, the less influence v_i has on u_j. Due to the denominator can't be zero, we define the denominator to be $|u_j| - H_{u_j} + 1$.

Lemma 1 *The runtime of Algorithm 1 is* $O(nl + n + m)$.

CMC performs the following operations on the nodes numbered from 1 to n: traverse l groups and find out the groups covered by each node. The runtime of the step is $O(nl)$. Then compute the number of activated members within the groups covered by each node via BFS method, so the runtime is $O(n + m)$. Hence, the runtime of the CMC algorithm is $O(nl + n + m)$.

3.2 Improved Reverse Influence Sampling Algorithm

The Improved Reverse Influence Sampling (IRIS) algorithm is improved on the basis of Reverse Influence Sampling (RIS) algorithm. The RIS algorithm

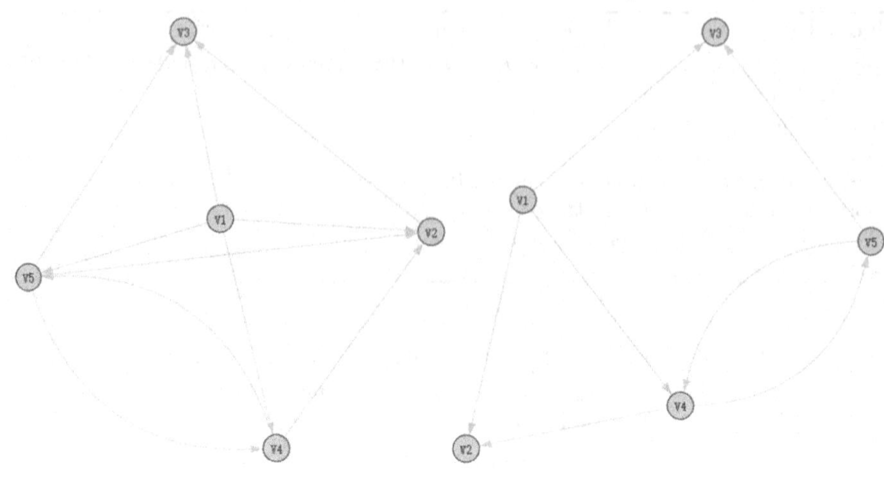

(a) An example of original graph (b) An example of sparse graph of (a)

Fig. 2. An example of a RR set generation

Algorithm 2. get_RRS algorithm

Input: An instance of GIM $G = (V, E, P, U)$.
Output: RR_set.

```
RR_set, new_nodes := Φ.
Get a random graph g from G.
Choose node v from g uniformly at random.
Add v into new_nodes.
repeat
Simulate influence spread, starting from new_nodes.
Add source nodes of new_nodes into RR_set.
Update new_nodes.
until new_nodes is empty.
return RR_set.
```

is divided into two steps: the process of generating RR (Reverse Reachable) sets and the process of selecting seed nodes. The first step is to randomly select node v in the original graph and traverse the entry edge of v. Each edge is inverted with the probability of p, or remains unchanged with the probability of $1-p$. Finally, a sparse reverse graph is generated. This helps to keep the high-probability edges, allowing a wider range of propagation. Simply speaking, the set of nodes that can reach node v with high probability is the RR set of node v. To take a simple example, Fig. 2a is the original social network graph, and there are 5 nodes and 10 directed edges. Figure 2b is the sparse graph of Fig. 2a, leaving 7 edges with high probability. The RR set of node v_2 is $\{v_2, v_1, v_4, v_5\}$, where each node has high probability to activate v_2.

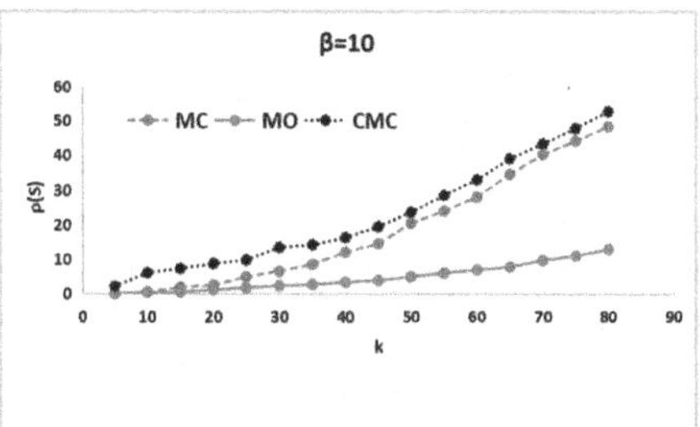

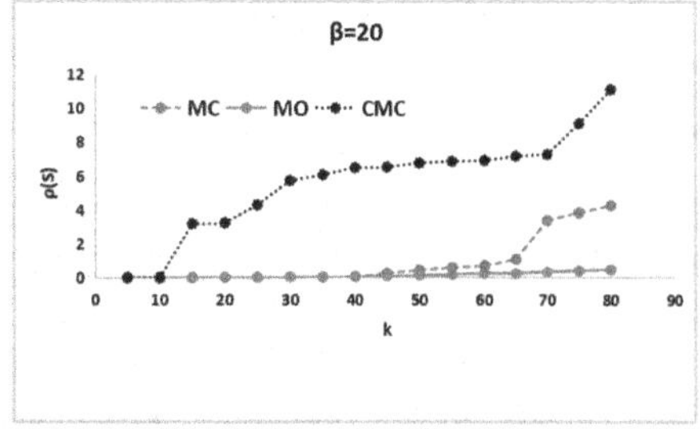

Fig. 3. Comparison of CMC, MC and MO under IC model for Dataset1

The second step of the RIS algorithm is to select the seed nodes covering maximum RR sets. Because covering more RR sets means affecting more nodes. The k nodes that cover most RR sets are the seed nodes we are looking for. But now the task is to activate maximum groups, not most nodes, and activating more nodes does not mean activating more groups. So we propose IRIS in order to solve GIM, we change the second step of RIS to choose k nodes that have maximum group coverage. In this way, the selected seed nodes can not only have certain propagation influence to activate more nodes, but also can activate more groups.

Lemma 2 *The runtime of Algorithm 3 is* $O\left(\Gamma\left(n+m\right)+knl\right)$.

The IRIS algorithm first forms Γ random sparse graphs of G, then randomly selects a node to generate a RR set in each subgraph. The runtime of the first step is $O\left(\Gamma\left(n+m\right)\right)$. Secondly iterate k times to select the node that covers the most groups in the RR sets. The runtime of the second step is $O\left(knl\right)$. Thus the runtime of the IRIS algorithm is $O\left(\Gamma\left(n+m\right)+knl\right)$.

Algorithm 3. The Improved Reverse Influence Sampling algorithm

Input: An instance of GIM $G = (V, E, P, U)$, the number of seed nodes k, Monte Carlo times t.
Output: the seed set S.
Set $S := \Phi$;
$R \leftarrow$generate t RR sets by Algorithm 2
for $i = 1$ to k **do**
Add the node that has the maximum group coverage in R into S.
Delete RR sets that contain S in R.
end for
return S.

4 Numerical Experiments

4.1 Experimental Setting

We used two data sets to perform experiments under the Independent Cascade (IC) model, including the undirected graph Dataset1 and directed graph Dataset2. Dataset1 collected in March 2020 is a social network of users from Asian (e.g. Philippines, Malaysia, Singapore) countries [25]. Nodes represent users of the music streaming service LastFM and links among them are friendships. Dataset2 consists of 9 snapshots of the Gnutella peer-to-peer file sharing network from August 2002 from SNAP. Nodes represent hosts in the Gnutella network topology and edges represent connections between the Gnutella hosts. For the convenience of the experiments, groups were randomly generated, and the probability of each edge was randomly generated. The Improved Reverse Influence Sampling (IRIS) algorithm is applied to directed graphs, so Dataset2 is available for the four algorithms, while Dataset1 is suitable to other algorithms except IRIS. Table 1 is the information of data sets used in our experiments.

Table 1. Datasets information

	Type	Nodes	Edges	Groups	Average group size
Dataset1	Undirected	7624	27806	198	34.01
Dataset2	Directed	6301	20777	234	33.84

Because k and β affect the objective function. Therefore we set the value of k from 5 to 80 at an interval of 5 for Dataset1 and Dataset2. Set the value of β to 10 and 20 for Dataset1, set the value of β to 5, 8, 10, 12, 15, 18 respectively for Dataset2. All programs were written in python3.7.

4.2 Experimental Results

As can be seen from Fig. 3, when the size of k grows, the number of activated nodes increases and hence does the number of activated groups. Besides, the number of groups activated decreases when β grows. For the undirected graph Dataset1, CMC outperforms MC and MO in general. MO performs worst, because MO aiming to seek k nodes with maximum out-degree does not focus on group activation. The performances of CMC and MC have little difference when $\beta = 10$, because the activation threshold is small, the two algorithms can find the key nodes to activate the majority of the groups. When $\beta = 20$, the difference between the experimental results of the two algorithms is widened, because the activation threshold increases, group activation becomes difficult, and the shortcomings of MC algorithm are also revealed.

As for the directed graph Dataset2, we can find that CMC and IRIS have better performance than MC and MO in average. From Fig. 4a CMC performs

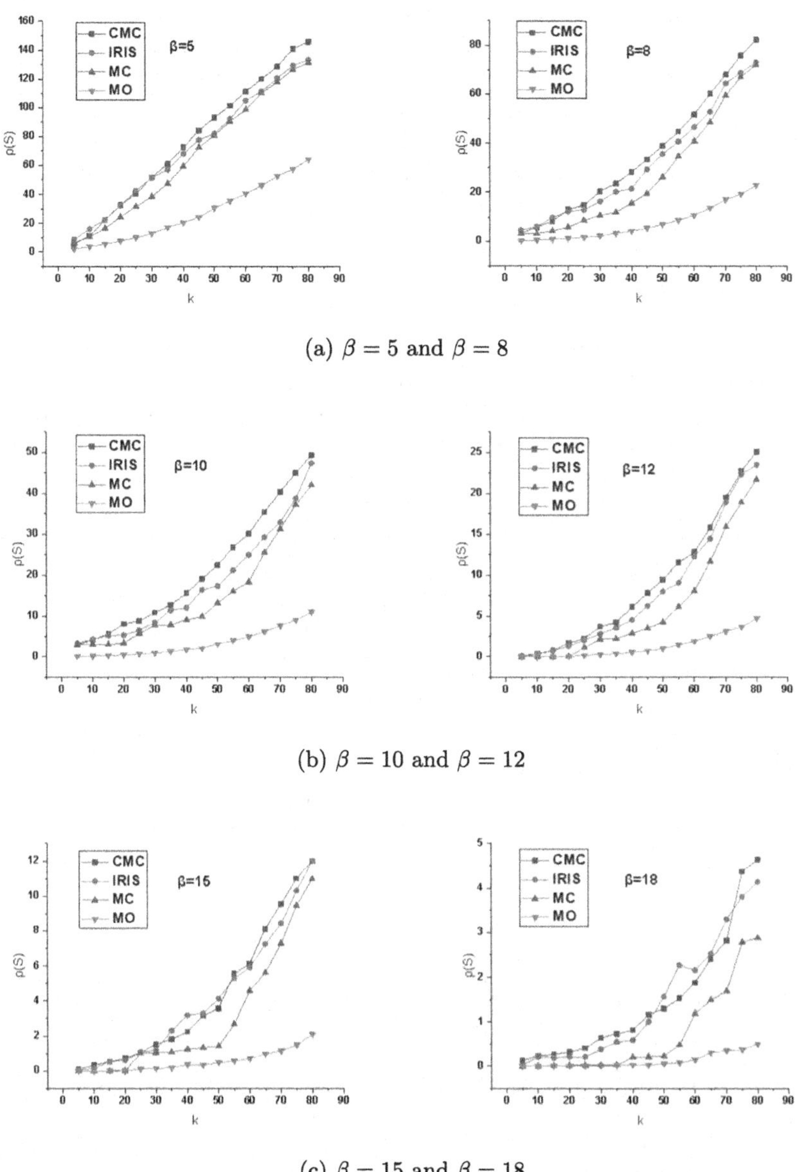

(a) $\beta = 5$ and $\beta = 8$

(b) $\beta = 10$ and $\beta = 12$

(c) $\beta = 15$ and $\beta = 18$

Fig. 4. Comparison of CMC, IRIS, MC and MO under IC model for Dataset2

best, IRIS is closer to MC, but slightly better than MC. While in Fig. 4b, the gap between IRIS and MC is widening, and IRIS is closer to CMC. Because IRIS not only focuses on seeking nodes which can cover more groups, but also attaches importance to propagation influence.

As demonstrated in Fig. 4c, our CMC algorithm has the best performance among all the algorithms in almost every instance except for some rare ones. The exceptional cases happen mainly because seed nodes obtained by IRIS differ in each time and the Reverse Reachable (RR) sets computed by IRIS focus on the influence of nodes outside the group, while CMC emphasizes the influence of nodes on members within the group.

5 Conclusion

In this paper, we proposed a heuristic algorithm called Complementary Maximum Coverage (CMC) based on analyzing the influence of the nodes over the groups to ensure the task of maximizing the number of groups activated. In addition, we also presented an algorithm called Improved Reverse Influence Sampling (IRIS) which is derived via improving the famous algorithm called Reverse Influence Sampling (RIS). Through experiments, we demonstrated that both CMC and IRIS outperform Maximum Coverage (MC) and Maximum Out-degree (MO) algorithms regarding the average number of activated groups under Independent Cascade model. Further, the CMC algorithm has better performance than IRIS in most cases besides the case when $\beta \geq 15$, while it runs significantly faster than IRIS in all instances. This indicates that CMC is the best among all the four algorithms. However, the deficiencies of CMC algorithm are that the effect is not significant when β is low and CMC is the third fast that it is slightly slower than MO and MC. We are currently analyzing the theoretical performance of CMC so as to provide an approximation ratio for the algorithm.

Acknowledgement. The authors are supported by National Natural Science Foundation of China (No.61772005) and Natural Science Foundation of Fujian Province (No.2017J01753).

References

1. Mary, M., Wu, L.: Internet trends 2018 (2018)
2. Domingos, P., Richardson, M.: Mining the network value of customers, pp. 57–66 (2001)
3. Kempe, D., Kleinberg, J., Tardos, E.: Maximizing the spread of influence through a social network, pp. 137–146 (2003)
4. Leskovec, J., Krause, A., Guestrin, C., Faloutsos, C., Vanbriesen, J.M., Glance, N.: Cost-effective outbreak detection in networks, pp. 420–429 (2007)
5. Goyal, A., Lu, W., Lakshmanan, L.V.S.: Celf++: optimizing the greedy algorithm for influence maximization in social networks, pp. 47–48 (2011)
6. Chen, W., Wang, Y., Yang, S.: Efficient influence maximization in social networks, pp. 199–208 (2009)

7. Wasserman, S., Faust, K.: Social Network Analysis: Social Network Analysis in the Social and Behavioral Sciences. Cambridge University Press, Cambridge (1994)
8. Estevez, P.A., Vera, P.A., Saito, K.: Selecting the most influential nodes in social networks, pp. 2397–2402 (2007)
9. Borgs, C., Brautbar, M., Chayes, J., Lucier, B.: Maximizing social influence in nearly optimal time, pp. 946–957 (2014)
10. Tang, Y., Xiao, X., Shi, Y.: Influence maximization: near-optimal time complexity meets practical efficiency, pp. 75–86 (2014)
11. Tang, Y., Shi, Y., Xiao, X.: Influence maximization in near-linear time: a martingale approach, pp. 1539–1554 (2015)
12. Nguyen, H.T., Thai, M.T., Dinh, T.N.: Stop-and-stare: optimal sampling algorithms for viral marketing in billion-scale networks, pp. 695–710 (2016)
13. Cao, T., Wu, X., Wang, S., Hu, X.: Oasnet: an optimal allocation approach to influence maximization in modular social networks, pp. 1088–1094 (2010)
14. Wang, Y., Cong, G., Song, G., Xie, K.: Community-based greedy algorithm for mining top-k influential nodes in mobile social networks, pp. 1039–1048 (2010)
15. Ji, J., Huang, L., Wang, Z., Li, H., Li, S.: A new approach to maximizing the spread of influence based on community structure. J. Jilin Univ. (Science Edition) **1**, 23 (2011)
16. Shuang, W.A.N.G., Bin, L.I., Xuejun, L.I.U., Ping, H.U.: Division of community-based influence maximization algorithm. Computer Engineering and Applications **2016**(19), 8 (2016)
17. Shang, J., Zhou, S., Li, X., Liu, L., Hongchun, W.: Cofim: a community-based framework for influence maximization on large-scale networks. Knowl. Based Syst. **117**, 88–100 (2017)
18. Xie, J., Szymanski, B.K., Liu, X.: SLPA: uncovering overlapping communities in social networks via a speaker-listener interaction dynamic process. In: 2011 IEEE 11th International Conference on Data Mining Workshops, pp. 344–349. IEEE (2011)
19. Qiu, L., Jia, W., Fan, X.: Influence maximization algorithm based on overlapping community. Data Anal. Knowl. Disc. **3**(7), 94–102 (2019)
20. Chen, Y.-C., Zhu, W.-Y., Peng, W.-C., Lee, W.-C., Lee, S.-Y.: CIM: community-based influence maximization in social networks. ACM Trans. Intell. Syst. Technol. (TIST) **5**(2), 1–31 (2014)
21. Huang, H., Shen, H., Meng, Z., Chang, H., He, H.: Community-based influence maximization for viral marketing. Appl. Intell. **49**(6), 2137–2150 (2019). https://doi.org/10.1007/s10489-018-1387-8
22. Bozorgi, A., Samet, S., Kwisthout, J., Wareham, T.: Community-based influence maximization in social networks under a competitive linear threshold model. Knowl. Based Syst. **134**, 149–158 (2017)
23. Zhu, J., Zhu, J., Ghosh, S., Weili, W., Yuan, J.: Social influence maximization in hypergraph in social networks. IEEE Trans. Netw. Sci. Eng. **6**(4), 801–811 (2018)
24. Zhu, J., Ghosh, S., Weili, W.: Group influence maximization problem in social networks. IEEE Trans. Comput. Soc. Syst. **6**(6), 1156–1164 (2019)
25. Rozemberczki, B., Sarkar, R.: Characteristic functions on graphs: birds of a feather, from statistical descriptors to parametric models (2020). arXiv preprint arXiv:2005.07959

Maximum Channel Access Probability Based on Post-Disaster Ground Terminal Distribution Density

Xingxing Hu[1,2(✉)], Demin Li[1,2(✉)], Chang Guo[1,2], Wei Hu[1,2], Lei Zhang[1,2], and Menglin Zhai[1,2]

[1] College of Information Science and Technology, Donghua University, Shanghai 201620, China
2181295@mail.dhu.edu.cn, deminli@dhu.edu.cn

[2] Engineering Research Center of Digitized Textile and Apparel Technology, Ministry of Education, Shanghai 201620, China

Abstract. In post-disaster relief, how to design an efficient emergency communication system (ECS) to provide emergency communication service and improve channel access probability still remains a challenge. In this paper, we use Thomas cluster process (TCP) to model the locations of ground terminals (GT) and propose a new scheme to maximize channel access probability. The proposed emergency communication infrastructure includes a hovering helicopter and a Unmanned Aerial Vehicle (UAV) to provide communication service for GTs. Different from the existed work, an adaptive speed cruise model is proposed for the UAV depending on distribution density of GTs. Then, an efficient dynamic channel resource schedule method is proposed for system with limited channel resource. The channel access probability is formed as non convex optimization problem. The original non-convex optimization problem is transferred into a convex problem by analyzing objective function. An interior-point method is adopted to solve this problem. Extensive simulations are performed to evaluate the model by optimizing the UAV speed in different regions. The results show that the proposed new scheme outperforms the one with constant cruise speed for UAV and static scheduling for channel resource allocation.

Keywords: Channel access probability · UAV · Ground terminal distribution density · TCP · Adaptive speed cruise · Resource schedule

1 Introduction

In order to quickly establish an efficient and reliable ECS, UAV has been used to assist emergency communication in [1]. The three typical cases of UAV-assisted wireless communication, including aerial base station (BS), relay [2] and information dissemination and data collection [3], are discussed in [4]. Researchers have done a lot of works based on these three application scenarios.

S. Chellappan et al. (Eds.): CSoNet 2020, LNCS 12575, pp. 164–175, 2020.
https://doi.org/10.1007/978-3-030-66046-8_14

In [5], authors are the first to propose a novel 3-D UAV-BS placement to maximize the number of covered users with different quality-of-service (QoS) requirements. They modeled the placement problem as a multiple circles placement problem and a low-complexity maximal weighted area algorithm was also proposed. In [6], authors adopted an air-to-ground (A2G) channel model that incorporated line-of-sight (LoS) and non-line-of-sight (NLoS) propagation. Channels experienced Rayleigh and Nakagami-m fading in the UAV-BSs network, respectively. The variation trend of average achievable rate with UAV distribution density was also analyzed and the results revealed that the coverage probability and average achievable rate decreased as the height of the UAV-BSs increased. In [7], an aerial network formed by multiple UAVs for assisting data relaying in disaster recovery was studied. The coverage probability of down-link user was analyzed and the optimal altitude of UAVs was achieved to maximize the capacity of ground network. However, the recent researches focus on the single factors. The model that considers both channel state and assignment is seldom studied.

In [8], an UAV was deployed to provide the fly wireless communication in a given geographical area. The system average coverage probability and sum-rate were analyzed when UAV was static and mobile, respectively. By using the disk covering problem and minimizing the number of stop points that the UAV needed to visit in order to completely cover the area, the minimum outage probability was obtained. In addition, in order to provide full coverage for the area of interest, the tradeoff between coverage and delay was discussed. In [9], Zhang *et al.* proposed a novel scenario that the service area was divided into two parts and covered by two UAVs, respectively. The difference from previous research is that authors took the channel access delay for establishing a full transmission between the vehicle and UAV into account. The coverage probability and achievable rate of a random vehicle located in the served area were derived by geometric analysis. Through changing related parameters, the optimal setting for the maximum coverage probability and achievable rate was obtained.

There are some problems need to be further optimized. First, the impact levels in the whole post-disaster area maybe different. More severely affected areas could become hotspots and a TCP is more suitable to model the locations of GTs rather than a Poisson point process (PPP). Second, UAV speed should be adjusted when it cruises the served area. According to the GT distribution densities of different regions, UAV should dynamic adjust its speed to increase the successfully access probability of each GT. Finally, a dynamic channel resource schedule should be made to further improve channel access. Different GT distribution densities require a flexible channel schedule constantly between aerial base stations. Above all, the contributions of this paper are listed as follows.

- First, in post-disaster area, a more suitable TCP rather than PPP is used to model the locations of GTs and each cluster has different GT distribution density. We propose an UAV adaptive speed cruise model based on GT distribution density.

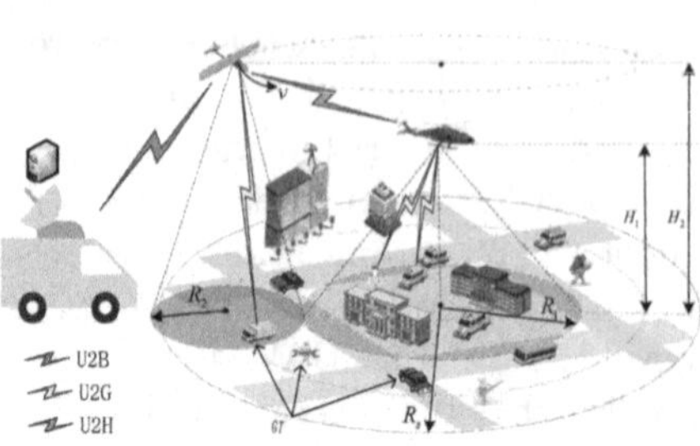

Fig. 1. Illustration of system model.

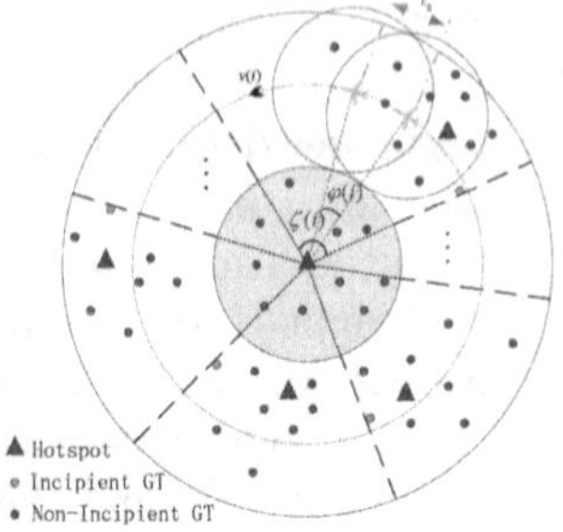

Fig. 2. Illustration of cruise model.

- Second, combining with channel state, we discuss the system channel access probability based on the channel resource availability. An efficient channel schedule method is proposed to alleviate resource competition.
- Finally, through transferring objective function and making mathematical approximations, the original non-convex problem is transformed into convex problem. The simulation results show the proposed new scheme achieves maximum channel access probability compared with the constant UAV cruise speed and static channel resource schedule.

2 System Model

2.1 Network Structure and GT Distribution

In order to quickly establish a local ECS, a hover flying helicopter (HFH) and an UAV are deployed to cover the worst heavily hit area and others, respectively. As shown in Fig. 1, according to the affected area and coverage of HFH and UAV, a local ECS is established to serve a circular post-disaster area with radius R_s. HFH's coverage is a circular area with radius R_1. The cruise flying UAV circles around HFH and its coverage is also a circle with radius R_2. By adjusting aircrafts' transmission powers or flight altitudes, the coverage of HFH and UAV is neither overlap nor gap. In order to ensure that GTs located on the edge of served area can be also covered, $R_s - (R_1 + 2R_2) \geq o$, where $0 \leq o \ll R_2$. Compared with center area, the other regions are less heavily hit. An UAV can be deployed quickly and efficiently scan those area to provide communication service for GTs. HFH and UAV can also communicate by H2U(U2H) link to exchange messages, such as adjusting both sides' coverage, and connect to the outside world through themselves or another one.

There would be many GTs in the ground of disaster area and all GTs are equipped with battery powered transceivers. These GTs mainly include emergency rescue vehicles, communication equipments of search and rescue personnel, phones of trapped person, sensors for environmental monitoring and so on. In general, densely populated areas, such as schools, hospitals, dwelling districts and so on, are more likely to be hotspots and need more emergency service after the impact of disaster. Thus, Poisson cluster process (PCP) [10] is more suitable to describe the location distribution of those hotspots and GTs. Based on the above analysis, the locations of hotspots are modeled by an independent PPP of density $\lambda^{hs} > 0$. And the locations of all GTs who are scattered around hotspots are modeled by a TCP. Unlike cellular network whose service areas are overlapping and complex, we assume these clusters are scattered and do not overlap. Thus, the probability density function (PDF) of TCP based scattered UEs around hotspot l with random distance vector Z, $f_Z(z) = \frac{1}{2\pi\sigma_{t,l}^2}\exp(-\frac{z^2}{2\sigma_{t,l}^2}), \quad z \in \mathbb{R}^2$, where $\sigma_{t,l}$ is the variance of cluster l formed by TCP. The distance from a GT to the center of cluster l is denoted as D. Then the distribution of D can be expressed as $\overline{F}_D(x) = \exp(-\frac{x^2}{2\sigma_{t,l}^2}), \quad x \geq 0$.

In our model, the impact level is different among the whole post-disaster area and the area covered by HFH is the worst heavily hit one. Therefore, the GTs densities among disaster area are also different. In Fig. 2, the disaster area covered by UAV is divided into I sector rings according to the clusters' locations. The beginning and ending bounds of sector ring are defined as the locations when UAV coves a cluster for the first time until it coves another. Incipient GT is the first one to be served in the cluster that UAV is going to serve. The average number of GTs in cluster i is $\mathcal{N}_i$, where $i = 1, ..., I$ and $\mathcal{N}_0$ for the HFH served cluster. We denote $\zeta_i(radian)$ as the central angle of sector ring i. In addition, considering the geometry, ζ_i satisfies $\sum_{i=1}^{I} \zeta_i = 2\pi$.

2.2 Channel Model

In this paper, we consider the Air-to-Ground channel which is dominated by Light-of-Sight (LoS) [11] links and the random access mechanism in MAC layer is adopted, such as IEEE 802.11 distributed coordination function protocol. When the HFH and UAV implement communication coverage, the SNR of ground terminal (GT) receiver must be greater than a threshold. Therefore, We use $g_j(r, \beta)$ [12] to represent the channel power gain of the communication link between the GT and HFH or UAV, $g_j(r, \beta) = \frac{\beta \cdot \beta_0}{H_j^2 + r^2}$, where β is the small scale fading in a certain distribution which subjects to Gamma distribution, β_0 denotes the channel power at the reference distance 1 m, H_j is the flying height of HFH or UAV (j = 1, 2, for the HFH and UAV, respectively). And r is the distance from GT to the horizontal projection point of the HFH or UAV. The channels in our model used are orthogonal. By this way, interference between channels is not considered. Thus, when implementing communication coverage, the SNR of the GT receiver must be greater than a threshold

$$SNR_j(\beta, r) = \frac{W_j \cdot g_j(r, \beta)}{\sigma^2} \geq \gamma_0, \tag{1}$$

where W_j is transmission power of aircraft j, σ^2 is the noise power of receiver, γ_0 is the SNR threshold.

2.3 Cruise Model

In our cruise model, the HFH hovers at a height H_1 above the central axis of the circular disaster zone. When UAV serves cluster i, it will adjust its speed to improve its quality of service. When UAV finishes its service for current cluster, it will maintain this speed $v(i)$ until it serves another cluster. With reference to the literature [13], we introduce the channel access delay $t_0(seconds)$ which indicates the minimum time for establishing a complete communication link with the UAV is t_0. Based on this assumption, within the time t_0, an overlapping area will appear as shown in Fig. 2. Only GTs in this overlapping area can establish complete communication links with the UAV. Since the UAV is fixed-wing, according to aerodynamics, it needs a certain speed to maintain it aloft, we denote by V_{min} and V_{max} the minimum and maximum speed of it, respectively. $\varphi(i)$ denotes the central angle of sector formed when UAV flies along the trajectory within time t_0. According to stochastic geometry analysis, the relation between $\varphi(i)$ and $v(i)$ is $\varphi(i) = \frac{v(i) \cdot t_0}{R_{12}}$, and $v(i) \leq V^a_{max}$, where $R_{12} = R_1 + R_2$. When the coverage area of UAV in time t is tangent to that in time $t + t_0$, V^a_{max} can be expressed as $V^a_{max} = \min(V_{max}, \frac{2R_{12}}{t_0} sin^{-1}(\frac{R_2}{R_{12}}))$.

3 Problem Formulation and Analysis

3.1 Channel SNR Threshold Probability

Considering the channel state information (CSI), we introduce a SNR threshold probability $P_{T,j}$ which is defined as the probability that a random GT satisfies the SNR condition when it picks up the detection signal sent by its corresponding aircraft j. The detail expression is

$$P_{T,j} = \mathbb{E}_r \left[\mathbb{P}(\frac{W_j \cdot g_j(r,\beta)}{\sigma^2} \geq \gamma_0)|r \right]. \tag{2}$$

In order to obtain the specific expression of $P_{T,j}$, we need to figure out the probability density function (PDF) of r.

First, it is necessary to calculate the area $S(i)$ of overlapping region when UAV flies over the sector ring i. As mentioned above, we assume $o \ll R_2$ to ensure GTs located on the edge of disaster area can be also covered. For simplicity of calculation, we assume $R_s \approx R_1 + 2R_2$ when o is very small. Thus, according to geometry, $S(i)$ can be approximated by

$$S(i) \approx 2R_2^2 \cos^{-1}\left(\frac{R_{12} \cdot \sin\frac{\varphi(i)}{2}}{R_2}\right) - 2R_{12} \sin\frac{\varphi(i)}{2}\sqrt{R_2^2 - R_{12}^2 \sin^2\frac{\varphi(i)}{2}}. \tag{3}$$

Based on reference [9], under the coverage of HFH, $f_{d_1}(r)$ denotes the PDF of r. It can be easily derived as $f_{d_1}(r) = 2r/R_1^2$ and the upper bound of r is R_1. Under the coverage of UAV, there are two geometric cases. By drawing the circle with radius r whose center is midpoint of the UAV trajectory during t_0, we denote by $f_{d_2}^i(r)$ the PDF of r, $f_{d_2}^i(r) = 2\pi r/S(i)$ and $0 \leq r \leq R_2 - R_{12}\sin\frac{\varphi(i)}{2}$.

In our proposed channel model, the total bandwidth B is divided into M orthogonal channels. By this way, interference between channels is not considered. In the case of small-scale fading, we choose Nakagami-m distribution. And its shape parameter s determines what distribution the channel obeys. According to the literature [13], the channel fading power gain β is subject to Gamma distribution and its PDF can be expressed as $f_g(\beta) = \frac{s^s\beta^{s-1}}{\Gamma(s)}e^{-s\beta}$, where $\Gamma(s) = \int_0^\infty x^{s-1}e^{-x}dx$. $s = \frac{N^2+2N+1}{2N+1}$ and N is a constant.

3.2 Channel Schedule and Cruise Efficiency

In terms of channel schedule, we assume there are M orthogonal channels that do not interfere with each other. η_i denotes the percentage of channels obtained by HFH when the UAV flies over the sector ring i. So, it is $1-\eta_i$ for the UAV and the total channel number obtained by HFH and UAV are $\eta_i \cdot M$ and $(1-\eta_i)\cdot M$, respectively. η_i is changeable when UAV flies over different areas because of the different GT distribution density.

We denote λ_i as the GT density of cluster i covered by UAV and λ_0 for center cluster covered by HFH, respectively. Considering the communication access threshold t_0, only GTs in the overlapping area covered by UAV and the area covered by HFH can communicate with the corresponding aircraft.

Lemma 1. *When $\overline{F}_D(x^*) \leq \varrho$, we assume all GTs clustered around its corresponding hotspot are located in the circle of radius x^*.*

Proof. In theory, GTs located in the cluster formed by TCP could appear anywhere away from center hotspot. And the only matter is the smaller and smaller probability when GT is gradually far away from hotspots. And this probability would approach to 0 when the distance is far enough. In practice, this limiting case is not going to happen. For example, in order to guarantee his normal work, a rescuer with communication equipment will not be too far from the hotspot. Then, emergency communication services is a kind of opportunistic access and we can not guarantee 100% completely coverage for all GTs. When $\overline{F}_D(x^*) \leq \varrho$, this error is within our acceptable range and x^* is the farthest distance from GT to its cluster center.

According to the average number of GTs of each cluster, the GT density of cluster i covered by UAV can be given by $\lambda_i = \frac{\mathcal{N}_i}{\pi \cdot x_i^2}$, $\quad i = 1, \cdots, I$. Considering GTs covered by HFH can establish uninterrupted communication links with HFH, there is not necessary to analysis the GT density in this cluster. Thus, when UAV serves cluster i, the detailed expression of η_i is presented as following formula $\eta_i = \dfrac{\mathcal{N}_0}{S(i)\cdot\lambda_i + \mathcal{N}_0}$. By dynamically adjusting η_i, it can effectively alleviate the channel resource competition between HFH and UAV when UAV serves different clusters.

As mentioned in the above section, it is necessary to consider the cruise efficiency of UAV. We denote by T_i the time that the UAV flies past the sector ring i at the speed $v(i)$ and the time constraint for the whole system is given as $\sum_{i=1}^{I} T_i \leq T_c$, where $T_i = \dfrac{\zeta(i)\cdot R_{12}}{v(i)}$ and T_c is a constant that denotes the duration of cruise cycle.

3.3 Maximum Channel Access Probability

When UAV serves cluster i, we denote by $P^U(i)$ the probability that a typical GT located in the cluster i can successfully connect to the UAV, and by $P^H(i)$ the probability that to the HFH. Thus, when UAV serves cluster i, the channel access probability is

$$P(i) = \sum_{\kappa=1}^{I}\left[P_{T,1}\cdot P^H(i) + P_{T,2}(i)\cdot P^U(i)\right]\cdot\delta(\kappa - i). \tag{4}$$

$\tau^H(i)$ and $\tau^U(i)$ are used to represent the probability that a GT covered by HFH or UAV when UAV flies over the sector ring i, respectively. And they can be expressed as following formulas

$$\tau^H(i) = \frac{2\pi R_1^2}{2\pi R_1^2 + \zeta(i)(R_s^2 - R_1^2)},\quad \tau^U(i) = \frac{2S(i)}{2\pi R_1^2 + \zeta(i)(R_s^2 - R_1^2)}. \tag{5}$$

In practice, because of limited channel resource, there will be competition for it. Assuming the number of channels is less than or equal to the number of GTs. And GTs in different cluster, even in the same one, will also fiercely compete for limited channel resource. Based on the above analysis, therefore, we define two variables denoted by $C^H(i)$ and $C^U(i)$ whose meanings are the number of channel per GT located in the clusters covered by the HFH and UAV, respectively. And the detailed expressions are presented as

$$C^H(i) = \frac{\eta_i M}{\mathcal{N}_0},\quad C^U(i) = \frac{(1-\eta_i)M}{\lambda_i\cdot S(i)}. \tag{6}$$

When UAV flies past sector ring i and then serves cluster i, the channel access probability $P(i)$ can be rewritten as

$$\begin{aligned} P(i) &= \sum_{\kappa=1}^{I} \left[P_{T,1} \cdot P^H(i) + P_{T,2}(i) \cdot P^U(i)\right] \cdot \delta(\kappa - i) \\ &= \sum_{\kappa=1}^{I} \Big[P_{T,1} \cdot \tau^H(i) \cdot C^H(i) \\ &\qquad + P_{T,2}(i) \cdot \tau^U(i) \cdot C^U(i)\Big] \cdot \delta(\kappa - i). \end{aligned} \tag{7}$$

Thus, when the UAV completes a cruise cycle, the system average channel access probability P is given as $\mathsf{P} = \frac{1}{I}\sum_{i=1}^{I} P(i)$.

Now, our objective function can be expressed as

$$\begin{aligned} P1: \max_{v(i)} \quad & \mathsf{P} \\ s.t. \quad & (18), & \text{(8a)} \\ & V_{min} \le v(i) \le V_{max}^{a}. & \text{(8b)} \end{aligned}$$

3.4 Problem Analysis

It is obvious that the first and second term of $P(i)$ are both related to $v(i)$. First, we consider the first term of $P(i)$. Because the numerator of the first term is a constant which is not related with $v(i)$, therefore, the first term can be simplified as $\Upsilon_1(i) = \dfrac{1}{S(i) \cdot \lambda_i + \mathcal{N}_0}$

Lemma 2. *There exists a unique $v^*(i)$ to make $\Upsilon_1(i)$ convex when $v(i) \le v^*(i)$.*

Proof. First, taking $\varphi(i)$ as our variable to obtain the first-order and second-order derivatives of $\Upsilon_1(i)$ which are expressed in following formulas

$$\Upsilon_1^{'}(i) = \frac{-\lambda_i S^{'}(i)}{(\lambda_i S(i) + \mathcal{N}_0)^2}, \quad \Upsilon_1^{''}(i) = \frac{\lambda_i \left[\lambda_i S(i) + \mathcal{N}_0\right] \cdot L_1(\varphi(i))}{(\lambda_i S(i) + \mathcal{N}_0)^4} \tag{9a}$$

where $L_1(\varphi(i)) = 2\lambda_i \left[S^{'}(i)\right]^2 - S^{''}(i)\left[\lambda_i S(i) + \mathcal{N}_0\right]$. It's easy to prove that $L_1(\varphi(i))$ is a monotonous non-increasing function and $L_1(0) > 0$, $L_1(\pi) < 0$. In fact, $\varphi(i)$ is much less than π. According to the monotony of the function, we can conclude that there is bound to be a speed $v^*(i)$ to make $L_1 = 0$. And $v^*(i)$ can be found by binary search algorithm. When $v(i) \le v^*(i)$, the $L_1 \ge 0$, so as $\Upsilon_1^{''}(i)$. Therefore, $\Upsilon_1(i)$ is convex.

Now, we consider the second term of $P(i)$ and rewrite the variables related with $v(i)$ as $\Upsilon_2(i) = \dfrac{Q(\varphi(i))}{S(i) \cdot \lambda_i + \mathcal{N}_0}$, where the details of $Q(\varphi(i))$ can be seen from following proof.

Algorithm 1. Interior point method solution for $P1$

Input: $\zeta(i)$: The central Angle of sector i; t: step length; μ: scale factor; ϵ_1, ϵ_2: error thresholds; $\beta 1$:backtracking line search parameter

Output: optimal $\mathbf{V}$

initial $r^{(0)} = 1$, $m = 0$, $V^{(0)}$

repeat

  repeat

    calculate Newton step_path $\triangle V_{nt}$ and decrement ℓ^2

    $\triangle V_{nt} = -\nabla^2 \chi_2(V^{(m)}, r^{(m)})^{-1} \nabla \chi_2(V^{(m)}, r^{(m)})$;

    $\ell^2 = \nabla \chi_2(V^{(m)}, r^{(m)})^T \nabla^2 \chi_2(V^{(m)}, r^{(m)})^{-1} \cdot \nabla \chi_2(V^{(m)}, r^{(m)})$;

    update step length: $t = t \cdot \beta 1$

    update $V^{(m+1)} = V^{(m)} + t \cdot \triangle V_{nt}$

    update $\mathbf{V} = V^{(m+1)}$

  until $\ell^2 \leq \epsilon_2$

  $r^{(m+1)} = \mu \cdot r^{(m)}$

until $||V^{(m+1)} - V^{(m)}|| < \epsilon_1$

return $\mathbf{V}$

Lemma 3. *Combining lemma* 1, *the* $\Upsilon_2(i)$ *is also convex when* $\frac{\beta_0 W_2}{\sigma^2} \geq 2R_2^2 \cdot \gamma_0$.

Proof. Taking $\varphi(i)$ as our variable to obtain the second-order derivative of $\Upsilon_2(i)$ and we can get $\Upsilon_2^{''}(i) = \frac{L_2(\varphi(i))}{[\lambda_i S(i) + \mathcal{N}_0]^3}$, where

$$\begin{aligned} L_2(\varphi(i)) = & \left[Q^{''}(\varphi(i))(\lambda_i S(i) + \mathcal{N}_0) - \lambda_i Q(\varphi(i)) S^{'}(i)\right] \\ & \times (\lambda_i S(i) + \mathcal{N}_0) - 2\lambda_i (\lambda_i S(i) + \mathcal{N}_0) \cdot S(i) \\ & \times \left[Q^{'}(\varphi(i))(\lambda_i S(i) + \mathcal{N}_0) - \lambda_i Q(\varphi(i)) S^{'}(i)\right], \end{aligned} \tag{10}$$

and $Q(\varphi(i)) = 1 - e^{-\frac{\gamma_0 \cdot \sigma^2}{\beta_0 W_2}(R_2 - R_{12} \sin \frac{\varphi(i)}{2})^2}$. When $\frac{\beta_0 W_2}{\sigma^2} \geq 2R_2^2 \cdot \gamma_0$, $Q(\varphi(i)) \leq 0$.

Now, we define two auxiliary functions to make further analysis of the two terms of $L_2(\varphi(i))$

$$\begin{aligned} h_2 &= -\lambda_i Q(\varphi(i)) S^{'}(i) \cdot [\lambda_i S(i) + \mathcal{N}_0], \\ h_3 &= 2\lambda_i S^{'}(i) Q^{'}(\varphi(i)) \cdot [\lambda_i S(i) + \mathcal{N}_0]. \end{aligned} \tag{11a}$$

It is obviously that h_2 and h_3 are both greater than 0. By scaling, $Q^{'}(\varphi(i)) < \frac{\gamma_0 \cdot \sigma^2}{W_2} \cdot (R_2 - R_{12} \sin \frac{\varphi(i)}{2})$. In addition, combining the physical significance of $\frac{\gamma_0 \cdot \sigma^2}{\beta_0 W_2}$ that it is a very small number. So, $Q(\varphi(i))$ can be approximated to $\frac{\gamma_0 \cdot \sigma^2}{\beta_0 W_2} \cdot (R_2 - R_{12} \sin \frac{\varphi(i)}{2})^2$ by Taylor formula. Then, $h_2 > h_3$ is easy to conclude. Therefore, $L_2(\varphi(i)) > 0$ and $\Upsilon_2(i)$ is convex.

Based on the above analysis, the first and second term of $P(i)$ are both convex. According to convex optimization theory, it is easy to confirm that $P(i)$ is also convex. Next, the interior point method and Newton method are used to solve the problem and obtain the optimal solution. $\chi_2(\mathbf{V}, r^{(m)})$ denotes the penalty function of problem $P1$ and the details are presented in Algorithm 1.

4 Simulation

4.1 Parameters Settings

Setting the flight height of HFH and UAV as 100 m and 200 m. The covering radius R_1 and R_2 are set as 450 m, 350 m, respectively. The whole disaster area is divided into 5 subregions which means $I = 5$. And the corresponding central angles are $[\pi/2, \pi/3, \pi/3, \pi/3, \pi/2]$ (radian). The variances $\sigma_{t,1} \sim \sigma_{t,5}$ are set as 65, and 85 for the center cluster covered by HFH, respectively. The average numbers of GTs for cluster 1–5 are set as $11, 13, 11, 15, 13$, and 44 for center one, respectively. t_0 is set as $1s$ and V_{max} and V_{min} are 80 m/s, 3 m/s. $b = 5$ Hz and other constants, such as $\mu, \varrho, \beta 1, \sigma_{t,0,\sigma_{t,I}}, \epsilon_1, \epsilon_2$ are set as $0.1, 10^{-6}, 0.8, 85, 65, 10^{-6}, 10^{-6}$, respectively.

4.2 Results Analysis

It can be seen from Fig. 3 that i): the maximum of $v(i)$ is more than 40 m/s and this increase of speed will be cut in other subregions. ii): the speeds of subregions whose center angles are identical are also tend to be different. In general, the UAV speed will increase with the increase of λ_i. For the first problem, we notice that UAV need to slow down in several subregions to improve channel access probability and speed up in other areas to satisfy the limitation of cruise cycle. Because of the larger center angles of subregion 1 and 5, speeding up in these two subregions will generate more benefit. Aimed to illustrate the second problem, we should review our objective function from global perspective to realize the fact that channel access probability will increase with the decrease of $v(i)$. First, greater λ_i means more GTs, which will lead to fiercer channel competition. Acceleration will reduce the amount of GTs served in each t_0. Thus, channel competition will be alleviated and the QoS is improved, so as channel access probability. Second, system will adjust the UAV speed of each subregion to achieve maximum channel access probability.

In Fig. 4, there are four maximum channel access probabilities under different conditions: constant speed and η which are adopted in [9], optimized η, optimized UAV speeds, optimized UAV speeds and η. First, when only the UAV speeds are optimized, the increment of channel access probability is 3.4% compared with [9]. Second, optimizing UAV speeds achieves 0.2% improvement when η is already optimized. The reason for this problem is that the UAV speed we used for non-optimized case is close to the optimal speed. Then, these two cases all achieve suitable channel schedule. Thus, the difference between these two increments is not vary distinct. Third, compared with constant channel schedule, the channel

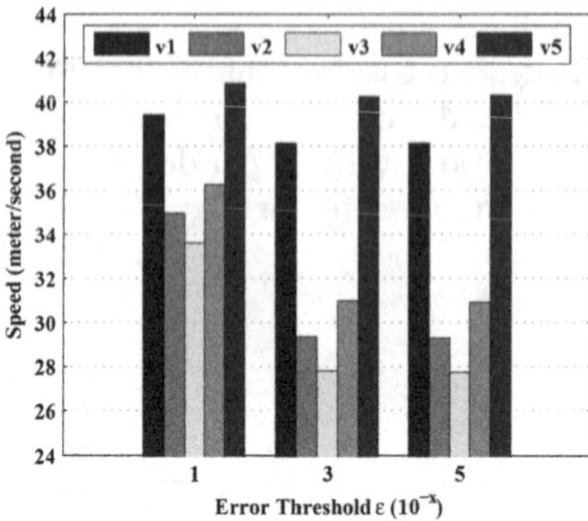

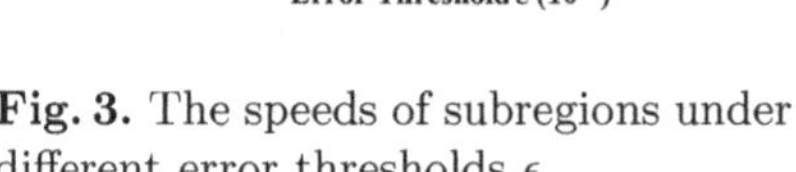

Fig. 3. The speeds of subregions under different error thresholds ϵ

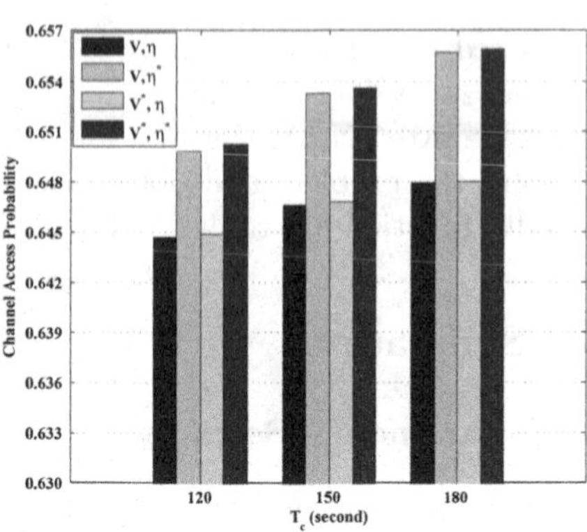

Fig. 4. The channel access probability under different optimization conditions.

access probability is distinctly improved by optimizing η. Fourth, when cruise cycle T_c increases, the channel access probability will increase correspondingly. It's easy to illustrate that UAV will have more time to establish more full communication links when T_c increases. Overall, all those channel access probabilities are less than the probability we can get at the V^* and η^*.

5 Conclusion

In this paper, we propose an adaptive UAV speed cruise model to provide communication service in post-disaster relief. TCP is introduced to model the location distribution of GTs, which is more suitable than PPP. By taking the channel state into account, we discussed the maximum channel access probability of the system under the condition of limited channel resources. And a flexible channel schedule was proposed to improve channel access probability. Simulation results show that channel access probability can be improved by adopting a dynamic channel schedule and optimizing the UAV speed of each subregion. Moreover, compared with constant UAV speed or channel schedule, the simulation results reveal that the proposed method performances well in coverage probability and achievable rate. In our future work, we will focus on dynamic adjustment of UAV flight height and further study the collaborative relay of multiple UAVs to improve the quality and efficiency of emergency communication system.

Acknowledgement. This work was supported in part by the NSF of China under Grants 71171045 and 61772130, in part by the Fundamental Research Funds for the Central Universities NO.2232020A-12, in part by the Innovation Program of Shanghai Municipal Education Commission under Grant No. 14YZ130, in part by the International S&T Cooperation Program of Shanghai Science and Technology Commission under Grant No. 15220710600, in part by the Fundamental Research Funds for the Central Universities NO.17D310404, and in part by the Special Project Funding for the

Shanghai Municipal Commission of Economy and Information Civil-Military Inosculation Project "Big Data Management System of UAVs" under the Grant NO.JMRH-2018-1042.

References

1. Arafat, M.Y., Moh, S.: Localization and clustering based on swarm intelligence in UAV networks for emergency communications. IEEE IoT J. **6**(5), 8958–8976 (2019). https://doi.org/10.1109/JIOT.2019.2925567
2. Feng, G., Wang, C., Li, B., Lv, H., Zhuang, X., Lv, H., Wang, H., Hu, X.: UAV-assisted wireless relay networks for mobile offloading and trajectory optimization. Peer-to-Peer Netw. Appl. **12**(6), 1820–1834 (2019). https://doi.org/10.1007/s12083-019-00793-5
3. Samir, M., Sharafeddine, S., Assi, C.M., Nguyen, T.M., Ghrayeb, A.: UAV trajectory planning for data collection from time-constrained IoT devices. IEEE Trans. Wirel. Commun. **19**(1), 34–46 (2020). https://doi.org/10.1109/TWC.2019.2940447
4. Zeng, Y., Zhang, R., Lim, T.J.: Wireless communications with unmanned aerial vehicles: opportunities and challenges. IEEE Commun. Mag. **54**(5), 36–42 (2016). https://doi.org/10.1109/MCOM.2016.7470933
5. Alzenad, M., El-Keyi, A., Yanikomeroglu, H.: 3-D placement of an unmanned aerial vehicle base station for maximum coverage of users with different QoS requirements. IEEE Wirel. Commun. Lett. **7**(1), 38–41 (2018). https://doi.org/10.1109/LWC.2017.2752161
6. Alzenad, M., Yanikomeroglu, H.: Coverage and rate analysis for unmanned aerial vehicle base stations with LoS/NLoS propagation. In: 2018 IEEE Globecom Workshops (GC Wkshps), pp. 1–7 (2018)
7. Guo, Z., Wei, Z., Feng, Z., Fan, N.: Coverage probability of multiple UAVs supported ground network. Electron. Lett. **53**(13), 885–887 (2017). https://doi.org/10.1049/el.2017.0800
8. Mozaffari, M., Saad, W., Bennis, M., Debbah, M.: Unmanned aerial vehicle with underlaid device-to-device communications: performance and tradeoffs. IEEE Trans. Wirel. Commun. **15**(6), 3949–3963 (2016). https://doi.org/10.1109/TWC.2016.2531652
9. Zhang, S., Liu, J.: Analysis and optimization of multiple unmanned aerial vehicle-assisted communications in post-disaster areas. IEEE Trans. Veh. Technol. **67**(12), 12049–12060 (2018). https://doi.org/10.1109/TVT.2018.2871614
10. Wang, X., Gursoy, M.C.: Coverage analysis for energy-harvesting UAV-assisted mmWave cellular networks. IEEE J. Sel. Areas Commun. **37**(12), 2832–2850 (2019). https://doi.org/10.1109/JSAC.2019.2947929
11. Saeedi, A., Azizi, A., Mokari, N.: Throughput maximization in poisson aerial base station based networks with coverage probability and power density constraints. Trans. Emerg. Telecommun. Technol. **29**(8), e3456 (2018)
12. Zeng, Y., Zhang, R.: Energy-efficient UAV communication with trajectory optimization. IEEE Trans. Wirel. Commun. **16**(6), 3747–3760 (2017). https://doi.org/10.1109/TWC.2017.2688328
13. Zhou, L., Yang, Z., Zhou, S., Zhang, W.: Coverage probability analysis of UAV cellular networks in urban environments. In: 2018 IEEE International Conference on Communications Workshops (ICC Workshops), Kansas City, MO, pp. 1–6 (2018). https://doi.org/10.1109/ICCW.2018.8403633

NLP and Affective Computing

Using Large Cliques for Hierarchical Dense Subgraph Discovery

Md Moniruzzaman Monir and Ahmet Erdem Sarıyüce(✉)

University at Buffalo, Buffalo, NY 14260, USA
{mdmoniru,erdem}@buffalo.edu

Abstract. Understanding the structure of dense regions in real-world networks is an important research area with myriad practical applications. Using higher-order structures (motifs), such as triangles, had been shown to be effective to locate the dense subgraphs. However, going beyond the triangle structure is computationally demanding and mostly overlooked in the past. In this work, we investigate the use of large cliques (up to 10 nodes) for dense subgraph discovery. Relying on the nucleus decomposition framework that finds hierarchical dense subgraphs, we introduce efficient implementations to instantiate the framework up to 10-cliques. We analyze various real-world networks and discuss the density pointers, dense subgraph distributions, and also the hierarchical relationships. We investigate the clique count distributions per vertex and report surprising behaviors that are not observed in the degree distributions. Our analysis shows that utilizing larger cliques can yield denser structures with more interesting hierarchical relations in several networks.

1 Introduction

Real-world networks have a sparse structure in the global level and contain dense regions in local neighborhoods [12]. Dense subgraphs are indicators for unusual behaviors and functional units. There are various applications, such as identifying the news stories from microblogging streams in real-time [2], finding price value motifs in the financial networks [8], detecting DNA motifs in biological networks [10], and locating spam link farms in web [7,11,14]. Dense regions are also used for visualization of complex graph structure [1,31].

Higher-order structures (or motifs) capture the network dynamics by considering a small set of nodes together. Triangle is the smallest non-trivial structure and has been heavily used in several models for network analysis [12]. However, considering larger structures is computationally expensive and thus mostly overlooked in the past. Previous works mostly focused on counting such structures by efficient heuristics [21] and sampling methods [13]. There are also some studies that finds a single optimum subgraph with respect to a given k-clique [28].

In this work, we analyze the impact of large cliques (up to 10 nodes) on the dense subgraph structure of networks. We use nucleus decomposition

S. Chellappan et al. (Eds.): CSoNet 2020, LNCS 12575, pp. 179–192, 2020.
https://doi.org/10.1007/978-3-030-66046-8_15

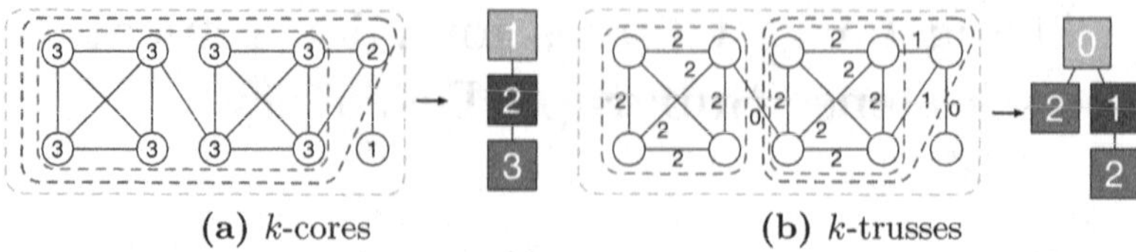

(a) k-cores (b) k-trusses

Fig. 1. Left depicts the k-core decomposition where core numbers are shown for each vertex with a hierarchy tree of different k-cores. Orange, blue, and red regions show the 1-, 2-, and 3-cores which are nested subgraphs, thus form the hierarchy by containment (1-core $\supseteq$ 2-core $\supseteq$ 3-core). Right shows the k-truss decomposition where truss numbers are shown for each edge with a hierarchy tree of different k-trusses. Entire graph is a 0-truss while five vertices in blue region form a 1-truss. There are also two 2-trusses and one of them is a subset of the 1-truss. (Color figure online)

[24,25], generalization of k-core [19,26] and k-truss decompositions [6,23,29,30], to find many subgraphs, of moderate density and with hierarchical relations, with respect to the large cliques. Informally, k-(r, s) nucleus, for fixed positive integers $r < s$, is a maximal subgraph where every r-clique participate in many s-cliques. Due to the computational challenges, existing implementations are bounded by (3, 4)-nucleus decomposition. We introduce practical algorithms for higher-order nucleus decompositions using large cliques and evaluate our algorithms through several experiments on a wide variety of real-world networks. We analyze various real-world networks and discuss the density pointers, dense subgraph distributions, and also the hierarchical relationships in a comparative way. Our statistical analyses of the density pointers and clique counts for the large (r, s) nuclei yield some interesting patterns. We observe that finer dense structures that are lost in larger structures can be identified by our algorithms, and there is an upper bound for higher-order nucleus decompositions where the results stop improving.

We consider a simple undirected graph $G = (V, E)$ where V is the set of vertices and E is the set of edges. We define k-clique as a complete graph among k vertices for $k > 0$, i.e., every vertex is connected to all other vertices. We first discuss k-core, k-truss, and nucleus decompositions.

k-core and k-truss Decompositions. k-core decomposition is a threshold-based hierarchical approach to decompose a network into nested subgraphs where the threshold k is set on the degree of a vertex to exploit the vertex-edge relationships. The idea of k-core was first introduced by Erdős and Hajnal [9] and rediscovered numerous times in different contexts [17,26]. k-core of G is a **maximal** and **connected** subgraph of G in which all nodes have degree at least k. The lowest possible value of k is 1 for any network because of the connectivity constraint. Core number of a node is the highest value of k such that it belongs to a k-core but not to any $(k+1)$-core. Figure 1a shows an example for the core numbers of vertices and the hierarchy in k-core decomposition.

k-truss decomposition extends the idea of k-core decomposition by changing the focus from vertex-edge relationship to edge-triangle relationship. k-truss of

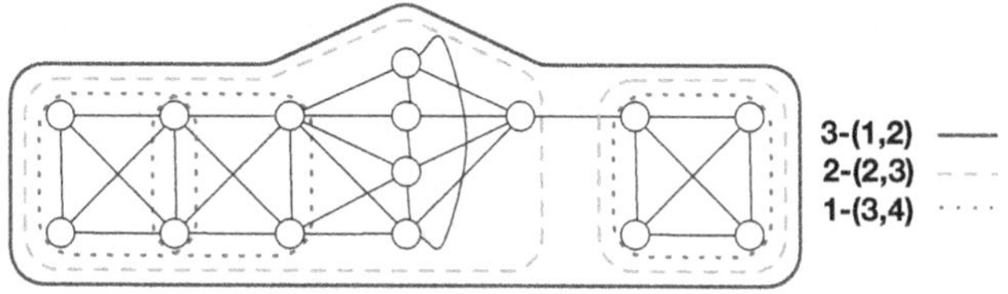

Fig. 2. Generalization of core and truss decompositions by nucleus decomposition. k-(1, 2) and k-(2, 3) nucleus decomposition represents k-core and k-truss, respectively. (1, 2) cannot detect a dense structure and reports the entire graph as a 3-(1, 2) nuclei while (2, 3) separates the 4-clique on the right and gives two 2-(2, 3) nuclei. However, (3, 4) can distinguish all the 4-cliques and report each as a 1-(3, 4) nuclei.

G is a **maximal** and **connected** subgraph of G in which every edge participates in at least k triangless [6,23,29,30]. Truss number of an edge is the highest value of k such that it belongs to a k-truss but not to any $(k+1)$-truss. Figure 1b shows an example for the truss numbers and the hierarchy in k-truss decomposition.

Nucleus Decomposition. k-core and k-truss decompositions are generalized by nucleus decomposition. It unifies the vertex-edge and edge-triangle relationships into r-clique and s-clique relationships where r, s are positive integers such that $r < s$. Informally, k-(r, s) nucleus of G is a **maximal** and **s-connected** subgraph of the r-cliques where each r-clique takes part in at least k s-cliques. We quote the definition of nucleus decomposition from [25].

Definition 1. *Let $r < s$ be positive integers.*

- *$R(G)$ and $S(G)$ are the set of r-cliques and s-cliques in G, respectively.*
- *s-degree of $R \in R(G)$ is the number of $S \in S(G)$ such that S contains R $(R \subset S)$.*
- *Two r-cliques R, R' are **s-connected** if there exists a sequence $R = R_1, R_2, ..., R_k = R'$ in $R(G)$ such that for each i, some $S \in S(G)$ contains $R_i \cup R_{i+1}$.*
- *Let k, r, and s be positive integers such that $r < s$. A k-(r, s) **nucleus** is a subgraph G' which contains the edges in the maximal union $S(G)$ of s-cliques such that*
  - *s-degree of any r-clique $R \in R(G')$ is at least k.*
  - *Any r-clique pair $R, R' \in R(G')$ are s-connected.*

As in the core and truss number definitions, we define the nucleus number of an r-clique, denoted k_s, as the largest k_s value such that the r-clique is a part of a k_s-(r, s) nucleus. Note that the values $r = 1$, $s = 2$ corresponds to the k-core and $r = 2$, $s = 3$ corresponds to the k-truss definition. Figure 2 shows a comparison of core, truss, and (3,4) nucleus subgraphs in a toy graph.

2 Algorithms and Implementation Details

In this section, we present the algorithms to generate nucleus decomposition using large cliques. Our implementation has two parts. First, we enumerate all k-cliques ($3 \leq k \leq 10$) of a graph for higher-order nucleus decompositions and save those cliques in disk. In the second part, we implement (r, s)-nucleus decomposition where $3 \leq r \leq 9$ and $s = r + 1$. As our main algorithmic goal is to construct the forest of nuclei using large cliques, we extend the previous framework of (3, 4)-nucleus decomposition introduced in [25]. But an extension of this framework for higher-order nucleus decompositions is non-trivial as the number of cliques grows exponentially for large values and managing those efficiently requires a careful implementation. Implementations for higher-order decompositions up to $(9, 10)$ nucleus available at http://sariyuce.com/largeND.zip.

2.1 Large Clique Enumeration

In Algorithm 1, we generate all k-cliques of a graph. We use **MACE** (MAximal Clique Enumerator) [18] code to enumerate all maximal cliques. This code takes O($|V||E|$) time for each maximal clique, where $|V|$ and $|E|$ are the number of vertices, and the number of edges in the input graph. In practice the code finds about 100,000 maximal cliques per second in sparse graphs, and the computation time increases almost linearly with the density of the graph. Finding all k-cliques from the list of maximal cliques is not trivial as there are many overlapping k-cliques in those maximal cliques. To solve this issue we initialize a hash table H (line 1 of Algorithm 1) where the key is generated by the id's of participating vertices in a k-clique, and the value is a boolean to show the existence of that k-clique. So, it will store all the enumerated k-cliques. In line 6, we create a bitmask of length n with k bits where n is the number of vertices in the maximal clique M. Instead of generating all permutations of the actual vertex id's, we generate all permutations of this bit mask to reduce computation time leveraging bitwise operations. In line 8, we initialize an empty array C for every permutation of the bitmask. We add a vertex from the maximal clique M into C if the corresponding bit value is 1. If C is not in the hash table H (enumerated for the first time), then we save C in H with value 1. Thus we prevent duplicates of k-cliques.

2.2 Higher-Order Nucleus Decompositions:

The framework of (r, s)-nucleus decomposition adopted a hypergraph version of classic Matula-Beck [19]. We extend this framework to design a generic (r, s)-nucleus decomposition. But as the number of cliques increases exponentially for large cliques in most of the datasets and maintaining these large lists is memory inefficient and intractable, we implement the algorithm case-by-case up to (9, 10)-nucleus decomposition to improve the runtime performance. We do not implement (r, s)-nucleus decomposition where $s > 10$ for practical purposes. We also ignore the nucleus decompositions where $s - r > 1$ since it has been shown that $s - r = 1$ is the best combination for the options with equal s [25].

We first get the list of all r-cliques and s-cliques by using Algorithm 1. Note that both r-cliques and s-cliques can be enumerated at the same time in Algorithm 1 by simply changing the inner part of the outer-most loop. This way we reduce the clique enumeration time which has a huge impact on the runtime when the number of cliques is very large. Also, we only store the r-cliques in a dynamic array for better scalability in terms of the memory space. The list of s-cliques is used only for faster s-clique counting (s-degree) for each r-clique. To save the s-degree of an r-clique, we create an index by using the id's of participating vertices in the r-clique. We use a hash table to store the index and s-degree of an r-clique in order to enable faster lookups. For utilizing the bucket data structure from the framework of (r, s)-nucleus decomposition we create another hash table to store the index of an r-clique and its position in the dynamic array where every r-clique is stored. So, in the bucket, we store the r-clique's position in the dynamic array and its s-degree. The bucket data structure uses linked lists for storing bucket contents and hash maps for finding the link list entry of any given r-clique. During the peeling process, we use the bucket sort for updating the s-degrees of r-cliques. In every iteration (line 6 of Algorithm 2), we choose the unprocessed r-clique with lowest s-degree and assign this value as its k_s-value. Then we find all s-cliques which contain this r-clique, check whether the neighbor r-cliques in those s-cliques are processed or not. If not processed and s-degrees of those neighbor r-cliques are greater than the s-degree of the current r-clique, then s-degrees of the neighbor r-cliques are decremented.

Algorithm 1: k-CliqueGen(G, k)

```
input  : G: graph, k: positive integer
output: list of all k-cliques

Initialize a hash table H
Enumerate all maximal cliques using MACE [18]
foreach maximal clique M do
    // M is an array of vertices
    n ← number of vertices in M
    if n ≥ k then
        b ← bitmask of k leading 1's and (n − k) trailing 0's
        for every permutation of b do
            C ← an empty array
            // C stores the clique vertices
            for i = 0 to n do
                if b[i] = 1 then add M[i] to C
            if C is not in the hash table H then
                save C in the hash table
```

```
Algorithm 2: set-k(G, r, s)
input  : G: graph, r < s: positive integers
output: k_s(.) : array of k_s indices for r-cliques
// fast clique enumeration by Algorithm 1
r-cliquesList, s-cliquesList ← list of r-cliques and s-cliques by k-CliqueGen(G,
  k)
// initialization
foreach r-clique R ∈ r-cliquesList do
    // using s-cliquesList for fast counting
    d_s(R) ← number of s-cliques containing R
    Mark R as unprocessed
    Save R in a hash table with d_s(R) value
// peeling
foreach unprocessed r-clique R with min. d_s(R) do
    k_s(R) = d_s(R)                  // nucleus number assigned
    Find set C of s-cliques containing R
    foreach s-clique S ∈ C do
        if any r-clique R' ⊂ S is processed then
            Continue
        foreach r-clique R' ∈ S do
            if d_s(R') > d_s(R) and R' ≠ R then
                d_s(R') = d_s(R') − 1
    Mark R as processed
```

3 Experiments

We evaluate our algorithms on various types of undirected simple real-world networks from different domains such as social networks (`Hamsterter`, `fb-Reed`, `fb-Simmons`, `fb-Caltech36`, `fb-Haverford76`, `fb-Swarthmore42`, `fb-USFCA72`), collaboration networks (`Jazz`, `Erdos992`, `DBLP_ds`, `DBLP_pp`, `DBLP_dm`), interaction networks (`PGP`, `Drug`), internet networks (`Caida`), and infrastructure networks (`PowerGrid`). All datasets are collected from SNAP [16], Konect [15], ICON [5], Network Repository [22], and Facebook100 dataset [27]. Key statistics of our datasets are summarized in Table 1. All experiments are performed on a Linux operating system (v. Linux 3.10.0-1127) running on a machine with Intel(R) Xeon(R) Gold 6130 CPU processor at 2.10 GHz with 192 GB memory.

We find three types of patterns for k-clique distribution in our datasets. The first pattern is shown in Figs. 3a and 3b where k-clique ($3 \leq k \leq 10$) count increases exponentially. This pattern is the most common, observed in 9 networks. In Fig. 3c, the second pattern is shown where the clique count shows some left-skew. In this pattern, the highest clique count is in the range between 1-clique to 10-clique. We observe this pattern in 5 networks (`Caida`, `fb-Reed`, `fb-Caltech36`, `fb-Simmons`, and `fb-Swarthmore42`). The last pattern, shown in Fig. 3d, is not so common as we find it in only 2 networks (`Erdos992` and `PowerGrid`). This pattern shows right-skew, and the clique count starts decreas-

Table 1. k-clique ($k \leq 10$) counts for the real-world graphs used in our experiments. Bold numbers indicate the largest k-clique counts of a dataset.

Dataset	$\|V\|$	$\|E\|$	$\|\triangle\|$	$\|K_4\|$	$\|K_5\|$	$\|K_6\|$	$\|K_7\|$	$\|K_8\|$	$\|K_9\|$	$\|K_{10}\|$
Jazz	198	2.7K	17.9K	78.4K	273.7K	846K	2.4M	6.3M	14.8M	**30.5M**
fb-Caltech36	769	16.7K	119.6K	460K	1.3M	2.7M	4.8M	6.9M	**8.2M**	7.9M
fb-Reed	962	18.8K	97.1K	233.2K	349.5K	**398.9K**	392.6K	349K	274.7K	181.9K
fb-Haverford76	1.4K	59.6K	627.9K	3.1M	9.5M	21.1M	37.4M	56.2M	74.2M	**87.5M**
Drug	1.5K	48.5K	569.5K	4.2M	21.8M	86.5M	268.3M	289.7M	288.7M	**408.6M**
fb-Simmons	1.5K	33K	168.6K	456.9K	962.1K	1.7M	2.6M	3.3M	**3.4M**	2.8M
fb-Swarthmore42	1.7K	61.1K	552.7K	2.3M	5.9M	10.6M	15.2M	18.4M	**19.4M**	17.7M
Hamsterster	2.4K	16.6K	53.3K	132.9K	298.1K	619.1K	1.2M	2M	3.2M	**4.5M**
fb-USFCA72	2.7K	65.3K	371.7K	1.2M	3M	7.6M	19.4M	48.2M	112.0M	**233.6M**
PowerGrid	4.9K	**6.6K**	651	90	15	2	0	0	0	0
Erdos992	6.1K	**7.5K**	1.6K	450	168	55	11	1	0	0
DBLP_ds	8.1K	23K	47.2K	148.4K	610.2K	2.5M	9.8M	33.3M	99.9M	**263.9M**
DBLP_PP	8.4K	22.9K	74.2K	436.1K	2.7M	15M	71.6M	300.8M	1.12B	**3.76B**
PGP	10.7K	24.3K	54.8K	238.6K	1M	3.8M	11.4M	27.9M	56.4M	**95.2M**
DBLP_dm	16.4K	33.9K	39.5K	63.5K	145.1K	342.5K	740.3K	1.4M	2.4M	**3.6M**
Caida	26.5K	53.4K	36.4K	53.9K	82.2K	102.1K	**104.1K**	87.5K	60.3K	33.9K

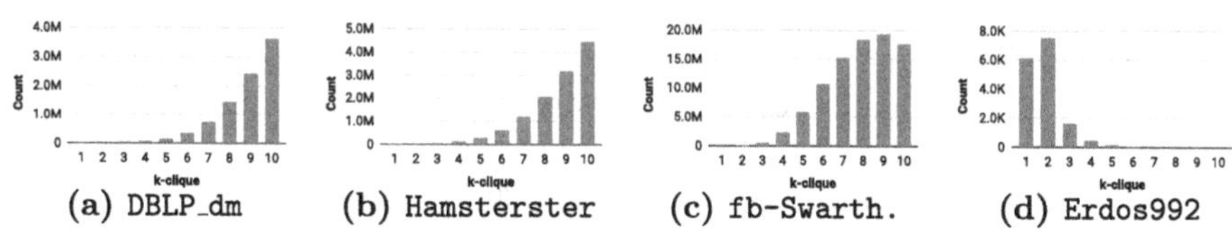

(a) DBLP_dm (b) Hamsterster (c) fb-Swarth. (d) Erdos992

Fig. 3. k-clique ($1 \leq k \leq 10$) distribution for DBLP_dm, Hamsterster, fb-Swarthmore42 and Erdos992 networks. x-axis is the value of k and y-axis is the count of k-cliques with that k value. Clique count increases exponentially in Fig. 3a and 3b which is the most common pattern observed in 9 networks. In Fig. 3c, we observe left-skewed distribution, which is found in 5 networks. The right-skewed behavior in Fig. 3d is not common, observed only in 2 networks.

ing after 2-cliques. Also, it is worth mentioning that there is no correlation between the clique distribution pattern and the size of a network (i.e., number of vertices and edges).

In the following, we present our analysis of higher-order nucleus decompositions with respect to various aspects. We first analyze the s-degree and k_s-value distributions and explain different behaviors observed in real-world networks. Then we investigate how the densest parts found by each higher-order nucleus decomposition change. Last, we look at the hierarchical relationships among nuclei in higher-order decompositions.

3.1 Analysis of s-degrees and k_s-values

Here we discuss the empirical patterns related to s-degrees and k_s-values that we find in our diverse datasets for higher-order nucleus decompositions. We analyze the large (r, s) nuclei and give comparisons for different r, s values.

s-degree Distributions. One of the most common macroscopic structural properties that are found in real-world networks is the heavy-tailed degree distribution [3,20]. There are very few highly connected nodes coexisting with a large number of lowly connected nodes. According to the clique definition, vertex is 1-clique and edge is 2-clique. So, vertex-edge relationships can be represented by (1, 2)-nucleus, and degree distribution of vertices can be thought of 2-clique frequency distribution of 1-cliques. Similarly, in (r, s)-nucleus decomposition, s-clique frequency of an r-clique is defined as the s-degree, i.e., the number of s-cliques containing the r-clique. We explore s-degree distribution of r-cliques from (3, 4) to (9, 10)-nucleus decompositions.

One interesting finding is that we do not observe any heavy-tailed s-degree distribution in the collaboration networks for higher-order nucleus decompositions (Figs. 4 and 5). In all other networks (except PGP), the heavy-tail pattern is observed up to (5, 6)-nucleus decompositions. After that, we observe Poisson distribution for most of the networks. We present Caida in Fig. 4 and DBLP-dm in Fig. 5 as a representative sample. In both figures, x-axis (binned) and y-axis represent s-degrees and the number of r-cliques, respectively. Other higher-order nucleus decompositions are not shown due to space constraints.

k_s-value Distributions. In (r, s)-nucleus decomposition, k_s-value is an important property of an r-clique encoding local structural information. k_s-values provide a more regular structure and distribution than the s-degrees. We analyze the k_s-values for all higher-order nucleus decompositions. At first, we explore the distribution of k_s-values concerning r-cliques from (3, 4) to (9, 10)-nucleus decomposition. Figure 6 presents the distributions for Drug network. Although the k_s-value distribution does not reveal any potential structural information, we notice that for most of the networks the range of k_s-values decreases gradually with larger r, s values, and the mass of the histogram is shifted to the right in the nucleus decompositions with larger r and s values. This indicates that most r-cliques have a large k_s-value in higher-order nucleus decompositions.

We also perform a vertex-centric analysis. The number of r-cliques that a vertex is a part of is an important measure. Figures 7 presents the results for PGP network. We discover that there are very few vertices with large r-clique

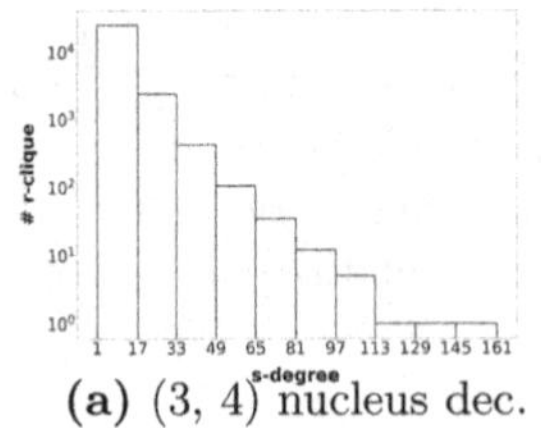

(a) (3, 4) nucleus dec.

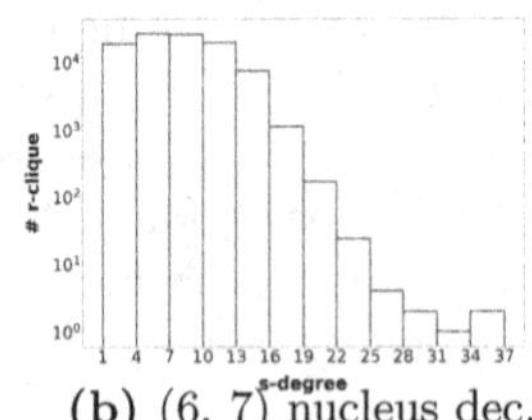

(b) (6, 7) nucleus dec.

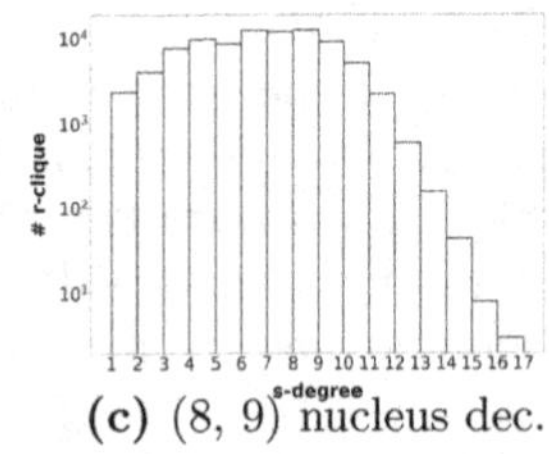

(c) (8, 9) nucleus dec.

Fig. 4. s-degree distribution of r-cliques for caida network, for r, s as (3, 4), (6, 7) and (8, 9). x-axis shows the s-degrees and y-axis denotes the counts of r-cliques in log scale. The histogram shows that there is a heavy-tail pattern up to (5, 6)-nucleus decomposition.

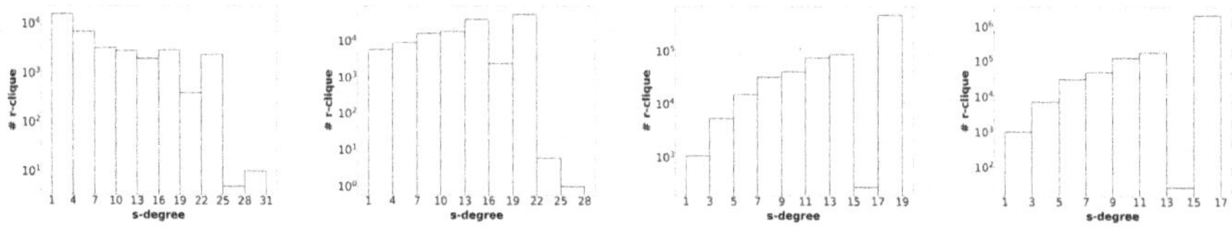

(a) (3, 4) nucleus d. **(b)** (5, 6) nucleus d. **(c)** (7, 8) nucleus d. **(d)** (9, 10) nucleus d.

Fig. 5. s-degree distribution of r-cliques for `DBLP_dm` network, for r, s as (3, 4), (5, 6), (7, 8) and (9, 10). x-axis shows the s-degrees and y-axis denotes the counts of r-cliques in log scale. The histogram shows that there is no heavy-tail pattern (similar behaviors observed for other collaboration networks).

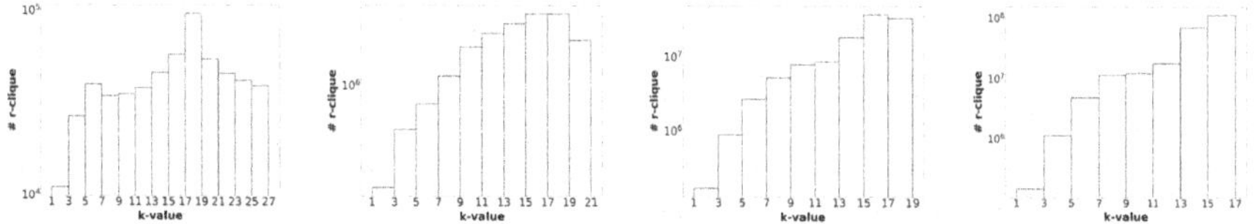

(a) (3, 4) nucleus d. **(b)** (5, 6) nucleus d. **(c)** (7, 8) nucleus d. **(d)** (9, 10) nucleus d.

Fig. 6. k_s-value distribution of r-cliques for `Drug` network. The x-axis (binned) is k_s-value and the y-axis is the number of r-cliques. We use logarithmic scale in y-axis to handle the skewness. The mass of the histogram is shifted to right in higher-order nucleus decompositions.

counts in nine networks. These vertices reflect the dense structure in the networks and number of such vertices remains constant in higher-order decompositions. But there is a huge decrease in the total number of vertices which are part of r-cliques in higher-order because of vertices that do not participate in any r-clique. Another interesting pattern that we uncover is the two distinct groups of the vertices in higher-order. One group has very high r-clique counts while the other group has very low r-clique counts. This indicates the existence of core-periphery structure in `DBLP_dm`, `DBLP_ds`, `Drug`, `Erdos992`, `Hamsterster`, and `Jazz` networks [4].

Being part of many r-cliques, a vertex has many k_s-values from those r-cliques. The k_s-value of a vertex in higher-order nucleus decompositions can be defined by the average, max, or min values of those k_s-values. We examine the distribution of those measure but there is no common pattern overall, neither for datasets nor for the varying r, s values.

3.2 Degeneracy Core

In the classic k-core decomposition, every vertex gets a k_s-value (core number) which reflects its significance in the network. The degeneracy of a graph is the maximum k-value such that the graph has a non-empty k-core. The core subgraph with maximum k-value is called the degeneracy core. As degeneracy core

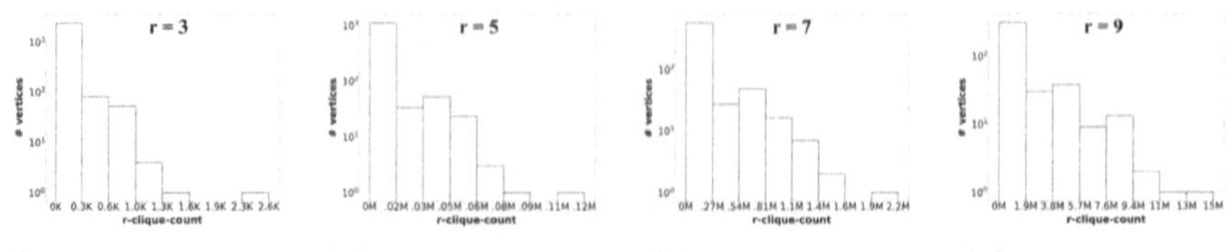

(a) # vertices: 2530 (b) # vertices: 1223 (c) # vertices: 673 (d) # vertices: 403

Fig. 7. Frequency distribution of r-cliques for vertices in PGP network. A few vertices have large r-clique counts and it remains constant in higher orders. There is a significant decrease in the number of vertices that are part of an r-clique in higher orders.

is a significant dense subgraph, we analyze it for higher-order nucleus decompositions. In (r, s)-nucleus decomposition, the k_s-value of an r-clique denotes that its s-degree is at least k_s. The r-cliques with the maximum k_s-value form the degeneracy core. We locate those cores by taking the induced subgraph of vertices that are part of those r-cliques. We uncover some interesting structural patterns in the degeneracy cores of higher-order nucleus decompositions. The expected behavior is that the size (vertex count) of the degeneracy core will decrease, and the density (fraction of internal edges with respect to the total possible edges) will increase with higher orders as fine-grained subgraphs will be found in a higher order which are lost in the larger structure. Surprisingly, the degeneracy core with the highest density is found in (3, 4)-nucleus decomposition for eight networks in our dataset. The size and density of the degeneracy core remain unchanged in higher orders for these networks. Table 2 presents the statistics of the densest degeneracy cores for all nucleus decompositions in each network. We only show the nucleus decompositions where going to larger r, s values yields a denser degeneracy core, i.e., the higher-order decompositions that do not results in denser degeneracy cores are not shown. We get the best degeneracy core in (4, 5)-nucleus decomposition for 5 facebook networks. Figure 8 presents the density and size behavior of all the k-cores in `fb-Haverford76`. **In several cases, it is possible to find denser structures with higher-order nucleus decompositions where r, s is larger than 3, 4.** In `fb-Reed` network, for instance, the size of the degeneracy core reduces from 33 to 19 and density increases from 0.6326 to 0.9766 when we go from (3, 4) to (4, 5)-nucleus decomposition. In `PGP` and `fb-USFCA72` networks, the best result is found in (5, 6)-nucleus decompositions. In `Drug` network, it is possible to find denser structures until the (8, 9)-nucleus decomposition.

3.3 Hierarchy Analysis

Nucleus decomposition summarizes the network as a forest of nuclei that shows a global hierarchical snapshot of dense subgraphs with containment relations. We analyze the forest of nuclei in higher-order nucleus decompositions to understand the hierarchical structure of a network for large r, s values. We use circle packing diagrams to visualize the forest of nuclei where each circle denotes a

Table 2. Vital statistics of the degeneracy cores. The quality of the degeneracy core is measured both in terms of size and density. For a network, size and density of the degeneracy core in higher-order decompositions are shown until the best degeneracy core is found. The smallest and densest degeneracy core is found in (3, 4)-nucleus decomposition for eight real-world networks.

Dataset	ND	Size	Density
Caida	(3, 4)	17	0.9926
DBLP_ds	(3, 4)	36	1.0
DBLP_pp	(3, 4)	45	1.0
DBLP_dm	(3, 4)	25	1.0
Jazz	(3, 4)	30	1.0
Hamster.	(3, 4)	25	1.0
Erdos992	(3, 4)	8	1.0
fb-USF.	(3, 4)	35	0.9832
	(4, 5)	35	0.9832
	(5, 6)	32	0.9940

Dataset	ND	Size	Density
fb-Simmons	(3, 4)	25	0.9633
	(4, 5)	24	0.9710
fb-Haverf.	(3, 4)	37	0.9309
	(4, 5)	30	0.9747
fb-Caltech36	(3, 4)	26	0.9661
	(4, 5)	23	0.9841
fb-Reed	(3, 4)	33	0.6326
	(4, 5)	19	0.9766
fb-Swarth.	(3, 4)	78	0.3876
	(4, 5)	51	0.5152

Dataset	ND	Size	Density
PGP	(3, 4)	35	0.9546
	(4, 5)	62	0.5124
	(5, 6)	29	0.9877
Drug	(3, 4)	59	0.8843
	(4, 5)	78	0.6417
	(5, 6)	42	0.9268
	(6, 7)	42	0.9268
	(7, 8)	42	0.9268
	(8, 9)	38	0.9445
PowerG.	(3, 4)	12	0.5455

(a) (3, 4), # nuclei: 46

(b) (4, 5), # nuclei: 82

(c) (5, 6), # nuclei: 137

Fig. 8. Size vs density plot of the nuclei (having more than 10 vertices) for `fb-Haverford76` network, for (3, 4), (4, 5) and (5, 6)-nucleus decompositions. In addition to the degeneracy core, we also show the leaf subgraphs and internal non-leaf ones in the nuclei hierarchy. The size of the degeneracy core reduces from 37 to 30 and its density increases from 0.9309 to 0.9747 for moving from (3, 4) to (4, 5)-nucleus decomposition. The degeneracy core remains unchanged for larger higher-order nucleus decompositions.

nucleus subgraph in the forest and the containment relationships are captured with nested circles. The size of the circle is proportional to the number of vertices in the corresponding nucleus, and the color of the circle represents the density (blue and red show density 0 and 1, respectively). Containment within each circle represents a level in the hierarchy. Any nucleus with less than 10 vertices are ignored. For most networks, we observe that denser structures can be obtained in higher-order decompositions with larger r, s values. However, this comes at the cost of losing hierarchical relationships. Figure 9 presents the visualizations for `fb-Simmons` network for all higher-order decompositions. Forest of (r, s)-nuclei can present the hierarchical structure at a finer granularity up to a certain higher-order decomposition. For most of the networks in our experiments, the hierarchical structure disappears after $(7, 8)$-nucleus decomposition.

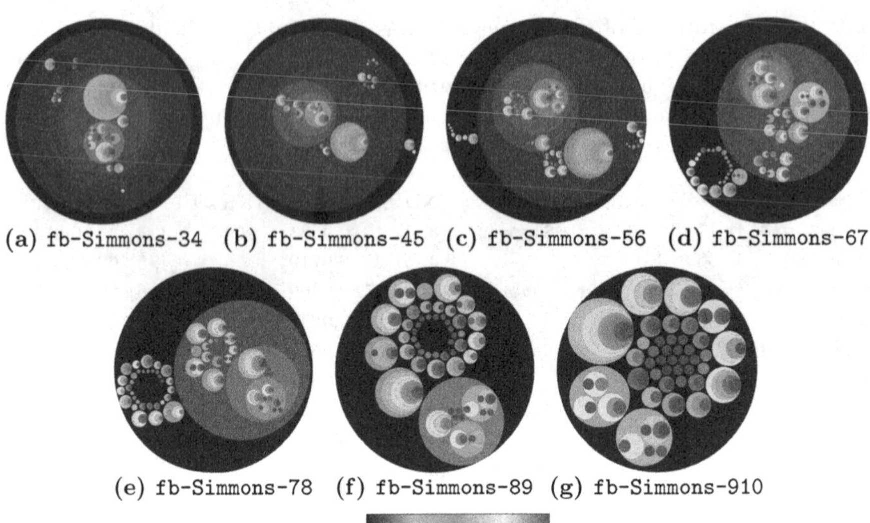

Fig. 9. (r, s)-nuclei forest in higher-order nucleus decompositions for `fb-Simmons`. The density is color coded. Each circle denotes a nucleus subgraph in the forest and the containment relationships are captured with nested circles. Any nucleus with less than 10 vertices are ignored. The leaves are mostly red with high densities. Finer dense structures that are lost in larger structures become visible in higher-order decompositions.

4 Conclusion

In this paper, we introduced an analysis for using large cliques in dense subgraph discovery. Relying on the nucleus decomposition, we implemented higher-order decompositions that can use up to 10-cliques and analyzed the resulting dense subgraphs and hierarchical relations for various real-world networks. Our analysis suggests that utilizing larger cliques can yield denser structures with more interesting hierarchical relations. For future work, we plan to investigate faster algorithms for large (r, s) nucleus decompositions.

Acknowledgments. Sariyuce was supported by NSF-1910063. This research used resources of the National Energy Research Scientific Computing Center (NERSC), a U.S. Department of Energy Office of Science User Facility operated under Contract No. DE-AC02-05CH11231.

References

1. Alvarez-Hamelin, J.I., Barrat, A., Vespignani, A.: Large scale networks fingerprinting and visualization using the k-core decomposition. In: NIPS, pp. 41–50 (2006)
2. Angel, A., Koudas, N., Sarkas, N., Srivastava, D., Svendsen, M., Tirthapura, S.: Dense subgraph maintenance under streaming edge weight updates for real-time story identification. VLDB J. 1–25 (2013). https://doi.org/10.1007/s00778-013-0340-z

3. Barabási, A.L., Albert, R.: Emergence of scaling in random networks. Science **286**(5439), 509–512 (1999)
4. Borgatti, S.P., Everett, M.G.: Models of core/periphery structures. Soc. Netw. **21**(4), 375–395 (2000)
5. Clauset, A., Tucker, E., Sainz, M.: The colorado index of complex networks (2016). https://icon.colorado.edu
6. Cohen, J.: Trusses: cohesive subgraphs for social network analysis. Technical report, National Security Agency Technical Report, Fort Meade, MD (2008)
7. Dourisboure, Y., Geraci, F., Pellegrini, M.: Extraction and classification of dense communities in the web. In: WWW, pp. 461–470 (2007)
8. Du, X., Jin, R., Ding, L., Lee, V.E., Jr., J.H.T.: Migration motif: a spatial-temporal pattern mining approach for financial markets. In: SIGKDD, pp. 1135–1144 (2009)
9. Erdős, P., Hajnal, A.: On chromatic number of graphs and set-systems. Acta Math. Hung. **17**(1–2), 61–99 (1966)
10. Fratkin, E., Naughton, B., Brutlag, D., Batzoglou, S.: Motifcut: regulatory motifs finding with maximum density subgraphs. Bioinformatics **22**(14), e150–e157 (2006)
11. Gibson, D., Kumar, R., Tomkins, A.: Discovering large dense subgraphs in massive graphs. In: VLDB, pp. 721–732 (2005)
12. Gleich, D.F., Seshadhri, C.: Vertex neighborhoods, low conductance cuts, and good seeds for local community methods. In: SIGKDD, pp. 597–605 (2012)
13. Jain, S., Seshadhri, C.: A fast and provable method for estimating clique counts using turán's theorem. In: WWW, pp. 441–449 (2017)
14. Kumar, R., Raghavan, P., Rajagopalan, S., Tomkins, A.: Trawling the web for emerging cyber-communities. In: WWW, pp. 1481–1493 (1999)
15. Kunegis, J.: Konect: the Koblenz network collection. In: Proceedings of the 22nd International Conference on World Wide Web, pp. 1343–1350. ACM (2013)
16. Leskovec, J., Krevl, A.: SNAP Datasets: stanford large network dataset collection (2014). http://snap.stanford.edu/data
17. Lick, D.R., White, A.T.: k-degenerate graphs. Can. J.Math. **22**(5), 1082–1096 (1970)
18. Makino, K., Uno, T.: New algorithms for enumerating all maximal cliques. In: Hagerup, T., Katajainen, J. (eds.) SWAT 2004. LNCS, vol. 3111, pp. 260–272. Springer, Heidelberg (2004). https://doi.org/10.1007/978-3-540-27810-8_23
19. Matula, D.W., Beck, L.L.: Smallest-last ordering and clustering and graph coloring algorithms. J. ACM **30**(3), 417–427 (1983)
20. Newman, M.E.: The structure and function of complex networks. SIAM Rev. **45**(2), 167–256 (2003)
21. Pinar, A., Seshadhri, C., Vishal, V.: Escape: efficiently counting all 5-vertex subgraphs. In: WWW, pp. 1431–1440 (2017)
22. Rossi, R.A., Ahmed, N.K.: The network data repository with interactive graph analytics and visualization. In: AAAI, pp. 4292–4293 (2015)
23. Saito, K., Yamada, T.: Extracting communities from complex networks by the k-dense method. In: IEEE ICDM Workshops, pp. 300–304 (2006)
24. Sarıyüce, A.E., Seshadhri, C., Pınar, A., Çatalyürek, Ü.V.: Finding the hierarchy of dense subgraphs using nucleus decompositions. In: WWW, pp. 927–937 (2015)
25. Sarıyüce, A.E., Seshadhri, C., Pınar, A., Çatalyürek, Ü.: Nucleus decompositions for identifying hierarchy of dense subgraphs. ACM Trans. Web **11**(3), 1–27 (2017)
26. Seidman, S.B.: Network structure and minimum degree. Social Netw. **5**(3), 269–287 (1983)
27. Traud, A.L., Mucha, P.J., Porter, M.A.: Social structure of facebook networks. Phys. A **391**(16), 4165–4180 (2012)

28. Tsourakakis, C.: The k-clique densest subgraph problem. In: International Conference on World Wide Web, WWW, pp. 1122–1132 (2015)
29. Verma, A., Butenko, S.: Network clustering via clique relaxations: A community based. Graph Partitioning and Graph Clustering **588**, 129 (2013)
30. Zhang, Y., Parthasarathy, S.: Extracting analyzing and visualizing triangle k-core motifs within networks. In: IEEE ICDE, pp. 1049–1060 (2012)
31. Zhao, F., Tung, A.: Large scale cohesive subgraphs discovery for social network visual analysis. In: PVLDB, pp. 85–96 (2013)

SqueezeBioBERT: BioBERT Distillation for Healthcare Natural Language Processing

Hongbin George Du[1] and Yanke Hu[2(✉)]

[1] University of Texas at Austin, Austin, TX 78712, USA
dugeorge21@utexas.edu
[2] Humana, Irving, TX 75063, USA
yhu@humana.com

Abstract. Healthcare text mining attracts increasing research interest as electronic health record (EHR) and healthcare claim data have skyrocketed over the past decade. Recently, deep pre-trained language models have improved many natural language processing tasks significantly. However, directly applying them to healthcare text mining won't generate satisfactory results, because those models are trained from generic domain corpora, which contains a word distribution shift from healthcare corpora. Moreover, deep pre-trained language models are generally computationally expensive and memory intensive, which makes them very difficult to use on resource-restricted devices. In this work, we designed a novel knowledge distillation method, which is very effective for Transformer-based models. We applied this knowledge distillation method to BioBERT [5], and experiments show that knowledge encoded in the large BioBERT can be effectively transferred to a compressed version of SqueezeBioBERT. We evaluated SqueezeBioBERT on three healthcare text mining tasks: named entity recognition, relation extraction and question answering. The result shows that SqueezeBioBERT achieves more than 95% of the performance of teacher BioBERT on these three tasks, while being 4.2X smaller.

Keywords: Natural language processing · Transformer · Deep learning · Knowledge distillation · Healthcare

1 Introduction

Healthcare text mining attracts increasing research interest as electronic health record (EHR) and healthcare claim data have skyrocketed over the past decade. Recently, deep pre-trained language models, such as BERT [2] and GPT [3], have improved many natural language processing tasks significantly. However, it won't give satisfactory results by directly applying those deep pre-trained language models to healthcare text mining. One important reason is that those models are trained from generic domain corpora, which contains a word distribution shift from healthcare corpora. Moreover, deep pre-trained language models

S. Chellappan et al. (Eds.): CSoNet 2020, LNCS 12575, pp. 193–201, 2020.
https://doi.org/10.1007/978-3-030-66046-8_16

are difficult to use on resource-restricted devices due to their huge computation complexity and memory consumption. It's very important to have embedded models that can directly inference on mobile for healthcare related apps in the US because: 1) it can provide better user experience at poor cell phone signal locations, and 2) it doesn't require users to upload their health sensitive information onto the cloud. In the US, health related data are only allowed to upload to the cloud by mobile apps being developed by certified institutes, which greatly suppresses the enthusiasm of developing healthcare mobile apps from individual developers. There are some model compression techniques developed recently for generic BERT [6–8], but there doesn't exist a small and efficient enough pre-trained language model in healthcare domain. In this work, we developed SqueezeBioBERT. SqueezeBioBERT has 3 transformer layers, and inference much faster while being accurate on healthcare natural language processing tasks. Our contributions are summarized as below:

- We designed a novel knowledge distillation method, which is very effective for compressing Transformer-based models without losing accuracy.
- We applied this knowledge distillation method to BioBERT [5], and experiments show that knowledge encoded in the large BioBERT can be effectively transferred to a compressed version of SqueezeBioBERT.
- We evaluated SqueezeBioBERT on three healthcare text mining tasks: name entity recognition, relation extraction and question answering. The result shows that SqueezeBioBERT achieves more than 95% of the performance of teacher BioBERT on these three tasks, while being 4.2X smaller.

2 Transformer Layer

As the foundation of modern pre-trained language models [2–4], transformer layer [1] can capture long-term dependencies of the input tokens with attention mechanism. A typical transformer layer contains two major components: *multi-head attention* (MHA) and *feed-forward network* (FFN).

2.1 Multi-head Attention

Practically, we calculate the attention function on a query set $\mathbf{Q}$, with key set $\mathbf{K}$ and value set $\mathbf{V}$. The attention function can be defined as below:

$$\mathbf{A} = \frac{\mathbf{Q}\mathbf{K}^T}{\sqrt{d_k}} \tag{1}$$

$$Attention(\mathbf{Q}, \mathbf{K}, \mathbf{V}) = softmax(\mathbf{A})\mathbf{V} \tag{2}$$

where d_k denotes the dimension of $\mathbf{K}$.

Multi-head attention will jointly train the model from different representation subspaces. It is denoted as below:

$$MultiHead(\mathbf{Q}, \mathbf{K}, \mathbf{V}) = Concat(head_1, ..., head_h)\mathbf{W} \tag{3}$$

where h denotes attention head number, $head_i$ is computed by Eq. (2), and W is the linear parameter weight.

2.2 Feed-Forward Network

After multi-head attention, a fully connected feed-forward network will follow, which is denoted as below:

$$FFN(x) = max(0, x\mathbf{W}_1 + b_1)\mathbf{W}_2 + b_2 \tag{4}$$

3 Knowledge Distillation

A very common way to boost the performance of a machine learning algorithm is to train several models, and then ensemble. Deep learning models are generally heavy neural networks, so it's normally considered too computationally expensive and inefficient to deploy the ensemble of deep neural networks in the production environment. [9] first proposed *Knowledge Distillation* and showed the possibility of compressing the function learned from a large complex model into a much smaller and faster model without significant accuracy loss [10]. As deep learning models are becoming more and more complex, knowledge distillation has shown its power of transferring the knowledge from a group of specialist networks to a single model [10–12].

Formally, *Knowledge Distillation* process can be defined as the process of minimizing the loss function between the a large teacher network $\mathbf{T}$ and a small student network $\mathbf{S}$ as below:

$$\mathcal{L}_{KD} = \sum_{x \in X} L(f^T(x), f^S(x)) \tag{5}$$

where L denotes the loss function to evaluate the difference between $\mathbf{T}$ and $\mathbf{S}$, x is the token input, X is the training set, f^T denotes the output of the teacher network $\mathbf{T}$ and f^S denotes the output of the student network $\mathbf{S}$.

4 BioBERT

BioBERT [5], with almost the same structure as BERT and pre-trained on biomedical domain corpora such as PubMed Abstracts and PMC full-text articles, can significantly outperform BERT on biomedical text mining tasks.

BioBERT has been fine-tuned on the following three tasks: Named Entity Recognition (NER), Relation Extraction (RE) and Question Answering (QA). NER is to recognize domain-specific nouns in a corpus, and precision, recall and F1 score are used for evaluation on the datasets listed in Table 1. RE is to classify the relationships of named entities, and precision, recall and F1 score are used for evaluation on the datasets listed in Table 2. QA is to answer a specific question in a given text passage, and strict accuracy, lenient accuracy and mean reciprocal rank are used for evaluation on BioASQ factoid dataset [24].

Table 1. BioBERT Named Entity Recognition evaluation datasets

Dataset	Entity type
NCBI Disease [13]	Disease
2010 i2b2/VA [14]	Disease
BC5CDR [15]	Disease/Drug
BC4CHEMD [16]	Drug
BC2GM [17]	Gene
JNLPBA [18]	Gene
LINNAEUS [19]	Species
Species-800 [20]	Species

Table 2. BioBERT Relation Extraction evaluation datasets

Dataset	Entity type
GAD [21]	Gene/Disease
EU-ADR [22]	Gene/Disease
CHEMPROT [23]	Protein

5 BioBERT Distillation

In this section, we developed a novel distillation method for BioBERT. Experiments show that knowledge encoded in the large BioBERT can be effectively transferred to the compressed version of SqueezeBioBERT.

Figure 1 shows the overview of the proposed knowledge distillation method. Supposing that the teacher BioBERT has M transformer layers and the student SqueezeBioBERT has N transformer layers, we distillated BioBERT both on transformer layers and task-specific layers.

Transformer layer distillation consists of multi-head attention distillation and feed forward network distillation. For multi-head attention distillation, we combine Eqs. (2), (3) and (5), and use the mean squared error (MSE) as the loss function since it's more suitable for regression tasks. Thus, the multi-head attention distillation process is denoted as below:

$$\mathcal{L}_{MHA} = \frac{1}{h}\sum_{i=1}^{h} MSE(M_i^T, M_i^S) \tag{6}$$

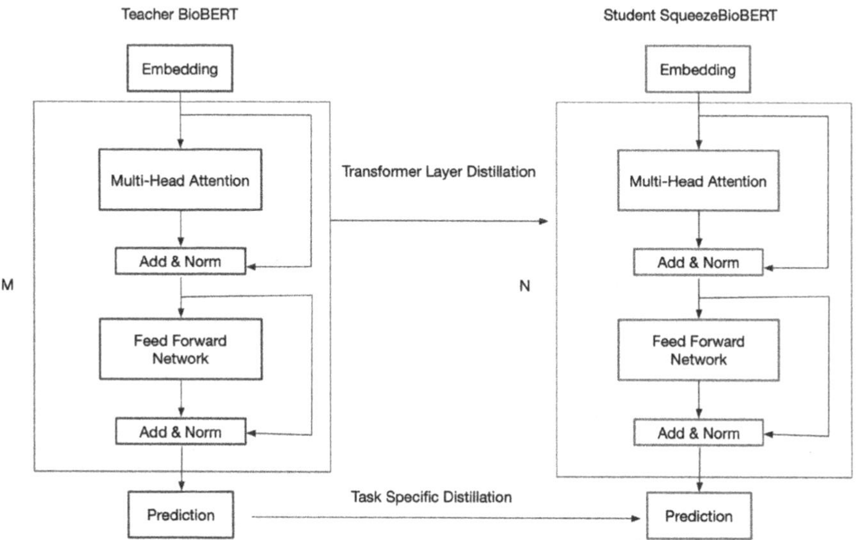

Fig. 1. The overview of distillation from BioBERT to SqueezeBioBERT

where h denotes the number of attention heads, M_i^S denotes the output of i-th student attention head, and M_i^T denotes the output of i-th teacher attention head.

For feed forward network distillation, we can use a single linear transformation W_{FFN} to transform the output of the teacher network into the student network. Thus, the feed forward network distillation process is denoted as below:

$$\mathcal{L}_{FFN} = MSE(O_{MHA}^T W_{FFN}, O_{MHA}^S) \tag{7}$$

For task-specific prediction layer distillation, we use *softmax cross-entropy* as the loss function, since it's more suitable for classification tasks. Thus, the task-specific prediction layer distillation is denoted as below:

$$\mathcal{L}_{pred} = -softmax(O_{FFN}^T)log(softmax(O_{FFN}^S)) \tag{8}$$

In summary, Eqs. (6), (7) and (8) describes the overall procedure of the BioBERT distillation process.

6 Experiments

We use BioBERT-Base v1.1 [25] as our source model, and distillated it to SqueezeBioBERT on the same three healthcare NLP tasks. BioBERT-Base v1.1

Table 3. Named Entity Recognition metrics comparison

Dataset	Metrics	BioBERT-Base v1.1	SqueezeBioBERT v1.0
NCBI Disease [13]	Precision	88.22	86.19
	Recall	91.25	88.42
	F1	89.71	87.74
2010 i2b2/VA [14]	Precision	86.93	83.97
	Recall	86.53	83.85
	F1	86.73	85.26
BC5CDR [15]	Precision	86.47	82.84
	Recall	87.84	84.94
	F1	87.15	85.23
BC4CHEMD [16]	Precision	92.80	89.83
	Recall	91.92	87.78
	F1	92.36	90.33
BC2GM [17]	Precision	84.32	82.46
	Recall	85.12	83.16
	F1	84.72	82.11
JNLPBA [18]	Precision	72.24	69.93
	Recall	83.56	81.67
	F1	77.49	75.09
LINNAEUS [19]	Precision	90.77	89.41
	Recall	85.83	84.29
	F1	88.24	85.15
Species-800 [20]	Precision	72.80	70.47
	Recall	75.36	74.38
	F1	74.06	72.73

Table 4. Relation extraction metrics comparison

Dataset	Metrics	BioBERT-Base v1.1	SqueezeBioBERT v1.0
GAD [21]	Precision	77.32	74.69
	Recall	82.68	81.61
	F1	79.83	77.04
EU-ADR [22]	Precision	77.86	75.37
	Recall	83.55	80.54
	F1	79.74	77.19
CHEMPROT [23]	Precision	77.02	75.79
	Recall	75.90	72.41
	F1	76.46	74.01

Table 5. Question answering metrics comparison

Dataset	Metrics	BioBERT-Base v1.1	SqueezeBioBERT v1.0
BioASQ 4b [24]	Strict Accuracy	27.95	27.31
	Lenient Accuracy	44.10	42.12
	Mean Reciprocal Rank	34.72	33.26
BioASQ 5b [24]	Strict Accuracy	46.00	43.58
	Lenient Accuracy	60.00	58.08
	Mean Reciprocal Rank	51.64	49.94
BioASQ 6b [24]	Strict Accuracy	42.86	41.83
	Lenient Accuracy	57.77	56.48
	Mean Reciprocal Rank	48.43	46.83

has 12 transformer layers and 109M weights. SqueezeBioBERT has 3 transformer layers and 26M weights.

NER results are show in Table 3, RE results are show in Table 4, and QA results are show in Table 5. From the results, we can see that SqueezeBioBERT is 4.2X smaller than BioBERT, but still achieves more than 95% accuracy performance of the teacher BioBERT on the three NLP tasks. This proves the efficiency of the proposed method of transferring knowledge encoded in the large BioBERT to the compressed version of SqueezeBioBERT.

7 Conclusion

Although recent deep pre-trained language models have greatly improved many natural language processing tasks, they are generally computationally expensive and memory intensive, which makes them very difficult to use on resource-restricted mobile or IoT devices. Embedded models that can directly inference on mobile is important for healthcare related apps in the US because: 1) it can provide better user experience at poor cell phone signal locations, and 2) it doesn't require users to upload their health sensitive information onto the cloud. In this paper, we designed a novel knowledge distillation method, which is very effective for compressing Transformer-based models without losing accuracy. We applied this knowledge distillation method to BioBERT, and experiments show that knowledge encoded in the large BioBERT can be effectively transferred to a compressed version of SqueezeBioBERT. We evaluated SqueezeBioBERT on three healthcare text mining tasks: name entity recognition, relation extraction and question answering. The result shows that SqueezeBioBERT achieves more than 95% of the performance of teacher BioBERT on these three tasks, while being 4.2X smaller.

Acknowledgement. This work was supported by Humana.

References

1. Vaswani, A., et al.: Attention is all you need. In: Advances in Neural Information Processing Systems (NeurIPS), pp. 5998–6008 (2017)
2. Devlin, J., Chang, M.-W., Lee, K., Toutanova, K.: BERT: pretraining of deep bidirectional transformers for language understanding. arXiv preprint arXiv:1810.04805 (2018)
3. Radford, A., Narasimhan, K., Salimans, T., Sutskever, I.: Improving language understanding by generative pre-training (2018)
4. Yang, Z., Dai, Z., Yang, Y., Carbonell, J., Salakhutdinov, R., Le, Q.V.: XLNet: generalized autoregressive pretraining for language understanding. arXiv preprint arXiv:1906.08237 (2019)
5. Lee, J., et al.: BioBERT: a pre-trained biomedical language representation model for biomedical text mining. Bioinformatics **36**, 1234–1240 (2019)
6. Sanh, V., Debut, L., Chaumond, J., Wolf, T.: DistilBERT, a distilled version of BERT: smaller, faster, cheaper and lighter. arXiv preprint arXiv:1910.01108 (2019)
7. Jiao, X., et al.: TinyBERT: distilling BERT for natural language understanding. arXiv preprint arXiv:1909.10351 (2019)
8. Sun, Z., Yu, H., Song, X., Liu, R., Yang, Y., Zhou, D.: MobileBERT: a compact task-agnostic BERT for resource-limited devices. In: Proceedings of the 58th Annual Meeting of the Association for Computational Linguistics (2020)
9. Bucilua, C., Caruana, R., Niculescu-Mizil, A.: Model compression. In: Proceedings of the 12th ACM SIGKDD International Conference on Knowledge Discovery and Data Mining, KDD 2006, New York, NY, USA, pp. 535–541. ACM (2006)
10. Hinton, G., Vinyals, O., Dean, J.: Distilling the knowledge in a neural network. arXiv preprint arXiv:1503.02531 (2015)
11. Urban, G., et al.: Do deep convolutional nets really need to be deep (or even convolutional)? In: Proceedings of the International Conference on Learning Representations (2016)
12. Ba, J., Caruana, R.: Do deep nets really need to be deep? In: Proceedings of the Advances in Neural Information Processing Systems, pp. 2654–2662 (2014)
13. Dogan, R.I., et al.: NCBI disease corpus: a resource for disease name recognition and concept normalization. J. Biomed. Inform. **47**, 1–10 (2014)
14. Uzuner, O., et al.: 2010 i2b2/VA challenge on concepts, assertions, and relations in clinical text. J. Am. Med. Inform. Assoc. **18**, 552–556 (2011)
15. Li, J., et al.: BioCreative V CDR task corpus: a resource for chemical disease relation extraction. Database **2016**, 1–10 (2016)
16. Krallinger, M., et al.: The CHEMDNER corpus of chemicals and drugs and its annotation principles. J. Cheminform. **7**, 1–17 (2015)
17. Smith, L., et al.: Overview of BioCreative II gene mention recognition. Genome Biol. **9**, 1–19 (2008). https://doi.org/10.1186/gb-2008-9-s2-s2
18. Kim, J.-D., et al.: Introduction to the bio-entity recognition task at JNLPBA. In: Proceedings of the International Joint Workshop on Natural Language Processing in Biomedicine and its Applications (NLPBA/BioNLP), Geneva, Switzerland, pp. 73–78 (2004). COLING. https://www.aclweb.org/anthology/W04-1213
19. Gerner, M., et al.: LINNAEUS: a species name identification system for biomedical literature. BMC Bioinform. **11**, 85 (2010). https://doi.org/10.1186/1471-2105-11-85
20. Pafilis, E., et al.: The SPECIES and ORGANISMS resources for fast and accurate identification of taxonomic names in text. PLoS One **8**, e65390 (2013)

21. Bravo, A., et al.: Extraction of relations between genes and diseases from text and large-scale data analysis: implications for translational research. BMC Bioinform. **16**, 55 (2015). https://doi.org/10.1186/s12859-015-0472-9
22. Van Mulligen, E.M., et al.: The EU-ADR corpus: annotated drugs, diseases, targets, and their relationships. J. Biomed. Inform. **45**, 879–884 (2012)
23. Krallinger, M., et al.: Overview of the BioCreative VI chemical-protein interaction track. In: Proceedings of the BioCreative VI Workshop, Bethesda, MD, USA, pp. 141–146. https://doi.org/10.1093/database/bay073/5055578 (2017)
24. Tsatsaronis, G., et al.: An overview of the BIOASQ large-scale biomedical semantic indexing and question answering competition. BMC Bioinform. **16**, 138 (2015). https://doi.org/10.1186/s12859-015-0564-6
25. https://github.com/naver/biobert-pretrained

A New Metric to Evaluate Communities in Social Networks Using Geodesic Distance

Sahar Bakhtar(✉), Mohammad Saber Gholami(✉), and Hovhannes A. Harutyunyan(✉)

Concordia University, Montreal, Canada
{s_bakhta,m_olamin,haruty}@encs.concordia.ca

Abstract. Community detection problem is a well-studied problem in social networks. A good community can be defined as a group of nodes that are highly connected with each other and loosely connected to the nodes outside the community. Regarding the fact that social networks are huge in size, having complete information of the whole network is almost impossible. As a result, the problem of local community detection has become more popular in recent years. In order to detect local communities, researchers mostly utilize an evaluation metric along with an algorithm to explore local communities. In this paper, the weaknesses of some well-known metrics are considered and a new metric to evaluate the quality of a community, only using local information, is proposed by using geodesic distance. The proposed metric can make a reasonable trade-off between the number of external edges and the density of the community. Furthermore, the experimental results of this study demonstrate that this metric could be useful in terms of evaluating the communities of real social networks.

Keywords: Social networks · Local community evaluation · Community evaluation metrics · Geodesic distance

1 Introduction

Social Networks have attracted remarkable attention in the past few years. They can capture the relationship between entities (such as people) in huge networks. Formally speaking, the social network could be represented as a graph $G = (V, E)$ in which V is the set of entities and E is the relationships among them. One problem of great interest in this domain is *community detection* in which the ultimate objective is to find dense communities within such networks. More precisely, a good community is a set of nodes in a graph that have many connections among them and are loosely connected to the other nodes of the network [7]. The process of community detection is a very important type of network data analysis and can reveal the hidden structures of the network. Detecting such

S. Chellappan et al. (Eds.): CSoNet 2020, LNCS 12575, pp. 202–216, 2020.
https://doi.org/10.1007/978-3-030-66046-8_17

structures in a network has many applications in complex networks, e.g., detecting common location users, discovering friends who share similar interests or occupations in a social network [9], and in biology [7], as well as the World Wide Web [4].

However, with the growth of social networks and their corresponding data size, handling the whole structure of the network seems to be impossible. Consequently, *local community detection* problem has attracted a great deal of attention from researchers in recent years. During the last few years, researchers have used different methods and algorithms to solve the problem of local community detection [11,12]. One of the popular methods to detect communities locally is Clauset's algorithms [2]. According to this method, a local metric that can represent the quality of a community is proposed and then this metric is used along with an incremental algorithm to detect the desired community. A number of studies have proposed such metrics and algorithms to locally detect communities [1,10,13]. However, none of the quality metrics proposed so far, are generally accepted to comprehensively evaluate the goodness of the detected communities.

Motivated by these facts, this paper aims to propose a comprehensive quality metric for community evaluation only using the local information. To this aim, the shortest distance among all pairs of nodes in a given community is normalized and used. The main contributions of this paper are as follows:

- Proposing a new metric which can evaluate the quality of any communities only employing the local information,
- This metric can be used to compare the results of different community detection algorithms, especially when the real (or ground-truth) communities of the network are not known,
- This metric can recognize overlapping nodes as well.

The remainder of this paper is structured as follows: Sect. 2 represents the literature review and discusses the most relevant studies. Section 3 proposes the new metric, while the aim of Sect. 4 is to present the experimental results and evaluation of the proposed metric. Finally, we conclude this study in Sect. 5 and give some ideas for possible future works.

2 Literature Review

During the last few years, because of the network growth and efficiency issues, having access to the global information of the network seems to be unlikely. As a result, many researchers have tried to find good communities based on local information by maximizing a quantitative value. Clauset [2] firstly introduced the problem of local community detection and defined 3 types of nodes in a graph (Fig. 1): $\mathcal{C}$ is the set of nodes inside the community, $\mathcal{B}$, or boundary nodes, is the set of nodes in the community that have connections with nodes outside $\mathcal{C}$, and $\mathcal{U}$ is the set of unknown nodes with at least one connection inside the community. According to the definition of the local community detection problem, only the introduced nodes are known to be used to evaluate the quality of the detected community. He defined R modularity as follows:

$$R = \frac{I}{T} \tag{1}$$

In (1), T is the number of edges with one or more endpoints in $\mathcal{B}$, while I is the number of those edges with at least one endpoint in $\mathcal{B}$ and neither endpoints in $\mathcal{U}$. Luo et al. [10] proposed another modularity, namely M, as follows:

$$M = \frac{E_{in}}{E_{out}} \tag{2}$$

In (2), E_{in} is the number of edges within the community, and E_{out} is the number of crossing edges or the edges that only have one endpoint in the community. Moreover, Chen et al. [1] proposed another modularity, namely L, as follows:

$$L = \frac{L_{in}}{L_{out}} \tag{3}$$

In (3), L_{in} and L_{out} are defined as follows:

$$L_{in} = \frac{E_{in}}{|\mathcal{C}|}, L_{out} = \frac{E_{out}}{|\mathcal{B}|} \tag{4}$$

In (4), $|\mathcal{C}|$ is the number of nodes inside the community and $|\mathcal{B}|$ is the number of border nodes. Although the three aforementioned metrics are quite well-known in the literature, they all have their own drawbacks when they are considered as a general quality metric for communities. To overcome those drawbacks, several research papers tried to propose different modularities. However, only a few considered the shortest path between pairs of nodes. Zhen-Qing et al. [19] proposed new modularity which considers the shortest path in the graph:

$$Q^d = \sum_{r=1}^{s}(\frac{L_r}{D_r} - \frac{\tilde{L_r}}{\tilde{D_r}}) \tag{5}$$

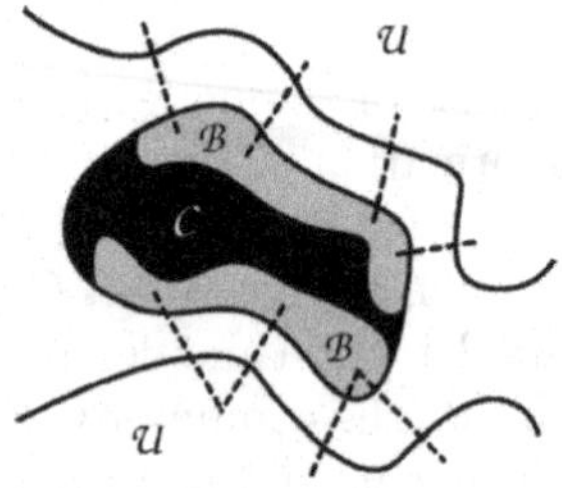

Fig. 1. Local community $\mathcal{C}$, its boundary $\mathcal{B}$, and the neighbors of the community $\mathcal{U}$ [2].

In (5), L_r is the number of edges in the community, and D_r is the average minimal path for all pairs of nodes within a given community. Similarly, $\tilde{L}_r$ and $\tilde{D}_r$ are the expected values for the same variables in a graph that is generated randomly. One issue with Q^d is the need for global information of the graph. To illustrate, to build a randomized graph, one needs to follow the same pattern in the degree distribution of the original graph. Similarly, Wu et al. [16] came up with an algorithm which works with closeness centrality:

$$C_c(v_i) = \frac{n-1}{\sum_{j \neq i}^{n} g(v_i, v_j)} \tag{6}$$

In (6), n is the number of nodes in the graph and $g(v_i, v_j)$ is the geodesic distance between node v_i and v_j. In the algorithm, firstly, the centrality of each node is calculated via its distance information, and *center nodes* are selected. Then, for each node of the graph, the most similar *center* is selected which demonstrates its community. These steps are repeated until convergence. Here, again, the same issue about using global information holds. Also, (6) is used to find center nodes and is not a quality metric for communities. Lastly, Lue et al. [13] tried to define new modularity in which there is no need for global information. Local modularity LQ is defined as follows:

$$LQ = \frac{e_c}{S} - (\frac{d_c}{2S})^2 \tag{7}$$

In (7), e_c is the number of edges within the detected local community, while d_c is the summation of degrees of all nodes belonging to that local community. Also, S is the number of edges that have one or two endpoints in the local community. No need to mention that this information is locally accessible. Besides, they proved that LQ is equivalent to modularities L and R, under certain conditions. However, they came up with an algorithm for multi-scale local community detection which works with LQ, it did not evaluate the performance of the metric solely.

The main goal of this study is to propose a comprehensive quality metric to assess communities only using local information. Although the proposed metric can be used to evaluate the quality of any communities, regardless of the algorithm (global or local), we only compare it with local metrics and modularities. The reason is that when global information is available, it would be more accurate to judge the quality of a community according to the structure of the whole network. In this study, three well-known local metrics, R, M, and L are employed to be compared with the proposed one. LQ is excluded because it is proved to be equivalent to modularities L and R, under certain conditions and the performance of LQ is not a target in their algorithm.

Moreover, some studies have tried to compare different community detection algorithms via assessing their detected community partitioning [3,6,8]. For example, Dao et al. [3] tried to estimate similarities between two detected community partitioning using the size density distributions of communities. Also, Jebabli et al. [8] proposed a new technique to compare the detected community partitioning with the ground-truth communities. However, in this paper we try to compare local community detection algorithms via comparing their detected communities. Obviously, only local information of detected communities is available which makes the process of evaluation and comparing more difficult.

3 Proposed Metric

In this section, some definitions and results which are necessary for the proposed metric, are represented. Then, the problem which this paper aims to address is explained. Next, the deficiencies of some well-known quality metrics are discussed and finally, the proposed metric is introduced.

3.1 Definitions and Auxiliary Results

In an undirected and unweighted graph $G = (V, E)$ in which V is the set of nodes and E is the set of edges, *Geodesic Distance* between nodes v_i and v_j ($gd(v_i, v_j)$), where $v_i, v_j \in V$ is the shortest path length between v_i and v_j. Calculating geodesic distance in a graph is of considerable importance and has many applications [15,17]. Besides, finding the geodesic distance from any node to all nodes in an arbitrary graph could be done via the simple BFS algorithm, starting from the source node. This could be done in $O(V + E)$. We denote the sum of the geodesic distance between every pair of nodes in a given graph $G = (V, E)$ as GD_G:

$$GD_G = \sum_{i<j, v_i, v_j \in V} gd(v_i, v_j) \tag{8}$$

Obviously, in a complete graph (K_n), the geodesic distance between every pair of nodes is 1. Also, a *path* (P_n) is a graph with n nodes in which the diameter is $n-1$. To normalize the geodesic distance, having its minimum and maximum values is necessary. We have proved that for a graph with n nodes, GD is minimized in a complete graph K_n and is maximized in a path P_n. GD_{min} and GD_{max} denote the minimum and maximum geodesic distances, respectively and are described as follows:

Proposition 1. *Among all graphs on n nodes, GD_{min} is achieved in a complete graph K_n, and $GD_{min} = n(n-1)/2 = \frac{n^2-n}{2}$.*

Proposition 2. *Among all connected graphs on n nodes, GD_{max} is achieved in a path P_n, and $GD_{max} = n(n-1)(n+1)/6 = \frac{n^3-n}{6}$.*

The formal proofs of Propositions 1 and 2 are omitted due to the space limit.

3.2 Problem Definition

This paper aims to propose a comprehensive quality metric to evaluate every detected community using local information. To evaluate a community detection algorithm, the detected community is compared with the real community of the network. Regarding this comparison, the most similar detected community to the real one is considered as the best-detected community. Here, one major problem arises when the real community of a network is unknown. As a result, no comparison can be done. The other problem of comparison with real communities is that all nodes have the same weight. For example, considering two communities detected by two different algorithms, each of which missed one node from the real community. Suppose one of the detected communities missed a node with degree 1 and the other missed an important node (for instance a center node). In this case, both of the detected communities are considered as the same, because the number of missing nodes for both is 1. Thus, it is crucial to have a comprehensive quality metric to assess the detected communities. Besides, proposing such metric for local community detection problem (in which only local information of the community is available) is more challenging, since the information in hand is much more limited.

A community can be considered a high-quality community based on two criteria: (1) the accuracy which compares the detected community with the real community and (2) the definition of a community which considers the density inside the community and its sparsity to the outside. It is noteworthy to mention that the proposed metric in this paper, works properly based on both criteria.

3.3 Drawbacks of Existing Metrics

Regarding the definition of communities in social networks, it is apparent that a community with a denser connection within $\mathcal{C}$ and a sparser connection with its neighbors in $\mathcal{U}$ is a high-quality community. Modularity R is the first local metric proposed by Clauset [2] in 2005 (refer to (1)). Modularity R employs the number of edges with at least one endpoint in $\mathcal{B}$ and no endpoints in $\mathcal{U}$ to control the density of a community. However, this information cannot represent the density of the whole community. Because edges within $\mathcal{C}$, which do not have any endpoints in $\mathcal{B}$ are the valuable information ignored by R. Considering that this information can be helpful to recognize the density of a community, losing it would reduce the generality of the modularity R.

Although the modularity M considers all the edges, the number of community nodes are neglected. In other words, only employing the number of edges inside the community, E_{in}, without considering the number of community nodes, $|\mathcal{C}|$, cannot perfectly demonstrate the density of the community. Assume two communities of size n and m with the same number of edges, where $n > m$. It can be concluded that the community with m nodes is the denser one. As a result, in addition to the number of edges, considering the number of nodes is crucial in order to represent the density of a community.

Chen et al. [1] discuss the deficiencies of the above-mentioned modularities using Fig. 2. Regarding Fig. 2, merging node O_i ($11 \leq i \leq 1$) increases the number of internal edges by one ($E_{in} + 1$ for M and $I + 1$ for R) while keeps the number of crossing edges unchanged. Thus, adding O_i leads to an increase in the metrics' scores. However, it is clear that the resulting community including O_1

to O_8 and O_9 to O_{11} has weak-linked outliers. In order to cover the presented drawbacks, Chen et al. [1] proposed the metric L as it is mentioned in (3). Metric L represents the density of the community by using the number of internal edges with regard to the number of nodes in the community. Chen et al. admitted that the metric L has some deficiencies, which is resolved by using an algorithm. In metric L, L_{in} can not perfectly show the density of the community, because the distribution of edges among nodes is neglected. According to the presented drawbacks, a new local metric to evaluate communities is proposed.

3.4 The Proposed Metric

Regarding the definition of a community, there is a need for a trade-off between maximization of the density inside the community and minimization of the number of crossing edges. Equation (9) represents the proposed geodesic distance metric (GDM_C) as a function of NGD for community C as follows:

$$GDM_C = \frac{X}{NGD_C} \tag{9}$$

In (9), NGD_C is the Normalized Geodesic Distance of C. Here, the geodesic distance of community C is normalized to be used in the modularity GDM_C, as follows:

$$NGD_C = \frac{GD_C - (GD_{C_{min}} - 1)}{GD_{C_{max}} - (GD_{C_{min}} - 1)} \tag{10}$$

In (10), GD_C is the geodesic distance of community C, $GD_{C_{min}}$ and $GD_{C_{max}}$ are the minimum and maximum values for the geodesic distance of community C of size $|C|$. Regarding (10), the value of geodesic distance for any community is normalized between 0 and 1. It is clear that for a complete community, a community with all possible edges among its nodes, the geodesic distance gives its minimum value, $GD_{C_{min}}$. As a result, the normalized geodesic distance for such communities would be 0. To avoid having 0 values, instead of $GD_{C_{min}}$, we use $GD_{C_{min}} - 1$. Furthermore, in (9), X is the parameter that controls the number of crossing edges and is described as follows:

$$X = \frac{E_{in}}{E_{in} + E_{out}} \tag{11}$$

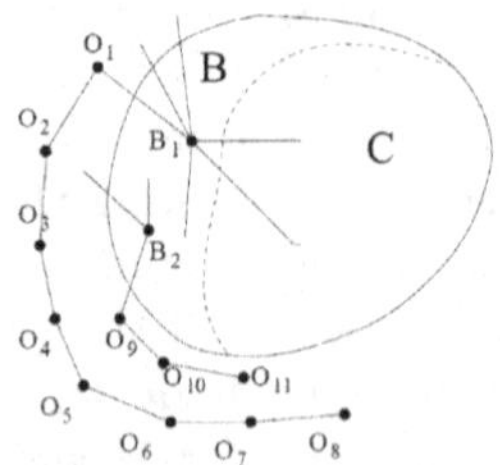

Fig. 2. Indicating the weakness of R and M [1].

Equation (11) represents the parameter X as a function of the number of internal edges E_{in} and the number of crossing edges E_{out}. In the proposed metric GDM, both X and NGD range between 0 and 1, which makes them comparable to be used together in a formula. In Eq. 9, NGD can perfectly capture the density inside a community and show how dense the community is, only using its local information. Also, parameter X can represent how much a community is separated from its neighbors. Thus, it is expected that the proposed metric acts satisfactory with maximizing the density inside the community and minimizing the number of external edges. In terms of complexity, the proposed GDM is more complex than the other local metrics. Since the proposed GDM is a comprehensive quality metric that is used only once to assess the quality of detected communities, there is not any concern about the high complexity of GDM.

4 Experimental Results

In this section, experimental results on Zachary Karate Club [18], Dolphins [14] and Football College [7] networks are presented. The experimental results show that metrics R, M, and L are designed to compare two communities with only one node difference. However, GDM is able to compare any two detected communities for a given node. In other words, GDM can assess detected communities resulted from different detection algorithms for a given node. Here, the research question is to compare the communities detected by different local community detection. However, no community detection algorithm is implemented and some selected communities are considered as example detected communities to be compared with the ground-truth communities.

Zachary Karate Club is a 34-node network which contains two groups of nodes that are members of two different clubs. These two groups are considered as two real communities of size 16 and 18 (RC_{16} and RC_{18}) for this network. Also, the Dolphins network with 62 nodes has two real communities of size 20 and 42. Moreover, Football college is a 115-node network that includes 11 real communities in which 8 nodes do not belong to any community [5].

In this paper, two experiments are designed and implemented. The structure of both experiments is according to the fact that the real communities must be given the highest scores in comparison with any other detected communities for the same given node.

4.1 The First Experiment

In the first experiment, assume that there is a real community RC_n of size n in a given dataset. Regarding real communities, at each step, one node from RC_n is chosen to be removed from the real community. Here, the removed node is still in the network but not in the real community. The resulted community after removing node y is denoted as $\{RC_n\} - y$. Considering $RC_n = \{a_1, a_2, \cdots, a_n\}$, the resulted communities from removing each member a_i $(0 \leq i \leq n)$ are $RC_n - a_1$, $RC_n - a_2$, $\cdots$, and $RC_n - a_n$. Also, at each step, one node from all over the

Table 1. Comparison of Karate Club real communities with the most similar communities to the real communities.

RC	Current community	R	M	L	GDM
RC_{16}	RC_{16}	0.714	3.3	1.03125	4.393
	$RC_{16} - \{3\}$	0.687	2.8	**1.12**	3.603
	$RC_{16} - \{5\}$	0.675	2.308	**1.077**	3.699
	$RC_{16} - \{6\}$	0.658	2.071	**1.105**	3.495
	$RC_{16} - \{7\}$	0.658	2.071	**1.105**	3.495
	$RC_{16} - \{11\}$	0.675	2.308	**1.077**	3.699
	$RC_{16} - \{13\}$	0.676	2.583	**1.033**	3.914
	$RC_{16} - \{17\}$	0.7	2.583	**1.205***	4.383
	$RC_{16} + \{9\}$	0.710	**3.4***	**1.2**	**4.585***
	$RC_{16} + \{10\}$	**0.722***	1.470	0.784	4.243
RC_{18}	RC_{18}	0.756*	3.5	1.555*	4.605
	$RC_{18} + \{3\}$	0.730	**4***	1.053	**5.072***
	$RC_{18} + \{20\}$	0.744	3.273	1.550	**4.732**

* Indicates the greatest score of the corresponding metric

network outside of RC_n is chosen to be merged into it. The resulted communities are RC_n+b_1, RC_n+b_2, $\cdots$ and RC_n+b_s, where $S = \{b_1, b_2, \cdots, b_s\}$ is the whole network outside of RC_n. In order to compare the above-mentioned communities with RC_n, the metrics R, M, L and GDM are calculated and compared with RC_n. It is expected that RC_n is given the highest scores from all four mentioned metrics. The purpose of using this experiment is to capture the most similar communities to the real communities, and compare them with the ground-truth communities. If a metric can give higher scores to the ground-truth communities in comparison with the values it is given to the most similar communities, the metric would be judged as a good metric.

Table 1 summarizes the results of the experiment on two communities of the Zachary Karate Club network (RC_{16} and RC_{18}). This table includes two categories for two real communities of this network. The first row of each category represents the metrics scores for RC_{16} and RC_{18} and the other rows contain the additions or deletions which are given higher scores than RC_{16}

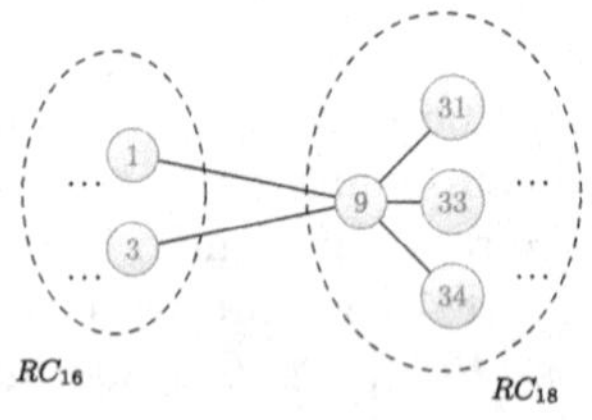

Fig. 3. The status of node 9.

or RC_{18} at least by one of the metrics. It is noteworthy to mention that the scores which are higher than that of real communities are shown bold and the maximum scores are denoted by a star. According to this table, since modularity R has only one wrong evaluation, i.e., it gave higher score to $RC_{16} + \{10\}$ rather than RC_{16}, it has the best performance. Regarding Table 1, GDM gives higher score to $RC_{16} + \{9\}$ rather than RC_{16}. For more illustration, adding node 9 into RC_{16} increases GDM by 0.192 (from 4.393 to 4.585). Figure 3 demonstrates the position of node 9 in the network. Regarding this figure, node 9 belongs to community RC_{18} with three connections to nodes 31, 33, and 34 in which node 34 is a core node for RC_{18}. On the other hand, node 9 is connected to RC_{16} with two edges to nodes 1 and 3 (with node 1 being a core node for RC_{16}). By comparing the connections of node 9 to the two real communities, it will be known that node 9 must belong to RC_{18} since removing 9 from RC_{18} increases the number of crossing edges by 1 and also weaken the density inside. However, it does not mean that if node 9 is added to RC_{16}, it would negatively affect RC_{16} since adding node 9 into RC_{16} increases the number of edges and nodes inside the community by 2 and 1, respectively. The reason is that node 9 is connected to the core node which does not let the density decline. All the above-mentioned reasons imply that the presence of node 9 into both communities can help them to be better communities But it is clear that removing node 9 from RC_{18} decreases the metric GDM more than 0.202 (It is decreased by 0.451, which is not mentioned in the table.). Thus, one may conclude that node 9 can be considered as an overlapping node, which can belong to both communities. This implies that GDM is able to recognize overlapping communities as well. In the same way, $RC_{18} + \{3\}$ and $RC_{18} + \{20\}$ are given higher scores than RC_{18} by GDM. Figure 4 and 5 illustrate the status of nodes 3 and 20 in the network and because of the same reasons as $RC_{16} + \{9\}$, they can also be referred to as overlapping nodes.

According to Table 1, in 8 cases, metric L results in higher values than that of RC_{16} (note the bold numbers). So, it can be concluded that the proposed metric can evaluate the quality of communities at least better than the L metric. Additionally, the same experiment is carried out on the other two networks. Table 2 indicates the number of wrong evaluation of the four metrics in Dolphins network. In this table, the first column shows the name and size of the real

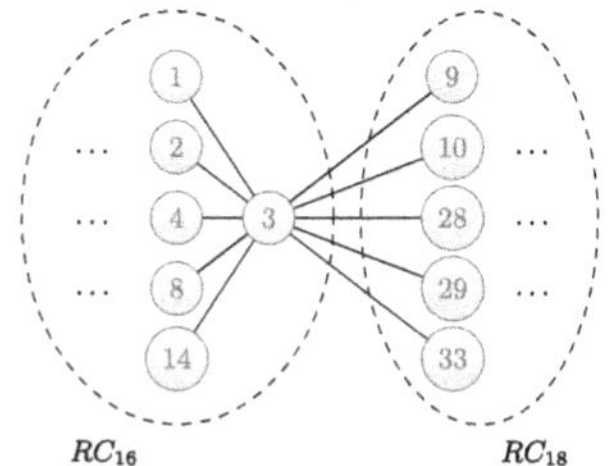

Fig. 4. The The status of node 3.

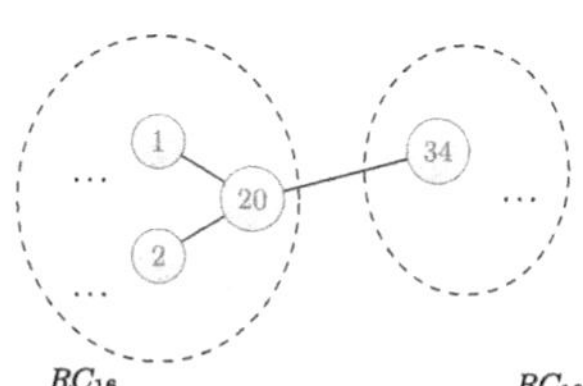

Fig. 5. The status of node 20.

Table 2. The number of wrong evaluation of the four metrics for Dolphins network in the first experiment.

RC	Metric	Adding	Removing
RC_{20}	R	0/42	5/20
	M	1/42	0/20
	L	6/42	13/20
	GDM	1/42	1/20
RC_{42}	R	0/20	38/42
	M	0/20	0/42
	L	4/20	26/42
	GDM	1/20	0/42

Table 3. The number of wrong evaluation of the four metrics for Football College network in the first experiment.

RC	Metric	Adding	Removing
RC_{13}	R	2/102	0/13
	M	2/102	0/13
	L	2/102	0/13
	GDM	1/102	0/13

communities and the second and third columns indicate the number of wrong evaluations of adding one node into the real community and removing one node from the real community. As can be seen from the table, metrics R and L have the worst performance in comparison with the other two metrics. Regarding Table 2, deletion is the most challenging part of this experiment for R and L. Figure 6 shows an example of removing one node from one real community of Dolphins network in which metric R cannot correctly assess the communities. Concerning this figure, removing node 5 from the community will make node 52 a new border node. Thus, this increases the number of crossing edges by 1 and also increases the number of edges with at least one endpoint in border nodes by 10. As a result, metric R is wrongly increased remarkably. Consequently, we can conclude that metric R is not a quality metric to be used independently to assess communities. However, metrics M and GDM perform satisfactorily for this network as well. Moreover, the same experiment is done on the Football College network which does not arise any challenge for any of the metrics. This network has 11 real communities in which only in one real community of size 13, metrics have wrong evaluations on addition steps, which can be taken into account as overlapping nodes. Table 3 summarize the number of wrong evaluation of metrics for this specific real community.

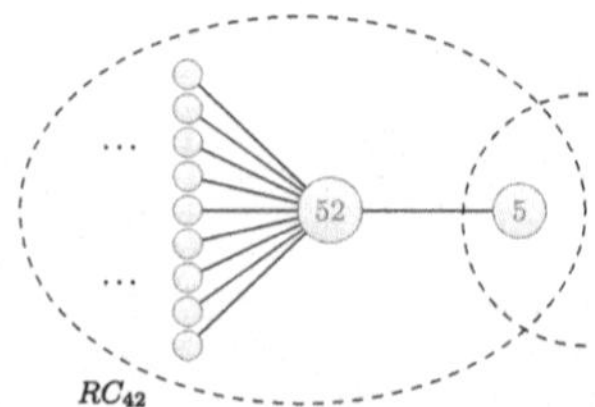

Fig. 6. An example of wrong assessment of communities by R modularity.

Table 4. The comparison of Football College real communities and the joint communities.

Community	R	M	L	GDM
$RC0_9$	0.59	1.44	1.44	50.164
$RC0_9 + RC1_8$	**0.605**	**1.533**	**1.533**	4.966
$RC0_9 + RC3_{12}$	**0.598**	**1.491**	**1.491**	3.306
$RC0_9 + RC6_{13}$	**0.6**	**1.5**	**1.5**	3.338
$RC0_9 + RC9_{12}$	**0.65**	**1.89**	**1.89**	5.154
$RC0_9 + RC10_9$	**0.592**	**1.451**	**1.451**	3.749
$RC1_8$	0.483	0.933	0.933	27.517
$RC1_8 + RC3_{12}$	**0.543**	**1.187**	**1.187**	0.0
$RC1_8 + RC4_9$	**0.542**	**1.185**	**1.185**	3.769
$RC1_8 + RC6_{13}$	**0.625**	**1.666**	**1.666**	5.167
$RC1_8 + RC7_8$	**0.487**	**0.95**	**0.95**	2.419
$RC1_8 + RC8_{10}$	**0.543**	**1.19**	**1.19**	2.845
$RC1_8 + RC9_{12}$	**0.551**	**1.226**	**1.226**	0.0
$RC1_8 + RC10_9$	**0.516**	**1.066**	**1.066**	0.0

4.2 The Second Experiment

To show the effectiveness of the proposed metric another experiment is designed and applied on the Football College network. In this experiment, two real communities are merged with each other and then the joint community is compared with each of the two real communities. The purpose of this experiment is to show that the three metrics R, M and L cannot perfectly capture the density inside the community. In this experiment, a wrong evaluation happens when a metric gives a joint community, a score higher than the two real communities which were used to construct the joint community. In this regard, Table 4 shows the wrong evaluation of metrics R, M, and L, only for two real communities of Football College network. In this table, the first column indicates the community, and the other four columns denoted the metrics scores for the corresponding communities. It should be mentioned that the real communities of Football College network are numbered from 0 to 10. So, $RC0_9$ denoted as the real community of number 0 and size 9. As it can be understood from the table, metrics R, M and L give the combined community higher scores than the real communities. Moreover, however, combined community, $RC1_8 + RC3_{12}$, results in a disconnected community, it earned higher scores than $DC1_8$ from the three metrics. Furthermore, the total number of wrong evaluation of the combined community

Table 5. The number of wrong evaluation of the four metrics for Football College network in the second experiment.

Dataset	R	M	L	GDM
Football College	77/110	78/110	78/110	0/110

experiment is indicated in Table 5 for four metrics. Respecting this table, among 110 possible comparisons, *GDM* has no wrong evaluation. However, the other three metrics *R*, *M* and *L* have 77, 78 and 78 wrong assessments, respectively. This experiment shows that the three above-mentioned metrics are designed to compare the same communities with only one node difference. However, the proposed metric in this paper is capable of comparing every community for a given node. This metric is aimed to assess the quality of detected communities instead of only comparing them with real communities. Since real communities of some real-world networks are unknown, there is a need for a comprehensive local quality metric to evaluate the quality of detected communities. Therefore, based on the results, analyses, and discussions, the contributions of this work could be summarized as follows:

- Considering geodesic distance as an auxiliary element showing the density inside a community, the proposed metric, *GDM*, can comprehensively evaluate the quality of a given community,
- Using *GDM* as a metric, it is easy to compare the quality of different detected communities for a given node,
- *GDM* is able to recognize overlapping nodes of communities,
- *GDM* is capable of measuring the quality of communities without using any algorithm,
- To evaluate the quality of detected communities, *GDM* can be used as an alternative instead of comparing them with real communities.

5 Conclusion and Future Work

This research proposes an evaluation metric to evaluate the quality of any community using the geodesic distance of the members of the community independent of any algorithm. In this study, the deficiencies and drawbacks of a number of well-known metrics are considered and according to those drawbacks, a new metric is proposed. The experimental results indicate that the *GDM* metric can be used as a comprehensive quality metric to assess detected communities from different detection algorithms. Considering the advantages of *GDM* metric compared to the other metrics, the following directions are also interesting for the future works:

- Employing big datasets to evaluate the proposed metric.
- Choosing some other metrics including global metrics to be compared with the *GDM*.
- Expanding *GDM* for directed or weighted networks.

References

1. Chen, J., Zaïane, O., Goebel, R.: Local community identification in social networks. In: 2009 International Conference on Advances in Social Network Analysis and Mining, pp. 237–242. IEEE (2009)
2. Clauset, A.: Finding local community structure in networks. Phys. Rev. E **72**(2), 026132 (2005)
3. Dao, V.-L., Bothorel, C., Lenca, P.: Estimating the similarity of community detection methods based on cluster size distribution. In: Aiello, L.M., Cherifi, C., Cherifi, H., Lambiotte, R., Lió, P., Rocha, L.M. (eds.) COMPLEX NETWORKS 2018. SCI, vol. 812, pp. 183–194. Springer, Cham (2019). https://doi.org/10.1007/978-3-030-05411-3_15
4. Dourisboure, Y., Geraci, F., Pellegrini, M.: Extraction and classification of dense communities in the web. In: Proceedings of the 16th International Conference on World Wide Web, pp. 461–470 (2007)
5. Evans, T.S.: Clique graphs and overlapping communities. J. Stat. Mech.: Theory Exp. **2010**(12), P12037 (2010)
6. Ghasemian, A., Hosseinmardi, H., Clauset, A.: Evaluating overfit and underfit in models of network community structure. IEEE Trans. Knowl. Data Eng. **32**, 1722–1735 (2019)
7. Girvan, M., Newman, M.E.: Community structure in social and biological networks. Proc. Natl. Acad. Sci. **99**(12), 7821–7826 (2002)
8. Jebabli, M., Cherifi, H., Cherifi, C., Hamouda, A.: Community detection algorithm evaluation with ground-truth data. Physica A: Stat. Mech. Appl. **492**, 651–706 (2018)
9. Lakhdari, A., Chorana, A., Cherroun, H., Rezgui, A.: A link strength based label propagation algorithm for community detection. In: 2016 IEEE International Conferences on Big Data and Cloud Computing (BDCloud), Social Computing and Networking (SocialCom), Sustainable Computing and Communications (SustainCom) (BDCloud-SocialCom-SustainCom), pp. 362–369. IEEE (2016)
10. Luo, F., Wang, J.Z., Promislow, E.: Exploring local community structures in large networks. In: 2006 IEEE/WIC/ACM International Conference on Web Intelligence (WI 2006 Main Conference Proceedings), WI 2006, pp. 233–239. IEEE (2006)
11. Luo, W., Lu, N., Ni, L., Zhu, W., Ding, W.: Local community detection by the nearest nodes with greater centrality. Inf. Sci. **517**, 377–392 (2020)
12. Luo, W., Zhang, D., Jiang, H., Ni, L., Hu, Y.: Local community detection with the dynamic membership function. IEEE Trans. Fuzzy Syst. **26**(5), 3136–3150 (2018)
13. Luo, W., Zhang, D., Ni, L., Lu, N.: Multiscale local community detection in social networks. IEEE Trans. Knowl. Data Eng. 1–1 (2019). https://doi.org/10.1109/TKDE.2019.2938173
14. Lusseau, D., Schneider, K., Boisseau, O.J., Haase, P., Slooten, E., Dawson, S.M.: The bottlenose dolphin community of doubtful sound features a large proportion of long-lasting associations. Behav. Ecol. Sociobiol. **54**(4), 396–405 (2003). https://doi.org/10.1007/s00265-003-0651-y
15. Price, B.L., Morse, B., Cohen, S.: Geodesic graph cut for interactive image segmentation. In: 2010 IEEE Computer Society Conference on Computer Vision and Pattern Recognition, pp. 3161–3168. IEEE (2010)
16. Wu, L., Bai, T., Wang, Z., Wang, L., Hu, Y., Ji, J.: A new community detection algorithm based on distance centrality. In: 2013 10th International Conference on Fuzzy Systems and Knowledge Discovery (FSKD), pp. 898–902. IEEE (2013)

17. Xiao, Y., Siebert, P., Werghi, N.: Topological segmentation of discrete human body shapes in various postures based on geodesic distance. In: Proceedings of the 17th International Conference on Pattern Recognition, ICPR 2004, vol. 3, pp. 131–135. IEEE (2004)
18. Zachary, W.W.: An information flow model for conflict and fission in small groups. J. Anthropol. Res. **33**(4), 452–473 (1977)
19. Zhen-Qing, Y., Ke, Z., Song-Nian, H., Jun, Y.: A new definition of modularity for community detection in complex networks. Chin. Phys. Lett. **29**(9), 098901 (2012)

Structuring Code-Switched Product Titles in Indonesian e-Commerce Platform

Ricky Chandra Johanes[1], Rahmad Mahendra[1(✉)], and Brahmastro Kresnaraman[2]

[1] Faculty of Computer Science, University of Indonesia, Depok, Indonesia
rahmad.mahendra@cs.ui.ac.id
[2] Bukalapak, Jakarta, Indonesia

Abstract. The product title in an e-commerce platform has a significant role in attracting consumers' attention to the product. Poor quality of a product title needs to be improved, leading to a need for text structuring on the product title. This research proposes an approach to structure e-commerce product titles that are written in code-switched style, i.e. a pipeline method that consists of four modules; chunking, language identification, promotion words identification, and reformation. The model used in the first three modules involves the Conditional Random Field model. The experiment is carried out to test the robustness of the pipeline system. The results showed the 49,14% for the WER and 82,61% for the BLEU score.

Keywords: Product title · e-Commerce · Code switching

1 Introduction

E-commerce has changed the majority of people's shopping behaviour from offline to online. With e-commerce platforms available on smartphones, shopping is only a few touches away. One of the main features in these platforms is the search engine, where customers can easily find the product they want by only entering a few words (search query) and the engine will return relevant products. The relevancy of products returned basically depends on two factors; the search engine's capability and the quality of the data.

Quality of the data refers to the quality of information available on the products, such as the titles, images, etc. Quality of the images refers to the fidelity of the image, or "clean" based on human judgment. For text-based information, it is not unlikely for it to be on a free-text form, where sellers can write virtually anything to name their products. This leads to potential typos, inappropriate punctuation marks, and other factors that can lower the quality of the data, which in turn lowers the relevancy of the products returned in the search results.

S. Chellappan et al. (Eds.): CSoNet 2020, LNCS 12575, pp. 217–227, 2020.
https://doi.org/10.1007/978-3-030-66046-8_18

When the product titles can be restructured into a more concise one with no unnecessary information, or in other words, the title represents only the basic idea of the product, it will increase its quality and discoverability. As a result, search queries that can match these titles are all virtually correct.

There are multiple ways to take advantage of this fact. First, it is possible to take the results and give them back to the seller as feedback or suggestion. With additional data as supporting evidence, sellers might reconsider to change the titles of the product and benefit from it. If this suggestion seems risky because there is a possibility that it will not meet the sellers well, it is also possible to save the results as metadata of the product in the database. By having a more concise form, it can be used in helping the discoverability of the product by including metadata in the search algorithm. It can also be utilized to find the most suitable catalogs or other forms of grouping.

Indonesia, the fourth most populous country in the world, recognizes Bahasa Indonesia (Indonesian language) as its official language. Nowadays, however, throughout the world - including Indonesia, it is common to communicate in English and adopt it as either their second or third language. English is also used in formal education, business, and - even if only some words - daily life. This also translates into its usage in the titles of products being uploaded into e-commerce platforms. For example, we found that sellers alternated between multiple languages in one utterance known as code-switching [9]. This is frequently found in titles of products in Indonesian e-commerce platforms, which also affects the quality of the data in those platforms.

As far as the authors have researched, there has not been other works on code-switched product titles in the e-commerce data. The contribution of this paper is to propose a pipeline that serves as a base framework for code-mixed English and Indonesian product titles.

2 Related Work

We review the relevant works in the following areas viz attribute extraction, text normalization, code-switching, and language identification.

Since the product title is in free text format, a number of works have attempts to extract structured information from them. Putthividhya and Hu [12] presented the named-entity recognizer that extracts the attributes and value from short product titles (e.g. `brand` from listing titles in clothing category). Mauge [6] proposed unsupervised method to discover product attributes and extract their values from product description. Then, the attributes were clustered using supervised Maximum Entropy algorithm. Melli [8] leveraged supervised linear CRF model to chunk the product title into semantically categorized sub-segments, for instance product brand term, product category term, merchant term, and offering feature term (e.g. subjective adjective promoting the product). Putra et al. [11] applied Named-Entity Recognition model in semi-supervised style using the number of features, such as lexical, position, word shape, and embedding, to extract the attributes of e-commerce products in book domain. Rif'at et al.

[14] worked on product titles from Indonesian e-commerce platform in which 16 different attribute labels were extracted using supervised CRF model.

Short text messages are typically ill-formed. The lexical normalization is common preprocessing task when working on social media data, like Twitter and SMS. Han [3,4] proposed a method for identifying and normalizing lexical variants and generates correction candidates based on morphophonemic similarity. Sridhar [17] applied unsupervised approach for lexical normalization by training a word embedding model from a large English corpora. Beckley [2] designed a system for English lexical normalization task consisting of three steps: creating a substitution list, building the rule based components, and constructing a sentence level reranker. Liu et al. [5] formulated the lexical normalization as a sequence labeling problem. They generated the character level alignment from standard to non-standard variant words leveraging the CRF model.

A few work addressed lexical normalization task on code-switched data. Singh et al. [15] worked on code-switched South Asian and English data. To normalize such code-switched text, they clustered words within the embedding space for the semantic features and Levenshtein distance for lexical features. Anab et al. [1] proposed a pipeline strategy to normalize code-switched Indonesian-English tweet. The pipeline consists of tokenization, language identification, lexical normalization, and translation. As the code-switched texts deal with multiple languages, the language identification is important step to process them. Mave et al. [7] examined word-level language identification on Hindi-English and Spanish-

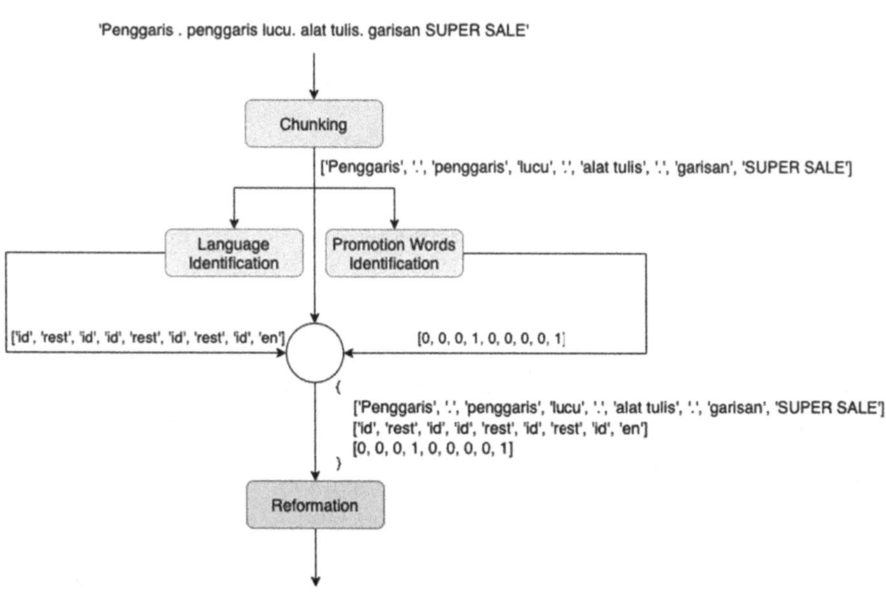

Fig. 1. An input-output example of pipeline model

English data. Soto and Hirschberg [16] performed joint learning to identify the language and to annotate the code-switch text with Part-of-Speech information.

3 Problem Formulation

The main objective of this study is to develop a system to structure the code-switched product title in a marketplace platform in order to improve the system performance and the user experience. We design a pipeline which consists of four modules, i.e. chunking, language identification, promotion words identification, and reformation. The pipeline takes the product title as the input and produce a list of keywords indicating the product in standard form of Indonesian language as the output. Figure 1 depicts the pipeline model with an example of the input and the output.

3.1 Chunking

Chunking module takes a single product title as the input, and then produces a sequence of chunks as the output. Due to non-standard writing style, misuse the whitespace become one of most common problem found in the text. Sometimes, two consecutive words that belong to different phrase are written without whitespace. Otherwise, a whitespace is introduced improperly so that a single word is separated as two tokens.

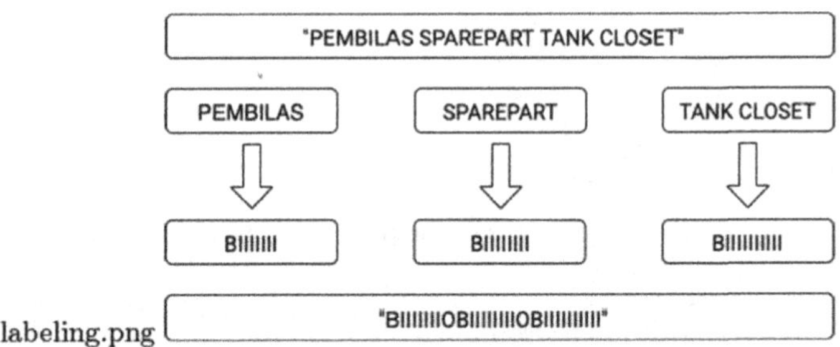

Fig. 2. An example of sequence labeling inside/outside

We approach chunking task as sequence labeling at the character level using the inside/outside chunk representation [13]. We use three different tags: **B** represents the beginning of a new chunk (a word or phrase), **I** indicates the current character being within the chunk (a word or phrase), and **O** indicates that the current character is outside of any chunks. Figure 2 depicts the example of sequence labeling done within a product title.

We use some features for the chunking classifier. The features set comprise of morphological information of a character (e.g. *current character*, *is alphabet*, *is numeric*, *is consonant*, *is vowel*, *is punctuation*, and *is uppercase*), the relative char position, and n-window character (n = 6). The sequence labeling algorithm used is Conditional Random Field (CRF) [18].

3.2 Language Identification

This module takes a sequence of chunks output from the chunking module as the input and then identifies the language code for each chunk. There are five possible values of the language code, i.e. "`en`", "`id`", "`mix`", "`rest`", and "`brand`". The label "id" and "en" are assigned for the chunk that was fully understood as an Indonesian and English word or phrase respectively. While, "mix" is assigned for the chunk that contains of more than one language. The label "brand" is assigned for the chunk that contains a specific individual's or company's brand, and "rest" is assigned for the chunk that does not belong to any language (e.g. proper name, number, measurement units).

We utilize several features for the language identification. The features set comprise of the current chunk in which the language code needs to be determined, morphological information of the current chunk (word or phrase), i.e. *is alphabet*, *is numeric*, *is capitalize*, *is uppercase*, *length*, *is contains digit*, *is contains punctuation*, then followed by relative chunk position. The model of this module is trained using Conditional Random Field.

3.3 Promotion Words Identification

This module proceeds a sequence of chunks that are the output of the chunking module. It identifies whether the chunks is the promotion words or not. We use some features for promotion words identification module. The features set comprise of the current chunk in which the promotion words code needs to be determined, morphological information of the current chunk, i.e. *is alphabet*, *is numeric*, *is capitalize*, *is uppercase*, *length*, *is contains digit*, *is contains punctuation*, then followed by the frequency of the words (according to the predefined threshold), and relative chunk position. The Conditional Random Field algorithm is performed to learn the model for this module.

3.4 Reformation

The reformation module takes the combination of outputs of first three modules in the pipeline: chunking, language identification, and promotion words identification and then reforms the chunk one by one independently. The approach used to reform is adjusted based on the language code. If the language code is either "brand" or "rest", there will be no action because there is not any complete brand corpus that has been built before and the chunk with language code "rest" is case-sensitive and the misuse is very difficult to be identified.

If the language code is "id", "en", or "mix", the chunk is validated by the dictionary. The dictionaries are Kateglo for Indonesian language and word list from Gutenberg Project for English. The resource for validating the chunk with label "mix" is English dictionary. We also leverage `googletrans`, a library built by `Google`, to identify the language of the text at word-level.

After validating with the dictionary or language detector library, the system then test to compare the chunk with each of the dictionary entries by counting their Levenshtein distance. The system return a word that has the smallest Levenshtein distance. If the distance is not zero, it means that word is not found in the dictionary. It is most likely misspelled word that needs to be normalized. Finally, when normal form of the word is not in Indonesian, it is translated using `googletrans`.

4 Experiments

4.1 Data Set

The data set for the experiment consists of the list of registered product titles by a number of sellers in Bukalapak, one of the e-commerce company in Indonesia. Those product titles are in Home and Living category. The data is considerably challenging as the product titles possesses either one of following characteristics, spelling errors, inappropriate usage of punctuation or capital letter, or the use of promotion words.

The gold-standard is constructed by employing two human annotators to tag 1003 product titles. The annotators are asked to conduct four sequential tasks, i.e. extracting list of words and phrases from the product titles, identifying whether extracted phrases are promotional buzz words, identifying the language code for the chunks in the product title, then reforming the word or phrase to the form that we expect.

The number of annotated chunks is 7,979. However, if we remove duplicate chunks, the numbers of unique chunks are only 5,529. Table 1 shows the example of annotated product title. Based on the example, we can see that chunk `YUUK` and `DI COMOT` are labeled as `undefined` which means that those chunks were expected to be removed because they do not convey meaningful information explaining the product, but simply used for promotion purpose.

Table 1. An example of annotated product title

Product Title:
"YUUK DI COMOT PELAMPUNG PEMBILAS SPAREPART TANK CLOSET"

Identified chunk	Language code	Promotion code	Reformed chunk
YUUK	id	1	undefined
DI COMOT	id	1	undefined
PELAMPUNG	id	0	Pelampung
PEMBILAS SPAREPART	mix	0	Pembilas Suku Cadang
TANK CLOSET	en	0	Tangki Kloset

Table 2 depicts that the language code with the highest number of chunks is "id", which has 3,693 chunks. However, if you delete duplicate chunks, there are only 2,609 of chunks with the language code "id" remain.

We also count the number of chunks that were categorized as promotion words and non-promotion words. There are 6870 chunks identified as non-promotion words, but only 5082 of them are unique. There are 1108 chunks identified as promotion chunks and only 447 of them are unique.

Table 2. Statistics of the data for language identification task

No	Language code	Number of chunk(s)	Number of unique chunk(s)
1	`en`	1.589	1.200
2	`id`	3.693	2.609
3	`mix`	106	97
4	`brand`	708	646
5	`rest`	1.123	1.031
6	`undefined`	759	23

Data Splitting. We split the data into 60% training set and 40% testing set using a stratified sampling.

4.2 Evaluation

We evaluate the performance of each proposed module and the pipeline as an integrated system. The first three modules (chunking, language identification, promotion words identification) are evaluated through feature ablation approach and measured by four metrics, i.e. accuracy, precision, recall, and f1-score. The reformation module is evaluated through accuracy metric by comparing the result of the chunk that was normalized by the module and the normalized chunk from annotated data. Moreover, the pipeline is evaluated using WER (Word Error Rate) and BLEU (Bilingual Evaluation Understudy) [10].

Chunking module is evaluated with an entity-level evaluation approach that was categorized into full-match and partial-match. To illustrate, suppose that a product title consists of three words. Full-match considers a word or phrase as true positive when the word or phrase was completely identified by the model and the index of each character of the word in the predicted word and the first product title is the same. Figure 3 depicts an example of the evaluation on chunking module.

Figure 3 shows that the result with full match approach is lower than the result with partial match approach. The reason of this is tied to how the system identifies two words as a chunk, sometimes it can fail and be identified as two chunks (from two words) instead of one chunk (consist of two words). We consider the partial match approach because it does not entirely fail to identify a single chunk by their character level features set. However, it cannot be denied that the expectation of the system is to have great results even within full match approach.

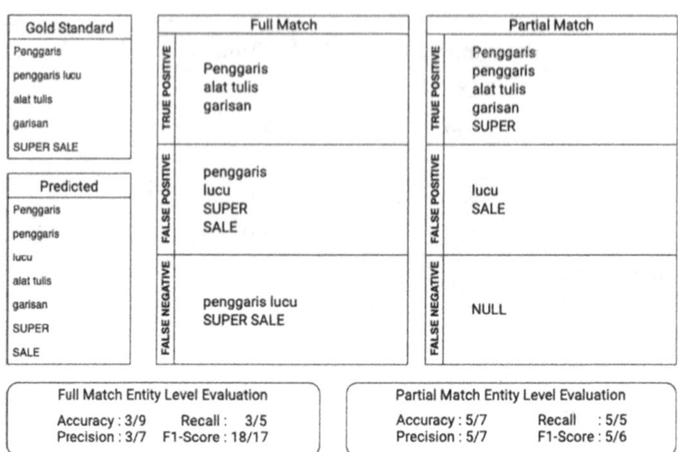

Fig. 3. An example of entity level evaluation on chunking module

4.3 Experimental Result

Chunking. Table 3 shows that several features contribute positively toward the chunk prediction. For precision metric, all of the features contribute positively, seen by both full match an partial match evaluation show no single result being higher when a feature was ablated. For recall and F1-Score metrics, bag of char and char morphology features contribute negatively, but relative position features contribute positively. Furthermore, 6-window char contribute positively on the f1-score when it is evaluated using partial match approach.

Table 3. Result of entity-level evaluation for chunking module (Full match/partial match)

Feature setting	Precision	Recall	F1-Score
All	49,39%/83,10%	51,69%/86,97%	50,51%/84,99 %
All - Bag of Char	49,31%/82,33%	**52,83%/88,22%**	**51,01%/85,17%**
All - 6-Window Char	44,35%/71,70%	**59,57%/96,30%**	**50,85%**/82,20%
All - Char Morphology	49,35%/81,70%	**53,77%/89,01%**	**51,46%/85,20%**
All - Relative Position	49,39%/83,09%	51,69%/86,97%	50,51%/85,16%

Language Identification. The chunk frequency features contribute negatively for language identification (from evaluation of precision and F1-Score). While, incorporating the dictionary lookup features can decrease the precision.

Table 4. Result of ablation study on the language identification module

Feature Setting	Precision	Recall	F1-Score
All	80.44%	60.25%	62.40%
All - Bag of Chunk	60.38%	55.20%	56.73%
All - Chunk Morphology	80.17%	50.37%	52.51%
All - Chunk Frequency	**80.77%**	60.06%	**62.63%**
All - Dictionary Lookup	**82.04%**	50.78%	52.56%
All - Relative Chunk Position	80.09%	60.06%	62.15%

Table 4 presents the result of feature ablation study for language identification experiment.

Promotion Words Identification. Table 5 shows that the chunk frequency and chunk morphology features contribute negatively to when predicting whether a chunk is a promotion word (from evaluation of precision and F1-Score metric).

Table 5. Result of ablation study on the promotion words identification module

Feature setting	Precision	Recall	F1-Measure
All	94.19%	82.70%	87.25%
All - Bag of Chunk	89.23%	75.81%	80.60%
All - Chunk Morphology	**94.47%**	82.62%	**87.29%**
All - Chunk Frequency	**94.48%**	82.62%	**87.29%**
All - Dictionary Lookup	94.19%	82.70%	87.25%
All - Relative Position	94.19%	82.70%	87.25%

Reformation. We find that 7452 chunks (93% of total chunks) chunks can be reformed properly with respect to the gold-standard.

Pipeline. The whole pipeline is evaluated by inserting each product title to the pipeline that had been defined, then comparing the result with the reformed result generated from the ground truth. Before the evaluation began, we had removed the `undefined` from the reformed result because, at the end, we expected those chunks identified as `undefined` removed.

The pipeline evaluation adapt two complementary settings: the micro average and the macro average. In the macro average evaluation, each title is evaluated independently, and then we calculate the average of the BLEU and WER values from all of the results. In the micro average evaluation, all of the titles is concatenated with a default delimiter (whitespace character), then the WER and BLEU scores are calculated. We obtain that the BLEU score are 82,61% (micro average evaluation) and 63,02% (macro average evaluation). On the other hand, the WER is 49,35% when evaluated using macro average and 49,14% using micro average.

5 Conclusion

In this paper, we have proposed a pipeline model comprising of four modules, i.e. chunking, language identification, promotion words identification, and reformation. We tested the pipeline strategy on 1003 annotated product titles from Indonesian e-commerce platform. Overall, the pipeline yields 82.61% for BLEU and 49.14% for WER.

We also evaluated the performance of each module independently. The performance of Conditional Random Field as supervised model is satisfying. Moving forward, we would like to utilize more product attributes and enhanced techniques in order to improve the performance evaluation result of the model.

Acknowledgment. This research was supported by the research grant from Universitas Indonesia, namely Publikasi Terindeks Internasional (PUTI) Saintekkes year 2020 no. NKB-2144/UN2.RST/HKP.05.00/2020.

References

1. Barik, A.M., Mahendra, R., Adriani, M.: Normalization of Indonesian-English code-mixed Twitter data. In: Proceedings of the 5th Workshop on Noisy User-generated Text, W-NUT 2019, pp. 417–424. Association for Computational Linguistics, Hong Kong (2019)
2. Beckley, R.: Bekli: a simple approach to Twitter text normalization. In: Proceedings of the Workshop on Noisy User-generated Text, pp. 82–86. Association for Computational Linguistics, Beijing (2015)
3. Han, B., Baldwin, T.: Lexical normalisation of short text messages: makn sens a #twitter. In: Proceedings of the 49th Annual Meeting of the Association for Computational Linguistics: Human Language Technologies, Portland, Oregon, USA, pp. 368–378 (2011)
4. Han, B., Cook, P., Baldwin, T.: Lexical normalization for social media text. ACM Trans. Intell. Syst. Technol. **4**(1), 1–27 (2013)
5. Liu, F., Weng, F., Wang, B., Liu, Y.: Insertion, deletion, or substitution?: Normalizing text messages without pre-categorization nor supervision. In: 49th Annual Meeting of the Association for Computational Linguistics: Human Language Technologies: Short-Papers, vol. 2, pp. 71–76. Association for Computational Linguistics (2011)
6. Mauge, K., Rohanimanesh, K., Ruvini, J.D.: Structuring E-commerce inventory. In: Proceedings of the 50th Annual Meeting of the Association for Computational Linguistics (Volume 1: Long Papers), Jeju Island, Korea, pp. 805–814 (2012)

7. Mave, D., Maharjan, S., Solorio, T.: Language identification and analysis of code-switched social media text. In: Third Workshop on Computational Approaches to Linguistic Code-Switching, pp. 51–61 (2018)
8. Melli, G.: Shallow semantic parsing of product offering titles (for better automatic hyperlink insertion). In: Proceedings of the 20th ACM SIGKDD International Conference on Knowledge Discovery and Data Mining, KDD 2014, pp. 1670–1678. Association for Computing Machinery, New York (2014)
9. Myers-Scotton, C.: Common and uncommon ground: social and structural factors in codeswitching. Lang. Soc. **22**(4), 475–503 (1993)
10. Papineni, K., Roukos, S., Ward, T., Zhu, W.J.: BLEU: a method for automatic evaluation of machine translation. In: Proceedings of the 40th Annual Meeting of the Association for Computational Linguistics, Philadelphia, Pennsylvania, USA, pp. 311–318 (2002)
11. Putra, H.S., Priatmadji, F.S., Mahendra, R.: Semi-supervised named-entity recognition for product attribute extraction in book domain. In: Proceedings of the The 22nd International Conference on Asia-Pacific Digital Libraries (2020)
12. Putthividhya, D., Hu, J.: Bootstrapped named entity recognition for product attribute extraction. In: Proceedings of the 2011 Conference on Empirical Methods in Natural Language Processing, Edinburgh, Scotland, UK, pp. 1557–1567 (2011)
13. Ramshaw, L.A., Marcus, M.P.: Text chunking using transformation-based learning. In: Armstrong, S., Church, K., Isabelle, P., Manzi, S., Tzoukermann, E., Yarowsky, D. (eds.) Natural Language Processing Using Very Large Corpora. TLTB, vol. 11, pp. 157–176. Springer, Dordrecht (1999). https://doi.org/10.1007/978-94-017-2390-9_10
14. Rif'at, M., Mahendra, R., Budi, I., Wibowo, H.A.: Towards product attributes extraction in Indonesian e-commerce platform. Computacin y Sistemas **22**(4), 1367–1375 (2018)
15. Singh, R., Choudhary, N., Shrivastava, M.: Automatic normalization of word variations in code-mixed social media text. arXiv preprint arXiv:1804.00804 (2018)
16. Soto, V., Hirschberg, J.: Joint part-of-speech and language ID tagging for code-switched data. In: Proceedings of the Third Workshop on Computational Approaches to Linguistic Code-Switching, pp. 1–10. Association for Computational Linguistics, Melbourne, July 2018
17. Sridhar, V.K.R.: Unsupervised text normalization using distributed representations of words and phrases. In: 1st Workshop on Vector Space Modeling for Natural Language Processing, pp. 8–16 (2015)
18. Sutton, C., McCallum, A.: An introduction to conditional random fields. Found. Trends Mach. Learn. **4**(4), 267–373 (2012)

Privacy and Security

Privacy Attack and Defense in Network Embedding

Chao Kong(✉), Baoxiang Chen, Shaoying Li, Yifan Chen, Jiahui Chen, Qi Zhou, Dongfang Wang, and Liping Zhang

School of Computer and Information,
Anhui Polytechnic University, Wuhu, China
kongchao@ahpu.edu.cn, {bxchen1996,shyli1996,yfchen1999,jhchen2000, qzhou1998,dfwang1998,lpzhang1980}@yeah.net

Abstract. Network embedding aims to learn the low-dimensional latent representations of vertices in a network. The existing works have primarily focused on various embedding methods for network data in general and overlooked the privacy security issue of them. For example, when a vertex is deleted from the network, it is easy to achieve the deleted relations by remaining embedding vectors. To address these issues, we propose choosing the node degree with selectivity to study the problem of privacy attack and defense in network embedding. While some existing works are addressed the data protection problem, none of them has paid special attention to combine network embedding with privacy security in such a deep way. Our solution consists of two components. First, we propose a new method named SANE, short for *Sampling Attack in Network Embedding* to utilize remaining vertex information to obtain the deleted relations between vertices as privacy attack. Second, we propose a new privacy defense algorithm named DPNE, short for *Differential Privacy in Network Embedding*, to employ obfuscation function to defend against attacks to prevent deleted related relations being recovered. The two components are integrated in a principled way for considering the node degree to classify the vertices into different levels for sampling. We conduct extensive experiments on several real-world datasets and one synthetic dataset covering the task of link prediction. Both quantitative results and qualitative analysis verify the effectiveness and rationality of our methods.

Keywords: Privacy attack and defense · Differential privacy · Network embedding

1 Introduction

With the popularization of search engines, recommender systems, and other online applications, a huge volume of network data from users has generated.

C. Kong and B. Chen—The two authors contributed equally to this work.

S. Chellappan et al. (Eds.): CSoNet 2020, LNCS 12575, pp. 231–242, 2020.
https://doi.org/10.1007/978-3-030-66046-8_19

To perform predictive analytics on network data, it is crucial to obtain the representations (i.e., feature vectors) for vertices. Network embedding aims to learn the low-dimensional latent representations of vertices in a network. Based on the vertex embeddings, standard machine learning techniques can be applied to address various predictive tasks such as link prediction, clustering, and so on. It is also well known in many research fields, including data mining [1], information retrieval [2], machine learning [3], etc. However, there is an increasing demand for data protection and data recovery, especially in social network scenario. Therefore, it is imperative and challenging to perform effective privacy attack and defense in network embedding task. As shown in Fig. 1(a), given a social network with all the embedding vectors, one user u_4 has been deleted. The intruder attempt to recover the relations related to u_4. A successful defense mechanism should obfuscate the remained relations in the embedding vectors of u_4's neighbors, which is shown in Fig. 1(b).

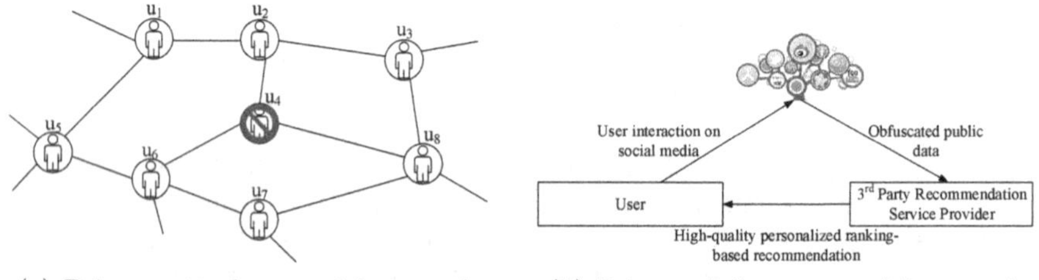

(a) Privacy attack on social network (b) Privacy defense on social network

Fig. 1. Privacy attack and defense scenario

Early studies mainly focus on the extraction of personal information due to the increased overall awareness of privacy protection [4]. In general, one type of attack named model inversion attacks [5]. The other type is the membership inference attack [6]. It aims to extract differences in the confidences of the outputs between data used during the training process and data that was not used. To protect user privacy, privacy-preserving data publishing has been widely studied to protect the private data by distorting the public data before its publication [7]. However, there is a trade-off between privacy and accuracy. On one hand, more distortion of user data leads to better privacy. On the other hand, it also makes the accuracy of the recommendation engine decreased.

Despite effectiveness and prevalence, we argue that these methods can be suboptimal for privacy protection in network embedding due to three primary reasons: 1) existing privacy attack and defense works are not tailored for network embedding, there is no optimization for network and embedding vectors; 2) existing attack techniques do not consider the differences between vertices in a network, it leads to meaningless computing cost; 3) current privacy defense in network embedding relies on retraining, which results in inefficient defense.

Is there a principled way to combine the merits of both kinds of approaches mentioned above? To the best of our knowledge, none of the existing works has paid special attention to combine network embedding with privacy attack and defense simultaneously. While this is our focus in this paper. We first propose SANE which utilizes node degree to select samples to train the classifier to predict the deleted privacy relations in the network. Second, we employ DPNE which aims to obtain an obfuscation function to ensure the minimum privacy leakage to create public embeddings. It means we do not need to refresh the embedding vectors after deleting the data.

The reminder of paper is organized as follows. We shortly discuss the related work in Sect. 2. We formally define the problem and describe the overview of our algorithm in Sect. 3, before delving into details of the proposed method in Sect. 4. We perform extensive empirical studies in Sect. 5 and conclude the paper in Sect. 6.

2 Related Work

Our work is related to the following research directions.

2.1 Network Embedding

As an effective and efficient network analytics method, network embedding (a.k.a. graph embedding) aims at converting the network data into a low dimensional space in which the network structural information and network properties are maximumly preserved [8]. The study of network embedding problem has become a hot topic in recent years and drawn more attention from both academia and industry. In recent years, there are three main types of network embedding methods including factorization-based methods [9,10], random-walk-based methods [11,12], and deep-neural-network-based methods [13,14].

Following the pioneering work of [15], the random-walk-based methods typically apply a two-step solution: first performing random walks on the network to obtain a "corpus" of vertices, and then employing word embedding methods to obtain the embeddings for vertices. Grover et al. [12] introduce the breadth-first sampling and depth-first sampling to change the method of random walk named node2vec. Tang et al. [11] proposed a method called LINE which considers the 2nd-order proximity in random walk to catch more implicit relations. However, Cao et al. [9] doubt whether the LINE can not obtain the deeper relations which just utilize the 2nd-order proximity. They proposed the GraRep which used factorization-based method to obtain high-order relations. Also, Wang et al. [13] used auto-encoder to extend LINE to deep networks to capture the high-order non-linear structure. Nevertheless, all of these methods are in the vertex domain which extracted spatial characteristics of topology, and found the neighbors that adjacent to each vertex. Kipf et al. [14] first used Fourier transformation to define the convolution in the graph, then combine the deep learning to propose the Graph Convolutional Network in the spectral domain. Although our proposed method are varied with these methods, it is independent of the algorithm used for training the embedding.

2.2 Membership Inference Attack

As we described before, we proposed the privacy attack in network embedding in this work as the transfer of general membership inference attack. Li et al. [16] first formulated the inference attacks which meant an adversary could infer the real value of a sensitive entry with high confidence. The basic idea is to extract differences in the confidences of the outputs for data used during training and data was no used. In social networks, Shokri et al. [6] used shadow model to constructed similar training datasets to target dataset to determine if the samples are in the training datasets. In the background of work of Shokri et al. [6], Jia et al. [17] proposed MemGuard to use utility-loss to defend with membership inference attack. This is an interesting game under the attack of membership inference. We choose to intrude noise with differential privacy to the datasets in network embedding to defend the membership inference attack.

2.3 Differential Privacy

According to the attacks considered, existing work can be classified into two categories. The first categorie is based on heuristic technique to protect ad-hoc defined user privacy [7]. The differential privacy [18] which we used in our defense belongs to the second category named uninformative principle [19]. The main contribution of differential privacy is to guarantee user privacy against attacks with arbitrary background knowledge. Sankar et al. [20] chose the conditional entropy as the metric to quantitatively measure privacy leakage. Instead, Calmon et al. [21] chose mutual information as the metric, and to design a privacy protection mechanism based on their measure. The benefits of differential privacy are obvious that it is stricter (i.e., against attacks with arbitrary background knowledge) than normal information-theoretic approaches.

In the privacy community, a few works focus on privacy across social media [22] and network embedding [23]. Most of there works are concentrated in normal databases which ignored the neonatal problem on online social media. Hence, our method offers a novel thought that combines privacy attack and defense in network embedding to deal with the online social media privacy problems.

3 Privacy Attack and Defense Approach

In this section, before we overview our proposed approach, we describe a formal definition of the network embedding problem.

3.1 The Problem Definition

In this paper, we assume $G = (V, E)$ to be an undirected, unweighted and connected network, where V and E denote the set of vertices and edges respectively. In the social networks, the vertices V are the users and the edges E are the friendship links between users. Hence, the privacy data in this scenario as shown in

Figs. 1(a) is the edges between each vertex. Let G be a network, the output of network embedding is computed as $\mathcal{E}(G)$, i.e., a mapping of each vertex to a fixed dimensional vector of d real numbers.

Further, when the vertex v_i is deleted, we denote the remaining network as G_{v_i}. Therefore, the remaining representation of network is $\mathcal{E}(G_{v_i})$. Because we only consider the vertex within a network, it can be shorthanded as $\mathcal{E}_{v_i}$. The $\mathcal{E}_{v_i}$ does not need to retraining, so there is no explicit information in deleted vertex v_i. However, the implicit information remains in the $\mathcal{E}_{v_i}$ which has been influenced by previously existing edges with v_i. When the remaining vertices retraining, we denote the representation of the network as $\mathcal{E}'_{v_i}$.

3.2 Overview of SANE

The privacy attack approach consists of three components as Figs. 2:

Step1. Difference Matrix Calculation. First, we calculate the $\mathcal{E}$ of the network, then remove a vertex v_i, we obtain the $\mathcal{E}_{v_i}$. After retraining, a new embedding $\mathcal{E}'_{v_i}$ is also obtained. Both of the distance matrices Δ_{v_i} and Δ'_{v_i} can be calculated between each vertex pair. We finally obtain the difference matrix by $Diff(\mathcal{E}_{V_i}, \mathcal{E}'_{V_i}) = \Delta_{V_i} - \Delta'_{V_i}$.

Step2. Feature Vectors Construction. In order to determine whether there is a relation between attacked vertex and other vertices, we need feature vectors to train a classifier. For each vertex in the remaining network, we calculate the distance changes to other vertices. The changes interval can be divided into different bins which means the dimension of the feature vector. The number of each bin represents the feature vector's value in this dimension.

Step3. Classifier Training. We use node degree to conduct sampling. In reality, vertex with high node degree contains more information and is more vulnerable to attack. Hence, we sort the node degree in order of high, medium and low to obtain different numbers of samples by $N_s = (\alpha + \beta + \gamma) * N$. For

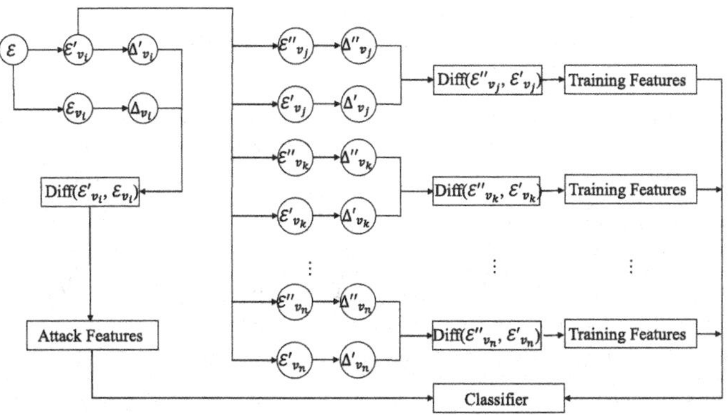

Fig. 2. Workflow of privacy attack

Algorithm 1. DPNE: Differential Privacy in Network Embedding Algorithm

Input: The remaining representation of network $\mathcal{E}_{v_i}$;
Output: Obfuscated representation of network $\hat{\mathcal{E}}_{v_i}$;
1: **for** Each vertex v_j in Remaining network G_{v_i} **do**
2: Obtain the embedding vector e_{v_j} of v_j;
3: Calculate the obfuscation function for v_j;
4: Get the cluster C of v_j, where $v_j \in C$;
5: Obfuscated the user's cluster C to $\hat{C}$ based on obfuscation function;
6: Randomly select a vertex $\hat{v}_k$ in cluster $\hat{C}$;
7: Obfuscate e_{v_j} to $\hat{e}_{v_j}$;
8: **end for**
9: **return** $\hat{\mathcal{E}}_{v_i}$

the retraining representation $\mathcal{E}'_{v_i}$ which has removed vertex v_i, we temporarily remove the sample vertex v_j to retraining a new representation $\mathcal{E}''_{v_j}$. Step 1 and Step 2 are performed for each sample to obtain the final training dataset for constructing the classifier.

3.3 Overview of DPNE

We now present the full DPNE algorithm in Algorithm 1. In this algorithm, the input is the remaining representation of network $\mathcal{E}_{v_i}$ after removing the vertex v_i. The result of this algorithm is to obtain the obfuscated representation. In lines 1–3, for each vertex v_j in the remaining network G_{v_i}, we first obtain its embedding vector e_{v_j} and calculate the corresponding obfuscation function to protect its private data. Specially, we cluster users into a limited and fixed number of groups according to their public data vector. Then, in lines 4–5, we utilize the obfuscation function to obfuscate its cluster C to $\hat{C}$. Finally, all the vertices in a cluster share the similar public data vectors, we randomly select one vertex $\hat{v}_k$ in the cluster $\hat{C}$ and leverage its public data vector as obfuscated embedding vector of v_j as shown in line 6–7. In the end, a whole new obfuscated representation of the network $\hat{\mathcal{E}}_{v_i}$ is obtained.

4 Modeling of Privacy Attack and Defense

We employ a node-degree-based sample to execute the attack and a differential-privacy-based method to defense this inference attack, as we defined in the previous section. When a vertex is deleted, the topological structure is changed, but the remaining information is still in the remaining embeddings. Efficient sampling of the remaining vertices can capture sufficient relations to construct a classifier to recover the deleted relations. The critical idea of defense is to learn an obfuscation function that can obfuscate the vertex to the public data vector. We propose a modeling of privacy attack method SANE and defense method DPNE in the following.

4.1 Sampling Attack via Node Degree

As we described before, inference attack is independent of the algorithm used for training the embedding. Hence, following the workflow of Fig. 2, we first calculate the difference matrix $Diff(\mathcal{E}_{V_i}, \mathcal{E}'_{V_i})$ by the distance matrices between each vertex by Eq. 1:

$$Diff(\mathcal{E}_{V_i}, \mathcal{E}'_{V_i}) = \Delta_{V_i} - \Delta'_{V_i}, \tag{1}$$

where Δ_{V_i} and Δ'_{V_i} are the distance matrices of remaining embeddings of network and the retraining embeddings of network respectively.

After we obtain different matrices, we start to construct feature vectors by calculating the distance changes. This step is to decide the dimension of the feature vector. It divides the range of changes into n bins. Through the hyper-parameter b, we create bins $b_1, b_2, ..., b_n$ that contain the same number of values. We repeat the above steps to create a training dataset for the classifier. In this step, sampling is necessary to decrease the meaningless computation. Node degree is the key to whether a vertex is vulnerable to attack. The vertices are arranged according to the node degree and divided into three parts: high, medium and low with three hyper-parameters α, β, γ as shown in Eq. 2:

$$N_s = (\alpha + \beta + \gamma) * N \quad s.t. \quad (\alpha + \beta + \gamma \leq 1), \tag{2}$$

where the N_s is the total number of samples, and N is the number of reaming vertices. By this equation, three hyper-parameters decide the number of samples in different node degrees, and more discuss about sampling will show in the empirical study. Finally, a classifier can be performed by these training data. Here, we employ the support vector machines as our classifier.

4.2 Privacy Defense via Differential Privacy

To protect the user data, it is necessary to keep two types of data: public data X and private data Y. The basic idea of privacy defense is to reduce the privacy leakage by obfuscating X to obtain $\hat{X}$ based on a probabilistic obfuscation function $p_{\hat{X}|X}$ through Eq. 3:

$$E_{\hat{X},X}(dist(\hat{X}, X)) \leq \Delta X, \tag{3}$$

where $dist(\hat{X}, X)$ is a distance metric obtained by ranking distance. ΔX limits the expected distortion to the obfuscation function $p_{\hat{X}|X}$. In summary, the final target is to learn the $p_{\hat{X}|X}$ that minimizes the privacy leakage under a given distortion budget ΔX.

Following the pioneering work [22], we use historical data to obfuscated another user's data by a clustering step. Calmon et al. [21] proved that privacy leakage ΔL becomes the mutual information between the released public data $\hat{X}$ and the specific private data Y as Eq. 4:

$$\Delta L = I(\hat{X}, Y) = \sum_{\hat{x}\in\hat{X}, y\in Y} p(\hat{x}, y) log \frac{p(\hat{x}, y)}{p(\hat{x})p(y)}. \quad (4)$$

We first combine the joint probability of $\hat{X}$ and Y with marginal probability $p_{\hat{X}}(\hat{x})$, $p_X(x)$ and $p_Y(y)$. Then, we remove the entropy of Y which is a constant for the private data. The following derivation can be obtained as:

$$\begin{aligned} I(\hat{X}, Y) = &\sum_{\hat{x}\in\hat{X}, x\in X, y\in Y} p_{\hat{X}|X}(\hat{x}|x) p_{X,Y}(x, y) \\ &\times log \frac{\sum_{x'\in X} p_{\hat{X}|X}(\hat{x}|x') p_{X,Y}(x', y)}{\sum_{x''\in X, y'\in Y} p_{\hat{X}|X}(\hat{x}|x'') p_{X,Y}(x', y')}. \end{aligned} \quad (5)$$

In Eq. 5, the optimal obfuscation function $p_{\hat{X}|X}$ is learned when minimized the $I(\hat{X}, Y)$ under a given distortion budget ΔX.

5 Empirical Study

To evaluate the performance of SANE and DPNE, we employ them to a representative application on three real-world networks and one synthetic network. Through empirical evaluation, we aim to answer the following research questions:

RQ1: How does SANE perform across different state-of-the-art network embedding methods in link prediction?
RQ2: After the introduction of DPNE, how do different state-of-the-art network embedding methods perform against inference attack in link prediction?

In what follows, we first introduce the experimental settings, and then answer the above research questions in turn to demonstrate the rationality of our methods.

5.1 Experiment Settings

Datasets. For the link prediction task, we utilize two types of datasets. *Facebook*[1], *Hamsterster*[2], and *DBLP*[3] are the real-world datasets. We use snowball sampling for both *Facebook* and *DBLP* datasets. The new network of *Facebook* has 2,000 vertices and 15,534 edges, and the new network of *DBLP* has 2,000 vertices and 8,057 edges. The *Hamsterster* is a social network for people who like hamsters which has 1,788 vertices and 12,476 edges. To better validate our methods, we use the Barabasi-Albert model [24] to construct synthetic scale-free networks. Following the step of pioneering work [23], we set the generated network with 1,000 vertices and a parameter of attachment of 5.

[1] http://konect.uni-koblenz.de/networks/facebook-wosn-links.
[2] http://konect.uni-koblenz.de/networks/petster-friendships-hamster.
[3] http://dblp.uni-trier.de/xml/.

Embedding Algorithms and Parameter Settings. As we introduced in Sect. 2, there are three main types of embedding algorithms. We choose the *LINE* and *node2vec* as the random-walk-based algorithm, the *GraRep* and *TADW* as the factorization-based algorithm, *GCN* and *SDNE* as the deep-neural-network-based algorithm. If not otherwise mentioned, we use the open-source tools OpenNE[4] to imply the network embedding algorithms with default parameters.

Evaluation Measures. For the link prediction task, there are established evaluation measures. We utilize *AUC*, *Precision@10*, *Macro-*F_1 and *Micro-*F_1 as metrics.

Table 1. Performance of the SANE on different networks and network embedding algorithms with and without the defense of DPNE. The value without parenthesis is the performance of embeddings directly under the DANE attack, and the value with parenthesis is the performance of embeddings which are defended by DPNE.

Network	AUC					
	LINE	node2vec	GraRep	TADW	GCN	SDNE
Barabasi	0.83 (0.77)	0.75 (0.68)	0.66 (0.63)	0.58 (0.52)	0.62 (0.55)	0.65 (0.60)
Facebook	0.72 (0.66)	0.74 (0.69)	0.94 (0.86)	0.87 (0.81)	0.73 (0.66)	0.77 (0.73)
Hamsterster	0.73 (0.62)	0.68 (0.61)	0.85 (0.80)	0.77 (0.71)	0.65 (0.55)	0.74 (0.67)
DBLP	0.76 (0.71)	0.66 (0.60)	0.95 (0.89)	0.87 (0.80)	0.68 (0.64)	0.66 (0.60)
Network	Precision@10					
	LINE	node2vec	GraRep	TADW	GCN	SDNE
Barabasi	0.52 (0.42)	0.33 (0.27)	0.32 (0.25)	0.41 (0.33)	0.27 (0.20)	0.31 (0.27)
Facebook	0.45 (0.32)	0.44 (0.37)	0.63 (0.60)	0.52 (0.44)	0.34 (0.29)	0.45 (0.41)
Hamsterster	0.33 (0.26)	0.28 (0.23)	0.41 (0.38)	0.29 (0.24)	0.22 (0.18)	0.25 (0.22)
DBLP	0.15 (0.11)	0.08 (0.07)	0.20 (0.15)	0.23 (0.21)	0.11 (0.09)	0.09 (0.07)
Network	Macro-F_1					
	LINE	node2vec	GraRep	TADW	GCN	SDNE
Barabasi	0.43 (0.31)	0.20 (0.15)	0.17 (0.13)	0.13 (0.10)	0.22 (0.13)	0.21 (0.17)
Facebook	0.34 (0.26)	0.25 (0.17)	0.33 (0.27)	0.31 (0.23)	0.23 (0.20)	0.28 (0.23)
Hamsterster	0.22 (0.21)	0.21 (0.17)	0.24 (0.20)	0.18 (0.15)	0.15 (0.11)	0.13 (0.11)
DBLP	0.14 (0.09)	0.08 (0.07)	0.18 (0.13)	0.17 (0.14)	0.09 (0.08)	0.07 (0.06)
Network	Micro-F_1					
	LINE	node2vec	GraRep	TADW	GCN	SDNE
Barabasi	0.49 (0.33)	0.21 (0.14)	0.17 (0.11)	0.13 (0.10)	0.15 (0.11)	0.17 (0.13)
Facebook	0.22 (0.15)	0.21 (0.16)	0.31 (0.26)	0.30 (0.21)	0.17 (0.14)	0.16 (0.13)
Hamsterster	0.24 (0.20)	0.23 (0.19)	0.15 (0.13)	0.13 (0.10)	0.12 (0.10)	0.13 (0.11)
DBLP	0.12 (0.09)	0.06 (0.06)	0.21 (0.14)	0.16 (0.12)	0.09 (0.08)	0.06 (0.06)

[4] https://github.com/thunlp/openne.

5.2 Performance Comparison (RQ1 & RQ2)

We evaluate the attack on several different networks and embedding algorithms to predict whether a vertex is connected with others, i.e., link prediction. The values outside bracket in Table 1 denote the performance of link prediction task after attacking the original networks by SANE which are trained without defense. The corresponding values in bracket illustrate the results with privacy protection by DPNE. Due to the space limitation, there is no demonstration in the hyper-parameter study. We tune the α, β, γ as 0.005, 0.0025, 0.0025 with the trade-off between the effectiveness and the efficiency.

Table 1 illustrates the performance comparison with and without privacy defense by DPNE after performing privacy attack by SANE on different networks and network embedding algorithms in link prediction task, where we have the following key observations: 1) the attack can recover substantial information of the removed vertex on many networks across several network embedding algorithms. Although in some networks it does not achieve good performance, it also obtains excellent value in several networks such as $AUC = 0.95$ in $DBLP$ with GraRep. It means that in practical situations, it is enough to identify an individual; 2) the embedding algorithm is independent with the inference attack, because the key to the performance of attack lies in the structure of the network rather than the effectiveness of the embedding algorithms. There is no embedding algorithm can perform best over all networks; 3) DPNE can decrease the performance of inference attack intensively (the values in bracket are smaller than the ones outside bracket). For some networks, it can decrease the performance by 0.1 in some metrics. From the trend of variation of performance in all networks across network embedding algorithms, DPNE plays an crucial role in privacy defense.

6 Conclusions

In this paper, we have studied the problem of privacy attack and defense in network embedding. It is a challenging task due to the difference of vertices and cost of retraining. We propose two methods to demonstrate the importance of defense in network embedding and the effectiveness of differential privacy in network embedding. We have illustrated our proposed method on three real-world networks and one synthetic network. Experimental results indicate that traditional network embedding methods are easy to attack, and the conscious defense of it can sharply decrease the effect of attacks.

In our future work, we plan to extend our work to handle the dynamic network embedding problems and deploy a distributed algorithm to support more efficient computation.

Acknowledgment. This work was supported by the National Natural Science Foundation of China Youth Fund under Grant No. 61902001, the Initial Scientific Research Fund of Introduced Talents in Anhui Polytechnic University under Grant

No. 2017YQQ015, the Major Project of Natural Science Research in Colleges and Universities of Anhui Province under Grant No. KJ2019ZD15, and the Natural Science Project of Anhui Education Department under Grant No. KJ2019A0158.

References

1. Chen, W., Liu, C., Yin, J., Yan, H., Zhang, Y.: Mining e-commercial data: a text-rich heterogeneous network embedding approach. In: 2017 International Joint Conference on Neural Networks, IJCNN 2017, Anchorage, AK, USA, 14–19 May 2017, pp. 1403–1410 (2017)
2. Seyler, D., Chandar, P., Davis, M.: An information retrieval framework for contextual suggestion based on heterogeneous information network embeddings. In: The 41st International ACM SIGIR Conference on Research & Development in Information Retrieval, SIGIR 2018, Ann Arbor, MI, USA, 08–12 July 2018, pp. 953–956 (2018)
3. Oluigbo, I., Haddad, M., Seba, H.: Evaluating network embedding models for machine learning tasks. In: Cherifi, H., Gaito, S., Mendes, J.F., Moro, E., Rocha, L.M. (eds.) COMPLEX NETWORKS 2019. SCI, vol. 881, pp. 915–927. Springer, Cham (2020). https://doi.org/10.1007/978-3-030-36687-2_76
4. Veale, M., Binns, R., Edwards, L.: Algorithms that remember: model inversion attacks and data protection law. CoRR, abs/1807.04644 (2018)
5. Papernot, N., McDaniel, P.D., Sinha, A., Wellman, M.P.: SoK: security and privacy in machine learning. In: 2018 IEEE European Symposium on Security and Privacy, EuroS&P 2018, London, United Kingdom, 24–26 April 2018, pp. 399–414 (2018)
6. Shokri, R., Stronati, M., Song, C., Shmatikov, V.: Membership inference attacks against machine learning models. In: 2017 IEEE Symposium on Security and Privacy, SP 2017, San Jose, CA, USA, 22–26 May 2017, pp. 3–18 (2017)
7. Fung, B.C.M., Wang, K., Chen, R., Yu, P.S.: Privacy-preserving data publishing: a survey of recent developments. ACM Comput. Surv. **42**(4), 14:1–14:53 (2010)
8. Cai, H., Zheng, V.W., Chang, K.C.-C.: A comprehensive survey of graph embedding: problems, techniques, and applications. IEEE Trans. Knowl. Data Eng. **30**(9), 1616–1637 (2018)
9. Cao, S., Lu, W., Xu, Q.: GraRep: learning graph representations with global structural information. In: Proceedings of CIKM, pp. 891–900 (2015)
10. Yang, C., Liu, Z., Zhao, D., Sun, M., Chang, E.: Network representation learning with rich text information. In: Proceedings of IJCAI (2015)
11. Tang, J., Qu, M., Wang, M., Zhang, M., Yan, J., Mei, Q.: Line: large-scale information network embedding. In: Proceedings of WWW, pp. 1067–1077 (2015)
12. Grover, A., Leskovec, J.: node2vec: scalable feature learning for networks. In: Proceedings of KDD, pp. 855–864 (2016)
13. Wang, D., Cui, P., Zhu, W.: Structural deep network embedding. In: Proceedings of the 22nd ACM SIGKDD International Conference on Knowledge Discovery and Data Mining, pp. 1225–1234. ACM (2016)
14. Kipf, T.N., Welling, M.: Semi-supervised classification with graph convolutional networks. arXiv preprint arXiv:1609.02907 (2016)
15. Perozzi, B., Al-Rfou, R., Skiena, S.: DeepWalk: online learning of social representations. In: The 20th ACM SIGKDD International Conference on Knowledge Discovery and Data Mining, KDD 2014, New York, NY, USA, 24–27 August 2014, pp. 701–710 (2014)

16. Li, C., Shirani-Mehr, H., Yang, X.: Protecting individual information against inference attacks in data publishing. In: Kotagiri, R., Krishna, P.R., Mohania, M., Nantajeewarawat, E. (eds.) DASFAA 2007. LNCS, vol. 4443, pp. 422–433. Springer, Heidelberg (2007). https://doi.org/10.1007/978-3-540-71703-4_37
17. Jia, J., Salem, A., Backes, M., Zhang, Y., Gong, N.Z.: MemGuard: defending against black-box membership inference attacks via adversarial examples. In: Proceedings of the 2019 ACM SIGSAC Conference on Computer and Communications Security, CCS 2019, London, UK, 11–15 November 2019, pp. 259–274 (2019)
18. Dwork, C.: Differential privacy. In: Proceedings of the Automata, Languages and Programming, 33rd International Colloquium, ICALP 2006, Venice, Italy, 10–14 July 2006, Part II, pp. 1–12 (2006)
19. Machanavajjhala, A., Kifer, D., Gehrke, J., Venkitasubramaniam, M.: L-diversity: privacy beyond k-anonymity. ACM Trans. Knowl. Discov. Data **1**(1), 3 (2007)
20. Sankar, L., Rajagopalan, S.R., Poor, H.V.: Utility-privacy tradeoffs in databases: an information-theoretic approach. IEEE Trans. Inf. Forensics Secur. **8**(6), 838–852 (2013)
21. du Pin Calmon, F., Fawaz, N.: Privacy against statistical inference. In: 50th Annual Allerton Conference on Communication, Control, and Computing, Allerton 2012, Allerton Park & Retreat Center, Monticello, IL, USA, 1–5 October 2012, pp. 1401–1408 (2012)
22. Yang, D., Bingqing, Q., Cudré-Mauroux, P.: Privacy-preserving social media data publishing for personalized ranking-based recommendation. IEEE Trans. Knowl. Data Eng. **31**(3), 507–520 (2019)
23. Ellers, M., Cochez, M., Schumacher, T., Strohmaier, M., Lemmerich, F.: Privacy attacks on network embeddings. CoRR, abs/1912.10979 (2019)
24. Barabási, A.-L., Albert, R.: Emergence of scaling in random networks. Science **286**(5439), 509–512 (1999)

Classifying Malware Using Function Representations in a Static Call Graph

Thomas Dalton(✉), Mauritius Schmidtler, and Alireza Hadj Khodabakhshi

Webroot, San Diego, USA
{tdalton,mschmidtler,ahadjkhodaba}@opentext.com

Abstract. We propose a deep learning approach for identifying malware families using the function call graphs of ×86 assembly instructions. Though prior work on static call graph analysis exists, very little involves the application of modern, principled feature learning techniques to the problem. In this paper, we introduce a system utilizing an executable's function call graph where function representations are obtained by way of a recurrent neural network (RNN) autoencoder which maps sequences of ×86 instructions into dense, latent vectors. These function embeddings are then modeled as vertices in a graph with edges indicating call dependencies. Capturing rich, node-level representations as well as global, topological properties of an executable file greatly improves malware family detection rates and contributes to a more principled approach to the problem in a way that deliberately avoids tedious feature engineering and domain expertise. We test our approach by performing several experiments on a Microsoft malware classification data set and achieve excellent separation between malware families with a classification accuracy of 99.41%.

Keywords: Neural networks · Representation learning · Malware detection · Function call graph · Reverse engineering

1 Introduction

Malware is often classified into families based on certain shared characteristics between samples. It is often very useful to distinguish between malware families in order to detect trends in malware infections over time and to attribute authorship. Traditionally, classifying malware has required teams of threat researchers to perform advanced reverse engineering techniques in order to identify various unique characteristics that define a family. However, cyber threats have exploded in recent years making it difficult for threat researchers to keep up. Malware in particular continues to grow in sophistication with new strains released daily. The practice of malware polymorphism renders traditional automated signature-based approaches ineffective for identifying novel instances of malware.

Webroot is an OpenText company.

S. Chellappan et al. (Eds.): CSoNet 2020, LNCS 12575, pp. 243–254, 2020.
https://doi.org/10.1007/978-3-030-66046-8_20

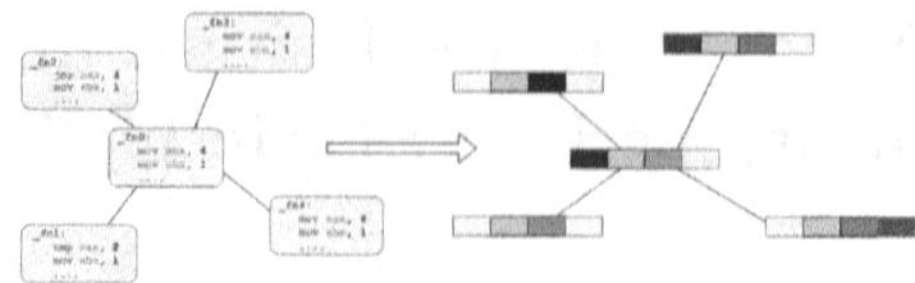

Fig. 1. Variable-length sequences of x86 instructions found in functions are embedded into fixed-length vectors using a GRU-based sequence-to-sequence autoencoder.

In this work, we propose a new approach to malware classification that is inspired by reverse engineering techniques yet requires no domain-specific feature engineering and is invariant to polymorphism. Specifically, we devise a function call-graph framework in which the function representations are learned. By framing the problem through the lens of representation learning, we are able to greatly improve automatic classification while also contributing to human insight which is helpful to determine authorship and intent. By incorporating rich, node-level representations as well as global, structural properties of an executable's call graph, we are able to classify malware families with very high accuracy. Our approach consists of several composite models aimed at learning robust function representations that when employed together form the full classification system.

2 Related Work

Call graphs are commonly used by malware analysts and reverse engineers to manually analyze and inspect executable files [14]. Indeed, many real-world data is naturally represented using graphs. Graphs have been successfully utilized in analyzing data from a wide variety of domains including social network link prediction [11], protein-protein interactions [1], and communication networks [12]. Due to their expressive ability, there is growing interest in applying machine learning techniques directly to graph-represented data to bypass tedious feature engineering. Graph kernels have been proposed to allow for kernel-based methods (such as support vector machines) to be applied directly to graph classification problems. Kernels based on the Weisfeiler-Lehman test of graph isomorphism have grown in popularity in recent years [21] owing to their relative simplicity and strong discriminative ability.

In prior works, call graphs have been used to automatically classify malware but typically these works employ relatively simple graph similarity measures such as graph edit distance or rely on heavy feature engineering involving summary statistics to describe functions in the graph [5,6,9,20]. We build on this call graph approach by incorporating certain representation learning techniques such as autoencoding and clustering [7] to obtain an improved function representation. By extending the well-established call graph strategies with a principled representation learning approach, we forego the tedious and heuristic feature engineering steps of prior work, giving us much better graph representations.

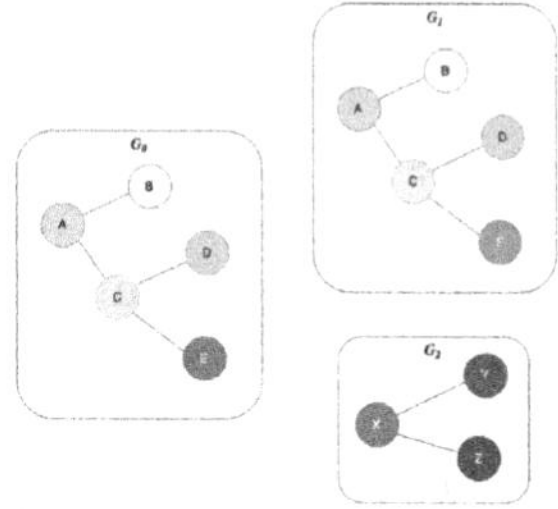

Fig. 2. G_0 and G_1 are considered similar since they both share a similar graph topology and near-identical vertex label sets. On the other hand, G_2 is considered very different from both G_0 and G_1 since it neither shares a graph topology nor a vertex set with the other graphs. The notion of graph "similarity" is clarified in Sect. 3.4

3 Call Graph Framework

A call graph describes the logical control flow of an executable file where functions (or subroutines) are expressed as vertices and edges represent a dependency or call relationship. Call graphs have proven to be extremely useful to security researchers for the analysis and classification of malicious software.

Actual	Predicted
mov edi, edi	mov edi, edi
push ebp	push ebp
mov ebp, esp	mov ebp, esp
sub esp, 48	sub esp, 24
lea ecx, 0x	lea ecx, 0x
push eax	<unknown>
push ecx	push ecx
call <addr>	call <addr>
pop ecx	pop ecx
...	...
...	...

Fig. 3. An example sequence decoding given a latent embedding. The decoder is able to re-create the original sequence with high accuracy, indicating that the latent embedding has captured sufficient information.

The main intuition behind the call graph approach to malware classification is that files sharing similar call graphs are likely to have been generated from the same family. By understanding the logical flow of the executable, we can gain significant insight into the intent of the malware. It is important, therefore, to represent the graph such that we capture rich vertex-level information as well as global, topological properties of the graph. The intuition is illustrated in Fig. 2.

3.1 Overview

We break the malware classification task down into three primary subtasks which we summarise here. In order to obtain a good whole-graph representation of the executable, it is important to first obtain high quality embeddings for the functions contained within the file. For this, we use a sequence-to-sequence autoencoder which captures the sequential nature of the ×86 code instructions into a low-dimensional, latent representation of the function (Fig. 1).

This function embedding helps to make our model more robust to polymorphic techniques since a perturbation in the ×86 instruction space results in a proportional perturbation in the embedding space. It can also be useful for identifying the specific functions that make the file malicious. This function embedding approach is one of the key differentiators between our approach and prior call graph approaches to malware classification.

Having obtained function represention, we cluster the embeddings to obtain discrete labels for the functions and re-label the graph vertices according to their respective cluster IDs. Finally, the whole-graph representation is obtained using a graph kernel inspired by the Weisfeiler-Lehman test of graph isomorphism. The message-passing property of the Weisfeiler-Lehman framework allow us to efficiently capture the global structure of the graph.

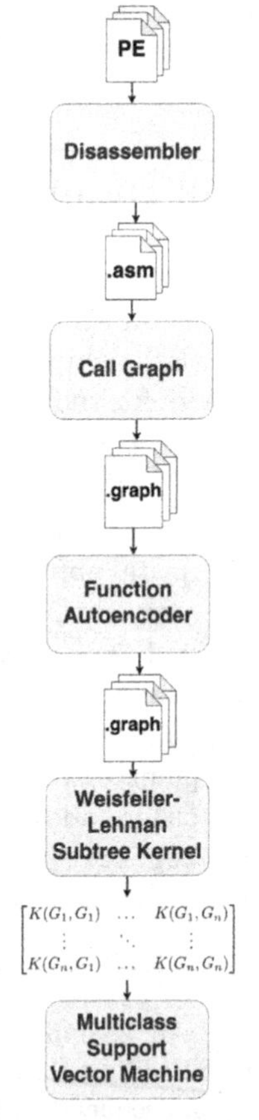

The executable binary files are disassembled into plain text `.asm` files using IDA [10], a popular disassembler widely used by security researchers. Due to the tendency of code sections to contain very long sequences (sometimes upwards of hundreds of thousands of instructions), we break up the sequences into functions or subroutines which provide natural delimiters much like sentences and paragraphs are in a document. These shorter length sequences enable us to use recurrent neural units such as long short-term memory (LSTM) or gated recurrent units (GRU) where the training samples are individual functions with sequences ranging from very short (fewer than 5 instructions) to as long as a few hundred instructions. By following the `call` instructions in the code, we can construct the file's call graph, $G = (\mathcal{V}, \mathcal{E})$ where vertices $v \in \mathcal{V}$ represent functions and edges $e = (v, v') \in \mathcal{V} \times \mathcal{V}$ represent a call dependency.

The model considers only portions of the executable containing valid ×86 code instructions. Traditionally, these code sections are identified by their section header name (e.g. `.text`, `.code`, etc.) but malware often obfuscates intent by using a packer which may result in non-standard section names such as `.brick` or `iuagwws`. In addition to all code found in the standard code sections, our approach also considers such nonstandard sections containing valid ×86 code to construct the call graph.

We make a distinction between two kinds of vertices: internal functions and external functions. Internal functions are those that are present in the executable and subsequently can be disassembled directly. External functions are those

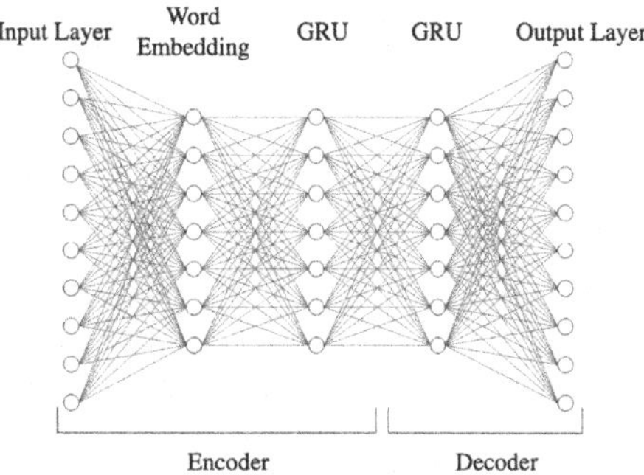

Fig. 4. The sequence-to-sequence autoencoder architecture. The left side of the network encodes the sequence into a fixed-length latent representation. The right side of the network decodes the latent representation back into the original sequence.

which are imported from external libraries and thus the code is not readily available for disassembly. Our graph therefore consists of edges between both internal and external functions. It is worth noting that executable files also contain sections that do not typically contain code such as `.data` or `.reloc`. While these sections provide additional data that is often quite useful for malware classification, we ignore any non-code data for the call graph construction task. It is possible to attribute the graph with the information contained in such non-code sections but that is beyond the scope of this work as our principle concern is that of malware classification using ×86 code representations.

A sequence-to-sequence [23] GRU-based [3] autoencoder architecture was chosen for the task of embedding variable-length sequences of ×86 code instructions into fixed-length, continuous vectors. The function embedding model is comprised of an encoder and a decoder with the encoder being responsible for compressing sequences into low-dimensional, latent representations. A decoder is used to decompress the fixed-length vector back into the original variable-length sequence. Because the autoencoder model must recreate the original sequence from its bottleneck representation, the model learns an efficient, latent representation of the original sequence. After the autoencoder model is trained, the decoder is discarded and only the encoder portion is used to encode new sequences. Sequence-to-sequence architectures have been used successfully in language modeling tasks such as machine translation. Often, the goal is to translate a sequence of words from one language, such as English, into another language, such as French. The input sequence is encoded into a bottleneck layer which captures a latent representation of the sequence irrespective of language. In machine translation tasks, the input and output sequences are usually composed of words drawn from disjoint vocabularies. However, our sequence-to-sequence task involves reconstructing the original input sequence from the bottleneck representation, so the same vocabulary is used for both the input and the output sequences. By reconstructing the original input sequence from the latent representation, the sequence-to-sequence network becomes an autoencoder.

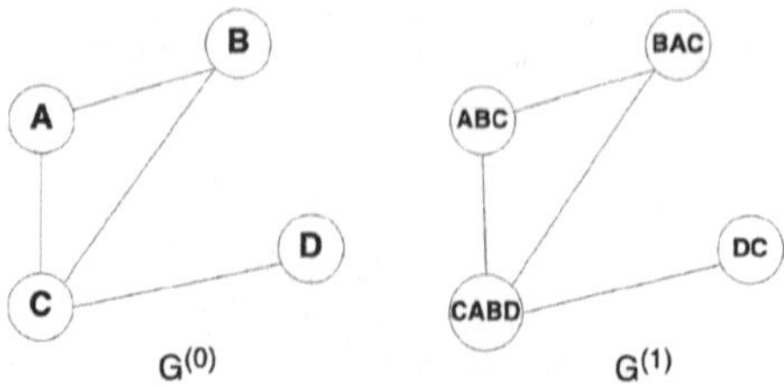

Fig. 5. For each iteration of the Weisfeiler-Lehman algorithm, a new label is generated for each vertex. The new label is derived by concatenating the labels of the adjacent vertices.

3.2 Function Representations

Given a GRU with the following definitions,

$$
\begin{aligned}
z_t &= \sigma_g(W_z x_t + U_z h_{t-1} + b_z) \\
r_t &= \sigma_g(W_r x_t + U_r h_{t-1} + b_r) \\
h_t &= (1 - z_t) \circ h_{t-1} + z_t \circ \sigma_h(W_h x_t + U_h(r_t \circ h_{t-1}) + b_h)
\end{aligned}
$$

the hidden representation of a sequence with length T is taken to be h_T.

During training, when the encoder receives the last token in the sequence $x_T =$ `<end>`, the decoder is initialized with $h_T^{(enc)}$, thus transferring the compressed sequence information to the decoder. In addition to the final hidden state of the encoder, the decoder is also supplied with the original input sequence with a one-step delay. That is, at time step t, the decoder receives the true input x_{t-1} for $t > 1$ where $x_0 =$ `<start>`. This technique of supplying the original sequence with a delay into the decoder is known as teacher forcing.

The decoder, therefore, is trained to predict the next token of the sequence given the hidden state of the encoder and the previous time step. This helps to greatly speed up the training of the autoencoder. An example decoding is illustrated in Fig. 3. After training is completed, the decoder portion of the model is thrown away and only the encoder is used to obtain latent representations for function sequences.

It is common for authors of malware to obfuscate the intent of a file by adding junk instructions such as no-op instructions. Because the function is represented in a latent space, it is relatively immune to such common obfuscation tactics which can often thwart signature-based or count-based solutions.

In our model, input sequences are tokenized as the full ×86 assembly instruction after replacing relative memory address locations with an `<addr>` string. The vocabulary is thus composed of the top 20,000 most common ×86 instructions found in the corpus plus the `<start>` and `<end>` tokens.

The sequence-to-sequence autoencoder network is constructed as in Fig. 4 with three hidden layers – two in the encoder and one in the decoder. The first hidden layer in the encoder is a fully connected layer for learning ×86 instruction embedding vectors of length 64. The weights in this layer can be pre-trained using a Word2vec [13], GloVe [16], or some other similar unsupervised word embedding technique. However in our experiments we observed no ill effects from initializing the weights randomly and learning the instruction embedding directly as part of the autoencoder training.

3.3 Function Clustering

Algorithm 1: Weisfeiler-Lehman Subtree Graph Kernel

```
Input: G, G', h
Output: k^(h)(G, G')
for i ← 1 to h do
    for v ∈ V do
        N_v = neighbors(v)
        S_v = sort(N_v)
        v, σ_v = hash(S_v)
    end
    for v' ∈ V' do
        N_v' = neighbors(v')
        S_v' = sort(N_v')
        v', σ_v' = hash(S_v')
    end
end

φ(G) = [c(G, σ_0), ..., c(G, σ_s)]
φ(G') = [c(G', σ_0), ..., c(G', σ_s)]

return ⟨φ(G), φ(G')⟩
```

Having obtained an ×86 instruction sequence encoder, we embed all internal functions found in the function call graph and attribute the vertices with their respective embeddings. External vertices representing imported functions or APIs remain non-attributed since we are unable to obtain function embeddings for these functions. They therefore retain their discrete external labels. The graphs then are composed of two types of vertices: internal functions with continuous attributes but arbitrary discrete labels and external functions with discrete labels but no continuous attributes. In order to carry out the graph classification task with established Weisfeiler-Lehman kernels, we must first obtain learned discrete labels for internal functions. We achieve this by clustering their continuous embeddings and labeling clusters according to their cluster identifier. We can then label the internal functions in the graph with their discrete cluster identifier. For the purposes of graph classification, our labels can be non-descriptive (e.g. $C_1, C_2, ...$) but it may be beneficial in future work to consider assigning descriptive cluster labels to aid humans in manual threat research analysis.

Even modestly-sized files can contain tens of thousands of individual functions so it is important to be able to scale our clustering task for many function samples. Thus, we use the popular mini-batch K-means clustering algorithm [19] as it is easily able to scale to many millions of samples. Using the so-called "elbow method", we found that $k = 7000$ was a reasonable choice for the number of clusters for our data sets. Although several hierarchical- and density-based clustering algorithms have been found to yield superior results over K-means, these algorithms are generally unable to scale to many samples.

3.4 Graph Classification

A graph kernel is a function that computes an inner product between graphs and can be thought of as a way to measure graph similarity. Graph kernels are widely studied since they allow kernel-based machine learning algorithms such as SVMs to be applied directly to graph-structured data. Most graph kernels are based on the Weisfeiler-Lehman test of graph isomorphism. Indeed, we employ the popular Weisfeiler-Lehman subtree kernel algorithm to obtain the whole-graph feature vector. Once a feature vector for the graph is obtained, we can compute a pairwise kernel matrix and train an SVM for malware classification.

Let the Weisfeiler-Lehman kernel with base kernel k be defined as

$$K_{WL}^{(h)}(G, G') = \sum_{i=0}^{h} \alpha_i k(G_i, G_i')$$

where $\{G_0, G_1, ..., G_h\}$ and $\{G_0', G_1', ..., G_h'\}$ are sequences of graphs that the Weisfeiler-Lehman algorithm generates from G and G' respectively after h iterations. For each iteration of the Weisfeiler-Lehman algorithm, each vertex obtains a new label by concatenating the labels of the adjacent vertices. This process is illustrated for one iteration of the algorithm in Fig. 5. The Weisfeiler-Lehman kernel, then, is simply the weighted sum of the base kernel function applied to the graphs generated by the Weisfeiler-Lehman algorithm. Let the subtree base kernel k be defined as the inner product between $\phi(G)$ and $\phi(G')$

$$k(G, G') = \langle \phi(G), \phi(G') \rangle$$

where $\phi(Q) = [c(Q, \sigma_0), c(Q, \sigma_1), ..., c(Q, \sigma_s)]$ and $c(Q, \sigma_i)$ is the count of vertex label $\sigma_i \in \Sigma^{(h)}$ occurring in the graph Q. The set of vertex labels obtained after h iterations of the Weisfeiler-Lehman algorithm is denoted as $\Sigma^{(h)}$. To compute the kernel matrix, we compute the pairwise kernels for all graphs as

$$K^{(h)} = \begin{bmatrix} k^{(h)}(G_1, G_1) & \dots & k^{(h)}(G_1, G_N) \\ k^{(h)}(G_2, G_1) & \dots & k^{(h)}(G_2, G_N) \\ \vdots & \ddots & \vdots \\ k^{(h)}(G_N, G_1) & \dots & k^{(h)}(G_N, G_N) \end{bmatrix}$$

Shervashidze, et al. (2011) have shown that for N graphs with n vertices and m edges, the Weisfeiler-Lehman subtree kernel of height h can be computed in $O(Nhm + N^2hn)$ time. This kernel matrix can be supplied directly to a one-versus-all support vector machine with Platt scaling in order to obtain the class probabilities [17].

4 Experiments

4.1 Setup

We performed three separate end-to-end experiments of our malware classifier system which is composed of the individually trained components below. Each component feeds into the next to form the final multiclass classifier system.

- Sequence-to-sequence autoencoder model
- K-means clustering model
- Weisfeiler-Lehman subtree kernel model

Table 1. Malware descriptions

Family name	Samples	Type
Ramnit	1263	Worm
Lollipop	2306	Adware
Kelihos_ver3	2931	Backdoor
Vundo	344	Trojan
Simda	33	Backdoor
Tracur	663	TrojanDownloader
Kelihos_ver1	382	Backdoor
Obfuscator.ACY	1158	Obfuscated Malware
Gatak	954	Backdoor

Ten percent of the original data set was withheld from training altogether, not seen by any of the individual sub-models and was used only for testing the composite classifier models. Ten percent of the training set was used for validation. Deep learning library Keras [4] was used to construct and train the sequence-to-sequence network. The network was trained on an NVIDIA Tesla K80 GPU. We used the GraKeL [22] implementation of the Weisfeiler-Lehman algorithm with three iterations to obtain the Weisfeiler-Lehman graphs and the kernel matrix. The scikit-learn [15] implementation for support vector machines based on LIBSVM [2] was used for the graph classification task with hyperparameters C and γ being obtained through grid search.

4.2 Data Set

We use the Microsoft Malware Classification data set [18] to evaluate our approach (Table 1). The data set consists of samples from nine different malware families. Each sample in the data set is composed of a pre-disassembled `.asm` file generated by IDA and a sanitized hexadecimal representation of the original executable. Our approach makes use of only the `.asm` and furthermore only takes advantage of the parsable code sections. Having obtained only the publicly available training set of 10,867 samples, we were able to extract function call graphs for 10,152 samples due, in part, to certain samples being packed or otherwise obfuscated.

Table 2. Results summary

Family Name	Precision	Recall	F1-Score	TP	FP	FN	TN	Support
Ramnit	0.970	0.995	0.982	382	12	2	2682	384
Lollipop	0.997	1.000	0.998	708	2	0	2358	708
Kelihos_ver3	1.000	1.000	1.000	861	0	0	2205	861
Vundo	0.989	1.000	0.994	93	1	0	2973	93
Simda	1.000	1.000	1.000	15	0	0	3051	15
Tracur	0.984	1.000	0.992	180	3	0	2886	180
Kelihos_ver1	1.000	0.967	0.983	87	0	3	2979	90
Obfuscator.ACY	1.000	0.974	0.987	368	0	10	2698	378
Gatak	1.000	0.992	0.996	354	0	3	2712	357

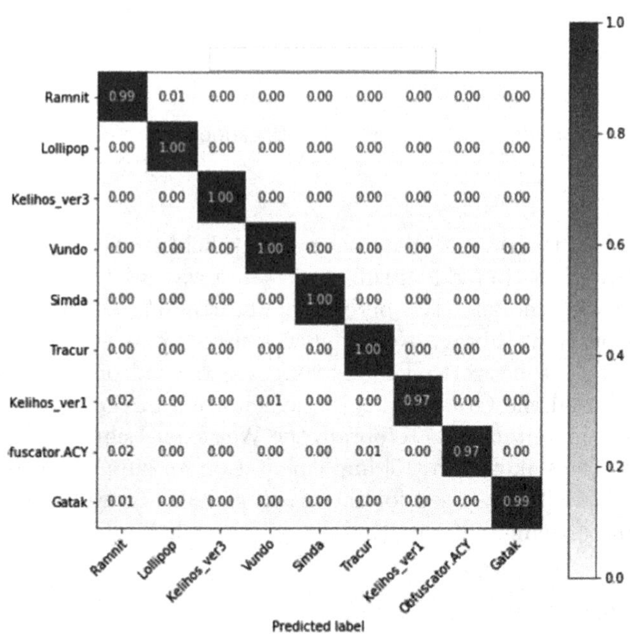

Fig. 6. Normalized confusion matrix

4.3 Results

We achieved a prediction accuracy of 99.41% in the malware family classification task (Fig. 6). Our approach outperforms other malware classifiers that involve extensive feature engineering or extract significantly more data from the executable such as non-code data [8,9,20]. Since we only use the code sections of the executable, we expect that incorporating additional data such as the `.rsrc` and `.idata` sections would help to further improve classification results. Table 2 summarizes the results across the three experiments.

5 Conclusion

In this work we applied several machine learning techniques to the problem of malware detection and achieved over 99% accuracy in the malware classification task using a composite model. A sequence-to-sequence autoencoder was used to obtain dense, latent representations of ×86 code which helped our model account for anti-malware evasion practices. We then clustered the function representations of the functions and obtained discrete function labels. Using the discrete labels, we constructed a function call graph where vertices represent functions and are labeled according to their cluster IDs. The Weisfeiler-Lehman graph kernel framework was used to obtain the Weisfeiler-Lehman graphs and to construct a kernel matrix which allowed us to ultimately perform the graph classification task using a support vector machine.

Acknowledgment. Special thanks to our colleague, Andrew Sandoval, for his valuable contributions and feedback throughout this work.

References

1. Airola, A., Pyysalo, S., Björne, J., Pahikkala, T., Ginter, F., Salakoski, T.: A graph kernel for protein-protein interaction extraction. In: Proceedings of the Workshop on Current Trends in Biomedical Natural Language Processing, pp. 1–9. BioNLP 2008, Association for Computational Linguistics, Stroudsburg, PA, USA (2008). http://dl.acm.org/citation.cfm?id=1572306.1572308
2. Chang, C.C., Lin, C.J.: LIBSVM: a library for support vector machines. ACM Trans. Intell. Syst. Technol. **2**, 27:1–27:27 (2011). software available at http://www.csie.ntu.edu.tw/~cjlin/libsvm
3. Cho, K., et al.: Learning Phrase Representations using RNN Encoder-Decoder for Statistical Machine Translation. arXiv e-prints arXiv:1406.1078, June 2014
4. Chollet, F., et al.: Keras. https://keras.io (2015)
5. Dam, K.H.T., Touili, T.: Malware detection based on graph classification. In: ICISSP (2017)
6. Dullien, T.: Graph-based comparison of executable objects (2005)
7. Goodfellow, I., Bengio, Y., Courville, A.: Deep Learning. The MIT Press, Cambridge (2016)
8. Hassen, M., Carvalho, M.M., Chan, P.K.: Malware classification using static analysis based features. In: 2017 IEEE Symposium Series on Computational Intelligence (SSCI), pp. 1–7, November 2017. https://doi.org/10.1109/SSCI.2017.8285426
9. Hassen, M., Chan, P.: Scalable function call graph-based malware classification. In: Proceedings of the Seventh ACM on Conference on Data and Application Security and Privacy, CODASPY 2017, pp. 239–248, March 2017. https://doi.org/10.1145/3029806.3029824
10. Hex-Rays: The ida pro disassembler and debugger. https://www.hex-rays.com/products/ida/, January 2011
11. Liben-nowell, D., Kleinberg, J.: The link prediction problem for social networks. J. Am. Soc. Inf. Sci. Technol. **58** (2003). https://doi.org/10.1002/asi.20591
12. Mesbahi, M., Egerstedt, M.: Graph theoretic methods in multiagent networks. Princeton University Press (2010)

13. Mikolov, T., Chen, K., Corrado, G., Dean, J.: Efficient estimation of word representations in vector space. arXiv preprint arXiv:1301.3781 (2013)
14. Murphy, G.C., Notkin, D., Griswold, W.G., Lan, E.S.: An empirical study of static call graph extractors. ACM Trans. Softw. Eng. Methodol. **7**(2), 158–191 (1998). https://doi.org/10.1145/279310.279314
15. Pedregosa, F., et al.: Scikit-learn: machine learning in Python. J. Machine Learn. Res. **12**, 2825–2830 (2011)
16. Pennington, J., Socher, R., Manning, C.: Glove: global vectors for word representation. In: Proceedings of the 2014 Conference on Empirical Methods in Natural Language Processing (EMNLP), pp. 1532–1543 (2014)
17. Platt, J.C.: Probabilistic outputs for support vector machines and comparisons to regularized likelihood methods. In: Advances In Large Margin Classifiers, pp. 61–74. MIT Press (1999)
18. Ronen, R., Radu, M., Feuerstein, C., Yom-Tov, E., Ahmadi, M.: Microsoft Malware Classification Challenge. arXiv e-prints arXiv:1802.10135, February 2018
19. Sculley, D.: Web-scale k-means clustering. In: Proceedings of the 19th International Conference on World Wide Web, pp. 1177–1178. WWW 2010, ACM, New York, NY, USA (2010). https://doi.org/10.1145/1772690.1772862
20. Searles, R., et al.: Parallelization of machine learning applied to call graphs of binaries for malware detection. In: 25th Euromicro International Conference on Parallel, Distributed and Network-based Processing (PDP), pp. 69–77. IEEE (2017)
21. Shervashidze, N., Schweitzer, P., Leeuwen, E.J.v., Mehlhorn, K., Borgwardt, K.M.: Weisfeiler-lehman graph kernels. J. Machine Learn. Res. **12**(Sep), 2539–2561 (2011)
22. Siglidis, G., Nikolentzos, G., Limnios, S., Giatsidis, C., Skianis, K., Vazirgiannis, M.: Grakel: a graph kernel library in python. arXiv preprint arXiv:1806.02193 (2018)
23. Sutskever, I., Vinyals, O., Le, Q.V.: Sequence to sequence learning with neural networks. In: Advances in Neural Information Processing Systems, pp. 3104–3112 (2014)

Characterizing the Cryptocurrency Market During Crisis

Kin-Hon Ho[1(✉)], Wai-Han Chiu[2], and Chin Li[3]

[1] Department of Computing, The Hang Seng University of Hong Kong, Sha Tin, Hong Kong
royho@hsu.edu.hk

[2] Department of Supply Chain and Information Management, The Hang Seng University of Hong Kong, Sha Tin, Hong Kong
memorychiu@hsu.edu.hk

[3] Hong Kong – Shenzhen Finance Research Centre, The Chinese University of Hong Kong, Sha Tin, Hong Kong
chinli@cuhk.edu.hk

Abstract. We conduct a network analysis with centrality measures, using historical daily close prices of top 120 cryptocurrencies between 2013 and 2020, to analyze the dynamic evolution and characteristics of the current cryptocurrency market. Our study has two primary findings: (1) the overall return correlation among the cryptocurrencies is weakening from 2013 to 2016 and then strengthening thereafter; (2) cryptocurrencies that are primarily used for transaction payment, notably BTC, dominate the market until mid-2016, followed by those developed for applications using blockchain as the underlying technology, particularly data storage and recording such as MAID and FCT, between mid-2016 and mid-2017. Since then, ETH has replaced BTC to become the benchmark cryptocurrencies. Interestingly, during the outbreak of COVID-19, QTUM and BNB have intermittently replaced ETH to take the leading positions, possibly due to their active community engagement during the pandemic.

Keywords: Cryptocurrency · Network analysis · Centrality measures · COVID-19

1 Introduction

Over the past two decades, there has been considerable work on how network analysis can be used to better understand the financial markets [1]. Network can be used to model the interactions among different financial assets such as stocks, currencies and commodities. One of the prominent techniques is the use of correlation-based network to understand and forecast the dynamics in the financial markets. In the network, nodes and edges represent financial assets and their correlations, respectively. Then, a network construction method is used to construct a less complex network. With this simplified network, centrality measures can be used to identify important or influential nodes or assets that play leadership roles in the financial markets. The aim of this paper is to

S. Chellappan et al. (Eds.): CSoNet 2020, LNCS 12575, pp. 255–266, 2020.
https://doi.org/10.1007/978-3-030-66046-8_21

apply network analysis with centrality measures to analyze the dynamic evolution and characteristics of the current cryptocurrency market. Using historical daily close price of top 120 cryptocurrencies between 2013 and 2020, our study has two primary findings: (1) the overall return correlation among the cryptocurrencies is weakening from 2013 to 2016 and then strengthening thereafter; (2) cryptocurrencies that are primarily used for transaction payment, notably BTC, are influential until mid-2016. Followed by this, the influential cryptocurrencies are those developed for applications using blockchain as the underlying technology, particularly data storage and recording such as MAID and FCT, between mid-2016 and mid-2017. Since then, ETH, and other strongly correlated cryptocurrencies such as ADA, NEO and OMG, have replaced BTC to become the benchmark cryptocurrencies. Interestingly, during COVID-19, QTUM and BNB have intermittently replaced ETH to take the leading positions, possibly due to their active community engagement during the pandemic.

With respect to cryptocurrency research, the work in [2] conducted a correlation analysis and discovered that those that were similar in codebases were positively correlated. The work in [3] used network analysis to analyze 16 cryptocurrencies by Minimum Spanning Tree (MST) and hierarchical tree methods. Their results revealed that ETH was the core node of the cryptocurrency network, while BTC was one of its branches. The evolution of the cryptocurrency market is studied in [5] and they found that cryptocurrencies that were identified as dominant were not always the most popular that were usually the ones with the highest capitalization (e.g., BTC and ETH). However, all these work focused either on a specific (or spliced) time period or on a very specific set of cryptocurrencies, which did not investigate the time-varying dynamic evolution of the cryptocurrency market as cryptocurrencies are entering the market at different times. Thus, we can identify which cryptocurrencies are influential during which periods of the market evolution, including the COVID-19 pandemic.

2 Data

The data used in our study is the time series of daily close prices of top 120 cryptocurrencies by market capitalization as of 14.08.2020. This sample of cryptocurrencies can be considered as a good representative of the cryptocurrency market since it represents over 90% of the total cryptocurrency market capitalization as of this date. Our data covers the period from 29.04.2013 to 14.08.2020, in total 2665 days, collected from http://coinmarketcap.com [13]. To begin our work, we transform the close price into logarithmic return by using the formula:

$$r_i(t) = ln\ p_i(t) - ln\ p_i(t-1) \tag{1}$$

where $r_i(t)$ and $p_i(t)$ are the return and close price of cryptocurrency i at day t.

3 Methodology

3.1 Cross-Return Correlation Coefficient Matrix

The input to construct a network for analysis is the return correlation among all pairs of the cryptocurrency. We create a cross-return correlation coefficient matrix using the

Pearson product-moment correlation for every pair of the cryptocurrency i and j where r_i represents the return vector of cryptocurrency i of a time period:

$$r_i c_{ij} = \frac{\langle r_i . r_j \rangle - \langle r_i \rangle \langle r_j \rangle}{\sqrt{\left(\langle r_i^2 \rangle - \langle r_i \rangle^2\right)\left(\langle r_j^2 \rangle - \langle r_j \rangle^2\right)}} \tag{2}$$

In this study, each time period corresponds to 182 days as we investigate the impacts of COVID-19 on the cryptocurrency market while setting the time period to be the current length or duration of the pandemic since the outbreak in the world (i.e. around 6 months). The result of the calculation is a $N \times N$ cross-return correlation coefficient matrix where N is the total number of the cryptocurrencies (i.e. $N = 120$ in this study).

3.2 Network Construction

When constructing a network, a node represents a cryptocurrency while an edge represents the return correlation between a pair of connected cryptocurrency nodes. A fully connected network is initially constructed, which often contains a large amount of redundant information. With the cross-return correlation coefficient matrix, we adopt MST to construct a less complex and undirected cryptocurrency network as it is robust, simple and includes all the cryptocurrencies for a complete analysis. The MST network is a graph constructed by linking N nodes with $N - 1$ edges without loops such that the sum of all edge distance is the minimum, i.e., the MST network uses the $N - 1$ linkage to extract the most important information from the cross-return correlation coefficient matrix. The distance of each edge in the network is derived by [6]:

$$d_{ij} = \sqrt{2(1 - c_{ij})} \tag{3}$$

where d_{ij} denotes the distance between nodes i and j. The distance function measures a distance between a pair of cryptocurrencies using their return correlation coefficients. The mapping between the return correlation coefficient and the distance function ranges from 0, for totally and positively correlated cryptocurrencies (i.e. when the return correlation coefficient is equal to 1), to 2 for totally anti-correlated cryptocurrencies (i.e. when the return correlation coefficient is equal to -1). For uncorrelated cryptocurrencies, the distance is $\sqrt{2}$. This transformation creates an $N \times N$ distance matrix from the $N \times N$ cross-return correlation coefficient matrix. Nevertheless, we have also performed evaluation using the networks constructed by other methods in [4] such as threshold network and plane maximum filter graph, and reached similar results and findings to the MST one, thus making our conclusions more reliable.

3.3 Moving Time Window Analysis

We adopt the moving time window approach to study the dynamic evolution of the cryptocurrency network. The reason for using this approach is that cryptocurrencies are entering the market at different times and we avoid restricting our work to only a specific set of cryptocurrencies in a specific time period when all their close prices have become available. The question to be researched is which cryptocurrencies are the influential ones during which periods of time. To look at the affiliation between the return of cryptocurrency i and j, we calculate the cross-return correlation coefficient matrix for all trading days across the investigated time period. The data is divided timewise into M windows $t = 1, 2, \ldots, M$ of width T corresponding to the number of daily returns included in each window. Several consecutive windows overlap with each other, the extent of which is dictated by the window step length parameter δT, describing the displacement of the window, measured also in trading days. The choice of window width is a trade-off between too noisy and too smoothed data for small and large window widths, respectively. Our results are calculated from daily stepped 182-day windows (i.e. 6 months). With 365 trading days a year in the cryptocurrency market, we use $\delta T = 1$ day and $T = 182$ days. Each time window thus contains at most 182 daily return observations. With these parameters, the overall number of windows is $M =$ 2483. This procedure allows us to more accurately reflect the structural changes of the cryptocurrency network using relatively small intervals between shifts while maintaining sufficiently large sample sizes of the cryptocurrency pricing data for calculating the cross-return correlation coefficient matrix for each shift.

4 Centrality Measures

To analyzing the network, we use the following five general centrality measures [14]:

- *Degree Centrality (DC)*: The degree centrality of node v is simply the total number of its immediate connected neighbor nodes. The degree centrality values are normalized by dividing the possible maximum number of edges in a network $N - 1$ where N is the number of nodes. DC measures the relative significance of a cryptocurrency, in terms of the number of edges upon it, that can directly affect the other cryptocurrencies. A cryptocurrency node with a higher DC score is likely to influent the behavior of more other cryptocurrencies that are directly connected to it.
- *Node Strength (NS)*: An extension to DC is to consider the correlation in addition to the number of their immediate neighbor nodes since a larger number of immediate connected neighbor nodes may not indicate a stronger correlation with these neighbor nodes. The node strength of node v is the sum of the correlation of v (i.e. edges) with all other nodes to which it is connected. Node strength measures how strong a cryptocurrency is correlated with the others and integrates the information of both its connectivity and the significance of its edges in terms of their total correlation. This is the normal generalization of the connectivity.
- *Betweenness Centrality (BC)*: The betweenness centrality of node v is the sum of the fraction of all-pairs shortest paths that pass through v. BC is used to quantify the control of a cryptocurrency node on information flow in the network. So, cryptocurrency nodes with high scores are considered as significant cryptocurrencies in terms of their roles in coordinating the information among cryptocurrencies. In other words, the higher the value, the more the node is likely to be an intermediate node or broker that transfers information from one node to another through it.

- *Closeness Centrality (CC)*: The closeness centrality of node v is the reciprocal of the sum of the shortest path distances from v to $N - 1$ other nodes. Since the sum of distances depends on the number of nodes in the network, closeness is normalized by the sum of minimum possible distances (i.e. $N - 1$). CC measures how close a cryptocurrency node to all other cryptocurrency nodes. The higher the score of a cryptocurrency node, the faster the cryptocurrency spread information from it to all others. Therefore, it represents the effectiveness of information propagation from a cryptocurrency to the others. Thus, if one cryptocurrency can reach others quickly, this cryptocurrency is at the central position in a network.
- *Eigenvector Centrality (EC)*: Node degree may not be a sufficient representation of how important or influential a node is, for it does not consider how important the neighbors of a node may be. As an example, one node may have a low degree centrality, but it may be connected with other nodes with very high DC or NS, so it can be, in some way, considered as influential. A measure that considers the degree of neighboring nodes when calculating the importance of a node is called eigenvector centrality. Compared to DC and NS, EC considers not only the number of or correlation strength to immediate neighbor nodes but also their importance. A cryptocurrency node with high EC typically connects to highly important neighboring nodes, thereby reflecting the importance of the node (i.e. located in the central).

5 Evaluation

5.1 Basic Properties of the Cross-Return Correlation Coefficient Distribution

The cross-return correlation coefficient c_{ij} reflects the correlation degree of the relative logarithmic return between cryptocurrencies i and j, while the distribution of the cross-return correlation coefficients shows the correlation distribution of the whole cryptocurrency market across the time period. Figure 1 shows the first four moments of the cross-return correlation coefficient distribution over all the 2483 time windows, namely mean, variance, skewness and kurtosis. The numbers below the x-axis are the number of emerged cryptocurrencies from our dataset at different periods of time. In terms of the mean correlation, it exhibits a V-shaped structure in overall. Since the market in early 2013 is relatively "narrow", which has much fewer cryptocurrencies (e.g. BTC, LTC, XRP and DOGE in our dataset) than the number of cryptocurrencies being exchanged today, they are generally correlated due to the strong influence of BTC on the others. More specifically, we observe a strong correlation between BTC and LTC (0.76 – 0.86) and a moderate correlation between BTC and XRP (0.35 – 0.5), and between BTC and DOGE (0.45 – 0.6), which keep the overall mean correlation high in general, even though other new cryptocurrencies that have low to moderate correlation with the others (0.25 to 0.5), are entering the market progressively. *The early stage of the cryptocurrency market exhibits a fairly strong correlation among the cryptocurrencies due to the strong influence of BTC on other cryptocurrencies.*

As time goes on, there is a sharp increase in the number of cryptocurrencies in the market since 2014 (66 in 2013 vs. 506 in 2014). There are approximately 6088 cryptocurrencies being traded with a total market capitalization of more than 338 billion

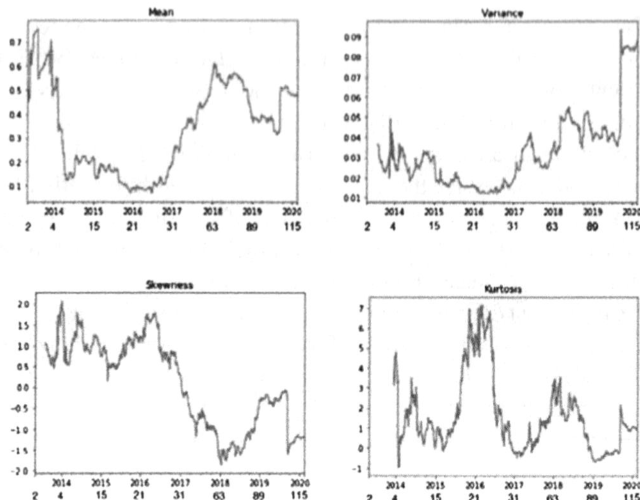

Fig. 1. The time-varying descriptive statistics of the cross-return correlation coefficients.

USD (as of 05.08.2020). These cryptocurrencies are created and used for a wide variety of applications, e.g. some are being used for transaction payment, while some are created for blockchain applications in different industries such as finance, healthcare and manufacturing. As shown by the valley in 2016 in Fig. 1, the low mean correlation indicates weak relationship whatsoever between many pairs of cryptocurrencies, e.g. cryptocurrencies that are being used for healthcare and manufacturing may not have any relationship with each other and therefore their prices or returns are likely to move individually. We observe that, during the valley period, the return correlation of about 75% of all the cryptocurrency pairs are very low, only between 0.0 and 0.2. *This reveals that the middle stage of the cryptocurrency market exhibits a relatively weak correlation among the cryptocurrencies, possibly due to a reason that many new cryptocurrencies are created and used for applications in many different industrial domains without reciprocal effects from the business and technology perspectives such that they act independently and their returns move individually.*

Starting from mid-2016, as shown in Fig. 1, the mean correlation of cryptocurrencies increases. A reason to explain this phenomenon is due to the two negative events or crises. First, in August 2016, Bitfinex announced that $72 million BTC was stolen from the company's customer's accounts. Immediately thereafter, bitcoin's trading price plunged by 20% [12]. Second, a crash in the cryptocurrency market as the price of BTC fell by about 65 percent during the month from 6 January to 6 February 2018 [7]. By September 2018, cryptocurrencies collapsed 80% from their peak in January 2018, making the 2018 cryptocurrency crash worse than the Dot-com bubble's 78% collapse. Furthermore, by November 2018, BTC fell by over 80% from its peak, having lose almost one-third of its value in the previous week. *Thus, the increase in the mean correlation reveals that, during the negative events such as crises, all affected cryptocurrencies are so highly correlated that the cryptocurrency market is dragging down as a whole. Therefore, similar to stock markets, any financial crisis can be observed and reflected by a prolonged increase of the market's cross-return correlation.*

5.2 Centrality Measures Evaluation

A node with large centrality may imply that it is important or influential in a network. The cryptocurrency nodes with the highest and the second highest centrality based on the MST network construction method are plotted in Fig. 2. Cryptocurrency nodes that are not among the two highest centrality values are not displayed in the figures to allow for better visualization of the influential cryptocurrencies. In general, these figures have reached similar results from which we can define 3 stages for the evolution of cryptocurrency market as highlighted by the three black dotted line boxes in Fig. 2, in which BTC dominates the first stage, followed by MAID and FCT in the second stage, and finally ETH takes the leading position in the third or the most recent stage. Some characteristics of these 3 stages are summarized in Table 1.

The first stage, from early 2013 to mid-2016, is mainly dominated by cryptocurrencies that are created for financial services. The most influential cryptocurrency is BTC, which is being used for transaction payment. Other cryptocurrencies, such as LTC, XRP, XLM, DOGE and BTS, serve similar financial purposes as BTC does. This confirms the findings in [8] that BTC and LTC are close to each other, and XLM, XRP, BTS and DOGE are within a community in the network.

The second stage, between mid-2016 and mid-2017, focuses on the use of blockchain technology in developing applications, particularly cloud data storage and recording by SC, MAID and FCT which have been identified influential cryptocurrencies. Cryptocurrencies with high market capitalization may not always be identified as influential (e.g. SC, MAID and FCT are ranked much lower than BTC which is ranked #1). The work in [9] reveals that MAID and FCT are ranked amongst the top 7 by their net-connectedness and PageRank to other cryptocurrencies, while MAID being the center of the network during the period. The work in [8] also find that MAID is one of the largest communities with respect to the number of cryptocurrencies in it, which includes FCT and SC. This transition of stages might also be triggered by the Bitfinex crisis that happens during mid-2016. Hence, not only an increase in mean correlation but also a change of influential cryptocurrencies may signal the occurrence of a crisis.

Finally, the third or recent stage since mid-2017 encourages adopting advanced blockchain features in applications such as smart contracts. ETH is the platform that supports smart contracts in the blockchain environment. Other cryptocurrencies, such as ADA, NEO and OMG, are strongly correlated with ETH as can be observed by their strong correlation among each other (0.8 – 0.87). Lastly, we consider closeness and betweenness centrality. The cryptocurrencies listed in Table 1 are again the closest to and being passed through by other nodes in the network during the stages they belong to. Cryptocurrencies among the highest rank in one centrality are likely to achieve the highest rank in most other centrality measures.

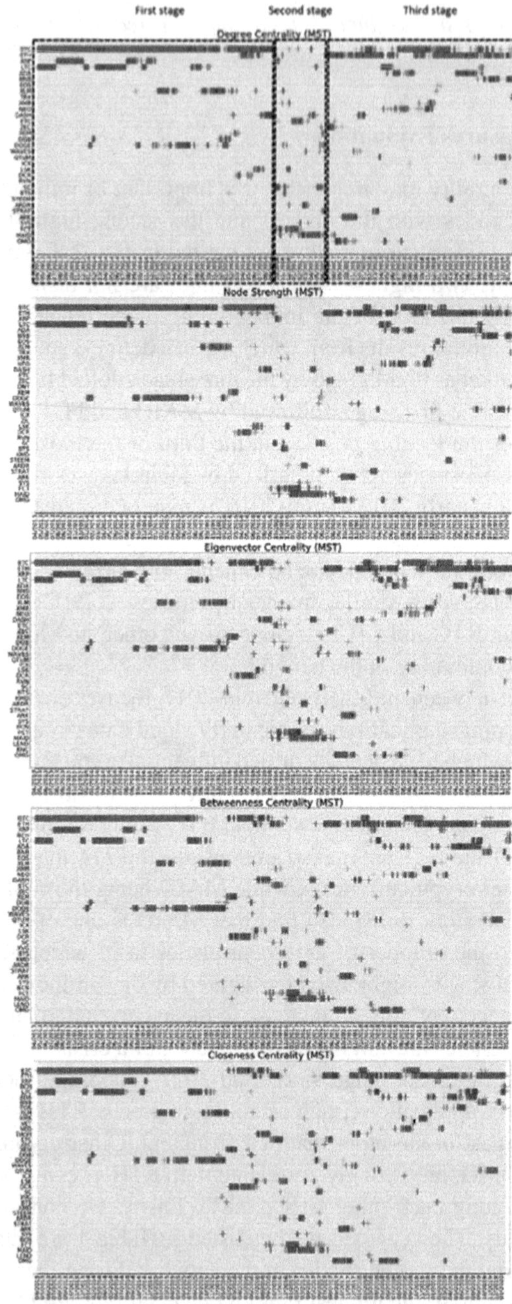

Fig. 2. Cryptocurrencies with the highest (red color) and the second highest (green color) on the five centrality measures in the cryptocurrency MST network. (Color figure online)

Table 1. A summary of 3 stages of the cryptocurrency market.

Stage	Cryptocurrencies with the two highest centrality measures	Main purpose of the cryptocurrencies
Early 2003 – Mid 2016	BTC, LTC, XRP, XLM, DOGE, BTS, DASH	Transaction payment
Mid 2016 – Mid 2017	MAID, FCT, SC, ARK	Cloud data storage and recording in blockchain networks
Since Mid 2017	ETH, ADA, NEO, OMG	Ethereum-based with smart contracts
During COVID-19	ETH, QTUM, BNB	Specific events

5.3 Changes on the Cryptocurrency Networks During Crisis

We investigate the dynamic changes on the cryptocurrency networks during two crises, namely (1) the 2018 cryptocurrency crash and (2) the COVID-19 in 2020. With respect to the 2018 cryptocurrency crash, Fig. 3 shows the networks before, during and after the cash. During the crash, BTC starts losing its dominant role to other cryptocurrencies, particularly ETH. After the crash, the network does not have any significant changes until the COVID-19 outbreak when the network changes, and QTUM and BNB are now located in the core part of the network, thus making them influential apart from the other cryptocurrencies such as BTC and ETH.

While ETH being identified as the leader, we find that, since the outbreak of COVID-19 in early 2020 (the rightmost part of Fig. 2), the most influential cryptocurrencies have been intermittently replaced by QTUM and BNB. First, QTUM, a platform that leverages ETH smart contract functionality along with the security of BTC network, has recently published its 2020 Quarter 2 report in which their most requested feature of Offline Staking code has been released to the community, which allows users to stake their QTUM from mobile, hardware and web wallets [10]. With the new objective of moving a lot of focus to the community, QTUM has also increased its online or social media community engagement, due to COVID-19 and many people staying home because of lockdowns, by hosting many Ask Me Anything (AMA) sessions, quizzes and key development updates. On the other hand, BNB has recently launched a $5-million COVID-19 relief champaign "Crypto Against COVID" by donating financial and medical resources to many countries in the world [11]. We believe that these COVID-19 related or aided events would have an influential impact in the community, which makes QTUM and BNB important cryptocurrencies that have attracted increasing public attention in recent months (the recent trend of their price movement is up). *Investors are advised to pay attention to those cryptocurrencies that provide any aids to the COVID-19 or other pandemic before making any trading decisions as the cryptocurrencies may benefit from providing aids during the epidemic.*

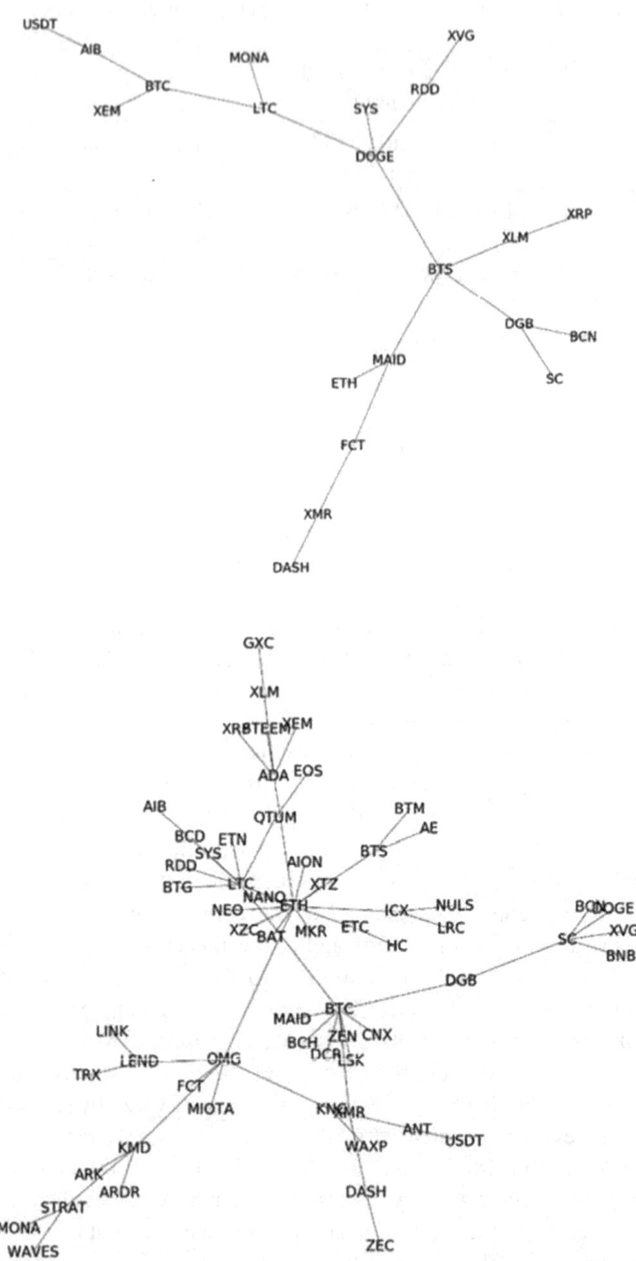

Fig. 3. Cryptocurrency network before the crash (top), during the crash (second from the top), after the crash or before COVID-19 (second from the bottom) and during COVID-19 (bottom).

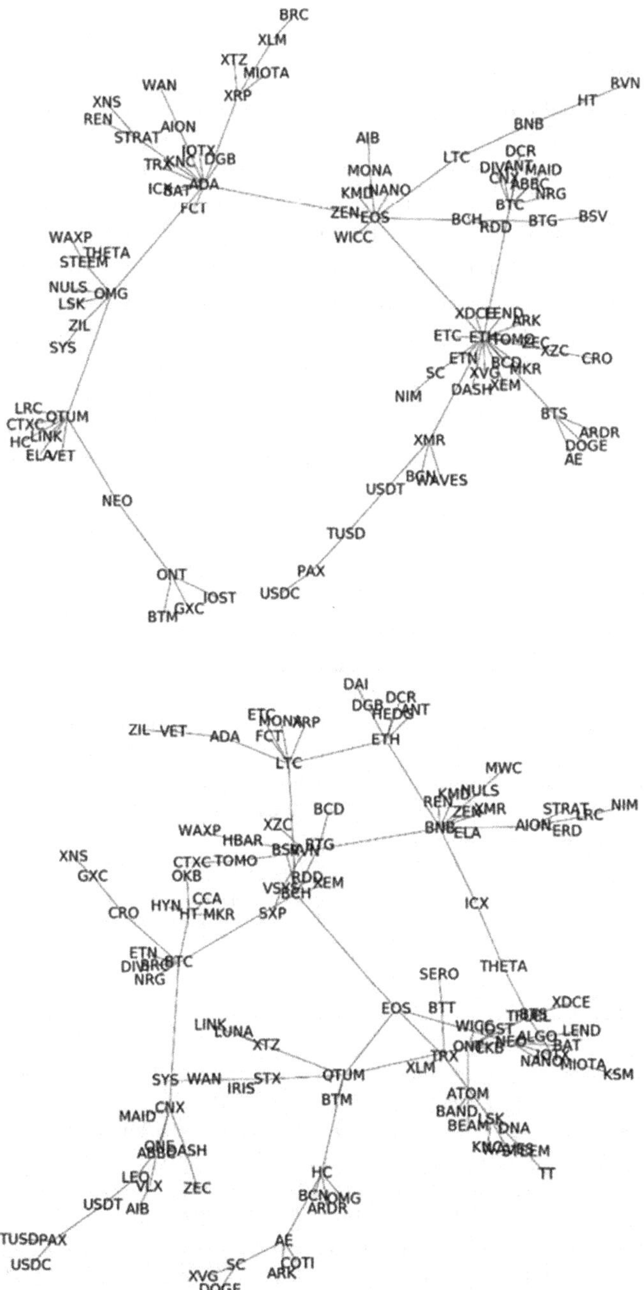

Fig. 3. *(continued)*

6 Conclusion

This paper analyzes the current cryptocurrency market using network analysis and centrality measures based on the time series daily close price of top 120 cryptocurrencies between 2013 and 2020. Our study has two primary findings: (1) the overall return correlation of the cryptocurrencies is weakening from 2013 to 2016, except for a very few pairs like BTC and LTC. (2) cryptocurrencies that are primarily used for transaction payment, notably BTC, dominate the market until mid-2016. Followed by this, the influential cryptocurrencies are those developed for applications using blockchain as the underlying technology, particularly data storage and recording such as MAID and FCT, between mid-2016 and mid-2017. Since then, ETH and other strongly correlated cryptocurrencies such as ADA, NEO and OMG, are taking leading positions in the network and have replaced BTC to become the benchmark cryptocurrencies. Interestingly, during the outbreak of COVID-19, QTUM and BNB have intermittently replaced ETH to take the leading positions, possibly due to their active community engagement during the pandemic.

References

1. Marti, G., et al.: A review of two decades of correlations, hierarchies, networks and clustering in financial markets. arXiv:1703.00485 (2020)
2. Burnie, A.: Exploring the interconnectedness of cryptocurrencies using correlation networks. In: Cyrptocurrency Research Conference, Cambridge, United Kingdom (2018)
3. Frances, C.J., Carles, P.G., Arellano, D.J.: The cryptocurrency market: a network analysis. Esic Mark. Econ. Bus. J. **49**(3), 569–583 (2018)
4. Boginski, V., Butenko, S., Pardalos, P.M.: Statistical analysis of financial networks. Comput. Stat. Data Anal. **48**(2), 431–443 (2005)
5. Papadimitriou, T., Gogas, P., Gkatzoglou, F.: The evolution of the cryptocurrencies market: a complex networks approach. J. Comput. Appl. Math. **376**, 112831 (2020)
6. Mantegna, R.N.: Hierarchical structure in financial markets. Eur. Phys. J. B **11**, 193–197 (1999). https://doi.org/10.1007/s100510050929
7. Cryptocurrency Bubble. https://en.wikipedia.org/wiki/2018_cryptocurrency_crash
8. Stosic, D., et al.: Collective behavior of cryptocurrency price changes. Phys. A **507**, 499–509 (2018)
9. Yi, S., et al.: Volatility connectedless in the cryptocurrency market: is Bitcoin a dominant cryptocurrency? Int. Rev. Financ. Anal. **60**, 98–114 (2018)
10. QTUM Q2 Review. https://blog.qtum.org/qtum-q2-review-2020-b8f67876f3a4
11. Coronavirus Relief: Cryptocurrency Aid Programs Launched to Combat Covid-19 Outbreak. https://news.bitcoin.com/coronavirus-relief-aid-cryptocurrency/
12. https://news.bitcoin.com/bitcoin-worth-282k-from-the-2016-bitfinex-hack-on-the-move/
13. CoinMarketCap. https://www.coinmarketcap.com
14. Centrality – NetworkX. https://networkx.github.io/documentation/stable/reference/algorithms/centrality.html

Two-Stage Framework for Accurate and Differentially Private Network Information Publication

Maneesh Babu Adhikari[1], Vorapong Suppakitpaisarn[2(✉)], Arinjita Paul[1], and C. Pandu Rangan[1]

[1] Indian Institute of Technology Madras, Chennai, India
adhimaneesh1998@gmail.com
{arinjita,prangan}@cse.iitm.ac.in
[2] The University of Tokyo, Tokyo, Japan
vorapong@is.s.u-tokyo.ac.jp

Abstract. We propose a novel mechanism to release an accurate and differentially private estimate of the link set of social networks. Differential privacy is one of the most common notations to quantify the privacy level of information publication. Several methods have been proposed to publish edge set information, among which one of the notable mechanisms is based on stratified sampling. While it is very scalable, social network information can be significantly altered by this technique. In fact, when we use mechanism based on stratified sampling, a totally random network may get published even when the input network is sparse. We aim to overcome this drawback in our work. We provide an efficient two-stage mechanism to control the edge set size and quality independently. To confirm the practical utility of our proposal, we apply it to the maximum matching problem when the edge information is spread between two different bipartite networks. We validate through experiments that the error induced by our framework is at least 20 times smaller than that of the original stratified sampling based mechanism when privacy level is 5. In addition, the computation time of our framework is 3 times shorter than the original method.

Keywords: Differential privacy · Stratified sampling · Maximum matching

1 Introduction

With the expeditious increase in the usage of online services, huge amounts of data are being generated everyday. Most of the generated data can be modelled as graphs, e.g., social network data, email data, etc. In these networks, people can be modelled as nodes and their interactions can be modelled as edges. The analysis of such data is pivotal in the spheres of medical research, fraud detection, recommendation engines, to name a few. However, the data owners are reluctant to share such data over privacy concerns of the users that are part of the network.

S. Chellappan et al. (Eds.): CSoNet 2020, LNCS 12575, pp. 267–279, 2020.
https://doi.org/10.1007/978-3-030-66046-8_22

Several anonymization techniques have been proposed to preserve privacy of individuals' data, but none of them provides mathematical guarantees with the availability of auxiliary information. Narayanan and Shmatikov in [1] proposed a technique to break the anonymity of naively anonymized Netflix data set using auxiliary information resulting in privacy loss of millions of users. Hence, it is important that the data is provably anonymized (even with access to auxiliary information) before it is released for research purposes. This motivates us to work with differential privacy to overcome the above discussed privacy risks.

The concept of differential privacy was formally introduced in [2] by Dwork. Differential privacy provides a mathematically provable guarantee of privacy preservation against linkage attacks, statistical attacks and leveraging attacks. It guarantees that the outcome of any analysis is equally likely, independent of the presence of any single entity in the data. Therefore, the risk of identifying private information with the availability of auxiliary information is nullified.

In this paper, we study the problem of publishing the link set of a social network. Several techniques have been proposed to achieve this, among which one of the notable mechanisms is based on stratified sampling [3]. While the computation time of this technique is quite short, social network information can significantly be altered by this technique. The published output network may be a completely random network independent of the input network when the input network is sparse.

1.1 Our Contribution

We introduce a stratified sampling based mechanism to publish an accurate estimate of the edge set with strong privacy guarantees. We propose a two-stage $[\varepsilon_1{:}\varepsilon_2]$-differentially private algorithm to release an anonymized, accurate estimate of the true edge set. In the first stage, we develop an ε_1-differentially private algorithm to sample an estimate of the size of the un-anonymized edge set. In the second stage, we present an ε_2-differentially private algorithm to sample an edge set of specific size sampled in the first step. The two-stage algorithm gives us a better control over the size of the edge set independent of its quality. It is particularly helpful when the resultant analysis on the published anonymized graph is highly sensitive to the number of edges. To show practical utilities of our proposed differential private mechanism, we consider a private variant of the maximum matching problem. The maximum matching size of a graph is highly sensitive to the presence or absence of edges in sparse graphs, although highly invariant in dense graphs. It gives us an ideal scenario to present the utility of our algorithm. We consider the setting in which two disjoint bipartite networks are connected by a set of inter-connecting (edges connecting nodes in different networks) edges. The node information of both networks and inter-connecting edge information is public whereas the intra-edge (edges connecting nodes in the same network) information of both the networks is private. We deal with the problem of finding the size of the maximum matching of the union of both the networks when one of the networks in anonymized. Comparing with the classical stratified sampling technique in [3], we present empirical results on the publicly available Moreno Crime dataset [4]. We also show results on networks synthesized from the R-MAT model [5]. We demonstrate drastic improvements in performance in sparse graphs when one of the input networks is anonymized with our proposed mechanism.

1.2 Related Works

There are several studies in literature aiming to protect if a particular person is in a social network (node differential privacy) [6–8]. Our discussion in this work focuses on hiding the information if an edge is in a graph or edge differential privacy [9]. Though we are not currently dealing with node differential privacy, we strongly believe that our framework can be extended to this privacy notation as well.

Several differential privacy works have been introduced to publish specific information of social networks. For example, Hay et al. [9] aims to output the degree distribution of an input graph, Kenthapadi et al. [10] aims to publish the shortest path length for all pairs of nodes, whereas Ahmed et al. [11] aims to output the eigenvectors of the input network's adjacency matrix. Although we experiment with the maximum matching size, our framework is not limited to any particular graph property. It outputs an accurate edge set of the social network and users can derive any network information from it.

There are some works which, similar to us, aim to publish an accurate estimate of the edge set to the users. Many of them are based on Kronecker graph [12–14]. While Kronecker graph can effectively capture global information of a social network like diameter, clusters, or degree distribution, we believe that it cannot capture properties that need local knowledge such as shortest path or maximum matching size. Therefore, techniques based on Kronecker graph and this work could be complementary to each other.

We rely on maximum matching size to show the accuracy of our proposal. Differentially private maximum matching is considered in several works such as [15–17]. They consider a situation in which one party holds all the information, and wants to release the maximum matching information from the entire social network they have. On the other hand, our experimental results focus on a situation when two parties want to exchange private information in order to calculate the maximum matching size.

2 Preliminaries

2.1 Differential Privacy [2]

We work with the concept of private databases to define differential privacy. A database is viewed as a collection of records with each record describing private information of some entity. Distance between two databases is defined as the number of records in which these two databases differ. Two databases d, d' are neighboring databases if they differ in exactly 1 record i.e, $\|d - d'\|_1 = 1$.

Definition 1. *Consider a randomized algorithm A which takes a database as input and outputs a member of $Range(A)$. We say that A is ε-differentially private if, for all neighboring databases d, d', and, for any $S \subseteq Range(A)$, we have* $\Pr[A(d) \in S] \leq e^{\varepsilon} \Pr[A(d') \in S]$. *where e is Euler's number.*

Informally, differential privacy bounds the amount by which output of an algorithm can change when a single record is either added or removed to/from a database. When a publication is under differential privacy, one cannot distinguish between two tables different by one record by the publication, and, hence, cannot know information of a particular person even though all other persons disclose their information.

We discuss an algorithm that satisfies the differential privacy notation. We begin by introducing l_1-sensitivity. Suppose D is the set of all possible databases, and the original information to be published from table $d \in D$ is $f(d)$.

Definition 2. *Let f be a function from a set of databases D to the set $\mathbb{R}^k$. The l_1-sensitivity of f is $\Delta f = \max_{\|d-d'\|_1=1} \|f(d) - f(d')\|_1$.*

The l_1 sensitivity of a function f is the maximum change in f obtained by the inclusion or exclusion of a single entity. In other words, it bounds the margin by which the output needs to be altered to hide the participation of a single entity.

Exponential Mechanism. Exponential mechanism was first introduced by McSherry and Talwar in [18]. It preserves ε-differential privacy when the output range S of an algorithm is discrete. It maps every (database, output) pair to a quality score given by the quality function $Q : D \times S \to \mathbb{R}$. Then, it samples and outputs an element $s \in S$ with likelihood proportional to $g(s) = \exp\left(\frac{\varepsilon Q(d,s)}{2\Delta Q}\right)$. Let $C = \sum_{s \subseteq S} g(s)$. The probability with which we output $s \subseteq S$ is then equal to $\Pr[s] = g(s)/C$. Intuitively, for some fixed database d, it is likely that the algorithm outputs an element of S with large quality score. We assign higher scores to preferred outputs and lower scores to bad outputs.

2.2 Differential Privacy vs Social Network Privacy

Social Networks like Facebook, Twitter, or Tinder can be modelled as graphs. Accounts (people) can be modelled as nodes and their relations can be modelled as edges. The analysis of these graph structures is pivotal to provide relevant recommendations and improve user experience. Such graph data has to be anonymized before publishing it for research purposes to preserve the privacy of users. Differential privacy can be extended to graph anonymization and provide a provable social network privacy.

We discuss the equivalence of neighboring databases in relation to graphs.

Definition 3 *(Edge Differential Privacy [14]). Graphs G and G' are said to be neighbors with respect to edge differential privacy if $\|E - E'\|_1 = 1$ where $G = (V, E)$ and $G' = (V, E')$.*

Based on the previous definition, differential privacy notion for graphs is similarly defined as follows:

Definition 4 *(Differential Privacy on Graphs). Consider a randomized algorithm A which takes a graph as input and outputs a member of Range(A). We say that A is ε-differentially private if, for all neighboring graphs G, G', and, for any $S \subseteq Range(A)$, we have* $\Pr[A(G) \in S] \leq e^{\varepsilon} \Pr[A(G') \in S]$.

Differential privacy hides the presence or absence of a data entity in neighboring databases by limiting the change in output introduced by that entity. In this case, neighboring databases are graphs that differ by one edge i.e., G and G' are neighboring graphs if G' can be obtained from G by adding or removing an edge. Because of this property, attackers cannot distinguish between a graph with a link and a graph without. The information whether two people are linked to each other is then protected if we have an algorithm that satisfies the notion of edge differential privacy.

2.3 Stratified Sampling

To sample an element according to a probability distribution, standard sampling technique [19] runs in linear time in the number of possible outcomes. If the number of possible outcomes is exponential in the input size, standard sampling is no longer tractable. Stratified sampling [3], however, takes advantage of the presence of homogeneous subgroups where the probability of any two outcomes in a homogeneous subgroup is same.

Let R be the finite set of possible outcomes and X be a discrete random variable defined on probability space (p, R), i.e., $p : x \in R \mapsto \Pr(X = x)$. Let $(R_0, R_1, ..., R_k)$ be a partition of R into k homogeneous subgroups. For any subgroup R_i and any two elements $x, x' \in R_i$, we have $p(x) = p(x')$. Now, according to stratified sampling, sampling from original distribution is same as:

1. Sampling a subgroup according to the relative subgroup probabilities using the standard sampling technique.
2. Sampling an element uniformly from the chosen subgroup in step 1.

The running time of sampling is greatly enhanced depending on the number of subgroups (denoted by k).

2.4 Matching Theory in Graphs (c.f. Chapter 7 of [20])

In this section, we introduce some basic graph definitions used in later sections.

Definition 5 *(Bipartite Graph). A graph $G = (V, E)$ is a bipartite graph if there exists a partition of V into X and Y such that there is no edge between two vertices in X and there is no edge between two vertices in Y.*

Definition 6. *A matching M of a graph $G = (V, E)$ is a subset of edges E such that no two edges have a common vertex. A matching M is said to be a maximum matching if there exists no other matching M' of G with larger number of edges.*

2.5 Previous Work on Differential Privacy by Stratified Sampling

In the forward message of [3], the goal is to communicate a differentially private estimate of the adjacent nodes of a specific node u in the graph $G = (V, E)$. Let U be the set of adjacent nodes of node u in graph $G = (V, E)$, i.e., for all $a \in V$, $(a, u) \in E \iff a \in U$ and let U^* be some approximation of U. The quality function for this mechanism is then defined as $Q(U^*) = |U \cap U^*| + |\overline{U \cup U^*}|$. The probability distribution is then calculated over the power set R of all nodes $V^- = (V \setminus \{u\})$ according to the above quality function. A set U^* is then sampled from R according to this probability distribution and is communicated as a differentially private estimate of U. From the definition of $Q(U^*)$, it can be observed that $Q(U^*) \in [0, |V^-|]$. The number of possible quality values is $|V|$, although the number of possible node sets U^* is exponential in $|V|$. Hence, stratified sampling can be used to sample U^* from R efficiently. The probabilities are calculated in log space since the exponents may otherwise blowup. The log space probability is given by $\ln(\Pr[U^*]) = \frac{\varepsilon Q(U^*)}{2\Delta Q} - \ln(C)$. The normalizing constant C can be calculated efficiently by calculating the number of node sets for each possible quality value. The normalizing constant C in this case turns out to be $C = (1 + \exp(\varepsilon/(2\Delta Q)))^{|V|-1}$ as described in [3]. C being in the form $(1 + A)^B$ makes it feasible to work in log space. The running time of this framework is linear in the total number of nodes, i.e. $\mathcal{O}(|V|)$.

3 Proposed Frameworks

In this section, we describe the working methodology of two differentially private frameworks. Each of the two frameworks can independently be used for computing the differentially private estimate of the edge set of any graph. Framework 1 is a direct extension of the mechanism in [3]. Framework 2 is a further extension of Framework 1 which gives us better control over the size of the differentially private edge set independent of its quality. We call Framework 2 as $[\varepsilon_1 : \varepsilon_2]$-differentially private algorithm indicating the dependence of the size of the private edgeset on ε_1 and its quality on ε_2.

3.1 Framework 1

In our framework, the goal is to communicate a differentially private estimate of the edges of graph $G = (V, E)$ when node information V is public. The mechanism described in [3] can easily be extended to reach that goal. Let E^* be the differentially private estimate of E. Then, the quality function is similarly defined as $Q(E^*) = |E \cap E^*| + |\overline{E \cup E^*}|$. The probability distribution is then calculated over power set S of all edges possible with vertex set V according to this quality function. We adopt the same sampling technique as described [3] and obtain differentially private estimate E^*. The running time of Framework 1 is linear in the total number of possible edges with $|V|$ nodes, which is $\mathcal{O}(|V|^2)$.

3.2 Framework 2

One of the main problems we encountered with Framework 1 was that

> the cardinality of $(E \Delta E^*)$ is often very high even when the privacy level is very high (ε is set to a very large value). If the analysis to be performed on private graph is very sensitive to addition or deletion of edges, then the private graph $G = (V, E^*)$ is not an ideal estimate of $G = (V, E)$.

So, we now propose a two stage mechanism to control the cardinality and quality of the differentially private edge set E^* independently.

- Algorithm Stage 1: Mechanism to output a differentially private estimate x of the size of the true edge set $|E|$.
- Algorithm Stage 2: Mechanism to output the differentially private estimate E^*, where $|E^*| = x$.

Algorithm Stage 1. This stage of the algorithm can be viewed as answering a query when the true answer is $|E|$. One might think that Laplace mechanism [2], one of the most common mechanisms, can be applied here. However, it cannot be applied to achieve differential privacy in this case, since it might output non-integral values whereas we need the output to be an integer that can be utilized in Stage 2 of the algorithm. Let E^t be the set of all possible edges in the graph $G = (V, E)$, i.e. $E^t = \{(u, v) : u, v \in V\}$. As the integer output x is always in $[0, |E^t|]$, the set of possible outputs is finite. The quality function for this mechanism is defined as $Q_1(x) = |E^t| - \text{abs}(x - |E|)$ where abs denotes the absolute value. The quality value $Q_1(x)$ deteriorates as we move away from the true value $|E|$ and is uniquely maximized when $x = |E|$. We adopt the same method as described in Framework 1 and work in log space. To calculate the log space probabilities, we need to obtain a closed form expression for the normalizing constant $C = \sum_{x=0}^{|E^t|} \exp\left(\frac{\varepsilon_1 . Q_1(x)}{2.\Delta Q_1}\right) = \frac{a^{|E^t|}}{a-1} \cdot \left[a + 1 - a^{-|E|} - a^{|E|-|E^t|}\right]$, where $a = \exp(\frac{\varepsilon_1}{2.\Delta Q_1})$. We ignore last two terms in RHS in the above expression as they are much smaller than $a + 1$. We now calculate the log space probabilities and sample the differentially private estimate x. Note that $\Delta Q_1 = 1$.

Algorithm Stage 2. In this stage of the algorithm, we need to output a differentially private edge set E^* from all possible edge sets of size x. We adopt the same quality function as described in Framework 1, which is $Q_2(E^*) = |E \cap E^*| + |\overline{E \cup E^*}|$. In order to sample a differentially private estimate E^*, we first need to find out the probability distribution over all possible edge sets of size x. The first task is to compute the normalizing constant efficiently in order to calculate the probabilities. We denote the quality value by q and the cardinality of intersection by i, i.e. $Q_2(E^*) = q$ and $|E \cap E^*| = i$. From the definition of Q_2, we obtain the equality $i = \frac{1}{2}(q + x + |E| - |E^t|)$. Hence, there exists an edge set of size x with quality value q if and only if $(q + x + |E| - |E^t|)$ is an even number along with other boundary conditions. If there exists an edge set with the above requirements, then such an edge set can be obtained by selecting i edges from E and remaining $(x-i)$ edges from $(E^t - E)$ respectively. Therefore, the number of such edge sets with quality q is given by $N(q) = \binom{|E|}{i}\binom{|E^t-E|}{x-i}$. The normalizing constant is then given by

$$C = \sum_q N(q) \cdot \exp\left(\frac{q\varepsilon_2}{2\Delta Q_2}\right) \tag{1}$$

The summation above is over all possible quality values q discussed in the previous paragraph. Unfortunately, Eq. (1) does not have a closed form expression. Since we are working in the log space, we approximate $\ln(C)$ instead of computing C which can later be used to compute the log space probabilities.

For all q, let us denote $s_q = N(q) \cdot \exp(\frac{q\varepsilon_2}{2\Delta Q_2})$ and $s_{\max} = \max_q s_q$. Then, $\ln(C) = \ln(s_{\max} \cdot \sum_q \frac{s_q}{s_{max}}) = \ln(s_{max}) + \ln\left(\sum_q \exp\left(\ln(s_q) - \ln(s_{\max})\right)\right)$. We only consider the terms for which $\ln(s_q) - \ln(s_{max}) \geq -\alpha$ for a large constant α and all the remaining terms are ignored. We used $\alpha = 650$ in our experiments ignoring all the values s_q for which the ratio s_q/s_{max} is less than e^{-650} which we think is a reasonably small value to neglect.

The second task is to sample an edge set according to this probability distribution. From the definition of Q_2, it can be observed that $Q_2(E^*) \in [0, |E^t|]$ i.e., the number of possible quality values is $(|E^t| + 1)$, although the number of possible edge sets is exponential. In relation to stratified sampling, a group of edge sets with same quality value can be viewed as a homogeneous subgroup since equal quality values induce equal probabilities. Sampling an edge set using stratified sampling is done as follows:

- Step 1: Sample a quality value q according to the relative homogeneous subgroup probabilities using the standard sampling technique.
- Step 2: Uniformly, sample an edge set of size x and quality value q.

Step 1 The probability $\Pr(q)$ associated with a homogeneous subgroup induced by quality q is the sum of probabilities of all edge sets with quality q. The probability associated with an edge set having quality q can be computed using $\Pr[s]$ as defined in Section II where $Q(d, s) = q$. Therefore, $\Pr(q) = N(q) \cdot \Pr[s]$ where s in an edge set with quality value q. The log space probability associated with a homogeneous subgroup with quality q is then given by

$$\ln(\Pr(q)) = \ln(N(q)) + \frac{\varepsilon_2 q}{2\Delta Q_2} - \ln(C) \tag{2}$$

The probability distribution over all possible quality values can be calculated in $\mathcal{O}(|E^t|)$ time and standard sampling can be done in $\mathcal{O}(|E^t|)$ time and space.

Step 2 The challenge is to sample an edge set E^* of size x and quality q uniformly from all possible edge sets when the original edge set is E. Recall that, when $|E \cap E^*| = i$, we have $i = \frac{1}{2}(q + x + |E| - |E^t|)$. For a given q and x, the size of intersection or the number of common edges in E and E^* is fixed to i. The probability of selecting some set of i edges from E without repetition is given by $1/\binom{|E|}{i}$. The remaining $(x-i)$ edges of E^* are then uniformly chosen from the set $(E^t - E)$. The probability of selecting some set of $(x-i)$ edges from $(E^t - E)$ without repetition is given by $1/\binom{|E^t-E|}{x-i}$.

We then publish the union of i and $(x-i)$ edges as our differentially private estimate E^*. We used the Fisher Yates Shuffling Algorithm [21] to randomly pick a few items from a large set without repetition. Note that $\Delta Q_2 = 1$.

4 Use Case on Bipartite Matching

To demonstrate the performance of our algorithm, we consider a private variant of the maximum matching problem. Maximum matching in bipartite graphs is a heavily studied area with immense practical importance. The size of maximum matching of a graph is highly sensitive to the presence or absence of edges in sparse graphs whereas it is highly invariant in dense graphs. It presents us with an ideal scenario to demonstrate the comparative utilities of our framework.

4.1 Problem Setting

We work in the similar setting as described in [3]. Assume that $G_1 = (X_1, Y_1, E_1)$ and $G_2 = (X_2, Y_2, E_2)$ are two node disjoint bipartite networks owned by organizations I_1 and I_2 respectively. Although every node belongs to one of the two bipartite networks, edges may span across both the networks. We denote the set of edges spanning across the two networks by $E_{12} \subseteq \{(u,v) \mid u \in X_1, v \in Y_2\}$ and $E_{21} \subseteq \{(u,v) \mid u \in Y_1, v \in X_2\}$. Our privacy assumptions are as follows:

- public information : $X_1, Y_1, X_2, Y_2, E_{12}, E_{21}$
- private information known only to I_1: E_1
- private information known only to I_2: E_2

We enable one of the organizations to compute the maximum matching size of the union of both the networks while hiding the intra-edge information of the other network from the organization. Suppose the organization to compute the maximum matching size is I_2, then I_2 will not know E_1 but its differentially private estimation of the set, denoted by E_1^*. It then must estimate the maximum matching size of $G_u = (X_1 \cup X_2, Y_1 \cup Y_2, E_u)$ where $E_u = E_1 \cup E_2 \cup E_{12} \cup E_{21}$.

4.2 Practical Utility

The problem setting is useful in many practical situations. Consider a situation when two institutions I_1 and I_2 want to see if a collaboration between them is beneficial to them or their customers. If they do not collaborate, their benefits are the maximum matching size of G_1 added by the maximum matching size of G_2, while the benefits are the maximum matching size of G_u when they collaborate.

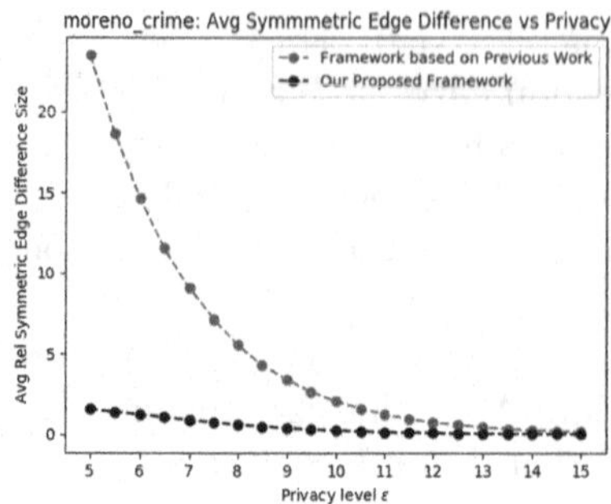

Fig. 1. Average relative symmetric edge difference ($|E_1 \Delta E_1^*|/|E_1|$) for $\varepsilon =$ 5 to 15, moreno crime dataset

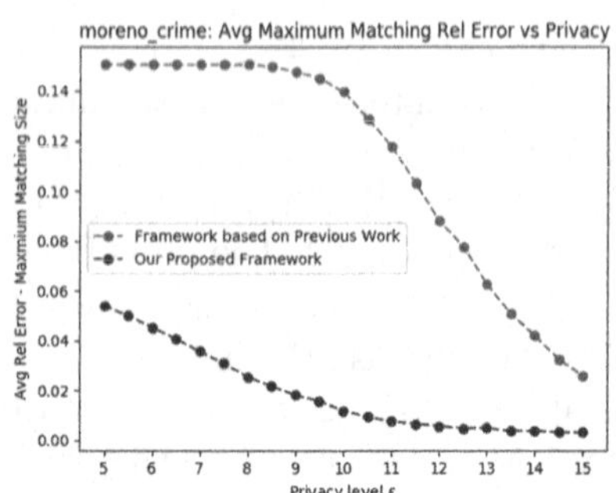

Fig. 2. Average relative maximum matching error for $\varepsilon = 5$ to 15, moreno crime dataset

We can consider I_1 and I_2 as two different university departments which are matching students with professors for graduate projects. The maximum matching size is then the number of students who are matched with their preferred professors. Two departments may then collaborate if the matching matching size is significantly increased by joining two social networks. On the other hand, we may want to protect if a link exists as students may not want to reveal if they prefer one professor over others. The same setting can be applied when two airlines wants to decide if they should have codeshare flights or when companies wants to decide if they should merge with each other.

5 Experimental Results

We apply the frameworks on E_1 to obtain the differentially private estimate E_1^* and then compute the maximum matching size of $G_u^* = (X_1 \cup X_2, Y_1 \cup Y_2, E_1^* \cup E_2 \cup E_{12} \cup E_{21})$. We refer to Framework 1 and Framework 2 in the above graph plots as 'Framework based on Previous Work' and 'Our Proposed Framework' respectively. All the experiments have been executed on Lenovo y50–70 machine with 16 GB RAM, using python 3.6 without parallel computations. Results in Figs. 1, 2, 3 are based on the publicly available moreno crime dataset [4] which is randomly divided into two bipartite networks with inter and intra edge connections as described in the above sections.

We first examine the variation of relative symmetric edge difference with privacy leverage in Fig. 1. In this figure, privacy leverage ε for Framework 2 indicates the summation of privacy levels at Algorithm stage 1 and stage 2 i.e., $\varepsilon = \varepsilon_1 + \varepsilon_2$. Our framework exhibits exponential improvements in the quality of differentially private edge set for smaller values of ε. We obtain better approximations with stronger privacy guarantees i.e., average relative symmetric edge difference is 1.56 for Framework 2 when compared to 23.49 for Framework 1 when $\varepsilon = 5$. Differentially private estimate in Framework 2 for $\varepsilon < 5$ is a bad approximation (but is still exponentially better than Framework 1) with relative error close to 2. Therefore, for an edge set publication, we recommend using $\varepsilon \geq 5$.

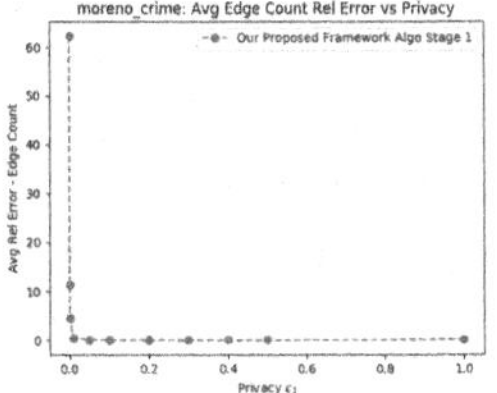

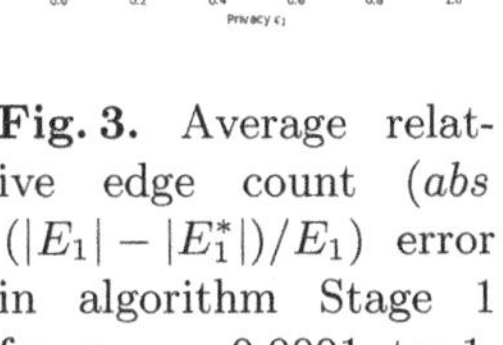

Fig. 3. Average relative edge count (*abs* $(|E_1| - |E_1^*|)/E_1$) error in algorithm Stage 1 for $\varepsilon_1 = 0.0001$ to 1, moreno crime dataset

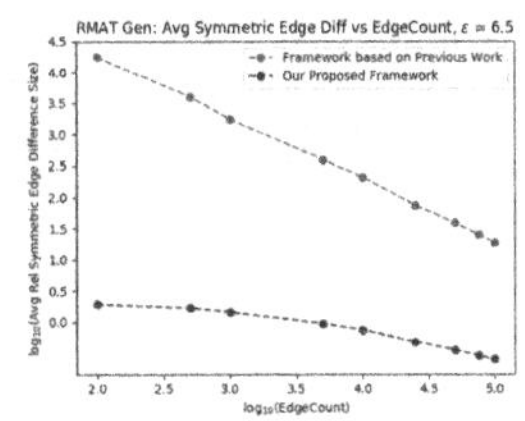

Fig. 4. Average relative symmetric edge difference $(|E_1 \Delta E_1^*|/|E_1|)$ vs total edge count $(|E^u|)$ for $\varepsilon = 6.5$, R-MAT generated graphs

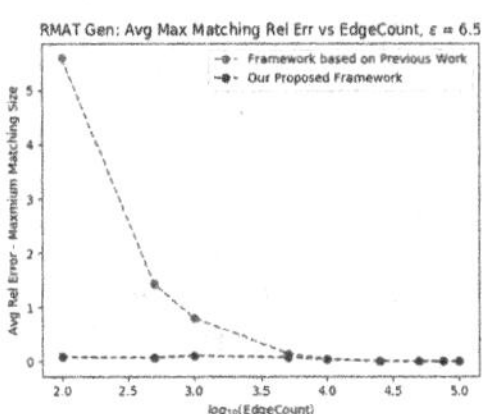

Fig. 5. Average relative maximum matching error vs total edge count$(|E_u|)$ for $\varepsilon = 6.5$, RMAT generated graphs

Figure 2 shows the relation between average relative maximum matching error and privacy leverage for ε between 5 and 15. Relative maximum matching error is as low as 0.05 for Framework 2 whereas it is 0.15 for Framework 1 when $\varepsilon = 5$. Average relative maximum matching error is quite small even for $\varepsilon < 5$ even though the symmetric edge difference is high owing to the fact that size of maximum matching can be same for completely different graphs. Figure 3 shows the variation of cardinality of differentially private edge set $|E_1^*|$ with privacy leverage ε_1 at stage 1 of the algorithm in Framework 2. We can see that the error is very small for any $\varepsilon_1 \geq 0.1$. Therefore, we propose to set value of $\varepsilon_1 = 0.1$.

We next report the results on the synthetic R-MAT [5] graphs. Multiple R-MAT graphs with constant number of nodes i.e., $|X_1 \cup X_2| = |Y_1 \cup Y_2| = 1024$ and edges ranging from 100 to 100000 have been generated. We further maintained the property that $|X_1| = |Y_1| = 512$ for the divided graphs with no further condition on the edges. We then examined the average relative symmetric edge difference and average relative maximum matching error as a function of edge cardinality of the union of graphs $|E_u|$ in Fig. 4 and Fig. 5 respectively. The relative symmetric edge difference is 0.94 for Framework 2 whereas it is 391.89 for Framework 1 when $|E_u| = 5000$ and $\varepsilon = 6.5$ proving the drastic improvement in performance we have achieved in relatively sparse graphs.

We also validated through our experimentation that Framework 2 is around 3 times faster then Framework 1.

6 Conclusions and Future Works

In this work, we consider the case where two parties own different parts of a social network. Their goal is to calculate certain network properties while preserving the information of their users. We propose a two-stage framework that can increase the accuracy of the calculation result by up to 20 times and reduce the computation time by 3 times.

In our work, we have considered a scenario when node information is public and edge information is private. But many cases even require the node information to be hidden. Also, a link might contain other information in addition to the person who are incident on it. We believe our mechanism can be extended to protect such private information, and we plan to do that in the future. We also plan to compare our mechanism with techniques other than stratified sampling, and work on different use case.

References

1. Narayanan, A., Shmatikov, V.: Robust de-anonymization of large sparse datasets. In: SP. IEEE **2008**, 111–125 (2008)
2. Dwork, C., McSherry, F., Nissim, K., Smith, A.: Calibrating noise to sensitivity in private data analysis. In: Halevi, S., Rabin, T. (eds.) TCC 2006. LNCS, vol. 3876, pp. 265–284. Springer, Heidelberg (2006). https://doi.org/10.1007/11681878_14
3. Roohi, L., Rubinstein, B.I., Teague, V.: Differentially-private two-party egocentric betweenness centrality. INFOCOM IEEE **2019**, 2233–2241 (2019)
4. "Crime network dataset - KONECT," April 2017. http://konect.uni-koblenz.de/networks/moreno_crime
5. Chakrabarti, D., Zhan, Y., Faloutsos, C.: R-MAT: a recursive model for graph mining. SDM SIAM **2004**, 442–446 (2004)
6. Ullman, J., Sealfon, A.: Efficiently estimating erdos-renyi graphs with node differential privacy. In: Advances in Neural Information Processing Systems 32: Annual Conference on Neural Information Processing Systems 2019, NeurIPS 2019, 8–14 December 2019, Vancouver, BC, Canada, 2019, pp. 3765–3775 (2019)
7. Day, W.-Y., Li, N., Lyu, M.: Publishing graph degree distribution with node differential privacy. ICDM **2016**, 123–138 (2016)
8. Kasiviswanathan, S.P., Nissim, K., Raskhodnikova, S., Smith, A.: Analyzing graphs with node differential privacy. In: Sahai, A. (ed.) TCC 2013. LNCS, vol. 7785, pp. 457–476. Springer, Heidelberg (2013). https://doi.org/10.1007/978-3-642-36594-2_26
9. Hay, M., Li, C., Miklau, G., Jensen, D.D.: Accurate estimation of the degree distribution of private networks. In: The Ninth IEEE International Conference on Data Mining, Miami, Florida, USA **6–9**(2009), pp. 169–178 (2009)
10. Kenthapadi, K., Korolova, A., Mironov, I., Mishra, N.: Privacy via the Johnson-Lindenstrauss transform, arXiv preprint arXiv:1204.2606 (2012)
11. Ahmed, F., Liu, A.X., Jin, R.: Publishing social network graph eigen-spectrum with privacy guarantees. In: IEEE Transactions on Network Science and Engineering, pp. 1–14 (2019)
12. Mir, D.J., Wright, R.N.: A differentially private estimator for the stochastic kronecker graph model. EDBT/ICDT Workshops **2012**, 167–176 (2012)
13. Li, D., Zhang, W., Chen, Y.: Differentially private network data release via stochastic kronecker graph. In: Cellary, W., Mokbel, M.F., Wang, J., Wang, H., Zhou, R., Zhang, Y. (eds.) WISE 2016. LNCS, vol. 10042, pp. 290–297. Springer, Cham (2016). https://doi.org/10.1007/978-3-319-48743-4_23

14. Paul, A., Suppakitpaisarn, V., Bafna, M., Rangan, C.P.: Improving accuracy of differentially private kronecker social networks via graph clustering. In: ISNCC 2020, 2020 (accepted)
15. Hsu, J., Huang, Z., Roth, A., Roughgarden, T., Wu, Z.S.: Private matchings and allocations. SIAM J. Comput. **45**(6), 1953–1984 (2016)
16. Varma, N., Yoshida, Y.: Average sensitivity of graph algorithms, arXiv preprint arXiv:1904.03248 (2019)
17. Huang, Z., Zhu, X.: Scalable and jointly differentially private packing. In: 46th International Colloquium on Automata, Languages, and Programming, ICALP 2019, July 9–12, 2019, Patras, Greece, ser. LIPIcs, 2019, pp. 73:1–73:12 (2019)
18. McSherry, F., Talwar, K.: Mechanism design via differential privacy. In: FOCS 2007. IEEE 94–103 (2007)
19. Cochran, W.G.: Sampling techniques. Wiley (2007)
20. Kleinberg, J., Tardos, E.: Algorithm design. Pearson Education (2006)
21. Durstenfeld, R.: Algorithm 235: random permutation. Commun. ACM **7**(7), 420 (1964)

Blockchain

A Privacy-Preserving Blockchain-based Information Shared Scheme in Smart-Cities

Yanping Wang[1], Xiaofen Wang[1], Pan Wen[1], Teng Hu[1,2], and Xiaosong Zhang[1](✉)

[1] University of Electronic Science and Technology of China, ChengDu 611731, Sichuan, China
johnsonzxs@uestc.edu.cn
[2] Institute of Computer Application, China Academy of Engineering Physics, Mianyang 621900, Sichuan, China

Abstract. Development of the Internet leads to a growing number of data. The data collected across the city is very useful for analysis and decision making. Data sharing is an important way to make good use of the valuable data. Since the data cannot be disclosed publicly in some cases, encrypted data sharing schemes are proposed. However, encryption causes a certain difficulty in data usage. In order to balance the data usage and privacy, this paper proposes a privacy-preserving blockchain-based data sharing scheme for smart cities, in which data is only shared to the authorized user. Moreover, the data accountability, trust and non-repudiability are provided by using blockchain, the access control and data confidentiality are enabled by using Attribute-Based Encryption (ABE), the Interplanetary File System (IPFS) system is used to mitigate the limitation of blockchain storage. Furthermore, the proposed scheme provides retrieval privacy to users, the interest record is obfuscated with other unrelated records to protect the user's privacy. The theoretical analysis and simulation are performed, and the results show that the proposed scheme is feasible.

Keywords: Data sharing · Blockchain · Smart contract · Privacy preserving · Access control

1 Introduction

Nowadays, urban areas lived more than half of the global population [1]. The high concentration is affecting people's living conditions, for example, urban concentration causes traffic jams and increase waste emissions etc. Smart cities are developed as a response to these problems, it aims to use technologies to improve outcomes across all aspects of city operations, and achieve precise and meticulous urban governance. As an intelligent responses to various needs that including healthcare, environmental protection, etc., smart cities devotes to improving

S. Chellappan et al. (Eds.): CSoNet 2020, LNCS 12575, pp. 283–294, 2020.
https://doi.org/10.1007/978-3-030-66046-8_23

the citizens' quality of life [2] through efficient and unified city operation and adjustment.

With the rapid development of Internet, data has become a core resource for urban development. Since the construction of smart cities requires massive data to achieve the rational allocation of resources, it necessary to collect data across citywide departments and platforms. However, if the data is stored in different databases that restricts access and use, the full value of the data cannot be extracted. In order to promote the construction of smart cities and break through information barriers, it's necessary to centralize the different data across citywide and integrate them into a unified standards. Thus, security and efficiency data sharing scenarios to help providing readily available access for authorities and citizens are important and significant to smart cites.

The blockchain [3,4] is a potential technology to extend the data sharing degree, which can technically promote the realization of a series of urban development goals. Compared with the traditional centralized architecture, the blockchain does not rely on specific central nodes to process and store data. And it has properties like accountability, trust and non-repudiability, which enables users to know where their data stores and what is happening to their data. However, since the blockchain is replicated on many nodes and become bloated, it's not the most suitable platform for sharing and storing large data. To solve this problem, some schemes [5,6] leverage cloud system to mitigate the storage limitation of blockchain, in which the large data is stored in cloud while the commitment and index are stored on-chain. This combination makes data sharing still benefits from blockchain. Since the cloud server cannot be considered completely reliable, Interplanetary File System (IPFS) [7], the distributed storage system is proposed recently, which provides an efficient content-address block storage model. After uploading a file to the IPFS system, it is available to the entire network, and the file can be tracked and identified through its content hash. Thus the risk of a single point failure can be avoided.

Privacy is, of course, a fundamental requirement for data sharing in smart city. To better balance the privacy and availability of data, the Attribute-Based Encryption (ABE) scheme [8,9] is utilised to achieve data access control in the public data sharing system, only the one who fulfills the required attribute can obtain the resource. The ABE makes data sharing effective and controllable, and can prevent data disclosure to a certain degree. However, even though the cryptographic schemes can prevent the content be leaked to other parties, but the network-level information (e.g., IP addresses) or access patterns (e.g., specific blocks) are still available to the public, the transaction information may be extracted by using network measures [10]. Considering that many of the privacy technologies were invented only a few years ago, the privacy is still an open issue, it is necessary to propose some new privacy-preserving scheme to achieve the privacy-preserving blockchain-based data sharing.

There are many researches [5,11] focusing on the security and privacy of user's data. However, they ignore the fact that when a user retrieves some specific data in a public environment, his privacy may be revealed. For example, if an attacker observed a given user visited a site immediately before receiving the donation, he/she can speculate that the user may make a donation; moreover, if the attacker subsequently tracked that this user checks whether the transaction has been posted to the blockchain, the attacker can almost confirm this suspicion.

In order to balance the data usage and privacy, this paper provided a privacy-preserving decentralized data sharing scheme, in which accountability, trust and non-repudiability is provided by using blockchain; the access is controlled by using ABE encryption; the distributed system, IPFS is used to mitigate the limitation of blockchain storage while still benefit from blockhain; and furthermore, the proposed scheme provides retrieval privacy to data requesters by using an oblivious transfer based scheme. Our work include two main contributions:

1. We propose a privacy-preserving data sharing scheme for smart cities, which ensures user's privacy while he/she retrieving data through Ethereum blockchain. Additionally, this scheme also achieves data confidentiality, accountability, trust, and non-repudiability.
2. Our scheme incorporates hash collusion and oblivious transfer, allowing smart contract returns multiple records that satisfy the search criteria, thereby hiding the interest record and protecting user privacy. The user only obtains the record that is permitted to him, while others cannot know which is the interest one. It's means even the user obtains multiple records, he/she cannot get other data except those that he/she has permission to decrypt.

The rest of the paper is organized as follow. In Sect. 2, the background is introduced. In Sect. 3, the objective and system model of the proposed solution is described. The proposal is defined in Sect. 4. Analysis and simulation of the proposed solution is in Sect. 5. In Sect. 6, the related work is surveyed. Finally, in Sect. 7, we draw our conclusion.

2 Preliminaries

In this section, the preliminaries of the proposed scheme is provided. We briefly introduce some cryptographic backgrounds and assumption as follows.

Hash Collusion: Hash operation maps different inputs into a unique, fixed-length value, it's one of the most common software operations. Let h represents the hash function, if $h(x_1) \neq h(x_2)$, the equation $x_1 \neq x_2$ holds. However, if $h(x_1) = h(x_2)$, the equation $x_1 = x_2$ may not hold. The later case is called the "hash collision", which means even though the hash outputs are the same, the two input values are likely to be different.

Oblivious Transfer(OT): OT is a two-party protocol between a sender and a receiver, the sender keeping oblivious to what information the receiver actually obtains. It was first proposed by Rabin [12] in 1981, where the sender S sends a message m to the receiver R, R receives the message m with a probability of 1/2. And Even et al. [13] extended the OT in 1985, they proposed the 1-out-of-2 OT, where the sender S has 2 messages m_0 and m_1, and the receiver R

inputs his choice b. When the OT process ends, S cannot obtain any valuable information about b, and R can only obtain m_b while knows nothing about m_{1-b}. Then, t-out-of-n oblivious transfer was presented, where the sender has messages $\{m_1, m_2, ..., m_n\}$ and the receiver has choices $\{\sigma_1, \sigma_2, ..., \sigma_n\}$. After a transfer, the receiver obtains messages $m_{\sigma_1}, m_{\sigma_2}, ..., m_{\sigma_n}$, while the sender know nothing about the receiver's choices.

Assumption: It's assumed the user has a certification key that allowing him to downloaded a $manifest$ file from smart contract. From the $manifest$ file he/she can know the required attribute set $\mathbb{P} = \{a_1, a_2, ..., a_n\}$ that can decrypt his interested record, and he/she can get the ABE private key SK from a attribute authority prior to the retrieval. When the user wants to retrieve data again after a long time, he/she needs to update the $manifest$.

3 Objectives and System Model

The objectives and system model of the proposed encrypted data sharing scheme are presented in this section.

3.1 Objectives

- **Authorization**: to prevent the data abuse, the data should only be obtained by the requesters whose attributes meet the access policy.
- **Accountability**: to prevent the misbehavior and solve possible legal controversies, accountability should be guaranteed, which means the one who uploads the data can be traced easily.
- **Retrieval privacy**: the user can obtain his interest record which is included in $\{ m_{\sigma_1}, m_{\sigma_2}, ..., m_{\sigma_n}\}$, and others cannot know which is the interest one. Let Pr represents the probability of other users know which record is the interested one, in order to protect requester's privacy, $n \geq 2$ should be satisfied, thus $Pr \leq \frac{1}{2}$.
- **Efficiency**: the cost in terms of gas consumption of smart contracts in the scheme is acceptable.

3.2 System Models

As shown in Fig. 1, the system framework for a blockchain-based privacy-preserving data sharing scheme is designed. The components used in this system are: attribute authority(AA), content manager(CM), data requester(DR), IPFS, smart contracts.

1. **Attribute authority**: The AA is an entity that takes charge of the system attributes management and key generation. Prior to the scenario execution, AA assigns keys to users according to his attribute.

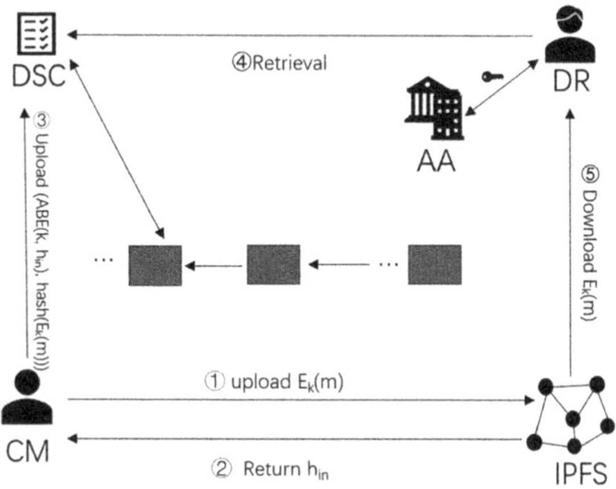

Fig. 1. The structure of the proposed scheme

2. **Content manager** : The content manager (always the owner of some resource) manages a specific type of data. CM is in charge of the data encryption, associates the ciphertext to the right policy, uploads the encrypted data on IPFS through a smart contract. Once the IPFS returns the hash index of the encrypted data to CM, it embeds the encrypted secret key and IPFS index h_{index} into an Ethereum transaction. Furthermore, CM is required to creates a description file called *manifest* file and send it to Ethereum blockchain.
3. **Data requester**: The Data requester, such as a doctor, who study a specific disease that needs data to support the research. DR owns some attributes, and he/she can request the attribute key from AA. DR invoke the smart contract to download required records and download the ciphertext from the IPFS.
4. **IPFS**: Interplanetary File System(IPFS) [14] is a peer-to-peer distributed file system that stores data in a distributed way. There is no central server, and single point failure can be avoided. Thus a resilient system of file storage and sharing can be provided. When CM uploads a file to the IPFS system, he/she can obtain a unique hash string, through which the ciphertext can be retrieved uniquely.
5. **Smart contract**: Smart contracts [15] are a kind of computer programs that defines transaction rules for participants. Once the smart contract formulated and deployed in Ethereum, it can be self-executed and self-verifed. In the proposed scheme, the smart contract is responsible for two jobs, 1) publish files on IPFS; and 2) provide the privacy-preserving data retrieval.

4 Our Proposal

In this section, the proposal is introduced. The proposed scenario can be carried out through the following five phases: Setup, Encrypt, Upload, Data retrieval, Decrypt.

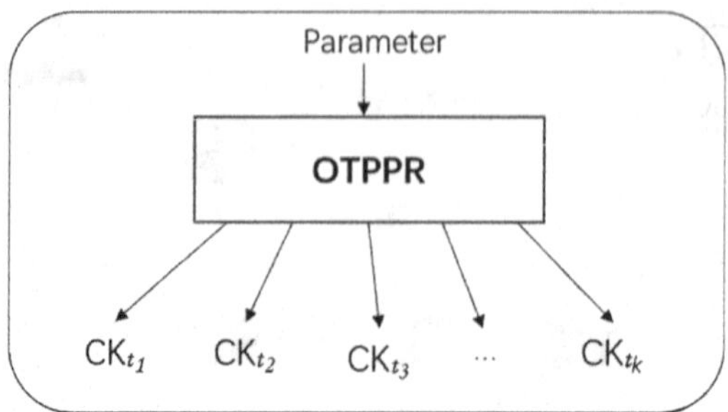

Fig. 2. The OT-based privacy preserving retrieval

Phase 1 Setup
This phase including two algorithms: the *Init* algorithm to initiate the public parameters PP and required key pairs (PK, MK), and the ABEGen algorithm to generate the ABE secret key SK for DR. Assuming the attribute set is $\mathcal{U}$, $|\mathcal{U}| = n$, let d represents the threshold, it means only when more than d attributes owned by the user satisfy the encryption policy, can he/she decrypt the cipher.

$AA.Init(\mathcal{K}) \rightarrow (PP, PK, SK)$: the Init algorithm inputs a security parameters $\mathcal{K}$, and outputs the public parameters $PP = \{g, p, G_1, \widehat{e}\}$, the public key $PK = \{G, T_1 = g^{\beta_1}, T_2 = g^{\beta_2}, ..., T_n = g^{\beta_n}, Y = \widehat{e}(g, g)^y\}$ and system master key $MK = \{\beta_1, \beta_2, ..., \beta_n, y\}$.

$AA.ABEGen(MK, w) \rightarrow SK$: the *ABEGen* algorithm inputs the master key MK and the encryption attribute set $w \sqsubseteq \mathcal{U}$ and chooses a $d-1$ degree polynomial function q that satisfies $q(0) = y$, then calculates:

$$D_i = g^{\frac{q(i)}{\beta_i}}, i \in w \tag{1}$$

$$SK = \{D_i\}_{i \in w} \tag{2}$$

Phase 2 Encrypt
CM first encrypts file F with a symmetric key k using the symmetric encryption algorithm such as AES, and then CM gets $CT = E_k(F)$. It's worth to note that every category of the file has a different symmetric key. CM chooses the attribute set w and encrypts the symmetric key k by the following ABE encryption algorithm. The detail encryption/decryption is referred to [8].

$CM.Encrypt(k, PK, w, r) \rightarrow CK$: The Encrypt algorithm first chooses a random number r, then it encrypts the symmetric key k under the attribute set w' and outputs the ciphered file:

$$CK = \{E = k \cdot Y^r, E_i = (T_i^r)_{i \in w}\} \tag{3}$$

Phase 3 Upload
In this phase, CM first uploads the encrypted file CT to the IPFS system. Then CM stores the encrypted key CK to smart contract.

1) CM uploads the encrypted file CT to IPFS

CM.Upload(CT) $\rightarrow h_{in}$: CM uploads the encrypted data CT to IPFS. As a return, CM obtains the output, the IPFS-hash h_{in} related to CT.

2) CM uploads the encrypted key CK to blockchain

CM.Upload($Eth_{CM}, ds, h_{in}, CK, hash(CT), w) \rightarrow manifest$: CM invokes the directory smart contract DSC through his Ethereum address Eth_{CM}, with the description ds, ciphertext $CK = E_{ABE}\{k\}$, the IPFS-hash h_{in}, the hash value $h(CT)$ as input. DSC stores $R = \{CK, h_{in}, hash(CT)\}$, and generates a unique location number for each record, represented by l_i. DSC stores the access attribute set w, the ds, and the l_i into the $manifest$ file.

Phase 4 Data retrieval

In this phase, CM can retrieve CK, which is generated by encrypting the key k.

The authorized DR firstly invokes DSC to download the $manifest$, in which he/she learns the unique location number l_i that his interest stores. Then, DR invokes the DSC to retrieve records. His/her privacy is protected by using the oblivious transfer based privacy preserving retrieval (OTPPR) showed in Fig. 2. The OTPPR outputs several records $\{CK_{t_1}, CK_{t_2}, CK_{t_3}, ..., CK_{t_n}\}$, which satisfy the search criteria, it provides privacy to DR by hiding the interest record in some unrelated records. Even through DR can obtain some unrelated records, he/she can't recover them without corresponding attributes. Thus the security of the unrelated data is ensured.

DR.Retrieve($Eth_{DR}, Eth_{DSC}, s, x, f, Str) \rightarrow \{CK_{t_1}, CK_{t_2}...\}$: DR ultimately obtains records $\{CK_{t_1}, CK_{t_2}...\}$ that include his interests CK_{t_i}. The DSC retrieves the record according to the input and sends those satisfy $h(l_i|x)_{i\in[s,f]} = Str$ to DR. s represents the start location of retrieval, and f represents the end location.

Phase 5 Decrypt

In this phase, DR first downloads the CT' from the IPFS, and then he/she verifies if the $hash(CT') = hash(CT)$. If holds, DR decrypts the symmetric key k from CK, then CM decrypts the file F from CT'.

DR.Decrypt($SK, CK) \rightarrow k$: In our assumption, if DR is an authorized requester who has the corresponding attributes, he/she can obtain the ABE private key $SK = D_i = \{g^{\frac{q(i)}{\beta_i}}\}_{i\in\precsim}$, p is a polynomial function with $q(0) = y$. The decryption algorithm outputs:

$$Y^s = e(E_i, D_i) = e(g, g)^{q(i)\cdot r} \tag{4}$$

$$k = CK/Y^r \tag{5}$$

Once DR obtained k, he/she can decrypt the file F with k using the symmetric encryption algorithm. DR gets $F = D_k(CT)$.

5 Theoretical Analysis and Simulations

In this section, we briefly discuss the properties of our scenario according to the proposed objectives (Sect. 3.1), which includes authorization, accountability, retrieval privacy. The simulation is also performed to demonstrate the feasibility of the proposed scheme.

5.1 Theoretical Analysis

Here, we discuss the properties of our scenario according to the proposed objectives (Sect. 3.1).

- **Authorization**
  The proposed scheme ensures authorized users to obtain the file F by using ABE encryption. CM can define which attributes is required in order to retrieve the F. The unauthorized user without the correct attributes key cannot obtained the symmetric key k. Only the user's attributes fulfill the associated policy can obtain the attribute key k, and can decrypt CT to obtain F. Therefore, the proposed scheme can achieve the authorization.
- **Accountability**
  Accountability is achieved by using smart contracts. Since the CT is uploaded to the blockchain, which is combined with its uploader's address. Once the disputes emerged, anyone can retrieve the uploader easily.
- **Retrieval Privacy**
  The retrieval privacy in the proposed scenario includes: the attribute of the retrieval user cannot be revealed, and the interest record cannot be predicted accurately. Firstly, the requester downloads the entire $manifest$ file, search the interest record location and attribute policy locally; Secondly, the requester uses the proposed privacy-preserving retrieval scheme to retrieve the $R = \{CK, h_{in}, hash(CT)\}$. Since the OTPPR scheme is used, the user can obtain at least two records, the probability of others know which is the user interest record is no more than $\frac{1}{2}$. During the retrieval phase, the requester did not expose his attributes, and the interested data is hidden in other records. Therefore, the proposed scheme achieved retrieval privacy to a certain degree.

Table 1. Smart contract cost test (Gasprice = 20Gwei, 1ether = 222.80 USD)

Function	Gas Used	Actual Cost(ether)	USD
Contract create	1215632	0.024313	5.416856
Setter_manifest	153617	0.003072	0.684517
Setter_R	250531	0.005011	1.116366

5.2 Simulations

The specific configuration of experimental platform and experimental environment are: 3.6 GHz Intel Core i7 with 16 GB RAM. The programming languages are python and solidity. We use Ganache v2.4.0 as the Ethereum blockchain environment to measure the gas cost of smart contract DSC.

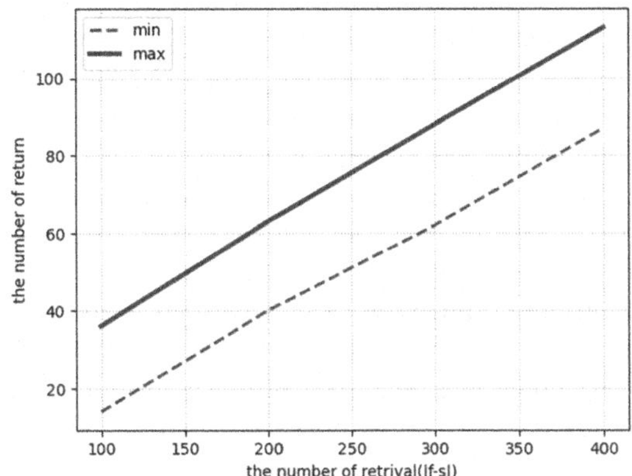

Fig. 3. The number of returned records

When we conducted the experiment, the gasPrice was set to 20 Gwei. And some of the smart contracts costs measured are shown in Table 1. The DSC is responsible for 1) upload $\{CK, hash(CT), h_{in}\}$ to blokhchain, and its cost is 0.005 ether; and 2) store the $manifest$, this operation costs 0.003 ether. The multiple executions costs of these operations are almost unchanged.

Each record $\{ds, w, l_i\}$ is 512-bit. When there are 10^4 records, the $manifest$ is about 4.5 M, it is feasible for users to download the entire file. We use hash function keccak256 to generate hash collisions to obtain multiple records, and masking the user's interest records. We set $|Str| = 3$ and measure the number of returned records vary from the value $f - b$, the result is shown in Fig. 3. The burlywood one represents the max number of the returned record, while the cornflowerblue one represents the min. When $f - s = 100$, it can be seen that the max number of return is 36 and the min is 14. It means that the requester can mask his interested record in other records, and the number of mask records is range from [13] .

6 Related Work

Smart cities include many aspects, such as smart healthcare, smart grid and smart transportation, etc. Blockchain has the properties like accountability, privacy, trust and non-repudiability, which can ensure data integrity, encourage individuals and organizations to share their data, achieve the transparent city management, and promote the trusted and secure implementation and development of smart cities [5].

There are many researches combined the blockchain with smart cities, for example, Alevtina [3] proposed a blockchain-based distributed Electronic Medical Records (EMR) storage and processing system. In [16], a smart healthcare system is presented, in which the physiological signals from the human body are protected based on blockchain technologies. In these researches, all the collected data is stored on the blockchain, the storage limitation of blockchain is the main problem. Laure and Martha [17] proposed a public blockchain-based data sharing scheme, in which large data is stored off the blockchain (such as stores in the cloud), and the encrypted link to the data is stored on-chain. The off-chain storage platform in Laure and Martha [17] can mitigate the storage pressure, it can provide a efficient data storage and sharing environment that can be used to play the role of off-chain database. However, just like the traditional centralized sever, their off-chain database cannot be considered completely reliable, and cannot prevent some attacks, such as the DDos attack. The decentralized storage system, IPFS, which is a peer-to-peer distributed file system that stores data in a distributed way [14], can be used to avoid the single point failure of cloud server.

Encrypting data before uploading it to the sharing platform is one of the main protective mechanisms recommended by the Cloud Security Alliance [18], which can balance the privacy and the execution payment of gas. However, encryption causes difficulties in the usage and access to data. In order to enable availability and controllability of the encrypted data, the attribute-based access control schemes [8,19] are proposed by leveraging attribute-based encryption. Yang et al. [9] indicates that the access policy may leak privacy, and they proposed a data access control scheme with privacy-preserving policy, in which the whole access policy can be hidden. These schemes can provide a good security and privacy for user data, however, they didn't consider the privacy of data requester.

The most similar work to this paper is Wang et al.'s work [20], they proposed a data storage and sharing scheme for decentralized storage systems, they aim to achieve fine-grained access control for data sharing, as well as solve the unreliable problem of the cloud, they employ a symmetric searchable encryption algorithm to smart contract to protect requester's privacy. However, since all requesters in their scheme own the same search key, and the smart contract can be viewed to all users, user's privacy may be revealed to adversaries who also have the search key.

Inspired by these papers, we proposed a data sharing scheme. The ABE encryption algorithm, decentralized IPFS system, and Ethereum are used to ensure data security; to provide requester privacy, the OTPPR scheme is used to hide the interest records to several records that satisfy the specific condition.

7 Conclusions

This paper provide a privacy-preserving distributed data sharing scheme for smart cities. The advantages can be concluded: 1) The content manager has the ability to decide who can get the data by specifying access policy, thus the access control is achieved; 2) Data is uploaded by smart contract, which provides reliability and accountability to prevent misbehavior and controversies; 3) The decentralized IPFS is used to solve the problem of single point of failure, and moreover, it also has a series of advantages such as low price and high throughput compare to traditional centralized storage system; 4) Although Ethereum provides pseudonymous to user, the logic of data retrieval is controlled by the smart contract, it is public, this could be a serious threat to privacy for both data and its requester. By hiding the interest record with other unrelated records, the proposed scheme can solve the privacy issue of retrieval data through smart contract.

However, the proposed scheme cannot provide the same privacy level. The proposed OTPPR scheme did return several records according to the input, but the number is not fixed. According to our experiments, if the retrieval input satisfies $f - s = 100, |str| = 3$, at least 14 records will be returned, and at most 36 records can be returned, thus the privacy level is different for different record. In future research, we will study methods that can return data evenly to improve the privacy of data retrieval.

Acknowledgment. This work was partly supported by Natural Science Foundation (U19A2066), Project of Chengdu Science and Technology (2019-YF09-00048-CG).

References

1. Bocquier, P.: World urbanization prospects: an alternative to the un model of projection compatible with the mobility transition theory. Demographic Res. **12**, 197–236 (2005)
2. Qin, H., Li, H., Zhao, X.: Development status of domestic and foreign smart city. Global Presence **9**, 50–52 (2010)
3. Alevtina, D., Xu, Z., Ryu, S., Michael, S., Wang, F.: Secure and trustable electronic medical records sharing using blockchain. In AMIA annual symposium proceedings, vol. 2017, p. 650. American Medical Informatics Association (2017)
4. Sultana, T., Almogren, A., Akbar, M., Zuair, M., Ullah, I., Javaid, N.: Data sharing system integrating access control mechanism using blockchain-based smart contracts for iot devices. Appl. Sci. **10**(2), 488 (2020)
5. Xie, S., Zheng, Z., Chen, W., Jiajing, W., Dai, H.-N., Imran, M.: Blockchain for cloud exchange: a survey. Comput. Electric. Eng. **81**, 106526 (2020)
6. Wei, P.C., Dahu Wang, Y., Zhao, S.K., Tyagi, S., Kumar, N.: Blockchain data-based cloud data integrity protection mechanism. Fut. Generation Comput. Syst. **102**, 902–911 (2020)
7. Huang, H., Lin, J., Zheng, B., Zheng, Z., Bian, J.: When blockchain meets distributed file systems: an overview, challenges, and open issues. IEEE Access **8**, 50574–50586 (2020)
8. Vipul, G., Omkant, P., Amit, S., Waters, B.: Attribute-based encryption for fine-grained access control of encrypted data. In Proceedings of the 13th ACM Conference on Computer and Communications Security, pp. 89–98 (2006)

9. Yang, K., Han, Q., Li, H., Zheng, K., Zhou, S., Shen, X.: An efficient and fine-grained big data access control scheme with privacy-preserving policy. IEEE Internet of Things J. **4**(2), 563–571 (2016)
10. Kumar, E.S.: Preserving privacy in ethereum blockchain. Ann. Data Sci. (2020)
11. Qi, F., He, D., Zeadally, S., Khan, M.K., Kumar, N.: A survey on privacy protection in blockchain system. J. Network Comput. Appl. **126**, 45–58 (2019)
12. Michael, O.R.: How to exchange secrets with oblivious transfer. In: IACR Cryptol. ePrint Arch., 2005(187) (2005)
13. Even, S., Goldreich, O., Lempel, A.: A randomized protocol for signing contracts. Commun. ACM **28**(6), 637–647 (1985)
14. Juan, B.: Ipfs-content addressed, versioned, p2p file system. arXiv preprint arXiv:1407.3561 (2014)
15. Wood, G., et al.: Ethereum: a secure decentralised generalised transaction ledger. Ethereum Project Yellow Paper **151**(2014), 1–32 (2014)
16. Zhao, H., Zhang, Y., Peng, Y., Xu, R.: Lightweight backup and efficient recovery scheme for health blockchain keys. In: 2017 IEEE 13th International Symposium on Autonomous Decentralized System (ISADS), pp. 229–234. IEEE (2017)
17. Laure, A.L., Martha, B.K.: Blockchain for health data and its potential use in health it and health care related research. In: ONC/NIST Use of Blockchain for Healthcare and Research Workshop. Gaithersburg, Maryland, United States: ONC/NIST, pp. 1–10 (2016)
18. Ilya, S., Sergey, Z.: A blockchain-based access control system for cloud storage. In: 2018 IEEE Conference of Russian Young Researchers in Electrical and Electronic Engineering (EIConRus), pp. 1575–1578. IEEE (2018)
19. Francesco, B., Vincenzo De, A., Gianluca, L., Lorenzo, M., Antonia, R.: An attribute-based privacy-preserving ethereum solution for service delivery with accountability requirements. In: Proceedings of the 14th International Conference on Availability, Reliability and Security, pp. 1–6 (2019)
20. Wang, S., Zhang, Y., Zhang, Y.: A blockchain-based framework for data sharing with fine-grained access control in decentralized storage systems. IEEE Access **6**, 38437–38450 (2018)

Verifiable Blockchain Redacting Method for a Trusted Consortium with Distributed Chameleon Hash Authority

Weilong Lv[1], Songjie Wei[1](✉), Shasha Li[1], and Minghui Yu[2]

[1] School of Computer Science and Engineering, Nanjing University of Science and Technology, Nanjing, China
swei@njust.edu.cn

[2] School of Science, Nanjing University of Science and Technology, Nanjing, China

Abstract. Blockchain is highly evaluated for its vantages of decentralization, anonymity, and information immutability, where the last one means historical data recorded on a blockchain ledger cannot be manipulated once committed under consensus. This guarantees the integrity and reliability of data on blockchain. However, when fake, illegal, expired or redundant transactions on a blockchain ledger need be corrected or removed, immutability disables blockchain from redacting or revoking data without violating consensus. As a complement, this paper proposes a chameleon-hash based design of a decentralized ledger redacting method for consortium blockchain. Considering the necessity of decentralized transaction redaction, that is, the trap door of the chameleon hash should not be generated and stored at a single node, the traditional chameleon hash is optimized for decentralization. The improved chameleon hash algorithm allows authority nodes in consortium blockchain cooperatively generating chameleon hash key pairs. Meanwhile, the usability and accountability of the proposed blockchain system are measured. Finally, the optimized chameleon hash algorithm is applied to construct a prototype chain enabling maintenance and compression of historical transactions. Experiments show that according to the ledger redacting method proposed, block data can be redacted and compressed for at least 30% with consistency, and the crucial phases of ledger redaction are less time-consuming compared with existing works, with no harm on security strength as before.

Keywords: Consortium blockchain · Chameleon hash · Blockchain redaction · Authority decentralization

1 Introduction

Blockchain is prevailing in every aspect as information technology innovation, with tremendous amount of news, research papers and application proposals booming. In a typical blockchain system, data falls into two categories: independent data not related to history, and dependent data that is related. In blockchain 1.0 represented by Bitcoin [1], blockchain system is mainly designed for recording and processing financial

S. Chellappan et al. (Eds.): CSoNet 2020, LNCS 12575, pp. 295–306, 2020.
https://doi.org/10.1007/978-3-030-66046-8_24

transactions. For the transfer records in blocks, there is no need to design redaction operations to reverse the transactions. On the one hand, because the transfer records are not independent data, there is a certain impact between their values and transactions in the neighboring blocks, which cannot be simply redacted or deleted. On the other hand, it is precisely due to the immutability characteristic of blockchain data that users are convinced to trust blockchain-based digital cryptocurrency. In blockchain 2.0 represented by Ethereum, users not only conduct financial transactions in the blockchain, but convert tangible and intangible objects in physical world into digital tokens and exchange, to achieve the so-called asset tokenization. There may exist situations where block data needs be redacted. For example, where in a blockchain-based intellectual property protection platform [2, 3], a users' intellectual property can be converted into a digital token and issued on blockchain. If the intellectual property regulation changes thereafter, the platform is obliged to redact it, to make data meet the new requirements by law.

Even from the perspective of national governance, blockchain should have the ability to redact data under specific conditions too. The EU's General Data Protection Regulation [4] establishes the right to be forgotten of personal privacy data at the legislative level for the first time, which means that individuals have the right to delete their personal data in a platform [5]. China's Blockchain Information Service Management Regulations require any blockchain information service provider to have emergency handling capabilities such as redaction and deletion of information prohibited by law. It is expected that in the near future, German and U.S. courts will soon have service providers with blockchains containing offensive contents convicted guilty [6]. Therefore, under certain conditions, allowing blockchain to redact problematic data is in line with national policy requirements and is conducive to the healthy development of the blockchain system in various countries.

Immutability is one of the major merits in blockchain. It means that historical data in past blocks cannot be manipulated once confirmed. Immutability guarantees the integrity and reliability of the historical data of the blockchain, but also prevents blockchain from redacting the historical data in question. In addition, because the current mainstream blockchain does not have data deletion and compression functions, the amount of data on chain continues to increase, resulting in a huge storage overhead and significant decrease in data processing efficiency. Therefore, it is necessary to find a way which adapting to the existing blockchain architecture to redact blockchain data, the core of which is the ledger redacting method applicable to the blockchain [7].

Current research on redactable blockchain is still in its infancy with only a few related proposals published. Most methods [8–10] are mainly based on the chameleon hash algorithm [11]. These methods store private subkeys of the chameleon hash on multiple nodes, the ledger redaction process achieves a certain degree of decentralization, but the generation or restoration of the keys still requires a centralized trusted node, so decentralization of these method is not sufficient.

The ledger redacting method proposed in this paper is not a customized design and development for a specific existing blockchain system. It does not rely on a specific blockchain architecture or a unique block structure. Actually, a practical ledger redaction function should not rely on any specification or assumption, but requires universality and compatibility across blockchain platforms and systems, and can redact a ledger without affecting the original integrity verification of the blockchain to ensure compatibility with the data and algorithms of the current mainstream blockchain systems. This paper adapts and revises the chameleon hash algorithm, and implements a distributed design for its key management, which realizes the redaction and verification of data on the chain that guarantees the original hash value.

As contributions, we improve and extend the traditional chameleon hash algorithm for blockchain data redaction. The new algorithm allows multiple nodes to cooperate and generate the public/private key pairs for the chameleon hash, ensuring the decentralization of the key generation and synchronization process; Aiming at the consortium blockchain, we use the improved chameleon hash algorithm to design a decentralized ledger redacting method, and propose a redactable consortium blockchain architecture. This method is mainly used to redact independent data in blocks. Performance evaluations with experiments and security analysis in theory on the proposed ledger redacting method demonstrate its superior advantages in block data compression ratio, execution overhead, and the security strength.

2 Chameleon Hash Algorithm

2.1 Mathematical Principles

Traditional blockchain guarantees data integrity with verifiable blocks and transactions relying on the collision difficulty of hash algorithm, while chameleon hash algorithm contains a trap door or a private key, which one may utilize to find collisions easily. In a chameleon hash function, there are two parameters: plaintext m and variable parameter r. After changing the plaintext, the equation $H(m, r) = H(m_2, r_2)$ can be established by changing the variable parameter. It mainly uses the following two properties of exponential operation: $g^a \times g^b = g^{a+b}$ and $(g^a)^b = g^{ab}$.

Calculating Chameleon Hash Value. The calculation formula of the chameleon hash value is $H(m, r) = g^m \times h^r$, where $h = g^x$, h is the public key, x is the private key, g is the public parameter, and m is the plaintext.

Forging new variable parameter r_2.. When knowing the private key x, bring $h = g^x$ into equation $H(m, r) = g^m \times h^r$, then get the equations $H(m, r) = g^m \times h^r = g^m \times g^{xr} = g^{m+xr}$ and $H(m_2, r_2) = g^{m_2} \times h^{r_2} = g^{m_2} \times g^{xr_2} = g^{m_2+xr_2}$. Since the two formulas have the same base and $H(m, r) = H(m_2, r_2)$, the new variable parameter r_2 can be forged by making the exponents equal. The new variable parameter $r_2 = (m + xr - m_2)/x$.

2.2 Algorithm Introduction

Krawczyk et al. [11] proposed the chameleon hash and signature algorithm in 2000. The chameleon hash algorithm proposed by Krawczyk et al. has five sub-functions which are described as follows:

- $pp \leftarrow \text{Setup}(\lambda)$: Input security parameter λ, output public parameter $pp = \{p, q, g\}$, where p, q satisfies $p = kq + 1$, and g is the generator of the multiplicative cyclic group Z_p^*;

- $\{h, x\} \leftarrow$ KeyGen(pp) : Input public parameter pp, output public key h and private key x, where x is an element randomly selected in the multiplicative cyclic group Z_q^*, and $h = g^x \mod q$;
- $CH \leftarrow$ Hash(h, m, r) : Input public key h, plaintext m, variable parameter r, output value of the chameleon hash $CH = g^m h^r \ mod\ p$, where m, r are elements of Z_q^*;
- $r_2 \leftarrow$ Forge(x, m, r, m_2) : Input private key x, original plaintext m, original variable parameter r, and new plaintext m_2, output a new variable parameter r_2 that matches m_2, where m, r, m_2 are elements of Z_q^*, and $r_2 = (m + xr - m_2)x^{-1} \mod q$;
- $0 or 1 \leftarrow$ Verify(h, m, r, CH) : Input public key h, plaintext m, variable parameter r, and the value of the chameleon hash CH, verify whether CH matches m, r. If yes, output 1; otherwise, output 0.

2.3 Algorithm Improvement

According to the above introduction, we may notice that the chameleon hash algorithm can directly replace the original hash function in blockchain, but such replacement requires the generation and use of keys being on a single trusted node. Decentralization is a critical characteristic for blockchain systems and applications. The overall process of transaction redaction operations should meet the decentralization characteristic as much as possible. Therefore, the original chameleon hash algorithm needs be improved.

Assume that there are w nodes in the consortium blockchain, of which n nodes are authority nodes with transaction redaction permissions. Make the system's private key $x = x_1 + x_2 + \ldots + x_n$, where $x_1, x_2, \ldots, x_n$ are the private subkeys corresponding to each authority node, and make the system's public key $h = g^{x_1 + x_2 + \ldots + x_n} = g^{x_1} g^{x_2} \ldots g^{x_n} = h_1 h_2 \ldots h_n$, where $h_1, h_2, \ldots, h_n$ are the public subkeys corresponding to each authority node. The improved algorithm is described as follows.

- $pp \leftarrow$ Setup(λ) : Input security parameter λ, output public parameter $pp = \{p, q, g\}$, where p, q satisfies $p = kq + 1$, and g is the generator of the multiplicative cyclic group Z_p^*;
- $\{h_i, x_i\} \leftarrow$ KeyGen(pp) : This function is called locally by each authority node. For the i th authority node, input public parameter pp, output the i th authority node's public subkey h_i and private subkey x_i, where x_i is an element randomly selected in the multiplicative cyclic group Z_q^*, and $h_i = g^{x_i} \ mod\ q$;
- $CH \leftarrow$ Hash(h, m, r) : Assume there are n authority nodes in the consortium blockchain. Input system's public key h, that is, the product of public subkeys of all authority nodes $h_1 h_2 \ldots h_n$, plaintext m, and variable parameter r, output the value of the chameleon hash $CH = g^m (h_1 h_2 \ldots h_n)^r \ mod\ p$, where m, r are elements of Z_q^*;
- $r_2 \leftarrow$ Forge(x, m, r, m_2) : Assume that k authority nodes have participated in the packaging process of a certain transaction. Input the system's private key x, that is, the sum of private subkey of the k authority nodes $x_1 + x_2 + \ldots + x_k$, original plaintext m, original variable parameter r, and new plaintext m_2, output a new variable parameter r_2 that matches m_2, where m, r, m_2 are elements of Z_q^*, $r_2 = (m + xr - m_2)x^{-1} \ mod\ q$, and $x = x_1 + x_2 + \ldots + x_k$;
- $0 or 1 \leftarrow$ Verify(h, m, r, CH) : Suppose a transaction that needs be redacted has k nodes involved in its packaging process. Input the system's public key h, that is, the

product of public subkeys of all authority nodes $h_1h_2 \ldots h_k$, plaintext m, variable parameter r, and the value of the chameleon hash CH, verify whether CH matches m, r. If yes, output 1; otherwise, 0.

2.4 Security Strength Analysis

The security analysis of the original algorithm is presented in [11]. This paper focuses on the security of the improved part of the algorithm.

Assume that there are n authority nodes in the consortium blockchain, among which the first i ($i \in [1, n)$) of the authority nodes are malicious nodes, and they know the public parameters $\{p, q, g\}$, the system's public key h, and their own private subkeys $\{x_1, x_2, \ldots, x_i\}$. In the improved chameleon hash:

$$\begin{aligned} H(m, r) &= g^m h^r \\ &= g^m (h_1 h_2 \ldots h_i h_{i+1} h_{i+2} \ldots h_n)^r \\ &= g^m (g^{x_1} g^{x_2} \ldots g^{x_i} h_{i+1} h_{i+2} \ldots h_n)^r \end{aligned}$$

If these malicious nodes want to forge a variable parameter r_2, so that $H(m, r) = H(m_2, r_2)$, without knowing the private subkeys of other authority nodes, for them:

$$\begin{aligned} H(m, r) &= g^m (g^{x_1} g^{x_2} \ldots g^{x_i} h_{i+1} h_{i+2} \ldots h_n)^r \\ &= g^{m+(x_1+x_2+\ldots+x_i)r} (h_{i+1} h_{i+2} \ldots h_n)^r \end{aligned}$$

Let $m' = m + (x_1 + x_2 + \ldots + x_i)r$, $h' = h_{i+1}h_{i+2} \ldots h_n$, then $H(m, r) = g^{m'}h'^r$, and similarly, $H(m_2, r_2) = g^{m_2'}h'^{r_2}$.

According to the variable substitution in the previous step, it is not difficult to find that its form is consistent with the original chameleon hash algorithm, so malicious nodes who want to calculate r_2 can only make $g^{m'}h'^r = g^{m_2'}h'^{r_2}$. Since the malicious nodes only know g, m', r, m_2', h', under this circumstance, if they want to forge r_2, the difficulty is equivalent to cracking the original chameleon hash algorithm, so the improved chameleon hash algorithm is secure as the original chameleon hash algorithm.

3 Ledger Redacting Method for Consortium Blockchain

3.1 Technical Route

In blockchain, each block is composed of a header and a body. The header includes data including a hash of the parent block, a timestamp, a Merkle root, etc. The body contains transactions with contents Tx and hashes H that determine the Merkle root in the block header. The block structure for Bitcoin as an example is shown in Fig. 1.

The integrity verification of the blockchain is mainly implemented by hash function. Miners perform hash calculation on the block headers of the parent blocks to ensure that new blocks can be connected to the parent blocks in an orderly manner. Miners perform hash calculations on the transactions to ensure that packaged transactions cannot be tampered with. In order to ensure the compatibility of the method with current mainstream

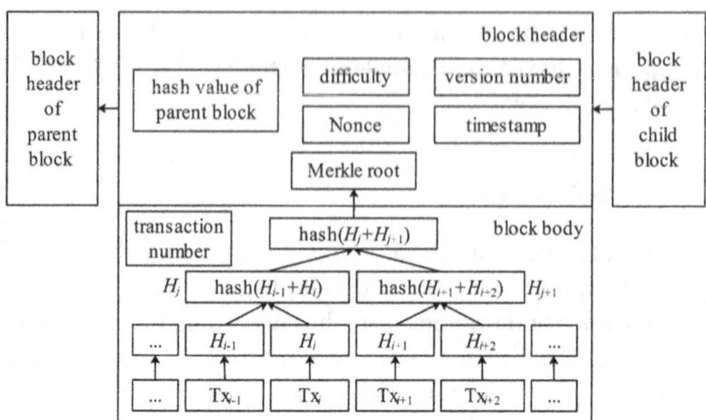

Fig. 1. Bitcoin block structure

blockchains, this paper expects that the ledger redacting method proposed does not rely on specific blockchain architecture and block structure as much as possible, and can redact the ledger without affecting the original integrity verification of the blockchain [12, 13].

We propose to replace the hash function of the transaction data hashes in the block body with the improved chameleon hash function. In such method, if the transaction to be redacted is in the i th block, the only need is to redact the transaction content of this transaction in the i th block, and then reforge the relevant variable parameter of this transaction in the i th block. Therefore, after the transaction content is changed, the hash value of this transaction is not changed. Specifically, in most cases, each transaction is in an irredactable state. When the i th transaction of the j th block needs to be redacted, the new transaction content m_i' will replace the original transaction content m_i in the block body. At this time, transaction i becomes transaction i'. Then use the pre-generated system's chameleon hash private key to forge a variable parameter r_i' that matches the transaction content m_i' and redact the relevant fields in the block body so that the relevant fields in the block body match the new transaction i'.

3.2 Key Generation Granularity of Chameleon Hash

Since the chameleon hash algorithm introduces the concept of public-private keys, for authority nodes, they need extra storage space to store data about public-private keys. At the same time, for a blockchain system, the synchronization and broadcast of public-private keys may bring in extra time overhead. If a pair of chameleon hash public-private keys are generated for each transaction, although this guarantee after the private key of a certain transaction is revealed, it will not affect the security of other transactions. However, this key generation granularity brings huge time and space costs, and greatly affects the efficiency of the blockchain system. The other extreme key generation granularity, i.e., the entire consortium blockchain only generates a single pair of chameleon hash public-private keys with trivial time and space overhead, but obviously if the private key of a certain transaction is revealed, all transactions in the consortium blockchain will be at the risk of being redacted.

Considering a compromise key generation granularity taking time periods as the key generation granularity. For each time interval, a pair of chameleon hash public-private keys is generated, and all transactions in all blocks generated during this time period use this pair of public-private keys to calculate the hash value. The time periods can be divided according to physical time, for example a pair of public-private keys for every few hours, days, months, etc. Or they can be divided according to virtual time, like a pair of public-private keys for every few blocks. The advantage of this kind of granularity is that the designer of the consortium blockchain can bargain security level and time and space costs by himself and flexibly set the key generation time suitable for his consortium blockchain. This paper adopts such kind of key generation granularity.

3.3 Accountability of Ledger Redacting Method

Considering the specificity of an ledger redaction operation, the system needs verify the identity of the operation proposer and maintain accountability when necessary. Therefore, this paper stipulates that the proposer must sign a redaction request [14] before broadcasting the operation. After receiving the proposal request, other authority nodes verify the identity of the proposer by comparing the ledger redaction request and signature, and store the proposal and signature locally as a redaction record. When a problem arises that requires accountability, the proposer can be found by comparing the redaction records in the local database, and using the signature as evidence to hold the proposer accountable. The fields of the redaction proposal will be described in detail in Sect. 3.4.

Authority nodes redaction records to facilitate accountability. Although this brings extra storage costs to the authority nodes, for the stability and accountability of the blockchain, the authority nodes are obliged to keep these records. At the same time, only authority nodes but not all nodes need to save these redaction records. For ordinary nodes, they still only need to store the main chain data. Therefore, the storage costs of ordinary nodes in the system is unchanged or relatively reduced.

3.4 Design of Ledger Redaction Operation Related Functions

This section details the specific design of ledger redaction operation related functions, including initialization of consortium blockchain, transaction packaging function, and transaction redaction function.

Initialization of the Consortium Blockchain. In the initialization phase of the consortium blockchain, in addition to performing the original operation of the blockchain initialization, system also executes the initialization function of the chameleon hash algorithm Setup(λ) to obtain the public parameter *pp*, and then stores the public parameter *pp* in the genesis block.

Transaction Packaging Function. Before transactions are packaged, all authority nodes should complete the generation operation of chameleon hash public-private subkeys and broadcast operation of the chameleon hash public subkeys. Each authority node calculates the system public key based on the public subkeys of other authority nodes. When the system public key has been calculated, the transaction packaging operation can be performed. The process is as follows.

1. Consortium blockchain system selects a miner in the authority nodes.
2. The miner generates a block. For each transaction data m_i, a variable parameter r_i is randomly selected, then the miner uses the system public key h that has been calculated before to execute the hash function $\mathrm{Hash}(h, m_i, r_i)$ to obtain the chameleon hash value CH_i of the i th transaction. The miner stores CH_i with the corresponding transaction data m_i and the variable parameter r_i in the block body, and stores the system's chameleon hash public key h of the block in the block header.
3. The miner connects this block to the previous block and broadcasts it.

Transaction Redaction Function. The transaction redaction process is as follows.

1. When a transaction content m_i needs to be redacted to m_i', an authority node in the consortium blockchain generates a transaction redaction proposal *redactTx* and broadcasts it to other authority nodes that have participated in the block generation for verification. The transaction redaction proposal contains the information of the publisher of the proposal *proposerID*, the block number of the transaction to be redacted *blockNum*, the transaction number *txNum*, the transaction content before the redaction m_i, the transaction content after the redaction m_i', the reason for the redaction *redactReason*, the signature of the proposer *proposerSig*, and the proposal state *proposalState*, that is

$$\begin{aligned} redactTx = \{ & proposerID, blockNum, txNum, m_i, m_i', \\ & redactReason, proposerSig, proposalState\}. \end{aligned}$$

Where the proposal state *proposalState* can be divided into three types: active, accepted and rejected. The initial state of proposal is active.

2. Other authority nodes will verify the correctness and rationality of the proposal after receiving *redactTx*. Correctness refers to whether the proposal is consistent with the signature, and rationality refers to whether the redaction operation of transaction i is reasonable. If a certain authority node thinks that the proposal is correct, it signs and broadcasts the verification pass message to other authority nodes. If all authority nodes agree to the proposal, each authority node changes the state of the proposal to accepted and returns its own chameleon hash private subkey x_i about the transaction to the proposal node. After the proposal node obtains all the private subkeys, it can calculate the crucial system private key x. If an authority node object to the proposal or the life cycle of the proposal has expired, each authority node changes the state of the proposal to rejected.
3. After obtaining all the private subkeys, the proposer executes the variable parameter forging function $\mathrm{Forge}(x, m_i, r_i, m_i)$ to obtain a new variable parameter r_i', replaces the variable parameter r_i about transaction i in the block, and finally broadcasts the transaction redaction message, that is, the accepted redaction proposal and the new variable parameter r_i'.

After ordinary nodes receive the transaction redaction message, they execute the hash verification function $\mathrm{Verify}\left(h, m_i', r_i', CH_i\right)$ to verify whether r_i', m_i' and CH_i match, and update the local block information if they match. After authority nodes receive the transaction redaction message, they first check whether there is a legal record of the transaction redacted in the local database, and then verify the integrity of the transaction. If the verification is successful, they update the local block information.

4 Performance Evaluation

In this section, performance analysis and evaluation are performed from two aspects: block compression ratio and running time of crucial phase. In order to specifically evaluate the performance of the proposed method, all programs are tested on a host configured with an Intel Core i7-8700 CPU, 16 GB memory, and a 1 TB hard drive.

4.1 Compression Ratio

In addition to the transaction contents and transaction hashes, the block data in the consortium blockchain also includes other data of the block. After some transactions are deleted, the transaction contents are deleted, but the transaction hashes, variable parameters and other data of the block still exist in the block. The concept of compression ratio *compressionRatio* in this paper refers to the ratio of the size of the new block after deletion $size_{newBlock}$ to the original block size before deletion $size_{oldBlock}$, that is

$$compressionRatio = \frac{size_{newBlock}}{size_{oldBlock}}$$

compressionRatio of a block is $[k\%, 100\%]$, $k \in [\min, 100]$. Obviously, when a block is not redacted, the value is 100%. The best (minimum) *compressionRatio* possible to achieve is $k\%$. For an empty block with no transaction, k is 100. For a block with the most number of transactions allowed, k is valued as min, which is always greater than 0.

We use Ethereum block data as a standard to construct experimental data. In Ethereum, the size of block header is 508 bytes, a block has an average of about 100 transactions, and a transaction takes up about 230 bytes of space. We try to perform a transaction deletion operation on a block with 100 transactions, and delete 1, 10, 50, and all transactions respectively. Theoretically, no matter how many transactions are deleted, the size of the block header will not change. This is because the transaction data is only stored in the block body and has nothing to do with the block header. The size of the block gradually decreases with more deleted transactions until it equals to $(size_r + size_{CH}) \times txCount$, where $size_r$ is the size of the variable parameter r, $size_{CH}$ is the size of the chameleon hash CH, and $txCount$ is the number of transactions. And *compressionRatio* can be expressed as

$$compressionRatio = \frac{size_{oldBlock} - txCount \times size_{tx}}{size_{oldBlock}}$$

In this experiment, $size_r = 32$ bytes, $size_{CH} = 32$ bytes, and $txCount = 100$, so after deleting all transactions, the block still has 6400 bytes, which is consistent with theory. Because the size of the block header data is constant and the variable parameter r and the chameleon hash value CH in the block will not be deleted, when the block is large enough, that is, the number of transactions is sufficient, this method's *compressionRatio* will be lower than 30%. The result of the compression ratio test is shown in Table 1.

Table 1. Compression ratio test

Delete x transactions	Size of block header	Size of block body	Ratio of deleted transactions to original transactions	Compression ratio
0	508 bytes	22677 bytes	0%	100%
1	508 bytes	22547 bytes	1%	99.4%
10	508 bytes	21070 bytes	10%	93.1%
50	508 bytes	14550 bytes	50%	64.9%
100	508 bytes	6400 bytes	100%	29.8%

4.2 Running Time of Crucial Phases

In order to realize the transaction redaction and compression function, this ledger redacting method introduces the chameleon hash algorithm on the basis of the traditional blockchain and adds related consensus and additional steps. Extra steps definitely increase the running time of the process related to the redaction operation. We conduct experiments to compare between the traditional blockchain, the redactable blockchain based on the chameleon hash, and the consortium blockchain proposed in this paper, mainly testing their running time in four crucial phases, that is, blockchain initialization, block generation, block synchronization, and transaction redaction. Since method [8] and method [10] are not much different in the algorithm aspect and the steps of the crucial phases, except that method [8] is selected for comparison. In this experiment, each blockchain has 15 nodes, and each block has an average of 100 transactions. The histogram of the running time of the crucial phases of the redactable consortium blockchain is shown in Fig. 2.

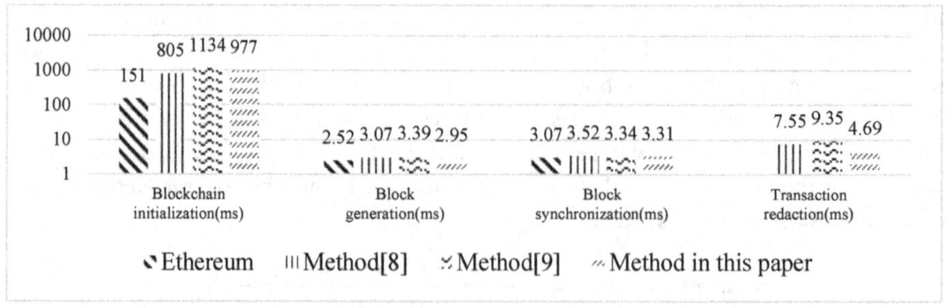

Fig. 2. The running time of the crucial phases of blockchain

In the blockchain initialization phase, since methods in [8, 9] and our method are all based on the chameleon hash algorithm, it is necessary to complete the initialization of the chameleon hash in the blockchain initialization phase and store the public parameters in the genesis block. Therefore, compared with the traditional blockchain, it bringsan in extra time cost of 800 ms.

In the block generation phase, all methods replace the parent block hash or the transaction hash in the traditional blockchain with the chameleon hash, and the other steps are not changed. Since the execution time of the chameleon hash is slightly longer than the traditional hash, the blockchain based on the chameleon hash increases the time costs by about 500 μs compared to the traditional blockchain, which is negligible.

The block synchronization phase mainly completes hash verification and block data storage. Using the chameleon hash algorithm, the verification sub-function of the chameleon hash is needed in the hash verification process. The running time of this sub-function is slightly longer than the verification sub-function of the traditional hash algorithm, so the method based on the chameleon hash increases the time cost of about 400 μs compared to the traditional blockchain, with less impact on block synchronization.

In the transaction redaction phase, this experiment attempts to redact all 100 transactions in a block. Since the traditional blockchain has no transaction redaction function, it is not experimented. Method [9] needs to complete multi-party computation at this phase. Its time costs is relatively high. Although method [9] requires no multi-party computation, it applies random number generation protocol and secret sharing technology to select the redactor. Its time costs is the highest. Our proposed method does not require multi-party computation or the selection of redactor, but only needs the chameleon hash system private key to forge new variable parameters to complete the redaction, with the lowest costs.

The comparison experiment shows that the chameleon hash algorithm has less impact on the consortium blockchain in terms of time overhead. Our proposed method is superior to other existing methods in the blockchain initialization, block generation and block synchronization phase, and it takes less time in the transaction redaction phase.

5 Conclusion

To support data redaction in consortium blockchain, this paper proposes a general-purpose redactable consortium blockchain architecture providing transaction redaction and block compression capabilities. The chameleon hash function is applied and improved to implement decentralized authorization for data redaction. We compare and benchmark the proposed design with other mainstream blockchain systems. The analyses and experiments show that our design of the redactable blockchain leads with lower time and space overhead, and more flexibility in authority node organization. The improved chameleon hash function executes in milliseconds, and achieves a blockchain data compression ratio of up to 30%.

Acknowledgement. Paper work is supported by China NSF fund No. 61802186, 61472189, Opinions expressed are those of the authors and do not necessarily reflect the views of the sponsors.

References

1. Nakamoto, S.B.: A peer-to-peer electronic cash system (2008)
2. Yang, F., Shi, Y., Wu, Q., et al.: The survey on intellectual property based on blockchain technology. In: 2019 IEEE International Conference on Industrial Cyber Physical Systems (ICPS), pp. 743–748. IEEE (2019)
3. Kraus, D., Boulay, C.: Blockchains: aspects of intellectual property law. Blockchains, Smart Contracts, Decentralized Autonomous Organizations and the Law. Edward Elgar Publishing (2019)
4. Regulation, P.: Regulation (EU) 2016/679 of the European Parliament and of the Council. REGULATION (EU), 679: 2016 (2016)
5. Cyberspace Administration of China. Blockchain information service management regulations (2019). http://www.cac.gov.cn/2019-01/10/c_1123971164.htm
6. Matzutt, R., Hiller, J., Henze, M., Ziegeldorf, J.H., Müllmann, D., Hohlfeld, O., Wehrle, K.: A Quantitative Analysis of the Impact of Arbitrary Blockchain Content on Bitcoin. In: Meiklejohn, S., Sako, K. (eds.) FC 2018. LNCS, vol. 10957, pp. 420–438. Springer, Heidelberg (2018). https://doi.org/10.1007/978-3-662-58387-6_23
7. Huang, K., Zhang, X., Mu, Y., et al.: Building redactable consortium blockchain for industrial Internet-of-Things. IEEE Trans. Industr. Inf. **15**(6), 3670–3679 (2019)
8. Ateniese, G., Magri, B., Venturi, D., et al.: Redactable blockchain–or–rewriting history in bitcoin and friends. In: Proceedings of IEEE European S&P, pp. 111–126. IEEE (2017)
9. Li, P., Xu, H., Ma, T., Mu, Y.: Research on fault-correcting blockchain technology. J. Cryptol. Res. **5**(5), 501–509 (2018)
10. Ashritha, K., Sindhu, M., Lakshmy, K.V.: Redactable blockchain using enhanced chameleon hash function. In: Proceedings of 5th International Conference on Advanced Computing & Communication Systems (ICACCS), pp. 323–328. IEEE (2019)
11. Krawczyk, H., Rabin, T.: Chameleon Hashing and signatures, US Patent, 2000-08-22
12. Crosby, M., Pattanayak, P., Verma, S., et al.: Blockchain technology: beyond bitcoin. Appl. Innov. **2**, 6–10 (2016)
13. Gao, W., Hatcher, W., Yu, W.: A survey of blockchain: techniques, applications, and challenges. In: 2018 27th International Conference on Computer Communication and Networks (ICCCN), pp. 1–11. IEEE (2018)
14. Hankerson, D., Menezes, A.: Elliptic Curve Cryptography. Springer, Boston (2011). https://doi.org/10.1007/978-1-4419-5906-5

Anomaly Detection for Consortium Blockchains Based on Machine Learning Classification Algorithm

Dongyan Huang[1(✉)], Bin Chen[1], Lang Li[1], and Yong Ding[2]

[1] Guangxi Key Laboratory of Wireless Wideband Communication and Signal Processing, Guilin University of Electronic Technology, Guilin 541004, Guangxi, China
huangdongyan-gua@163.com

[2] Guangxi Key Laboratory of Cryptography and Information Security, Guilin 541004, Guangxi, China
stone_dingy@126.com

Abstract. Although the consortium blockchains commonly adopt consensus algorithms with Byzantine fault tolerance (such as practical Byzantine fault tolerance (PBFT)), its consensus efficiency will be degraded by the existence of malicious nodes or behaviors. However, the existing researches mainly focus on the detection of malicious behaviors for public blockchains, but are rare about consortium blockchains. In this paper, an anomaly detection model based on machine learning (ML) classification algorithm is proposed for consortium blockchains that adopt PBFT. Besides, a two-stage process is proposed to reduce the resource consumption for anomaly detection. The data needed for proposed model only has two dimensions and is convenient to obtain. The results of experiment show that ML is very effective in anomaly detection for consortium blockchains. Specifically, the algorithms with the highest accuracy are convolutional neural networks (CNN), k-nearest neighbor (KNN) and support vector machines (SVM) in turn. However, KNN and SVM are more suitable because resource consumption of both algorithms are one third of CNN, and the accuracy rates are above 0.9 which is 0.9% lower than CNN.

Keywords: Consortium blockchain · Machine learning · Anomaly detection · PBFT · Supervised learning

1 Introduction

In 2008, Satoshi proposed the concept of Bitcoin [1] which marked the emergence of blockchain technology. Blockchain technology can be divided into pub-

Supported by Guangxi Key Research and Development Program (Guike AB20238026); Guangxi Science and Technology Base and Talent Special Project of China (Guike AD19110042);Guangxi Natura Science Foundation of China (2018GXNSFDA281054,2018GXNSFAA281232); Guangxi Key Experimental Director Fund of Wireless Broadband Communication and Signal Processing (GXKL06160111).

S. Chellappan et al. (Eds.): CSoNet 2020, LNCS 12575, pp. 307–318, 2020.
https://doi.org/10.1007/978-3-030-66046-8_25

lic blockchains, consortium blockchains and private blockchains according to the degree of decentralization. Generally, a consortium blockchain is made up of different organizations or entities, providing security management functions such as member management, authorization, monitoring, and auditing. Therefore, the consortium blockchains have the characteristics of lower cost and higher efficiency, which make them more suitable for commercial application [2] than public blockchains.

The security and consistency in the blockchains are guaranteed by the consensus algorithms. Considering the requirements of commercial applications for security and performance, the consortium blockchains generally adopt the Byzantine fault tolerance (BFT) [3] algorithm (such as practical Byzantine fault tolerance (PBFT) [4]) for consensus [5]. Compared with the "Proof-of-X" [1,6,7] consensus algorithms, the PBFT algorithm does not require nodes to perform competitive accounting-related calculations [8], so its consensus efficiency is higher. By testing the implementation of the PBFT algorithm of the Hyperledge Fabric project which is an open source project of IBM, it is known that the throughput of PBFT can be maintained at more than 12,000 times per second (TPS) [9].

Since the participants of consortium blockchain come from different organizations, there is no completely trust among them. Although the consensus algorithm such as PBFT has certain fault tolerance, the existence of malicious or faulty nodes will degrade the TPS of consortium bolckchains [10]. If malicious nodes can be detected quickly and accurately and isolated from other honest nodes in the network, the consensus efficiency and reliability of the consortium blockchain will be improved. Machine learning (ML) provides a new way to detect the malicious nodes. With the help of ML, computers can learn the laws and patterns of data, and then dig the potential and valuable information within the data [11].

The application of ML to network anomaly detection is a hot spot of current researches [12–16]. Ahmen *et al.* [12] summarized the technology of abnormal traffic detection from three aspects: statistics, ML (classification and clustering) and information theory. Liang *et al.* [13] used one-hot encoding to encode the original network packets in the data set, reconstructed the dimensions to form two-dimensional data, used the GoogLeNet network for feature extraction and learning, and finally trained the classifier model for detection. Jia *et al.* [14] proposed an improved detection algorithm based on K-means hierarchical iteration, which reduces the data dimension of K-means clustering through targeted feature selection, and after multiple iterations of attribute reduction K-means clustering. Sun *et al.* [15] used an improved support vector machines (SVM) classification algorithm to detect abnormalities in the wireless sensor networks. Chen *et al.* [16] analyzed and compared network abnormal traffic detection based on ML.

The application of ML algorithms to blockchain networks anomaly detection is still rare, and most of them are for public blockchains [17–19]. Pham *et al.* [17] used three unsupervised learning methods, including K-means clustering,

Mahalanobis distance, and unsupervised SVM to detect anomaly in the Bitcoin transaction network, Yin *et al.* [18] used 13 supervised learning classification algorithms for estimating the proportion of cybercriminal entities in the Bitcoin network, Wu *et al.* [19] used one-class SVM to detect phishing scams on Ethereum via Network. However, the research about consortium blockchains is still blank.

By combining ML, this paper focuses on anomaly detection and malicious nodes or behaviors detection for consortium blockchains that adopt PBFT consensus algorithm. First, a complete consortium blockchain platform based on Fabric 0.6 [20] is set up; and then in order to obtain the data required for anomaly detection, the malicious behaviors or nodes in the consensus process are simulated; finally, four ML algorithms including KNN, NaiveBayes, SVM and CNN are adopted to identify abnormal nodes.

The main contributions of this paper are summarized as follows:

1. An anomaly detection model based on ML classification algorithm is proposed for consortium blockchains that adopt PBFT.
2. Furthermore, a two-stage process is proposed to reduce the resource consumption for anomaly detection.
3. The effectiveness of the proposed anomaly detection model is validated by extensive experiments on Fabric 0.6. Experimental results demonstrate that the proposed model can detect malicious node in the consortium blockchain with high accuracy. It should be pointed that the proposed model is also suitable for other similar consortium blockchains.

The remainder of this paper is organized as follows. Section 2 presents the overall detection framework of the anomaly detection model. In Sect. 3, we present the technical details of the proposed anomaly detection model. Then we evaluate the anomaly detection performance of the proposed model on consortium blockchain in Sect. 4. Finally, conclusions and discuss future work are given in Sect. 5.

2 System Model

2.1 PBFT Consensus Algorithm

The experiment is based on the consortium blockchain platform of Fabric 0.6, which adopts PBFT as consortium algorithm. In 1999, Miguel Castro and Barbara Liskov proposed PBFT, which reduces the complexity of original BFT from exponential level to polynomial level. So the BFT algorithm becomes more practical.

In PBFT, the nodes are divided into one primary node and several replica nodes. The consensus process is: the client sends a request to the primary node, the primary node broadcasts the request to other replica nodes, all nodes execute the request sent by the client, and send the result back to client. If the client receives the same result from at least f+1 different node, it will take the result as the final response. Therefore, PBFT can operate normally if no more than one third of nodes are malicious. The specific steps of the PBFT consensus are shown in Fig. 1(f = 1 in the figure).

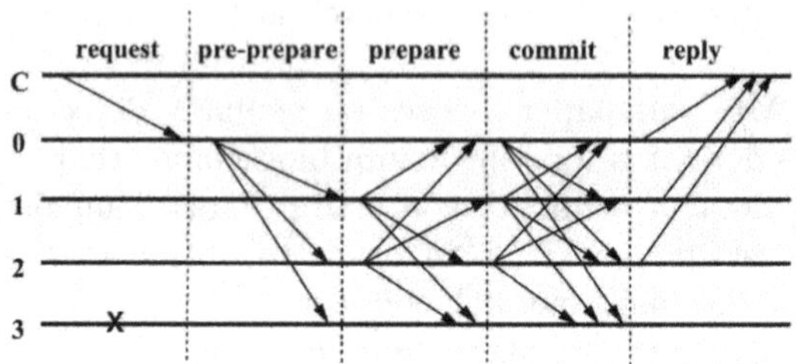

Fig. 1. Implementation process of PBFT consensus algorithm [6]

In the Fig. 1, C is the client, 0, 1, 2, and 3 are four nodes. Node 0 is the primary node and node 3 is down. The specific steps are as follows:

1. Request: Client C sends a request to primary node 0.
2. Pre-prepare: The primary node 0 receives the request sent by the client and performs verification. After the verification is passed, the request is sent to nodes 1, 2, and 3 by broadcasting, otherwise the request is discarded.
3. Prepare: Nodes 1, 2, and 3 will verify after receiving the broadcast request. After the verification is passed, the request will be sent to other nodes by broadcasting, otherwise the request will be discarded. Node 3 cannot broadcast due to downtime. If the node receives 2f (f=1 at this time) prepare messages, the node's prepare phase is completed.
4. Commit: The node enters the commit phase when the prepare phase is completed. At this time, the node broadcasts the client request and the message that the node has been committed. Node 3 cannot broadcast due to the downtime. The node will verify after receiving the request. When the node receives 2f+1 (Including your own) commit message, the node commit phase is completed.
5. Reply: After the node commit phase is completed, the client request will be executed and the execution result will be returned to the client. Node 3 cannot broadcast due to downtime. If the client receives f+1 identical commit messages, the client sends the request has reached the consensus of the whole network.

PBFT adopts a view change mechanism to promote the consensus process by replacing failed primary nodes.

2.2 Network Anomaly Detection Model

The PBFT consensus algorithm can tolerate a certain number of abnormal nodes, but when the number of the abnormal nodes exceeds the upper tolerance limit, consensus speed will slow down. The proposed anomaly detection model focuses on how to identify malicious nodes when the number of abnormal nodes is larger than the maximum number of malicious nodes.

The experiment chooses the time interval data between adjacent phases in the PBFT three-phase consensus. These data have the characteristics of easy access, less data dimension and real-time response to network conditions. However, when the primary node applies for a block, only the primary node broadcasts messages to other nodes in the pre-prepare phase, so only the data related to the primary node can be obtained, which cannot represent the whole consortium blockchain network. Therefore, the anomaly detection model does not use the data of this phase. Instead, experiment select the time interval data of prepare and commit phases which can represent the entire consortium blockchain network.

When performing anomaly detection, if the maliciously delay nodes are identified directly, the time data of each node in the process of PBFT consensus need to be obtained. At this time, as the number of nodes in the consortium blockchain network increases, the resources required to obtain these data will gradually increase. In order to reduce resource occupation, first, the experiment obtains the data of single node for malicious delay detection. If malicious delay is detected, the data of all nodes are used to identify malicious delay nodes. This can ensure that on the premise of detecting malicious delay nodes, further reducing resource occupation. The specific steps are shown in Fig. 2.

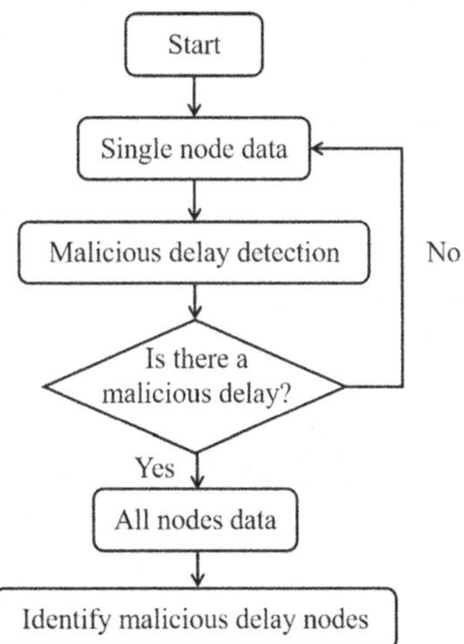

Fig. 2. Flow chart of anomaly detection

According to the literatures [12–19], when using ML for anomaly detection, the accuracy of neural network and supervised learning methods is higher than unsupervised learning methods. In terms of operating speed, the speed of supervised learning and unsupervised learning is faster than neural network algorithms. Considering the accuracy and running speed, we selected three supervised learning algorithms and one neural network algorithm to detect the abnormalities in the consortium blockchains.

The popular supervised learning algorithms are: NaiveBayes, SVM and KNN. The NaiveBayes algorithm is based on statistical data, according to the conditional probability formula to calculate the probability that the current feature sample belongs to a certain category, and finally selects the largest probability category; SVM algorithm finds a (N-1)-dimensional hyperplane in N-dimensional space to classify the data; the KNN algorithm classifies the data by finding the category to which most of the K nearest samples in the feature space belong.

The local connection, weight sharing, and down-sampling operation of CNN can effectively reduce the complexity of the network, reduce the number of training parameters, make the model invariant to translation, distortion and scaling to a certain extent, and CNN has strong robustness and fault tolerance, is also easy to train and optimize.

Supervised learning requires using labeled data for training. Therefore, it is necessary to obtain normal data and abnormal data. First, obtain normal data without malicious delay. In which, the abnormal data is the time interval data of adjacent phases in the consensus process when there is malicious delay. The delay is divided into fixed delay and random delay. Fixed delay is added to study the detection effect of anomaly detection under different delay conditions, and then determine the malicious delay range. Random delay is to simulate the real consortium blockchains network, so as to test the detection effect of anomaly detection algorithm in the real consortium blockchains network.

First, different labels are added to the normal data and abnormal data in the experiment, and then four algorithms including CNN, KNN, NaiveBayes and SVM are used for training anomaly detection model, after that the accuracy of different algorithms are calculated. Accuracy is the proportion of correctly classified data to the total data. So, the closer it is to one, the better the algorithm is.

In the model, CNN algorithm uses three full connection layers, and the stochastic gradient descent parameters are as follows: learning rate is 0.01, momentum parameter is 0.9, and learning attenuation value is 1e−5, which is included for backward compatibility to allow time inverse decay of learning rate; KNN algorithm sets the number of neighbors is five, and Euclidean distance is used; SVM algorithm uses linear kernel function, and the regularization parameter $C = 0.86$; the NaiveBayes algorithm uses Gaussian model and Bernoulli model.

3 Experiment Procedure

In the experiment, the consortium blockchain platform was first built, and then 4, 7, 10, and 13 nodes were created under the local area network.

3.1 Retrieve Data

During the experiment, f nodes in the consortium blockchain network with 3f+1 nodes will be down, where f = 1,2,3,4, and then get:

1. The time interval data of prepare phase and commit phase of each node, when the remaining nodes work normally, one of the nodes applies for a block.
2. The time interval data of prepare phase and commit phases of each and all nodes, when one of the remaining nodes is delayed in the prepare phase and commit phase, one of the nodes applies for a block.

There are two kinds of delay: fixed delay and random delay. The fixed delay is in the case of 4 nodes used to determine the specific delay range of malicious delay. The delay data is taken every 25 ms in the 100 ms–300 ms interval of prepare phase. According to the analysis of the data obtained under the normal working conditions, it is found that the time interval of the prepare phase is about 10 times that of the commit phase. Therefore, in the commit phase, the experimental delay is one over ten of the prepare phase. The random delay is to simulate the real network situation. It is a random delay of 100 ms–300 ms in the prepare phase and 10 ms–30 ms in the commit phase.

During the experiment, 100,000 pieces of data were obtained from each node. The label of normal data is 1, which represents the data when f nodes are down, and the other nodes are not delayed. The label of abnormal data is 0, which represents f nodes are down and one node delays. To prevent data imbalance from affecting the accuracy of anomaly detection, the ratio of normal data to abnormal data is 1:1.

3.2 Train ML Classification Algorithm Models

There are several steps to train the ML algorithm models in the experiment:

1. Determine the delay range:
   During the experiment, the fixed delay data obtained from the consortium blockchain network of 4 nodes are used for model training, and the range of anomaly detection is determined according to the training results.
2. Malicious delay detection:
   The models are trained by using the random delay time data of a single node obtained from the consortium blockchain network with 4, 7, 10 and 13 nodes respectively. Then, we record experiment results.
3. Identify malicious delay nodes:
   The experiment uses the random delay time data of all nodes obtained from consortium blockchain network with 4, 7, 10 and 13 nodes to train models. And the experiment results are recorded.

In the above three cases, the ratio of training set and test set is 8:2.

4 Experiment Results

The experiment results of determining delay range, malicious delay detection and determining malicious delay nodes are recorded in the experiment, as well as the resource occupation of training algorithm model and using trained model for anomaly detection. The specific experiment results are as follows:

4.1 Determine the Delay Range

The experiment results of 4 nodes consortium blockchain network with a fixed delay: (the horizontal axis in the figure represents the delay, and the vertical axis represents the accuracy).

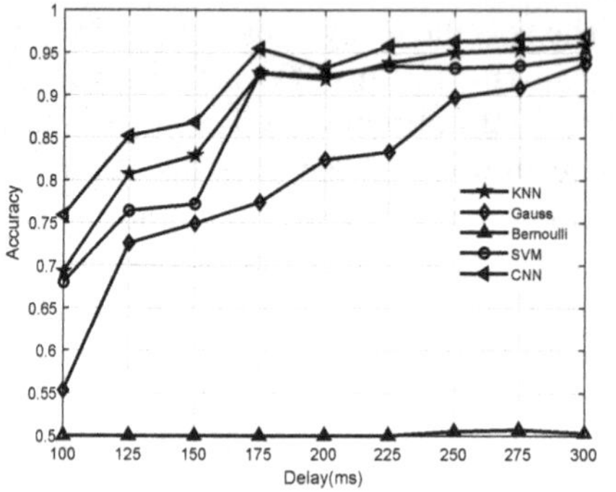

Fig. 3. Experiment results of node n1

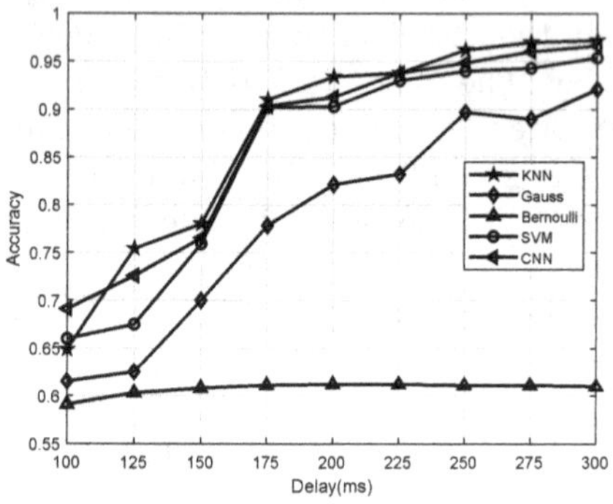

Fig. 4. Experiment results of node n2

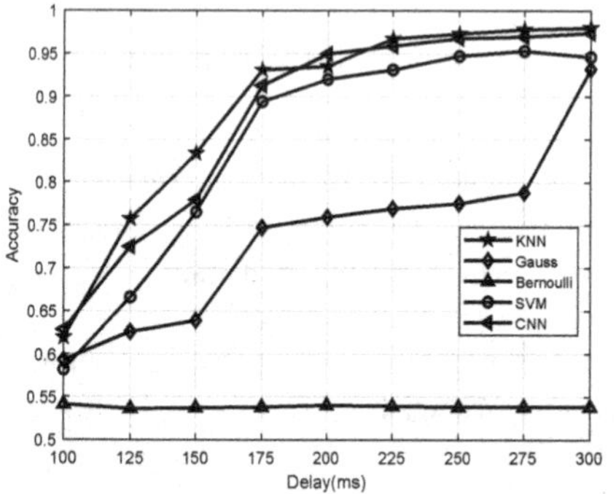

Fig. 5. Experiment results of node n3

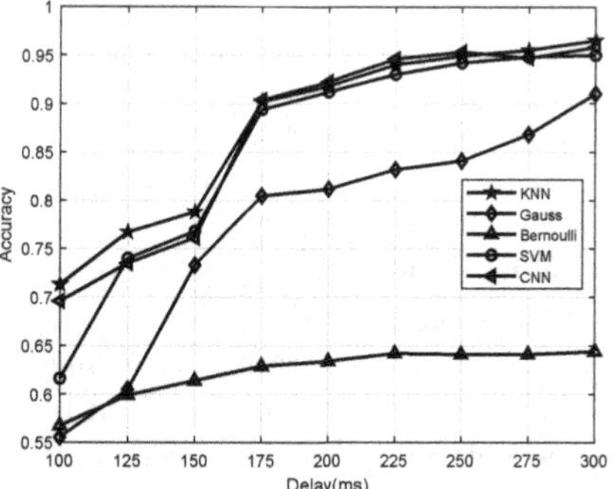

Fig. 6. Experiment results of node n4

Figure 3, 4, 5 and Fig. 6 show the experiment results of anomaly detection by 4 nodes in the range of 100 ms–300 ms with increasing delay. The experiment results show that with the increasing delay of 4 nodes, the algorithm accuracy of CNN, KNN, SVM and Gaussian model also increases. The average accuracy of CNN is 0.06% higher than KNN, KNN is 2.6% higher than the SVM, SVM is 8.08% higher than the Gaussian model, Gaussian model is 29.87% higher than the Bernoulli model. However, the accuracy of the Bernoulli model is basically stable.

4.2 Malicious Delay Detection

Experiment results of malicious delay detection in consortium blockchain network with 4,7,10,13 nodes under random delay condition: (the horizontal axis in the figure represents the number of nodes, the vertical axis represents the accuracy).

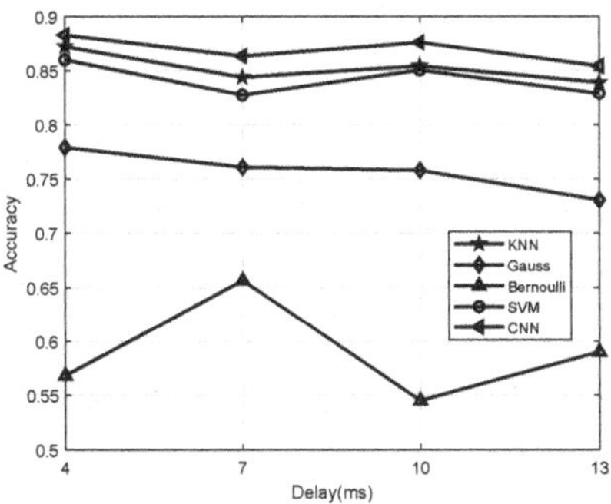

Fig. 7. Experiment results of malicious delay detection in multi-nodes consortium blockchain network

Figure 7 shows the experiment results of malicious delay detection for 4, 7, 10 and 13 nodes' consortium blockchain network with random delay in the range of 100 ms–300 ms. The experiment results show that the average accuracy of CNN is 1.67% higher than KNN, KNN is 1.07% higher than SVM, SVM is 8.49% higher than Gaussian model, and Gaussian model is 16.7% higher than Bernoulli model.

4.3 Identify Malicious Delay Nodes

Experiment results of identifying malicious delay nodes in consortium blockchain network with 4,7,10,13 nodes under random delay: (the horizontal axis in the figure represents the number of nodes, and the vertical axis represents the accuracy).

Figure 8 shows the experiment results of identifying malicious delay nodes in the consortium blockchain network of 4, 7, 10 and 13 nodes with random delay in the range of 100 ms–300 ms. The experiment results show that the average accuracy of CNN is 0.9% higher than KNN, KNN is 0.29% higher than SVM, SVM is 6.84% higher than Gaussian model, and Gaussian model is 22.3% higher than Bernoulli model.

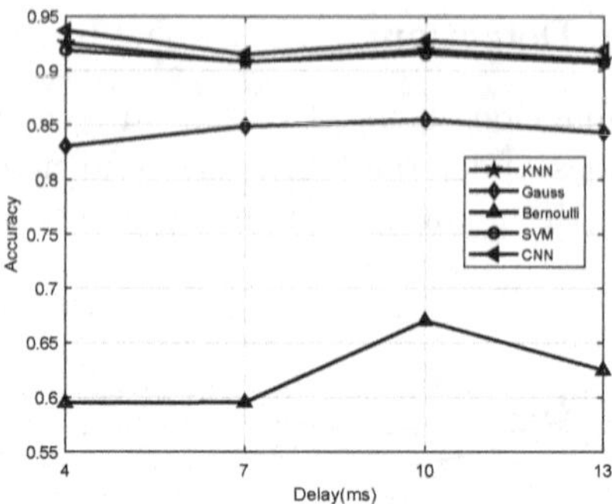

Fig. 8. Experiment results of identifying malicious delay nodes in multi-nodes consortium blockchain network

4.4 Memory Resource Usage When Training Algorithm Models

Table 1 shows the memory resources consumed by CNN, SVM, KNN, and NaiveBayes algorithm when training models. It can be seen from the table that the CNN consumed the most memory resources during training, which consumed 285.9 MB of memory. SVM and KNN consumed 89.7 MB and 95.7 MB of memory respectively. The NaiveBayes consumes the least memory, which is 64.7 MB.

Table 1. The memory resource is occupied during training.

Algorithm	Memory resource usage
CNN	285.9 MB
SVM	89.7 MB
KNN	95.7 MB
NaiveBayes	64.7 MB

4.5 The Size of Algorithm Models and Memory Resource Usage During Anomaly Detection

Table 2 shows the size of the trained CNN, SVM, KNN and NaiveBayes algorithm model and the memory resources consumed in anomaly detection. Among them, the KNN algorithm model is the largest, which is 2.99 MB, SVM and CNN are 595 KB and 33.1 KB respectively. The NaiveBayes algorithm model is the smallest, with 1KB. In anomaly detection, the CNN algorithm model occupies the most memory, which is 30.6 MB, SVM and KNN algorithm models occupy 24.6 MB and 28.2 MB respectively, and the NaiveBayes algorithm model occupies the least memory, which is 19.2 MB.

Table 2. The size of algorithm models and the memory resource usage when anomaly detection.

Algorithm	Algorithm model size	Memory resource usage
CNN	33.1 KB	30.6 MB
SVM	595 KB	24.6 MB
KNN	2.99 MB	28.2 MB
NaiveBayes	1 KB	19.2 MB

Overall, the accuracy of CNN, KNN and SVM is relatively close and significantly higher than NaiveBayes. The ML algorithm can distinguish the normal and abnormal data collected from the experiment, and can classify the new data well.

5 Conclusion

In this paper, an anomaly detection model based on ML classification algorithm is proposed for consortium blockchains that adopt PBFT. Four ML algorithms are selected for the model, which is more reliable than one algorithm, the data of the proposed model is two dimensions and is easy to obtain. Therefore, the proposed model is practical. Specifically, the model uses two stages to identify malicious delay nodes, which consumes less resource than obtaining all nodes' data directly. The experimental results show that the CNN algorithm achieves the highest accuracy among the algorithms but also requires a lot of resources during training. The accuracy of KNN and SVM approaches to that of CNN while consuming far less resources. Furthermore, the accuracy of CNN, KNN and SVM models is stable in different network size. The proposed model is useful for improving the reliability and consensus efficiency in the consortium blockchain network when the malicious nodes are removed. The proposed model mainly focuses on malicious delay. The detection model that applies to more types of malicious behavior will be explored in our future work.

References

1. Nakamoto, S.: Bitcoin: a peer-to-peer electric cash system. https://bitcoin.org/bitcoin.pdf
2. Huang, B.T., Cai, L.: Blockchain decryption: building the next generation Internet based on credit. Tsinghua University Press, Beijing, China (2016)
3. Lamport, L., Shostak, R., Pease, M.: The Byzantine generals problem. ACM Trans. Program. Lang. Syst. **4**(3), pp. 382–401 (1982). https://doi.org/10.1145/357172.357176
4. Castro, M., Liskov, B.: Practical Byzantine fault tolerance. In: Symposium on Operating Systems Design and Implementation, New Orleans, USA (1999). https://doi.org/10.1145/571637.571640

5. Lin, I.C., Liao, T.C.: A survey of blockchain security issues and challenges. IJ Network Secur. **19**(5), pp. 653–659 (2017). https://doi.org/10.6633/IJNS.201709.19(5).01
6. King, S., Nadal, S.: PPCoin:peer-to-peer crypto-currency with proof-of-stake. http://ppcoin.org/static/ppcoin-paper.pdf
7. Larimer, D.: Delegated Proof-of-Stake(DPoS). Bitshare White Paper, Blacksburg (2014)
8. Pahlajani, S., Kshirsagar, A., Pachghare, V., et al.: Survey on private blockchain consensus algorithms. In:1st International Conference on Innovations in Information and Communication Technology (ICIICT), Chennai, India (2019). https://doi.org/10.1109/ICIICT1.2019.8741353
9. Liu, X.F.: Research on performance improvement of Byzantine fault tolerant consensus algorithm based on dynamic authorization.Unpublished MS dissertation, Zhejiang University, Hangzhou, China (2019)
10. Miller, A., Xia, Y., Croman, K., et al.: The honey badger of BFT protocols. In: Computer and Communications Security, vol 24, pp. 31–42. Vienna, Austria (2016). https://doi.org/10.1145/2976749.2978399
11. Zhou, J., Zhu, J.W.: Machine learning classification problem and algorithm research. Software **40**(7), 205–208 (2019)
12. Ahmen, M., Mahmood, A.N., Hu, J.: A survey of network anomaly detection techniques. J. Network Comput. Appl. **60**, 19–31 (2016). https://doi.org/10.1016/j.jnca.2015.11.016
13. Liang, J., Chen, J.H., Zhang, X.Q., et al.: Anomaly detection based on single heat coding and convolutional neural network. J. Tsinghua Univ. (Natural Science Edition) **59**(07), 523–529 (2019)
14. Jia, F., Yan, Y., Zhang, J.Q.: Network anomaly detection based on K-means clustering feature reduction. J. Tsinghua Univ. (Natural Science Edition) **58**(02), 137–421 (2018)
15. Miao, X.D., Liu, Y., Zhao, H.Q., et al.: Distribute online one-class support vector machine for anomaly detection over networks. IEEE Trans. Cybernetics **49**, 1475–1488 (2019). https://doi.org/10.1109/TCYB.2018.2804940
16. Chen, S., Zhu, G.S., Qi, X.Y., et al.: Research on network abnormal traffic detection based on machine learning. Inf. Commun. **180**(12), 44–47 (2017)
17. Pham, T., Lee, S.: Anomaly detection in Bitcoin network using unsupervised learning methods. arXiv: Learning (2016)
18. Yin, H.S., Vatraou, R.: A first estimation of the proportion of cybercriminal entities in the bitcoin ecosystem using supervised machine learning. In:2017 IEEE International Conference on Big Data (Big Data), Boston (2017). https://doi.org/10.1109/BigData.2017.8258365
19. Wu, J.J., Yuan, Q., Lin, D., et al.: Who are the phishers? phishing scam detection on ethereum via network embedding. IEEE Transactions on Systems, Man, and Cybernetics: Systems, pp. 1–11 (2019). https://doi.org/10.1109/TSMC.2020.3016821
20. Androulaki, E., Barger, A., Bortnikov, V., et al.: Hyperledger Fabric: a distributed operating system for permissioned blockchains. In: EuroSys 2018: Proceedings of the Thirteenth EuroSys Conference, Porto, Portugal (2018) . https://doi.org/10.1145/3190508.3190538

Fact-Checking, Fake News and Malware Detection in Online Social Networks

Behavioral Analysis to Detect Social Spammer in Online Social Networks (OSNs)

Somya Ranjan Sahoo[1], B. B. Gupta[1](✉), Chang Choi[2], Ching-Hsien Hsu[3], and Kwok Tai Chui[4]

[1] Department of Computer Engineering, National Institute of Technology Kurukshetra, Kurukshetra, India
somyaranjan.sahoo@gmail.com, gupta.brij@gmail.com

[2] Gachon University, Seongnam-si, Republic of Korea
enduranceaura@gmail.com

[3] Asia University, Taiwan and CS, Chung Hua University, Hsinchu, Taiwan
robertchh@gmail.com

[4] The Open University of Hong Kong, Kowloon, Hong Kong
jktchui@ouhk.edu.hk

Abstract. The faster and regular usage of Web 2.0 technologies like Online Social Networks (OSNs) addicted to millions of users worldwide. This popularity made target for spammers and fake users to spread phishing attack, viruses, false news, pornography and unwanted advertisements like URLs, images and videos etc. The present paper proposes a behavioral analysis-based framework for classifying spam contents in real time by aggregating machine learning techniques and genetic algorithm. The main procedure of the work is, firstly based on social networks spam policy, novel profile based and content-based features are proposed to facilitate spam detection. Secondly, accumulate a dataset from various social networks like Facebook, Twitter, and Instagram including spam and non-spam profiles. For suitable feature selections, we have used a genetic algorithm and various classifiers for decision making. In order to attest the effectiveness of our proposed framework, we have compared with existing techniques.

Keywords: Online social networks · PSO · Facebook · Machine learning

1 Introduction

Due to the busy schedule of a human being, people use OSNs such as Facebook, Twitter and Instagram for their communication, sharing of thoughts with their friends, post messages, share valuable views and discuss hot topics. These websites play an important role in people's daily life [1–3]. Unfortunately, these activities of social platform become a new gateway for social spammers to achieve their goals such as spreading malware, posting spam content, and doing other illicit activities. Basically, social spammer spotting is a binary classification approach using feature analysis. In order to improvise the performance, suitable feature selections are required. The spreading of malicious content

S. Chellappan et al. (Eds.): CSoNet 2020, LNCS 12575, pp. 321–332, 2020.
https://doi.org/10.1007/978-3-030-66046-8_26

degrades user performance, experience, and various functions at server site such as analysis of user behavior, database server and resource recommendation. Therefore, it becomes desirable to develop a framework for detecting spammer and their activities. Currently, there have been few solutions developed by academicians and industry to detect spammer and their behavior in a social network platform. These solutions are either ineffective due to public feature analysis and manual selection of features [4, 5].

This paper investigates spammer in the social platform by analyzing public and private features by using suitable feature selection based on genetic algorithm and machine learning approach. Meanwhile, in order to improve the performance of the proposed framework, we utilize various social network information and label dataset by using API and crawler to guide the machine learning approach easily. We empirically evaluate the proposed framework on real-world dataset and depict the benefit of the proposed framework. The remaining parts of the paper are organized as follows. In Sect. 2, we reviewed related work for spammer detection. Section 3 describes our proposed framework and suitable feature selection approach. In Sect. 4, we describe an analysis of result and comparative work with others. Finally, in Sect. 5, we conclude our paper and some future research direction.

2 Related Work

Detection of social spammer becomes a hot subject in industry and academic field. Spam is an unwanted message spread through a social network platform. In recent years, many methods and frameworks have been proposed by academician to detect spammer on OSNs including feature analysis, social graph-based analysis and various optimization techniques. In [6], the author used support vector machine to classify the malicious content from a legitimate one. He analyzed app similarity and post name similarity content spread through various users as advertisements. In [7], the author analyzes the user characterization based on the user interaction with their followers. After collecting various features from different profiles, author used a machine learning method to separate spammer contents. The author in [8], identified the spammer content in twitter profile by analyzing the behavior of the user and generated trust score based on profile features. In [9], the author evaluated 4 different features using 16 online learning algorithms and chooses the best-suited algorithm to detect spammer in machine learning environment. The author uses nonnegative matrix factorization based integral framework for spammer detection in social media by implementing collaborative factorization principle [10]. In [11], the author uses extreme learning machine based supervised machine for spammer detection. A set of features are extracted by the crawler and process these datasets using extreme machine learning approach.

In [12], author proposed a trust rank based on URLs posted by various users using direct message principle. An invitation graph scheme proposed for detecting Sybil nodes in various social network platforms to analyze profile characteristics [13, 14]. In [15], the author proposed a model called COLOR + to detect spammer accounts in a social network in mobile devices by analyzing messages shared by the users. The approach proposed in [16, 17] analyze user behavior pattern according to the data interest and user behavior in a different group to detect spammer in a social network. The author identifies various kinds of anomalies using past behavior that deviates from the current one. In [18], the author observed the model that stores various processes related to information processing in a social platform for detecting spammer. If the observation lie-down below the threshold, it said to be anomalous. After exploring all the above articles, we conclude that spammer on OSNs can be very harmful for social users and their information. They need to be detected and removed at users end. After all, we came to the conclusion that we need some suitable feature extraction algorithm and optimization technique for better feature selections to helps spammer detection.

3 Spammer Detection Framework

Spammer detection framework is depicted in Fig. 1. We collected dataset from various social networks like Facebook, Twitter, and Instagram by using our crawler and API. The dataset divided into two different sets called training data and testing data. Each dataset contains various features associated with different profiles through feature extraction mechanism.

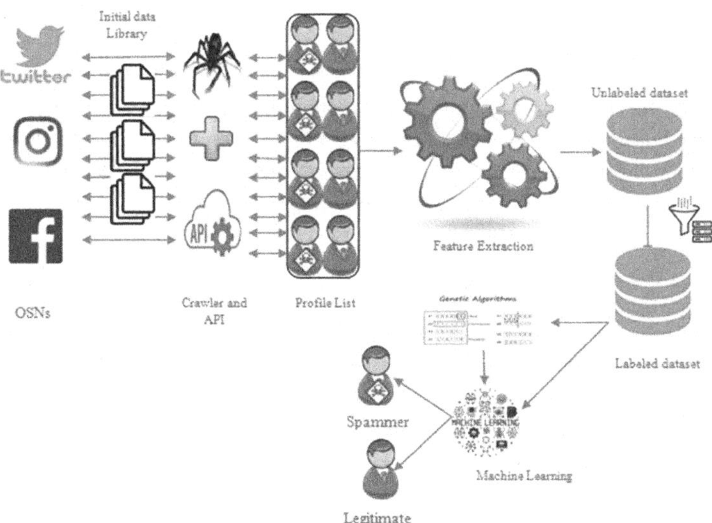

Fig. 1. Spammer Detection Framework

3.1 Data Collection

We collected dataset from various social networks by using crawler and API. Crawler runs on chrome extension to extract profile content and user information related to user profiles. API boosts up the performance of crawler to extract private information about the user. We collected more than 2500 profile information on each social network depicted in Table 1. The dataset contains both spammers as well as legitimate profile information. In addition, we collect some profile activities based on privacy principle applied to social networks.

Table 1. Collected dataset for our framework

Online Social networks	Total Profiles (Spammer + Legitimate)	Spammer	Legitimate
Facebook	3635	1523	2112
Twitter	6558	3123	3435
Instagram	2667	1083	1584

3.2 Training and Test Set Data

The collected dataset separated into two different sets called training set and test set. To obtain the model we have to conduct some experimental analysis of training data, whereas to determine the level of accuracy of the trained model testing data used. For an experimental approach, we used 10-cross-validation technique to separate the dataset into training and test sets.

3.3 Preprocessing

Transforming the raw information into a perceivable format, preprocessing is required in a machine learning approach. To detect the spammer in OSNs, our proposed model needs preprocess the generated content using various approaches like data streaming, folding approach, stopwatch removal, and tokenization.

3.4 Manual Feature Selections

Features are required as a reference to separate spammer from legitimate. Based on related work mentioned above, we select some profile and content-based features for our proposed model. We analyze the most popular features related to user profiles. For the feature extraction, we use web crawler run on chrome extension. Various features used in this research are depicted in Table 2.

3.5 Suitable Feature Selection Using GA

To detect suspicious profiles in OSNs is a challenging task. By analyzing suitable user profile and content-based features related to a user account is highly necessary for observation. The manual selection of features leads to lower accuracy and higher training time in a machine learning environment. To overcome the above issues, we used GA (Genetic algorithm) for a better selection of features. Genetic algorithms are based on evolution and natural selections to solve different diverse types of problem. The entire process of GA covered 5 different stages called initial population, selection, mating, crossover, and mutation. The algorithm starts with individuals' selection of chromosomes called population. Each chromosome consists of a sequence of genes that could be various characteristics of individual users. In the next phase crossover is used to produce next level chromosomes. At later, mutation is used to find various suitable combinations.

Table 2. Selected features from Facebook, Twitter and Instagram

Features		
Facebook	Twitter	Instagram
#Profile ID	#Profile ID	#Profile ID
#Profile Name	#Number of Tweets	#Profile name
#All friends	#Number of followers	#Number of hashtag
#Number of following	#Number of Followings	#Number of URLs shared
#Number of pages liked	#Replies on Tweets	#Sharing videos
#Number of events	#Media content shard	#Number of live video updates
#Number of participating user group	#Number of re-tweets	#Sharing stories
#Post shared	#Direct message send	#Sharing images
#Photos and #video shared	#Number of URLs shared	#Sharing notifications
#Number of tag and #Hashtag	#Back ground image	#Number of likes
#New post, #Recent post like	#Default profile view	
#Profile with photo guard	#Translator used	
#Current Location share	#Number of Hashtags	

Similar processes are carried out to find final level of features that are suitable and gives better output describes in algorithm 1. The related experimental analysis for selecting various features shows in Fig. 2. Fitness of every individual is calculated using matching percentage of every population with the normal sample.

$$Fitness(X) = \frac{A_i}{A} \tag{1}$$

Where,

A_i = number of chromosomes matching individuals

A = Total size of the chromosomes

We tested Euclidian and Minkowski distance measure formula in genetic algorithm in different trial to calculate the distance between parent and new chromosomes. To detect the malicious content, Euclidian formula also used. The distance between two chromosomes can be calculated by using Eq. (2).

$$D(X, Y) = \sqrt{(X_1 - Y_1) + (X_2 - Y_2) + \ldots (X_N - Y_N)} \tag{2}$$

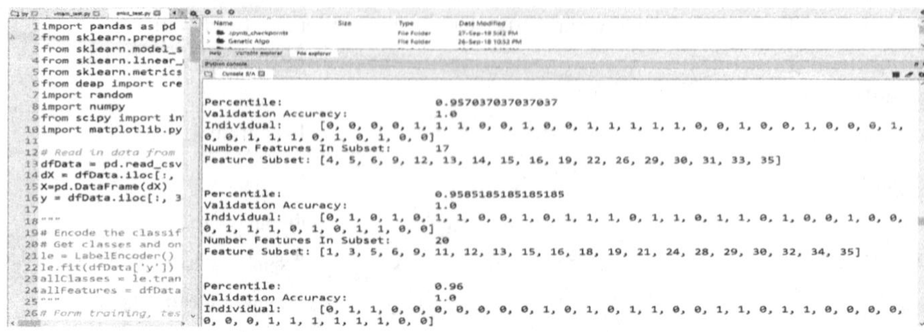

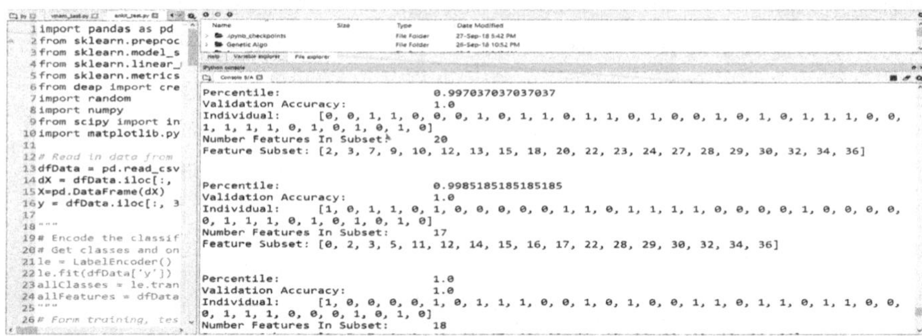

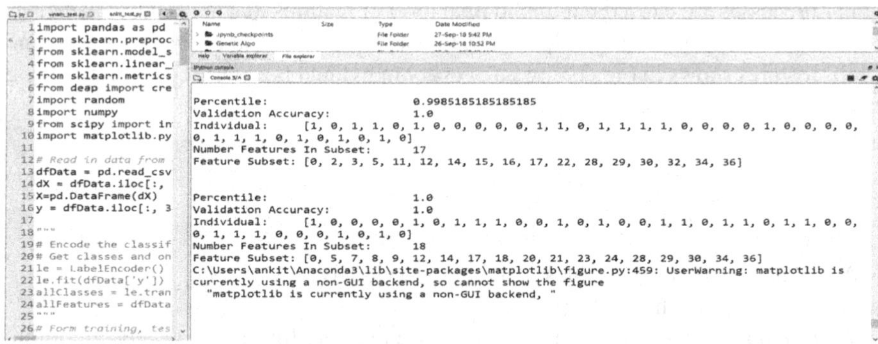

Fig. 2. Feature selection based on Genetic algorithm

To calculate the power value between chromosomes, we use Minkowski distance measure formula using p-norm dimension depicted in Eq. (3).

$$\mathrm{D(X,\ Y)} = \left(\sum\nolimits_{i=0}^{N}\left(|X_i - Y_i|^p\right)\right)^{\frac{1}{2}} \tag{3}$$

Algorithm: Feature selection using Genetic Algorithm (GA)

1. Choose 'N' number of different individuals from training set
2. On continuous features run binning algorithm
3. Select random individuals from 'N' for initial population
4. For specific number of generations do
5. For choose size of population
6. Select two individuals (parents) i.e. N_1 and N_2
7. Apply crossover to produce new individual called N_3
8. Use mutation over crossover
9. Compute distance $d^1$and d^2 i.e. from (N_3 to N_1) and (N_3 to N_2)
10. Compute fitness of old and new populations as F_1, F_2 and F_3 respectively.
11. If (d_1<d_2) and (F_1>F_2) then
12. Replace N_1 with N_3
13. else
14. If (d_2< = d_1) and (F_1>F_3) then
15. Replace N_2 with N_3
16. End if
17. End if
19. End for
20. End for
21. Extract the best for operation.

3.6 Classification Based on Machine Learning Approach

The targeted classifier produced the outputs as spammer and legitimate using various features extracted by our crawler. We used various classifiers, namely Support vector machine (SVM), Random forest, bagging, J48, decision tree and Logistic Regression. To evaluate predictive models, we use 10-fold cross validation by partitioning original sample into training set and test set. The evaluation result in the form of precision, recall, true positive rate, false positive rate and ROC area observed for decision making.

4 Experiment and Result Analysis

We use different social networks dataset, which contains more than 2500 user information's. Our crawler run on chrome extension extracts profile information along with date and time of every activities posted by the user. In the evaluation process, we consider confusion matrix for spammer detection. The proposed approach is evaluated various metrics, namely true positive rate, true negative rate, precision, recall and F-score related to classifiers. Accuracy is the ratio of total correctly classified instances of both classes over total instances in the dataset and expressed as,

$$\text{Accuracy} = \frac{\textit{True positive} + \textit{True negative}}{\textit{True positive} + \textit{True negative} + \textit{False positive} + \textit{False Negative}} \tag{4}$$

$$\text{Precision} = \frac{\textit{True positive}}{\textit{True positive} + \textit{False Positive}} \tag{5}$$

$$\text{True positive rate (TPR)} = \frac{\textit{True positive}}{\textit{True positive} + \textit{False negative}} \tag{6}$$

4.1 Data Analysis

We observed that, by using various characteristics analysis, the follower of legitimate users is more as compared to the spammers in twitter account. But, the number of likes by the user for any event is more by spammers. As expected, spammers spread more advertisements and fraudulent information's in different social network to attract users. After all, Random forest classifier gives higher accuracy as compared to other classifications. But, in Logistic regression, false positive rate is less in Twitter dataset depicted in Table 3, Table 4 and Table 5.

Table 3. Experimental analysis of Facebook dataset

Resultant								
Different Classifications	TP rate	FP Rate	Precision	Recall	F-measure	MCC	ROC Area	PRC Area
Random Forest	.994	.011	.989	.994	.992	.983	.999	.999
Bagging	.994	.012	.989	.994	.991	.982	.998	.998
JRip	.992	.014	.986	.992	.989	.978	.991	.986
J48	.991	.013	.988	.991	.990	.979	.991	.987
PART	.987	.012	.988	.987	.988	.975	.993	.991
Random tree	.985	.017	.984	.985	.984	.968	.984	.977
Logistic	.957	.008	.992	.957	.975	.955	.995	.995
SVM	.893	.017	.896	.893	.890	.898	.899	.898

Table 4. Experimental analysis of Twitter dataset

Resultant								
Different Classifications	TP rate	FP Rate	Precision	Recall	F-measure	MCC	ROC Area	PRC Area
Random Forest	0.993	0.003	0.997	0.993	0.995	0.989	1.000	1.000
Bagging	0.990	0.006	0.995	0.990	0.993	0.984	0.998	.997
JRip	0.995	0.004	0.996	0.995	0.996	0.990	0.995	.995
J48	0.993	0.006	0.995	0.993	0.994	0.986	0.995	.994
PART	0.992	0.010	0.991	0.992	0.991	0.981	0.994	.991
Random tree	0.996	0.007	0.994	0.996	0.995	0.989	0.995	.992
Logistic	0.985	0.014	0.986	0.985	0.986	0.980	0.985	.985
SVM	0.896	0.010	0.891	0.896	0.893	0.885	0.896	.893

Table 5. Experimental analysis of Instagram dataset

Resultant								
Different Classifications	TP rate	FP Rate	Precision	Recall	F-measure	MCC	ROC Area	PRC Area
Random Forest	.973	.018	.963	.961	.971	.968	.962	.962
Bagging	.942	.019	.946	.939	.949	.943	.959	.942
JRip	.962	.011	.959	.956	.960	.962	.932	.953
J48	.981	.011	.980	.981	.982	.986	.989	.984
PART	.967	.012	.968	.977	.958	.952	.963	.961
Random tree	.975	.016	.974	.975	.974	.978	.964	.967
Logistic	.967	.012	.962	.957	.965	.965	.965	.965
SVM	.873	.016	.872	.879	.870	.878	.879	.878

4.2 Performance Analysis

We evaluate our proposed framework by using various classifications and compared the analysis with some existing approaches. Particularly our experimental approach in the form of accuracy is higher as compared to other state of art techniques. It reaches higher accuracy above 99% in all social network platforms. Likewise, the precession of various analyses is higher as compared to other approaches . Especially, by using genetic algorithm, accuracy in every case increases by 12% to 15% as compared to normal feature selection. The selection of suitable features from group of all features by GA achieved higher detection rate. In all experimental approach, SVM produces lower accuracy due to structured dataset. Comparative analysis of various classifications in different social platforms with other existing approaches like Ameen et al., (2017) [19], Ala'm et al., (2017) [20] and Herzallah et al., (2017) [21] depicted in Fig. 3, Fig. 4, Fig. 5 and Fig. 6.

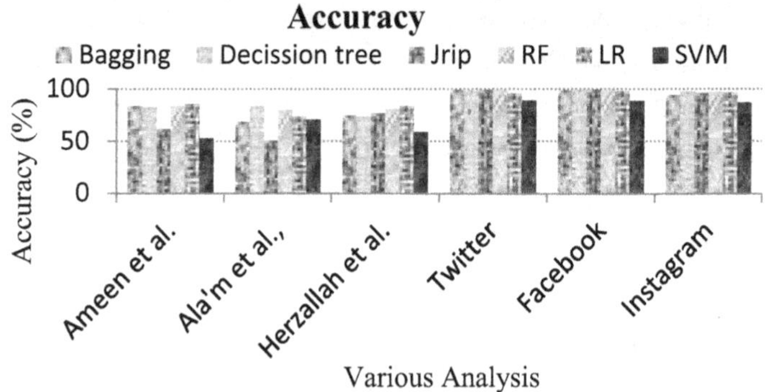

Fig. 3. Comparative analysis of Accuracy

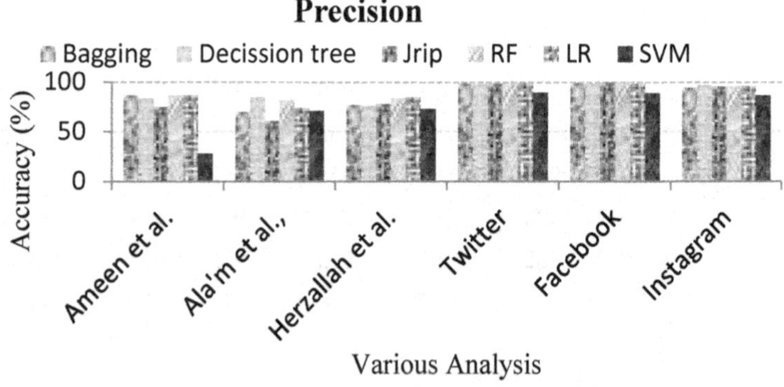

Fig. 4. Comparative analysis of Precision

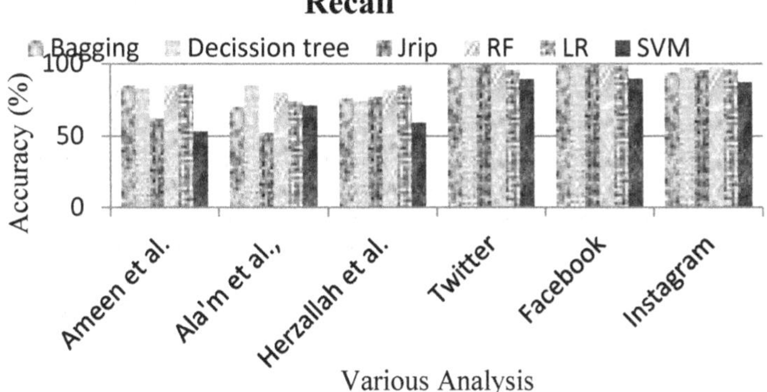

Fig. 5. Comparative analysis of Recall

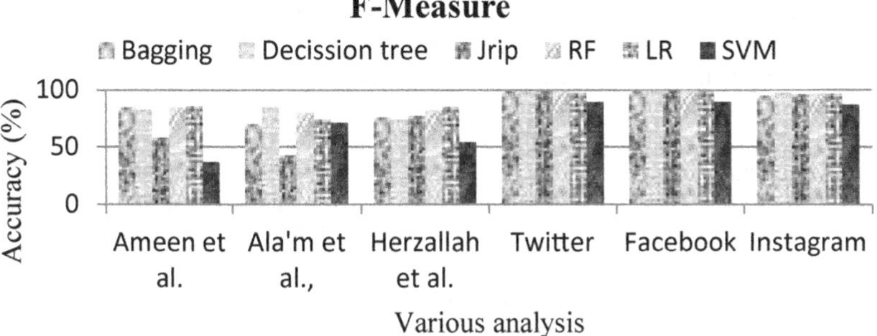

Fig. 6. Comparative analysis of F-Measure

5 Conclusion and Future Work

The paper presents a Genetic algorithm-based feature selection approach with machine learning classifier to detect spammers in social network platform. A set of content and behavioral features are collected from Twitter, Facebook and Instagram using our crawler. By investigating various user behaviors, we provided a detection mechanism to detect spammer content in OSNs. Through a set of experiment and rating with a real-world dataset, proposed framework produces better accuracy and detection rate as compared to other frameworks. Next, we plan to extend our proposed framework in the following aspects. Firstly, we consider other private features related to the users account to detect spammer. Secondly, we wish to improve the detection rate by using other optimization approaches. Finally, design an online detection mechanism, which automatically detect the spammer behavior in social network platform.

References

1. Zhang, Z., Gupta, B.B.: Social media security and trustworthiness: overview and new direction. Fut. Generation Comput. Syst. **86**, 914–925 (2018)

2. Gupta, B.B., Gupta, S., Gangwar, S., Kumar, M., Meena, P.K.: Cross-site scripting (XSS) abuse and defense: exploitation on several testing bed environments and its defense. J. Inf. Priv. Secur. **11**(2), 118–136 (2015)
3. Zhang, Z., Sun, R., Zhao, C., Wang, J., Chang, C.K., et al.: CyVOD: a novel trinity multimedia social network scheme. Multimedia Tools Appl. **76**(18), 18513–18529 (2017)
4. Brezinski, K., Guevarra, M., Ferens, K.: Population Based Equilibrium in Hybrid SA/PSO for Combinatorial Optimization: Hybrid SA/PSO for Combinatorial Optimization. Int. J. Softw. Sci. Comput. Intell. (IJSSCI) **12**(2), 74–86 (2020)
5. Harrath, Y., Bahlool, R.: Multi-objective genetic algorithm for tasks allocation in cloud computing. Int. J. Cloud Appl. Comput. (IJCAC) **9**(3), 37–57 (2019)
6. Sahoo, S.R., Gupta, B.B.: Classification of various attacks and their defence mechanism in online social networks : a survey. Enterp. Inf. Syst. pp. 1–33 (2019). http://doi.org/10.1080/17517575.2019.1605542
7. Sahoo, S.R., Gupta, B.B.: Classification of spammer and non-spammer content in online social network using genetic algorithm-based feature selection. Enterprise Inf. Syst. 710–736 (2020). http://doi.org/10.1080/17517575.2020.1712742
8. Singh, M., Bansal, D., Sofat, S.: Who is who on twitter–spammer, fake or compromised account? a tool to reveal true identity in real-time. Cybern. Syst. **49**(1), 1–25 (2018)
9. Sahoo, S.R., Gupta, B.B.: Fake profile detection in multimedia big data on online social networks. Int. J. Inf. Comput. Secur. 303–331 (2020). http://doi.org/10.1504/IJICS.2020.105181
10. Yu, D., Chen, N., Jiang, F., Fu, B., Qin, A.: Constrained NMF-based semi-supervised learning for social media spammer detection. Knowl.-Based Syst. **125**, 64–73 (2017)
11. Sahoo, S.R., Gupta, B.B.: Popularity-based detection of malicious content in facebook using machine learning approach. In: First International Conference on Sustainable Technologies for Computational Intelligence, pp. 163–176. Springer, Singapore (2020)
12. Gyongyi, Z., Garcia-Molina, H., Pedersen, J.: Combating Web spam with trust rank. In: Proceedings of the Thirteeth International Conference on Very Large Data Bases, vol. 30, VLDB 2004, pp. 576–587 (2004)
13. Xue, J., Yang, Z., Yang, X., Wang, X., Chen, L., Dai, Y.: Votetrust: leveraging friend invitation graph to defend against social network sybils. In: Proceeding of the 32nd IEEE International Conference on Computer Communications, INFOCOM 2013 (2013)
14. Alweshah, M., Al Khalaileh, S., Gupta, B.B., Almomani, A., Hammouri, A.I., Al-Betar, M.A.: The monarch butterfly optimization algorithm for solving feature selection problems. Neural Comput. Appl. 1–15 (2020)
15. Sahoo, S.R., Gupta, B.B.: Hybrid approach for detection of malicious profiles in twitter. Comput. Electric. Eng. **65–81**, 2019 (2019). https://doi.org/10.1016/j.compeleceng.2019.03.003
16. Ahmed, M., Mahmood, A.N., Hu, J.: A survey of network anomaly detection techniques. J. Network Comput. Appl. **60**, 19–31 (2016)
17. Jain, A.K., Gupta, B.B.: Towards detection of phishing websites on client-side using machine learning based approach. Telecommun. Syst. **68**(4), 687–700 (2018)
18. Kaur, R., Kaur, M., Singh, S.: A novel graph centrality based approach to analyze anomalous nodes with negative behavior. Procedia Comput. Sci. **78**, 556–562 (2016)
19. Ameen, A.K., Kaya, B.: Detecting spammers in twitter network. Int. J. Appl. Math. Electron. Comput. **5**(4), 71–75 (2017)
20. Ala'M, A.-Z., Faris, H. et al.: Spam profile detection in social networks based on public features. In: 2017 8th International Conference on Information and Communication Systems (ICICS), pp. 130–135. IEEE (2017)
21. Herzallah, W., Faris, H., Adwan, O.: Feature engineering for detecting spammers on twitter: Modelling and analysis. J. Inf. Sci. 0165551516684296 (2017)

A Multi-feature Bayesian Approach for Fake News Detection

Mario Casillo[1], Francesco Colace[1(✉)], Dajana Conte[2], Massimo De Santo[1], Marco Lombardi[1], Serena Mottola[3], and Domenico Santaniello[1]

[1] DIIn, Università degli Studi di Salerno, Fisciano (Salerno), Italy
{mcasillo,fcolace,desanto,malombardi,dsantaniello}@unisa.it
[2] DIPMAT, Università degli Studi di Salerno, Fisciano (Salerno), Italy
dajconte@unisa.it
[3] Dipartimento di Studi Economici e Giuridici, Università degli Studi di Napoli Parthenope, Naples, Italy
serena.mottola@uniparthenope.it

Abstract. In a world flooded with information, often irrelevant, lucidity is power. Never as in this historical period can anyone, thanks to new technologies, participate as a protagonist in the debates raised about events and issues that affect our society. In this flood of information, remaining lucid and knowing how to discriminate between real and false becomes fundamental. In this scenario, a leading role is played by Fake News, information that is partly or entirely untrue, divulged through the Web, the media, or digital communication technologies. Fake news is characterized by an apparent plausibility, the latter fed by a distorted system of public opinion expectations, and by an amplification of the prejudices based on it, which facilitates its sharing and diffusion even in the absence of verification of the sources. Fake News is becoming a severe problem that affects various sectors of society: medicine, politics, culture, history are some of the areas that suffer most from the phenomenon of fake news, which can often generate significant social problems. This paper will introduce a probabilistic approach to determining the degree of truthfulness of the information. The system is based on the definition of some features, identified after an analysis of fake news in the literature through NLP-based approaches and statistical methods. The specified features will highlight the syntactic, semantic, and social features of the information. These features are combined in a Bayesian Network, previously trained on a dataset composed of fake news, to provide a probabilistic level of the truthfulness of the information analyzed. The proposed method has been tested in some real cases with very satisfactory results.

Keywords: Bayesian network · Fake news · Natural language processing

S. Chellappan et al. (Eds.): CSoNet 2020, LNCS 12575, pp. 333–344, 2020.
https://doi.org/10.1007/978-3-030-66046-8_27

1 Introduction

Social networks allow us to spread information straightforwardly: anyone can share the news with a potentially worldwide audience. This possibility has revealed a problem related to the nature of the news we read online: the phenomenon of Fake News. Thanks to mobile devices, we are always connected to the internet, and we receive a copious amount of data every day, which may or may not tell real facts. With the term Fake News, we mean news intentionally false and proposed in such a way as to persuade those who read it of its authenticity [1]. The fake news spread on the web has become a "social" problem [2], so much so that it could even influence the outcome of political elections as it happened in the United States in 2016 or the evolution [3].

Fake News can be presented in different ways and for other purposes. Some of these, for example, are: News that aims to direct network traffic to specific platforms, which generate profit from users' visits. This kind of information usually proposes facts that have no correspondence with reality.

News that concerns news that is false in the facts or that proposes opinions. In this case, in the news, and net the point of view of the writer. News based on false content and based on humor. Fake News of this kind is hosted by sites that declare their nature but still have many readers who believe in what is published. It is difficult to say with certainty whether the news is false. Some characteristics and recurrent elements in a Fake News are the sensationalistic tones of the title and the text, retouched images, or created ad hoc. This text reports the information in a confused and approximate way.

Based on a real fact, the news could be modulated to be made viral or to promote its propagation. The news may be retouched and, therefore, that it is only partially true. An example could be information accompanied by a modded image or a real image inserted concerning false information. It may also happen that a news item is written in tones that persuade the reader to interpret the fact as if it were true. In this regard, it is necessary to specify that the net's information always has (at least) an objective for which it was written. You may find news intended to inform you, for example, about an event, a problem, or a person. This kind of news typically does not contain opinions but only reports the facts in an objective way. Instead, there is information written precisely to persuade the reader of a specific point of view. In this case, the writer supports his thesis, neglecting others, and giving partial information. There is also frequent advertising news, content that aims to sell a service, a product, or even promote a political candidate. Some news may fall into the category of propaganda. In this case, the communicator wants to promote a cause and actively involve the reader in it. This kind of information is widely used by dictators or terrorists who, focusing on emotions (especially fear), create a distorted view of reality by misrepresenting the facts. Another type of news is the so-called Raw information, i.e., content that is not edited, not interpreted, and not disclosed before it is published; the objective of this kind of information is to document and provide a recording of an event.

Fake News has found in Social Media an excellent vehicle to spread quickly and as widely as possible. The new tools offered by the network have allowed anyone to write on the web. Facebook and Twitter have made it possible to exchange information on a much larger scale than could be done with traditional means of communication. For example, CMS, such as WordPress, have given the possibility to create a site with great ease. It would be wrong to claim that Social Media provide fake news; they are the privileged means of diffusion used by those who produce them.

The creators of false news do not address a casual audience; thanks to the advent of targeted advertising, they can focus their attention on the most susceptible and vulnerable users who, in turn, will spread the news itself.

The research on how Fake News propagates through Social Networks shows that the element that most influences Fake News's propagation is the precision with which are chosen those who will share the news first. So comes into play a "witness effect," according to which you trust information read on Social Networks because it is someone close, with similar interests and similar opinions to have done the same. In this case, we are led to share news to feel "connected" and protagonists. With the sharing (and the comments, like, share that follows), you feel the emotion to be the first to know certain information. Therefore, the key to success for Fake News is to find a set of users who can believe the proposed information, that comment, and share it.

Fake News is becoming a severe problem that affects various sectors of society: medicine, politics, culture, history are some of the areas that suffer most from the phenomenon of fake news, which can often generate significant social problems. In this paper, we will introduce a probabilistic approach for the determination of the degree of truthfulness of news. The process is based on the definition of some features, identified after an analysis of fake news in the literature through NLP-based approaches and statistical methods. The specified features will highlight the syntactic, semantic, and social features of the news. These features are combined in a Bayesian Network, previously trained on a dataset composed of fake news, to provide a probabilistic level of the truthfulness of the news analyzed. The proposed method has been tested in some real cases with very satisfactory results. The paper is so organized: the next section will introduce some related works. In section three, the proposed approach is described, while section four will show the obtained results. Some conclusions will end the paper.

2 Related Works

In literature, various approaches aim to automatically determine the truthfulness of news. Most of these are classification approaches based on Machine Learning techniques such as Deep Learning [9]. Alternatively, some researchers have applied other approaches based, for example, on data mining techniques, such as time series analysis, and have exploited external resources (e.g. knowledge bases), to predict the class of documents or events, or to assess their credibility [10]. In this context, artificial intelligence is currently considered a tool of primary importance in discerning between true and false information [4]. In particular, deep learning, with its complex neural networks, is proving to be able to overcome the results obtained with other methodologies: Classifiers Naive Bayes, SVM, Random Forest, etc. [5]. All these techniques are characterized to consider as a starting point the extraction of features of news that describe their meta-information. Some examples are:

- *Source*: the author of the news
- *Headline*: text that describes, in short, the main topic of the article and has the main purpose to capture the readers' attention
- *Body*: main text containing the details of the news
- *Attachments (images/video)*: part of the content of news that provides visual cues to better frame the story and its context

Based on these basic features, you can recognize more specific ones, which can be divided into:

- *Linguistic based*: lexical features, syntactic features, semantic features [6].
- *Visual based*: features related to visual elements such as images and video [7].

To these can also be added features of the social context (Context-Based Features), often decisive in the process of analysis on the truthfulness of news [8]:

- *User-based*: features of users who interact with online news; these features can be divided into two levels: individual and group.
- *Post-based*: features related to the emotions or opinions of users towards news and expressed through posts on social networks; these features can be divided into post level, group level, and temporal level.
- *Network-based*: features based on the characteristics of the Network used by users to spread the news, i.e. the properties of the network on which the news is shared.

From this data usually Detection Techniques will be developed. Among these, machine learning algorithms have proved to be extremely useful to analyze fake news, especially thanks to supervised learning. Below are listed the main classification methods used in the literature [14,17]:

- Support Vector Machines (SVM)
- Random Forest
- Decision Tree
- Logistic Regression
- Conditional Random Field (CRF)
- Hidden Markov Models (HMM)

As mentioned earlier, Deep Learning is one of the most widely explored research topics. The most widely adopted paradigms are based on Recurrent Neural Networks (RNN) or Convolutional Networks (CNN). In the context of fake news, the first adoption of RNN for voice detection is reported in [11]. Chen et al.

[13] have instead proposed CNN to solve the classification of the truthfulness of tweets.

The approach proposed in this article, instead, aims to introduce mechanisms based on probabilistic techniques, the Bayes networks, to determine the degree of truthfulness of news. An approach of this type can show what is happening in the classification process allowing, if necessary, to modify the operational flow. In the next paragraph, the proposed approach will be presented in detail.

3 Proposed Approach

As previously said, there is high interest in the development of systems able to identify fake news. The economic and social impact that fake news can potentially have in our societies drives governments and companies to develop automated systems for the immediate identification and removal of fake news. The identification process can involve many aspects and now there is no single shared methodology. The approach proposed in this article aims to consider fake news from three different points of view: syntactic, semantic, and social. Each of these aspects has representative features able to describe the textual content and characterize it. The objective is to have a reference model able to describe in its main features fake news and allow the identification of others. It is therefore proposed to design and implement a system that starting from fake news is able to provide a syntactic, semantic, and social description. Such information will then be used to train a Bayesian network that will be able to provide, with a certain probability, the degree of fake news. The system works in two phases. In the first, through the analysis of a series of news labeled as false, the system provides to train a Bayesian network properly designed [12]. In particular, its nodes assume weights through the acquisition of the various cases subjected to analysis. At the end of the training phase, the Bayesian network is able to represent, in probabilistic terms, fake news through the frequency of appearance of some syntactic, semantic, and "social" characteristics [15,16]. The general schema is described in Fig. 1. In the second phase, the Bayesian network thus obtained can then be used as a filter to analyze news and classify them. Some news are inserted into the system that through the analysis of their main characteristics and the Bayesian network previously trained, returns a probability on the falsity of the information. The functioning of this part of the system is described in Fig. 2. Below will be detailed the various modules present in the schemes previously introduced.

4 The Syntactic Analyzer

The purpose of this module is to extract some syntactic indexes that can contribute to the definition of a model for the identification of fake news. These indexes will feed the Bayesian network adopted: for each of these indexes will be created nodes whose states are the range of possible values that can be assumed. The parameters that have been considered are the following:

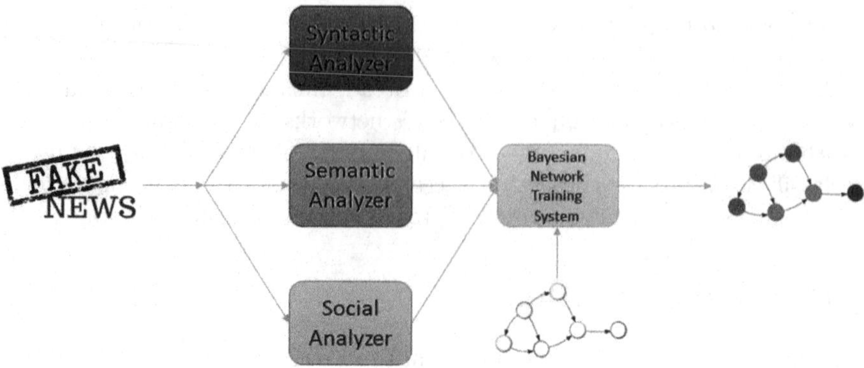

Fig. 1. The proposed approach: the training phase.

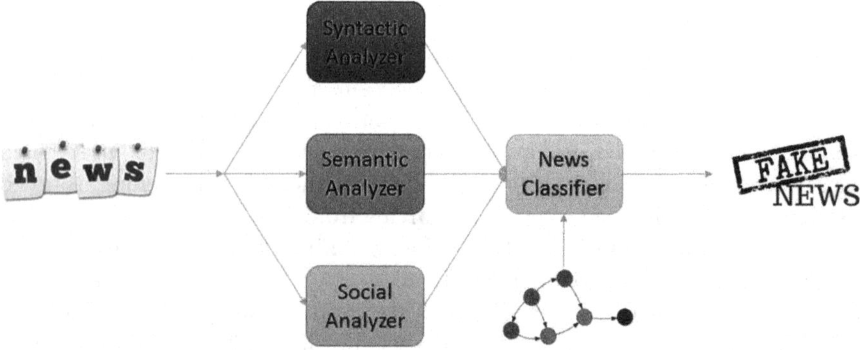

Fig. 2. The classification phase.

- The number of characters in the news. Usually, fake news is characterized either by a very low number of characters or by an excessive length. Five possible ranges have been defined: up to 100 characters, from 100 to 300 characters, from 300 to 500 characters, from 500 to 700 characters, over 700 characters.
- The Flesch Index: The Flesch Index is used to measure the readability of a text in English. It is also commonly referred to as Flesch-Kincaid (F-K) from the name of the scholars Rudolf Flesch and J. Peter Kinkaid who empirically deduced it in the 1970s during a survey developed for the United States Navy on the average level of education. The way to calculate this index is as follows:

$$F = 206.835 - (84.6 * S) - (1.015 * P) \tag{1}$$

  Where
  - F is readability
  - S is the average number of syllables per word
  - P is the average number of words per sentence

Table 1. Flesch Index Score.

F	School level	Notes
100.00–90.00	5th grade	Very easy to read
90.0–80.0	6th grade	Easy to read
80.0–70.0	7th grade	Fairly easy to read
70.0–60.0	8th & 9th grade	Plain English
60.0–50.0	10th to 12th grade	Fairly difficult to read
50.0–30.0	College	Difficult to read
30.0–10.0	College graduate	Very difficult to read
10.0–0.0	Professional	Extremely difficult to read

Table 2. Gunning fog Index range.

Fog Index	Reading level by grade
17	College graduate
16	College senior
15	College junior
14	College sophomore
13	College freshman
12	High school senior
11	High school junior
10	High school sophomore
9	High school freshman
8	Eighth grade
7	Seventh grade
6	Sixth grade

Scores can be interpreted as shown in the Table 1. In general fake news are either very complex (range 30–60) or very simple (range 70–100).

- The Gunning fog Index: In linguistics, the Gunning fog index is a readability test for English writing. The index estimates the years of formal education a person needs to understand the text on the first reading. The Gunning fog index is calculated with the following algorithm:
  - Select a passage (such as one or more full paragraphs) of around 100 words. Do not omit any sentences;
  - Determine the average sentence length. (Divide the number of words by the number of sentences.);
  - Count the "complex" words consisting of three or more syllables. Do not include proper nouns, familiar jargon, or compound words. Do not include common suffixes (such as -es, -ed, or -ing) as a syllable;

- Add the average sentence length and the percentage of complex words; and
- Multiply the result by 0.4.

The complete formula is:

$$GI = 0.4 * [(words/sentences) + 100 * (ComplexWords/Words)] \quad (2)$$

The range of GI index is reported in Table 2. In general the fake news have either fog index between 14 and 17 or between 6 and 9.

5 The Semantic Analyzer

This module aims to extract semantic features from the news. In particular, the idea is to understand from the analysis of documents if there are semantic features able to testify the truthfulness of news. The features that have been considered are the following:

- Topic: fake news is usually linked to topics that are trending topics at a given time. Topics such as politics, health, star system, economy are most affected by fake news. This index, therefore, returns 1 in the case of a potentially attractive topic for fake news. 0 in all other cases. The determination of the topic, in case of lack of this information, will be done through an approach presented in [20].
- Fake News Similarity: the mixed graph of terms is a graph that is able to represent a textual document through the most recurrent words and their links [21]. In particular, this graph measures both the number of occurrences of a word and the number of possible co-occurrences with others present in the document. Through the construction of a Mixed Graph of Terms obtained from the analysis of previously labeled news, it is possible to compare those obtained from news whose truthfulness is to be verified. The system is able, in this way, to return a degree of similarity with respect to fake news. The range of values that the system returns the following values: Similar, Neutral, Dissimilar
- Sentiment Extraction: through the approach introduced in [22] it is possible to label a text document with the sentiment expressed by the person who wrote it. Through an analysis linked once again to the generation of a mixed graph of terms, the system can automatically determine the degree of positivity or negativity associated with the news. In particular, the system will provide value 1 if the sentiment is negative and 0 if the sentiment is positive. In general, fake news is characterized by negative sentiment.

Also in this case these indexes will feed some nodes, and the relative states, present within the Bayes network.

6 The Social Analyzer

In this case, aspects related to social network dynamics will be considered. In particular, the following parameters will be considered:

- Number of likes or shares obtained from the news. In general, fake news is characterized by a high number of shares. In this case, the considered range is the following: Low Sharing if there are less than 100 shares or like, from 100 to 300 shares or like average, over 300 high sharing.
- Number of comments to the News: generally fake news is characterized by a high number of comments. In this case, the range considered is as follows: Low Number of Comments if there are less than 50 comments, Low Average Number of comments from 50 to 200 comments, High Average Number of comments from 200 to 500 comments, High Number of comments over 500 comments.

Each index previously introduced is a node of the Bayes network that will act as a classifier as shown in Fig. 3. The node states are the ranges previously introduced in the definition of each index.

7 Experimental Results

To verify the effectiveness of the proposed methodology, it was tested both on datasets in the literature and on one related to the COVID topic created by collecting news from Twitter in the period March 2020 and July 2020. The following datasets in the literature have been selected: LIAR [15] and CREDBANK [19]. The main features of the datasets are described below:

- *LIAR*: this dataset was obtained using the API of the PolitiFact.com website. It includes 12,836 short human-labeled statements: each statement has been assigned a truth value ranging from "True" to "Pants on Fire". The statements collected are related to different contexts (press releases, television or radio interviews, speeches in election campaigns, etc.) and mainly date back to the period between 2007 and 2016. The dataset is divided into training files (10,240 statements), validation (1,284 statements), and testing (1,267 statements) and has features compatible with the previously introduced scheme.
- *CREDBANK*: it is a dataset of about 60 million tweets collected between mid-October 2014 and the end of February 2015. All tweets are linked to more than 1,000 news events, each of which has been evaluated for credibility by 30 Amazon Mechanical Turk commentators.

After having properly set the Bayes networks, according to the specifications of the various datasets, the data were analyzed in terms of Precision, Recall, and F Score. After this phase of validation of the proposed methodology, we have built our own dataset (UNICO) collecting data from Facebook and Twitter. In particular, posts were taken that reported the following hashtags: #covid19, #covid, #coronavirus, #stayhome, #staysafe, #pandemic, #socialdistancing

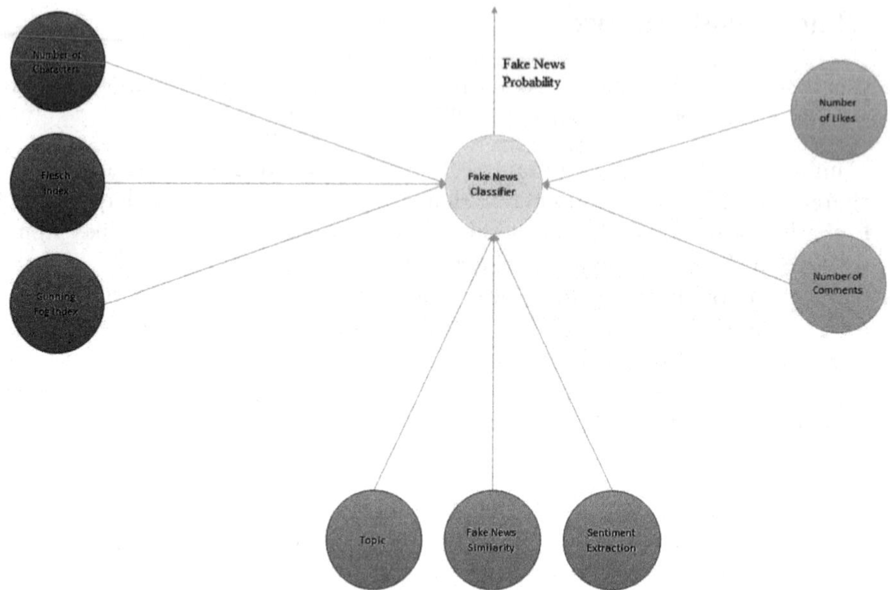

Fig. 3. Bayesian network classifier.

Table 3. Obtained results.

Dataset	Precision	Recall	F Score
LIAR	0,81	0,84	0,82
CREDBANK	0,78	0,81	0,79
UNICO	0,83	0,89	0,86

9265 tweets have been collected and a group of 25 students, Ph.D. students and professors from the University of Salerno have labeled them.

The training set was obtained by selecting 75% of the dataset, 6950 posts, while the test set is obviously composed of the remaining 2315 posts. The Bayesian network has been customized to the case study. The obtained results are described in Table 3.

The results obtained are satisfactory. In particular, the system works better when analyzing longer posts focused on certain topics.

8 Conclusions

In this article a methodology for the identification of fake news has been presented. The approach chosen was probabilistic and uses a Bayesian network as classifier. The proposed approach has been used on standard datasets or taken in real contexts. In both cases the results were satisfactory.

Future developments are the introduction of more indexes for the modeling of a fake news and a better construction of lexicons based on the topics covered. Further development could be the use of this approach in real time allowing an immediate classification of fake news in social media.

References

1. Tandoc Jr., E.C., Lim, Z.W., Ling, R.: Defining "Fake news": A typology of scholarly definitions. Digit. Journalism **6**(2), 137–153 (2018). https://doi.org/10.1080/21670811.2017.1360143
2. Baccarella, C.V., Wagner, T.F., Kietzmann, J.H., McCarthy, I.P.: Social media? it's serious! understanding the dark side of social media. Eur. Manag. J. **36**(4), 431–438 (2018). https://doi.org/10.1016/j.emj.2018.07.002
3. Abd-Alrazaq, A., Alhuwail, D., Househ, M., Hai, M., Shah, Z.: Top concerns of tweeters during the COVID-19 pandemic: a surveillance study. J. Med. Internet Res. **22**(4), e19016 (2020). https://doi.org/10.2196/19016
4. Ahmed, H., Traore, I., Saad, S.: Detection of online fake news using N-gram analysis and machine learning techniques (2017)
5. Girgis, S., Amer, E., Gadallah, M.: Deep learning algorithms for detecting fake news in online text. In: Paper presented at the Proceedings - 2018 13th International Conference on Computer Engineering and Systems, ICCES 2018, pp. 93–97 (2019) https://doi.org/10.1109/ICCES.2018.8639198
6. Afroz, S., Brennan, M., Greenstadt, R.: Detecting hoaxes, frauds, and deception in writing style online. In: ISSP 2012 (2012)
7. Jin, Z., Cao, J., Zhang, Y., Zhou, J., Tian, Q.: Novel visual and statistical image features for microblogs news verication. IEEE Trans. Multimedia **19**(3), 598–608 (2017)
8. Shu, K., et al.: Fake news detection on social media: a data mining perspective. ACM SIGKDD Explor. Newsl. **19**(1), 22–36 (2017)
9. Meel, P., Vishwakarma, D.K.: Fake news, rumor, information pollution in social media and web: a contemporary survey of state-of-the-arts, challenges and opportunities. Exp. Syst. Appl. **153**, 112986 (2020). https://doi.org/10.1016/j.eswa.2019.112986
10. Bondielli, A., Marcelloni, F.: A survey on fake news and rumour detection techniques. Inf. Sci. **497**, 38–55 (2019)
11. Qawasmeh, E., Tawalbeh, M., Abdullah, M.: Automatic identification of fake news using deep learning. In: 2019 6th International Conference on Social Networks Analysis, Management and Security, SNAMS 2019, pp. 383–388 (2019) https://doi.org/10.1109/SNAMS.2019.8931873
12. De Stefano, C., Fontanella, F., Marrocco, C., di Freca, A.S.: A hybrid evolutionary algorithm for Bayesian networks learning: an application to classifier combination. In: Di Chio, C. (ed.) EvoApplications 2010. LNCS, vol. 6024, pp. 221–230. Springer, Heidelberg (2010). https://doi.org/10.1007/978-3-642-12239-2_23
13. Chen, Y.C., Liu, Z.Y., Kao, H.Y.: IKM at SemEval-2017 Task 8: convolutional neural networks for stance detection and rumor verification. In: Proceedings of the 11th International Workshop on Semantic Evaluation (SemEval-2017) 2017
14. Rubin, V.L., et al.: Fake news or truth? using satirical cues to detect potentially misleading news. In: Proceedings of the Second Workshop on Computational Approaches to Deception Detection (2016)

15. Cordella, L.P., De Stefano, C., Fontanella, F., Scotto di Freca, A.: A weighted majority vote strategy using Bayesian networks. In: Petrosino, A. (ed.) ICIAP 2013. LNCS, vol. 8157, pp. 219–228. Springer, Heidelberg (2013). https://doi.org/10.1007/978-3-642-41184-7_23
16. De Stefano, C., Fontanella, F., Scotto Di Freca, A. A novel Naive Bayes voting strategy for combining classifiers. In: Proceedings - International Workshop on Frontiers in Handwriting Recognition, IWFHR, pp. 467–472 (2012)
17. Vosoughi, S., Mohsenvand, M.N., Roy, D.: Rumor Gauge: predicting the veracity of rumors on Twitter. ACM Trans. Knowl. Discov. Data **11**(4), 1–36 (2017). https://doi.org/10.1145/3070644. Article 50
18. Wang, W.Y.: 'liar, liar pants on fire': A new benchmark dataset for fake news detection. arXiv:1705.00648 (2017)
19. Mitra, T., Gilbert, E.: Credbank: a largescale social media corpus with associated credibility annotations. In: ICWSM 2015 (2015)
20. Colace, F., De Santo, M., Greco, L., Napoletano, P.: Text classification using a few labeled examples. Comput. Hum. Behav. **30**, 689–697 (2014)
21. Colace, F., De Santo, M., Greco, L., Napoletano, P.: Improving relevance feedback-based query expansion by the use of a weighted word pairs approach journal of the association for. Inform. Sci. Technol. **66**, 2223–2234 (2015)
22. Colace, F., Casaburi, L., De Santo, M., Greco, L.: Sentiment detection in social networks and in collaborative learning environments. Comput. Hum. Behav. **51**, 1061–1067 (2015)

Propagation of Fake News on Social Media: Challenges and Opportunities

Saqib Hakak[1], Wazir Zada Khan[2], Sweta Bhattacharya[3], G. Thippa Reddy[3], and Kim-Kwang Raymond Choo[4(✉)]

[1] Faculty of Computer Science, Canadian Institute for Cybersecurity, University of New Brunswick, Fredericton, Canada
saqib.hakak@unb.ca

[2] Faculty of CS and IS, Jazan University, Jazan, Saudi Arabia
wazirzadakhan@jazanu.edu.sa

[3] School of Information Technology and Engineering, Vellore Institute of Technology, Vellore, India

[4] Department of Information Systems and Cyber Security, University of Texas at San Antonio, San Antonio, TX 78249-0631, USA
raymond.choo@fulbrightmail.org

Abstract. Fake news, particularly with the speed and reach of unverified/false information dissemination, is a troubling trend with potential political and societal consequences, as evidenced in the 2016 United States presidential election, the ongoing COVID-19 pandemic, and the ongoing protests. To mitigate such threats, a broad range of approaches have been designed to detect and mitigate online fake news. In this paper, we systematically review existing fake news mitigation and detection approaches, and identify a number of challenges and potential research opportunities (e.g., the importance of a data sharing platform that can also be used to facilitate machine/deep learning). We hope that the findings reported in this paper will motivate further research in this area.

Keywords: Fake news mitigation · Social media · Opportunities · Future challenges

1 Introduction

Social media platforms are widely used by individuals and communities to post user-generated content, communicate and keep in touch with each other, and to learn of events across the globe. However, such platforms can also be (ab)used to disseminate fake or misleading news (also referred to as misinformation or disinformation) [7,23], as evidenced in the current COVID-19 pandemic [2,3,9] (e.g., intentionally manipulated information that can potentially lead to vaccine hesitancy [8,16]).

A simplified example of how fake news propagate through social media platforms is depicted in Fig. 1. As shown in the figure, fake news can be generated

S. Chellappan et al. (Eds.): CSoNet 2020, LNCS 12575, pp. 345–353, 2020.
https://doi.org/10.1007/978-3-030-66046-8_28

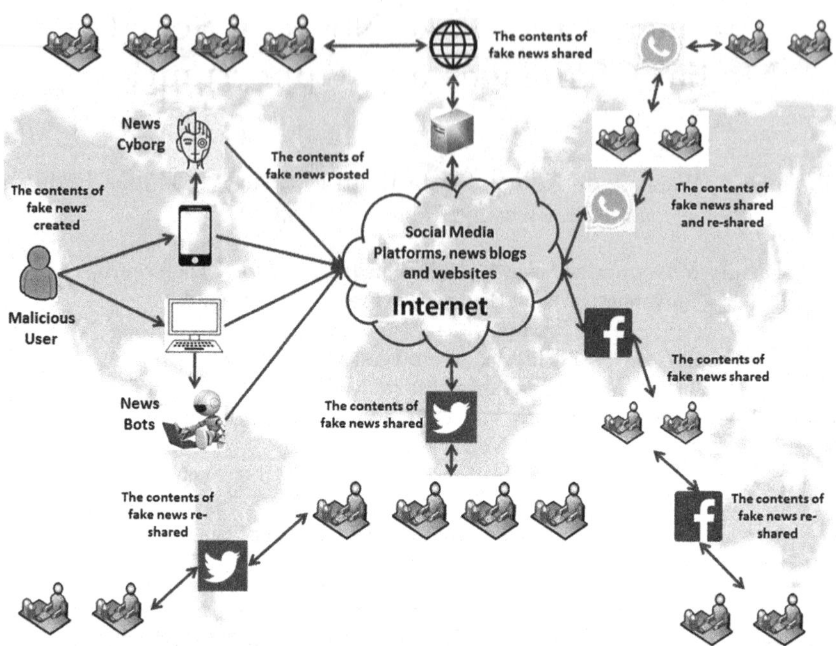

Fig. 1. Fake news propagation

by social bots, trolls and cyborgs. This should not be surprising, since the cost of accessing social media is (extremely) low and creating fake accounts is trivial (in terms of effort and cost). When these fake social media accounts are controlled by computational algorithms they become social bots. These social bots can be used to perform various tasks, ranging from creating fictitious information to facilitating misinformation/disinformation, and so on. Unlike social bots, trolls are generally human users behind their keyboard contributing to misinformation/disinformation campaigns, say using deep fake technologies [14], for a broad range of reasons (e.g., boredom, politically or ideologically-motivated). In the context of cyborgs, accounts are created by human users who then use computer algorithms to carry out fake news related activities on the social network.

The speed and reach of such fake news can have broad political and societal impacts. Given the potential, and in some cases significant, political and societal consequences, it is not surprising that there have been extensive efforts in designing approaches to detect fake news, including those on social media [11,21,26]. However, detecting fake news remains challenging for a number of reasons. For example, a tweet may contain information that is not entirely fictitious or fake (e.g., partial truth about a particular presidential candidate). Hence, do we consider this tweet to be fake news? In addition to the content (e.g., authenticity), we may have to understand the intent. In the former, we can attempt to fact-check the content, although this is not always trivial or practical. Similarly establishing intent may not always be straightforward.

The (ongoing) interest in fake news detection is also partly evidenced by the number of literature review and survey articles on the topic [5,20,28]. Seeking to complement these existing articles, we will review existing approaches designed to detect and mitigate fake news, as well as the associated challenges.

In the next section, we will review the potential mitigation approaches.

2 Potential Detection and Mitigation Approaches

Fake news is not new [12,27], although the popularity of social media platforms have made it easier to carry out misinformation/disinformation campaigns and to a broader audience target. Examples of existing fake news detection and mitigation approaches are outlined in Table 1, and associated datasets shown in Table 2.

Table 1. A snapshot of example fake news detection approaches

Study	Methods Used	Evaluation metric	Limitations
[13]	Multivariate Time Series	Detection speed of fake news, Propagation of fake news, Accuracy, Precision, Recall and F-score	Semi-supervised learning techniques not implemented, PU (Positive Unlabelled) learning algorithm not implemented
[15]	Supervised AI Model	Accuracy, Precision, Recall and F-score	Evaluations hybridized algorithm not performed, Optimization algorithm not implemented to enhance performance of existing models
[18]	CSI, Capture	User log, User activity and User vector, Accuracy and F-score	Reinforcement learning and crowd sourcing not implemented
[22]	Recurrent Neural Network (RNN), Long Short Term Memory (LSTM)	Accuracy, Precision, Recall, F1	N/A
[24]	Bayesian Approach	Learning about users, Users engagement in flagging, Robustness against spammers	N/A
[26]	Gibbs Sampling	Accuracy, Precision, Recall, F1	N/A

Kaur et al. [10] proposed a multi-level voting ensemble model. In their approach, the dataset used is split into two parts, namely: 67% of the dataset used for training and the remaining 33% used for testing. In the feature extraction phase, three feature extraction techniques (i.e., Term Frequency-Inverse

Table 2. Fake news datasets used in studies outlined in Table 2

	Kaggle	Liar	ISOT	Buzzfeed	Politifact	Twitter	NELA-GT-2018	Other sources
Y.Liu et al. [13]	✗	✗	✗	✗	✗	✓	✗	Weibo
F.Altunbey et al. [15]	✗	✗	✓	✓	✗	✗	✗	Random Fake News
N.Ruchansky et al. [18]	✗	✗	✗	✗	✗	✗	✗	✗
K.Shu et al. [22]	✗	✗	✗	✓	✓	✗	✗	✗
S.Tschiatschek et al. [24]	✗	✗	✗	✗	✗	✗	✗	Facebook Graph
S.Yang et al. [26]	✗	✓	✗	✓	✗	✗	✗	✗

Document Frequency (TF-IDF), Count-Vectorizer (CV) and Hashing-Vectorizer (HV)) are applied, and numerical features from a textual document are extracted using tokenization, counting and normalization. Subsequently in the next phase, classification algorithms are chosen and the retrieved features are fed to the classification phase to facilitate fake news identification. In order to learn and identify relevant patterns, various machine learning (ML) models are evaluated based on performance metrics. The models used include Logistic Regression, Passive Aggressive, Stochastic Gradient Descent, MultinomialNB, Support Vector Classifier, Multi-Layer Perceptron, Linear Support Vector Classifier, AdaBoost, Gradient Boosting, Decision Tree, and Voting Classifiers. These models are integrated to propose a multi-level voting model to improve the accuracy to reduce the classifiers' training time.

In [15], the authors attempted to distinguish fake news from authentic ones, using a three-tier pre-processing approach. First, the tokenization technique breaks the text into smaller chunks (referred to as tokens), which removes all types of punctuation. Filers are then deployed to eliminate all terms having numerical values. Then, a case converter is used to convert all texts to lower case format and finally an N-chars filter is used to delete all words having less than predefined N characters. The second level of data pre-processing removes "stop-words". In English grammar, stop words are basically words that do not convey any meaningful information, but they are used for sentence construction or to connect information (e.g., conjunctions, prepositions, and pronouns) The third level of pre-processing includes the stemming process, wherein all the adjectives, verbs, adverbs and noun words are transformed to their basic form but retaining their original meaning. As an example, words like connection, connectivity, connected belong to the root word connect. Following the data pre-processing step, a feature engineering technique entitled Vector Space Method (SVM) is applied to select the most significant features from the high dimensional dataset and text mining is then undertaken. The process helps to convert text document to vectors and the value of each word is assigned a weight using various methods like Term Frequency - Inverse Document Frequency (TF-IDF), Inverse

Document Frequency (IDF), Term Frequency (TF) or classical binary format. Finally, the extracted data is subjected to 23 different supervised artificial intelligence algorithms to detect fake news, and the algorithm(s) with the highest accuracy is/are identified. A key limitation of this work is the lack of exploring or designing new and hybrid algorithms, such as those using hyperparameter optimization techniques.

In [13], the limitations of using machine learning algorithms in detecting fake news were explored. It is a known fact that the predictions of machine learning algorithms generally depend on news' characteristics, which are often insufficient. The news being collected at an early stage often has incomplete information; thus, resulting in lower accuracy in fake news detection. Thus, the authors classified news propagation paths. Specifically, the proposed framework models propagation path for each new story, represented as a multivariate time series. Each tuple or row in the multivariate time series is a numerical vector, which depicts the character of the person responsible for spreading the fake news. A time series classifier is built, consisting of recurrent and convolutional networks that identify different variations in user characteristics. The proposed framework was shown to be capable of detecting fake news with better accuracy and speed, in comparison to several other competing techniques. However, the study did not consider user characteristics or identify users who are easy believers and would potentially spread fake news faster. Another limitation of the study is the lack of empirical evaluation involving any semi-supervised or hybrid machine learning algorithm to evaluate the effectiveness of the proposed framework.

In [18], the authors identified three main characteristics of fake news, namely: "text" of the article, the "response" to the article, and the "source" (e.g., users who disseminate the fake news). The study integrates all of these three characteristics to develop a model to facilitate accurate and automated prediction of fake news. The model comprises three modules. The first module is a "Capture" module based on the text and responses for the articles using a Recurrent Neural Network. The third module is an integration of capture and score, which classifies whether an article is fake or authentic. The results generated from the CSI results in more relevant representation of user behaviour, texts and also achieves more accurate results in comparison to conventional approaches. However, the model did not include human users in the learning process which could potentially yield more accurate results. In addition, reinforcement learning and related technologies are not used to train the algorithms.

Tschiatschek et al. [24] presented an algorithm (referred to as DETECTIVE), designed to detect fake news. This algorithm performs Bayesian inference to determine whether the news is fake with a certain confidence level, as well as jointly learning the user's flagging accuracy over time. The authors attempted to minimize the spread of misinformation by stopping the propagation of fake news in the network. In the proposed algorithm, a small subset of k news is selected from a given set and is sent to an expert for reviewing. Only after the news is labeled as fake by the expert will it be blocked. In their evaluation, the authors used the social circle's Facebook graph that consists of 4,039 users (nodes) and

88,234 edges, computed from survey data collected by using a Facebook app for identifying social circles.

Shu et al. [22] designed a system (referred to as FakeNewsTracker) in order to detect fake news. The proposed system works in two steps, namely: (fake) news collection and fake news detection. In the first step, the authors proposed a strategy for collecting fake news in a periodic manner to update the repository. The verified fake news and true news were collected from fact-checking websites like PolitiFact on a daily basis. Tweets related to the fake/real news were also gathered by using the Twitter's advanced search API. Moreover, social engagements of users including retweet, replies of tweet and favorites were also gathered using Twitter's APIs. Finally, information about the followers and followees of the users who were engaged with the fake news were also collected. Such information collectively is used to facilitate the extraction of relevant user features in the detection task. For the second step, the authors proposed the social article fusion (SAF) model that classifies fake news by leveraging the linguistic features of news content and features of social context. An auto encoder is used to capture the text content of the news articles in the lower dimensional space. The SAF model combines the features generated by the auto-encoder and social context recurrent neural network. In the experiments, the authors used deep long short term memory (LSTM) networks with two layers comprising 100 cells at each layer and 200-dimensional word embeddings with an input vocabulary of 5000 words in the encoder. Two layers of LSTMs with 100 cells in each layer are also used for the decoder. The word embeddings are initialized randomly and they were learned along with the network. The experiments are performed with some variations of SAF framework, including SAF, in which both news article contents and social engagements are leveraged, SAF/A in which only social context is utilized and SAF/S in which only news article content is used.

Yang et al. [26] studied the problem of unsupervised fake news detection with unreliable social engagements, and proposed a framework called unsupervised fake news detection (UFD) framework. The latter allows one to extract user opinions on the news by analyzing their engagements on social media. A Bayesian probability graphical model is also built. An efficient approach called collapsed Gibbs sampling was proposed for the detection of fake news and estimation of the users' credibility simultaneously. The truth estimation of each news is first randomly initialized to either 0 or 1 and then based on the initial truth estimations, the counts of each verified and unverified users are calculated. Subsequently, the sampling process is conducted for a number of iterations. The experiments were performed on two real world social media datasets, and the performance of the proposed framework compared with those of other approaches.

3 Concluding Remarks

While there are many challenges associated with social media, a pressing issue faced by our society is identifying misinformation/disinformation, particularly during pandemics (e.g., COVID-19) and events of national interest (e.g., elections).

In this article, we briefly reviewed the extant literature on fake news detection, and identified a number of challenges and potential research agendas.

3.1 Data Diversity and Dynamicity

There are many potential data sources, ranging from printed and digital news media to websites (e.g., government and private sector websites) to blogs to social and online media, and so on. The diversity of data sources, data types (e.g., texts, videos, and pictures), and dynamic nature of news contents compound the challenges of verification. This is further complicated by advances in deep fake technologies (e.g., FakeApp and DeepFaceLab software), which have been reported used to generate fake videos and shared via social media platforms [1,14].

This reinforces the importance of designing tools that can deal with the diversity of data sources, types, and dynamicity. For example, can data owners and platform owners work collaboratively to share intelligence to facilitate timely detection of fake news on their platforms (e.g., blogs, websites, and social media services)?

3.2 Data Sharing Platforms

In the literature, a number of datasets (e.g., LIAR dataset [25], and datasets from Kaggle; see also Table 2) have been used to train different machine and deep learning models [6,17,19]. However, the accuracy of these models is not consistent across different datasets, partly due to the lack of comprehensive and representative datasets that sufficiently reflect the dynamic nature of (fake) news content. Similar to the observations reported in [4] for Internet of Things (IoT) research, existing datasets for fake news research tend to be limited in terms of training samples, narrowly focus, not being up-to-date, etc. Hence, this reinforces the importance of developing a community platform that collects and integrates data from different public sources (e.g., social media), as well as government sources. Such a platform can also to facilitate data sharing and machine/deep learning (e.g., federated or transfer learning algorithms) training and analysis to more effectively detect ongoing misinformation/disinformation campaigns in real-time.

References

1. Ahmed, S.: Who inadvertently shares deepfakes? analyzing the role of political interest, cognitive ability, and social network size. Telematics Inform, p. 101508 (2020)
2. Wasim, A., Josep, V.-A., Joseph, D., Seguí, F.L.: Dangerous messages or satire? analysing the conspiracy theory linking 5G to COVID-19 through social network analysis. J. Med. Internet Res. (2020)
3. Oberiri, D.A., Omar, B.: Fake news and covid-19: modelling the predictors of fake news sharing among social media users. Telematics Inform. p. 101475 (2020)

4. Mandrita, B., Junghee, L., Choo, K.K.R.: A blockchain future for internet of things security: a position paper. Digital Commun. Netw. **4**(3), 149–160 (2018)
5. Bondielli, A., Marcelloni, F.: A survey on fake news and rumour detection techniques. Inf. Sci. **497**, 38–55 (2019)
6. Samara, C., et al.: Detection of bots and cyborgs in twitter: a study on the chilean presidential election in 2017. In: International Conference on Human-Computer Interaction, pp. 311–323. Springer (2019)
7. Chesney, R., Citron, D.: Deepfakes and the new disinformation war: the coming age of post-truth geopolitics. Foreign Aff. **98**, 147 (2019)
8. Gellin, B.: Why vaccine rumours stick-and getting them unstuck. The Lancet **396**(10247), 303–304 (2020)
9. Saqib, H., Wazir, Z.K., Imran, M., Choo, K.K.R., Shoaib, M.: Have you been a victim of covid-19-related cyber incidents? survey, taxonomy, and mitigation strategies. IEEE Access, **8**, 124134–124144 (2020)
10. Sawinder, K., Parteek, K., Kumaraguru, P.: Automating fake news detection system using multi-level voting model. Soft Comput. 1–21 (2019)
11. Dhruv, K., Jaipal, S.G., Gupta, M., Varma, V.: Mvae: multimodal variational autoencoder for fake news detection. In: The World Wide Web Conference, pp. 2915–2921 (2019)
12. David, M.J., et al.: The science of fake news. Science **359**(6380), 1094–1096 (2018)
13. Yang, L., Yi-Fang, B.W.: Early detection of fake news on social media through propagation path classification with recurrent and convolutional networks. In: Thirty-Second AAAI Conference on Artificial Intelligence (2018)
14. Yang Liu and Yi-Fang Brook Wu: Fned: a deep network for fake news early detection on social media. ACM Trans. Inf. Syst. (TOIS) **38**(3), 1–33 (2020)
15. Feyza Altunbey Ozbay and Bilal Alatas: Fake news detection within online social media using supervised artificial intelligence algorithms. Physica A: Stat. Mech. Appl. **540**, 123174 (2020)
16. Neha, P., Eric, A.C., Hourmazd, H., Gunaratne, K.: Social media and vaccine hesitancy: new updates for the era of covid-19 and globalized infectious diseases. Human Vaccines & Immunotherapeutics, pp. 1–8 (2020)
17. Jorge, R., et al.: A one-class classification approach for bot detection on twitter. Comput. Secur. **91**, 101715 (2020)
18. Natali, R., Seo, S., Liu, Y.: CSI: a hybrid deep model for fake news detection. In: Proceedings of the 2017 ACM on Conference on Information and Knowledge Management, pp. 797–806 (2017)
19. Giovanni, C.S., Munif, I.M., Jake, R.W.: Detecting social bots on facebook in an information veracity context. In: Proceedings of the International AAAI Conference on Web and Social Media, vol. 13, pp. 463–472 (2019)
20. Sharma, K., Qian, F., Jiang, H., Ruchansky, N., Zhang, M., Liu, Y.: Combating fake news: a survey on identification and mitigation techniques. ACM Trans. Intell. Syst. Technol. (TIST) **10**(3), 1–42 (2019)
21. Kai, S., Limeng, C., Suhang, W., Lee, D., Liu, H.: Defend: explainable fake news detection. In: Proceedings of the 25th ACM SIGKDD International Conference on Knowledge Discovery & Data Mining, pp. 395–405 (2019)
22. Shu, K., Mahudeswaran, D., Liu, H.: Fakenewstracker: a tool for fake news collection, detection, and visualization. Comput. Math. Organ. Theory **25**(1), 60–71 (2019)
23. Shu, K., Sliva, A., Wang, S., Tang, J., Liu, H.: Fake news detection on social media: a data mining perspective. ACM SIGKDD Explorations Newsletter **19**(1), 22–36 (2017)

24. Sebastian, T., Adish, S., Manuel, G.R., Arpit, M., Andreas, K.: Fake news detection in social networks via crowd signals. In: Companion Proceedings of the The Web Conference 2018, pp. 517–524 (2018)
25. William, Y.W.: liar, liar pants on fire: a new benchmark dataset for fake news detection. arXiv preprint arXiv:1705.00648 (2017)
26. Yang, S., Shu, K., Wang, S., Renjie, G., Fan, W., Liu, H.: Unsupervised fake news detection on social media: a generative approach. Proc. AAAI Conf. Artif. Intell. **33**, 5644–5651 (2019)
27. Reza, Z., Xinyi, Z., Kai, S., Huan, L.: Fake news research: theories, detection strategies, and open problems. In: Proceedings of the 25th ACM SIGKDD International Conference on Knowledge Discovery & Data Mining, pp. 3207–3208 (2019)
28. Xichen, Z., Ali, A.G.: An overview of online fake news: characterization, detection, and discussion. Inf. Process. Manage. **57**(2), 102025 (2020)

Multidimensional Analysis of Fake News Spreaders on Twitter

Maneet Singh[1(✉)], Rishemjit Kaur[2], and S.R.S. Iyengar[3]

[1] Indian Institute of Technology Ropar, Rupnagar, India
2018csz0008@iitrpr.ac.in

[2] CSIR-Central Scientific Instruments Organization, Chandigarh, India
rishemjit.kaur@csio.res.in

[3] Indian Institute of Technology Ropar, Rupnagar, India
sudarshan@iitrpr.ac.in

Abstract. Social media has become a tool to spread false information with the help of its large complex network. The consequences of such misinformation could be very severe. The paper uses the Twitter conversations about the scrapping of Article 370 in India to differentiate the spreaders of fake news from the general spreaders. Various features were used for comparison such as bot usage, patterns and emotions in tweets posted by bots, heterogeneity among the spreaders, and geographic as well as demographic characteristics. The bots were found to be relatively more indulged in spreading fake tweets by conversing more through replies. The tweets related to bots engaged in spreading fake news are more emotionally loaded especially with anger, disgust and trust than tweets posted by any other bots. The people living outside India played a major role in the dissemination of fake news on Article 370. The social connections as well as demographic features do not distinguish the fake news spreaders on the platform, although the fewer number of older people were found among the fake news spreaders. This may help in automating the detection of fake news spreaders.

Keywords: Spreaders · Fake news · Twitter · Bots

1 Introduction

The social media platforms offer the medium to its users to connect with the people across the globe, sharing news or expressing views on national and international issues. Just like every other technology, social media also has its pros and cons. Social networking sites like Facebook and Twitter are heavily used for spreading false information [1]. The consequences of this misinformation could be degrading the image of a public figure [2], affecting public health due to false health claims [3] and manipulating the minds of voters, which can be very harmful to any society [4]. Due to these adverse effects, several measures to control the spread of such false information have been taken by social networking

S. Chellappan et al. (Eds.): CSoNet 2020, LNCS 12575, pp. 354–365, 2020.
https://doi.org/10.1007/978-3-030-66046-8_29

platforms such as suspending the accounts merely responsible for such activities [5], removing posts that are fact-checked as false [14] and improvising the news feeds to its users [6]. Since malicious users continue to use the online platforms for their atrocious agenda [7], there is a need to implement better solutions that may help in further regulating the spread of fake news.

Besides the malicious users present on online platforms, there are also other sources that play a vital role in the dissemination of fake news on social media such as bots and fake news websites. The bots on online platforms could be either good or bad, where good bots may help in giving future warnings for a natural disaster such as earthquake [28] and bad bots may behave like humans with the purpose to deceive them [27]. There are certain websites that are tagged as fake news websites as they often share low credible content [28].

There has been a considerable amount of work that has attempted to analyze the spread of misinformation on social media platforms using various characteristics such as the content [12], user behaviour [16], spreading pattern [17], etc. The diffusion of false news on Twitter happens more rapidly than true news and is mainly aided by the novelty of content [8]. The majority of misinformation spread during the U.S. Presidential Elections held in 2016, was by very few websites as well as users and the political affiliation was directly associated with the level of exposure and consumption of fake news [9]. Shao et al. [10] developed an application named Hoaxy for tracking misinformation on Twitter. Although the tweets sharing fake news and the tweets related to fact-checking are similar in terms of popularity, the tweeters of both kinds of tweets, however, can be differentiated concerning their level of involvement on the platform. Various measures such as layer ratio, characteristic distance and structural heterogeneity associated with the propagation networks, could help in differentiating fake news from real news. The re-tweeting of fake news is mainly dominated by indirect followers whereas the same is not valid in case of real news [11]. The Australian Presidential Elections 2016 observed the side effects of using the misinformation to promote the candidate by its own followers [12]. Zollo et al. [13] used data from Facebook and observed that the sharing of news is associated with one's ideology i.e. people likes to share contents that strengthen their own opinion even though those content are of low credibility. The recent pandemic COVID-19 has also fallen victim to the misinformation campaigns executed by malicious users on various platforms like Facebook, Twitter and YouTube [14]. There are studies which use several features of fake news to develop automated methods for detection of fake news using only the content [18] or content as well as other user-based attributes on the platform [16]. Recent studies [34,35] have shown that linguistic features, personality as well as writing style may help in recognizing fake news spreaders.

The bots on Twitter use various strategies such as mentioning high profile Twitter accounts in their tweets and actively tweeting during the early stages of a post to boost the popularity of fake news at the beginning [17]. The tool Bot Electioneering Volume developed by Yang et al. [19] was used during the 2018 US midterm elections to visualize the activities of accounts that have a larger probability of being bots on Twitter. The tool identified that conservative bots were more active in tweeting election-related tweets than the liberal bots. The demographics of Twitter users such as age and gender explicitly obtained from their profile can be linked with the sharing of fake news [2,20]. The female users and the ones with higher age are more likely to share and trust fake news. Besides the demographic features, the country of the users on the Twitter platform might help in figuring out the fake news spreaders [21].

There exists a huge amount of flow of misinformation on social media about the abrogation of Article 370 and 35A from Jammu & Kashmir by dividing it into two Union Territories namely Jammu & Kashmir and Laddak [15]. The focus of our paper is in studying the spreaders of fake news related to Article 370 by comparing them with the general spreaders i.e. those that discuss Kashmir or Article 370 similar to the fake tweets but their contents are real or at least not fact-checked to be fake. In this study, we have taken a multi-dimensional view of the spread of fake news by bringing together a comprehensive set of features. The bots present among the fake news spreaders are compared with the bots among the general spreaders in terms of proportion as well as emotions and spreading patterns of their tweets. The geographical distribution, social connections and demographics of both kinds of spreaders are also compared with each other to assess the possibility of isolating fake news spreaders on Twitter.

2 Methodology

The proposed approach for differentiating fake news spreaders on Twitter is shown in Fig. 1.

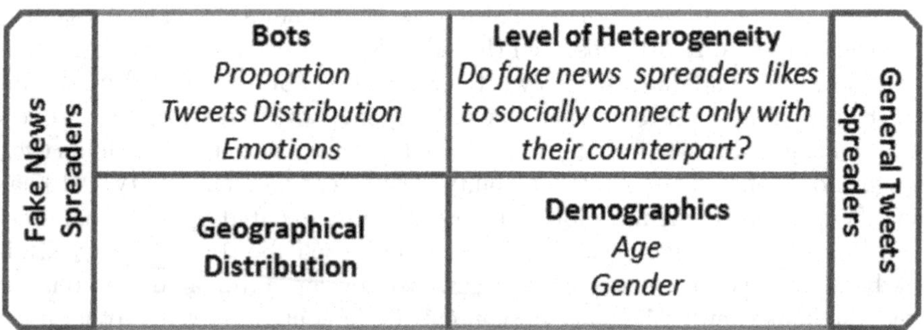

Fig. 1. Comparison of fake news spreaders and general tweets spreaders

2.1 Data Collection

As the goal of our study is to analyze the spreaders of fake news on Twitter, therefore it was required to first identify tweets containing fake news content.

The detection of fake news is a challenging task because of the lack of existence of a universal approach that can accurately classify the given tweet as fake or not. There are various fact-checking websites such as altnews, smhoaxslayer, factly, boomlive and facthunt that are dedicated to verifying the authenticity of the news shared on the online platforms for the Indian context. These websites were manually searched for tweets related to the scrapping of Article 370. The tweets obtained from websites were then searched on Twitter using their content and the twitter handle mentioned, resulting in seventeen unique tweets that were tagged as fake from 5th August 2019 to 31st August 2019. Further, 1428 accounts sharing these fake tweets were collected using Twitter REST API. In parallel, we also collected 1455 spreaders of general tweets (tweets containing keywords 'Kashmir' or 'Article 370') who tweeted during the same period. It was ensured that the accounts posting general tweets were different from the fake news accounts. The general tweets were also manually verified for credibility to ensure that they are not fake. The process of data collection is also shown in Fig. 2. The details such as tweets from the timeline, list of friends and their location (as obtained from their profile) of all the spreaders were also extracted.

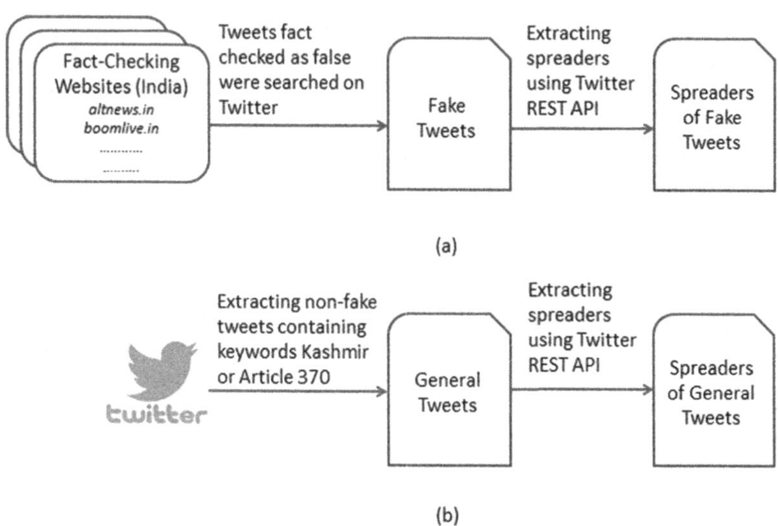

Fig. 2. Extraction of (a) fake news spreaders and (b) general tweets spreaders. The fact-checking websites were used for obtaining fake news and Twitter was used for extracting the spreaders.

2.2 Detection of Bots

There have been several studies that highlight the use of bots in spreading misinformation on social media [17,19]. Hence, it is essential to detect the presence of bots in the spreaders of fake tweets as well as general tweets. Wi et al. [24]

developed a machine learning model (better known as Botometer API), that uses thousands of features of the given twitter account to predict its likelihood of being a bot. Thus, using the Botometer API, the bot score was computed for all the spreaders present in our dataset. A given twitter account was classified as a bot if the bot score had a minimum value of 0.5 [20].

2.3 Measurement of Emotional Content

According to Plutchik [22], there are eight different emotions in human beings namely anger, anticipation, disgust, fear, joy, sadness, surprise and trust. The level of all these emotions was identified in the recent tweets (obtained from the timeline) of bots present in both kinds of spreaders with the help of the NRC Emotion Lexicon [23]. The NRC dictionary consists of 14181 words and the corresponding emotion(s) associated with each word. Thus, for every tweet, based on the number of words used, a normalized word count for every emotion was computed.

2.4 Measuring Heterogeneity Between Fake and General Spreaders

A network was constructed using the social connections among the spreaders of fake tweets as well as general tweets. The nodes in the network represent the Twitter accounts of the spreaders and connections between the nodes corresponds to their follower-following relationship as obtained from their Twitter profile. The communities present in the network were then extracted using the Louvain community detection algorithm [29]. After obtaining the communities, a heterogeneity score of the network [26] was computed using Eq. 1 where C denotes the set of communities having at least five nodes, C_i denotes the ith community, n_{if} and n_{gf} represents the number of spreaders of fake tweets and general tweets in ith community respectively. The heterogeneity score produces a value between 0 and 1, where zero would mean the fake news spreaders are only connected to other fake news spreaders and same will be true for general spreaders, whereas the score of one would indicate that both kinds of spreaders are equally connected with each other.

$$H = \frac{1}{\sqrt{2} * |C|} \sum_{i=1}^{|C|} \sqrt{1 - \frac{1}{(|C|)^2} [n_{if}^2 + n_{ig}^2]} \tag{1}$$

2.5 Extracting Demographic Characteristics

Wang et al. [25] developed an M3 model to predict three demographic characteristics for any Twitter user. First, it predicts the gender of the user as either Male or Female. Second, it predicts the age group of the user into four categories- less than 18, from 19 to 29, from 30 to 39 and greater than or equal to 40. Third, whether the given twitter account is operated by an individual or an organization. For our analysis, all three characteristics were predicted for both kinds of spreaders using the m3inference library.

3 Results and Discussions

3.1 Bots

In this section, we will discuss various characteristics such as proportion, tweets distribution and emotions of bots available among the spreaders of fake news and general spreaders.

Proportion of Bots. The bot scores for fake and general tweets spreaders were calculated and their distributions were compared using the probability density function as shown in Fig. 3. The area under the curve below bot score of 0.5 is more for the spreaders of general tweets and vice versa. A two-sample t-test was conducted to compare the proportion of bots. The number of bots involved in spreading fake news was relatively more than the number of bots in the general spreaders ($t = 5.15$ and $p < 0.0001$).

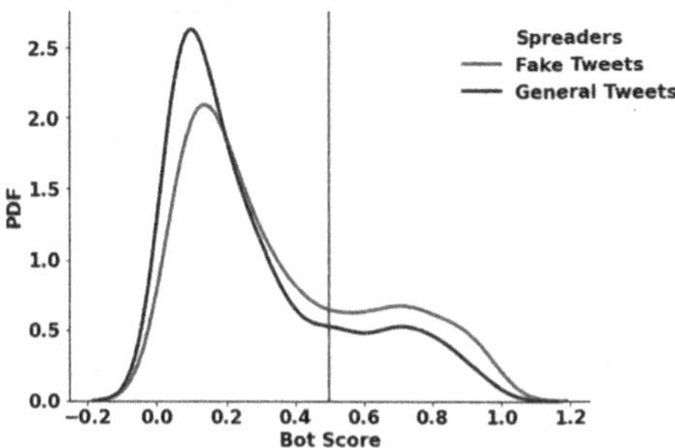

Fig. 3. The probability distribution function of bot scores for spreaders of fake and general tweets. The vertical line $x = 0.5$ (threshold for tagging the account as bot) is drawn to partition the distribution for humans and bots.

Tweets Distribution of Bots. The posts on Twitter could be in various forms such as retweets, replies or quoted tweets. The type of tweets commonly used may vary from one user to another. The tweeting behaviour based on the kind of tweet used in the timeline is shown in Fig. 4 for bots of both the spreaders. The bots of fake news spreaders are relatively more involved in conversations through replies($t = 2.24$ and $p < 0.05$) and posting original content ($t = 4.22$ and $p < 0.0001$), whereas bots of general spreaders merely like to share tweets ($t = 3.56$ and $p < 0.001$). There are previous studies which claim that the humans retweet more than bots [17,31], whereas our study moves one step further by saying that the general bots retweet more than the fake bots, thus our claims might guide in extracting fake bots from the overall bots present on Twitter.

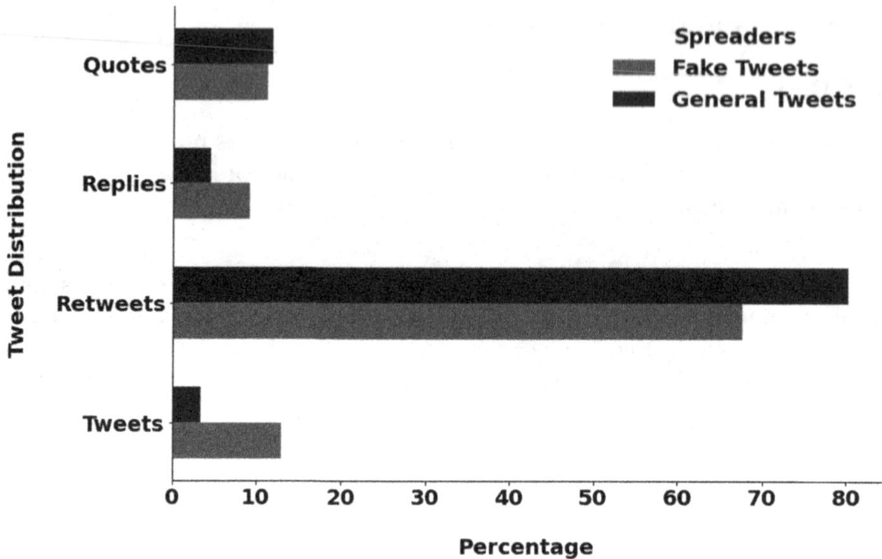

Fig. 4. The share of different types of tweets such as original tweets, retweets, replies and quotes for bots present in the spreaders of fake tweets and general tweets.

Emotions in Bots. The eight different kinds of emotions present in the tweets of bots of both the spreaders were compared with each other (Fig. 5). The mean proportion of every emotion category is higher in fake news spreaders and the difference is significant [32] in case of anger (ES $=$ 0.46 and $p < 0.05$), disgust (ES $=$ 0.45 and $p < 0.05$) and trust (ES $=$ 0.46 and $p < 0.05$). The result of observing higher anger and disgust are in line with previous research that compares fake news with real news [30]. The presence of certain kind of emotions being present in the tweets of the spreaders of fake news that are likely bot might help in future studies as useful features for detection of bots involved in spreading fake news on social media.

3.2 Heterogeneity Between Fake and General Spreaders

The follower's network of the spreaders of both the fake tweets and general tweets is shown in Fig. 6 (a). The heterogeneity score for the network comes out to be 0.89. The high value of heterogeneity denotes that both kinds of spreaders are almost equally connected with each other. Thus in terms of connections on social media, the fake news spreaders cannot be isolated as they are very well connected within the platform, which may be due to the fact that fake news spreaders incorporates both intentional as well as unintentional users [33].

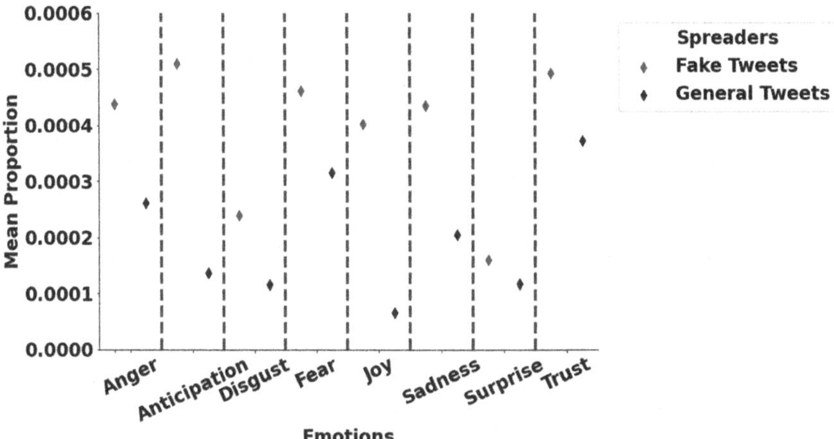

Fig. 5. Presence of eight different emotion categories in the tweets of bots of both fake and general spreaders. The mean values for all kinds of emotions are highlighted for bots present in both the spreaders.

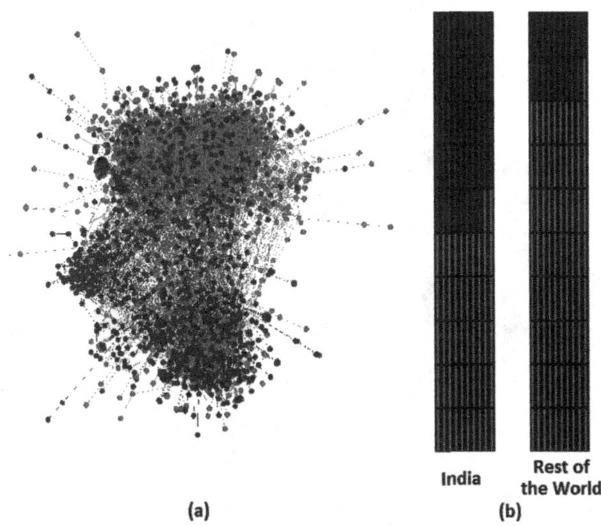

Fig. 6. (a) Followers Network of spreaders of fake (blue) and general tweets (red). The edge between the two nodes indicates that at least one of them follows the other on Twitter. (b) Comparing the ratio of spreaders of fake tweets (blue) and general tweets (red) in the users from India and Rest of the World. (Color figure online)

3.3 Geographical Distribution of Spreaders

The geographical distribution of spreaders that discussed scrapping of Article 370 on Twitter was analysed, using the country information obtained from the location field of their profile on the platform (Fig. 6 (b)). The distribution of both the spreaders is significantly dominated by general spreaders ($t = 6.75$ and $p < 0.0001$) for users belonging to India and fake spreaders ($t = 8.75$ and $p < 0.0001$) for users from rest of the world.

3.4 Demographics of Spreaders

The role of demographic features in spreading fake news was also evaluated as shown in Fig. 7. The percentage of factors like different age groups, gender and organization in fake and general spreaders was compared. None of the factors shown significant difference except that users having age greater than or equal to forty are dominated by general spreaders ($t = 2.4$ and $p < 0.05$). Thus people with varying demographics are involved in spreading fake news on Twitter.

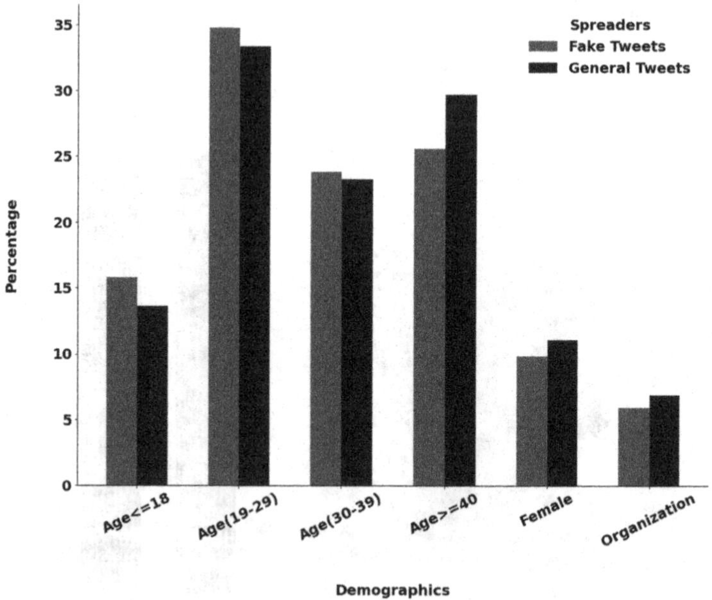

Fig. 7. Comparing the percentage(y-axis) of each demographic feature (x-axis) of fake and general spreaders. The age is divided into four categories and for simplicity, only the percentage of females is shown.

4 Conclusion

The concern regarding the spread of misinformation on social media platforms persists even though several measures are being adopted by the platforms itself as well as fact-checking websites and the governments of various countries. Our study attempts to distinguish fake news spreaders on Twitter from the general spreaders using the discussions held on the platform regarding the scrapping of Article 370 by the Government of India. The tweets sharing fake news were extracted using the information published on various fact-checking websites of India. Thus using the tweets mentioned in the websites, the spreaders of fake tweets are compared with the general spreaders. The proportion of bots is more in case of spreaders of fake tweets thus highlighting the issue of the massive use of bots in spreading misinformation on online platforms. The tweeting behaviour of bots used for fake news dissemination is different from the general bots as they relatively post more original content and get indulged in replies. The emotion categories like anger, disgust and trust are comparatively more in the tweets of the spreaders of fake news. The fake news spreaders are highly blended with the general tweets spreaders on Twitter, thus making it difficult to segregate them using only the connections among the users. As far as age is concerned, users on social media having age greater than forty are less active in spreading misinformation online. Such results using data from the Indian context should motivate the researches to perform a more detailed analysis of the behaviour of fake news spreaders using cross-national data. The online users indulged in spreading misinformation may be unintentional, therefore the social media platforms must take measures such as providing the fact check meter on the tweets having sensitive content to regulate the spread of misinformation.

References

1. Lazer, D.M., et al.: The science of fake news. Science **359**(6380), 1094–1096 (2018)
2. Bergmann, E.: Populism and the politics of misinformation. Safundi **21**(3), 251–265 (2020)
3. Ayoob, K.-T., Duyff, R.L., Quagliani, D.: Position of the American dietetic association: food and nutrition misinformation. J. Am. Diet. Assoc. **102**(2), 260–266 (2002)
4. Grinberg, N., Joseph, K., Friedland, L., Swire-Thompson, B., Lazer, D.: Fake news on Twitter during the 2016 US presidential election. Science **363**(6425), 374–378 (2019)
5. Thomas, K., Grier, C., Song, D. and Paxson, V.: Suspended accounts in retrospect: an analysis of twitter spam. In: Proceedings of the 2011 ACM SIGCOMM Conference on Internet Measurement Conference, pp. 243–258 (2011)
6. Mike, A.: The partnership press: Lessons for platform-publisher collaborations as Facebook and news outlets team to fight misinformation (2018)
7. Pennycook, G., McPhetres, J., Zhang, Y., Lu, J.G., Rand, D.G.: Fighting COVID-19 misinformation on social media: experimental evidence for a scalable accuracy-nudge intervention. Psychol. Sci. **31**(7), 770–780 (2020)

8. Vosoughi, S., Roy, D., Aral, S.: The spread of true and false news online. Science **359**(6380), 1146–1151 (2018)
9. Grinberg, N., Joseph, K., Friedland, L., Swire-Thompson, B., Lazer, D.: Fake news on Twitter during the 2016 US presidential election. Science **363**(6425), 374-378 (2019)
10. Shao, C., Ciampaglia, G.L., Flammini, A. and Menczer, F.: Hoaxy: a platform for tracking online misinformation. In: Proceedings of the 25th International Conference Companion on World Wide Web, pp. 745–750 (2016)
11. Zhao, Z., et al.: Fake news propagates differently from real news even at early stages of spreading. EPJ Data Sci. **9**(1), 1–14 (2020). https://doi.org/10.1140/epjds/s13688-020-00224-z
12. Kušen, E., Strembeck, M.: Politics, sentiments, and misinformation: An analysis of the Twitter discussion on the: Austrian presidential elections. Online Soc. Netw. Media **5**(2018), 37–50 (2016)
13. Zollo, F., Quattrociocchi, W.: Misinformation spreading on Facebook. In: Lehmann, S., Ahn, Y.-Y. (eds.) Complex Spreading Phenomena in Social Systems. CSS, pp. 177–196. Springer, Cham (2018). https://doi.org/10.1007/978-3-319-77332-2_10
14. Brennen, J.S., Simon, F., Howard, P.N., Nielsen, R.K.: Types, sources, and claims of Covid-19 misinformation. Reuters Inst. **7**, 1–3 (2020)
15. Kashmir Rumour Mill On Social Media Goes Into Overdrive. https://economictimes.indiatimes.com/news/politics-and-nation/kashmir-rumour-mill-on-social-media-goes-into-overdrive/articleshow/70636473.cms?from=mdr. Accessed 14 Aug 2019
16. Castillo, C., Mendoza, M. and Poblete, B.: Information credibility on twitter. In: Proceedings of the 20th International Conference on World Wide Web, pp. 675–684 (2011)
17. Shao, C., Ciampaglia, G.L., Varol, O., Yang, K.C., Flammini, A., Menczer, F.: The spread of low-credibility content by social bots. Nature Commun. **9**(1), 1–9 (2018)
18. Giachanou, A., Rosso, P., Crestani, F.: Leveraging emotional signals for credibility detection. In: Proceedings of the 42nd International ACM SIGIR Conference on Research and Development in Information Retrieval, pp. 877–880 (2019)
19. Yang, K.C., Hui, P.M., Menczer, F.: Bot electioneering volume: Visualizing social bot activity during elections. In: Companion Proceedings of The 2019 World Wide Web Conference, pp. 214–217 (2019)
20. Shu, K., Wang, S., Liu, H.: Understanding user profiles on social media for fake news detection. In: 2018 IEEE Conference on Multimedia Information Processing and Retrieval (MIPR), pp. 430–435. IEEE (2018)
21. Linvill, D.L., Boatwright, B.C., Grant, W.J., Warren, P.L.: The Russians are hacking my brain! investigating Russia's internet research agency twitter tactics during the 2016 United States presidential campaign.". Comput. Hum. Behav. **99**, 292–300 (2019)
22. Plutchik, R.: A general psychoevolutionary theory of emotion. In: Theories of Emotion, pp. 3–33. Academic Press (1980)
23. Mohammad, S.M. and Turney, P.D.: Nrc emotion lexicon. Natl. Res. Counc. Canada 2, (2013)
24. Davis, C.A., Varol, O., Ferrara, E., Flammini, A., Menczer, F.: Botornot: a system to evaluate social bots. In: Proceedings of the 25th International Conference Companion on World Wide Web, pp. 273–274 (2016)

25. Wang, Z., et al.: Demographic inference and representative population estimates from multilingual social media data. In: The World Wide Web Conference, pp. 2056–2067 (2019)
26. Lužar, B., Levnajić, Z., Povh, J., Perc, M.: Community structure and the evolution of interdisciplinarity in Slovenia's scientific collaboration network. Plos one **9**(4), e94429 (2014)
27. Wald, R., Khoshgoftaar, T.M., Napolitano, A., Sumner, C.: Predicting susceptibility to social bots on twitter. In: 2013 IEEE 14th International Conference on Information Reuse & Integration (IRI), pp. 6–13. IEEE (2013)
28. de Lima Salge, C.A., Berente, N.: Is that social bot behaving unethically? Commun. ACM **60**(9), 29–31 (2017)
29. Blondel, V.D., Guillaume, J.-L., Lambiotte, R., Lefebvre, E.: Fast unfolding of communities in large networks. J. Stat. Mech. Theor. Exp. **2008**(10), 10008 (2008)
30. Paschen, J.: Investigating the emotional appeal of fake news using artificial intelligence and human contributions. J. Prod. Brand Manage. (2019)
31. Shu, K., Mahudeswaran, D., Wang, S., Lee, D., Liu, H.: Fakenewsnet: a data repository with news content, social context and dynamic information for studying fake news on social media. arXiv preprint arXiv:1809.01286 8 (2018)
32. Mann, H.B., Whitney, D.R.: On a test of whether one of two random variables is stochastically larger than the other. Ann. Math. Stat. 50-60 (1947)
33. Ardèvol-Abreu, A., Delponti, P., Rodríguez-Wangüemert, C.: Intentional or inadvertent fake news sharing? Fact-checking warnings and users' interaction with social media content. El profesional de la información (EPI) 29(5), (2020)
34. Cardaioli, M., Cecconello, S., Conti, M., Pajola, L. and Turrin, F.: Fake news spreaders profiling through behavioural analysis. In: CLEF (2020)
35. Giachanou, A., Ríssola, E.A., Ghanem, B., Crestani, F., Rosso, P.: The role of personality and linguistic patterns in discriminating between fake news spreaders and fact checkers. In: Métais, E., Meziane, F., Horacek, H., Cimiano, P. (eds.) NLDB 2020. LNCS, vol. 12089, pp. 181–192. Springer, Cham (2020). https://doi.org/10.1007/978-3-030-51310-8_17

Detection of Sybil Attacks in Social Networks

Allan Lobo[(✉)], Yukta Mandekar, Sonali Pundpal, and Bidisha Roy

St. Francis Institute of Technology, University of Mumbai, Mumbai, India
allanlobo10@gmail.com, mandekar.yukta99@gmail.com,
sonalipundpal1998@gmail.com, bidisharoy@sfit.ac.in

Abstract. The advent of the Internet revolutionized communication between people in different geographical locations. It has brought about a reduction in the turnaround time, for exchange of information between people, from days to seconds. Social networks have become an important part of life. They provide a platform for people to connect and communicate with one's kith. As they have an important role in communication, social networks are under the threat of cyber-attacks. Sybil attacks are a form of security breach where the network is infiltrated with forged identities. Multiple duplicate identities are created by malicious users to flood the system with fake information, negatively influencing the performance of the system. These attacks make the system look unreliable. This paper builds on Asadian and Javadi's [1] work of detecting sybil nodes in a network. They proposed using Jaccard index as a similarity measure which is then used by Louvain algorithm to divide the dataset into communities. Apart from the two usual communities in which nodes are allocated, Honest and Sybil, this paper introduces a third community, the Questionable community, where suspicious nodes are assigned. This allows the nodes to be quarantined and keep tabs on their activities without removing them from the network and risking loss of goodwill. We then explore the Honest community using L2 Norm and those found below a threshold are assigned to the Questionable community. This refines the results found in the first part of the system. The results obtained are promising and should provide favorable results in real time systems. The system presented in this paper returns a precision value of 0.98, equal to SICTF and Improved KD-Tree method [2] and returns a recall value of 0.94, which is better than other methods available.

Keywords: Social network · Jaccard Index · Louvain algorithm · Sybil attack · Similarity score · L2 norm · Interaction score

1 Introduction

The Internet has changed the way people communicate forever. The shift from letters which would take days/weeks to the Internet which takes minutes/seconds has been a boon to people's lives. Waiting for important and time-sensitive communication is no longer a concern, nor is casually communicating with kith and kin in far off areas.

With the gaining popularity of the Internet, Internet security has become a major concern. Communicating with strangers across the Internet, has increased the risks that Internet users face. The type, volume and magnitude of attacks have increased exponentially through the years. Some well-established attacks are ransom wares, which require

S. Chellappan et al. (Eds.): CSoNet 2020, LNCS 12575, pp. 366–377, 2020.
https://doi.org/10.1007/978-3-030-66046-8_30

a key to recover the system and data, or viruses which destroy all information, or attacks which compromise the privacy and integrity of correspondence between users or attacks which prevent users from accessing services.

With the rise of social networks, a common type of attack which has arisen is called sybil attack. It is seen in peer to peer networks or in platforms which are primarily used for interaction between users. Malicious users are known to operate multiple identities in the network, feeding inaccurate information and blending into the network by connecting to multiple users. This in turn negatively influences the reputation of the system as it affects the authenticity of the information available. A lay user or an observer of the network is unable to distinguish between fake and real identities.

The repercussions of sybil attacks in networks usually depends on the size, reputation and influence of the social network in people's lives. For example, Twitter is a social networking site where people message (tweet) and share their views with each other. On this platform, between the first and second US Presidential Election debates in 2016, 1/3 of Pro-Donald Trump twitter tweets and 1/5 of Pro-Hillary Clinton tweets were produced by sybil identities, which resulted in drowning real identities and swaying public opinion [3]. 19% of the total tweets produced in this election, were by sybil identities [4]. Similar trends have been seen in elections around the world. In 2019, the Spanish general elections were affected by online sybil identities swaying public opinion for and against candidates [5]. Sybil identities have also played key roles in online social network battles on the most pressing national and international issues around the world by campaigns of disinformation. The consequences of these activities have spilled into the offline world, causing riots and strikes. The most severe sybil attacks indirectly lead to loss of human life and substantial financial losses.

Various authors have proposed techniques to counter the problem of sybil attack. Some of them are, SybilBelief: a semi-supervised learning approach for structure-based sybil detection [6], Sybil Defender: It leverages network topologies and identifies sybil nodes using random walks [7], SICT and Improved KD-Tree method [2], Random Walk-based(RW) and Loop Belief Propagation (LBP) are applied iteratively to nodes in the system [8]. These techniques face challenges which we have tried to overcome.

The work which we present in this paper is an extension of the work done by Asadian and Javadi where they have classified nodes based on their interactions by assigning them to communities using Louvain algorithm [1].

In this paper, we have pursued a two-pronged approach. In the first part, bottom-up approach, we calculate the Jaccard Index similarity of each node, with every other node in the dataset. The similarity measure calculates the strength of the links between node pairs. The Jaccard Index similarities of all node pairs are then used by Louvain algorithm as weights, in a graph to form communities [9].

After the forming of node communities, a similarity score is calculated between each community pair. Setting a threshold value, communities are divided and labelled into Honest and Sybil communities. Communities which do not have a strong likeness or pull to either the Honest or Sybil communities, or nodes which are mutually placed in both communities are brought together and placed in the Questionable community. The Questionable community is a quarantined or suspicious nodes community which has been separated to limit its exposure to the system and to remain attentive to the activities of its members. In the second part, top-down approach, we explore the Honest communities and perform a rigorous analysis of strength of node links amongst members of the same community. In this part, L2 Norm [10] is calculated as the similarity measure for all node pairs in a community. Setting a threshold value, link strength of node pairs below the threshold, are put in the Questionable community.

The present study returns a precision value of 0.98, equal to SICTF and Improved KD-Tree method [2], and returns a recall value of 0.94, which is better than all other methods available.

The present system is important because not only does it form communities with node interactions using Louvain algorithm, but improves the solution by finding sybil nodes in Honest communities using L2 Norm interaction scores. It creates a provision to detect questionable behavior of nodes who can then be quarantined. The system is also able to detect similar member types based on their interactions in the networks, which have applications in the business and sales front of a company.

Paper Structure. The paper consists of 7 sections. Section 1 introduces the project. Section 2 consists of work that has been previously done. Section 3 details the challenges identified with the previous work. Section 4 gives an overview of the system and details the process of the system execution. Section 5 displays the results obtained and describes the performance evaluation parameters of the system. Section 6 concludes the paper and explains the future scope of the system.

2 Related Work

Neil Zhenqiang Gong et al. proposed a method called SybilBelief, a semi-supervised learning approach for structure-based sybil detection. This method takes a set of honest and a set of sybil nodes as its input and then begins to propagate the label information. This method is also resilient to noise [6].

In 2013, Wei Wei, Fengyuan Xu, Chiu C. Tan, Qun Li proposed a method named Sybil Defender, which leverages network topologies. This method detects and defends the system against sybil nodes. In this method the identification happens using random walks. Here it is said that the walks originating from Honest communities ends in Honest communities and vice versa. Therefore, the walks with origin in Sybil communities will be shorter as the sybil nodes are comparatively very low in number. This process is repeated iteratively and can detect sybil nodes even when the number of sybil nodes introduced by each attack edge is low [7].

Renuga Devi and M. Hemalatha proposed a method that uses Connectivity Threshold. The method also makes use of Improved KD-Tree method. These two algorithms together focus on getting the connection threshold values. Now if a node's connection strength exceeds this connection threshold value then the node is deemed to be sybil and those below the threshold are called honest nodes. This method focusses on mainly using SICT and Improved KD-Tree method and gives an accuracy of 96% [2].

In 2015, Binghui Wang, Jinyuan Jia, Le Zhang, and Neil Zhenqiang Gong proposed a novel structure-based approach called Local Rule-based Propagation for Detection of Sybil Nodes (SybilSCAR). In this method, Random Walk-based (RW) and Loop Belief Propagation-based (LBP) methods are merged together and are applied iteratively to every node in the system. Here, a local rule is applied which helps the system declare the label information for propaganda. After this, a new local rule is deigned which is thereafter applied to check for sybil nodes [8].

In 2018, Hooman Asadian and Hamid Haj Javadi proposed a method that uses user interaction as a parameter to detect the sybil nodes. In this method, firstly an un-weighted graph is converted to a weighted one and are then formed into communities using Louvain algorithm. The interactions between various nodes in a network is considered as a prime deciding factor to distinguish between honest and sybil nodes [1].

Zhuhua Cai and Christopher Jermaine proposed a hierarchical model called the latent community (LC) model in 2011. This model forms groups and makes a community of the inputted identities, which loosely connects to the rest of the graph. This model's major drawback is the fact that it might not work properly in a distributed environment since it looks for more closely knit communities that enable it to form groups [11].

Javier Pastor-Galindo *et al.* proposed an approach in which their aim was to spot political social bots in twitter. The method used is called BASTION, Big Data Mining for Social Bot Identification. The data is collected, then passed for analysis where the relevant features are picked and used for user identification. Thereafter, it is passed for Knowledge Extraction [5].

3 Challenges Identified

In most proposed solutions as explained in Sect. 2, the system assumes that all the data is available in a centralized manner, which makes it hard to work with a more distributed dataset. The present system, uses Louvain algorithm to form communities [1]. It uses modularity as a parameter to place the nodes in either Honest or Sybil communities. This enables the system to be able to group nodes even if the data is distributed.

There are high chances of an honest node getting misclassified as a sybil node, since there is no mechanism available that double-checks the allocation of nodes in a community. In the present system, we have made sure to verify the allocation of nodes in the Honest communities to make sure that no sybil nodes are missed in the process. The biggest challenge in this project is to attain a 100% accuracy rate, since it is practically impossible to detect a sybil node if it has mingled too well with the Honest community. The better an identity blends in the environment with other users, the more secure and dominant it becomes in terms of spreading of information.

Solutions proposed by other authors have classified nodes in a dataset as Honest or Sybil. But there is always some suspicion about few users due to their interactions in a social network. Nodes which are well integrated in the system are difficult to decipher if they are genuine users or not. These generally get listed as sybil nodes in most approaches proposed since there is no definitive reason for it to be classified as a safe and genuine user. This negatively affects the reputation of a social network, as misclassifying significant number of genuine users as sybil identities can cause a loss of goodwill and discontent among users operating on the social network. To overcome such difficulties, the present study has introduced a third community called Questionable community.

There are two types of sybil attack. A lone attacker or a group of attackers working simultaneously. When a group of attackers are working, detecting individual nodes is inefficient. Using Louvain community detection algorithm, detecting one node can help us detect other nodes in the same cluster based on the interactions with each other [9].

4 System Overview

The flowchart representing the workflow of the system is shown below in Fig. 1.

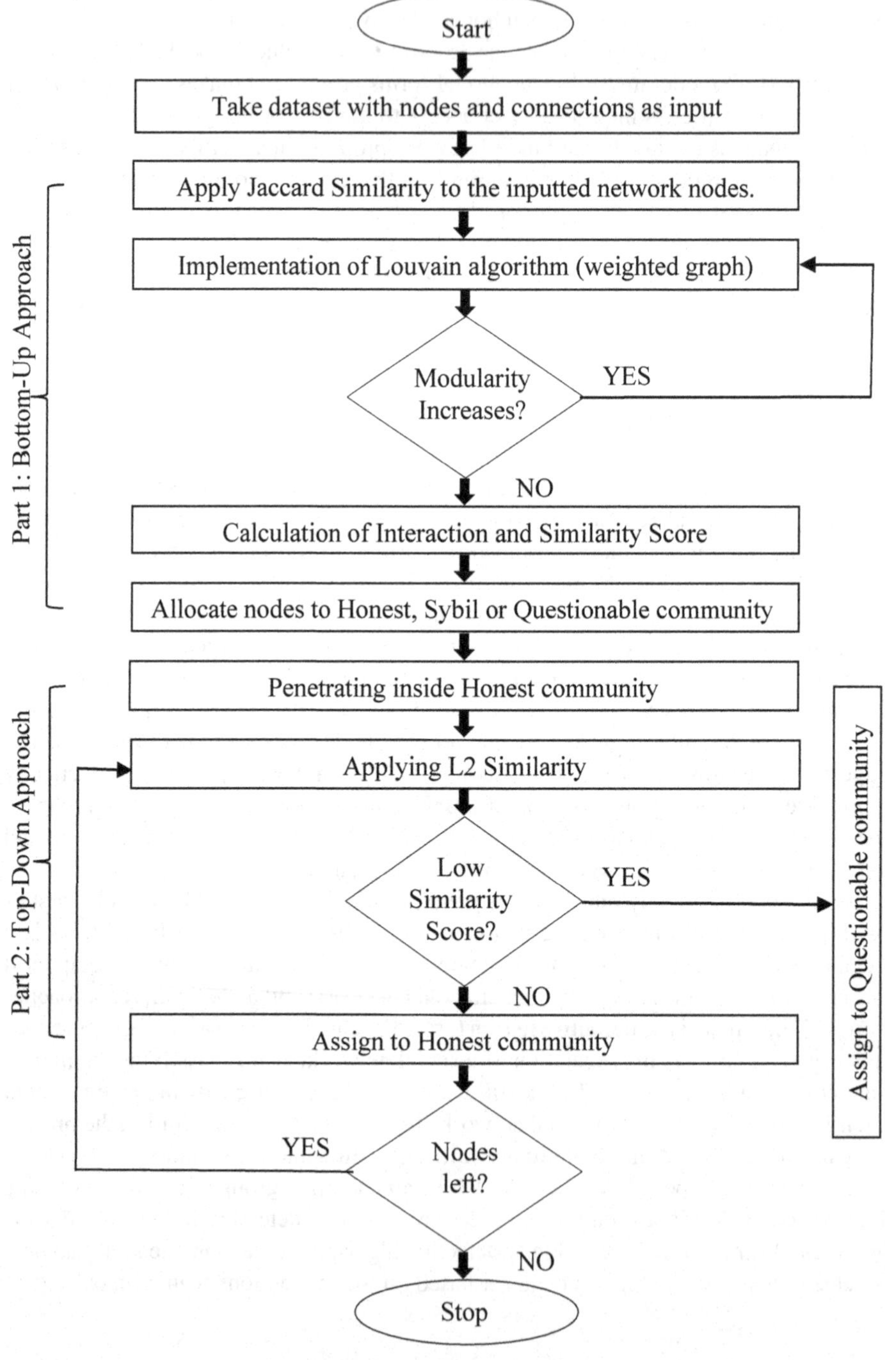

Fig. 1. Workflow of the system

A dataset was simulated based on interactions and exchange of information of a small closed community. The nodes and their network with which they interact with were taken in the dataset as an unweight graph. The users in the dataset correspond to the nodes while the interaction between node pairs forms the edges.

We use *like* interactions between users, on posts posted on each other's social network pages, to calculate the link strength of edges between two nodes or users. This is done by using Jaccard Index [1]. The link strength or similarity between node pairs denotes the structural similarity between them. It will be used to cluster nodes in communities, being used as weights in the input graph.

The Eq. (1) is used to find the Jaccard Index similarity of node pairs.

$$J(\mathrm{A},\mathrm{B}) = \frac{|\mathrm{A} \bigcap \mathrm{B}|}{|\mathrm{A} \bigcup \mathrm{B}|} = \frac{|\mathrm{A} \bigcap \mathrm{B}|}{|\mathrm{A}| + |\mathrm{B}| - |\mathrm{A} \bigcap \mathrm{B}|} \tag{1}$$

Where **J (A, B)** is the Jaccard Similarity value found, and **A, B** are nodes of the dataset whose link strength are being calculated.

Figure 2 shows a networkx graph. It shows the weighted graph of the input network. It is a representation of all the nodes linked to each other using the weights generated by Jaccard Similarity.

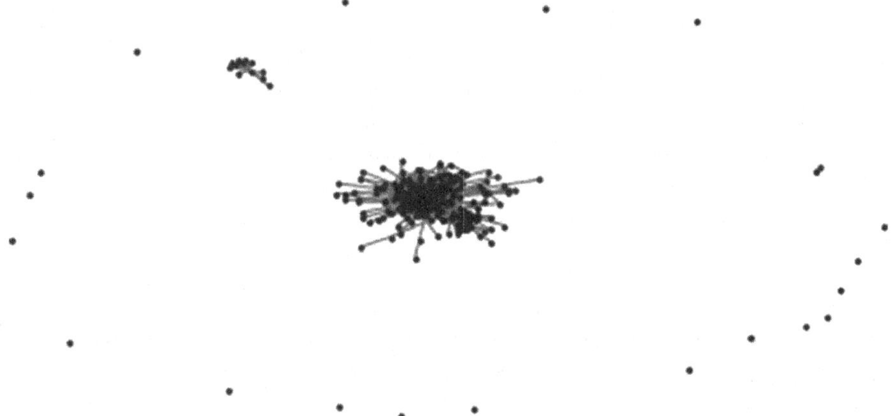

Fig. 2. Weighted graph of input network.

This graph is used as an input parameter in Louvain algorithm to form communities of similar or identical nodes. We use Louvain algorithm, as it is an efficient greedy method for identifying communities in both small and large networks. It is useful in distributed networks to optimally group or cluster nodes.

Louvain algorithm starts by searching for small communities by locally optimizing modularity. All the nodes in one community are aggregated and are treated as a single entity or node in the following iteration of the algorithm. In the following iteration, a new network is formed by pooling similar nodes (previously small local communities) in new communities. This cycle is repeated iteratively until the modularity value is at its highest value and a hierarchy of communities are produced.

Modularity ranges from –1 to 1, and is calculated as the sum of edges inside the communities to the sum of edges outside communities. The optimum value of modularity, theoretically, gives us the best possible grouping of nodes in a network. But due to networks being very large, and calculating node pair interactions of all the nodes in the network with every other node is impractical and infeasible, heuristic algorithms are employed to make it efficient.

The Eq. (2) details how the modularity is calculated for each iteration of Louvain algorithm.

$$Q \equiv \frac{1}{2m} \sum\nolimits_{ij} \left[A_{ij} - \frac{k_i k_j}{2m} \right] \partial \left(c_i, c_j \right) \tag{2}$$

In Eq. (2), $\boldsymbol{Q}$ stands for the modularity value to be found for Louvain algorithm, $\boldsymbol{A_{ij}}$ represents the node link strength or edge weights between nodes $\boldsymbol{i}$ and $\boldsymbol{j}$, $\boldsymbol{k_i}$ and $\boldsymbol{k_j}$ correspond to the total weights of edges or node pair links attached to nodes $\boldsymbol{i}$ and $\boldsymbol{j}$ respectively, $\boldsymbol{m}$ gives the aggregate of all the edge weights in the graph, $\boldsymbol{c_i}$ and $\boldsymbol{c_j}$are the communities which contain the nodes;

Louvain algorithm is made up of two phases that are repeated iteratively. In the first phase, each node in the network graph is assigned its own community. Then the change in modularity is calculated for each node $\boldsymbol{i}$, by removing it from its own community and inserting it in neighboring communities of $\boldsymbol{i, j}$. The second phase begins by building a new network. The nodes in this network were communities in the previous iteration, which have been aggregated. Self-loops on a node in the new network represent links between nodes of the same community, as present in the previous iteration. Links between multiple nodes of one community to nodes of another community in the previous iteration, are now represented by a single weighted edge between the new nodes (which were communities in the previous iteration). These two phases undergo repeated iterations, till an optimum value of modularity is computed.

Communities formed in Louvain algorithm consists of nodes which have strong link strength or similarity with other nodes in the community [1]. The score of the interaction between two nodes should be above a certain limit or threshold for it to be called a strong interaction.

The Eq. (3) summarizes the calculation of the Link strength

$$LinkStrength(\mathrm{A, B}) = \left\{ \begin{array}{ll} Strong & |IndicatorScore| \geq ITH \\ Weak & |IndicatorScore| < ITH \end{array} \right\} \tag{3}$$

Here ***A, B*** are nodes in a given network, ***ITH*** is the interaction threshold. It decides on placement of nodes in a community.

Figure 3 given below shows the different communities formed by Louvain algorithm identified by their differing color.

After the communities are formed, the similarity score between communities in the graph is calculated. The similarity score calculated for this network was done using

Fig. 3. Communities formed using weighted network graph by louvain algorithm (Color figure online)

Jaccard index, with all the notations being the same, however this time instead of node pair similarity, we calculate community pair similarity. If the similarity score is above a certain threshold value the communities are considered to be of similar state.

The Eq. (4) shows the mathematical form used to distinguish the state of communities [1].

$$Similarity(\mathrm{A}, \mathrm{B}) = \left\{ \begin{array}{ll} Similar & InteractionScore(\mathrm{A}, \mathrm{B} > STH) \\ Dissimilar & InteractionScore(\mathrm{A}, \mathrm{B} \leq STH) \\ N/A & NoInteraction(\mathrm{A}, \mathrm{B}) \end{array} \right\} \quad (4)$$

In this equation, ***A*** and ***B*** are communities in the network whose state is being evaluated. ***STH*** is the Similarity Threshold which is the cutoff value below which communities are known to be dissimilar.

We then assign an Honest/Sybil label to a community based on the interactions of few nodes in the community. Accordingly, all other communities are labelled depending on their similarity to each other. Nodes which are in conflicting communities, Honest and Sybil, are assigned to a third community called the Questionable community for further analysis of their behavior in the network. This community is specifically created as a quarantined or suspicious node community.

We have now found out Honest, Sybil and Questionable communities and their nodes. This completes the first part of the detection of sybil nodes by the system. We now move on to the second part of the study where we strive to provide a more refined solution. Specifically, we will focus our activity in the Honest communities, where malicious nodes might still be operating undetected.

A top down approach is implemented wherein a further check is done in the Honest communities to guarantee accurate and reliable solutions. We compare interactions of nodes with the rest of the nodes in a community using L2 Norm [10].

The Eq. (5) shows how the interaction is calculated for two nodes in an Honest community.

$$L2(\mathrm{A},\ \mathrm{B}) = \frac{|\mathrm{A} \cap \mathrm{B}|}{\sqrt{|\mathrm{A}| \cdot |\mathrm{B}|}} \tag{5}$$

Here, **L (A,B)** is the L2 Norm value found, and **A, B** are nodes of the dataset whose interaction score is being calculated.

The L2 Norm gives us the level of interaction a node has with other nodes in the community. The interaction score of each node is aggregated. Similar technique is undertaken for all Honest communities. We set a threshold value for all the interaction scores of Honest community nodes. Nodes below the threshold are assigned to the Questionable community for further analysis.

5 Results and Performance Evaluation Parameters

5.1 Results

In Fig. 4. the networkx graph shows the three segments, in which the nodes have been labelled, according to their interaction in the system. The first segment of nodes are honest nodes represented by green, whose usage of the network is benevolent and appropriate. The second segment are the sybil nodes shown by red dots, whose malicious behavior is detected during system execution. The final segment, the Questionable community, represented by blue, can run in the system but has to be put under restrictions and oversight.

Fig. 4. A refined solution is presented by the system after the top-down approach (Color figure online)

5.2 Performance Evaluation Parameters

To examine the performance of the system proposed in this paper, parameters such as precision and recall are taken. Precision and recall are useful as they measure the success of prediction when the classes are very imbalanced.

1. **Precision** - The precision metric shows the accuracy of positive class, that is the degree of closeness of a capacity to the quantity's true value. In this paper, precision gives us a measure of the total number of honest nodes actually being correctly predicted as honest [2].

$$\Pr ecision = \frac{TP}{TP + FP} = 0.98 \tag{6}$$

2. **Recall** - Also known as sensitivity, Recall shows how good a model is in detecting a positive class. In this case, it shows how successful the model is in predicting honest nodes and keeping the network safe and secure [2].

$$\mathrm{Rec}all = \frac{TP}{TP + FN} = 0.94 \tag{7}$$

In Eqs. 6 and 7, **True** denotes honest nodes whereas **False** denotes sybil nodes. **TP** stands for True Positive value which signifies nodes which are actually Honest and are predicted as Honest by the system. **FP** is False Positive value which means nodes which are actually Sybil but are predicted as honest by the system. **TN** is True Negative conveys nodes that are Honest but are predicted as Sybil. Finally, **FN** stands for False Negative which signifies nodes that are Sybil and are predicted as Sybil by the system.
Figure 5 and 6 are a comparison of precision and recall values resulting from the Present System and solutions proposed by other authors.

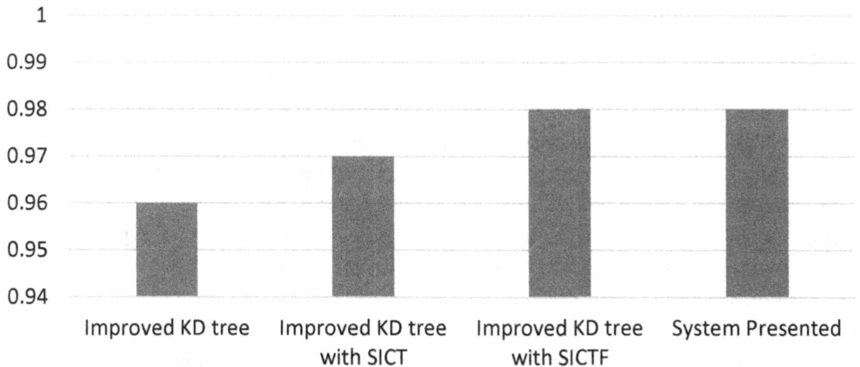

Fig. 5. Comparison of precision values, between the present system and other solutions

The present study returns a precision value of 0.98, and a recall value of 0.94.

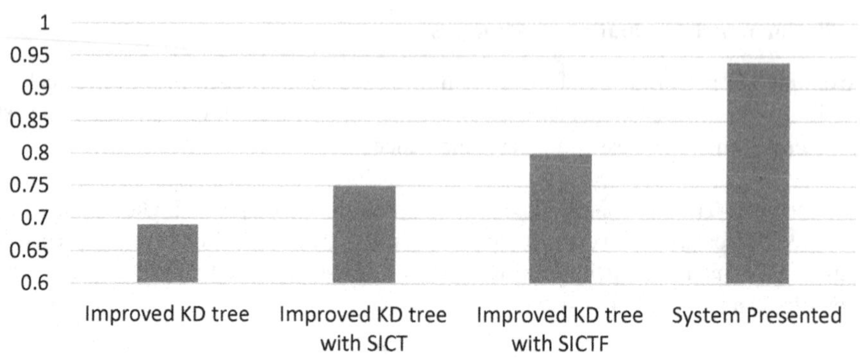

Fig. 6. Comparison of recall values, between present system and other solutions

6 Conclusion

Detection of sybil nodes is of vital importance in the working of social networks. Presence of such sybil identities destabilizes and reduces the authenticity and credibility of a network. Since the last 10 years, intensity of sybil attacks have grown and it has reached a juncture where not only does it greatly affect interactions online and offline, but sways opinions through disinformation. The magnitude of sybil identities are so large, they have started destabilizing systems. With this outlook, it is an optimum time to introduce the system proposed in this paper in social networks, and identify and bar sybil nodes in the network. As the sybil identities grow, distinguishing between real and sybil identities becomes more difficult. The proposed system is resource friendly and can be run with favorable results on real time systems. It identifies sybil identities based on their behavior and interactions.

The system presented uses Jaccard similarity for edge strength, and groups them in communities using Louvain algorithm. These communities are labeled as Honest, Sybil or Questionable communities. The Questionable community allows the nodes to be quarantined without removing them from the network and risking loss of goodwill. The first part of the project can be run on any network, large or small with ease. It helps identify and label nodes faster, which is beneficial for operations with real-time data. For a more refined solution, the system works with nodes in the Honest community using L2 norm, identifying any misclassifications caused by the down-up approach using Louvain algorithm and interaction score. The second part of the system proposed can be implemented in more vital and restrictive network environments

The system presented in this paper returns a precision value of 0.98, equal to SICTF and Improved KD-Tree method [2], but returns a recall value of 0.94, which is better than all other methods available.

The future scope of this system will be to link various social networks together, through data sharing, with necessary consent. This will give users a single online identity, which will drastically reduce the number of sybil identities present in social networks and keep check the disinformation which is spread on these networks. The system can also include more parameters to calculate the link strength between nodes in the network. For example, comment analysis, type of content shared, time spent online, Geo or IP tagging can be incorporated. Additional privacy control options should be available to network users, giving them the power to control their visibility and security.

References

1. Asadian, H., Javadi, H.H.S.: Identification of Sybil attacks on social networks using a framework based on user interactions. Secur. Priv. **1**(2), e19 (2018)
2. Devi, R.R., Hemalatha, M.: Sybil Identification in Social Networks using SICT and SICTF algorithms with improved KD-Tree. J. Theor. Appl. Inf. Technol. **56**(2), 443–451 (2013)
3. Kollanyi, B., Howard, P.N., Woolley, S.C.: Bots and Automation over Twitter during the Second U.S. Presidential Debate. Data Memo 2016.2. Oxford,UK: Project on Computational Propaganda (2016)
4. Bessi, A., Ferrara, E.: Social bots distort the 2016 U.S. Presidential election online discussion. 21(11), (2016). https://doi.org/10.5210/fm.v21i11.7090
5. Pastor-Galindo, J.: Spotting political social bots in Twitter: A use case of the 2019 Spanish general election. arXiv:2004.00931 [cs.SI]. (2020)
6. Gong, N.Z., Frank, M., Mittal, P.: SybilBelief: a semi-supervised learning approach for structure-based sybil detection. IEEE Trans. Inf. Forensic Secur. **9**,.976–987 (2014)
7. Wei, W., Xu, F., Tan, C.C., Li, Q.: SybilDefender: a defense mechanism for sybil attacks in large social networks. IEEE Trans. Parallel Distrib. Syst. **24**, 2492–2502 (2013)
8. Wang, B., Jia, J., Zhang, L., Gong, N.Z.: Structure-based sybil detection in social networks via local rule-based Propagation. IEEE Trans. Netw. Sci. Eng. pp. 1–1 (2018) https://doi.org/10.1109/tnse.2018.2813672
9. Ghosh, S., et al.: Distributed Louvain Algorithm for Graph Community Detection. In: 208 IEEE International Parallel and Distributed Processing Symposium, Vancouver, BC (2018)
10. Spertus, E., Sahami, M., Buyukkokten, O.: Evaluating similarity measures: a large-scale study in the Orkut social network. In: Proceedings of the ACM SIGKDD International Conference on Knowledge Discovery and Data Mining, pp. 678–684 (2005) https://doi.org/10.1145/1081870.1081956
11. Cai, Z., Jermaine, C.: The Latent Community Model for Detecting Sybil Attacks in Social Networks. VLDB 2011, Seattle, WA Copyright VLDB Endowment, ACM (2011)

Differential Privacy Approach to Solve Gradient Leakage Attack in a Federated Machine Learning Environment

Krishna Yadav[1], B. B. Gupta[1(✉)], Kwok Tai Chui[2], and Konstantinos Psannis[3]

[1] Department of Computer Engineering, National Institute of Technology Kurukshetra, Kurukshetra, Haryana, India
krishna.nitkkr1@gmail.com, gupta.brij@gmail.com
[2] The Open University of Hong Kong, Kowloon, Hongkong, China
jktchui@ouhk.edu.hk
[3] University of Macedonia, Thessaloniki, Macedonia, Greece
kpsannis@uom.edu.gr

Abstract. The growth of federated machine learning in recent times has dramatically leveraged the traditional machine learning technique for intrusion detection. Keeping the dataset for training at decentralized nodes, federated machine learning have kept the people's data private; however, federated machine learning mechanism still suffers from gradient leakage attacks. Adversaries are now taking advantage of those gradients and can reconstruct the people's private data with greater accuracy. Adversaries are using these private network data later on to launch more devastating attacks against users. At this time, it becomes essential to develop a solution that prevents these attacks. This paper has introduced differential privacy, which uses Gaussian and Laplace mechanisms to secure updated gradients during the communication. Our result shows that clients can achieve a significant level of accuracy with differentially private gradients.

Keywords: Federated learning · Machine learning · Intrusion detection · Differential privacy · Gradient leakage

1 Introduction

In the past few years, we can see the massive increment in the computational resources in smartphones. Modern days smartphones are powered up by high GPU and memory spaces. Due to this computational infrastructure, researchers and developers have embedded several smartphone applications, which are fueled up by the machine and deep learning algorithms. The evolution of machine learning algorithms has extensively leveraged modern apps intelligence, making people's life a lot easier. These algorithms need large amounts of data to be trained to make an intelligent decision. Initially, people were not concerned about their data being exported to large organizations, but as time progressed, several data breaches have occurred, leading to the transfer of people's private data to the adversaries [1, 2]. Adversaries are then using personal data to

S. Chellappan et al. (Eds.): CSoNet 2020, LNCS 12575, pp. 378–385, 2020.
https://doi.org/10.1007/978-3-030-66046-8_31

launch phishing attacks and even blackmail the people [3]. In the case of the Intrusion detection system (IDS), researchers are exporting people's network traffic datasets to build an intelligent IDS for early detection of malicious traffic in people's smartphones [4]. When these types of network traffic datasets get leaked during a data breach, they have served as a baseline to launch more devastating attacks to the users [5]. To solve these problems, and keep people's data private in 2017, Google introduced federated machine learning [6]. Federated machine learning does not export the people's data to the server and trains the machine learning models in their smartphone with their locally generated dataset. Results show that federated machine learning provided the same level of intelligent decision making as with traditional machine learning. Federated machine learning was introduced to solve people's privacy issues; however, this approach was entirely not private. If the adversaries have control over the server where the unencrypted updated gradients from the clients were sent to be averaged or merely intercepting the gradients during federated communications, adversaries were able to reconstruct the dataset present across people's smartphones. Authors at [7] developed a gradient attack algorithm that reconstructed the MNIST dataset with significant accuracy. Moreover, the author at [8] used cosine similarity loss and some optimization methods to rebuild the images by taking the knowledge of shared gradients to the server during federated learning.

This paper uses a differential privacy approach to add noise to the gradients being shared with the server for averaging. We have used two noises, i.e., Gaussian and Laplace noise. In our experimentation, we added three noise levels, i.e., low noise, medium noise, and high noise to the gradients, and saw their accuracy. We have further compared how a differential privacy approach affects a model's accuracy than the non-differential method. We have also discussed how our differential privacy approach gives the adversaries no chance to perform gradient leakage attacks.

The rest of the paper is organized as follows: Sect. 2 gives an overview of work that has been done to solve gradient leakage attacks in federated machine learning. Section 3 gives the reader an introductory background on differential privacy. Section 4 provides an overview of our proposed approach. Section 5 and Sect. 6 discusses the experimentation and results. Finally, Sect. 7 concludes the paper.

2 Related Work

In this paper, we experiment with different possible noise mechanisms that can be used to achieve differential privacy in a federated machine learning environment; however, in literature, we can find some amount of work that is being carried out in differential privacy. Authors at [9] have proposed two mechanisms, i.e., Random sub-sampling and Distorting, to hide the gradients of each client, which later is sent to the server for aggregation. They followed the Gaussian mechanism to distort the sum of all the updated gradients at the client-side. Their proposed differentially private approach achieved more than 90% accuracy which was only 5% less than the non-differential privacy approach. Authors at [9] achieved a reasonable amount of accuracy; however, authors at [10] stated that the traditional differential privacy approach carried out by [9] led to significantly decreased accuracy, so they came with a hybrid approach where they combined differential privacy and secure multiparty computation (SMC) to mask the gradients. Their proposed approach is more reliable than the author at [9] since combining differential privacy with SMC will reduce the growth of noise injected during federated training as the number of clients increases. Authors at [11] realized that the traditional differential privacy approach creates a lot of noise in the updated gradients in federated training, which have 10s of digits after a decimal point. To solve this problem they came with a LDP-Fed mechanism that first provides a differential privacy guarantee to the updated gradients and then selects and filters the perturbing gradients in the server. Their approach is very effective for precision sensitive gradients value; however, filtering the gradients will require extra effort and computation and may lead to the delay in communication during federated training. Authors at [12] have used the bayesian differential privacy mechanism for preserving the gradients. Their proposed mechanism leads to the addition of a lower amount of noise, which ultimately has increased the accuracy of the model with reduced communication rounds. Authors at [13] have proposed a differential privacy mechanism (NbAFL), which adds the artificial noise to the gradients being updated. They first proved that their proposed mechanism satisfied the principles of differential privacy and did various performance analysis of the model after the gradients were obfuscated with noise.

Most of the literature's work introduces the differential privacy on image, text, and health datasets. Our research work is a pioneer in the literature that applies differential privacy in the intrusion detection dataset to the best of our knowledge. Detecting intrusion is a sensitive and rapid process. Unlike most of the work described in the literature, which requires higher communication rounds to achieve reasonable accuracy after adding noise to the updated gradients, our proposed approach does not require higher communication rounds, perturbing techniques as described in [11] and can achieve a good amount of accuracy in detecting intrusion.

3 Background

In this section, we introduce the definition of differential privacy, give a brief discussion about the Gaussian and Laplace mechanism. We further will discuss the use of these mechanisms in achieving differential privacy.

3.1 Differential Privacy

Differential privacy was introduced to permit statistical analysis of the dataset without revealing the private information of an individual inside a dataset [14]. For any two neighboring dataset D_1 and D_2, a randomized mechanism M is said to be differentially private if the outcome, i.e., C from a mechanism M such that $C \in$ Range(M) and $\|D_1 - D_2\| \leq 1$ where $\|D_1 - D_2\|$ is the distance between two datasets D_1 and D_2. Equation 1 below represents a differentially private equation. Here, D_1 is a measure of the dataset's size and $\|D_1 - D_2\|$ gives an idea about the difference in the record between two datasets, D_1, and D_2.

$$Pr\left[M(D1) \in C\right] \leq exp(\varepsilon)\, Pr\left[M(D2) \in C\right] + \delta \tag{1}$$

In the above equation, δ controls the amount of additive noise. There is a theoretical difference between (ε, 0) and (ε, δ). (ε, 0) means that for every D_1, the output $M(D_1)$ observed is likely to be equally observed for all the data in a dataset. When the observed output is expected to be the same, an adversary may infer valuable information from the output, and we will not be able to achieve higher privacy. (ε, δ) for dataset D_1 the output with the mechanism $M(D_1)$ is unlikely to be observed for the dataset D_2. When δ has a higher value greater than zero, we may add a significant level of noise, and a reasonable amount of privacy of the data can be achieved. To keep track of the amount of privacy one can reach by varying the value of δ, we have a privacy loss parameter. For a given output $\varepsilon \backsim M(D_1)$, adversaries may produce a dataset D_2 such that D_1, D2 ∈ D, then the privacy loss is defined as:

$$\mathcal{L}exp(\varepsilon)\ M(D1)\ ||\ M(D2)\ =\ ln\left(\frac{Pr[M(D1)=\varepsilon]}{Pr[M(D2)=\varepsilon]}\right) \tag{2}$$

Privacy loss can also be defined as an essential random variable that keeps track of noise being added from any random mechanism.

In differential privacy, we can use any Randomized algorithm(M) with dataset D and range R such that M: D → Δ(R) such that on input, let's say, d ∈ D, the randomized algorithm M produces output M(d) = r with probability $(M(d))_r$ for each r ∈ R. Randomization algorithms such as Gaussian, Laplace, exponential, and Bayesian can be used to achieve differential privacy, however, in our approach, we have used only two of those algorithms, i.e., Gaussian and Laplace which is discussed below.

3.2 Laplace Mechanism

Laplace mechanism is derived from Laplace distribution where for a value x, Laplace distribution is $Lap(x|\mu, b) = \frac{1}{2b}\exp\left(\frac{-|x-\mu|}{b}\right)$. In the equation, μ tells us about the position of distribution, i.e., whether positive or negative, and b is an exponential scale parameter which gives an idea about the distribution of a laplacian noise [14]. The parameter b depends upon two things, i.e., ε and Δf. Here Δf is a sensitivity, which is the change in output obtained when the same function is applied for both dataset D_1 and D_2.

$$\Delta f\ = max\, D1,\ D2|f(D1) - f(D2)| \tag{3}$$

For a randomized function f: D → R, the laplace mechanism is defined as: M(d, f(.), ε) = f(d) + Lap(Δf/ε), where Lap(Δf/ε) is a laplacian noise.

3.3 Gaussian Mechanism

Let f: D → R be a randomized function with its sensitivity Δf. The Gaussian mechanism with a parameter σ adds noise $N(0, I\sigma^2)$. Then gaussian mechanics is defined as M(d) = f(d) + $N(0, I\sigma^2)$ where $\sigma > \Delta f\sqrt{2\,log\frac{1.25}{b}} \Big/ \varepsilon$. The noise $N(0, I\sigma^2)$ is obtained from a Gaussian distribution. For additional information on the Gaussian mechanism and Gaussian distribution, we encourage the readers to [14].

4 Proposed Approach

4.1 Differentially Private SGD Algorithm

Our proposed algorithm is described in Algorithm 1. Our central intuition in the proposed algorithm was to mask the gradients generated by each device with noise obtained from differential privacy mechanisms in federated communication. In algorithm 1, initially, all the nodes receive the global model initialized with some weight to their respective parameters. In the case of the SGD classifier, the parameter is a learning rate η. The global dataset D is divided into local datasets across each node, which is denoted by d_n. The received global model is trained on each client's local dataset, i.e., d_n, and the weight of the parameter, i.e., W_{weight} is obtained. The obtained weight is then masked with the noise factor F_{noise} produced by mechanisms, such as Gaussian and Laplace. Each client's masked weights are then sent to the server for averaging, and $W_{average}$ denotes the average weight. The $W_{average}$ is again obfuscated at the server side with differential privacy mechanisms and sent to different clients. The obfuscation of weight at the server side will prevent the adversaries from gaining knowledge from the gradients if they can intercept the gradients during federated communication.

Algorithm 1. Federated averaging along with the addition of noise

Procedure Server()
    W_{all_nodes}= Receive_weight()
    $W_{average} \leftarrow \frac{1}{n}\sum_{k=1}^{n} W_k$
    Set weight of $M_{global} \leftarrow W_{average} + F_{noise}$
    Send(M_{global})

Procedure Node()
    D← Local dataset divided into mini datasets
    M_{global}=Receive(global_model)
    for all each node in K in parallel **do**
        Train M_{global} with their respective dataset d_n
        $W_{weight} = W_{weight} - \eta\Delta l(W_{weight}, d_n)$
        $W_{updated\_weight} \leftarrow W_{weight} + F_{noise}$
        Send_weight($W_{updated\_weight}$)

5 Experimentation

Our experimentation was performed on a machine having a core i5 processor with a clock speed of 3.4 GHz, 8 GB of RAM, and 2 GB of the graphics card. The experimentation was fully performed in Python. We have used the Diffprivlib library developed by IBM to implement differentially private mechanisms [15]. To validate our approach, we take the NSL-KDD dataset for federated machine learning. NSL-KDD dataset is considered as a benchmark dataset for building an intrusion detection system [16]. NSL-KDD contains

125,973 records in KDDTrain+ file. We divided records in this file among ten nodes, and the distribution of our dataset was performed in a Non-IID manner. The distribution of the dataset among ten nodes is described in Table 1. We only made ten nodes in our experimentation and went up to 100 communication rounds due to computational infrastructure limitations. However, the result obtained is very reliable.

Table 1. Distribution of KDDTrain+ among 10 nodes.

Dataset	Attack type	Number of instances
Node1	Neptune, smurf	40466
Node2	Land, teardrop	6107
Node3	Pod, back	6315
Node4	Portsweep, nmap	8938
Node5	Ipsweep, satan	11135
Node6	Imap, warezmaster	5420
Node7	Ftp_write, guess_passwd	5442
Node8	Multihop, spy	5402
Node9	Phf, warezclient, buffer_overflow	6135
Node10	Loadmodule, perl, rootkit	5411

6 Result and Discussion

We added three levels of noise during federated communication, i.e., low, medium, and high to achieve differential privacy. The epsilon value was set to 0.05, 0.01, 0.005 to achieve low, medium, and high noise levels. The obtained accuracy with two different noise mechanisms is presented in Table 1. As gaussian noise depends upon three parameters, i.e., sensitivity(Δf), delta(δ), and epsilon(ε), we set the $\Delta f = 1$ and threshold value to $\delta = 0.7$. For Laplace noise and gaussian noise, the experiment was conducted without any change in parameter value mentioned above. Table 1 shows that we can achieve the highest accuracy of 96.37% by adding a sufficiently adequate amount of noise to the gradients. We also see that to achieve the highest level of privacy, we can use a high amount of noise to the gradients, but it will significantly decrease the accuracy and even requires a large communication round for loss function to be converged. The addition of the low or high amount of noise to the gradients depends upon the type of machine learning problem we are dealing with. A medical health record in federated machine learning may need the highest amount of differential privacy. In contrast, privacy will not be the highest preference in a movie or text recommendation system. Table 2 represents the differential privacy result obtained with the Laplace mechanism; however, there was no significant difference in accuracy and communication round for these two mechanisms, i.e., Laplace and Gaussian. Hence, we can choose any noise mechanism to achieve differential privacy in a federated environment.

Table 2. Accuracy of nodes under different level of noise

Noise	Communication round	Accuracy
Gaussian mechanism		
Low	29	96.37
Medium	64	92.24
High	95	86.39
Laplace mechanism		
Low	26	95.64
Medium	60	92.01
High	89	86.08

We also experimented with the Gaussian mechanism with different epsilon(ε) values to get knowledge about the obtained accuracy by varying noise levels. We set the range $\varepsilon = \{10^{-3}, 10^{-2}, 110^{-1}, 1\}$, and the accuracy obtained is shown in Fig. 1. Figure 1 depicts the lower value of ε leads to higher differential privacy, but lower accuracy and increase in the value of ε compromises the differential privacy; however, we can get sufficient accuracy. Figure 1 also gives a comparison of the variation of accuracy with differentially private and non-private approaches.

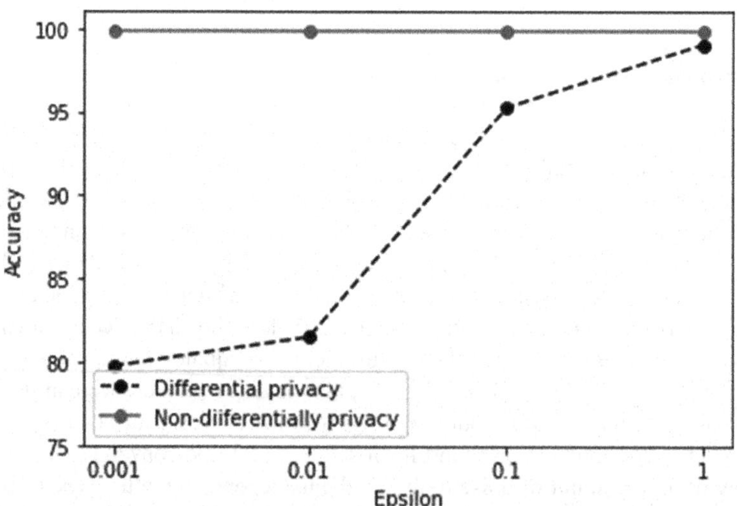

Fig. 1. Accuracy versus epsilon(ε) for a differentially private and non-private approach.

7 Conclusion

In this paper, we discussed two differentially private mechanisms, i.e., Gaussian and Laplace, to achieve differential privacy in a federated environment. The result shows that the mechanisms used produces a significant amount of accuracy without giving the adversaries the chance to share the gradients during federated communication. However, in an intrusion detection system built using a federated approach for smartphones, a false negative of even 5% can lead to a huge loss. In this type of system where accuracy is an utmost preference, in the coming future, we are planning to develop a sophisticated technique that can solve the gradient leakage attack without compromising the accuracy during federated communication.

References

1. Gupta, S., Gupta, B.B.: Detection, avoidance, and attack pattern mechanisms in modern web application vulnerabilities: present and future challenges. Int. J. Cloud Appl. Comput. (IJCAC) **7**(3), 1–43 (2017)
2. Kumar, A.: Design of secure image fusion technique using cloud for privacy-preserving and copyright protection. Int. J. Cloud Appl. Comput. (IJCAC) **9**(3), 22–36 (2019)
3. Jain, A.K., Gupta, B.B.: Towards detection of phishing websites on client-side using machine learning based approach. Telecommun. Syst. **68**(4), 687–700 (2018)
4. Jiang, F., et al.: Deep learning based multi-channel intelligent attack detection for data security. IEEE Trans. Sustain. Comput. **5**, 204–212 (2018)
5. Ramos, J., Nedjah, N., de Macedo Mourelle, L., et al.: Visual data mining for crowd anomaly detection using artificial bacteria colony. Multimed. Tools Appl. **77**(14), 17755–17777 (2018)
6. Cheng, K., et al.: Secureboost: a lossless federated learning framework. arXiv preprint arXiv:1901.08755 (2019)
7. Wei, W., et al.: A framework for evaluating gradient leakage attacks in federated learning. arXiv preprint arXiv:2004.10397 (2020)
8. Geiping, J., et al.: Inverting gradients–how easy is it to break privacy in federated learning?. arXiv preprint arXiv:2003.14053 (2020)
9. Geyer, R.C., Tassilo, K., Moin, N.: Differentially private federated learning: a client level perspective. arXiv preprint arXiv:1712.07557 (2017)
10. Truex, S., et al.: A hybrid approach to privacy-preserving federated learning. In: Proceedings of the 12th ACM Workshop on Artificial Intelligence and Security (2019)
11. Truex, S., et al.: LDP-fed: federated learning with local differential privacy. In: Proceedings of the Third ACM International Workshop on Edge Systems, Analytics and Networking (2020)
12. Triastcyn, A., Boi, F.: Federated learning with Bayesian differential privacy. In: 2019 IEEE International Conference on Big Data (Big Data). IEEE (2019)
13. Wei, K., et al.: Federated learning with differential privacy: algorithms and performance analysis. IEEE Trans. Inf. Forensics Secur. **15**, 3454–3469 (2020). https://doi.org/10.1109/TIFS.2020.2988575
14. Dwork, C., Roth, A.: The algorithmic foundations of differential privacy. Found. Trends Theor. Comput. Sci. **9**(3-4), 211–407 (2014)
15. Holohan, N., et al.: Diffprivlib: the IBM differential privacy library. arXiv preprint arXiv:1907.02444 (2019)
16. Dhanabal, L., Shantharajah, S.P.: A study on NSL-KDD dataset for intrusion detection system based on classification algorithms. Int. J. Adv. Res. Comput. Commun. Eng. **4**(6), 446–452 (2015)

A Novel Approach for Fake News Detection in Vehicular Ad-Hoc Network (VANET)

Akshat Gaurav[1(✉)], B. B. Gupta[1(✉)], Arcangelo Castiglione[2], Kostas Psannis[3], and Chang Choi[4]

[1] Department of Computer Engineering, National Institute of Technology Kurukshetra, Kurukshetra, Haryana, India
akshatgaurav470@gmail.com, gupta.brij@gmail.com
[2] University of Salerno, Fisciano, Italy
arcastiglione@unisa.it
[3] University of Macedonia, Thessaloniki, Macedonia, Greece
kpsannis@uom.gr
[4] Gachon University, Seongnam, Republic of Korea
enduranceaura@gmail.com

Abstract. In Vehicular ad-hoc network (VANET) vehicles communicate with other vehicles and with the RSU(Road Side Unit). It provides safety and other help to the drivers and the passengers of the vehicles. It is important for Intelligent Transport Systems, hence in recent years the Industrial sector and researchers give it special importance and did much research for its development. In VANET vehicle nodes exchange messages to gain information to make the travel efficient for the passengers of the vehicle. But sometimes attacker start broadcasting the fake news about the surroundings like information of fake accident of traffic jam which in turn produce a negative impact on the safety a efficiency of vehicle. In this paper, we have introduced an entropy-based approach to detect fake news. The attacker uses the spoofed IP address for broadcasting the fake news packets, so we use the entropy of the source IP address for the identification of fake news packets.

Keywords: VANET · Fake news · Entropy · IP spoofing

1 Introduction

An intelligent transportation system (ITS) [1] is a new area of research developed in recent years. VANET which is the subgroup of MANET is a part of ITS. VANET is a combination of mobile vehicles and roadside stationary units (RSU). Each vehicle is equipped with an On-Board Unite (OBU). Which is responsible for its communication with other vehicles or with RSU [2]. In the VANET communication takes place among the mobile vehicles (V2V) or between vehicle and stationary RSU (V2I) [3]. In V2V communication, vehicles share their basic

S. Chellappan et al. (Eds.): CSoNet 2020, LNCS 12575, pp. 386–397, 2020.
https://doi.org/10.1007/978-3-030-66046-8_32

information such as speed, position, etc. with other vehicles. The main purpose of this communication is to provide additional information to the driver of the vehicle. In V2I communication the information which is important to the driver of the vehicle like the nearest petrol pump, nearest hospital, etc. are shared between vehicles and RSU. Figure 1 represents the basic VANET scenario in which moving vehicles communicating with each other and with the RSU. Each vehicle or RSU uses Dedicated Short-range communication of 5.9 GHz to connect to the other vehicle or RSU in the range of 1 km [4]. The main aim of VANET is to provide safety and reliable service to the people in the vehicle.

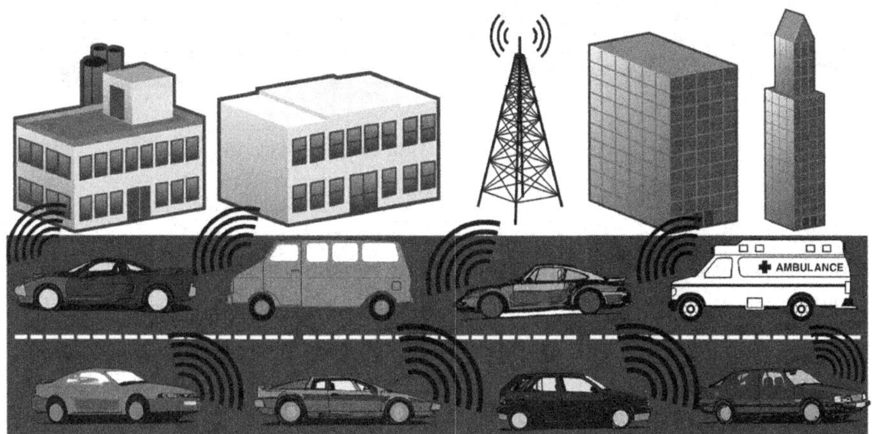

Fig. 1. Basic VANET scenario

VANET works in infrastructure less network so it is vulnerable to different cyber attacks. The attacks in the VANET are mainly classified as inter-vehicle attacks and intra-vehicle attacks [5]. In inter-vehicle attack attacker attacks on the communication among the vehicles and, in intra-vehicle attacks attacker tries to interrupt the communication between the vehicle and RSU. Broadcasting of fake news about the road conditions or neighbouring conditions is one of the cyber-attacks. In this attack, malicious users flood the network with fake news packets, due to this the legitimate vehicles and RSU not recives the correct and important information this attack is similar to the fake news broadcasting attack on social networking sites [6,7]. Figure 2 represent the attack scenario, attacker 1 broadcast many spoofed fake news packets which firstly, misguides the legitimated user and secondly, consumes the victim's resources so it is not able to communicate with the RSU. Attacker 2 sends a large number of packets to RSU, which it turn overload the network of RSU and it is not available to the other vehicles.

In this paper, we propose entropy base detection of fake news packets in VANET. According to our proposed approach, each vehicle and RSU calculate

Fig. 2. Generation and propagation of fake news in VANTE

the entropy of incoming packets and compare it with the threshold value and then decides whether the packets are malicious or legitimate. Major contributions of the paper are as follows:

- The proposed approach uses an entropy bases approach to detect fake news packets in VENET.
- The proposed approach is generic i.e. it is independent of transmitted data type or the routing protocol.

The remaining paper is organized as follows. Related work is given in Sect. 2. Proposed approach is explained in Sect. 3. Section 4 presents the result and finally Sect. 5 gives the conclusion.

2 Related Work

Xiao et al. [8] proposed a method to detect fake news in IoV. It uses the concept of edge computing and blockchain concepts to detect fake news. In this scheme, the IoV network is divided into the edge machines and host virtual machines. Edge machines consist of RSU and host virtual machines consist of vehicle nodes. The main advantage of this approach is that it requires less evidence to detect the fack news so its response time is less comparatively less.

Ozbay et al. [9] proposed a two-step method for the detection of fake news. In the first step, the given unstructured data set is converted into structured data set, and in the second step twenty-three supervised artificial learning techniques are used to detect fake news. But the main issue is that for different datasets the precision, F-measure, and recall values, of each artificial learning algorithm are different.

Zhou et al. [10] prosed a SimilarityAware FakE (SAFE) news detection method for the detection of fake news. In this approach firstly by using neural networks textual and visual content of the news is extracted then these contents are jointly analyzed for the detection of fake news. The main limitation of this approach is that it only compares the textual and visual features of the news but if the attacker intelligent fabricated the news item then this approach will not work efficiently.

Raghuwanshi et al. [11] proposes a method in which each vehicle maintains a table to store the IP address of its neighbors. If the receiving packet's source IP address is not from the table then it is considered as a fake packet, also if the number of packets sends by the neighbor is more than the threshold then blacklist that node. But the problem in this type of method is that it consumes a large amount of memory.

Khan et al. [12] proposes a way in which nodes work in a mutually cooperative manner. Each node monitors its neighboring node behavior and if it behaves maliciously then it reports to the certifying authority. But in this, each node has to do extra work of monitoring its neighbor this will consume its resources and bandwidth.

Verma et al. [13] proposes a bloom filter based node monitoring. In this method, the Edge node creates a database of the IP of the source of UDP messages that are entering the network domain or leaving the network domain. Then the information is shared with all the vehicle nodes in the domain if the same IP address is kept on repeating then it is considered as a malicious node. But as we know deletion is not possible from bloom filter so as time increases the memory requirements of the system increases and the system becomes unmanageable.

Sinha et al. [14] proposes a method in which neighboring nodes corporate with each other to detect the attack packets. Each node calculates the upper limit of the received packet with the help of the replay of the "Hello" request from its neighbor. If the number of received messages is more than the upper limit then they are discarded. But the selection of the upper limit of the messages is an issue and if the malicious node starts transmitting false upper limit value then detection accuracy reduced.

Kumar et al. [15] proposes a clustering based attack detection technique (MMPDA). Each cluster consists of a cluster head and some verifier nodes which monitor its neighboring nodes, and if any node misbehaves then the cluster head takes action on that node. But if the cluster head starts behaving maliciously the there is no way to correct it or eliminate cluster head from the cluster.

Singh et al. [16] proposes a RSU controlled detection method EAPDA for detecting malicious node. RSU monitors each node in its range and if any node behaves maliciously then it informs all the other nodes about it and blacklists the malicious node [16]. But if an attacker hacks the RSU then, there is no method to stop the malicious traffic.

Quyoom et al. [17] also uses RSU based method to identify the malicious nodes, RSU identifies the malicious nodes and give their location information to all other nodes. This approach has the same limitation as that of the previous approach.

RoselinMary et al. [18] also proposed an RSU controlled detection algorithm (APDA). In this algorithm, the RSU decides with the help of the velocity and transmission frequency of the vehicle node whether the node is malicious or not. If frequency and velocity are high then the node is considered as a malicious node. But if the malicious node keeps on changing its velocity then the efficiency of this approach is reduced.

Gandhi et al. [19] proposes RSU controlled detection algorithm (RRDA). In this algorithm RSU use hop-count to differentiate attack packets from the normal traffic. RSU compares the hop-count of the packets generated by each vehicle with a predefined threshold and, if its value is more than the threshold then those packets are discarded. But this approach not able to detect the malicious user inside the cluster.

Mokdad et al. [20] proposes a packet delivery ratio based detection method. The packet delivery ratio is also a good parameter to measure the malicious node. In the presence of a malicious node the packet delivery ratio is decreased, so measuring the packet delivery ratio detection of the malicious node is easy. But this approach is not efficient under low-rate flooding attacks.

Choudhari et al. [21] proposes a trust-based detection approach (DADCQ) that uses the packet delivery rate to differentiate attack packets from normal packets. DADCQ analyzes the packet delivery ratio and if its value is more than the threshold then the node's trust value is reduced and the lowest trust value nodes are considered as attacker nodes. This approach is also less efficient for low rate flooding attack.

Mejri et al. [22] proposed an entropy-based detection method. In this method, the packet emission entropy is measured. During the attack period, the entropy value increases because attackers generate a large number of packets to flood the victim node. The difference in entropy values is used to detect the attack. But in this approach, there is no way to differentiate attack traffic from the flash crowd. 'Flash crowd' is a scenario in which legitimate users generating a large amount of traffic like at the time of the accident. So the proposed approach can consider this traffic as the attack traffic and hence loss of information takes place.

3 Proposed Approach

3.1 Definition and Theorems

Definition 1. *The probability of random variable X which can take n different values is given by*

$$P(x) = \frac{x}{\sum_{i=0}^{i=n} x_i} \tag{1}$$

Definition 2. *The entropy of a random variable is defined according to Shannon's entropy formula. If X is a random variable which can take n discrete values then its entropy is given by the formula*

$$H(X) = -\sum_{i=1}^{n} Px_i \times \log(Px_i) \tag{2}$$

where H(X) is the entropy of random variable and $P(x_i)$ *represents the probability of random variable at each event.*

Theorem 1. *The entropy of source IP address during normal scenario is less than the entropy of source IP address at the time of the attack.*

$$H(X_{normal}) < H(X_{Attack}) \tag{3}$$

Proof. According to the Jensen's inequality [23] for monotonically increasing convex function, the following equation holds good.

$$E[f(x)] \geq f(E[x]) \tag{4}$$

where f(x) is a monotonically increasing convex function and E[x] is the expectance value.

Let $P_1 = \{P_1^1, P_2^1 ..., P_n^1\}$ represents the set of the source IP address receives during normal operation and $P_2 = \{P_1^2, P_2^2 ..., P_n^2\}$ represents the ser of source IP address receives during the fake news attack scenario. During a fake news attack scenario source IP addresses are more randomly distributed than the normal scenario because in a fake news attack attacker uses packet spoofing. The rate of transferring packets is also more during the fake news attack scenario than the normal operation. So from equations entropy of in fake news attack is represented as a monotonically increasing convex function and entropy during a normal scenario is a monotonically increasing concave function. So according to Jensen's inequality.

$$H^2(X) > H^1(X) \tag{5}$$

where $H^2(X)$ represents entropy of fake news attack scenario and $H^1(x)$ represents entropy of normal scenario.

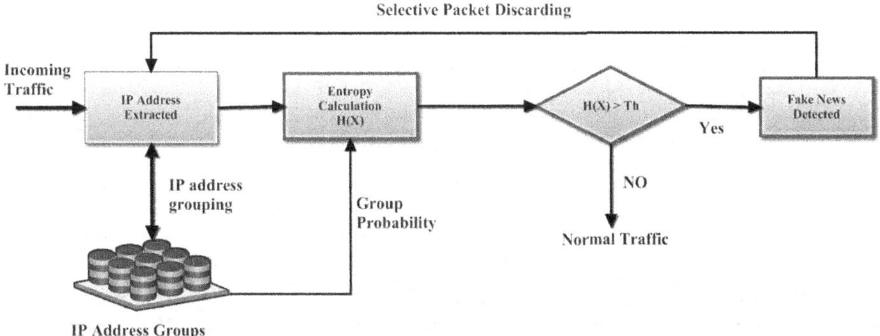

Fig. 3. Block diagram of proposed approach

3.2 Proposed Approach

Our proposed approach uses a proactive individual filtering method. The block diagram of our proposed approach is represented in Fig. 3. In this scheme each node analysis the incoming traffic in the following steps:

- Source address extraction - Our main aim is to identify fack news traffic for this we use the source IP address of the incoming packet. Each incoming packet is grouped according to the source IP address. If for an IP address a group is present then the counter of the group is increased, but if the IP address does not belong to any present group then a new group is formed for it.
- Entropy calculation - The Probability of each group is calculated according to the Eq. 1 and then its overall entropy is calculated.
- Comparison - The calculated Entropy value is compared with the predefined threshold value. If its value is more than the threshold then it is assumed that traffic is due to a fake traffic.
- Selective Packet Discarding - If fake news traffic is detected then the vehicle node starts the filtering process. For filtering, the vehicle node blacklist all the IP address belongs to the group with the highest probability of occurrence. So during the next time slot, all the packets from the blacklist IP address are dropped by the vehicle node.

3.3 Description of Algorithm

This section gives a detailed explanation of the algorithm that is executed in each vehicle. The attributes used in the algorithm are defined in the Table 1.

Table 1. Attributes used in algorithm

Term	Explanation
Gi	i^{th} group
p_i	Probability of i_{th} packet
H	Entropy of the system
Th	Threshold for Entropy
T	Threshold

According to Eq. 1 for k_{th} incoming packet IP address is extracted and it is placed in the group G_i. But if no group is present for the IP address then a new group $Gn + 1$ is formed and it is placed in it. Then using Eq. 1 and 2 probability and entropy (H) of the group are calculated. The entropy is compared with the predefined threshold value (Th). As in the fake news attack scenario source IP address are randomly distributed, so it entropy value is higher than the threshold value. If fake news traffic is detected then vehicle node selects the group G_i which has highest probability of occurrence. All the IP address belongs to the group G_i are considered as malicious source so in next time slot all the packets from these IP address are discarded. This process of selective discarding is repeated in each time slot.

Algorithm 1: Algorithm to Analysis Incoming traffic

```
Input : Incoming Packets
Output : Weather Packet containing fake news or not
Start
for Every incoming packet (P_k) do
    P_k → IP_k,IP address is extracted
    if IP_k ∈ G then
        Place the packet in the appropriate group according its IP address;
        Calculate the Entropy H;
    end
    else
        Create a new group G_{n+1} and place P_k in it.;
        Calculate the Entropy H;
    end
    if H > Th then
        Fake news traffic detected;
        G_i = max.of {G_1, G_2, ..G_n}
        IP address in group (G_i) are Blacklisted;
    end
    else
        IP address in the group (G_i) are Legitimate ;
    end
end
END
```

4 Results and Discussion

We use OMNET++,SUMO, and Veins for the simulation of our proposed approach. OMNET++ is a discrete event simulator that is used to analyze the events and generating the results. SUMO is used to generate mobile vehicles and roads. Venis provides the interface between ONMET++ and SUMO. The simulation parameters used by us for the implementation of proposed approach are represented in the Table 2

Table 2. Simulation Parameters Used

Term	Value
Simulation Area	$250 \times 250\ m^2$
Simulation Time	200 s
Routing Protocol	Random
Traffic Generation	Random
Becon Rate(normal node)	5 s
Becon Rate(attacker)	1 s
MAC Layer	802.11p
Network Interface	OMNET++
Network Mobility Framework	Veins
Traffic Generator	SUMO

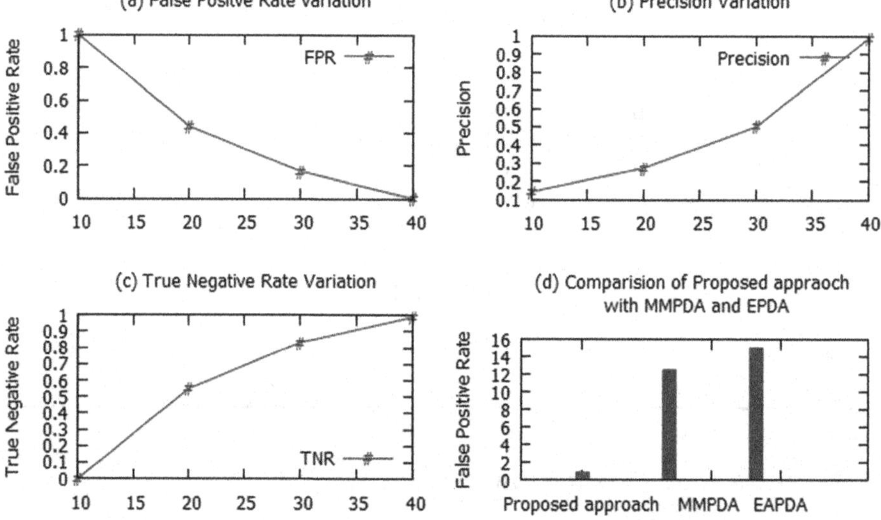

Fig. 4. Performance analyse of proposed approach

We use following parameters to analyse the performance of our proposed approach.

- False Positive Ratio - It defines the percentage of fake news packets that are not filtered by our proposed approach. In our proposed approach if the entropy value is more than the threshold value then vehicle node keeps on dropping the packet in the group of highest probability of occurrence. So in our proposed approach as the time passes the FPR value decreases, this is represented in Fig. 4.

- True Negative Rate - It gives the percentage of dropped fake news packets. As explained above in our proposed approach the vehicle node drops the packets of the group which have the highest probability of occurrence in the time slot, so the TNR value in our proposed approach is keep on increasing with the time as represented in the Fig. 4.
- Precision - It measures the accuracy of the proposed approach. In our proposed approach the precision value is keep on increases with the time because vehicle node keep on filtering the fake news packets in each time slot.
- Comparison – To show that our proposed approach efficiently detects the fake news packets in VANET, we compare it with other flood detection techniques MMPDA and EAPDA. MMPDA uses a clustering approach for the detection of malicious nodes and EAPDA uses RSU based detection of malicious nodes. From Fig. 4 it is clear that our proposed approach detects the malicious nodes more accurately as compared to the other two methods.

5 Conclusion

In this paper, we proposed an entropy-based method to detect fake news in VANET. Entropy is the measure of the randomness of the source's IP address, so the entropy of the source's IP address during the broadcasting of the fake news is higher than the entropy of normal traffic. We use this variation of entropy to differentiate the fack news packets from normal traffic. Each incoming packet is grouped according to the source IP address and then entropy is calculated. If the entropy is more than the threshold value then all the IP addresses in the group of highest probability of occurrence are considered as malicious and packets generated from those IP addresses are discarded. The proposed approach is evaluated using precision, true negative rate, and false-positive rate. High precision and low false-positive ratio show that our proposed approach detects the fake news traffic efficiently. Our future work will be focused on testing the proposed approach with more and different attack scenarios.

References

1. Hussain, M.M., Beg, M.S.: Using vehicles as fog infrastructures for transportation cyber-physical systems (t-cps): Fog computing for vehicular networks. Int. J. Softw. Sci. Comput. Intell. (IJSSCI) **11**(1), 47–69 (2019)
2. Mirsadeghi, F., Rafsanjani, M.K., et al.: A trust infrastructure based authentication method for clustered vehicular ad hoc networks. Peer-to-Peer Network. Appl., 1–17 (2020)
3. Kolandaisamy, R., et al.: A multivariant stream analysis approach to detect and mitigate ddos attacks in vehicular ad hoc networks. Wireless Communications and Mobile Computing 2018 (2018)

4. Jiang, D., Taliwal, V., Meier, A., Holfelder, W., Herrtwich, R.: Design of 5.9 GHz dsrc-based vehicular safety communication. IEEE Wireless Commun. **13**(5), 36–43 (2006)
5. Sakiz, F., Sen, S.: A survey of attacks and detection mechanisms on intelligent transportation systems: Vanets and IoV. Ad Hoc Netw. **61**, 33–50 (2017)
6. Zhang, Z., Sun, R., Zhao, C., Wang, J., Chang, C.K., et al.: CyVOD: a novel trinity multimedia social network scheme. Multimedia Tools Appl. **76**(18), 18513–18529 (2017)
7. Chaudhary, P., Gupta, B.B., Gupta, S.: Cross-site scripting (XSS) worms in Online Social Network (OSN): taxonomy and defensive mechanisms. In: 2016 3rd International Conference on Computing for Sustainable Global Development (INDIACom), pp. 2131–2136. IEEE, March 2016
8. Xiao, Y., Liu, Y., Li, T.: Edge computing and blockchain for quick fake news detection in IoV. Sensors **20**(16), 4360 (2020)
9. Ozbay, F.A., Alatas, B.: Fake news detection within online social media using supervised artificial intelligence algorithms. Physica A: Stat. Mech. Appl. **540**, 123174 (2020)
10. Zhou, X., Wu, J., Zafarani, R.: Safe: Similarity-aware multi-modal fake news detection. arXiv preprint arXiv:2003.04981 (2020)
11. Raghuwanshi, V., Lilhore, U.: Neighbor trust algorithm (nta) to protect vanet from denial of service attack (dos). Int. J. Comput. Appl. **140**(8), 8–12 (2016)
12. Khan, U., Agrawal, S., Silakari, S.: Detection of malicious nodes (dmn) in vehicular ad-hoc networks. Procedia Comput. Sci. **46**, 965–972 (2015)
13. Verma, K., Hasbullah, H., Kumar, A.: Prevention of dos attacks in vanet. Wireless personal communications **73**(1), 95–126 (2013). https://doi.org/10.1007/s11277-013-1161-5
14. Sinha, A., Mishra, S.K.: Queue limiting algorithm (qla) for protecting vanet from denial of service (dos) attack. Int. J. Comput. Appl. Technol. **86**(8), 14–17 (2014)
15. Kumar, S., Mann, K.S.: Detection of multiple malicious nodes using entropy for mitigating the effect of denial of service attack in vanets. In: 2018 4th International Conference on Computing Sciences (ICCS), pp. 72–79. IEEE (2018)
16. Singh, A., Sharma, P.: A novel mechanism for detecting dos attack in vanet using enhanced attacked packet detection algorithm (EAPDA). In: 2015 2nd International Conference on Recent Advances in Engineering & Computational sciences (RAECS), pp. 1–5. IEEE (2015)
17. Quyoom, A., Ali, R., Gouttam, D.N., Sharma, H.: A novel mechanism of detection of denial of service attack (dos) in vanet using malicious and irrelevant packet detection algorithm (mipda). In: International Conference on Computing, Communication & Automation, pp. 414–419. IEEE (2015)
18. RoselinMary, S., Maheshwari, M., Thamaraiselvan, M.: Early detection of dos attacks in vanet using attacked packet detection algorithm (APDA). In: 2013 International Conference on Information Communication and Embedded Systems (ICICES), pp. 237–240. IEEE (2013)
19. Gandhi, U.D., Keerthana, R.: Request response detection algorithm for detecting dos attack in VANET. In: 2014 International Conference on Reliability Optimization and Information Technology (ICROIT), pp. 192–194. IEEE (2014)
20. Mokdad, L., Ben-Othman, J., Nguyen, A.T.: Djavan: detecting jamming attacks in vehicle ad hoc networks. Perform. Eval. **87**, 47–59 (2015)

21. Choudhari, D.P., Dorle, S.S.: Maximization of packet delivery ratio for DADCQ protocol after removal of eavesdropping and ddos attacks in VANET. In: 2019 10th International Conference on Computing, Communication and Networking Technologies (ICCCNT), pp. 1–8. IEEE (2019)
22. Mejri, M.N., Ben-Othman, J.: Entropy as a new metric for denial of service attack detection in vehicular ad-hoc networks. In: Proceedings of the 17th ACM International Conference on Modeling, Analysis and Simulation of Wireless and Mobile Systems, pp. 73–79 (2014)
23. Ruel, J.J., Ayres, M.P.: Jensen's inequality predicts effects of environmental variation. Trends in Ecol. Evol. **14**(9), 361–366 (1999)

Metadata Security Measures for Protecting Confidential Information on the Cloud

Mamta[1], B. B. Gupta[1(✉)], Kwok Tai Chui[2], and Konstantinos Psannis[3]

[1] Department of Computer Engineering, National Institute of Technology Kurukshetra, Kurukshetra, Haryana, India
er.mamta.dabra@gmail.com, gupta.brij@gmail.com

[2] The Open University of Hong Kong, Kowloon, Hong Kong, China
jktchui@ouhk.edu.hk

[3] University of Macedonia, Thessaloniki, Macedonia, Greece
kpsannis@uom.edu.gr

Abstract. In recent times, unprotected metadata resulted in many serious security breaches on a shared cloud storage, which clearly depicts the need to protect this crucial information about the original data. Encryption seems to be the obvious solution to this issue. But it makes all the processing on data infeasible, it requires us to download both the data as well as the associated metadata and perform decryption locally to further process it, which defeats the purpose of using the cloud storages. There are many instances where we need metadata information for efficient processing of data. Therefore, there is a need to develop a technique that can enable selective retrieval of this metadata information without actually revealing anything about it in the plaintext form. In this paper, the authors will present one such technique based on key-policy design framework of attribute-based encryption.

Keywords: Metadata encryption · Key-policy attribute-based encryption · Information retrieval

1 Introduction

The advent of information technology has changed the way we use, share and store data. The extent of penetration of information technology in our life can be gauzed from the fact that information about any aspect of a person's life whether his/her professional profile or his/her relationship status. Everything is available over the Internet, but such wide availability of information has a flip side also. Same information could be used for committing serious crimes like cyber theft and bullying. To prevent such problems, sensitive data is often stored in encrypted form. But apart from confidential data there is a data which is often ignored even by experts, leave alone a common man, and such ignorance has caused many security breaches even at the upper echelons of government, and this data is called metadata. In simple terms, we can define metadata as the data about data. If we consider a simple text file the name of the file, name of the author, updation history etc. constitute metadata. Although the information contained in metadata

S. Chellappan et al. (Eds.): CSoNet 2020, LNCS 12575, pp. 398–410, 2020.
https://doi.org/10.1007/978-3-030-66046-8_33

seems trivial, yet it has potential to wreak havoc. Predicament faced by UK government during Iraq war is the classical example of such scenario. During Iraq war, UK government submitted a report to United Nations regarding security situation in Iraq. But metadata of that file showed that the report was written by a US research scholar, and the UK government has simply copied his work [1]. This situation resulted in the national embarrassment. The UK government suffered from this shame because of ignorance, but there may be the cases where one can attempt to change that metadata information. To avoid such misuse of the critical information the only measure to protect is the encryption. Further, an unprotected metadata can reveal your location, line of work, place of work and in some cases even your health related data, and this information could be used by a malicious person for performing social engineering and other cyber-attacks.

To secure any sensitive information the obvious solution that strikes to everyone's mind is the encryption. Encryption of metadata information solves the issue of privacy. However, the authorized person may want to process this encrypted metadata information to get the information about the original data. For this purpose, there is a need for a technique through which only the authorized users can selectively get the required information. To fulfill this need, a combination of attribute-based encryption and searchable encryption is proposed to efficiently retrieve the data files using metadata information but without actually revealing the metadata in the plaintext.

Key Contributions

Following are the key contributions of the paper:

- The proposed scheme provides an efficient mechanism for metadata security and retrieval.
- The proposed scheme is efficient in terms of constant size secret key, trapdoor and number of pairing operations. Hence, saves channel bandwidth, results in reduced cost and enables fast search as compared to the state-of-the art schemes in the literature.
- The above claims are justified both theoretically by calculating and comparing the storage and computational cost of the proposed scheme with state-of-the art schemes in the literature as well as practically by implementing the proposed scheme using JPBC library in JAVA.

The rest of the paper is organized as follows: Sect. 2 presents the related work. Section 3 provides an overview of the proposed scheme by briefly describing the building blocks, the algorithms and the entities involved in the proposed scheme. Section 4 describes the construction steps of the proposed scheme in detail along with the correctness proof of the scheme. Section 5 and 6 covers the performance and complexity analysis of the proposed scheme respectively. Finally, Sect. 7 concludes the paper and provide directions for the future work.

2 Related Work

In the literature there exists several such techniques which enables fine-grained search and retrieval of data files using the metadata information [2–11]. All these techniques use attribute-based encryption scheme as their underlying technique, and are sometimes called the attribute-based searchable encryption (ABSE) scheme is a technique. It enables secure search over encrypted metadata items stored on the shared cloud storage managed by the third party. It is the combination of attribute-based encryption (ABE) and searchable encryption (SE) with the inherent benefits of fine-grained access control and expressive searching capabilities in multi-user setting. There are two design frameworks in which one can use ABE to construct ABSE scheme. The first is key-policy ABE (KP-ABE) [12] and the other is ciphertext-policy ABE (CP-ABE) [13]. In the CP-ABE design framework, the attributes are associated with the users and the access policy is associated with ciphertext of the metadata. While in the KP-ABE design framework the attributes are embedded in the ciphertext of the metadata and the access policy is embedded in the secret key of the user. In this paper, we have used KP-ABE design framework to develop an efficient technique for retrieving the encrypted data files using encrypted metadata items.

3 Scheme Preliminaries

This section presents the preliminaries of the proposed scheme which are required to understand its construction. Here, we will have a brief overview of the basic building blocks like the bilinear maps and the type of the access structure used in the proposed scheme. Further, we will present the definition of different algorithms involved in the proposed scheme under the heading system definition and also provide the details of the different entities involved in the scheme under the heading system framework.

Bilinear Map: Let G, G_T be the source and target cyclic groups of prime order p and g be the generator of the source group G. Let e be the symmetric bilinear map between G and G_T, $e : G \times G \rightarrow G_T$, which satisfies the following properties:

- $\forall l = g^a \in G, m = g^b \in G : e(g^a, g^b) = e(g, g)^{ab}$ where $a, b \in Z_p$.
- $e(g, g)$ is the generator of the target group, G_T, if g is the generator of source group G.
- $\forall l, m \in G$; $e(l, m)$ is efficiently computable.

The structure of the access policy is general represented by a tree where the attributes are present at the leaves and the internal nodes represents the threshold gates [5]. For assigning the secret values, we have also used the bottom-up approach like [5] which was proposed by Emura et al. [14].

3.1 System Definition and Framework

The system is composed of the following probabilistic polynomial time algorithms:

SystemInitialization$(1^k, Att, MD) \rightarrow [PP, MSK]$: This algorithm will take security parameter k, attribute universe Att and Universe of metadata items MD as input and outputs the public parameters PP and master secret key MSK.

AssignCredentials$(PP, MSK, \gamma_u) \rightarrow SK_u$: This algorithm takes PP, MSK and access policy γ_u for user u as input and returns the secret key for that user.

MetadataEncryption$(PP, md \in MD, \xi) \rightarrow C$: This algorithm encrypts the metadata item under the set of attributes ξ.

RetrievalToken$(PP, SK_u, md \in MD) \rightarrow TK$: Data user will use this algorithm to generate the retrieval token for the metadata item, *md* which will be given to the server of shared cloud to retrieve the location of the data file corresponding to the metadata item.

Retrieve$(C, TK) \rightarrow (0, \perp)/(1, R)$: This algorithm will take the ciphertext C for the metadata item and the retrieval token TK for the metadata and performs search for that metadata item without decrypting it. If a match is found then it return 1 and the corresponding reference of the original data file else, it returns 0 and null.
Correctness: The proposed scheme is correct if the following condition holds:

$$\left(Retrieve(C, TK) = 1 \middle| \begin{array}{l} PP \\ C \\ TK \end{array} \right) \tag{1}$$

System Framework
The system is composed of the following four entities as shown in Fig. 1:

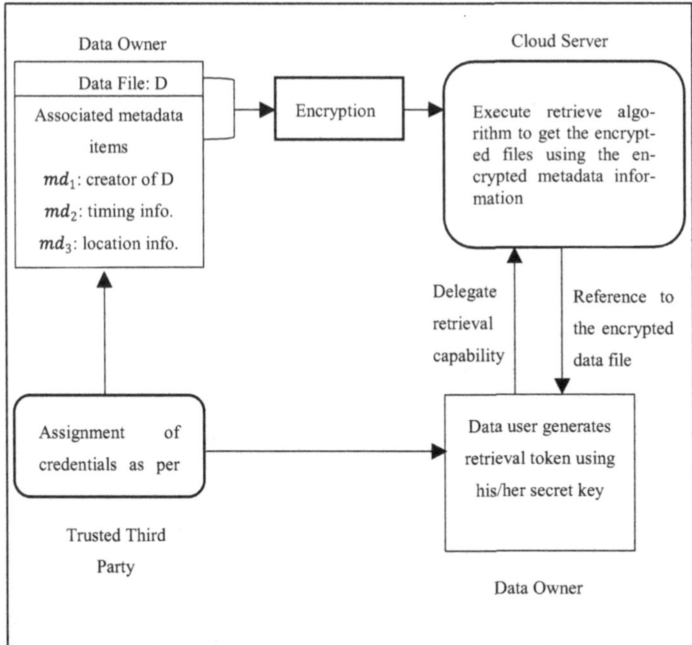

Fig. 1. System framework of the proposed scheme

The data owner, who wants to outsource their data in an encrypted form for the purpose of sharing it with multiple users in a differential manner. The data users, who wants to retrieve the data stored by the data owner at the cloud server; a trusted third party (TTP), who grants essential credentials to the data owners and data users; a cloud server, which stores the encrypted data and retrieves required data files on the behalf of data user by using the retrieval token and executing the retrieve operation over all the encrypted metadata items. The cloud server is assumed to be honest i.e. it correctly executes the retrieve algorithm, but at the same time it is curious in the sense that it tries to learn as much as possible. But the proposed scheme must ensure that it will no information in any form to the cloud storage server neither about the metadata items nor about the original data file.

4 Detailed Construction

The proposed scheme executes the retrieve algorithm only for the authorized users. If it founds the user to be unauthorized the retrieve algorithm gets terminated at that instance. The notations used in the construction and the comparative analysis of the proposed scheme are given below in Table 1.

The detailed construction steps involved in the proposed scheme are as follows:

$SystemInitialization\left(1^k, Att, MD\right)$:
Let G and G_T be the source and target cyclic groups of prime order, $p : |p| = k$ respectively and g be the generator of source group,G. Let $e : G \times G \rightarrow G_T$ be the bilinear map between G and G_T. Let $Att = \{att_1, att_2, \ldots att_n\}$ be the attribute universe and MD be the universe of all the metadata items:$MD = \left\{md_1, md_2, \ldots md_{|MD|}\right\}$, where each $md \in \{0, 1\}^*$. Define a hash function $H : \{0, 1\}^* \rightarrow Z_p$. Now, randomly choose $x, y, z \overset{\$}{\leftarrow} Z_p$ and compute $X = g^x, Y = g^y, Z = g^z$. For each attribute $att_j \in Att$, TA randomly selects $s_j \leftarrow Z_p^*$ and sets $S = \{s_j\}_{att_j \in Att}$ and compute $T_j = g^{s_j} | att_j \in Att$ and $T = \{T_j\}_{\forall att_j \in Att}$. Finally outputs the public parameters $PP = (p, G, G_T, g, e, Att, W, H, X, Y, Z, T)$ and Master Secret Key $MSK = (x, y, z, S)$

$Assigncredentials(PP, MSK, \gamma_u)$:
It is run by the TTP. This algorithm is used to assign the secret key to a particular user, where γ_u represents the access policy of that user u and T_{γ_u} represents the respective access tree for γ_u. First of all, TTP gets $T_{\gamma_u}^{ext} \leftarrow AddDummyNode\left(T_{\gamma_u}\right)$. Then, TTP calls $AssignedValue(S, T_{\gamma_u}^{ext})$ to get secret of the root of access tree $T_{\gamma_u}^{ext}$ as s_T and secret of the dummy nodes of $T_{\gamma_u}^{ext}$ as $S_D = \left\{s_{d_j}\right\}|_{\forall d_j \in D_{T_{\gamma_u}^{ext}}}$ and publishes the public values of γ_u as $\mathcal{T}_{\gamma_u} = \left(S_D, V_{T_{\gamma_u}} = g^{s_T}, T_{\gamma_u}^{ext}\right)$. TTP selects a random element $t_u \overset{\$}{\leftarrow} Z_p$ for that particular user and computes:

$$K_1 = g^{\frac{xz+t_u}{s_T}}, K_2 = g^{t_u} \tag{2}$$

Output: $SK_u = (K_1, K_2, \gamma_u)$

Table 1. Notations used in the proposed scheme

Notation	Description
$\|G\|$,$\|G_T\|$	Length of source (G) and target group (G_T) elements respectively in case of symmetric bilinear pairing
$\|G_1\|$, $\|G_2\|$, $\|G_T\|$	Length of source (G_1, G_2) and target group (G_T) elements respectively in case of asymmetric bilinear pairing
$\|Z_p\|$	Length of an element in a group of integers of prime order, p
H	Collision resistant one-way hash function
P	Bilinear pairing operation
E, E_T	Exponent operation in source and target group respectively
S, N	# of attributes associated with users and access policy respectively
U	# of authorized users in the system
m	# of possible values an attribute can take
k	# of keywords in case of a multi-keyword search scheme
γ_u, T_{γ_u}	Access policy assigned to a user, u, and the corresponding access tree
$T_{\gamma_u}^{ext}$	Extended access tree after adding dummy nodes
Att	Attribute universe
MD	Metadata items universe
s_{d_j}	Secret value assigned to the dummy nodes
s_T	Secret value assigned to the root node
Δ_{att_j}	Product of the Lagrange coefficients for each of the attribute, att_j in $T_{\gamma_u}^{ext}$
Δd_j	Product of the Lagrange coefficients for each of the dummy node, d_j in $T_{\gamma_u}^{ext}$

For the details of the *AddDummyNode*, *AssignedValue* and *MST* algorithms readers are suggested to refer article [3].

$MetadataEncryption(md \in MD, PP, \xi)$:
It is run by the data owner. This algorithm encrypts the metadata item under a set of attributes ξ. The data owner selects two random values:t_e and $t_{e'} \xleftarrow{\$} Z_p$ and computes:

$$C_0 = g^{t_e}, C_1 = X^{t_e + t_{e'}} Y^{H(md) t_{e'}}, C_2 = Z^{t_{e'}}, \left\{C_{3,j} = T_j^{t_e}\right\}_{\forall att_j \in \xi} \quad (3)$$

$RetrievalToken(SK_u, PP, md)$:
It is run by the data user. This algorithm generates the token that will be used in retrieval of the desired data files by the cloud server, and is thereby referred as retrieval token md by using the secret key SK_u of the data user. The data user selects a random value:$t_q \xleftarrow{\$} Z_p$ and computes:

$$D_1 = \left(XY^{H(md)}\right)^{t_q}, D_2 = Z^{t_q}, K_1' = K_1^{t_q}, K_2' = K_2^{t_q} \quad (4)$$

Output:$TK = \left(D_1, D_2, K_1^{'}, K_2^{'}, \gamma_u\right)$
Retrieve(C, TK) :
It is run by the cloud server. This algorithm data files corresponding to the token shared by the data user. This algorithm executes only if $\gamma_u(\xi) = 1$. Otherwise, it returns $\perp$. The cloud server calls $MST\left(\xi, T_{\gamma_u}^{ext}\right)$ algorithm to get $\left(T_{\gamma_u}^{\xi}, \{\Delta_{att_j}\}|_{\forall att_j \in \xi}, \{\Delta_{d_j}\}|_{\forall d_j \in D_{T_{\gamma_u}^{\xi}}}\right)$ as output. The cloud server can get the $\{s_{d_j}\}_{\forall d_j \in D_{T_{\gamma_u}^{\xi}}}$ corresponding to ξ from $\mathcal{T}_{\gamma_u}$ and computes:

$$Q_1 = \prod_{\forall att_j \in \xi} \left(C_{3,j}\right)^{\Delta_{att_j}} = \prod_{\forall att_j \in \xi} (g)^{t_e s_j \Delta_{att_j}} = g^{t_e\left(\sum_{att_j \in \xi} s_j \Delta_{att_j}\right)} \tag{5}$$

$$Q_2 = \prod_{\forall d_j \in D_{T_{\gamma_u}^{\xi}}} (C_0)^{S_{d_j} \cdot d_j} = g^{t_e\left(\sum_{d_j \in D_{T_{\gamma_u}^{\xi}}} s_{d_j} \cdot d_j\right)} \tag{6}$$

If $\gamma_u(\xi) = 1$ then $\sum_{att_j \in \xi} S_j \Delta_{att_j} + \sum_{d_j \in D_{T_{\gamma_u}^{\xi}}} S_{d_j} \cdot d_j = S_T$. Hence, $Q = Q_1 \cdot Q_2 = g^{t_e s_T}$
Output:

$$\begin{cases} (1, R), if \frac{e(C_1, D_2)}{e(C_2, D_1)} = \frac{e\left(Q, K_1^{'}\right)}{e\left(C_0, K_2^{'}\right)} \\ (0, \perp), otherwise \end{cases} \tag{7}$$

Correctness Proof:
In Eq. (7), from L.H.S. compute $e(C_1, D_2)$ and $e(C_2, D_1)$

$$\begin{aligned} e(C_1, D_2) &= e\left(g^{x(t_e + t_{e'})} g^{yH(w)t_{e'}}, g^{zt_q}\right) \\ &= e(g, g)^{xt_e zt_q} e(g, g)^{xzt_q t_{e'}} e(g, g)^{yH(w)zt_q t_{e'}} \end{aligned}$$

$$\begin{aligned} e(C_2, D_1) &= e\left(g^{zt_{e'}}, \left(g^x g^{yH(w)}\right)^{t_q}\right) \\ &= e(g, g)^{zt_{e'} xt_q} e(g, g)^{xyH(w)t_q t_{e'}} \end{aligned}$$

Output:$C = \left(\xi, C_0, C_1, C_2, C_{3,j}\right)$Now in Eq. (7), from R.H.S. compute $e\left(Q, K_1^{'}\right)$ and $e\left(C_0, K_2^{'}\right)$:

$$e\left(Q, K_1^{'}\right) = e\left(g^{t_e s_T}, \left(g^{\frac{xz + t_u}{s_T}}\right)^{t_q}\right) = e(g, g)^{t_e xzt_q} e(g, g)^{t_e t_u t_q}$$

$$e\left(C_0, K_2^{'}\right) = e\left(g^{t_e}, \left(g^{t_u}\right)^{t_q}\right) = e(g, g)^{t_e t_u t_q}$$

$$\frac{e(C_1, D_2)}{e(C_2, D_1)} = e(g, g)^{xt_e zt_q} = \frac{e\left(Q, K_1'\right)}{e\left(C_0, K_2'\right)} \tag{8}$$

Hence from Eq. (8) the proposed scheme is correct.

5 Performance Analysis

To evaluate the performance, we have implemented the proposed scheme in JAVA using Netbeans-8.1 IDE and java pairing based cryptography library (JPBC) [15] on a 64-bit windows-10 system with Intel core i3 processor 2.00 GHz and 4 GB RAM. In JPBC to instantiate Bilinear map we have used Type A pairing constructed on elliptic curve, $y^2 = x^3 + x$ over a field F_q, where $q \equiv 3 mod 4$ is some prime. In this pairing both G_1 and G_2 are the group of points from $E\left(F_q\right)$ and hence it is called symmetric pairing. The size of the base field is set to be 512-bit which offers a security equivalent to 1024-bit DLOG [15] and the order, p of source group G and target group G_T is set to be 160-bit. To demonstrate the performance, we have varied the number of attributes in the attribute universe, the access policy and in the set ξ from 10 to 50 with a step length of 10 and in each step the experiment has been executed many times to find the average time taken by each algorithm which is listed below in Table 2.

Table 2. Average execution time (second) of the algorithms of the proposed scheme where the number of attributes in attribute universe, access policy and the set ξ are kept same.

Algorithm	10	20	30	40	50
System Initialization	1.2013562	1.447362	1.611378	1.820817	2.012344
Assign Credentials	0.0514958	0.051394	0.051544	0.051869	0.051771
Metadata Encryption	0.2486007	0.442674	0.580226	0.702572	0.879705
Retrieval Token	0.0963208	0.096336	0.096085	0.09626	0.096053
Retrieval	0.3444418	0.50067	0.705373	0.852511	0.981253

From Table 2 we have observed that the *System Initialization*, *Metadata Encryption* and *Retrieve* are comparatively more expensive than the rest of the algorithms for the same number of attributes. However, among these algorithms *Setup* and *GenIndex* are executed only once and the *Retrieve* algorithm is executed over the cloud server which has plenty of resources, hence they does not significantly affect the overall performance of the scheme as compared to the algorithm like *Retrieval Token* which is executed quite frequently.

For the better demonstration of the experimental results, we have plotted the average execution time taken by each algorithm against the number of attributes in Fig. 2. Figure 2-a) shows that the average execution time of *System Initialization* algorithm increases linearly with the number of attributes because of the component, T_j which corresponds to the number of attributes.

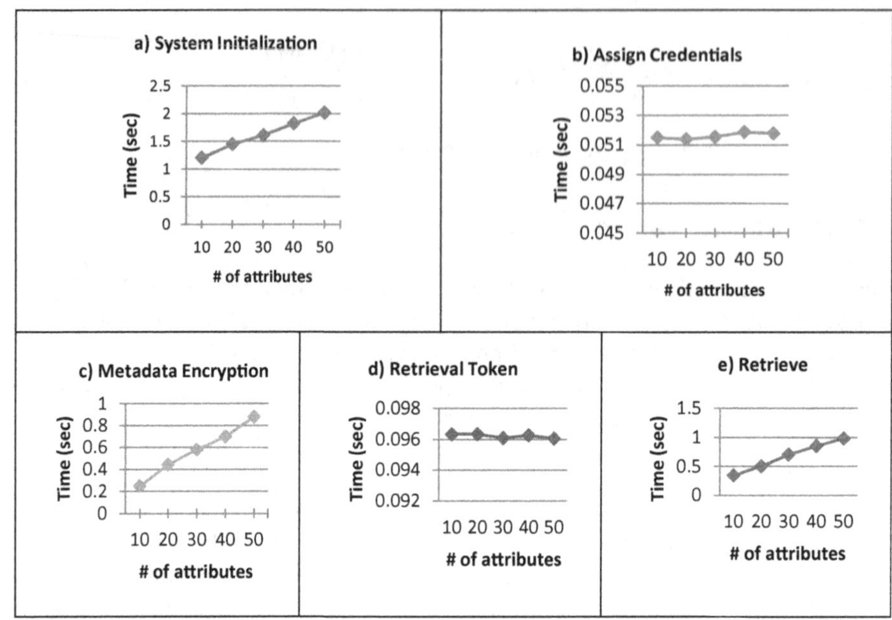

Fig. 2. Average execution time of the proposed scheme

Figure 2-b) shows the average execution time of *Assign Credentials* algorithm. Since the secret key assigned to the user is independent of the number of attributes and will always have two fixed components, so this algorithm will take constant time.

Figure 2-c) shows that the average execution time of *Metadata Encryption* algorithm increases linearly with the number of attributes because of the component, $C_{3,j}$ which corresponds to the number of attributes.

Figure 2-d) shows that the average execution time of *Retrieval Token* algorithm is independent of the number of attributes because the trapdoor is generated using secret key of the user which in turn is independent of the number of attributes.

In Fig. 2-e) it is observed that there is a slight increase in the average execution time of *Retrieve* algorithm because internally it computes Q_1 and Q_2 where the number of exponentiation and mutiplication operations in $Q_1 = \prod_{\forall att_j \in \xi} (C_{3,j})^{\Delta_{att_j}}$ and $Q_2 = \prod_{\forall d_j \in D_{T^{\xi}_{\gamma_u}}} (C_0)^{S_{d_j} \cdot d_j}$ increases with the increase in number of attributes. However, the total number of pairing operations are always constant and are independent of the number of attributes as compared to the most of existing attribute based searchable encryption schemes in literature [16–22]. Hence, the overall time increases linearly with the number of attributes but the rate with which it increases is very low as compared to schemes like [16–22].

6 Asymptotic Complexity Analysis

This section gives the asymptotic complexities of various algorithms: Assign Credentials, Metadata Encryption, Retrieval Token, Retrieve of the proposed scheme with the existing schemes in a comparative manner.

Table 3 presents the storage and the computational complexity of the proposed scheme and the other similar schemes in the literature in a comparative manner.

The storage cost in the above table is computed in terms of number and size of the group elements involved in the scheme, while the computational cost is computed in terms of the number and type of operations involved in the scheme.

As it can be observed from Table 3, the proposed scheme achieves constant size for the secret key as well as for the trapdoor, while in the existing schemes it is dependent on the number of attributes involved. These theoretical claims were further justified by the experimental results shown in Fig. 2 where we got a straight line for the assign credentials (Fig. 2 b) and for the retrieval token (Fig. 2 d), which denotes that these algorithms take constant time irrespective of the change (increase/decrease) in number of attributes in the system. While in the state of the art schemes shown in the above table this cost varies with the number of attributes and hence their complexity is more than the proposed scheme. Further, in the search algorithm, we obtained constant number of pairing operations and these pairing operations are relatively quite expensive than the normal exponentiation and other operations. As we are able to keep the pairing operations constant, it results in fast search at the cloud server end. Since, none of the existing techniques have simultaneously achieved constant size for the secret key, retrieval token and the constant number of pairing operations. Thus making the proposed scheme efficient both in terms of the storage as well as the computational cost as compared to the existing schemes.

7 Conclusion

Metadata may contain sensitive and crucial information about the data, therefore in addition to encryption of the data files, the metadata information also needs be encrypted. However, encryption makes the metadata information inaccessible. Therefore, in this paper a fine-grained encryption scheme has been proposed through which this sensitive metadata information can be processed without decryption and without revealing any information about it in the plaintext. The proposed scheme is efficient in terms of the fast retrieval capability as the number of pairing operations are constant. Further, the size of the user secret key and the retrieval token are also constant which save the channel bandwidth and thus further ensures the efficiency of the proposed scheme.

Table 3. Comparisons of Asymptotic complexities

Ref.	Algorithm	Storage Cost	Computational Cost
[16]	*Assign Credentials*	$2N\|G_2\|$	$2NE$
	Metadata Encryption	$1\|G_2\| + \left\|\{0, 1\}^{logp}\right\|$	$2P + 4E + 3H$
	Retrieval Token	$1\|G_1\| + 2\|G_T\| + \left\|\{0, 1\}^{logp}\right\|$	$2P + 1E + 2H$
	Retrieve		$(\xi + 1)P + \xi E_T + 2H$
[17]	*Assign Credentials*	$(2N)\|G\|$	$3NE + NH$
	Metadata Encryption	$(\xi + 3)\|G\|$	$(\xi + 4)E + \xi H$
	Retrieval Token	$(2N + 2)\|G\|$	$(2N + 2)E$
	Retrieve		$(2\xi + 2)P + \xi E_T$
[18]	*Assign Credentials*	$3N\|G\|$	$4NE$
	Metadata Encryption	$(\xi + 3)\|G\| + \left\|\{0, 1\}^{2logp}\right\| + 1\|G_T\|$	$(\xi + 4)E + 1E_T + 4H$
	Retrieval Token	$2N\|G\|$	$4N^2E + 1H$
	Retrieve		$1P + \xi E$
[19]	*Assign Credentials*	$N\|G\| + N\|Z_p\|$	NE
	Metadata Encryption	$(\xi + 1)\|G\| + 2\|G_T\|$	$2P + \xi E + 1E_T + 3H$
	Retrieval Token	$(N + 1)\|G\| + 1\|Z_p\|$	$(2N + 2)E + 1H$
	Retrieve		$2\xi P + 2\xi E_T$
[20]	*Assign Credentials*	$(2N + 4)\|G\| + 1\|Z_p\|$	$(2N + 6)E$
	Metadata Encryption	$k\|G_T\| + (\xi + 2)\|G\|$	$(\xi + 2)E + 2kE_T + kH$
	Retrieval Token	$(2N + 2)\|G\|$	$2E + 1H$
	Retrieve		$(2\xi + 2)P + \xi E_T + 1H$
[21]	*Assign Credentials*	$(2N)\|G\|$	$(2N + 1)E + NH$
	Metadata Encryption	$(\xi + 3)\|G\| + 1Z_p$	$(\xi + 4)E + (\xi + 2)H$
	Retrieval Token	$(2N + t + 1)\|G\|$	$(2N + t + 1)E + (t + 1)H$
	Retrieve		$(2\xi + 2)P + \xi E_T + tE$
[22]	*Assign Credentials*	$(2N)\|G\|$	$3NE$
	Metadata Encryption	$(\xi + 1)\|G\| + 2\|G_T\|$	$1P + (\xi + 4)E + 2E_T + 2H$
	Retrieval Token	$(2N + 2)\|G\|$	$(2N + 2)E + 2H$
	Retrieve		$(\xi + 1)P + 2E + 2H$
Proposed Scheme	*Assign Credentials*	$2\|G\|$	$2E$
	Metadata Encryption	$(\xi + 3)\|G\|$	$(\xi + 4)E + 1H$
	Retrieval Token	$4\|G\|$	$5E + 1H$
	Retrieve		$\xi E + 4P$

References

1. "Government 'intelligence' report on Iraq revealed as Plagiarism." https://fas.org/irp/news/2003/02/uk020603.html
2. Xu, L., Li, J., Chen, X., Li, W., Tang, S., Wu, H.-T.: Tc-PEDCKS: towards time controlled public key encryption with delegatable conjunctive keyword search for Internet of Things. J. Netw. Comput. Appl. **128**, 11–20 (2019)
3. Li, C., Zhang, Z., Zhang, L.: A novel authorization scheme for multimedia social networks under cloud storage method by using MA-CP-ABE. Int. J. Cloud Appl. Comput. (IJCAC) **8**(3), 32–47 (2018)
4. Chaudhari, P., Das, M.L.: Privacy preserving searchable encryption with fine-grained access control. IEEE Trans. Cloud Comput. (2019)
5. Mamta, Gupta, B.B.: An efficient KP design framework of attribute-based searchable encryption for user level revocation in cloud. Concurr. Comput. Prac. Exp. **32**(18), e5291 (2020)
6. Mamta., Gupta, B.B.: Secure fine-grained keyword search with protection from key abusers in the cloud. In: 2019 IEEE 8th Global Conference on Consumer Electronics (GCCE), pp. 679–683 (2019). https://doi.org/10.1109/gcce46687.2019.9015302
7. Mamta, Gupta, B.B., Ali, S.T.: Dynamic policy attribute based encryption and its application in generic construction of multi-keyword search. Int. J. E-Serv. Mob. Appl. 11(4), 16–38, 2019. https://doi.org/10.4018/ijesma.2019100102
8. Gupta, B.B.: An efficient KP design framework of attribute-based searchable encryption for user level revocation in cloud. Concurr. Comput.: Pract. Exp. **32**(18), e5291 (2020)
9. Mamta, Gupta, B.B.: An attribute-based keyword search for m-Health networks. J. Comput. Virol. Hacking Tech, 1–16 (2020)
10. Olakanmi, O.O., Dada, A.: An efficient privacy-preserving approach for secure verifiable outsourced computing on untrusted platforms. Int. J. Cloud Appl. Comput. **9**(2), 79–98 (2019)
11. Panica, S., Irimie, B., Petcu, D.: Enabling and monitoring platform for cloud-based applications. Int. J. High Perform. Comput. Netw. **12**(4), 328–338 (2018)
12. Goyal, V., Pandey, O., Sahai, A., Waters, B.: Attribute-based encryption for fine-grained access control of encrypted data. In: Proceedings of the 13th ACM Conference on Computer and Communications Security, pp. 89–98 (2006)
13. Bethencourt, J., Sahai, A., Waters, B.: Ciphertext-policy attribute-based encryption. In: 2007 IEEE Symposium on Security and Privacy (SP 2007), pp. 321–334 (2007)
14. Emura, K., Miyaji, A., Nomura, A., Omote, K., Soshi, M.: A ciphertext-policy attribute-based encryption scheme with constant ciphertext length. In: Bao, F., Li, H., Wang, G. (eds.) ISPEC 2009. LNCS, vol. 5451, pp. 13–23. Springer, Heidelberg (2009). https://doi.org/10.1007/978-3-642-00843-6_2
15. De Caro, A., Iovino, V.: jPBC: java pairing based cryptography. In 2011 IEEE Symposium on Computers and Communications (ISCC), pp. 850–855 (2011)
16. Khader, D.: Attribute based search in encrypted data: ABSE. In: Proceedings of the 2014 ACM Workshop on Information Sharing & Collaborative Security, pp. 31–40 (2014)
17. Zheng, Q., Xu, S., Ateniese, G.: VABKS: verifiable attribute-based keyword search over outsourced encrypted data. In: 2014 proceedings of Infocom, pp. 522–530. IEEE (2014)
18. Zheng, Q., Wang, X., Khan, M.K., Zhang, W., Gupta, B.B., Guo, W.: A lightweight authenticated encryption scheme based on chaotic scml for railway cloud service. IEEE Access **6**, 711–722 (2017)
19. Ye, J., Wang, J., Zhao, J., Shen, J., Li, K.-C.: Fine-grained searchable encryption in multi-user setting. Soft. Comput. **21**(20), 6201–6212 (2016). https://doi.org/10.1007/s00500-016-2179-x
20. Li, J., Lin, X., Zhang, Y., Han, J.: KSF-OABE: outsourced attribute-based encryption with keyword search function for cloud storage. IEEE Trans. Serv. Comput. **10**(5), 715–725 (2017)

21. Ameri, M.H., Delavar, M., Mohajeri, J., Salmasizadeh, M.: A key-policy attribute-based temporary keyword search scheme for secure cloud storage. IEEE Trans. Cloud Comput. (2018)
22. Zhu, B., Sun, J., Qin, J., Ma, J.: Fuzzy matching: multi-authority attribute searchable encryption without central authority. Soft. Comput. **23**(2), 527–536 (2017). https://doi.org/10.1007/s00500-017-2849-3

XSSPro: XSS Attack Detection Proxy to Defend Social Networking Platforms

Pooja Chaudhary[1], B. B. Gupta[1(✉)], Chang Choi[2], and Kwok Tai Chui[3]

[1] Department of Computer Engineering, National Institute of Technology Kurukshetra, Kurukshetra, India
pooja.ch04@gmail.com, gupta.brij@gmail.com
[2] Gachon University, Seongnam-si, Republic of Korea
enduranceaura@gmail.com
[3] The Open University of Hong Kong, Kowloon, Hong Kong, China
jktchui@ouhk.edu.hk

Abstract. Social Platforms transpired as the fascinating attack surface to explode multitude of cyber-attacks as it facilitates sharing of personal and professional information. XSS vulnerability exists approximately in 80% of the social platforms. Hence, this paper presents an approach, XSSPro, to defend social networking platforms against XSS attacks. XSSPro operates through isolating the JavaScript code in the external file and performs decoding operation. The context of each injected JS code is identified and then similar scripts are grouped together to optimize the performance of XSSPro. Finally, extracted scripts are matched against the XSS attack vector repository to detect XSS attack. If matched then it is refined by using XSS APIs, otherwise, the response is XSS free and sent to the user. Experimental results revealed that XSSPro achieved an accuracy of 0.99 and is effective against thwarting XSS attack triggered using new features of the built-in code language with low false alarm rate.

Keywords: Cross site scripting (XSS) · Social networking platforms (SNPs) · XSS API · Code injection vulnerability · Malicious JS code

1 Introduction

In this era, everything and everyone around the globe is connected through the internet. This brings out the platform of opportunities and businesses to prosper and grow. This scenario is fueled with the inception of social networking platforms (SNPs) as it facilitates sharing of information that is publically visible to everyone on the network. As per a report, about 80% of daily active internet users visits their social accounts on a daily basis. SNP [1] offers a digital place to internet users where they own their social accounts, initiate new connection with other users on the network, post their personal or any other information that is shared with the connected ones. Fascinating social platform includes Facebook with around 2.7 billion active users [2], YouTube, WhatsApp, Instagram, Twitter to name a few. Since it is a treasure trove of useful information,

S. Chellappan et al. (Eds.): CSoNet 2020, LNCS 12575, pp. 411–422, 2020.
https://doi.org/10.1007/978-3-030-66046-8_34

hence the most enthralling platform for the attackers to abuse latent vulnerabilities [3] such as Cross Site Scripting (XSS). XSS [4, 5] comes from the family of code injection vulnerabilities in which attacker inserts malign script code into any web application. At the time when any user access the application then this script is rendered by the browser, resulting in XSS attack.

XSS attack has 3 distinct classes [5]: Stored XSS, Reflected XSS and DOM based XSS attack. In Stored XSS, attacker permanently stores the malign script code into the web applications with a goal to infect large number of users. Reflected XSS initiates when attacker send a crafted link with malign code to victim so that when he clicks the link then server reflects back the malicious code in the response which gets processed by the browser. DOM based XSS attack is trigged using scripts with hidden malicious code that makes illegitimate modifications in the DOM tree of the web page. This attack may be triggered with an intent to steal sensitive credentials of the victim or it may initiated as the initial step to launch more advanced and sophisticated cyber-attacks such as Distributed Denial-of-Service (DDoS) attack. Therefore, there is a need to emphasize on the solutions to alleviate the XSS attack on the social media platforms.

In this article, we design a XSS attack detection and mitigation approach, XSSPro that acts as the proxy between the browser and server to detect and prevent social media applications from XSS attack. To achieve this task, we extract and isolate the vulnerable/malign JavaScript (JS) code into external file. To bypass the traditional XSS filters, attackers use encoding of JS scripts, hence, we perform decoding followed by the identification of scripts background. It might be possible that attacker injects similar type of malicious scripts at the vulnerable points in the application; therefore, instead of handling each class of similar scripts individually, we implements script grouping using Levenshtein distance so that processing overhead can be reduced. Additionally, the decoded and grouped scripts are compared with the blacklisted XSS attack vectors. If match is found then, code refining is performed. Otherwise, HTTP response is XSS free and sent it to the user.

1.1 Literature Review

In this section, the key contributions of the various researchers have been highlighted briefly. Pelizzi [6] proposed a client-side XSS filter, XSSFilt, which could discover non-persistent XSS vulnerabilities. This filter identifies and thwarts portions of address URL from giving an appearance in web page. Galán et al. [7] designed a multi-agent system to defend against stored XSS attack through perform automatic scanning of the web applications. Gupta et al. [4] design a client-server framework to alleviate all kinds of XSS attack through performing runtime tracking and string matching operations of malicious scripts. However, it incurs processing overhead and time consumption. To mitigate DOM based XSS attack, variance between the expected web ape and received web page is identified to secure applications in cloud computing environment in [8].

Zhang et al. [9] design an approach using GMM models that are modeled using the dataset containing features corresponding to normal and injected payload web page. Rao et al. [10] proposed a technique named as XSSBuster, that mitigate all kinds of XSS attack through processing HTML and JavaScript code separately. However, still there are prevalent issues these techniques such as high processing and computational overhead, high rate of false positive in attack detection, requiring major portion of code modifications at the browser and/or server side, and are not competent enough to handle DOM based XSS attack. Moreover, less attention is focused towards securing the social media platforms against XSS attack. Hence, to overcome some of the major challenges, authors have designed a proxy called as XSSPro to defend social networking platforms against XSS attack.

The layout of rest of the article is: Sect. 2 comprehensively describes the modules comprising our proposed approach. Section 3 highlights the implementation setup detail and provides details of performance assessment of proposed approach. Finally, Sect. 4 concludes our article.

2 Proposed Work

This section comprehensively describes the key modules of the XSS detection approach. The novelty of this approach lies in the fact that it not only identify and neutralizes the effects of simple XSS attack but it also recognized the encoded or obfuscated JS attack vectors. Next sub-section presents the abstract view of the proposed approach.

2.1 Abstract Design Outline

Authors have designed an approach named as XSSPro (XSS Proxy) to alleviate the XSS attack on the real world social networking platforms. The key objective of XSSPro is to transform the vulnerable HTTP response web page such that the new modified version maintains the application logic by moving entire JavaScript code to a separate file. Then, it analyzes these files to uproot latent attack pattern from untrusted input locations. Figure 1 depicts the abstracted version of XSSPro.

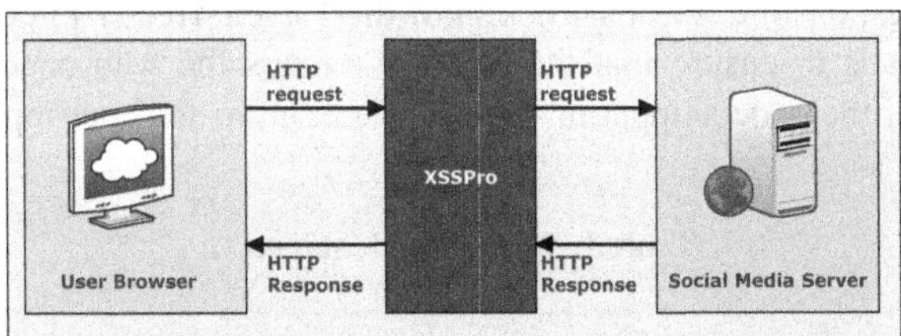

Fig. 1. Abstract design outline of XSSPro

XSSPro operates as the proxy between the client and server side to ignore the modifications at both side. It mainly performs following operations: a) parsing and extraction of JS code into separate external file; b) decoding of extracted JS code to identify partial script injection and obfuscated malign attack vectors; c) determining background information and grouping of extracted scripts; d) testing and refining of code. The entire working procedure of XSSPro is illustrated in the following section.

2.2 Detailed Design Outline

This section furnishes the comprehensive architectural detail of XSSPro. It discuss the sophisticated working of each module, how they process web page to produce the output in required format & how they support other modules to accomplish the respective goal. Figure 2 shows the detailed design overview of XSSPro. To accomplish the desired goal, XSSPro comprises following modules:

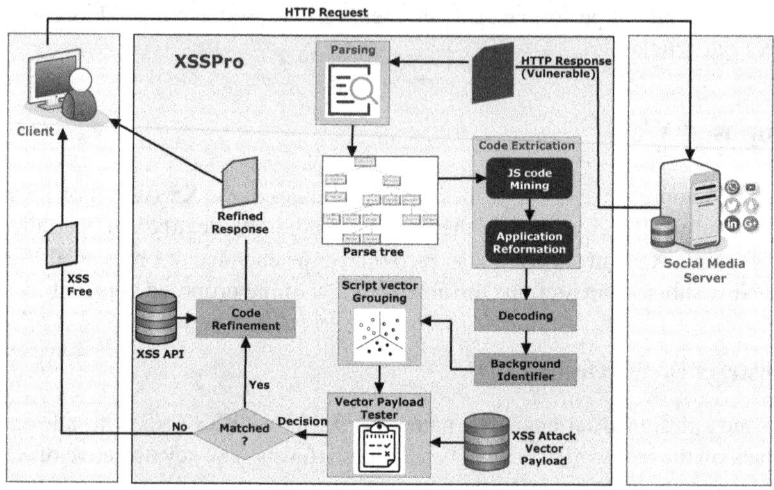

Fig. 2. Detailed design outline of XSSPro

Parsing. This module is the first component to receive the vulnerable HTTP response web page. It is responsible for construction of the Parsed Tree (PT) corresponding to that web page. It is to ensure that the browser renders the web page correctly. For instance, consider the code snippet in Table 1. Here, untrusted user input is applied at

Table 1. Sample Code snippet

<html>
<body>
<div name = "val" onClick = "my()" > Click Me!!! </div>
<script>
function my() {
document.getElementByName("val").innerhtml = "hello" + "$_GET('name')" + "you are" + "$_GET('age')" + "years old";}
</script>
</body></html>

S_GET('name') and $_GET('age'). The parse tree generated for the above code snippet is shown in Fig. 3. Each node of the tree represents HTML tags or text. This tree will be processed to determine script node embedded in to the web page.

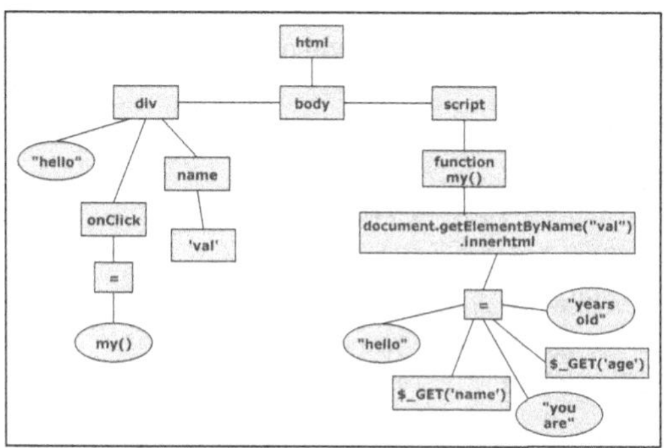

Fig. 3. Parsed tree of above code snippet

Code Extrication. In this module, the extracted parsed tree is processed for isolating the vulnerable JS code into the external file. This task is performed using 2 components: JS code mining and application reformation.

- *JS code mining:* This component is responsible for extracting the JS code from the parsed tree. To ease this task, we perform Depth First Search (DFS) between the nodes having value <script> and </script> . Each identified path denotes the JS code and is then forwarded to the next component which performs the application code rectification.
- *Application reformation:* This component performs the code reformation to achieve the JS code separation task. It receives the extracted JS code from JS code mining component. This component aims at shifting this code to a separate file say, JS_file. It then forwards this file and modified HTTP response web page to the next module. Algorithm 1 is implemented for code extrication.

Decoding. This module is responsible for applying the decoding operation on the extracted JS code. To bypass the traditional XSS filter, attacker employs smarter ways to inject malign code. In most of the cases, attacker use encoding of the attack vectors to forge deployed filters. Therefore, to detect such ambiguous, partially crafted and obfuscated attack vector, we perform decoding operation with respect to the determined encoding method. For instance, to hide `<script>` tag attacker may encode it as `<script>`. So to reverse this we conduct decoding.

Background Identifier. This component is responsible for the determination of the background information of the vulnerable source. It accepts the decoded vulnerable JS code and then uses it to determine the theme of the injected location in the web page. Algorithm 2 is implemented to identify the background information.

Script Vector Grouping. This module carries out the grouping of similar scripts. Attacker might inject the similar scripts at multiple locations.

```
Algorithm 1: Code Extrication
Input: Parse Tree (V, E)
Output: JS code external file and modified HTTP response
Start
JS_rep ← NULL;
For Each v ∈ V
  If (v.value == "<script>") then
      p ← DFS(v);
      While (p.value!= "</script>")
          JS_rep ← p.value ;
      End while
  End If
End For
For Each output statement
  X ← Check if output string is an HTML Tag;
  If (X) then
      For each (<script>... </script>)I pair ∈ JS_rep
        JS_file ← Content between (<script>... </script>);
          H_RES ← Include pointer to JS_file;
      End For Each
  End If
End For Each
Return JS_file, H_RES
End
```

Therefore, to reduce the time for code refining we conduct grouping of similar scripts. This component implements algorithm 3 for grouping the extracted attack vectors payloads depending on their similarity ratio. Consequently, a template is generated that describes the attack vectors in compressed form. Consider the example as shown below:

```
<script> alert(48a$bc); </script>
<script> alert(48xv&ez); </script>
```

Then the compressed template will be `<script> alert(48-S-); </script>` where S is the placeholder.

Vector Payload Tester . This module is responsible for identification of the XSS attack. It receives clustered JS attack vectors and it compares them with the externally available XSS attack vector payload repository. This repository contains the blacklisted attack vectors to trigger the XSS attack. If any match is identified between the blacklisted XSS vectors and extracted JS code then it indicates the presence of malicious attack vector and denote XSS attack. In this case, the modified response is sent to the code refinement module. Otherwise, the received response is XSS free and sent to the user without any modifications.

Algorithm 2: Background Identifier

Input: decoded JS code file
Output: Background information of each untrusted source.

```
Start
Background identifier: BI_1| BI_2|...|BI_N;
JS_Dec ← List of decoded JS code;
B_log ← NULL;
For Each S_I ∈ JS_Dec
        C_I ← BI(S_I);
        B_log ← C_I ∪ B_log;
End For Each
For Each C_I ∈ B_log
        If (S_I ∈ String) then
           f: C_I ↦ String;
        Else if (S_I ∈ Numeric) then
           f: C_I ↦ Numeric;
        Else if (S_I ∈ Regular expression) then
           f: C_I ↦ RegExp;
        Else if (S_I ∈ Literal) then
           f: C_I ↦ Literal;
        Else if (S_I ∈ Variable) then
           f: C_I ↦ Variable;
        End If
End For Each
B_log ← newvalue(C_I);
Return B_log
End
```

Code Refinement. This module accepts the identified malicious attack vectors as its input. It applies filtering to the malign script code to accomplish code refinement with the help of XSS Filtering APIs. This is done to halt the execution of injected malicious string and triggers malicious effects.

Next section elaborates in detail the implementation details and observed experimental results followed by the performance evaluation.

3 Experimental Outcomes and Assessment

In this section, we elaborate the implementation details and discuss the experimental evaluation of our proposed approach on different social networking platforms.

3.1 Implementation Layout

We have implemented XSSPro in java using Apache Tomcat server [11] as the backend, for mitigating the effect of XSS vulnerabilities. In this work, we have tested the efficacy of the XSSPro on four distinct social networking platforms i.e. Oxwall [12], HumHub [13], Elgg [14], and Ning [15]. Initially, we verified the performance of the proposed approach against five open source available XSS attack repositories [16–20], which includes the list of old and new XSS attack vectors. Very few XSS attack vectors were able to bypass our proposed approach. We utilize HtmlUnit [21] HTML parser to create the parse tree for extraction of malicious JS code. To avoid the modifications at the client and server side, the XSSPro is designed to be implemented as the XSS detection proxy between browser and server. The experiment background is simulated with the help of a normal desktop system, comprising 3.2 GHz processor, 8 GB DDR RAM and Windows 7 operating system.

```
Algorithm 3: JS Attack payload vectors grouping
Input: JS payload vector with identified background information
Output: Grouped Template of Attack Vector Payloads
Threshold (δ):= 0;
Start
JS_file ← list of traversed attack vectors;
G_Rep ← NULL;
V_I ← 0
For Each attack vector A_I ∈ JS_file
      Equate(A_I , A_I+1);
      V_I ← Levenshtein_distance(A_I , A_I+1);
      If (V_I > δ)
            Approve (A_I , A_I+1);
              Create group template GT ∈ (A_I , A_I+1);
             G_Rep ← GT ∪ G_Rep;
      Else
             Abandon (A_I , A_I+1);
             Select next pair (A_I+1, A_I+2);
      End If
End For Each
Return G_Rep
End
```

3.2 Experimental Results

For the XSS detection, we inject the XSS attack vector payload at the injection points in the tested social platforms. This is achieved for evaluating the XSS attack detection capability on such platforms of applications. In terms of accuracy, we estimate what percent of "unsurprisingly arising" XSS attack vectors are alleviated by XSSPro. In terms of performance, we evaluate the performance-related issues of executing our framework on a variety of web page-loading and JavaScript standards. Figure 4 highlights the observed results of XSSPro on the four social networking platforms.

We have also calculated the XSS detection rate of XSSPro by dividing the number of attacks detected (i.e.# of True Positives) to the number of XSS attack vectors injected on each tested social platform. Figure 5 highlights the detection rate of all four applications.

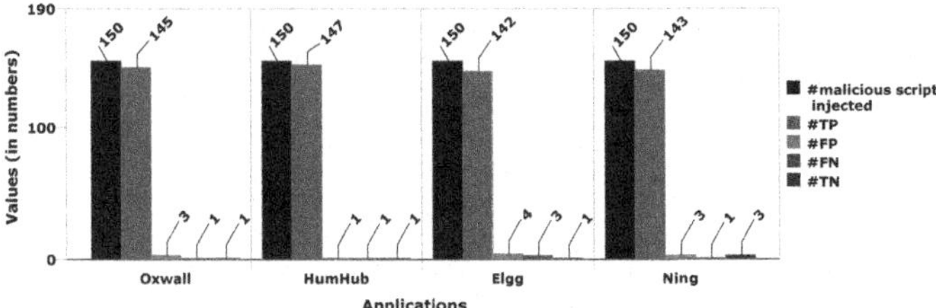

Fig. 4. Observed outcomes of XSSPro on different social platforms

Here, it is clearly reflected that the proposed approach is achieving the highest detection rate of 0.98 on HumHub social networking platform followed by the Oxwall and Ning platform with a detection rate of 0.97. Moreover, XSSPro is achieving a lowest detection rate of 0.95 on Elgg platform. In the next sub-section, we have evaluated the performance analysis of XSSPro through F-measure.

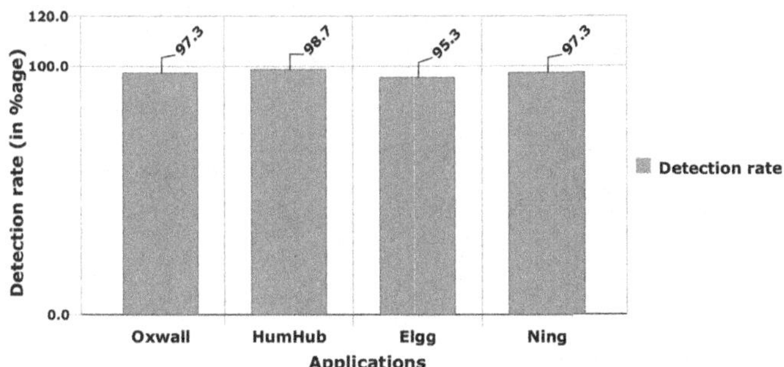

Fig. 5. Detection rate of XSSPro on different social platforms

3.3 Performance Assessment Using F-Measure

This section describes the performance evaluation of XSSPro using F-measure as the statistical analysis method. F-measure generally analyzes the performance of system by calculating the harmonic mean of precision and recall. The analysis conducted reveals that our approach exhibits high performance as the observed value of F-measure in all the social platforms is 0.9. Therefore, XSSPro exhibits 90% success rate in all the four social networking applications. Figure 6 displays the observed results of precision, recall, and F-measure.

$$precision = \frac{TruePositive(TP)}{TruePositive(TP) + FalsePositive(FP)} \tag{1}$$

$$recall = \frac{TruePositive(TP)}{TruePositive(TP) + FalseNegative(FN)} \tag{2}$$

$$F - measure = \frac{2 * precison * recall}{precision + Recall} \tag{3}$$

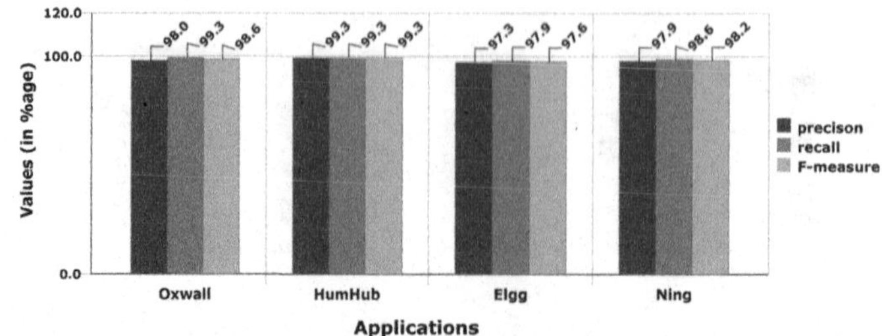

Fig. 6. Performance assessment evaluation outcomes

$$FPR = \frac{FalsePositive(FP)}{FalsePositive(FP) + TrueNegative(TN)} \tag{4}$$

Figure 7 represents the observed False Positive Rate (FPR) of XSSPro on each tested social networking platform. Although, XSSPro is achieving the similar False Positive rate on HumHub and Ning social platform, nevertheless, it achieves the highest detection rate of 0.99 on Humhub and lowest on Ning i.e. 0.97.

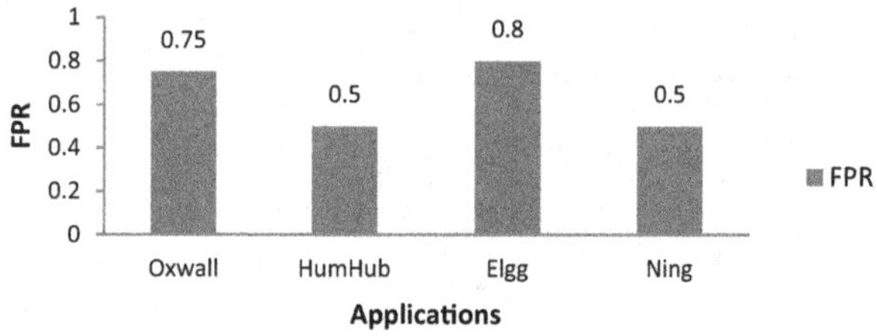

Fig. 7. Observed FPR on different tested platforms

3.4 Comparative Assessment

Here, authors have compared the XSSPro (proposed approach) with the other approaches stated in the literature. Table 2 shed highlights the comparative study on the basis of some pre-defined parameters: XSS Class defended (XCD indicates XSS class defended- S (stored), R (Reflected), and D (DOM-based), Partial injection detection (PID indicates partial malicious code injection detection), Obfuscated code detection (OCD indicates detection of ambiguous script code injection), code amendments (CA indicates any kind of alterations at client or server side), script background identification (SBI indicates identification of background of injected malicious code before refining the response).

Table 2. Comparative analysis of our approach with existing literature

Parameters →	XCD			PID	OCD	CA		SBI
Approaches ↓	S	R	D			Client	Server	
[6]	×	√	×	×	×	×	√	×
[7]	√	×	×	×	√	×	√	√
[4]	√	√	×	√	√	√	√	×
[8]	×	×	√	√	×	√	×	√
[9]	√	√	×	×	×	√	×	×
[10]	√	√	×	√	×	√	×	×
XSSPro	**√**	**√**	**×**	**√**	**√**	**×**	**×**	**√**

4 Conclusion

Indeed, Social networking platforms are treasure troves of personal and professional information. Thereby, it is one of the most captivating attack surfaces for the adversaries to stimulate multiple attacks such as XSS. In this article, authors have designed XSSPro, to alleviate XSS attack on real world social networking sites. It performs extraction and decoding of malicious JS Code and then resolves the background details of these scripts. Additionally, it implements scripts grouping based on the Levenshtein distance to reduce the time for code refining in HTTP response. Finally, it equates extracted JS code with the blacklisted XSS attack vectors. If attack vector identified then it executes code refinement with the help of XSS API otherwise, response is XSS free and forwarded to the user. The experimental results has proclaimed the efficiency of XSSPro in detecting new XSS attack vector payload without requiring any kind of alterations at the browser or server side. As a part of our future work, we will attempt to integrate XSSPro for mitigating the effects of XSS against applications in the mobile cloud computing environment and moreover we will enhance the capabilities of XSSPro to defend against DOM based XSS attack.

References

1. Fire, M., Goldschmidt, R., Elovici, Y.: Online social networks: threats and solutions. IEEE Commun. Surv. Tutorials **16**(4), 2019–2036 (2014)
2. Gupta, B.B., Gupta, S., Gangwar, S., Kumar, M., Meena, P.K.: Cross-site scripting (XSS) abuse and defense: exploitation on several testing bed environments and its defense. J. Inf. Priv. Secur. **11**(2), 118–136 (2015)
3. Sahoo, S.R., Gupta, B.B.: Classification of various attacks and their defence mechanism in online social networks: a survey. Enterp. Inf. Syst. **13**(6), 832–864 (2019)
4. Gupta, S., Gupta, B.B., Chaudhary, P.: A client-server JavaScript code rewriting-based framework to detect the XSS worms from online social network. Concurr. Comput. Pract. Exper. **31**(21), e4646 (2019)

5. Rodríguez, G.E., Torres, J.G., Flores, P., Benavides, D.E.: Cross-site scripting (XSS) attacks and mitigation: a survey. Comput. Netw. **166**, 106960 (2020)
6. Pelizzi, R., Sekar, R.: Protection, usability and improvements in reflected XSS filters. In: Proceedings of the 7th ACM Symposium on Information, Computer and Communications Security, Seoul, Korea (2012)
7. Galán, E., Alcaide, A., Orfila, A., Blasco, J.: A multi-agent scanner to detect stored-XSS vulnerabilities. In: 2010 International Conference for Internet Technology and Secured Transactions pp. 1–6. IEEE November 2010
8. Chaudhary, P., Gupta, B.B., Yamaguchi, S.: XSS detection with automatic view isolation on online social network. In: 2016 IEEE 5th Global Conference on Consumer Electronics, pp. 1–5. IEEE October 2016
9. Zhang, J., Jou, Y.T., Li, X.: Cross-site scripting (XSS) detection integrating evidences in multiple stages. In: Proceedings of the 52nd Hawaii International Conference on System Sciences January 2019
10. Rao, K.S., Jain, N., Limaje, N., Gupta, A., Jain, M., Menezes, B.: Two for the price of one: a combined browser defense against XSS and clickjacking. In: 2016 International Conference on Computing, Networking and Communications (ICNC), pp. 1–6. IEEE February 2016
11. Apache tomcat server. https://tomcat.apache.org/download-80.cgi
12. Oxwall social networking platform. https://developers.oxwall.com/download
13. Humhub social networking site. https://www.humhub.org/en
14. Elgg social networking engine. https://elgg.org
15. Ning: social networking platform. https://www.ning.com/
16. Rsnake. XSS Cheat Sheet 2008. http://ha.ckers.org/xss.html
17. HTML5 Security Cheat Sheet. http://html5sec.org/
18. XSS vectors available. http://xss2.technomancie.net/vectors/
19. Gupta, S., Gupta, B.: PHP-sensor: a prototype method to discover workflow violation and XSS vulnerabilities in PHP web applications. In: Proceedings of the 12th ACM International Conference on Computing Frontiers, pp. 1–8 (2015)
20. @XSS Vector Twitter Account. https://twitter.com/XSSVector
21. HtmlUnit parser. https://sourceforge.net/projects/htmlunit/files/htmlunit/

Information Spread in Social and Data Networks

COVID-19: What Are Arabic Tweeters Talking About?

Btool Hamoui[1(✉)], Abdulaziz Alashaikh[2], and Eisa Alanazi[1]

[1] Center of Innovation and Development in Artificial Intelligence, Umm Al-Qura University, Makkah, Saudi Arabia
s43680523@st.uqu.edu.sa, eaanazi@uqu.edu.sa

[2] Computer and Networks Engineering Department, University of Jeddah, Jeddah, Saudi Arabia
asalashaikh@uj.edu.sa

Abstract. The new coronavirus outbreak (COVID-19) has swept the world since December 2019 posing a global threat to all countries and communities on the planet. Information about the outbreak has been rapidly spreading on different social media platforms in unprecedented level. As it continues to spread in different countries, people tend to increasingly share information and stay up-to-date with the latest news. It is crucial to capture the discussions and conversations happening on social media to better understand human behavior during pandemics and alter possible strategies to combat the pandemic. In this work, we analyze the Arabic content of Twitter to capture the main discussed topics among Arabic users. We utilize Non-negative Matrix Factorization (NMF) to discover main issues and topics based on a dataset of Arabic tweets from early January to the end of April, and identify the most frequent unigrams, bigrams, and trigrams of the tweets. Eventually, the discovered topics are then presented and discussed which can be roughly classified into COVID-19 origin topics, prevention measures in different Arabic countries, prayers and supplications, news and reports, and finally topics related to preventing the spread of the disease such as curfew and quarantine. To our best knowledge, this is the first work addressing the issue of detecting COVID-19 related topics from Arabic tweets.

Keywords: COVID-19 · Twitter · Topic discovery · Arabic

1 Introduction

In recent years, social networks have become a remarkable source of information, reflecting societies interest and reactions about a specific topic. Analyzing the content and the diffusion of social networks information has been shown useful and increasingly used in many fields to characterize an event of interest, e.g., political, sports, or medical events. Lately, it was worthwhile to direct this capability

This work was supported by King Abdulaziz City for Science and Technology. Grant Number: 5-20-01-007-0033.

S. Chellappan et al. (Eds.): CSoNet 2020, LNCS 12575, pp. 425–436, 2020.
https://doi.org/10.1007/978-3-030-66046-8_35

toward the pandemic spread of corona virus. Consequently, an expedited research effort has been applied on analyzing social networks contents and activities during the pandemic spread to help recognize and characterize the social response [1].

In the meanwhile, with coronavirus infection spreading around the world, Arabic countries have been suffering from the outbreak of COVID-19 as the rest of the world. Nowadays, many individual's activities and conversations related to the pandemic are carried out through social media platforms such as Facebook, Twitter, Instagram, etc. Twitter is one of the most famous social media platforms that has a strong growth in the Arabic region, the number of posts reaches 17 million tweets per day according to the Arab social media report [2].

Due to its overwhelming usage and popularity, tweet content mining can potentially provide valuable information during health crises. Several studies have shown that Twitter can be exploited as a valuable data source for detecting and managing the outbreaks [3,4]. Recently, the rise of coronavirus cases in the Arabic countries has led to an escalating discussions related to the COVID-19 pandemic on social media platforms. Therefore, identifying the main concerns, thoughts, and topics regarding the coronavirus crises might be useful to assist public health professionals and social scientists. The main goal of this paper is employing text mining techniques to get an overview of the most discussed topics by Arabic tweeters during the pandemic. Particularly, we use Non-negative Matrix Factorization (NMF) to identify latent COVID-19 related topics in Arabic tweets.

2 Related Work

There has been a growing body of work aiming at mining content related to the COVID-19 pandemic. A study done by Alshaabi et al. [5] analyzed tweets in the context of COVID-19 by extracting 1,000 unigrams in 24 languages from tweets posted in early 2020 and compared it with the ones used a year ago. The authors observed that the first peak was around January 2020 and the second peak was in early March. Li et al. [6] performed an analysis (on Twitter and Weibo) by tracking the change of topic trends, sentiments, and emotions to understand the public attitude towards coronavirus crisis. The vast majority of the previous studies have been on English Twitter content. Recently, some studies (e.g., [7] and [8]) gave attention to analyzing Arabic Twitter content during the pandemic. A dataset of Arabic tweets, ArCOV-19, collected from January 27th, 2020 to March 31st, 2020 [7]. The sentiment analysis of Arabic tweeters in Saudi Arabia toward the preventive measures to combat COVID-19 were conducted in [8].

Various works have been done to extract topics from Twitter with varieties of algorithms. Prier et al. [9] explored tobacco-related tweets from health-related tweets by applying (LDA) algorithm. Besides, (LDA) algorithm employed by Sokolova et al. [10] to identify election-related events tweets. Alternatively, NMF can be employed to extract topics from text. It has been frequently used to analyze tweets' text. Geo-tagged tweets were analyzed by detecting trending topics

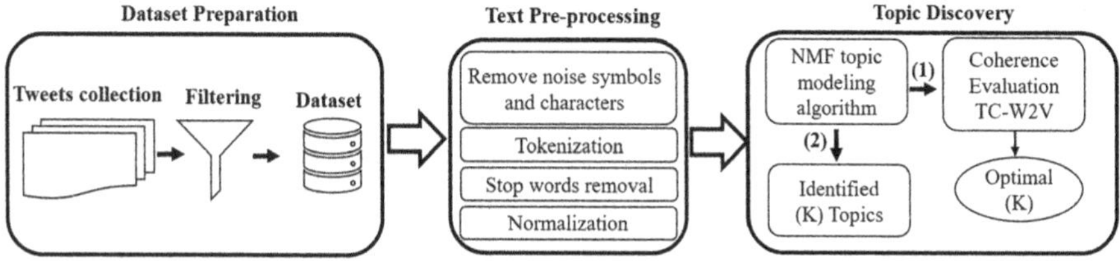

Fig. 1. Methodology workflow

using NMF for urban monitoring in certain areas in Indonesia [11]. Moreover, Klinczak and Kaestner [12] showed that the result of NMF on Twitter data yeilded better performance over the other two clustering algorithms, k-means, and k-medoids.

3 Methodology

This section describes the workflow of the methodology adapted for this study and explains the main steps. The workflow is depicted in Fig. 1 and is composed of the following steps: 1) Dataset preparation, 2) Text pre-processing, and 3) Topics discovery and themes identification, which involves: NMF for topic modelling, Topic model coherence evaluation employing word2vec, and Exploratory topic discovery.

3.1 Dataset Preparation

We use the dataset of the Arabic Twitter COVID-19 collection[1] [13], which contains 3,934,610 Arabic tweets related to COVID-19. The original dataset was collected through Twitter's streaming API and covers the time span from January 1, 2020 to April 30, 2020. Figure 2 illustrates the COVID-19 collected tweets frequency per day. To build a better-quality potential dataset for the experiment, certain filtration and cleaning are applied on the tweets collection to remove noise from the data:

- Filtering non-Arabic tweets: many tweets founded were multilingual tweets, since the Arab users may post tweets written in different languages besides Arabic. Therefore, we opted to filter out the multilingual tweets. The non-Arabic tweets were identified using the language field in the tweets metadata.
- Filtering out the retweets: the retweets were removed from the dataset to eliminate the duplicated content tweets.
- Filtering out short tweets: the tweets with one or two words usually could be ambiguous, hence, this will not provide meaningful information. Therefore, the tweets with less than three words were filtered out.

Applying the previous filtering steps, we ended up with 2,426,850 tweets.

[1] Available at: https://github.com/SarahAlqurashi/COVID-19-Arabic-Tweets-Dataset.

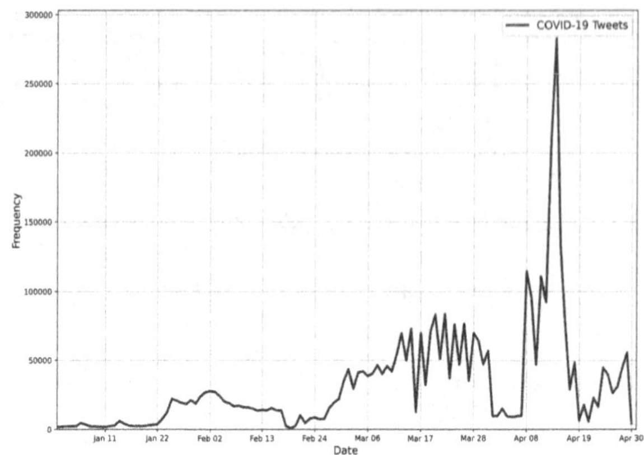

Fig. 2. COVID-19 Tweets Frequency per day

3.2 Text Pre-processing

The pre-processing involved applying several steps to the entire dataset with the aim of reducing the amount of trivial noise to clean the data. The following text pre-processing techniques were applied: First, the cleaning step is performed to remove noise data, in which we remove mentions, URLs links, emojis, punctuation, Non-alphabetic characters, and non-Arabic words. The hashtags were also removed yet maintaining its content in tweets. Furthermore, the Arabic vowel diacritics, 'Tashkeel' تشكيل: : 'Tashkeel [14] are diacritical marks appeared above or below each letter, used in the Arabic to affect the way of Arab pronunciation were removed; to unify the shape of tweeted words' format. Second, we performed tokenization on every tweet where each word was tokenized. Third, stop words removal was applied. For example the Arabic prepositions {من, الى, على, في, ...etc.}, along with other common words in Arabic that have no polarity significance in tweets were deleted. Lastly, we applied normalization to convert multiple forms of a letter into one uniform letter. To unify the form of 'Alef' and the form of 'Taa Marbotah', we replaced {أ, إ, آ} with {ا} and replace {ة} with {ه}. We also applied an extra normalization to the word virus, as it is pronounced in two different ways, as "Fairus" or "Firus". The word virus in Arabic was converted from فايروس to فيروس.

3.3 Topic Discovery and Themes Identifying

NMF for Topic Modelling. Non-negative Matrix Factorization (NMF) is an unsupervised technique for reducing the dimensionality of non-negative matrices [15]. It has been successfully applied in the field of text mining to identify topics [16]. Our study utilizes (NMF) according to its ability to give semantically meaningful results. A study done by O'callaghan et al. [17] found that

NMF produces more coherent topics than other popular topic modelling technique such as the latent Dirichlet al.location (LDA) model. To apply NMF, the pre-processed tweets are transformed to log-based Term Frequency-Inverse Document Frequency (TF-IDF) vectors, where each row corresponds to a term and each column to a document [18]. NMF based on (TF-IDF) values approves its usefulness since it can account for the importance of a word to a document within a collection of texts [17,19].

Topic Model Coherence Evaluation Employing Word2vec. According to the difficulty of defining the similarity measure in high-dimensional sparse vector space, we incorporated the potential of word embedding techniques to determine the number of topics. We opted to use Topic Coherence-Word2Vec (TC-W2V) metric, presented in [17], that measures the coherence between words assigned to a topic via Word2Vec. Word2Vec basically consists of a model to represent words as vectors. It is one of the most promising techniques in NLP that captures the meaning of the words [20].

We employed word2vec by training our model based on the 2,426,850 collected tweets using the Skipgram algorithm with a dimension of 200. To build the model[2], we used a small window of size 3 since the maximum length of a tweet is 280 characters, and we set the minimum word count to 10. The word vectors were produced using the Gensim package in Python. Given the trained word2vec model, we explored 11 words that have arisen and used frequently during COVID-19 pandemic such as {covid, mask, Wuhan, quarantine}, and visualize it's relevant words (top most 20 words similar) that have the same meaning, as shown in Fig. 3. As observed, Fig. 3 shows that the words {علاج, "treatment"}, {عقار, "drug"}, {ترياق, "antidote"}, {مصل, "serum"} are the words closest vector of "Vaccine" as an example. Figure 3 illustrates that the model was able to capture the similarity of the meaning of words.

After the word2vec model has been constructed, we trained the NMF model for different values of k, the number of topics. Then, we calculated the average TC-W2V for each model across all topics by extracting the similarity between all top-n words pairs in each topic from the word2vec model. The final NMF model trained with the highest average TC-W2V. As shown in Fig. 4, the highest average value was 0.3504 with $k = 11$. Hence, we trained the NMF model with the optimal number of topics using the scikitlearn implementation of NMF (including NNDSVD initialization) with k equal to 11.

4 Result and Analysis

4.1 Unigrams, Bigrams and Trigrams Frequency over Time Exploration

Basic unigrams, bigram and trigram frequency analysis over time will reflect the change of Arabic tweeters trends and concerns during the pandemic. After

[2] Available at: https://github.com/BatoolHamawi/COVID19Word2Vec.

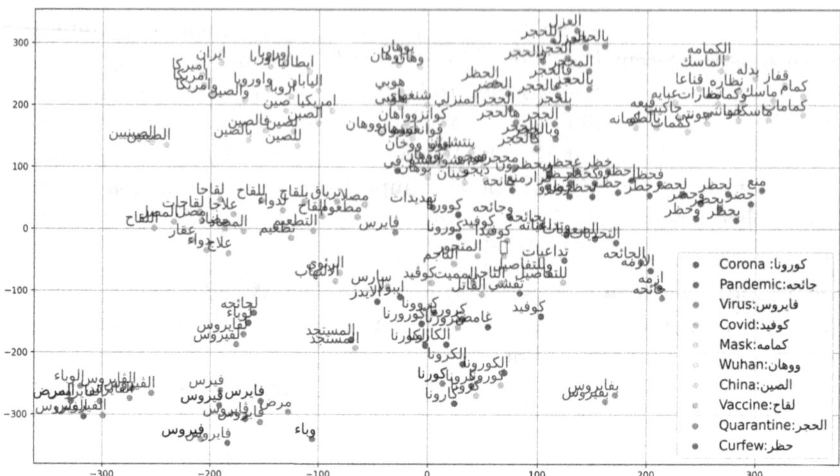

Fig. 3. t-SNE reduced visualization for 20 words closest to the chosen words that are related to the pandemic in the trained Word2vec Arabic Covid-19 model.

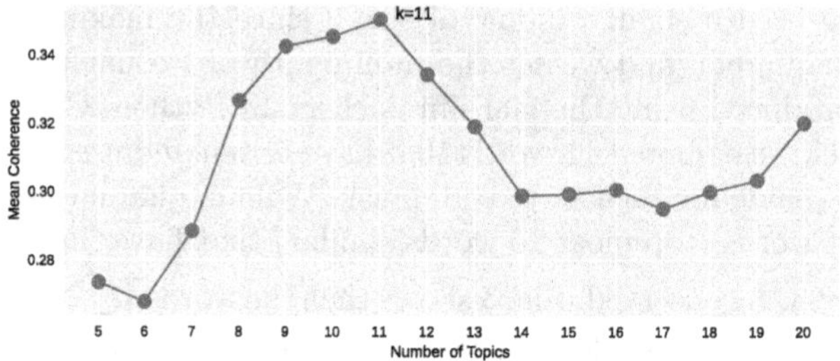

Fig. 4. Average TC-W2V for k from 5 to 20

applying the pre-processing steps, we constructed unigrams, bigrams and trigrams frequency table for the entire pre-proccessed dataset that resulted with 2,426,850 tweets. Then, we analyzed the frequency of each gram over the whole dataset, and explored the topmost unigrams, bigrams and trigrams over weeks. Figures 5 and 6 are the plots of grams frequency per day. In the plotting analysis, the series of grams counts smoothed by moving average to clearly presented the n-grams frequency over days and weeks. For unigram frequency, we investigated the volume of specific words appeared in the Arabic tweet content in January and associated with COVID-19 pandemic; كورونا، وباء، ووهان, which stand for "corona", "epidemic", and "Wuhan", respectively. Figure 5(A) plots the number of occurrences of these words. An increase is clearly noticed over the last two weeks of the January and reached the highest occurrences on the 25th January.

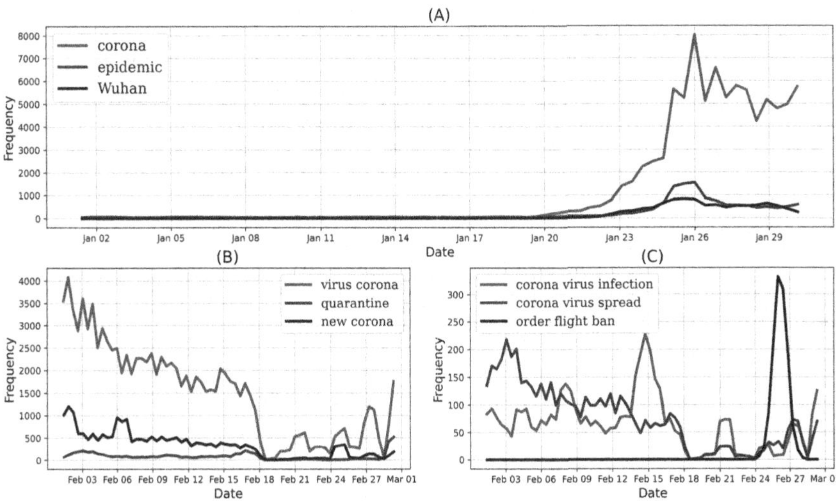

Fig. 5. COVID-19 n-grams frequency for January and February. (A) COVID-19 related words in January, (B) bi-grams frequency in February, and (C) trigrams frequency in February

Table 1. Top 10 bigrams and trigrams.

Bigram	Bigram (Ar)	Frequency	Trigram	Trigram (Ar)	Frequency
virus corona	فيروس كورونا	461443	new corona virus	فيروس كورونا مستجد	31068
home quarantine	حجر منزلي	136004	corona virus spread	انتشار فيروس كورونا	27324
curfew	حظر تجول	101077	corona virus new	فيروس كورونا جديد	23543
Ministry of health	وزارة صحة	60712	world health organization	منظمة صحة عالمية	22787
New corona	كورونا جديد	49870	virus corona outbreak	تفشي فيروس كورونا	18920
Corona epidemic	وباء كورونا	49252	home quarantine activity	فعاليات حجر منزلي	18651
new corona	كورونا مستجد	37985	new corona virus	جديدة فيروس كورونا	17148
Virus spread	انتشار فيروس	34908	new virus infection	اصابة فيروس كورونا	13222
World health	صحة عالمية	32951	facing virus corona	مواجهة فيروس كورونا	12188
Health quarantine	حجر صحي	32667	new virus infection	اصابة جديدة فيروس	10052

With respect to bigrams and trigrams, Table 1 presents the top 10 most co-occurrences bigrams and trigrams identified from the overall tweets in the pre-processed dataset. From the constructed bigrams and trigrams table, we manually crafted a list of bigrams and trigrams. Then, we tracked daily frequency for each of them by combining the identified bigrams and trigrams with its corresponding grams that have the same meaning. In February 2020, the news about coronavirus started to disseminate over Arabic countries. The bi-grams "corona virus", فيروس كورونا, and "corona covid", كورونا كوفيد , appeared mostly at the first week of the month, while the bi-gram "quarantine", الحجر الصحي, started to increase over the last days in February as shown in Fig. 5(B). Similarly,

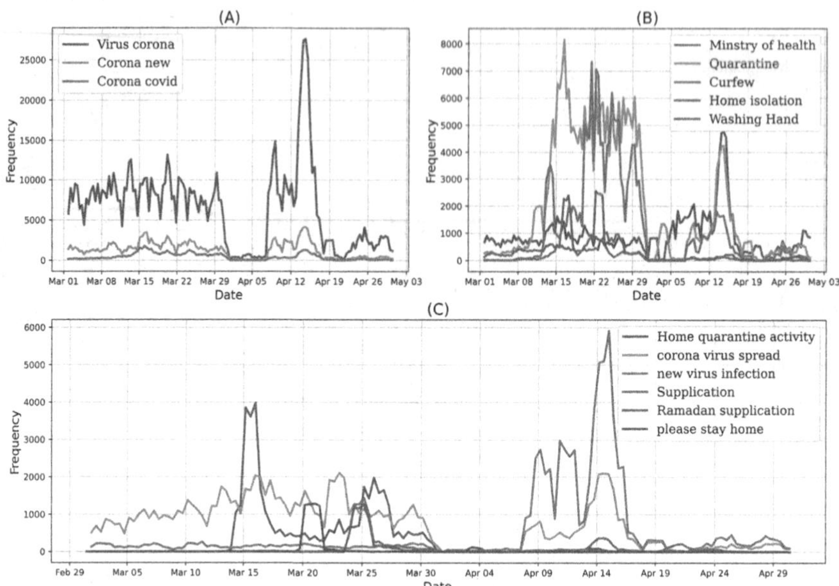

Fig. 6. COVID-19 top bi-grams and trigrams frequency for both March and April. (A) bi-grams related to coronavirus, (B) bi-grams of Health ministry, and preventive measures, and (C) the top trigrams frequency for both March and April

Fig. 5 (C) shows the evolution of the top three trigrams in February. The trigram "corona virus infection", اصابه بفيروس كورونا, had the highest occurrences in the second week. While corona virus spread, انتشار فيروس كورونا, started with the higher occurrences in the first week of February. We also noticed that the trigram order flight ban, نطالب بوقف الطيران, was the most frequent trigram at the end of February.

In March 2020, the number of infections with Corona virus was increasing rapidly in Arabic countries, and so the tweets about the virus. We tracked the bi-grams and trigrams for both March and April 2020 as done previously. The bigrams list was separated into two lists: bi-grams related to coronavirus, and bi-grams that include the "Ministry of Health" bi-gram and four bigrams about prevention measures as shown in Fig. 6 (A) and (B). In terms of bigrams frequency related to coronavirus, Fig. 6 (A) shows that there was stability in the pattern of bigrams in March comparing to April. Regarding the second list, the bi-grams quarantine, الحجر الصحي, and curfew, حظر التجول, they appeared as the topmost frequent bi-grams from the second week of March to the end of the fourth week. However, these bi-grams appeared during April albeit less frequently as shown in Fig. 6 (B). Moreover, the bigrams "washing hand", غسل اليدين, and "Home isolation", العزل المنزلي, were mostly used in March, while their frequency went down during April. The topmost frequent bigram in April was "Ministry of

Health", وزارة الصحة, and it has higher frequency compared with March. In terms of trigrams frequency in March, the trigram "home quarantine activities", فعاليات الحجر المنزلي, was the most frequent trigram in March as shown in Fig. 6 (C). Although this trigram was the sixth top frequent trigram in the entire dataset as listed in Table 1, it appeared only a few times over April. The trigram "corona virus spread "انتشار فيروس كورونا" was used more frequently in March than April. However, the trigram "corona virus infection", اصابة بفيروس كورونا was the highest frequent trigram in April, and it appeared in higher occurrences comparing to March. The rest trigrams which include supplications "oh God, remove the affliction", اللهم اكشف البلاء, "Allah, let our lives be extended so that we live to see the holy month of Ramadan", اللهم بلغنا رمضان reached the highest in March, and continued to appear over April with lower frequency. Moreover, the trigram "please stay at home", تكفون اقعدوا بيوتكم, appeared in March only.

Overall, the presented analysis demonstrates how the COVID-19 pandemic has dominated the Arab conversations over months with different phases; awareness phase, taking the action phase, and evaluation phase. In response to the news about the outbreak of coronavirus in China, some words related to coronavirus were mentioned in the posted tweets in the last ten days of January. The awareness phase about the virus continued to increase in February, the "coronavirus" and "corona COVID" co-occurrences expressed people awareness regarding the new virus alongside fears from virus spread by asking to stop the flight from and to China. During March, the lockdown measures were implemented in most Arabic countries [21]. The partial curfew was announced and imposed by authorities in different Arabic countries, such as Saudi Arabia, Kuwait, Jordan, and Egypt. Consequently, a shift towards discussing the precautionary measurements such as "quarantine", "curfew", and "home isolation" were observed and reached its peak in March. Besides, Arab tweeters encouraged each other to stay at home and increase prayers to God, which reflects the Arab attitude to take actions and combat the pandemic. Although, the lockdown measures implementation was extended to April, and some Arabic countries imposed the 24 h curfew [21], the discussion tendency in tweets content change to another phase. Notably, Arab users were more attentive to monitor and evaluate the number of infections, the situation of virus spread, and following up the impact of the precautionary measures with the Ministry of Health.

4.2 Exploratory Topic Discovery

We analyzed the 11 topics extracted from tweets using the NMF described earlier in Sect. 3.3. The distributions and the top-7 terms associated with each topic shown in Table 2. To provide an overview of the main discussed topics regarding the coronavirus in Arabic tweets, we inspected 1,000 chosen tweets from each topic along with top frequent bigrams and trigrams. Then, we manually analyzed with two Arabic native speakers volunteers the sets of the common bigrams, trigram, and overall 11,000 tweets. We observed the following:

- Topic 1: Preventive measures taken against the virus, staying at home, and protection from coronavirus infection. The most frequent countries mentioned in the tweets were Saudi Arabia, Egypt, Lebanon, China, Jordan and Oman.
- Topic 2: About quarantine, its impact on individuals, and quarantine activities. Moreover, appealing to increased charitable donations.
- Topic 3: Corona is a global epidemic, suspension school, and the coronavirus epidemic.
- Topic 4: About China, flight cancellations from and to China, and discussion about spreading the virus in Wuhan city.
- Topic 5: About curfew- tweeters mostly mentioned Kuwait, Saudi Arabia, and Jordan in the tweets. Moreover, appeals to stay at home mostly written in Gulf dialect such as "Please stay home!", "تكفون اقعدو بيوتكم".
- Topic 6: It is mainly about coronavirus spread in Egypt. Most of the tweets were written in Egyptian local dialect.
- Topic 7: Supplications. Asking God for relief and protection from illnesses, such as may Allah save us, and protect Muslims. Examples of trigrams founded: "حمانا الله وإياكم" and, "حفظ الله الجميع".
- Topic 8: About the latest News. The tweets that belonged to this topic mainly showed statistics and, number of cases, the number of new cases every day, and the number of deaths caused by coronavirus in different cities and countries.
- Topic 9: Ramadan Supplications, such as "اللهم بلغنا رمضان," which mean O' Allah, let our lives be extended so that we live to see the holy month of Ramadan.
- Topic 10: The main topics founded are about: facing the spread of coronavirus, and corona out-breaks.

Table 2. Identified topics and their components

Topic	Topics identified	Keywords	Distribution
1	Prevention measures in different countries	السعوديه ، الكويت ، الاردن ، لبنان ، فيروس ، كورونا ، مصر Saudi Arabia, Kuwait, Jordan, Lebanon, virus, corona, Egypt	17.95%
2	Quarantine	حجر ، صحي ، ، منزلي ، عزل ، واجب ، بيت ، خليك quarantine, healthy, house, isolation, must, home, stay	6.76%
3	Corona is a global pandemic	وباء ، عالم ، عالمي ، اخطر ، دول ، مرض ، ناس epidemic, global, globally, the most dangerous, countries, disease, people	5.37%
4	China	الصين ، ووهان ، وفيات ، ارتفاع ، صينيه ، امريكا ، عالم China, Wuhan, deaths, higher, Chinese, America, world	15.17%
5	Curfew	قرار، الكويت، السعوديه ، حظر، تجول ، اجباري، حضر Curfew, wandering, compulsory, lockdown, decision, Kuwait, Saudi Arabia	4.55%
6	Coronavirus in Egypt	مصر ، كورونا، زمن، عشان، اخطر ، خايف ، علاج Egypt, corona, time, because, danger, afraid, treatment	9.31%
7	Supplications	الله ، يكفينا ، مسلمين ، نسال ، شاء ، حسبي ، كارونا Allah, away from, Muslims, we ask, will, suffices, corona	13.49%
8	Latest News	تسجيل ، ارتفاع ، حاله ، اصابه ، جديده ، وفاه ، تعلن Record, increase, case, infections, new, death, announce.	5.46%
9	Ramadan Supplications	اللهم ، رمضان ، شعبان ، يارب ، بلغنا ، مسلمين ، اسقام O Allah, Ramadan, Shaaban, O Lord, we have reached, ailments	3.76%
10	Coronavirus spread	تفشي ، مواجهة ، وقاية، فيروس، كورونا، مستجد، انتشار Outbreak, confrontation, prevention, virus, corona, novel, spread.	10.89%
11	Ministry of Health announcements	صحة ، وزارة ، منظمة ، تعلن ، حالات ، وزير ، عالمية Health, ministry, organization, announce, cases, minister	7.24%

- Topic 11: About the World Health Organization, Ministry of Health announcements in different countries, and health care workers on the front-line (health heroes).

5 Conclusion

This paper presents a preliminary analysis and topic extraction of Arabic tweets posted during COVID-19 pandemic from January to April 2020. An analysis of the topmost frequent bi-grams and trigrams showed change in topic over time. The topics were extracted utilizing the Non-negative Matrix Factorization (NMF) methods. Our results demonstrate the power of NMF in detecting meaningful topics that we believe will give great insights to the current discussions and conversations happening on Arabic Twitter. In the near future, we plan to consider the sentiment of the Arabic users to the current pandemic using deep learning techniques.

References

1. Culotta, A.: Towards detecting influenza epidemics by analyzing Twitter messages. In: Proceedings of the First Workshop on Social Media Analytics, pp. 115–122 (2010)
2. Mourtada, R., Salem, F.: Citizen engagement and public services in the Arab world: the potential of social media. In: Arab Social Media Report Series, 6th edn, June 2014
3. de Quincey, E., Kostkova, P.: Early warning and outbreak detection using social networking websites: the potential of Twitter. In: Kostkova, P. (ed.) eHealth 2009. LNICST, vol. 27, pp. 21–24. Springer, Heidelberg (2010). https://doi.org/10.1007/978-3-642-11745-9_4
4. Morin, C., Bost, I., Mercier, A., Dozon, J.-P., Atlani-Duault, L.: Information circulation in times of Ebola: Twitter and the sexual transmission of Ebola by survivors. PLoS Currents **10** (2018)
5. Alshaabi, T., et al.: How the world's collective attention is being paid to a pandemic: Covid-19 related 1-gram time series for 24 languages on Twitter. arXiv preprint arXiv:2003.12614 (2020)
6. Li, X., Zhou, M., Wu, J., Yuan, A., Wu, F., Li, J.: Analyzing COVID-19 on online social media: trends, sentiments and emotions. arXiv preprint arXiv:2005.14464 (2020)
7. Haouari, F., Hasanain, M., Suwaileh, R., Elsayed, T.; ARCOV-19: the first Arabic COVID-19 Twitter dataset with propagation networks. arXiv, arXiv-2004 (2020)
8. Alhajji, M., Al Khalifah, A., Aljubran, M., Alkhalifah, M.: Sentiment analysis of tweets in Saudi Arabia regarding governmental preventive measures to contain COVID-19 (2020)
9. Prier, K.W., Smith, M.S., Giraud-Carrier, C., Hanson, C.L.: Identifying health-related topics on Twitter. In: Salerno, J., Yang, S.J., Nau, D., Chai, S.-K. (eds.) SBP 2011. LNCS, vol. 6589, pp. 18–25. Springer, Heidelberg (2011). https://doi.org/10.1007/978-3-642-19656-0_4
10. Sokolova, M., et al.: Topic modelling and event identification from Twitter textual data. arXiv preprint arXiv:1608.02519 (2016)

11. Sitorus, A.P., Murfi, H., Nurrohmah, S., Akbar, A.: Sensing trending topics in twitter for greater Jakarta area. Int. J. Electr. Comput. Eng. **7**(1), 330 (2017)
12. Klinczak, M.N., Kaestner, C.A.: A study on topics identification on Twitter using clustering algorithms. In: 2015 Latin America Congress on Computational Intelligence (LA-CCI), pp. 1–6. IEEE (2015)
13. Alqurashi, S., Alhindi, A., Alanazi, E.: Large Arabic Twitter dataset on COVID-19. arXiv preprint arXiv:2004.04315 (2020)
14. Zerrouki, T., Balla, A.: Tashkeela: novel corpus of Arabic vocalized texts, data for auto-diacritization systems. Data Brief **11**, 147 (2017)
15. Lee, D.D., Seung, H.S.: Learning the parts of objects by non-negative matrix factorization. Nature **401**(6755), 788–791 (1999)
16. Kuang, D., Yun, S., Park, H.: SYMNMF: nonnegative low-rank approximation of a similarity matrix for graph clustering. J. Global Optim. **62**(3), 545–574 (2015)
17. O'callaghan, D., Greene, D., Carthy, J., Cunningham, P.: An analysis of the coherence of descriptors in topic modeling. Expert Syst. Appl. **42**(13), 5645–5657 (2015)
18. Salton, G., Buckley, C.: Term-weighting approaches in automatic text retrieval. Inf. Process. Manage. **24**(5), 513–523 (1988)
19. Greene, D., Cross, J.P.: Exploring the political agenda of the European parliament using a dynamic topic modeling approach. arXiv preprint arXiv:1607.03055 (2016)
20. Mikolov, T., Chen, K., Corrado, G., Dean, J.: Efficient estimation of word representations in vector space. arXiv preprint arXiv:1301.3781 (2013)
21. Abbas, N.: These Arab Countries Are Now In Lockdown, 2020. https://www.forbesmiddleeast.com/industry/healthcare/in-numbers-the-global-ventilator-shortage. Accessed 20 Aug 2020

MIDMod-OSN: A Microscopic-Level Information Diffusion Model for Online Social Networks

Abiola Osho(✉), Colin Goodman, and George Amariucai

Kansas State University, Manhattan, KS 66506, USA
{aaarise,c3544g,amariucai}@ksu.edu
http://www.cs.ksu.edu/

Abstract. As online social networks continue to be commonly used for the dissemination of information to the public, understanding the phenomena that govern information diffusion is crucial for many security and safety-related applications. In this study, we hypothesize that the features that contribute to information diffusion in online social networks are significantly influenced by the type of event being studied. We classify Twitter events as either informative or trending and then explore the node-to-node influence dynamics associated with information spread. We build a model based on Bayesian Logistic Regression for learning and prediction and Random Forests for feature selection. Experimental results from real-world data sets show that the proposed model outperforms state-of-the-art diffusion prediction models, achieving 93% accuracy in informative events and 86% in trending events. We observed that the models for informative and trending events differ significantly, both in the diffusion process and in the user features that govern the diffusion. Our findings show that followers play an important role in the diffusion process and it is possible to use the diffusion and OSN behavior of users for predicting the trending character of a message very early, long before being able to count the number of reactions.

Keywords: Social networks · Information diffusion · Bayesian learning · Classification and regression · Dimensionality reduction/feature selection

1 Introduction

Online social networks (OSN) have become increasingly important for the dissemination of information for public health, as well as during disasters and crises. While the dissemination of accurate information may protect the general public and potentially save lives, the spread of false or inaccurate information is detrimental to public health and safety in those contexts. During a time when the spread of misinformation is an increasingly serious problem, it is important to study the creation and spread of information, as well as opinion formation in

S. Chellappan et al. (Eds.): CSoNet 2020, LNCS 12575, pp. 437–450, 2020.
https://doi.org/10.1007/978-3-030-66046-8_36

OSNs. To effectively establish this phenomenon, it is essential that we identify the key features that contribute to the repost and eventually, the spread of information in OSNs. Information is said to propagate, or diffuse, when it flows from one individual or community in a network to another. In the case of Twitter, diffusion can be seen as an action to share a Tweet with a user's followers with (i) no other new content added, called Retweet or (ii) new content added, called a Quote. Most studies in analyzing information diffusion focus on the overall spread of information by focusing on event detection and the spread of the event across the network without comprehensively evaluating the diffusion process on a microscopic level – i.e., the factors that influence diffusion, differences in the spread of information in varying Twitter events and the information dissemination process. It is usually hard to assess why some information disseminates and other does not, but it is safe to assume that the features and/or the contexts of messages that go "viral" and those that do not must differ to some extent. In crises/trending Twitter events, the volumes of messages and interaction grow exponentially within a short time. This kind of interaction explosion is expected to impact the prediction model in a different way than when the spread is over a longer period. We assume that building a temporal pattern of a user's online behavior – like the time of day when the user creates or reacts to tweets versus when the tweets get retweeted – is important, as this behavior can be exploited for targeted information spread.

Existing models for predicting information diffusion observe diffusion on a holistic level across trending events or hashtags. Many of these studies are focused on finding super-seeders, or influential nodes, based on the assumptions that the influence of the feature vector will be static across event types. The feature vector is a combination of attributes, possibly specific to user, message, network, and/or interaction, that contribute to an account's online persona. In this study, we hypothesize that the features that contribute to information diffusion in online social networks are significantly influenced by the type of event being studied. We classify Twitter events as (1) informative for topics relating to general knowledge and which have not attained viral status, and (2) trending for topics that can be described as viral, breaking news, hot topics, or crises. We describe a topic to be trending if there are observed sharp spikes in the rate of posts relating to the topic instead of a gradual growth observed over a period of time. Similar to studies on predicting extremism [4] and temporal dynamics [6] in social networks, we build a model that predicts diffusion using features learned from Twitter data. We go the extra mile by exploring the node-to-node influence dynamics associated with information spread and use this knowledge to propose a crowdsourcing approach for early detection of virality before the message spreads within the network. The proposed model is built on Bayesian Logistic Regression (BLR) for learning and prediction, and Random Forests (RF) for feature selection. These two statistical models have been observed to perform sufficiently well in predicting information spread in online social networks. The contributions of the paper are as follows:

- We introduce the node-to-node feature analysis stochastic model MIDMod-OSN for learning the diffusion process by combining a set of network, interaction, semantic and temporal features.
- We identify the optimal subset of features needed to efficiently predict information diffusion in Twitter events.
- We draw conclusions regarding the best time to tweet, as well as the most important user attributes that contribute to achieving maximum retweetability, and in turn maximum diffusion, in the network.
- We employ the MIDMod-OSN model for predicting the virality of a post long before this would even be possible by counting user reactions; in the process, we rely on a novel implicit form of crowdsourcing.
- We make the replicability of our results possible and straightforward, by building a tool to crawl the Twitter Search API using user IDs, and building a database encoded using JSON based on key-value pairs, with named attributes and associated values, and making both publicly available.

The paper is organized as follows. Section 2 reviews the related work on information diffusion in social networks. Section 3 describes our general approach, classification algorithms and evaluation metrics. Section 4 describes the data collection, the experiment setup and the feature set, and presents our results. Section 5 describes crowdsourcing on Twitter and how to predict if a post will go viral, before information about the reaction count can be extracted. Finally, Sect. 6 gives conclusions and insights into possible future works.

2 Previous Work

Methods for predicting information diffusion depend greatly on efficient topic and event detection, as well as feature selection. Within the vast literature on diffusion in networks relevant to our study, we provide a brief overview on information propagation and diffusion prediction models, with some details on recent work in feature selection for information diffusion.

Information Diffusion and Prediction Models. The information diffusion process can be observed through the diffusion graph and rate of adoption of the information by the nodes in the graph. The diffusion graph shows influence in the network, which is important for viral marketing [2,3,14], crisis communication [1] and retweetability [9]. Generally, influence analysis models have focused on relationship strength based on profile similarity and interaction activity [16], and the mechanisms responsible for network homogeneity [8].

Predictive models like the independent cascade (IC) model [7] make use of submodular functions to approximate the selection of most influential nodes where people observe the choices of others while ignoring their personal knowledge. The linear threshold model (LT) described in [5], deals with binary decisions where a node has distinctly mutually exclusive alternatives and an inactive node is activated by its already activated neighbors, if the sum of influence degrees exceeds its own threshold. Asynchronous IC and LT (AsIC and AsLT respectively) defined in [11,12] introduced a time delay parameter before a parent node can activate an inactive child node. Some other studies like [15] propose a model based on Partial Differential Equations (PDE) by introducing a diffusive logistic to model to predict temporal and spatial patterns in Diggs, an online social news aggregation site.

Feature Selection for Information Diffusion. [6] introduced a variant of the AsIC model called the T-BAsIC framework that assigns a fixed value for a real time-dependent function for each link, without fixing the diffusion probability. In [4], the authors leverage a mixture of metadata, network and temporal features in detecting users spreading extremist ideology and predict content adopters and interaction reciprocity in social media. Given the temporal relevance of tweets, [13] hypothesize that the probability that an audience member reacts to a message depends on factors such as his daily and weekly behavior patterns, his location and timezone, and the volume of other messages competing for his attention.

Instead of focusing on the diffusion of trending events, our model seeks to show the difference between the diffusion models of informative and trending Twitter events, as it relates to the volume of posts, features influencing diffusion and time to post for maximum spread. The proposed model is then applied in the early detection of virality by using an implicit crowdsourcing approach to predicting the likelihood that a tweet will receive enough attention in the network for it to become trending.

3 Model and Method

In this section, we describe the dataset and data gathering process, learning and feature selection algorithms, as well as the evaluation metrics for our microscopic-level information diffusion model for online social networks (*MIDMod-OSN*).

Table 1. Data distribution

Event type	Topic	# Users	# Edges	# Tweets	Diffused/not Diffused ratio
Informative	Health benefits of coffee	50919	1100270	2958382	40/60
	Mental health	29362	3224330	4030412	
Trending	2018 Kansas elections	15339	2509255	24188962	52/48
	2018 Government shutdown	12581	2549136	14513377	

3.1 Dataset Description

Due to the number of features being examined, we needed the complete metadata of Tweet and user JSON (JavaScript Object Notation) objects. For the purpose of future research requiring Twitter JSON objects, we created a tool that crawls the Twitter Search API using the usernames or IDs of a set of seed users and made it publicly available on GitHub. The tool creates a relationship graph built around the seed users and their followers. Since it is almost impossible to have the complete Twitter graph, the sub-graph generated is as representative as it can be. For each of the 4 topics we are exploring, we randomly select 50 users and build a followership relationship around them for up to depth 2. The user (or node, used interchangeably throughout the remainder of this paper) information is then used to build a database crawled over a 30-day period, by collecting all the tweets created by users in the sub-graph during this time period.

For this study, we classify these events into two categories: informative and trending. We then examine two topics for each event. The topics defined are (1) Informative: (1.1) Health benefit of coffee, (1.2) Mental health and (2) Trending: (2.1) 2018 Kansas elections, (2.2) 2018 Government shutdown. The data and network distribution for the dataset can be found in Table 1. We associate each topic with a bag of words that are deemed important to the topic by creating a list of words frequently used with or associated with the topic. A tweet is said to be relevant to a topic if and only if it contains one or more of the predefined keywords. For example, 60 key words were used to identify tweets belonging to the topic of *health benefit of coffee*. The data is split into: (1) a training set used for parameter estimation and (2) a test set to assess the performance of the model, using an 80%–20% training-test data split and performance of the training models obtained using the k-fold cross validation technique, with $k = 10$ folds.

Information Spread Behavior: In a directed network $G = (V, E)$ with no self-links (communities within the graph might contain cycles), V is the set of nodes and $E(\subset V \times V)$ is the set of edges. For each node $v \in V$, we denote U as the set of v's followers and W as the set of v's friends, *i.e.*, $U = \{u; (v, u) \in E\}$ and $W = \{w; (w, v) \in E\}$, respectively. Similar to [11], we assume $AsIC$ with the time delay function associated with information diffusion along the edge. At time t each node v gets a chance to activate (get a reaction through retweet, favourite, quote or reply) its follower u. If node u is not activated by time $t + \delta$, then node v looses the competition for activating u to any other node v' that attempts to activate u between $t + \delta$ and the time of u's activation. For simplicity, we assume that activation is restricted to a node's interaction with the network, but in reality, this will not always be the case, as activation is not solely dependent on the network activities but could be from sources external to the network itself, thereby causing delay in activation.

3.2 Learning and Feature Estimation Models

The model we propose takes a pair of users with established followership relationship and extracts a set of attributes classified as: Network, Interaction, Semantic and Temporal. We adopt two off-the-shelf machine learning models: Bayesian Logistic Regression and Random Forests due to the good performance of both models in similar settings, as observed in [6] and [4]. First, we use the attributes described in Table 2 to train our model based on BLR. By removing features that are highly correlated and those with minimal effect on the predictability of the model, we select a subset of the original features by using RF as a filter. The BLR model is then re-trained with the selected feature set and evaluated to determine the predictive abilities of the selected features.

We perform node-to-node influence analysis by examining feature performance between two users with established followership relationship. We extract attributes from our dataset and organize them as: Network, Interaction, Semantic and Temporal. The features are estimated for both the source and destination nodes, with an associated binary label depicting diffusion along the edge between them. For each user, we learn 27 features, and a social homogeneity (common to two users, showing an overlap in the sets of users they relate with, i.e. common friends and followers) by adopting the features of [6] (excluding the temporal feature) and introducing new ones. Since each observation is a pair of users given as source and destination, the input to the learned model is a vector of 55 features along with a diffusion label per data point. For the temporal dimension, we study the creation, consumption and forwarding of content by splitting a 24-h period into 6 h interval (i.e., 0:00–5:59 am, 6:00–11:59 am, 12:00–5:59 pm, 6:00–11:59 pm) and learn a model for each time period. Overall, we learn 4 temporal models for each pair of users, to observe how the post and reactions to post behaviors change across different time periods in a day.

The prediction capabilities of the learned model are tested based on its abilities to predict if there is diffusion across an edge given the learned model. We employ standard machine learning evaluation metrics: Precision, Recall and F1 score, to measure the predictability of the model.

4 The Diffusion Prediction Experiment

In this section, we describe our experimental setup, and the results obtained for each phase of our model, and then make comparisons with state-of-the-art prediction models. Finally, we discuss the time to tweet paradigm based on our observations.

4.1 Experimental Setup

We perform a supervised learning task where we train the model using the attributes from a pair of nodes with an established followership relationship and label the interaction between them as either diffused or not diffused. An

Table 2. Features extracted for each user to serve as input variables to the learning model

Feature class	Feature	Description
Network	Avg # of followers	Higher follower count means higher reach
	Avg # of friends	Average number a user follows
	Ratio of followers-to-friends	Balance in user's network
Interaction	Volume of tweets	Normalized over account's lifetime
	Social homogeneity	Depicts common friends and followers
	Ratio of directed tweets	% of user's posts directed at others
	Active interaction	Established interaction between users
	Mention rate	Gives volume of posts directed at the user
	Ratio of retweet-to-tweet	% of user's posts with retweet
	Tweets with hashtags	# of original posts have hashtags
	Retweets with hashtags	User reacts to posts with hashtags
	# of retweets by account	Assume account is a bot if ratio is high
	Avg tweets per day	Gives insight into how active the user is
	Avg # of mentions	Shows how interesting others find the user
	Ratio of mentions-to-tweet	% of posts containing @ or RT
	Tweets containing URL	# of user's original tweet contain URLs
	Retweets containing URL	User reacts to posts with URLs
	Tweets containing media	% of user's original tweet with media
	Retweets containing media	User reacts to posts with media
	Presence of user description	User's profile has description (bio)
	Ratio of favorited-to-tweet	% of user's tweets endorsed by others
Semantic	Presence of keywords	User has tweeted about the topic or not
	Positive polarity of tweets	% of tweets with positive sentiment
	Negative polarity of tweets	% of tweet with negative sentiment
Temporal	Ratio of tweets/time	% of posts within a time period
	Tweets with retwt/time	% of tweets with retweet in a time period
	Ratio of retweet/time	% of reactions produced in a time period
	Avg time before retweet	Avg time elapsed getting a reaction

edge is said to be diffused if and only if the destination user (in Twitter terms: *follower*) has at any point forwarded his friend's (*followee's*) messages on the topic being examined. The attributes learned are said to be representative of users' network, interaction, participation, role and importance in the spread of information to other nodes in the network. As previously stated, these attributes are learned over four different time intervals. After learning these features, we fit a regression function that maps the learned user attributes to the likelihood of diffusion between the nodes. Given the directed nature of the Twitter graph, the learning task is non-deterministic, as switching the source and destination nodes may produce a different mapping between the input and output variables. The feature selection framework is initialized to first learn a function with the same set of attributes, secondly rank the features in decreasing order of importance, and third retrain the model using the 15 most important features.

4.2 Diffusion Prediction Model

Firstly, we observed that the volume of tweets across a 30-day period varied widely for informative and trending events. As shown in Table 1, it can be established that even though the combined number of users observed in the trending events is 2.8 times less than the number of users across informative events, we were still able to record 5.5 times more tweets over informative events. We note that in our dataset, trending events generate up to 15 times more tweets than informative events with the same network size. This sort of data projection will be sufficiently affected by the impact of the topic. For instance, one can forecast such data growth for trending events with wide reach like political and health topics but not in lifestyle. Other factors that will impact the data projection include time of day, and external sources like coverage in traditional media.

Table 3. Model evaluation of MIDMod-OSN in predicting diffusion of posts from different event types compared with state-of-the-art.

Event type	Model	Precision	Recall	F1
Informative	55 feat.	0.91	0.96	0.93
	top-15	0.87	0.94	**0.91**
	top-10	0.85	0.90	0.87
	Guille et al.	0.87	0.85	0.86
Trending	55 feat.	0.87	0.84	0.86
	top-15	0.89	0.90	**0.89**
	top-10	0.87	0.90	0.88
	Guille et al.	0.89	0.88	0.88

In Table 3, we show the performance of our models, averaged out across topics in each event class, given the performance metrics previously highlighted. Using the F1 measure, the model achieved 93% accuracy in prediction in informative events and 86% in trending events. The simplified models, based on the 15 most important feature for training, showed a 90% prediction accuracy in informative events and 89% in trending events. Results in the present study are consistent with the prediction results for trending events in past literature. Also, we see that both models with 55 and top-15 features, perform considerably better than the state-of-the-art diffusion prediction model proposed by Guille et al. [6]. Our hypothesis that increasing the feature vector space by learning more attributes from the Twitter JSON objects will make the predictive model more robust is proved correct as we were able to record a 7% increase from the model of Guille et al. It might be argued that a 7% increase is not enough to justify the increase in computation time and resources caused by the increase in feature space, however, we oppose this argument with the feature selection phase, introduced solely for maximizing diffusion prediction by utilizing the features that will directly impact the information spread. For a small cost in accuracy, reducing the input variables by 72% (top-15 features) will give a prediction accuracy of 91%, which is only a 2% reduction in predictive power (when compared with all 55 features). In like manner, an 81% reduction (top-10 features) yields a prediction accuracy of 87%, constituting a 6% reduction in accuracy. The trade-off in adopting the top-10 features is significant, and as such, we adopt the top-15 important features as the optimal set of features necessary for diffusion prediction without incurring expensive computational costs.

Contrary to expectations, it is observed that learning all possible features in trending events impacts prediction accuracy negatively. Due to the consistently changing pattern of interactions and behavior in trending events, increasing the number of features learned brings about over-fitting caused by the exponential growth in the data needed for training. We are able to mitigate the impact of over-fitting in the model using the k-fold cross validation technique, with k set to 10. Nonetheless, it will be detrimental to suggest that learning these features is of no value, as we are convinced that feature selection over several topics will be useful in building a template of attributes for a pre-trained prediction model. The accuracy of the prediction model is consistent with previous studies that have focused on Trending events.

Cross Testing Between Models. To further show that the performance of the models is not biased to topic domains, we tested the informative model with a political related topic and trending model with an health related topic. On testing both models with data from new topics (not used for training and in new topic domains), we observed results similar to those reported earlier with F1 score of 90% for informative and 89% for trending events. This confirms that the models will perform comparably regardless of topic domain. To ascertain that there is indeed a difference between the informative and trending models, we evaluated the informative model with data from trending topics and evaluated the trending model with data from informative topics. The objective is to test if the knowledge gained from one model can be used in making predictions in the other. The outcome of predicting the diffusion of trending posts using a trained informative model produced an F1 score of 82%, while we observed an F1 score of 78% from predicting informative posts using a trained trending model. This result is not totally surprising, due to the irregular pattern associated with posts and users contributing to trending topics.

4.3 Feature Selection Framework

Considering that the goal of the feature analysis task of this study is to identify the optimal set of features necessary to maximize diffusion prediction, we trained an RF model using a 10-fold cross-validation technique that achieved an ROC score of 99% in both informative and trending events. We select the top 15 features, rather than the traditional top 10 (for reasons highlighted in Section 4.2), and report these features in Table 4.

Table 4. Ranking of the top 15 optimal features that should be maximized for maximum diffusion or minimized for containment

Informative	Trending
Dest (destination node) tweets containing URL	Social homogeneity
Src (source node) ratio of retweet/time	Dest active interaction
Src volume of tweet	Src avg # followers
Dest tweets with retweet/time	Src ratio of favorited-to-tweet
Social homegenity	Src mention rate
Dest tweets containing media	Src ratio of retweet/time
Src ratio of retweet-to-tweet	Src volume of tweet
Src ratio of tweet/time	Src active interaction
Src tweets with retweet/time	Src tweets containing URL
Dest retweets with hastags	Src ratio of retweet-to-tweet
Dest ratio of retweet/time	Src ratio of mentions to tweet
Src retweets with hastags	Src avg tweets per day
Src retweet containing URL	Src ratio of mentions-to-tweet
Src avg tweets per day	Dest ratio of mentions-to-tweet
Dest # of retweets by account	Dest volume of tweets

Given two users, we observed that the attributes of the followers (destination nodes) account for 40% of the optimal subset of features, in informative events, and for 20% in trending events. In recent happenings in online social networks, it has been observed that discussions and threads that impact trending events are not usually trending in nature. For instance, the much publicized propaganda campaign during the U.S. 2016 elections targeted users on both sides of the political divide by exposing them to opinions formulated over time, using hashtags and shortened URLs. Irrespective of the type of event, social homogeneity and source's (1) ratio of retweet per time period (2) volume of tweets over account's lifetime (3) ratio of retweets to tweets (4) average number of tweets, prove to be important in the information diffusion process.

We notice that the follower's features are powerful enough to impede diffusion in informative events but these abilities diminish as the event becomes trending. As topics become viral, the number of followers a user has ranks third in trending events. Combining it with a high ratio of retweets to tweets, mention rate, and active interaction from followers, will boost the user's reach. It is inadequate to assign importance to an account across all networks and topics, as seen in [10], if the authority it wields vary with changing topic, event and social network. It is paramount that the relevance of a user be decoupled across social networks, especially Twitter, since a considerable number of users maintain a level of anonymity. For instance, a user will not run a web search on an account to confirm the authenticity of its posts before reacting on Twitter. Also, a user that is authoritative on health-related issues on Twitter might be an unreliable source of health-related posts on Facebook. Throughout this research, we demonstrated that the role of the followers in diffusion prediction is more than just a contribution to the follower count of the sender, and should combine the effectiveness of the interaction of each follower with their friend. Our results show that the influence a user wields in a network is an aggregate of his influence over each of the nodes in the network.

4.4 Time to Tweet

The results from our experiment validate our assumptions that the extent to which messages diffuse will be significantly influenced by the time when they are created. As observed in the top-15 most important features, see Table 4, for both the follower and followee in the network, the time period where most of their messages (original tweets and reaction) fall are crucial to propagation. Experimental results show that more than 75% of informative posts fall into the 2nd (6:00–11:59 am) and 4th (6:00–11:59 pm) time periods, but those of trending posts are in the 3rd (12:00–5:59 pm) and 4th (6:00–11:59 pm) time periods. It is interesting to note that both Twitter event types got considerable attention during the 4th time period as this for most people is a time to catch up with the day's activities. However, we observed that the best time to tweet an informative message on Twitter for maximum diffusion is in the 2nd time period, while trending is in the 4th. We speculate that the contrast in peak diffusion times can be due to the reactive nature of trending events, occurring mostly after the day's activities, unlike the active nature of informative events, where a user is mostly putting opinion out.

5 Crowdsourcing for Early Trending Topic Detection

In this section we discuss the concept of crowdsourcing in OSNs, and why it is important. We describe the experiment and experimental results on adopting MIDMod-OSN for crowdsourcing the early detection of trending topics.

5.1 Using MIDMod-OSN for the Early Detection of Trending Topics

Individuals and organizations looking to use Twitter as an advertising or political campaign platform will find it useful to know ahead of time if a newly created message or hashtag will become trending, in order for them to maximize the attention for personal gain or minimize negative exposure. Similarly, organizations attempting to neutralize the spread of misinformation during crisis scenarios could monitor users' reactions to previously identified harmful-misinformation-carrying messages, and predict whether these messages will become viral before this determination can be done via standard methods, like counting tweets.

In the past, individuals and organizations have used OSNs like Twitter as an avenue to obtain ideas in a crowdsourcing context. In this section, we apply the MIDMOD-OSN model to view a user's reaction to a post as an implicit contribution towards crowdsourcing, where users' posts and reactions to posts serve as a form of criticism or validation, report on crisis and event, advert of product and service, protest, or even political campaign. While some users react to posts from all event types (trending and informative), others only react (share, quote, favorite, reply or retweet) to tweets that are trending or about to attain the trending status because of the need to share or contribute to hot topics. This kind of users can serve as discriminants in the model that predicts the trending character of a message. The goal of the prediction task is to show that the diffusion behavior and OSN behavior of users is useful for predicting the trending character of a message when the reaction count is unavailable.

5.2 Experiment Design and Results

For this experiment, we are interested particularly in evaluating the usefulness of users' reactions to predicting message virality. It is for this reason that we must avoid (1) including specific message features in the classifier and (2) including – explicitly or implicitly – counts of tweets relating to a specific message. The first requirement fits naturally with our previous model, which only relies on user, rather than message features. To satisfy the second requirement, we must construct an experiment that treats each user interaction with the message independently of all others. That is, we purposely make a prediction of virality from each user interaction, rather than combining all user interactions into a single model.

Our model predicts if a message will go viral or not, by including the diffusion property *diffuse/not diffuse* of the message as an independent variable during the training phase. We examine how users on Twitter relate with posts of their friends by building a classifier to distinguish user interactions based on the virality status of the message. For a message m, where $m \in \{1, \ldots, M\}$, spread over a network with n interactions, we train a model that predicts the virality status of the message based on the diffusion behavior observed along each one of the n links along which the message propagates. This results in n distinct predictions. The overall predicted output is calculated as the majority virality status observed across the n interactions. We select 1000 messages –500 each– from trending and informative event types and evaluate the MIDMod-OSN's ability to predict if a message will go viral or not. We run the experiment with 10000 users. With this fraction of the network, we were able to show that to a certain degree that the diffusion behavior and OSN behavior of users is useful for predicting the trending character of a message without having to count the number of reactions. The prediction model saw precision, recall and F1 scores of 65%, 75%, and 70% respectively. We should note here that when attempting to predict message virality, one should consider a more comprehensive model, including message attributes and a joint treatment of all user reactions to a specific message. Nevertheless, the results of this experiment demonstrate that crowdsourcing (at least part of) the detection mechanism is not without merit.

6 Conclusion and Future Work

Predicting information diffusion will continue to be an active research area due to the fast growing importance of online social networks. In this paper, we studied the problem of identifying features that impact diffusion in different types of Twitter events. We created the MIDMod-OSN model and trained it using 55 features extracted directly from the Twitter REST API and outperformed the prediction power of state-of-the-art models. We further established that a prediction model based on the top-15 most important features, selected by our feature selection framework, is optimal in correctly predicting diffusion, achieving an AUC score of 96% in both event types. Our main theoretical contribution is distinguishing between Informative and Trending Twitter events, and teasing out differences in information diffusion patterns. Even though they are generally overlooked, informative posts make up a big chunk of messages shared on social networks. We showed the differences between the pattern of interaction between users when exchanging these kinds of posts and trending posts. Additionally, we establish the divergence in features influencing reaction to post, with 40% of the top ranked features belonging to the followers in informative events and 20% in trending events. From our results, we infer that for an influence maximization model to be effective, it needs to combine centrality concepts for control, efficiency and activity. Future work may include more complex prediction tasks, involving the use of latent user and message attributes for predicting user reactions to posts based on the user's perceived veracity of the post in OSNs.

Acknowledgment. This work was supported in part by the U.S. National Science Foundation under grants No. 1527579 and 1619201.

References

1. Acar, A., Muraki, Y.: Twitter for crisis communication: lessons learned from japan's tsunami disaster. Int. J. Web Based Communities **7**(3), 392–402 (2011)
2. Chen, W., Wang, C., Wang, Y.: Scalable influence maximization for prevalent viral marketing in large-scale social networks. In: Proceedings of the 16th ACM SIGKDD International Conference on Knowledge Discovery and Data Mining, pp. 1029–1038. ACM (2010)
3. Domingos, P.: Mining social networks for viral marketing. IEEE Intell. Syst. **20**(1), 80–82 (2005)

4. Ferrara, E., Wang, W.-Q., Varol, O., Flammini, A., Galstyan, A.: Predicting online extremism, content adopters, and interaction reciprocity. In: Spiro, E., Ahn, Y.-Y. (eds.) SocInfo 2016. LNCS, vol. 10047, pp. 22–39. Springer, Cham (2016). https://doi.org/10.1007/978-3-319-47874-6_3
5. Granovetter, M.: Threshold models of collective behavior. Am. J. Sociol. **83**(6), 1420–1443 (1978)
6. Guille, A., Hacid, H., Favre, C.: Predicting the temporal dynamics of information diffusion in social networks. arXiv preprint arXiv:1302.5235 (2013)
7. Kempe, D., Kleinberg, J., Tardos, É.: Maximizing the spread of influence through a social network. In: Proceedings of the Ninth ACM SIGKDD International Conference on Knowledge Discovery and Data Mining, pp. 137–146. ACM (2003)
8. Lewis, K., Gonzalez, M., Kaufman, J.: Social selection and peer influence in an online social network. Proc. Natl. Acad. Sci. **109**(1), 68–72 (2012)
9. Neppalli, V.K., Medeiros, M.C., Caragea, C., Caragea, D., Tapia, A.H., Halse, S.E.: Retweetability analysis and prediction during hurricane sandy. In: ISCRAM (2016)
10. Rao, A., Spasojevic, N., Li, Z., Dsouza, T.: Klout score: measuring influence across multiple social networks. In: 2015 IEEE International Conference on Big Data (Big Data), pp. 2282–2289. IEEE (2015)
11. Saito, K., Kimura, M., Ohara, K., Motoda, H.: Generative models of information diffusion with asynchronous timedelay. In: Proceedings of 2nd Asian Conference on Machine Learning, pp. 193–208 (2010)
12. Saito, K., Nakano, R., Kimura, M.: Prediction of information diffusion probabilities for independent cascade model. In: Lovrek, I., Howlett, R.J., Jain, L.C. (eds.) KES 2008. LNCS (LNAI), vol. 5179, pp. 67–75. Springer, Heidelberg (2008). https://doi.org/10.1007/978-3-540-85567-5_9
13. Spasojevic, N., Li, Z., Rao, A., Bhattacharyya, P.: When-to-post on social networks. In: Proceedings of the 21th ACM SIGKDD International Conference on Knowledge Discovery and Data Mining, pp. 2127–2136. ACM (2015)
14. Subramani, M.R., Rajagopalan, B.: Knowledge-sharing and influence in online social networks via viral marketing. Commun. ACM **46**(12), 300–307 (2003)
15. Wang, F., Wang, H., Xu, K.: Diffusive logistic model towards predicting information diffusion in online social networks. In: 2012 32nd International Conference on Distributed Computing Systems Workshops (ICDCSW), pp. 133–139. IEEE (2012)
16. Xiang, R., Neville, J., Rogati, M.: Modeling relationship strength in online social networks. In: Proceedings of the 19th International Conference on World Wide Web, pp. 981–990. ACM (2010)

Nonsubmodular Constrained Profit Maximization from Increment Perspective

Liman Du, Shengminjie Chen, Suixiang Gao, and Wenguo Yang(✉)

School of Mathematical Sciences,
University of Chinese Academy of Science, Beijing 100049, China
yangwg@ucas.edu.cn

Abstract. The growing importance of online social networks where people share information with others leads to the emergence of viral marketing, a new way to promote the sales of products. A derivation of classical Influence Maximization (IM) problem is the Profit Maximization (PM) problem that we focus on in this paper. We propose the PM problem with a cardinality constraint in order to make the problem closer to the real world. Without a fixed and pre-determined budget for seed selection, the profit spread metric of PM considers the total benefit and cost. The difference between influence spread metric and profit spread metric is that the latter is no longer monotone and lose the property of submodularity in general. Due to the natural form as the difference between two submodular functions, the profit spread metric admits a DS decomposition. What matters is that we design a Marginal increment-based Prune and Search (MPS) algorithm. From the perspective of marginal increment, MPS algorithm can compute profit spread more directly and accurately. Extensive experiments demonstrate the effective and outperformance of our algorithm.

Keywords: Profit maximization · Nonsubmodularity · Social network

1 Introduction

Due to their fast development, Online Social Networks (OSNs) become powerful mediums for spreading innovations. The market of OSNs advertisement is growing explosively. A managing partner of a consulting firm claimed in [1] that the e-commerce industry in the U.S. was worth approximately $500 billion in 2018 and had been one of the fastest growing areas of the economy.

In OSNs, users can share their opinions about an event or a promoted product with other users, and this kind of information dissemination is in unprecedented prosperity nowadays. In the IM problem, a positive integer k is given and the problem aims to find a set of k seeds which maximizes the total number

Supported by National Natural Science Foundation of China under Grant No. 11991022 and No. 12071459. We would like to express our appreciation to the anonymous reviewers who have helped to improve the paper.

S. Chellappan et al. (Eds.): CSoNet 2020, LNCS 12575, pp. 451–463, 2020.
https://doi.org/10.1007/978-3-030-66046-8_37

or expected number of active nodes in a social network. In [2], Kempe et al. firstly consider the issue of choosing influential sets of individuals as a discrete optimization problem, prove the problem is NP-hard under both Independent Cascade (IC) model and Linear Threshold (LT) model and propose a greedy algorithm which yields (1–1/e)-approximation due to the submodularity and monotone properties of the influence spread. As shown in [3], computing exact influence in general networks under the LT model is #P-hard. Many follow-up, such as [4–9], further study IM problem in term of improving efficient implementation of algorithms, extending the maximization from a practical view and so on. When an OSN provider is hired to conduct the viral marketing campaign, it not only receives commission from the advertiser but also pay for the information propagation. Therefore, the OSN provider needs to account for both the benefit and cost of influence spread to maximize its profit. As an extension of IM, Tang J. et al. propose the PM problem whose aim is to find all the nodes that can maximize the profit in online social networks and define a general profit metric that can be expressed as the difference between benefit function and cost function in [11,12]. Given that the benefit function is the total benefit brought by all the nodes activated, it is a submodular function. As for cost function, it is also submodular when it represents the total cost incurred by the whole active nodes, different from the budget constraint studied by previous works. Therefore, profit metric is a nonsubmodular and non-monotone function.

A lot of studies in [13–15] focus on submodular optimization while nonsubmodular optimization has been attracting more scholars' attention for many years. As summarized in [16], there are many approaches to solve nonsubmodular optimization problems. One of them is DS decomposition mentioned in [17–20]. As shown in [17,18], every set function $f : 2^X \rightarrow R$ can be expressed as the difference of two monotone nondecreasing submodular functions g and h, i.e., $f = g - h$, where X is a finite set. Based on the theorem, many algorithms such as the modular-modular algorithm and iterated sandwich algorithm are proposed.

We observe some real marketing process and come to the conclusion that although the vast majority of companies select some users to help them promote products, the number of selected users is severely limited. The reason may be that excessive marketing not only bring profit but also incur greater cost. In this paper, we formulate the profit maximization problem with a cardinality constraint and accurately explain the profit function from the marginal increment perspective. The constrained profit maximization (CPM) problem aims to select at most k nodes such that the total profit generated by activated nodes is maximized. Different from existing common methods, we can obtain the marginal gain of profit from the perspective of marginal increment. Generally speaking, the profit spread function is neither submodular or monotone. Hence the CPM problem is a kind of nonsubmodular optimization problem. Due to its definition, profit function can be naturally expressed as the difference between two submodular functions. Therefore, we design a Marginal increment-based Prune and Search (MPS) algorithm. A algorithm whose goal is reducing the search space is devised in the pruning phase and two algorithms inspired by the classic greedy algorithm and the DS decomposition method respectively are designed for selecting seed nodes.

The rest of this paper is organized as follows. In Sect. 2, we propose our formulation of the nonsubmodular CPM problem. Then, we derive MPS algorithm, a two-phase algorithm based on marginal increment method, in Sect. 3. Our experiment settings are introduced in Sect. 4 and results confirm the effectiveness of MPS algorithm. Concluding remarks and suggestions on the future works are given in Sect. 5.

2 Problem Formulation

2.1 Constrained Profit Maximization

In this section, we give CPM problem as follows. It should be emphasized that the marginal increment and CPM problem is not restricted by the diffusion model, and we take IC model for example. Given a directed graph $G = (V, E, P)$, a constant k, benefit b_v and cost c_v for each node $v \in V$, CPM problem aims to find a seed set S which includes at most k nodes to maximize the return profit.

We formulate the profit function from the perspective of marginal increment and describe the profit function value as accurate as possible. For the given directed graph $G = (V, E, P)$, nodes in V represent users and edges in E represent the connections among users. Each node v is associated with benefit b_v and cost c_v. For any directed edge $< u, v >\in E$, refer to v as a neighbor of u and refer to u as an inverse neighbor of v. Denote $N_u = \{v : v \in V, < u, v >\in E\}$. Let $p_{u,v}$, associated with each edge $< u, v >\in E$, represents the activate probability from node u to node v. The diffusion process starts with a given set $S \subseteq V$ which includes all the active nodes. When a node u firstly becomes active, for each node $v \in N_u$, it has a single chance to activate v and succeeds with probability $p_{u,v}$. The diffusion process ends when there are no more nodes can be activated. Denoted $\phi(S)$ as the profit generated by a seed node set S. It is obvious that $\phi(S) = \beta(S) - \gamma(S)$, where $\beta(S)$ is the benefit of influence spread generated by a seed set S and $\gamma(S)$ is the total spread cost incurred by the whole nodes activated by S. The goal of constrained profit maximization problem is to find a seed set S satisfying $|S| \leq k$ to maximize the profit $\phi(S)$. Then, we will discuss more details about $\phi(S)$.

Property 1. $\phi(S) = \beta(S) - \gamma(S)$ is a non-submodular and non-monotone function in general.

2.2 Analysis of Profit Function

In this section, we will analyze the property of benefit function and cost function respectively from the perspective of marginal increment. The analysis will assist us reacquainting profit function.

Marginal Increment. Before discussing more details about benefit function and cost function, we recall some definitions about marginal increment provided in [21,22] as follows.

Definition 1. *Suppose that $f : 2^V \to R$ is non-negative set function, where V is the ground set. For any subset A of V, $\triangle_v f(A) = f(A \cup \{v\}) - f(A)$ is called the marginal gain of $v \in V \backslash A$ at A. In addition, $\triangle_B f(A) = f(A \cup B) - f(A)$is defined as the marginal gain of $B \subseteq V \backslash A$ at A.*

It is well-known that for a non-negative set function $f : 2^V \to R^+$ defined on the ground set V, f is a monotone function if $f(A) \leq f(B)$ for any $A \subseteq B \subseteq V$ and is submodular, if $f(A)+f(B) \geq f(A \cup B)+f(A \cap B)$ for any $A, B \subseteq V$. According to above definitions, we can easily infer two properties. One is that for a given set $S \subseteq V$ and any subset $A \subseteq S$, $f(S) = f(S\backslash A)+\triangle_A f(S\backslash A) = f(A)+\triangle_{S\backslash A} f(A)$ for any given set function f. The other is that when f is monotone, $\triangle_A f(S\backslash A) \leq \triangle_B f(S\backslash B)$ and $\triangle_{S\backslash A} f(A) \geq \triangle_{S\backslash B} f(B)$ for any subset $A \subseteq B \subseteq S$.

Benefit Spread Function. At first, we formulate the benefit spread function from the perspective of marginal increment. According to the result of Jiang T. et al. in [11,12], it is obvious that benefit spread function $\beta(S)$ of influence spread generated by a seed set S is the benefit brought by all the nodes activated. Then, let $b_v^X \in (0, b_v]$ be the benefit spread of $v \in V$ with seed node set X, and for any $v \in V$, $b_v^{\emptyset} = 0$. Denote $\triangle b_v^X(u) = b_v^{X\cup\{u\}} - b_v^X$ as the marginal gain of the profit on node v when a new node u is selected as seed node. Then following formulas are proposed to calculate $\triangle b_v^X(u)$, the marginal gain of benefit spread function at node v.

Property 2. The marginal gain $\triangle b_v^X(u) = \left(b_v - b_v^X\right) p_{u,v} b_u^X$ for any $v \in N_u$ and for any $w \in N_v$, we have

$$\triangle\, b_w^X(u) = \frac{b_v - b_w^X}{1 - p_{(u,v)} b_v^X} p_{v,w} \triangle\, b_v^X(u)\,. \tag{1}$$

Furthermore, if a node can be reachable from node u, we can update the marginal gain according to the topology order in recursive manner and we define $\triangle b_w^X(u) = 0$ for node w which is unreachable from node u.

Then, we can conclude that the objective function of benefit spread can be expressed as

$$\beta(X) = \sum_{v \in V} b_v^X = \sum_{v \in V} \sum_{u \in X} \triangle b_v^{X^u}(u)\,, \tag{2}$$

where X^u is the set of nodes that have already activated before node u. Denote $X = \{v_1, v_2, \ldots, v_{\widehat{k}}\}$ as a node set which contains all the nodes that can be selected as seed, $\widehat{k} = |X|$, $X^k = \{v_1, v_2, \ldots, v_k\}$, $k = 1, 2, \ldots, \widehat{k}$ and $X^0 = \emptyset$ for convenience. Then $\beta(X)$ can be rewritten as $\beta(X) = \sum_{k=1}^{\widehat{k}} \triangle_k \beta\left(X^{k-1}\right)$, where $\triangle_k \beta\left(X^{k-1}\right) = \sum_{v \in V} \triangle b_v^{X^{k-1}}(v_k)$. We also have a property of $\beta(X)$ as follows.

Property 3. $\beta(X) = \sum_{v \in V} \sum_{u \in X} \triangle b_v^{X_u}(u) = \sum_{k=1}^{\widehat{k}} \triangle_k \beta\left(X^{k-1}\right)$ is submodular and monotone decrease with $b_v^{X^{k-1}}$, for any $v \in V$ and $k = 1, 2, ..., \widehat{k}$

Cost Function. We have formulated and analyzed the property of benefit spread function, and it is time to turn to the cost spread function. Generally speaking, the cost function changes during the spread process. The cost of influence propagation induced by a seed set X is the total cost incurred by all the nodes activated. Therefore, from the marginal increment perspective, let c_v^X be the cost spread of $v \in V$ with seed node set X. Denote $\triangle c_v^X(u) = c_v^{X \cup \{u\}} - c_v^X$ as the marginal gain of the cost on node v when a new node u is selected as seed node, and for any $v \in V$, if $v \notin X$, $c_v^{\emptyset} = 0$. We formulate the cost spread function as

$$\gamma(X) = \sum_{v \in V} c_v^X = \sum_{v \in V} \sum_{u \in X} \triangle c_v^{X^u}(u), \tag{3}$$

where X^u is the set of nodes that have already activated before node u. Let $X = \{v_1, v_2, \ldots, v_{\widehat{k}}\}$ represent the node set that includes all the candidate nodes, $\widehat{k} = |X|$, $X^k = \{v_1, v_2, \ldots, v_k\}$, $k = 1, 2, \ldots, \widehat{k}$ and $X^0 = \emptyset$. Then $\gamma(X) = \sum_{k=1}^{\widehat{k}} \triangle_k \gamma\left(X^{k-1}\right)$, where $\triangle_k \gamma\left(X^{k-1}\right) = \sum_{v \in V} \triangle c_v^{X^{k-1}}(v_k)$. We can see that another property of cost function $\gamma(X)$ can be proposed as follows.

Property 4. $\gamma(X) = \sum_{k=1}^{\widehat{k}} \triangle_k \gamma\left(X^{k-1}\right)$ is submodular and monotone decrease with $c_v^{X^{k-1}}$, for $v \in V$, and $k = 1, 2, \ldots, \widehat{k}$.

3 Algorithm for Constrained Profit Maximization Problem

We devise a marginal increment-based two-phase algorithm MPS for CPM problem. One of the highlights of the MPS algorithm is that benefiting from the method of marginal increment, we can compute the benefit spread function and cost spread function more accurately. At the first phase of MPS, we use Modified Iterative Prune (MIP) algorithm to reduce search space. Then, we can select seed nodes by one of the two different algorithms proposed in Sect. 3.3.

3.1 Marginal Increment Computation

First of all, we consider $\phi(X) = \beta(X) - \gamma(X)$, where $\beta(X)$ and $\gamma(X)$ is the total benefit and cost of all the nodes activated respectively. From the perspective of marginal increment, for any $X \subseteq V$ only containing seed nodes, the benefit and cost can be expressed as $\beta(X) = \sum_{v \in V} b_v^X = \sum_{v \in V} \sum_{u \in X} \triangle b_v^{X^u}(u)$, $\gamma(X) = \sum_{v \in V} c_v^X = \sum_{v \in V} \sum_{u \in X} \triangle c_v^{X^u}(u)$. We design two algorithms to compute $\beta(X)$ and $\triangle \beta^X(u)$ respectively. And the method for computing $\gamma(X)$ and $\triangle \gamma^X(u)$ is the same as that for computing $\beta(X)$ and $\triangle \beta^X(u)$. Inspired by some existing studies of nonsubmodular optimization, there are several ways to deal with $\phi(X)$. It should be emphasized that this profit spread metric can be viewed as the difference between two submodular functions. Therefore, algorithm based on DS decomposition can be used naturally. We propose a two-phase framework to solve the CPM problem, which includes pruning phase and search phase.

Algorithm 1. Marginal Increment for computing $\beta(X)$

Input: $G(V,E)$, IC model and candidate set $X = \{u_1, u_2, \ldots, u_k\}$, $b_v^{X^i}$ for any $v \in V$
Output: function value $\beta(X)$
Initialize $i = 0$ and $b^{X^i} = \{..., b_v^{X^i}, ...\}$
for $u_i \in X$ **do**
update $b^{X^i} = \{..., b_v^{X^i}, ...\}$ with $b_v^{X^i} = b_v^{X^{i-1}} + \left(1 - b_v^{X^{i-1}}\right) p_{u_i,v} b_{u_i}^{X^{i-1}}$ for each $v \in V$ according to the topological order
end for
$\beta(X) = \sum_{v \in V} b_v^{X^k}$
return $\beta(X)$

Algorithm 2. Marginal Increment for computing $\triangle\beta^X(u)$

Input: a reference set $X \subseteq V$ and a node $u \in V \backslash X$
Output: marginal gain $\triangle\beta^X(u)$
for $v \in V$ **do**
compute $\triangle b^X(u) = \{..., \triangle b_v^X(u), ...\}$ with $\triangle b_v^X(u) = \left(1 - b_v^X\right) p_{u,v} b_u^X$ according to the topological order
end for
$\triangle\beta^X(u) = \sum_{v \in V} \triangle b_v^X(u)$
return $\triangle\beta^X(u)$

3.2 Pruning Phase

Considering the constraints of PM problem mentioned in [12], the marginal profit gain is bounded below by the smallest benefit gain less the largest cost gain and bounded above by the largest benefit gain less the smallest cost gain. Apparently, for any node $v \in V$, if the lower bound of marginal profit gain is positive, v may be selected in an optimal solution of PM. Similarly, a node v cannot be selected in an optimal solution when its marginal profit gain is bounded up by a negative number. Starting with $A_0 = \emptyset$, $B_0 = V$, $t = 0$, algorithm mentioned in [12] extends the idea in an iterative manner and return A_t as A^*, B_t as B^* when they are converged. It is proved that for any global maximizer S^* of a unconstrained profit problem, it holds that $A_t \subseteq A_{t+1} \subseteq A^* \subseteq S^* \subseteq B^* \subseteq B_{t+1} \subseteq B_t$ for any $t \leq 0$. Therefore, only the nodes in $B^* \backslash A^*$ need to be further examined for seed

Algorithm 3. Modified Iterative Prune (MIP)

start with $A_0 \leftarrow \emptyset$, $B_0 \leftarrow B$ and $t = 0$
repeat
  $A_{t+1} \leftarrow A_t \cup \{u : \triangle\beta^{B_t \backslash \{u\}}(u) - \triangle\gamma^{A_t}(u) > 0 \text{ and } u \in B_t \backslash A_t\}$
  $B_{t+1} \leftarrow B_t \backslash \{u : \triangle\beta^{A_t}(u) - \triangle\gamma^{B_t \backslash \{u\}}(u) < 0 \text{ and } u \in B_t \backslash A_t\}$
  $t \leftarrow t + 1$
until $A_t = A_{t+1}$ and $B_t = B_{t+1}$
return A_t as A^*, B_t as B^*

selection. However, when a cardinality constraint is added, the problem becomes more difficult. In order to make the computation easier, we remove some nodes in V to obtain a node set $B \subset V$ satisfying the condition that the size of $S^* \backslash B$ is as small as possible. And based on it, we design Modified Iterative Prune (MIP) algorithm. It requires skill to choose an appropriate start baseline B. Many methods mentioned in [23] can be studied further more. In the experiments, we adopt two different strategies and compare their performance.

3.3 Search Phase

Considering the natural DS decomposition form of profit function, we propose two algorithms in the search phase. One practical algorithm is the Marginal Increment Greedy Algorithm shown as Algorithm 4. The other available method is the Improved Modular-Modular algorithm given as Algorithm 5.

Marginal Increment Greedy Algorithm. Given a directed graph $G(V, E)$ where V represents the whole user and E is the set of their relations. After conducting MIP algorithm, we can obtain A^* and B^*. As above discussion reveals, all the nodes in A^* has a non-negative marginal profit gain and may be selected as seed node for CPM problem while every $v \in V \backslash B$ cannot be contained in any optimal seed node set. If $|A^*| \leq k$, the seed node set X is initialized as A, else $X = \emptyset$. In each iteration, MIGA algorithm selects node u which has the largest marginal profit gain $\triangle\phi^X(u) = \triangle\beta^X(u) - \triangle\gamma^X(u)$ and adds it into X. Repeat the process until no node left has positive marginal gain or $|X| > k$. In the meanwhile, we propose another algorithm, which is based on the ModMod procedure and also be combined with MIP algorithm to solve the CPM problem.

Improved Modular-Modular Algorithm. The ModMod procedure introduced by Iyer and Bilmes in [17] aims to optimize set function expressed as the difference between submodular functions. And given that only nodes in B^* should be considered for CPM, we can obtain two modular upper bounds of $\gamma(Y)$ which are both tight at a given set X^t for any $Y \subseteq V$ as

Algorithm 4. Marginal Increment Greedy Algorithm (MIGA)

Input: $G(V,E)$, a constant k, A^*, B^*
Output: a set of k nodes $X \subseteq B^*$

```
if |A*| ≤ k then
    X = A*
else
    X = ∅
end if
while |X| ≤ k do
    u ← arg max_{u∈B*} (△β^X(u) − △γ^X(u))
    update △β^X(u) and △γ^X(u)
    if △β^X(u) − △γ^X(u) ≤ 0 then
        return X
    end if
    X ← X ∪ {u}
end while
return X
```

$$\gamma(Y) \leq m^1_{X^t}(Y) = \gamma(X^t) - \sum_{u \in X^t \backslash Y} \triangle\gamma^{B^* \backslash \{u\}}(u) + \sum_{u \in Y \backslash X^t} \triangle\gamma^{X^t}(j), \quad (4)$$

$$\gamma(Y) \leq m^2_{X^t}(Y) = \gamma(X^t) - \sum_{u \in X^t \backslash Y} \triangle\gamma^{X^t \backslash \{u\}}(u) + \sum_{u \in Y \backslash X^t} \triangle\gamma^{\emptyset}(j). \quad (5)$$

For convenience, we denote $m_{X^t}(Y)$ represent above two tight upper bound, i.e., $m_{X^t}(Y)$ can be explained as $m^1_{X^t}(Y)$ or $m^2_{X^t}(Y)$. Let π be any permutation of V that places all the nodes in $X^t \subseteq V$ before the nodes in $V \backslash X^t$. Let $S^\pi_i = \{\pi(1), \pi(2), \ldots, \pi(i)\}$ be a chain formed by the permutation, where $S^\pi_0 = \emptyset$ and $S^\pi_{|X^t|} = X^t$. Define $h^\pi_{X^t}(\pi(i)) = \beta(S^\pi_i) - \beta(S^\pi_{i-1})$. Then, $h^\pi_{X^t}(Y) = \sum_{v \in Y} h^\pi_{X^t}(v)$ is a lower bound of $\beta(Y)$ for any $Y \subseteq V$ tight at X^t.

Algorithm 5. Improved Modular-Modular Algorithm (IMM)

```
Initialize t ← 0
if |A*| ≤ k then
    X^0 = A*
else
    X^0 = ∅
end if
repeat
    choose the permutations of X^0, X^t\X^0, B*\X^t and concatenate them as π
    X^{t+1} ← arg max_{Y⊆B*} h^π_{X^t}(Y) − m_{X^t}(Y)
    t ← t + 1
until |X^t| > k or X^t = X^{t−1}
Return X^t
```

4 Experiments

In this section, we conduct experiments on three data sets to test the effectiveness of MPS algorithm for optimizing ϕ, and compare it with other different algorithms. When cost function represents the total cost of seed nodes, i.e. $\phi(X) = \sum_{v \in V} b_v^X - \sum_{u \in X} c(u)$, we can view it as a special case of $\phi(X)$.

4.1 Experiment Setup

A synthetic graph and two real-world social graphs are used in our experiment. We will describe them more precisely in the following. We can see a wide variety of relationship can be represented by these social graphs.

Synthetic: This is a relatively small acyclic directed graph randomly generated with 2708 nodes and 5278 edges.

Facebook: The Facebook data set consists of 4039 users and 88234 edges collected from survey participants and has been anonymized.

Wikipedia: The Wikipedia data set is generated by a voting activity, containing 7115 nodes and 103689 edges. Nodes in the network represent wikipedia users and a directed edge from node i to node j represents that user i voted on user j.

All the data sets come from Stanford Large Network Dataset Collection and only have the relationship between two nodes. We use the Independent Cascade propagation model. For ease of comparison, we have some assumption as follows. For the propagation probability, we use a trivalency model in [21], selecting a value from $(0.1, 0.01, 0.001)$ at random. And the profit of each node is set to be 1. The strategies we use in the experiment include:

Random: It randomly selects k nodes. We run the algorithm 10 times and take their average value as the expected profit.

MaxDegree: We select top k nodes according to their degree.

MGIA: We conduct the MIGA algorithm where $A^* = \emptyset$ and $B^* = V$.

MPS with B^1: It includes two phases. MIP algorithm is conducted and the MIGA is carried out subsequently. In the pruning phase, all the nodes are sorted according to their degree and top 500 nodes is included in B.

MPS with B^2: This algorithm is similar to MPS with B^1 mentioned above while each node in the start baseline B has at least two adjacent edges.

The algorithms are all implemented in MATLAB and the experiments are carried out on a machine with an Inter Core i5-6200U 2.30 GHz CPU and 8 GB memory. The running time of MPS algorithm is greatly sensitive to the choice of B and under above setup the MPS algorithm takes several hours in average.

4.2 Exprement Result

In this section, we value the effectiveness of MPS. First of all, we compare the effect of two different start baseline. Then, we show the relation of cost and profit spread value. The last but not least is the comparison with other seed nodes selection algorithms.

In Fig. 1, we can see that different start baselines can produce different effect on the effectiveness of MPS algorithm. Due to the different definitions of B^1 and B^2, it is inevitable that more potential seed nodes are excluded from B^1, resulting in a small profit spread value in Facebook and Wikipedia. And in Fig. 2, it is obvious that the change speed of profit spread value decreases with the increasing cost. Judging from this result, the constraint of seed node set's size is important when the cost is not small. The Fig. 3 illustrates that MPS outperforms other algorithms excluding MIGA. And the difference between MIGA and MPS with B^2 is small. It should be noted that the difference is smaller in Wikipedia network than in Facebook network. Therefore, MPS may perform better in a network which contains more nodes and edges. We can also arrive at a conclusion that MPS will perform better with the a more ideal start baseline B_0.

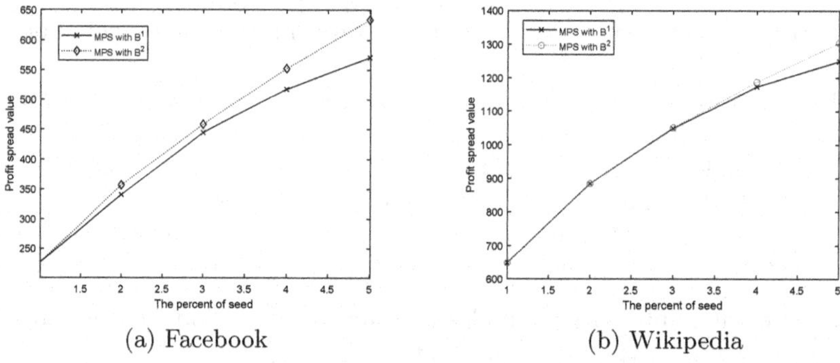

(a) Facebook (b) Wikipedia

Fig. 1. Profit spread value versus different prune start baseline

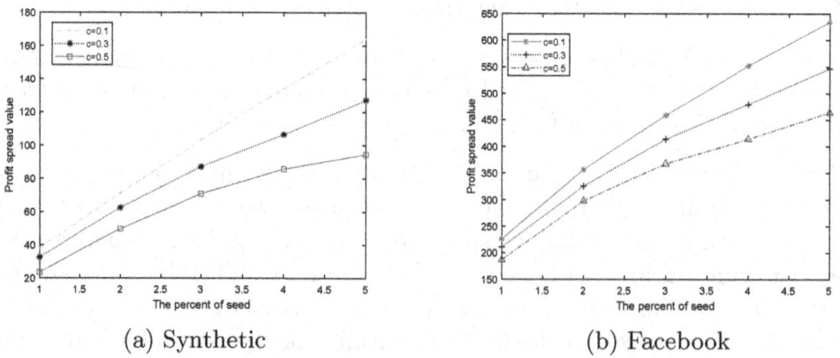

(a) Synthetic (b) Facebook

Fig. 2. Profit spread value versus different cost

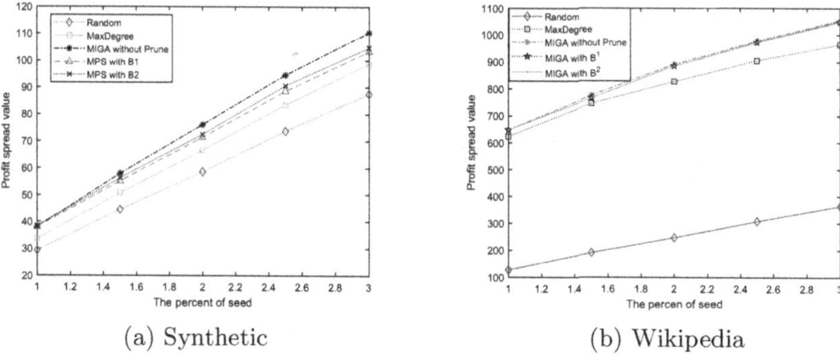

(a) Synthetic (b) Wikipedia

Fig. 3. Comparison with other methods

5 Conclusion and Future Works

In this paper, we have studied the CPM problem and formulate it from an incremental marginal gain perspective. Given that the objective function of CPM problem lacks submodularity in general, we design MPS algorithm to optimize the profit function. In the first phase, MIP algorithm is used to reduce the search space. The MIGA and IMM algorithm are devised in the second phase to select at most k seed nodes. Based on the marginal increment method, these algorithms calculate the profit function as accurate as possible. Experimental results show that our MPS algorithm substantially outperform some other algorithms, and it is also perform well with submodular profit metric after a few adjustments.

Several research directions of CPM problem deserve further study. The first and most problem is how to select the baseline of MIP algorithm. We can see that B in MIP algorithm directly affects the algorithm's efficiency and performance and MPS algorithm is feasible in large-scale social networks with a ideal B. Therefore, the property of a ideal baseline B need to be studied. Beyond that, more efforts on study whether MPS algorithm can generate a constant approximation is significant.

References

1. George D.: Google, Facebook and Amazon are the only winners in Ecommerce. https://www.entrepreneur.com/article/328478. Last accessed 5 Sep 2020
2. Kempe, D., Kleinberg, J., Tardos, E.: Maximizing the spread of influence through a social network. In: 9th ACM SIGKDD International Conference on Knowledge Discovery and Data Mining, pp. 137–146. ACM, New York (2003)
3. Chen, W., Wang, C., Wang, Y.: Scalable influence maximization for prevalent viral marketing in large-scale social networks. In: ACM SIGKDD International Conference on Knowledge Discovery and Data Mining, pp. 1029–1038. ACM, New York (2010)

4. Kempe, D., Kleinberg, J., Tardos, É.: Influential nodes in a diffusion model for social networks. In: Caires, L., Italiano, G.F., Monteiro, L., Palamidessi, C., Yung, M. (eds.) ICALP 2005. LNCS, vol. 3580, pp. 1127–1138. Springer, Heidelberg (2005). https://doi.org/10.1007/11523468_91
5. Kimura, M., Saito, K.: Tractable models for information diffusion in social networks. In: Fürnkranz, J., Scheffer, T., Spiliopoulou, M. (eds.) PKDD 2006. LNCS (LNAI), vol. 4213, pp. 259–271. Springer, Heidelberg (2006). https://doi.org/10.1007/11871637_27
6. Even-Dar, E., Shapira, A.: A note on maximizing the spread of influence in social networks. In: Deng, X., Graham, F.C. (eds.) WINE 2007. LNCS, vol. 4858, pp. 281–286. Springer, Heidelberg (2007). https://doi.org/10.1007/978-3-540-77105-0_27
7. Borgs, C., Brautbar, M., Chayes, J., et al.: Maximizing social influence in nearly optimal time. In: 25th ACM-SIAM Symposium on Discrete Algorithms, pp. 946–957. Society for Industrial and Applied Mathematics, USA (2014)
8. Youze, T., Xiaokui, X., Yanchen, S.: Influence maximization: near-optimal time complexity meets practical efficiency. In: the 2014 ACM SIGMOD International Conference on Management of Data (SIGMOD 2014), pp. 75–86. ACM, New York (2014)
9. Youze, T., Yanchen, S., Xiaokui, X.: Influence maximization in near-linear time: a martingale approach. In: The 2015 ACM SIGMOD International Conference on Management of Data (SIGMOD 2015), pp. 1539–1554. ACM, New York (2015)
10. Goyal, A., Lu, W., Lakshmanan, L.V.S.: SIMPATH: an efficient algorithm for influence maximization under the linear threshold model. In: 13th International Conference on Data Mining, Vancouver, BC, pp. 211–220. IEEE (2011)
11. Tang, J., Tang, X., Yuan, J.: Profit maximization for viral marketing in online social networks: algorithms and analysis. IEEE Trans. Knowl. Data Eng. **30**(6), 1095–1108 (2018)
12. Tang, J., Tang, X., Yuan, J.: Towards profit maximization for online social network providers. arXiv:1712.08963 (2017)
13. Lee, J., Mirrokni, V., Nagarajan, V., Sviridenko, M.: Maximizing nonmonotone sub-modular functions under matroid or knapsack constraints. SIAM J. Disc. Math. **23**(4), 2053–2078 (2010)
14. Gupta, A., Roth, A., Schoenebeck, G., Talwar, K.: Constrained non-monotone submodular maximization: offline and secretary algorithms. In: Saberi, A. (ed.) WINE 2010. LNCS, vol. 6484, pp. 246–257. Springer, Heidelberg (2010). https://doi.org/10.1007/978-3-642-17572-5_20
15. Feldman, M., Naor, J., Schwartz, R.: A unified continuous greedy algorithm for submodular maximization. In: 52nd Annual Symposium on Foundations of Computer Science (FOCS 2011), USA, pp. 570–579. IEEE Computer Society (2011)
16. Wu, W., Zhang, Z., Du, D.Z.: Set function optimization. J. Oper. Res. Soc. China **7**(2), 183–193 (2019)
17. Iyer, R., Bilmes, J.: Algorithms for approximate minimization of the difference between submodular functions, with applications. In: 28th Conference on Uncertainty in Artificial Intelligence (UAI 2012), Arlington, Virginia, pp. 407–417. AUAI Press (2012)
18. Narasimhan M., Bilmes J.: A submodular-supermodular procedure with applications to discriminative structure learning. In: 21st Conference on Uncertainty in Artificial Intelligence (UAI 2005). arXiv:1207.1404

19. Bai W., Bilmes J.: Greed is still good: maximizing monotone submodular + supermodular functions. In: Dy, J., Krause, A. (eds.) 35th International Conference on Machine Learning (ICML 2018). LNCS, vol. 80. pp. 304–313. PMLR (2018)
20. Li, X., Du, H.G., Pardalos, P.M.: A variation of DS decomposition in set function optimization. J. Comb. Opt. **40**(1), 36–44 (2020). https://doi.org/10.1007/s10878-020-00560-w
21. Yang, W., et al.: Marginal gains to maximize content spread in social networks. IEEE Trans. Comput. Soc. Syst. **6**(3), 479–490 (2019)
22. Yang, W., Zhang, Y., Du, D.-Z.: Influence maximization problem: properties and algorithms. J. Comb. Opt. **40**(4), 907–928 (2020). https://doi.org/10.1007/s10878-020-00638-5
23. Erkol, Ş., Castellano, C., Radicchi, F.: Systematic comparison between methods for the detection of influential spreaders in complex networks. Sci. Rep. **9**, 15095 (2019). https://doi.org/10.1038/s41598-019-51209-6

BNnet: A Deep Neural Network for the Identification of Satire and Fake Bangla News

Abdullah Al Imran[1(✉)], Zaman Wahid[2], and Tanvir Ahmed[3]

[1] American International University-Bangladesh, Dhaka, Bangladesh
abdalimran@gmail.com

[2] Daffodil International University, Dhaka, Bangladesh
jaman35-953@diu.edu.bd

[3] University of Central Florida, Orlando, USA
tanvir.ahmed@ucf.edu

Abstract. Misleading and fake news in rapidly increasing online news portals in Bangladesh has become a major concern to both the government and public lately, as a substantial amount of incidents have taken place in different cities due to unwarranted rumors over the last couple of years. However, the overall progress of research and innovation in detecting fake and satire Bangla news is yet unsatisfactory considering the prospects it would bring to the decision-makers of Bangladesh. In this study, we have amalgamated both fake and real Bangla news from quite a pool of online news portals and applied a total of seven prominent machine learning algorithms to identify real and fake Bangla news, proposing a Deep Neural Network (DNN) architecture. Using a total of five evaluation metrics: Accuracy, Precision, Recall, F1 score, and AUC, we have discovered that DNN model yields the best result with an accuracy and AUC score of 0.90 respectively while Decision Tree performs the worst.

Keywords: Bangla · Fake news identification · Text classification · Natural Language Processing · Deep Neural Network

1 Introduction

Reading news online has become increasingly popular over the last few years in Bangladesh, superseding the traditional way of getting updated with contemporary incidents by reading hard-copies of newspapers delivered to one's door every morning. In proportion to the fact, online news portals have significantly been increased in numbers adapting to the modern way of revenue generation of which the potential is underlined exponentially. However, to attract visitors in websites, it is often a practised approach of using satire and misleading headlines, even by the well-established and prominent newspaper companies in Bangladesh. Back in 2015 in Bangladesh, a news posted on a renowned online news portal

S. Chellappan et al. (Eds.): CSoNet 2020, LNCS 12575, pp. 464–475, 2020.
https://doi.org/10.1007/978-3-030-66046-8_38

was shared by millions of people as they read that their most favorite actor, Abdur Razzak, is no more. Nonetheless, a few percentage of people could get the subtlety that the actor is dead in the latest movie he was doing, not in real life. The panic in people sustained over weeks, however the practise of publishing satire and fake news with an incredible technique of making the news seemingly true to increase the website traffic is substantially sky-rocketed at times. While having over 1000 newspapers published online daily from Bangladesh, finding genuine news have become quite difficult out of the inundation of fake and satire news.

Over the years, Natural Language Processing, a branch of Artificial Intelligence, has been playing key roles in understanding written languages and providing insightful solutions to respective problem domains on demand, especially of detecting fake news. While the advancement of leveraging machine learning techniques in the prediction of fake and satire news in English is laudable, the progress for the Bangla news is not yet substantial. In this study, we have applied seven prominent machine learning and NLP algorithms: Logistic Regression, Naive Bayes, Decision Tree, Random Forest, K-Nearest Neighbors, Support Vector Machine, and Deep Neural Network, to identify satire and fake Bangla news and find out the best model in terms of performance. Using web scraping techniques, we have formed a dataset collecting both fake and real news from various online news portals of Bangladesh, The Daily Star, Jagonews, BDNews24, for example. To evaluate the model performance, we have used five major evaluation metrics namely Accuracy, Precision, Recall, F1 Score, and Area under the ROC curve (AUC). After a comparative analysis of the results of the experiment, we have found Deep Neural Network as the best classifier of predicting fake Bangla news with an accuracy and AUC score of 0.90, respectively. However, due to the poorest performance with an accuracy and AUC score of 0.86, respectively, the Decision Tree classifier is labeled as the least performer in the detection of satire and fake Bangla news.

The findings of this study can be utilized by the experts in not only detecting the satire, fake Bangla news spreading throughout the country but also finding out the major companies involved in this kind of practice to take appropriate actions. Not limiting the prospects, software engineers and researchers can build tools to provide more reliable filtered news to the public, reducing the negative consequences it would bring otherwise. The rest of the paper is divided and organized in the following sections: Related Works, Data Description, Data Preprocessing, Methodology, Result & Analysis, and Conclusion and Future Work.

2 Related Works

Being a low-resourced language, Bangla does not have very rich literature in the domain of Natural Language Processing (NLP). In this section, we briefly discuss the existing applications of NLP and it's advancements that are relevant to this study.

Abu Nowshed et al. [1] applied the Naive Bayes classifier to classify the category or group of Bangla news articles based on the news code of the International

Press Telecommunications Council (IPTC). To prepare the dataset, they have built a web crawler and extracted texts from different web pages. In the preprocessing phase, they tokenized the words, removed the stopword, and applied a light-weight Bangla stemmer. They used the Inverse Document Frequency (IDF) method for feature extraction. Finally, a Naive Bayes classifier was trained on the preprocessed dataset to classify the news categories. They presented the evaluation of the model by using a Recall-Precision graph.

RN Nandi et al. [2] performed a study on content-based recommendation systems for Bangla news using doc2vec, Latent Semantic Analysis (LSA), and Latent Dirichlet allocation (LDA) algorithm. In their study, they have performed qualitative and quantitative experiments on a large Bangla news corpus which has more than 3,00,000 uncategorized articles and a human-generated triplet dataset. Their findings have shown that doc2vec can provide more contextual recommendations than LSA and LDA and also yields an outperforming accuracy (=91%) on the human-generated triplet dataset. For the quantitative experiment, they have trained a t-SNE model to project the word vectors into a lower dimension and visualized the clusters in a 2D space.

Ankita Dhar et al. [3] used two similarity measure techniques namely cosine similarity, and euclidean distance, and five classification algorithms namely J48, Naive Bayes, Naive Bayes Multinomial, Random Forest, Simple Logistic to classify Bangla text documents from multiple domains such as Business, State, Medical, Sports, and Science texts. They have used the TF-IDF feature extraction techniques to extract features from 1000 text documents. 50% of the total documents from each of the five domains have been used for training and the rest of the documents have been used for testing purposes. They found that between the two distance measures, cosine similarity yields the recognition accuracy (=95.80%). Whereas, among the five classifiers, Naive Bayes Multinomial resulted in the highest precision score (=90.80%).

Zahrul Islam et al. [4] performed a study on the readability of Bangla news articles for children where they have observed children news articles in Bangla based on four difficulty levels. For building a news corpus, they crawled data from the children news articles of four popular news sites in Bangladesh and one from West Bengal. Using the data they built the news corpus that was categorized by the ages of children. To build a corpus for representing the child level difficulty, they collected data from textbooks of grade two to grade ten that have been used for teaching at different school levels in Bangladesh. For feature selection, they have used Lexical and Information-Theoretic based features. Finally, they used 80% of the corpus to train a Support Vector Machine (SVM). The rest of the 20% data has been used for assessing the model's performance. Their model achieved an accuracy of 85.60% and an F-Score of 84.46%.

Mustakim Al et al. [5] aimed to measure the similarity of Bangla news articles and hence assign the article to its respective topic. To build the corpus, they collected 7134 news articles from 200 different topics from the "The Daily Prothom Alo" using a web crawler. For measuring the similarity, they have used Bi-grams with Latent Dirichlet Allocation (LDA) algorithm. They also applied the Doc2Vec method and showed a comparison of performance between LDA and Doc2Vec. They found that LDA cosine similarity gives a 95.15% similarity which is almost close to the human interpreter whereas Doc2Vec performed poorly and gave only a 68.54% similarity score. Later in this study, they used the train LDA model to classify the news articles to their respective topics.

Anirudha et al. [6] proposed a way to calculate similarity and apply summarization on Bangla news documents by applying various data mining techniques, making a crawler to crawl 993 news articles from popular newspaper websites in Bangladesh. Their study was divided into two major parts: finding similar documents using DBSCAN and summarizing selected documents depending on priority values assigned to the preprocessed sentences. To find the similarity among the documents, they have used the cosine similarity. For evaluation, they used the N-gram units between human-made summary and algorithm produced summary (ROUGE-N) method to evaluate the performance of the methods. They found that the TF method got the best precision score (=0.4503), and the TF-IDF method got the best recall score (=0.5354).

Md. Majharul et al. [7] proposed a new methodology for Bengali news document summarization that outperformed the existing works. Their approach incorporates the sentence frequency technique for redundancy elimination and sentence clustering technique based on cosine similarity ratio among sentences. To ensure the maximum coverage of information in the summary, it takes sentences from each cluster based on the volume of the cluster. They have used two human-generated summary data sets for training and testing the system. Their methodology yielded an average Precision, Recall, and F-measure score of 0.608, 0.664, and 0.632 respectively which outperformed the state-of-the-art performance for Bengali news summarization.

From the above study, we can observe that most of the studies include common NLP applications such as newsgroup or topic classification, content-based recommendation, text summarization, and language form classification [10]. However, narrowly focusing on the identification of originality of Bangla news vital to shape and control the social aspects of Bangladesh is yet unexplored; which we are trying to explore in this study proposing a DNN architecture.

3 Data Description

The data has been collected using web scraping from various Bangla news portals. Initially, we have listed 43 websites of Bangla news portals among which 25 are real, renowned, and validated news portals and 18 are fake and sarcastic news portals. The attributes we have considered to prepare the dataset are discussed in Table 1. Table 2 includes a few examples of news titles with corresponding categories and labels.

The entire dataset contains 500 observations that include the aforementioned 4 attributes. We have collected news from 31 unique categories. In total there are 257 observations labeled as "Real" news and 243 observations labeled as "Fake"

Table 1. Description of the dataset

Attribute	Description	Discussion
Title	The title of the news article	The title can be the primary indicator for classifying the news
Category	The category of the news article	The category may also help us in the classification process and further analysis
Description	The first paragraph of the news article	Usually, the first paragraph contains an overview of the entire article. It will help us extract important features
Class	The class label (Real/Fake) for the article	We set a class label manually for each observation. It is our target class for the supervised classification problem

Table 2. Example of few news titles

Title	**Translation**	**Category**	**Label**
অস্ত্রোপচারের পর ভালো আছেন কাদের	Kader is fine after the surgery	Politics	Real
এইচএসসির ফলাফল ১৯ জুলাই! পাশের হার ৩০%!	HSC results on July 19! The pass rate is 30%!	Education	Fake
তাসকিনের বিরুদ্ধে বউ পেটানোর অভি-যোগ!	Taskin accused of beating his wife!	Sports	Fake
গভীর নলকূপের পানির বিশুদ্ধতা নিয়ে আশঙ্কা	Concerns about the purity of deep tube well water	Latest News	Real

news. The dataset is well balanced and distributed to be used for a supervised classification task.

4 Data Preprocessing

Data preprocessing is one of the most crucial processes of a Data Mining experiment, especially in the Natural Language Processing (NLP) tasks. The malformation and unstructuredness of text data throw extra preprocessing challenges when the data is collected from various internet sources using web scraping. In this phase, we have performed three preprocessing tasks namely denoising, normalization, and stemming.

4.1 Denoising

When the data is scraped from various web pages, it usually brings up extra noises such as HTML tags, extra spaces, character encoding, and escape characters. These extra noises must be cleaned to make the data usable, called the process "denoising". To clean the noises found in our dataset such as '\r', '\n', HTML tags: '<br>', '<p>' and extra white-spaces, we have written a hard-coded program to automate the process of denoising.

4.2 Normalization

While processing unstructured text data, normalization generally refers to a process that puts a sequence of words on equal footing and allows processing to proceed uniformly. Depending on the language, text data requires different types of text normalization such as case conversion, removing punctuations, accent marks, diacritics, removing stop words, and sparse terms. In the case of our Bangla textual data, we have applied two normalization techniques: i) punctuation removal, ii) stop word removal. Listing all the 20 punctuation marks available in Bangla language, we applied a removal function over the entire dataset as well as a removal operation for a total of 398 Bangla stop words.

4.3 Stemming

A stem is the portion of a word that is left after removing its prefixes and suffixes [8], and the process is called stemming. However, it is useful for dealing with sparsity issues as well as standardizing the vocabulary. In this study, we have applied a rule-based Bengali stemmer that was proposed and developed by MR Mahmud et al. in their Bangla NLP research [9].

5 Methodology

5.1 Feature Extraction

One of the core steps for a typical NLP task is to transform the raw or annotated text into numeric features, which gives the machine learning models a simpler and focused view of the text. In this study, we have performed two types of feature extraction:

1. Applying the TF-IDF technique with Bag-of-Words to extract numeric features from the textual columns such as "Title", and "Description".
2. Applying One-Hot Encoding to encode and extract features from the categorical column, "Category".

After performing all the feature extraction steps, we have merged all the features to finalize the preprocessed dataset which is ready for modeling. All the feature extraction steps and algorithms are briefly discussed below.

5.1.1 Bag-of-Words (BoW): BoW takes a text document as input and outputs a table where each row corresponds to a document and each column represents a unique word. The entries are the frequency counts of each word in each document, which is calculated by using the following formula:

$$TF = \frac{Number\,of\,occurrence\,of\,a\,word}{Total\,words\,in\,a\,document} \quad (1)$$

5.1.2 Term Frequency-Inverse Document Frequency (TF-IDF): In TF-IDF, the term TF refers to Term Frequency which is the frequency of the word in the current document (output of the BoW model) and the term IDF refers to Inverse Document Frequency which is the score of the words among all the documents. The inverse term frequency of a word is calculated by using the following formula:

$$IDF\,(word) = \frac{Total\,number\,of\,documents}{Number\,of\,documents\,containing\,the\,words} \quad (2)$$

And, the TF-IDF is the product of these two frequencies, TF and IDF:

$$TF - IDF = TF \times IDF \quad (3)$$

While applying the TF-IDF technique, we set a value of 0.01 to the "min_df" parameter which means that when building the vocabulary it will ignore terms that have a document frequency strictly lower than the given threshold. After applying TF-IDF, we have got 673 features as a result.

5.1.3 One-Hot Encoding: One-Hot Encoding, also known as a 1-of-K encoding scheme, is a popular categorical value encoding and feature extraction method that takes a categorical column having 'n' categories and constructs 'n' different binary features for each category. Applying the method to the "Category" column consisting of 31 unique news categories, the one-hot encoder yielded 31 new features for each of the categories.

5.1.4 Splitting the Preprocessed Data: After performing all the feature extraction processes, we have merged all the features to construct the final preprocessed dataset containing 704 features in total. Using the 80:20 ratio for the train-test split, we used 400 and 100 observations respectively for the training and testing of the models.

5.2 Classification Algorithms

In this study, we have explored 7 different machine learning algorithms of different genres. From the probabilistic genre we have used Logistic Regression (LR) and Naive Bayes (NB); Decision Tree (DT) and Random Forest (RF) has been picked from the tree-based genre; K-Nearest Neighbors (KNN) is from distance-based and Support Vector Machine (SVM) from the kernel-based genre.

Apart from these traditional algorithms, we have also employed a Deep Neural Network approach. The deep neural network is a neural network with multiple intermediate layers which learns the complex patterns from an enormous volume of data. In a DNN, there are three types of layers: an input layer, intermediate or hidden layers, and an output layer. Each layer contains a bunch of neurons or nodes which are the basic unit of a neural network. In terms of the DNN architecture, every adjacent layer is fully connected to one another, meaning every neuron in the layer is connected to every neuron in the adjacent layers. Between each layer, there is a component called the activation function which performs the functional mappings between the inputs and response variable making the network non-linear. In this study, we have built a DNN architecture with an input layer, an output layer, and five intermediate hidden layers. The input layer contains 704 neurons, the first, second, third, fourth, and fifth hidden layer contains 512, 256, 128, 64, and 32 neurons respectively, whereas the output layer contains only one neuron since we have a binary output. The "Sigmoid" activation function has been used between the fifth hidden layer and the output layer. In all other layers, we have used the "ReLU" activation function. All the parameters were fine-tuned to ensure the best prediction performance. The following Fig. 1 represents our proposed DNN architecture.

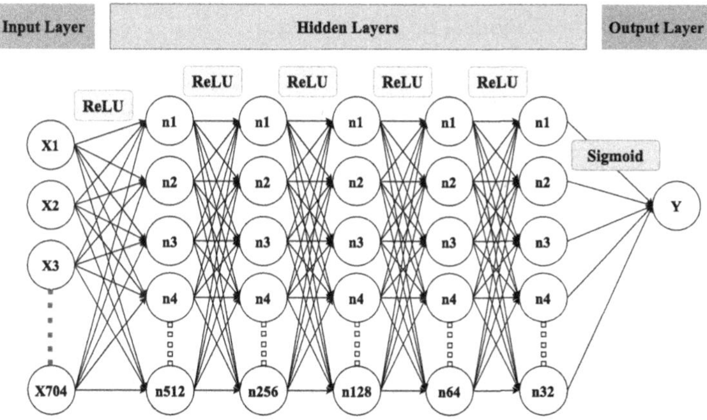

Fig. 1. DNN architecture used in this study

5.3 Evaluation Metrics

To mathematically derive the evaluation metrics, we have used the notations of the confusion matrix such as True Positives (TP), True Negatives (TN, False Positives (FP), and False Negatives (FN). The 5 evaluation metrics we have used to assess the predictive performance of the models are given below:

1. $Accuracy = \frac{TP+TN}{TP+TN+FP+FN}$
2. $Precision = \frac{TP}{TP+FP}$
3. $Recall = \frac{TP}{TP+FN}$
4. $F1\,Score = 2 \times \frac{(Precision \times Recall)}{Precision + Recall}$
5. *Area Under the ROC Curve (AUC)* = AUC score is calculated from the Receiver Operating Characteristic (ROC) curve. A ROC curve plots the performance of a binary classifier under various threshold settings; this is measured by true positive rate and false positive rate. AUC is the area enclosed by the ROC curve. The range of possible AUC values is [0, 1]. A perfect classifier has AUC = 1 and a completely random classifier has AUC = 0.5.

6 Result and Analysis

This section briefly discusses the experimental results and shows a comparative analysis of the performance of the models. The experimental results have been recorded for each of the models with the five aforementioned evaluation metrics. The predictive performance of the models has been measured on the test data which is 20% (=100 observations) of the entire data. However, we have noted an additional validation performance while using a validation set for tuning the hyperparameters of the DNN model. The following Table 1 shows the predictive performance for all the 7 models on the test data.

Table 3. Results & comparative analysis of the seven models

Classifier	Accuracy	Precision	Recall	F1 Score	AUC
LR	0.87	0.87	0.88	0.87	0.87
NB	0.80	0.88	0.71	0.78	0.80
DT	0.76	0.78	0.75	0.76	0.76
RF	0.86	0.80	**0.96***	0.88	0.86
KNN	0.88	0.87	0.90	0.89	0.88
SVM	0.86	0.85	0.88	0.87	0.86
DNN	**0.90***	**0.89***	0.92	**0.90***	**0.90***

From the above table we can see that except recall, in all other evaluation metrics DNN model performs the best (accuracy = 0.90, precision = 0.89, f1-score = 0.90, auc = 0.90). The DNN algorithm also yielded a validation accuracy of 0.89 which is very consistent with the test accuracy. Whereas, the DT algorithm performs the lowest score in every evaluation criteria. A different scenario can be observed in the performance of the RF model. The RF model has yielded the best recall score (=0.96) which takes a very important consideration. We can have a clear comparative overview of the models performance in the following Fig. 2.

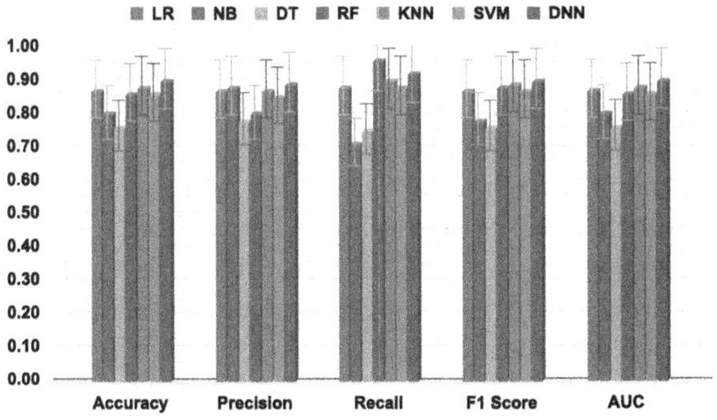

Fig. 2. Predictive Performances of the models.

Every evaluation metric has it's objective and importance according to the problem. That is why all the evaluation metrics may not have equal importance for evaluating the performance of a predictive model. In terms of our news classification problem, we have two primary considerations: (i) reducing the misclassification rate of the fake news, (ii) finding the best model that has a good balance between the false positive rate and false-negative rate.

Hence, for (i) we should pay attention to recall scores to assess the efficacy of reducing the misclassification rate. A recall is the ratio of the correctly classified fake news by the model to all which is a fake news in reality. From the above Fig. 1, we can see that, in terms of recall score, the RF model is the best (=0.96) performer.

For (ii), we should consider the AUC score to find the best-balanced classifier. For binary classification problems, AUC describes the trade-off between the true positive rate and the false positive rate which gives information about how the classifier is as compared to random guesses. AUC is a better metric for binary classifiers since it does not get biased on the size of test data. Figure 3 represents the ROC curves for each model along with its AUC score.

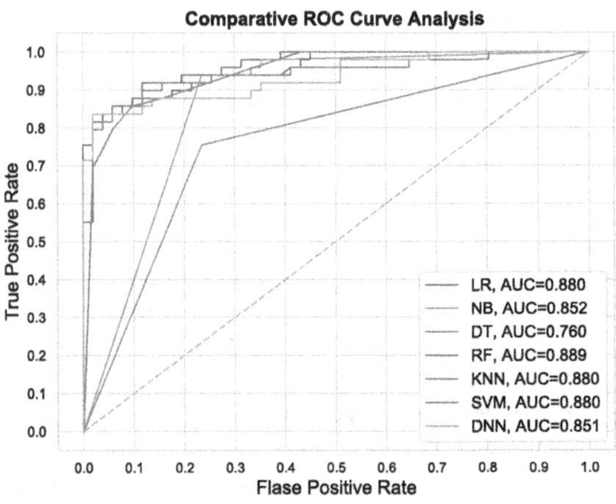

Fig. 3. Comparative ROC curve analysis

From the above Fig. 3, we can see that the ROC curve of the DNN model is very consistent at various thresholds settings. Also it yields the best AUC score (=0.90). So, by taking the best AUC score into account, we can consider the DNN model as the best balanced model for the news classification problem.

For qualitative analysis, we have projected the preprocessed high-dimensional data into a two-dimensional space using t-Distributed Stochastic Neighbor Embedding (t-SNE) algorithm. t-SNE is a non-linear algorithm for dimensionality reduction algorithm which is especially well suited for visualizing high-dimensional data in a lower dimension. It projects the high-dimensional data to a lower-dimensional space by minimizing the divergence between two distributions: a distribution that measures pairwise similarities of the input objects and a distribution that measures pairwise similarities of the corresponding low-dimensional points in the embedding. Hence, it tries to find patterns in the data by identifying observed clusters based on the similarity of data points and preserve the group of local data points that are close together. A t-SNE visualization will help us to perform the qualitative analysis and understand the relationship and distance between the "Fake" and "Real" news clusters. The following Fig. 4 shows the t-SNE visualization on a 2D space for all the data.

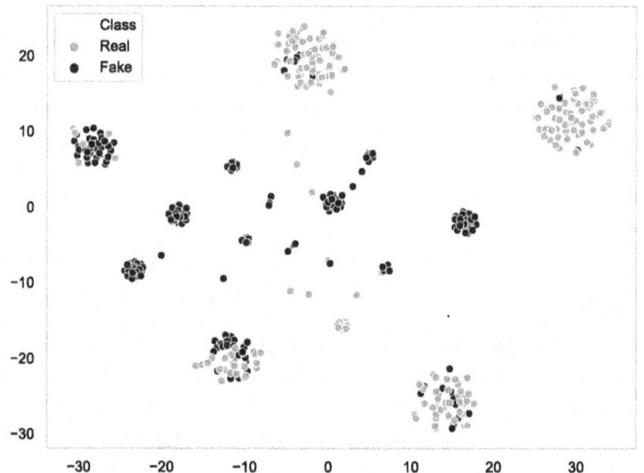

Fig. 4. Fake and real news clusters

From Fig. 4, we can observe that most of the "Real" and "Fake" news articles have common features in between them and lie very close within their own cluster. Each cluster maintains a significant distance which helped our classifiers to yield promising results.

7 Conclusion and Future Work

Our primary goal, in this study, was to classify satire and fake Bangla news on a web-scraped corpus of fake and real news from popular Bangladeshi online news portals. While serving this purpose we've investigated seven different, prominent machine learning algorithms and performed a comparative analysis to find out the best model among them in terms of overall performances and experimental results. Our experimental results show despite the fact that Random Forest performs highest for the efficacy of reducing the misclassification rate as the Recall Score is 0.96, the proposed DNN is labeled as the best classifier yielding superior performance in the rest of the four evaluation metrics, especially the AUC score of 0.90. Surprisingly, Decision Tree performed poorly as the lowest; the score in every metric is less than 0.77 which is a substantial difference from the others.

References

1. Chy, A.N., Seddiqui, M.H., Das, S.: Bangla news classification using Naive Bayes classifier. In: 16th International Conference Computer and Information Technology. IEEE (2014)
2. Nath Nandi, R., Arefin Zaman, M.M., Al Muntasir, T., Hosain Sumit, S., Sourov, T., Jamil-Ur Rahman, Md.: Bangla news recommendation using doc2vec. In: 2018 International Conference on Bangla Speech and Language Processing (ICBSLP). IEEE (2018)
3. Dhar, A., Dash, N., Roy, K.: Classification of text documents through distance measurement: an experiment with multi-domain Bangla text documents. In: 2017 3rd International Conference on Advances in Computing, Communication & Automation (ICACCA) (Fall). IEEE (2017)
4. Islam, Z., Rahman, R.: Readability of Bangla news articles for children. In: Proceedings of the 28th Pacific Asia Conference on Language, Information and Computing, pp. 309–317 (2014)
5. Mouhoub, M., Al Helal, M.: Topic modelling in Bangla language: an LDA approach to optimize topics and news classification. CIS **11**, 77 (2018)
6. Paul, A., et al.: Bangla news summarization. In: Nguyen, N.T., Papadopoulos, G.A., Jędrzejowicz, P., Trawiński, B., Vossen, G. (eds.) ICCCI 2017. LNCS (LNAI), vol. 10449, pp. 479–488. Springer, Cham (2017). https://doi.org/10.1007/978-3-319-67077-5_46
7. Haque, Md.M., Pervin, S., Begum, Z.: Automatic Bengali news documents summarization by introducing sentence frequency and clustering. In: 2015 18th International Conference on Computer and Information Technology (ICCIT). IEEE (2015)
8. Liu, B.: Web Data Mining: Exploring Hyperlinks, Contents, and Usage Data. Springer, Heidelberg (2007). https://doi.org/10.1007/978-3-540-37882-2
9. Mahmud, Md.R., Afrin, M., Razzaque, Md.A., Miller, E., Iwashige, J.: A rule based Bengali stemmer. In: 2014 International Conference on Advances in Computing, Communications and Informatics (ICACCI). IEEE (2014)
10. Parves, A.B., Al Imran, A., Rahman, Md.R.: Incorporating supervised learning algorithms with NLP techniques to classify Bengali language forms. In: Proceedings of the International Conference on Computing Advancements. ACM (2020). https://doi.org/10.1145/3377049.3377110

Graph-Based Supervised Clustering in Vector Space

Lily Schleider[1,2(✉)], Eduardo L. Pasiliao[1,2], and Qipeng P. Zheng[1,2]

[1] University of Central Florida, Orlando, FL 32816, USA
lily.schleider@knights.ucf.edu
[2] Air Force Research Laboratory, Munitions Directorate, Eglin AFB, FL 32542, USA

Abstract. Neural Networks are able to cluster data sets and our goal was to figure out how well the neural network clustered. The MNIST data set was ran through a neural network and the distances were extracted from both the feature and output layer. Five different distances were used on both layers. K-means clustering was used assess the clustering performance of each layer in the neural network. Results conveyed that the feature layer was not as proficient at clustering when compared to the output layer. The type of distance did not make a significant difference for clustering. These conclusions can be derived from qualitative observation of the cluster graphs. By observing the clustering performance of the different layers in the CNN, we are able to gain insight on the neural network.

Keywords: Neural networks · Feature layer · Output layer · Clustering

1 Introduction

Machine learning allows computers to "learn" from a training data set so it can make decisions and/or predictions. Neural networks are a fundamental aspect of machine learning. They work by recognizing patterns. A convolutional network applies a filter over the images and create a feature map. Convolutional neural networks (CNN) can have multiple filters and multiple feature maps. A max-pooling layer is applied in between filter convolutions in order to keep the most significant features while reducing the dimensions. The feature map created by the convolutions allow the machine to learn traits in the data set. Once the convolutions and maxpooling is done, everything is flattened into one dimension that is fully connected, which is the output layer.

Mao and Jain [3] designed a Linear Discriminant Analysis (LDA) network, Sammon's projection network, a Kohonen-Based Nonlinear Projection Network (NP-SOM), and a Nonlinear Discriminant Analysis Network (NDA). All of these networks utilize adaptive learning and are ideal for data sets where patterns

S. Chellappan et al. (Eds.): CSoNet 2020, LNCS 12575, pp. 476–486, 2020.
https://doi.org/10.1007/978-3-030-66046-8_39

change over time. They found that the NP-SOM was the best at data visualization while the Sammon's network was the best at maintaining cluster shape, data structure, and inter-pattern distances. The NDA was the best at classifying and the results from this paper were consistent with other analysis.

Research has been done that compares the performance between auto-learned features from Deep Convolutional Neural Networks (DCNN) and hand-crafted features. Their goal was to find a noninvasive method for detecting Circulating Tumor Cells in a wide variety of cancer types. The DCNN is trained from positive, negative, and false positive data sets. The false positives are classified into either hard or easy using K-means clustering method. The hard samples are added to the negative data set. The hard-false positive samples are given more weight during training in order to allow the classification boundary to get closer to the hard samples. They use sigmoid activation function in their convolutional layers. The hand-crafted features are made by using the Histogram of Gradients and Histogram of Color in the Support Vector Machine. It took the DCNN longer to run but it also performed better than the hand-crafted features. The DCNN also reduced the redundancy in the samples [4].

Pradheep and Srinivasan's [5] paper introduces diagonal based feature extraction and compares it to horizontal and vertical feature extraction. They used images of off-line handwritten letters that were written by different people as their data set. These images were scanned and had to be pre-processed before feature extraction. The features are extracted by moving across the diagonals in each zone, which are size 10×10 pixels. Each zone gets 19 sub features and they are averaged to get a single value of the entire zone. Next, a feed forward back propagation neural network executes the classification. They use log sigmoid activation function. This paper concluded that the diagonal feature extraction had a 97.84% accuracy and worked better than vertical or horizontal method.

K-means clustering organizes observations into clusters based on their means. The k in k-means clusters is the number of clusters you are trying to organize the data into. The algorithm selects a random 10 data points at first (we can call these the initial clusters). It then measures the distance between every other point and the initial cluster and groups it with the nearest of the initial clusters. It then finds the total variance in each of the clusters. It repeats these steps until the variation in each cluster is close to each other. If we wanted to find the best k, then we would plot the reduction in variation using different values of k and see where there is significant reduction of variance and choose that k. This is called an elbow plot. In our case, the MNIST data set has its predetermined clusters so we know $k = 10$ [2].

The primary focus of this paper is to determine how well the both the feature layer and the output layer of the CNN is able to cluster using k-means clustering. This would allow us to see at which stage the clustering is most effective and can give us an insight as to why it does. We can see how significant different layers and different distances are for the CNN to cluster. This would give us more information on CNNs and how they work.

2 Experiment

2.1 Dataset

The specific data set we worked with came from the Modified National Institute of Standards and Technology (MNIST) database. It consists of 60,000 training images and 10,000 testing images. The images are black and white and have handwritten digits 0–9 with a white background. Each image is 28×28 pixels. We had to have the images in forms of arrays so we could find the distance between the images. The arrays had numbers ranging from 0–255 with smaller numbers representing lighter shades and larger numbers representing darker shades. For example, the white background of the images would have 0's. We divided the numbers by 255 so we could normalize the numbers and have them be between 0–1.

Our goal was the figure out which images have edges in between them. The edges represent similarities between the images. Once we find the similarities, we can cluster the images based on their digit (Fig. 1).

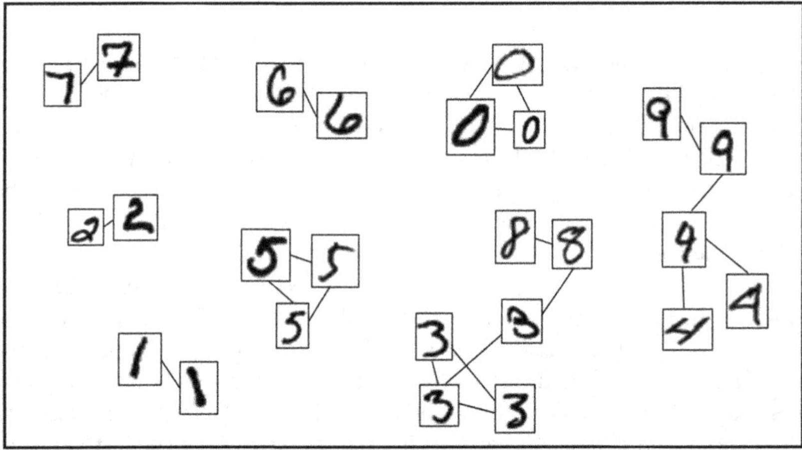

Fig. 1. This is a representative diagram. Notice how certain numbers have edges with other numbers that are a different digit (a 3 has an edge with an 8). This is an example of false alarms. There are also edges that should exist but do not (two 4's do not have an edge). This is an example of missed detection.

Our first step was the run the MNIST data through a CNN so we can extract the distances in both the feature layer and the output layer. The images were in the form of an array so we can find the distances easily. We used 5 different types of distances: dot product, Euclidean distance, Minkowski distance, Manhattan distance, and Chebyshev distance. We use these distances to create a k-means clustering graph. Jupyter Notebook was used for the clustering and Spyder was used for the CNN and distances. The Scikit-learn library was used for the clustering and Keras was used for the CNN (Fig. 2).

2.2 Distances

$$\boldsymbol{v}_i \qquad \leftarrow \text{Image vector } i \tag{1}$$

$$\mathrm{D}_p(\boldsymbol{v}_i, \boldsymbol{v}_j) = \left(\sum_k |\boldsymbol{v}_{ik} - \boldsymbol{v}_{jk}|^p\right)^{1/p} \qquad \leftarrow \text{Minkowski distance} \tag{2}$$

$$\mathrm{D}(\boldsymbol{v}_i, \boldsymbol{v}_j) = \sum_k |\boldsymbol{v}_{ik} - \boldsymbol{v}_{jk}| \qquad \forall i \leq j \leftarrow \text{Manhattan distance} \tag{3}$$

$$\mathrm{D}(\boldsymbol{v}_i, \boldsymbol{v}_j) = \left(\sum_k |\boldsymbol{v}_{ik} - \boldsymbol{v}_{jk}|^2\right)^{1/2} \qquad \forall i > j \leftarrow \text{Euclidean distance} \tag{4}$$

$$\mathrm{D}(\boldsymbol{v}_i, \boldsymbol{v}_j) = \max_k |\boldsymbol{v}_{ik} - \boldsymbol{v}_{jk}| \qquad \forall i \leq j \leftarrow \text{Chebyshev distance} \tag{5}$$

$$\mathrm{D}(\boldsymbol{v}_i, \boldsymbol{v}_j) = \sum_k (\boldsymbol{v}_{ik} \cdot \boldsymbol{v}_{jk}) \qquad \forall i \leq j \leftarrow \text{Dot product distance} \tag{6}$$

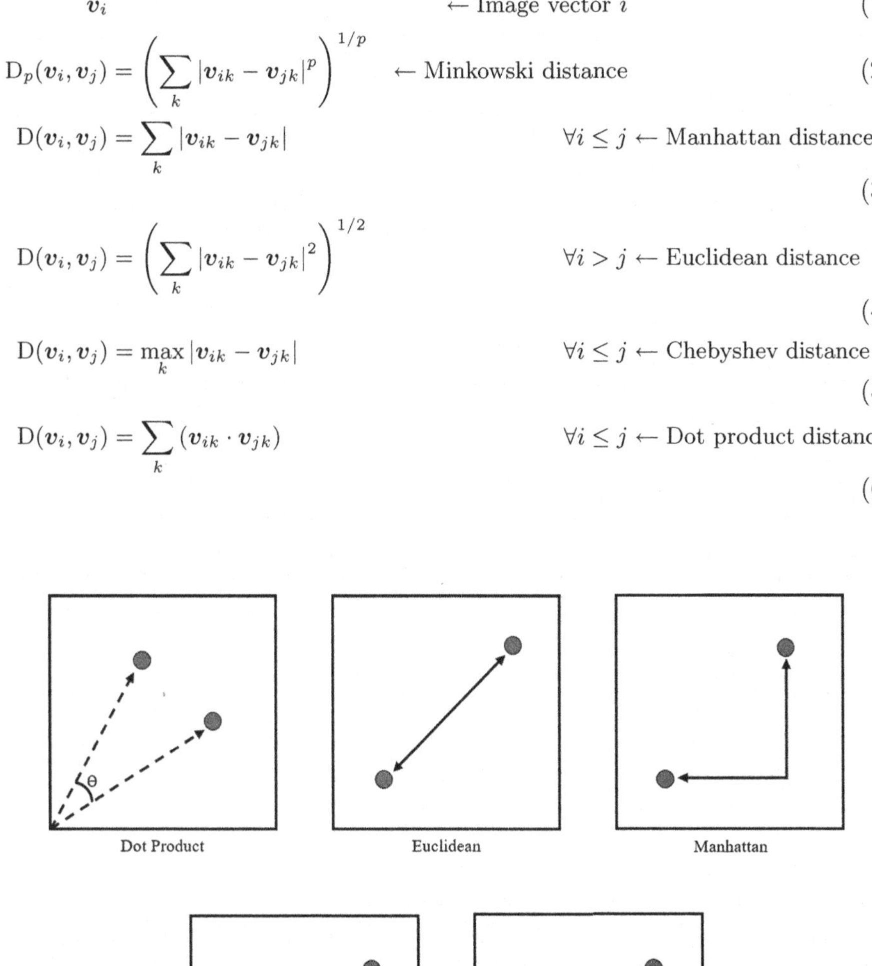

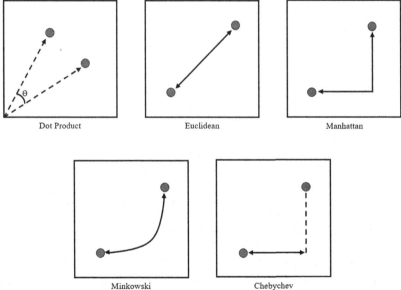

Fig. 2. Visual representation of the different type of distances that were used [1].

The dot product (6), also known as the scalar product, uses the length of two vectors and the angle between them. The Euclidean distance (4) finds the direct distance between two points in the vector space. The Manhattan distance (3) is similar except it only measures along vertical and horizontal axes with right angles. It is also known as the city block distance because it measures as if it is traveling across a city block grid. The Chebychev distance (5) calculates either the x distance or y distance depending on which is greater. It is also known as the chessboard distance. The Euclidean, Manhattan, and Chebychev distances are subsets of the Minkowski distance (when $p = 2$, $p = 1$ and $p = \infty$, respectively). The Minkowski distance (2) is determined in a normed vector space and can take in any p value. For our Minkowski distance, we used $p = 3$.

2.3 Convolutional Neural Network

Keras was used to create the CNN. The CNN was trained using the MNIST dataset. The CNN consists of a convolution layer, maxpooling layer, flatten layer, and two dense layers. The activation function relu was used in the convolutional and the first dense layer. Relu is a common activation function in neural networks and is defined as $y = max(0, x)$. The softmax activation was used in the last dense layer. Softmax is a normalized exponential function. It creates a normalized probability distribution. The feature layer and output layer were extracted and the distances were found for both of them. The flatten layer was retrieved from the flatten layer while the output layer was retrieved from the second dense layer.

3 Data and Results

The output layer distances were able to be clustered much better than the feature layer distances. We can use qualitative observations to see that the feature layer muddles the clustering while the output layer does a much better job at clustering. The clustering can be judged based on the clarity and distinctness of the clusters in the graph. A more distinct graph indicates better clustering.

The clustering from the feature layer displays errors and shows a lack of accuracy (Fig. 3, 4, 5, 6 and 7). There aren't any definite clusters. From the output layer clustering we can tell that the clusters are clear and defined (Fig. 7–8). Each digit has a clear cluster. The clustering is still not perfect. In the dot product distance metric, you can see that there is still some misclustering. For example, a zero is being misclustered as a 5 (Fig. 12). Overall the output layer was able to be clustered very well (Figs. 9, 10 and 11).

By qualitative observations of the graph, we can see that once we reach the output layer, the neural network was very good at clustering the MNIST data set, but it was not 100% accurate. As we saw, the output layer still made a couple of errors. The main difference between the layers is that there is a softmax function in the output layer, which was the key difference in improved clustering. There was only a significant difference in clustering when using dot product with the output layer. That was the only distance that made a couple of clustering errors. Other than that, the distance did not make a overwhelming difference.

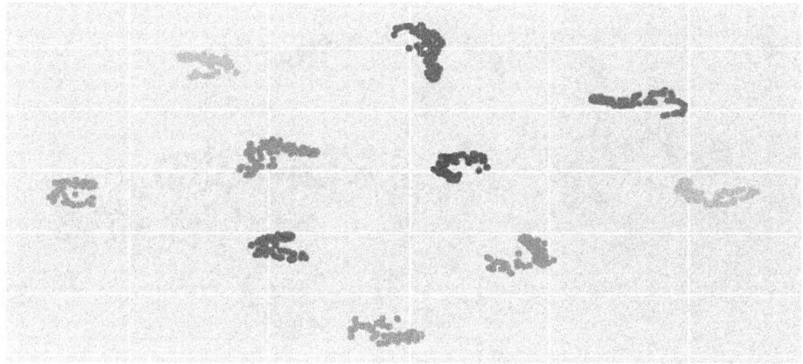

Fig. 3. Dot product on feature layer

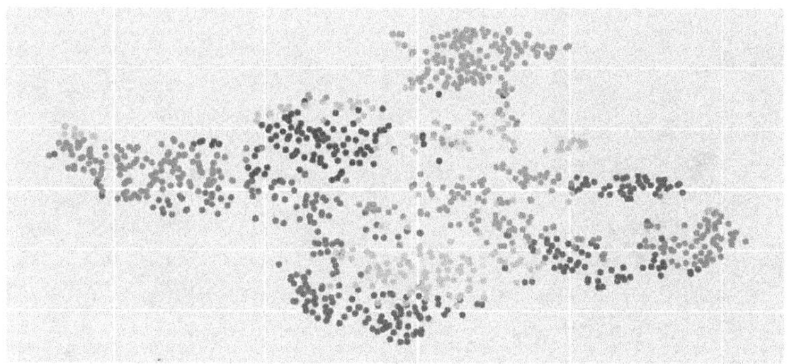

Fig. 4. Euclidean distances on feature layer

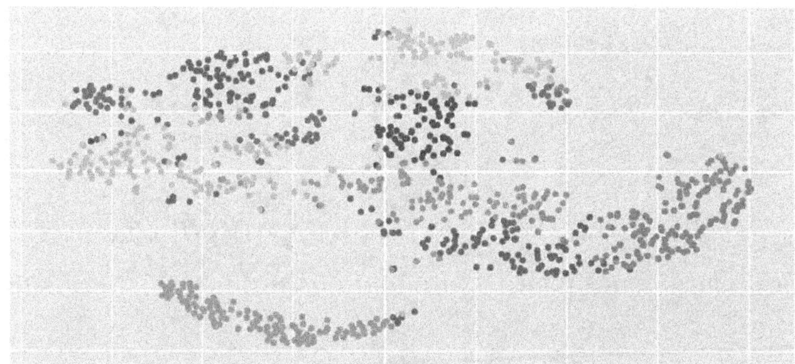

Fig. 5. Minkowski distances on feature layer

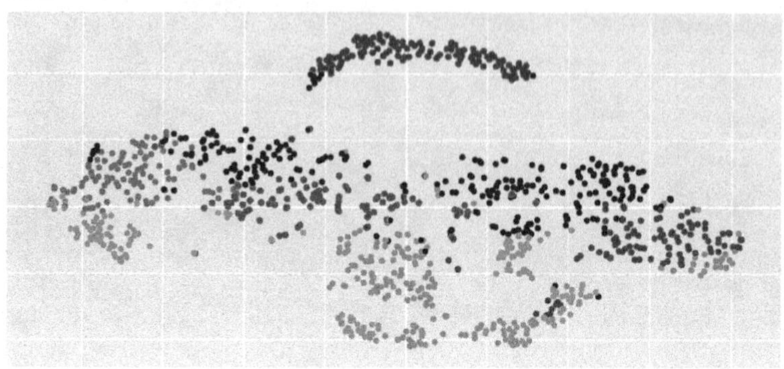

Fig. 6. Manhattan distances on feature layer

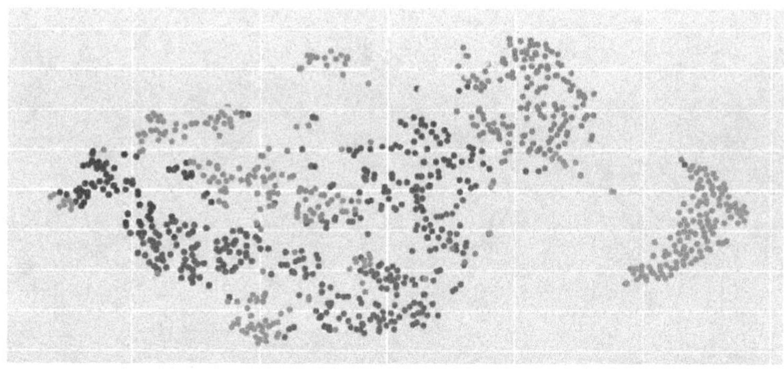

Fig. 7. Chebyshev distances on feature layer

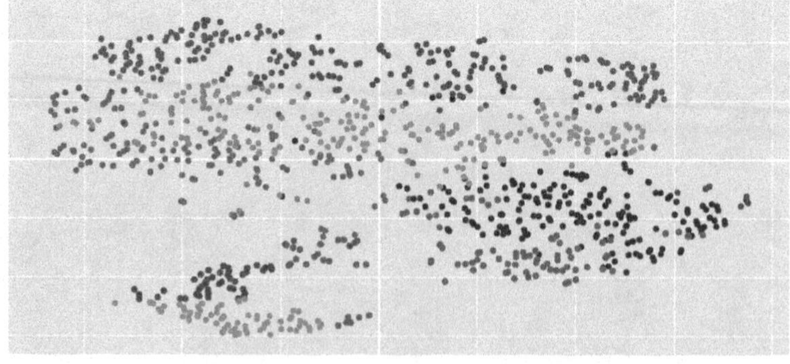

Fig. 8. Dot product on output layer

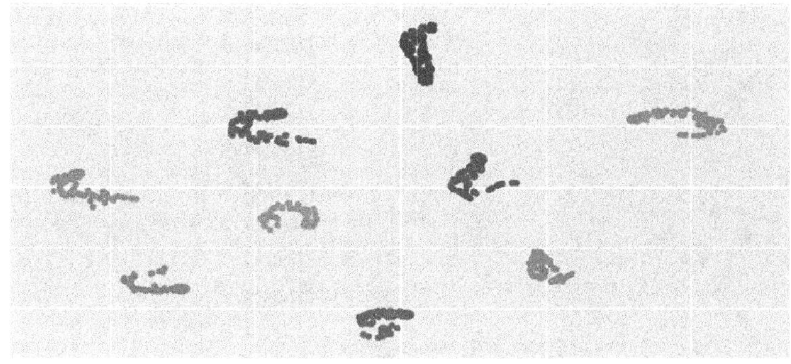

Fig. 9. Euclidean distances on output layer

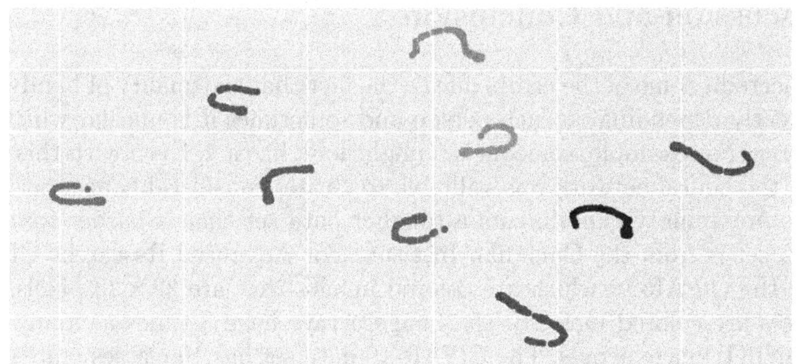

Fig. 10. Minkowski distances on output layer

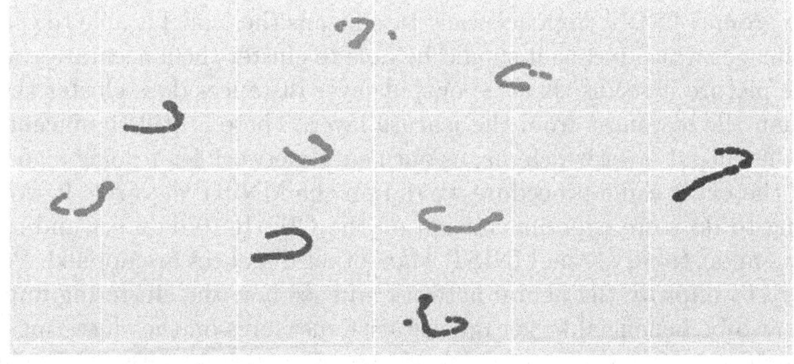

Fig. 11. Manhattan distances on output layer

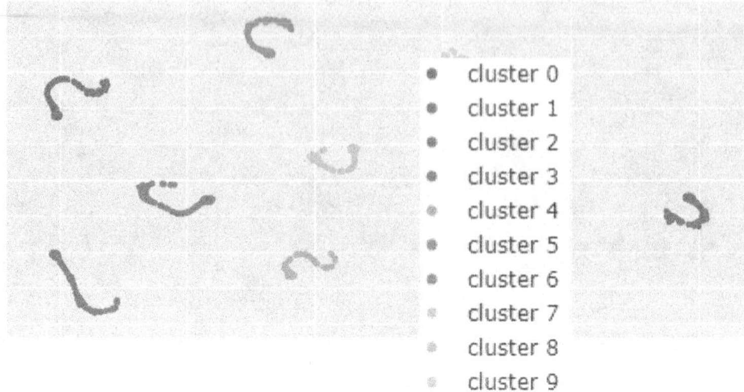

Fig. 12. Chebyshev distances on output layer

4 Discussion and Conclusion

We can accredit some of the errors due to the fact that the quality of handwriting varies greatly depending on each person and sometimes it is unclear which digit was written. For example, someone's 9 might look like a 4. Even with this varied data set, the neural network was still able to cluster considerably accurately. We did some preliminary experiments a tougher data set that is harder to cluster. The data set is from the Canadian Institute For Advanced Research (CIFAR). We used the CIFAR-10 which are colored images that are 32×32 pixels. Since the images are colored in RGB, the image arrays have 3 times as many layers as the MNIST image arrays. The CIFAR-10 data set has 10 classes (categories). Some examples of the classes are cats, fish, trucks, etc. (Figs. 13 and 14).

Unlike MNIST, these data sets are not center oriented meaning the objects are not always in the center of the image, so it is harder to classify and cluster. Neural networks have low accuracy rates on CIFAR compared to MNIST. MNIST had an accuracy rate of 98% while the CIFAR-10 data set had an accuracy rate around 45%. A high accuracy rate means the model is able to correctly identify images which means it should be able to cluster them accurately as well. From the picture it seems that the output layer distances does cluster the data better than the distances from the feature layer. There is still significant muddling in the output layer which means out neural network isn't doing a good job. We used the exact same procedure we did on the MNIST data set. It would be interesting to do more experimentation on the CIFAR-10 data set and see if it follows a similar trend as the MNIST when other distances are applied. Perhaps we can try to improve the neural network and see how the clustering improves. It would also be beneficial to get quantitative measures on the clustering charts so we can do a deeper comparison. We also want to include optimization models to find the best metric for clustering. Our current ideas involve using Gurobi optimizer to minimize false positives and missed detection.

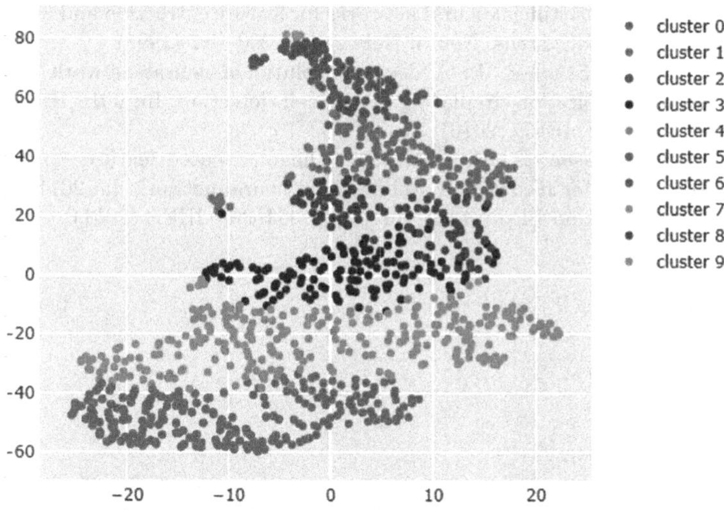

Fig. 13. Minkowski distances on flatten layer CIFAR10

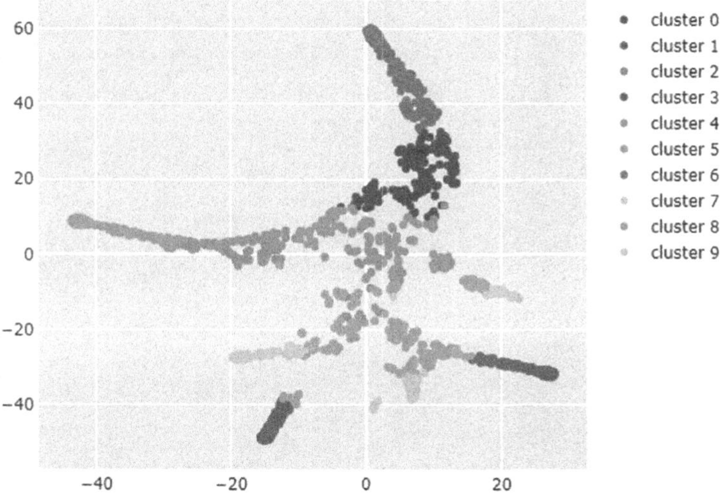

Fig. 14. Minkowski distances on output layer CIFAR10

References

1. Measuring distance or similarity. Packt Subscription
2. Likas, A., Vlassis, N., Verbeek, J.J.: The global k-means clustering algorithm. Pattern Recogn. **36**(2), 451–461 (2003). https://doi.org/10.1016/S0031-3203(02)00060-2. http://www.sciencedirect.com/science/article/pii/S0031320302000602. Biometrics

3. Mao, J., Jain, A.K.: Artificial neural networks for feature extraction and multivariate data projection. IEEE Trans. Neural Netw. **6**(2), 296–317 (1995)
4. Mao, Y., Yin, Z., Schober, J.: A deep convolutional neural network trained on representative samples for circulating tumor cell detection. In: 2016 IEEE Winter Conference, pp. 1–6. IEEE (2016)
5. Pradeep, J., Srinivasan, E., Himavathi, S.: Diagonal based feature extraction for handwritten character recognition system using neural network. In: 2011 3rd International Conference on Electronics, vol. 4, pp. 364–368. IEEE (2011)

Collective Behavior of Price Changes of ERC-20 Tokens

Henri T. Heinonen[1(✉)], Alexander Semenov[2], and Vladimir Boginski[3]

[1] University of Jyväskylä, Jyväskylä, Finland
henri.t.heinonen@jyu.fi
[2] University of Florida, Gainesville, FL, USA
asemenov@ufl.edu
[3] University of Central Florida, Orlando, FL, USA
vladimir.boginski@ucf.edu

Abstract. We analyze a network constructed from tokens developed on Ethereum platform. We collect a large data set of ERC-20 token prices; the total market capitalization of the token set is 50.2 billion (10^9) US dollars. The token set includes 541 tokens; each one of them has a market capitalization of 1 million US dollars or more. We construct and analyze the networks based on cross-correlation of tokens' returns. We find that the degree distributions of the resulting graphs do not follow the power law degree distribution. We cannot find any hierarchical structures nor groupings of ERC-20 tokens in our analysis.

Keywords: Token · Cryptocurrency · Cross correlation matrix · Degree distribution

1 Introduction

1.1 History and Terminology

Econophysicists have studied complex financial systems using concepts and methods originally developed for studying physical systems [5,10]. Such methods have also been used to study the collective behavior of price changes of various cryptocurrencies [12].

In 2009, Bitcoin started the revolution of a new form of money and introduced the concept of a blockchain - a special case of a Distributed Ledger Technology (DLT). 'Bitcoin' (with capital 'B') is a protocol and a network. The native currency of the blockchain started by Satoshi Nakamoto is known as 'bitcoin' (with lower case 'b'). The blockchain has split (or forked) into various other blockchains, and their names and currency units differ (BTC for Bitcoin, BCH for Bitcoin Cash, and BSV for Bitcoin SV). The monetary value between these different currencies varies a lot. Their respective blockchain protocols follow different rules. These different splits of the same blockchain all have the same genesis block (the first block of the entire chain) and the same blocks after the genesis block until the block that caused the split event.

S. Chellappan et al. (Eds.): CSoNet 2020, LNCS 12575, pp. 487–498, 2020.
https://doi.org/10.1007/978-3-030-66046-8_40

There are also completely separate blockchains since the beginning of the chain: for example, Litecoin and Bitcoin do not have the same genesis block. These completely separate blockchains can be using different rules and/or different hashing algorithms (e.g., Litecoin and Bitcoin) or they can be using the same rules and/or the same hashing algorithms (e.g., Namecoin and Bitcoin).

Ethereum blockchain introduced Turing-complete smart contracts that can be used to create programs that can be run in the supercomputer of the decentralized and distributed network. These smart contracts can be used to create new tokens. Tokens can also have monetary value. The most popular platform for tokens is the Ethereum blockchain and its Ethereum Virtual Machine (EVM) that supports smart contracts. Users are usually creating smart contracts with Solidity language. The ERC-20 standard is for creation of tokens with some basic properties. It is the most used standard for making new tokens. The ERC-20 standard gives three optional (token name, symbol, number of decimals) and six mandatory rules (totalSupply, balanceOf, transfer, transferFrom, approve, allowance) for the tokens [14].

We are using the term 'coin' to describe the native currency of a blockchain; litecoin (LTC) is the coin of Litecoin blockchain. We are using the term 'token' to describe an asset that is constructed by the methods of smart contracts; EOS (EOS) is one of the many ERC-20 tokens of Ethereum blockchain and CryptoKitties is a smart contract with non-fungible tokens following the ERC-721 standard.

Previous studies suggest that prices of some stocks are correlated [1], as are prices of cryptocurrencies [12]. Construction and analysis of networks based on correlations, or causal relationships between the characteristics of the financial instruments may be useful for such kind of applications as portfolio selection. Although there were studies on analysis of cryptocurrency cross-correlations, these studies concentrated on overall cryptocurrency market, and have not dealt with relations between Ethereum tokens. In order to fill this gap, in this paper we construct and study the network between the tokens built on the Ethereum platform.

1.2 Literature Review

The econophysics book by Richmond et al. [10] introduces statistical physics, probability theory, and correlation functions. It looks at the behaviour and evolution of financial systems from the perspective of physics - or econophysics. Yet another introduction to econophysics is the book by Mantegna and Stanley [5].

The graph theory book by Bollobás [2] gives an introduction to modern graph theory.

There are lots of methods to analyze financial time series. For example, Podobnik et al. [8] use several methods to analyze the properties of volume changes $|\tilde{R}|$, and their relationship to price changes $|R|$. They analyze 14,981 daily recordings of S&P 500 Index over the period of 1950–2009, and find power-law cross-correlations between R and $|\tilde{R}|$ by using detrended cross-correlation analysis (DCCA) method [9]. This method is suitable for investigating power-law cross correlations between two simultaneously recorded nonstationary time series.

Stosic et al. [12] analyze cross correlations between price changes from data of 119 different cryptocurrencies and 200 simultaneous days in the time period from August 26, 2016 to January 18, 2018. They use methods of random matrix theory and minimum spanning trees. They find that the cross correlation matrix shows non-trivial hierarchical structures and groupings of coin/token pairs. However, they do not find such hierarchy in the partial cross correlations. They discover that most of the eigenvalues in the spectrum of the cross correlation matrix do not agree with the predictions of random matrix theory. The minimum spanning tree of cross correlations reveals distinct community structures that are quite stable. They find that the minimum spanning tree of coins and tokens consists of five communities. The conclusion is that the results represent genuine information about the cryptocurrency market, because similar communities are found for different random measurements or time periods and choices of coins and tokens or set N. It is also indicated that the communities have very different properties than the average properties of the minimum spanning tree. An application could be a lower risk cryptocurrency portfolio where cryptocurrencies are selected from distinct communities.

Boginski et al. [1] study a network representation, the market graph, of the stock market. They conduct the market graph statistical analysis and find out that it follows the power-law model. They detect cliques and independent sets in the market graph.

Plerou et al. [7] use random matrix theory methods to analyze the cross-correlation matrix C of stock price changes of the largest 1000 US companies for the period from 1994 to 1995. Their finding is that the statistics of most of the eigenvalues in the spectrum of C agree with the predictions of random matrix theory. They also find some deviations for the largest eigenvalues.

Plerou et al. [6] analyze cross correlations between price fluctuations of different stocks using methods of random matrix theory (RMT). They use two large databases for calculating cross-correlation matrices C of returns constructed from three different US stock periods. They test the statistics of the eigenvalues λ_i of C against a null hypothesis, which is a random correlation matrix constructed from mutually uncorrelated time series. Their finding is that a majority of the eigenvalues of C fall within the RMT bounds $[\lambda_-, \lambda_+]$ for the eigenvalues of random correlation matrices. They test the eigenvalues of C within the RMT bound for universal properties of random matrices. The result implies a large degree of randomness in the measured cross-correlation coefficients.

Soloviev and Belinskiy [11] construct indicators of critical and crash phenomena for cryptocurrencies. They combine the empirical cross-correlation matrix with the random matrix theory to examine the statistical properties of cross-correlation coefficients, the evolution of the distribution of eigenvalues and corresponding eigenvectors of the global cryptocurrency market. The data is the daily returns of 24 cryptocurrencies price time series from 2013 to 2018. A collective effect of the whole market is reflected by the largest eigenvalue. The proposed economic mass and the largest eigenvalue of the matrix of correlations can act like quantum indicator-predictors of falls in the cryptocurrency market.

Liang et al. [4] do a comparative analysis of cryptocurrency, foreign exchange, and stock. They took the daily close prices for about four years and construct the correlation matrices and asset trees of the markets. They conduct comparisons on volatility, centrality, clustering structure, robustness, and risk. They find that the cryptocurrency market is more fragile than the others based on the robustness and the clustering structure. For example, the clusters in the cryptocurrency market have no evident rules and they change more rapidly. For comparison, the clusters in stock market correspond to geographical regions or business sector, and the clusters in foreign exchange market match nicely with the geographical regions.

Conlon et al. [3] explore the dynamics of the equal-time cross-correlation matrix of multivariate financial time series. They examine the eigenvalue spectrum over sliding time windows and find that the dynamics of the small eigenvalues oppose those of the largest eigenvalues.

It is not known why most of the eigenvalues [12] in the spectrum of the cross correlation matrix in cryptocurrency market do not agree with the universal predictions of random matrix theory. This is in sharp contrast to the predictions for other financial markets. We investigate Ethereum's ERC-20 tokens and their network graphs to learn if similar results hold for such a subset of all the cryptocurrencies. Our research question is thus: What kind of hierarchical structures and groupings do the network graphs show for ERC-20 tokens?

2 Methods

2.1 Returns and Cross Correlations

To calculate the price change (or return) of a token over a time scale Δt, let us define $Y_i(t)$ as the price of a collection of tokens $i = 1, \ldots, N$ at time t. We analyze returns, defined as

$$R_i(t) \equiv \frac{Y_i(t+\Delta t) - Y_i(t)}{Y_i(t)} = \frac{Z_i(t)}{Y_i(t)}. \tag{1}$$

The problem with Eq. (1) is that it is sensitive to scale changes when using long time horizons [5].

The equal-time cross correlation matrix is

$$C_{ij} \equiv \langle R_i(t) R_j(t) \rangle. \tag{2}$$

$C_{ij} = 1$ is a perfect positive correlation, $C_{ij} = -1$ is a perfect negative correlation, and $C_{ij} = 0$ means no correlation [12].

2.2 Basic Concepts from Graph Theory

Let us define a graph $G = (V, E)$ with a set of n vertices nodes $V = \{1, ..., n\}$ and a set of m edges $E \subset V \times V$, $|V| = n$ and $|E| = m$. Each edge $e \in E$ of the graph G has a weight $W(e) \in \mathcal{R}$ Nodes of the graph are formed by tokens for particular calendar year, weight of the edge (i, j) is equal to correlation of returns for tokens i and j. If $(i, j) \in E$, then vertices i, and j are called adjacent. If every two vertices are adjacent, the graph is called complete. Neighborhood $\mathcal{N}(v)$ of a vertex v is a set of all nodes v' adjacent to v, i.e. $v' \in \mathcal{N}(v)$ for all $(v, v') \in E$. Then, the degree of v, $\deg(V) = |\mathcal{N}(v)|$. For any subset of vertices $S \subseteq V$, $G[S] = (S, (S \times S) \cap E)$ denotes the *subgraph* induced by S on G. A vertex belonging to S is referred to as a group vertex, vertices in $V \backslash S$ are considered to be the non-group vertices. Group $G[S]$ is called *clique* if the *subgraph* induced by S is complete.

3 Results

We have collected historical data on price changes for all Ethereum's ERC-20 tokens with market capitalization higher than 1 million US dollars (USD) listed at the website Coingecko.com. Figure 1 displays log-rank plot of its market capitalization. In total, we collected data for 541 tokens, their total market capitalization is 50.2 billion USD. Overall, there were 866 cryptocurrencies with market capitalization higher than 1 million USD. The used data set did not include ether (ETH) coin itself, but it is interesting to observe that total market capitalization of Ethereum tokens exceeds that of ether, which is about 42 billion USD at the time of collection.

In order to compute correlation networks, we took the tokens that have price data for the full calendar year. In this case, it resulted in 4 tokens in 2016, 8 tokens in 2017, 111 tokens in 2018, and 333 tokens in 2019. We have computed the Pearson correlation coefficient between returns of these tokens; distributions of the resulting correlations for the two calendar years are shown in Figs. 2 and 3. We created a "sliced" network by keeping only the edges formed by correlations with a value higher than the 95th percentile. As a result, we obtained three networks as described in Table 1.

Table 1. Characteristics of the networks for 3 years. We omit the years 2015, and 2016 due to insufficient amount of data. The density and diameter are reported for the giant component.

Year	#nodes	#edges	#components	Giant component size	Density	Diameter
2017	8	2	6	3	0.66	2
2018	111	306	56	55	0.2	4
2019	333	2781	143	185	0.16	7

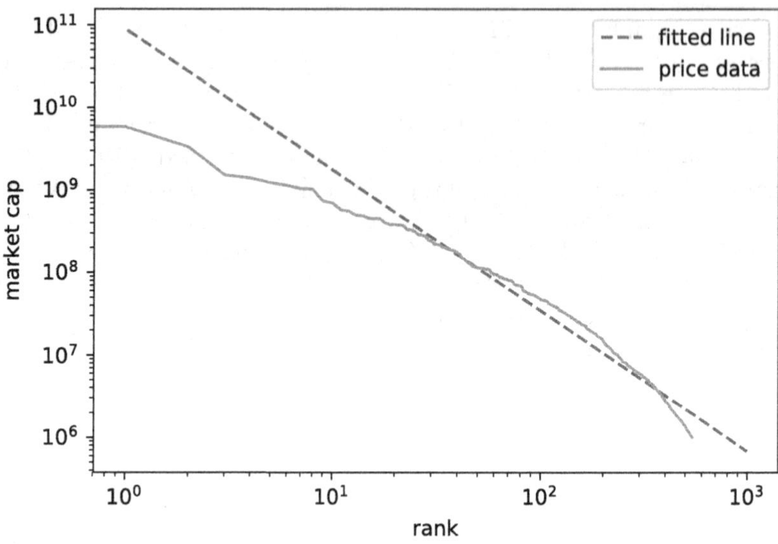

Fig. 1. Log-rank plot of the market capitalizations of collected tokens. The plot shows the market capitalization of 541 ERC-20 tokens; from these, only 9 have market capitalization more than 1 billion USD. Dashed line shows the line fitted to the log-rank plot ($\gamma = -1.71, R^2 = 0.95$)

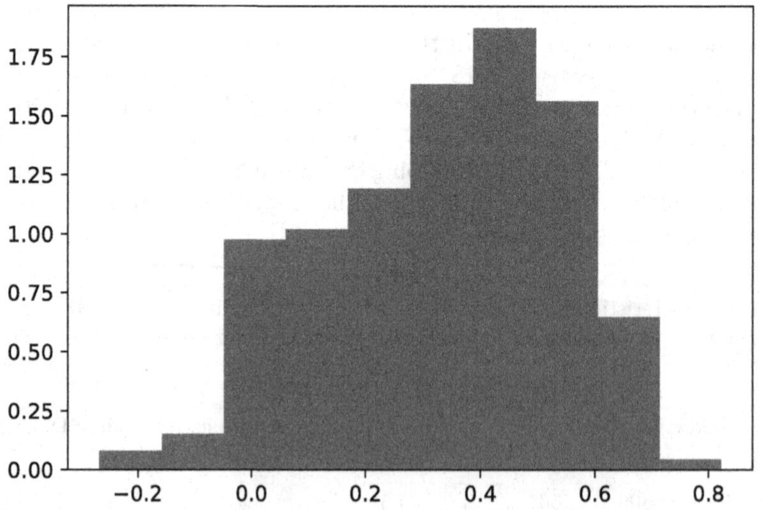

Fig. 2. The distribution of correlations for tokens of the year 2018.

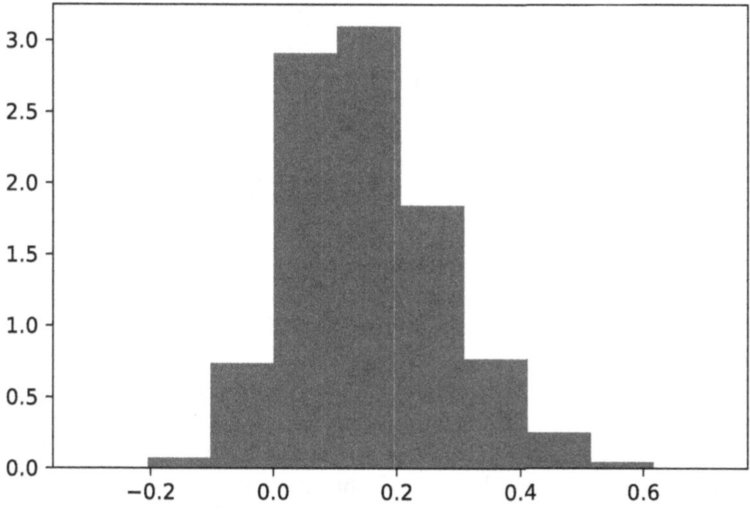

Fig. 3. The distribution of correlations for tokens of the year 2019.

Figures 4 and 5 show degree distributions for the networks for the years 2018 and 2019. Figures 6 and 7 show the network graphs of the tokens for the years 2018 and 2019. Also, it is interesting to observe, that graph for the year 2019 has a maximum clique size of 33 (tokens OMG, SNT, GNT, AE, BLZ, POLY, MKR, ZRX, POWR, REQ, DNT, ELF, BNT, TNB, SNGLS, CND, GVT, QSP, OCN,

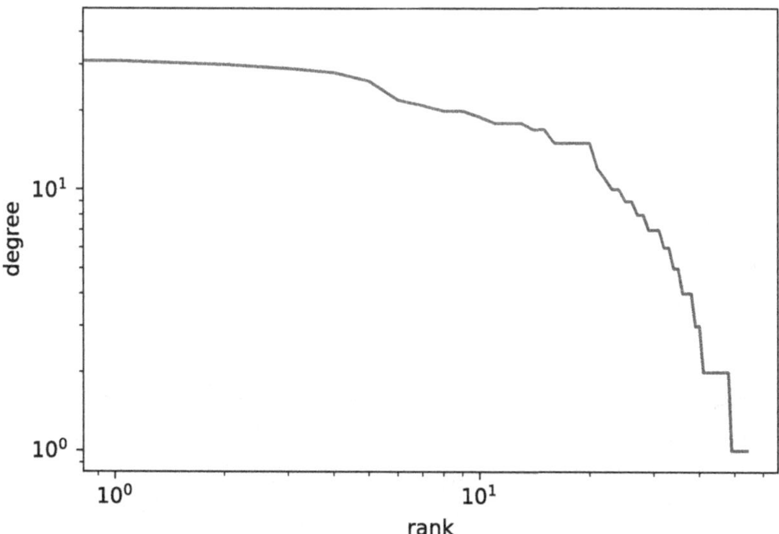

Fig. 4. The log–rank plot of degree distribution for the year 2018.

WPR, AMB, LOOM, VIBE, MFT, STMX, QKC, VIB, GNO, BCPT, POE, WTC, YOYOW, LRC), and graph for the year 2018 has a maximum clique size of 14 (tokens BNT, CVC, POWR, OMG, LEND, STORJ, SALT, RCN, RDN, KNC, QSP, WINGS, SNM, REQ).

4 Discussion

According to Liang et al. [4] the clusters in the cryptocurrency market have no evident rules and they change more rapidly than clusters in the foreign exchange and stock markets. Do the network graphs show any hierarchical structures and groupings of ERC-20 tokens in our analysis? We can see from Figs. 4 and 5 that degree distributions do not exhibit power-law behavior, that is found in many real-world graphs, including correlation networks [1]; however, there are many nodes having equally high degree. Top ten nodes with the highest degree for the years 2018 and 2019 are shown in Table 2. Total market capitalization of the ten tokens with the highest degree for the year 2018 is equal to 2.36 billion USD, and that of 2019 is equal to 2.35 billion USD, however, only two tokens are presented in both data sets: OMG and BNT.

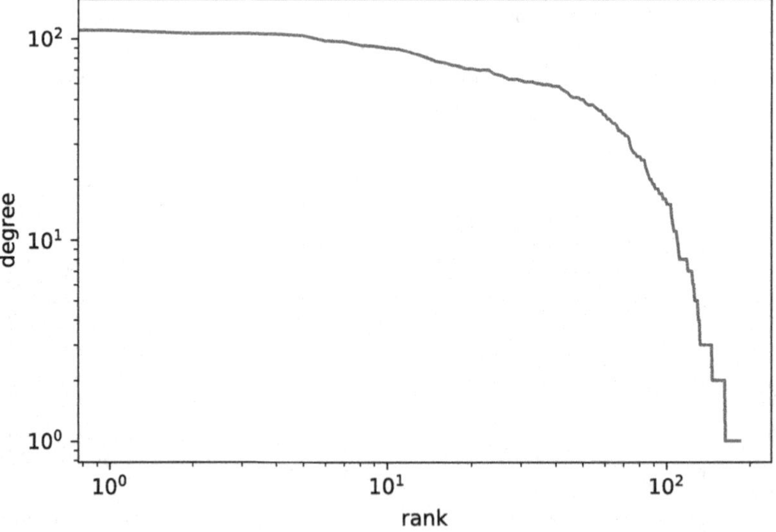

Fig. 5. The log–rank plot of degree distribution for the year 2019.

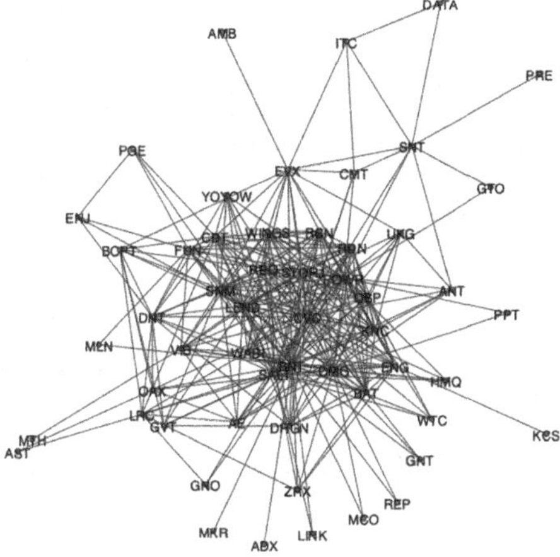

Fig. 6. The network graph of the tokens of the year 2018.

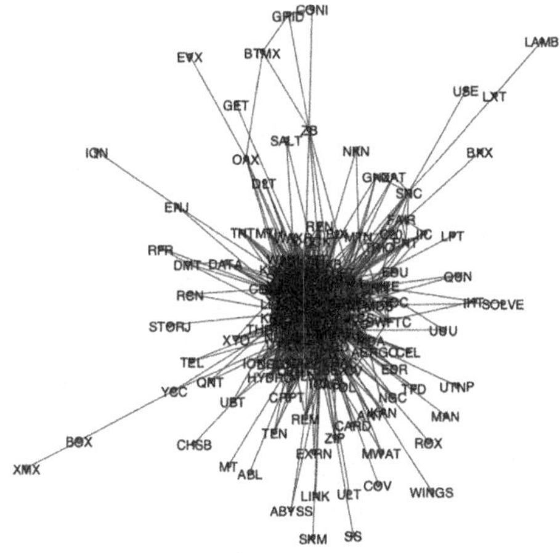

Fig. 7. The network graph of the tokens of the year 2019.

One of the limitations of our study is the limited number of tokens; although, we have collected data on 541 tokens, our largest size graphs (for the years 2018 and 2019) have only 111 and 333 nodes, respectively. In future research it would be of interest to construct the networks on shorter-term price data; for example, for each 3 months, instead of one year. The Eq. (1) we used for calculating the returns is sensitive to scale changes for long time horizons [5].

Table 2. The top 10 nodes by degree for the years 2018 and 2019.

Year 2018			Year 2019		
Name	Degree	Description	Name	Degree	Description
BNT	41	Continuous liquidity and asynchronous price discovery	OMG	125	Layer-2 scaling solution for transferring value on Ethereum
CVC	31	Identity verification services	SNT	111	Status is an open source messaging platform and mobile interface to interact with DApps; the Status Network Token is a modular utility token that fuels the Status network
POWR	30	Allow access and usage of the Power Ledger Platform	GNT	107	The Golem Network Token is designed to ensure flexibility and control over the future evolution of the project; Golem is the first truly decentralized supercomputer
OMG	29	Layer-2 scaling solution for transferring value on Ethereum	MKR	107	Token for governing the Maker Protocol - the smart contracts that power Dai
LEND	28	Token for global peer-to-peer lending market	AE	106	ternity blockchain is an Erlang-based scalable smart contract platform; the Aeternity Ethereum contract expired on 2019-09-02 rendering all ERC-20 AE tokens non-transferable
SALT	26	Token for a platform for lending and borrowing	BLZ	104	An external token to represent on exchanges for customers to easily obtain to use the Bluzelle service; it is a token that bridges the Bluzelle native token (BNT) with ETH coin
SNM	22	Token on the Sonm computing power marketplace	POLY	98	Token for Polymesh, which is an enterprise-grade blockchain built for security tokens
QSP	21	Token used as the payment method for code security audits	BNT	97	Continuous liquidity and asynchronous price discovery
REQ	20	Token for participating the the Request Network, which is a decentralized network for payment requests	ELF	93	Token for a multi-chain parallel computing blockchain framework
KNC	20	Economic Facilitation, Governance, and Treasury Funds on Kyber Based Networks	ZRX	92	Token for 0x open protocol that enables the peer-to-peer exchange of assets on the Ethereum blockchain

5 Conclusions

In this paper, we made the first attempt at constructing and analyzing the network of cryptocurrencies based on their price fluctuations. Interestingly, we found that the global connectivity structure of this network does not follow a power law degree distribution that was observed for networks of stocks constructed using a similar approach [1]. Instead, the shape of our network's degree distribution resembles the one found for the Facebook social network graph [13] (although the size of the Facebook network is clearly much larger), which is an interesting observation that might be worth looking into in future work.

Furthermore, our research question was: "What kind of hierarchical structures and groupings do the network graphs show for ERC-20 tokens?" We have constructed the network from the tokens built on the Ethereum platform, but we cannot find such hierarchical structures/groupings in our analysis. Nevertheless, our preliminary results can serve as a starting point for more in-depth analysis of collective behavior of cryptocurrencies price fluctuations via network-based approaches.

References

1. Boginski, V., Butenko, S., Pardalos, P.M.: Statistical analysis of financial networks. Comput. Stat. Data Anal. **48**(2), 431–443 (2005). https://doi.org/10.1016/j.csda.2004.02.004. http://www.sciencedirect.com/science/article/pii/S0167947304000258
2. Bollobás, B.: Modern Graph Theory. GTM, vol. 184. Springer, New York (1998). https://doi.org/10.1007/978-1-4612-0619-4
3. Conlon, T., Ruskin, H., Crane, M.: Cross-correlation dynamics in financial timeseries. Phys. A: Stat. Mech. Appl. **388**(5), 705–714 (2009). https://doi.org/10.1016/j.physa.2008.10.047. http://www.sciencedirect.com/science/article/pii/S0378437108008960
4. Liang, J., Li, L., Chen, W., Zeng, D.: Towards an understanding of cryptocurrency: a comparative analysis of cryptocurrency, foreign exchange, and stock. In: 2019 IEEE International Conference on Intelligence and Security Informatics (ISI), pp. 137–139 (July 2019). https://doi.org/10.1109/ISI.2019.8823373
5. Mantegna, R.N., Stanley, H.E.: An introduction to econophysics: correlations and complexity in finance (2000)
6. Plerou, V., Gopikrishnan, P., Rosenow, B., Amaral, L.A.N., Guhr, T., Stanley, H.E.: Random matrix approach to cross correlations in financial data. Phys. Rev. E **65**, 066126 (2002). https://doi.org/10.1103/PhysRevE.65.066126. https://link.aps.org/doi/10.1103/PhysRevE.65.066126
7. Plerou, V., Gopikrishnan, P., Rosenow, B., Nunes Amaral, L.A., Stanley, H.E.: Universal and nonuniversal properties of cross correlations in financial timeseries. Phys. Rev. Lett. **83**, 1471–1474 (1999). https://doi.org/10.1103/PhysRevLett.83.1471. https://link.aps.org/doi/10.1103/PhysRevLett.83.1471
8. Podobnik, B., Horvatic, D., Petersen, A.M., Stanley, H.E.: Cross-correlations between volume change and price change. Proc. Natl. Acad. Sci. **106**(52), 22079–22084 (2009). https://doi.org/10.1073/pnas.0911983106. https://www.pnas.org/content/106/52/22079

9. Podobnik, B., Stanley, H.E.: Detrended cross-correlation analysis: a new method for analyzing two nonstationary time series. Phys. Rev. Lett. **100**, 084102 (2008). https://doi.org/10.1103/PhysRevLett.100.084102. https://link.aps.org/doi/10.1103/PhysRevLett.100.084102
10. Richmond, P., Mimkes, J., Hutzler, S.: Econophysics and Physical Economics. No. 9780199674701 in OUP Catalogue. Oxford University Press (2013). https://ideas.repec.org/b/oxp/obooks/9780199674701.html
11. Soloviev, V.N., Belinskiy, A.: Complex systems theory and crashes of cryptocurrency market. In: Ermolayev, V., Suárez-Figueroa, M.C., Yakovyna, V., Mayr, H.C., Nikitchenko, M., Spivakovsky, A. (eds.) ICTERI 2018. CCIS, vol. 1007, pp. 276–297. Springer, Cham (2019). https://doi.org/10.1007/978-3-030-13929-2_14
12. Stosic, D., Stosic, D., Ludermir, T.B., Stosic, T.: Collective behavior of cryptocurrency price changes. Phys. A: Stat. Mech. Appl. **507**, 499–509 (2018). https://doi.org/10.1016/j.physa.2018.05.050. http://www.sciencedirect.com/science/article/pii/S0378437118305946
13. Ugander, J., Karrer, B., Backstrom, L., Marlow, C.: The anatomy of the Facebook social graph. arXiv preprint arXiv:1111.4503 (2011)
14. Vogelsteller, F., Buterin, V.: Eip-20: Erc-20 token standard. https://web.archive.org/web/20200812054202/eips.ethereum.org/EIPS/eip-20. Accessed 15 Oct 2020

A Cutting Plane Method for Least Cost Influence Maximization

Cheng-Lung Chen[1], Eduardo L. Pasiliao[2], and Vladimir Boginski[1](✉)

[1] University of Central Florida, Orlando, FL 32816, USA
vladimir.boginski@ucf.edu
[2] Air Force Research Laboratory, Eglin AFB, FL 32542, USA

Abstract. We study the least cost influence maximization problem, which has potential applications in social network analysis, as well as in other types of networks. The focus of this paper is on mixed-integer programming (MIP) techniques for the considered problem. The standard arc-based MIP formulation contains a substructure that is a relaxation of the mixed 0-1 knapsack polyhedron. We give a new exponential class of facet-defining inequalities from this substructure and an exact polynomial time separation algorithm for the inequalities. We report preliminary computational results to illustrate the effect of these inequalities.

Keywords: Mixed-integer programming · Influence maximization · Social networks · Valid inequalities

1 Introduction

Intricate connections between entities in many natural and man-made systems form large complex networks. Of particular interest in the area of network science is gaining insight into the dynamic behavior of spreading or influence processes in complex networks. For instance, in social network analytics, optimal initiation of the processes of spreading information, opinions, and/or influence, may play an important role in designing competitive marketing strategies. Accordingly, there is an increasing trend in studying influence and information propagation in social networks (see, e.g., [4,12]). Granovetter [7] propose the linear threshold model to describe the propagation process in social network, in which the resistance of an individual to influence and influence strength to others are quantified as threshold and influence factor, respectively. The term "active" is adopted to represent the state of individual behavior being influenced if the summation of influence factors from all the connections in social network exceeds the threshold. There are many variants of this problem related to optimally determining the most influential nodes (people), in order to trigger the propagation process and reach a desired penetration rate. Kempe et al. [11] consider the *Influence*

This material is based on work supported by the AFRL Mathematical Modeling and Optimization Institute.

S. Chellappan et al. (Eds.): CSoNet 2020, LNCS 12575, pp. 499–511, 2020.
https://doi.org/10.1007/978-3-030-66046-8_41

Maximization Problem (IMP), which they formulate as a discrete stochastic optimization problem. They adopt two models for diffusion processes, namely, the *linear threshold* and the *independent cascade* models. The goal is to activate some users initially and use them to influence as many other users as possible by the end of the propagation process. They show that it is NP-hard to both approximate and solve the problem to optimality. Another similar problem introduced by Chen [3] is referred to as the *Target Set Selection Problem* (TSSP). In TSSP, the decision is to find the minimum number of users required initially in order to activate the entire network through the propagation process. Chen showed that the problem is NP-hard to approximate and gives a polylogarithmic lower bound on the approximation ratio. Recently, a new problem named *Least Cost Influence Maximization Problem* (LCIM) has been introduced in [5]: it involves the combination of individual incentives (e.g., discounts, payments, free sample products) with peer influence together to activate nodes and prompt influence propagation in a social network. The goal of LCIM is to determine the required minimum cost of partial incentives given to the key opinion leaders.

Despite the fact that the aforementioned problems share certain similarities, the challenges of finding an exact optimal solution can be very different when these problems are formulated by mathematical optimization models. In this paper, we consider the LCIM problem and formulate it as a mixed-integer programming problem to study its polyhedral structure. We assume that all the parameters are deterministic and the influence propagation occurs in discrete time steps. From a practical point of view, the assumption of deterministic linear threshold depends on the accuracy of estimation of influence factor and threshold parameters. Machine learning and data mining techniques may enable one to obtain accurate predictions on those parameters from massive amounts of data available nowadays. A similar assumption on deterministic linear threshold model can be found in [10], where the authors consider targeted and budgeted influence maximization in social networks and give an iterative greedy algorithm to solve the problem. Most of the previous studies on social network optimization problems mainly focus on developing heuristic and approximation algorithms. Existing studies on exact integer programming methods for influence maximization problems are relatively limited. Raghavan and Zhang [15] study the Weighted Target Set Selection problem (WTSSP) in which each node is associated with a unique cost in the objective function for initial activation. They give a compact and tight extended formulation for WTSSP on tree graphs and later show it is also tight on directed acyclic graphs. To apply this extended formulation to general graphs, they design a branch-and-cut algorithm that includes a separation for cycle elimination constraints. Wu and Küçükyavuz [17] study the two-stage stochastic influence maximization problem where the second-stage cost function is submodular. They develop a delayed constrained generation algorithm with strong optimality cuts that utilizes the submodularity and demonstrate its effectiveness in extensive computational results. Nannini et al. [14] propose a branch-and-cut algorithm and heuristic branch-cut-and-price algorithms for robust influence maximization, where node thresholds and arc influence factors are subject to budget uncertainty. They show that optimization for a worst-case scenario robust solution is NP-hard. Fischetti et al. [6] present a novel set covering formulation for generalized LCIM. They propose strengthened generalized propagation inequalities and show that they dominate the cycle elimination constraints in the original formulation. A price-cut-and-branch algorithm with heuristic separation for the proposed inequalities and column generation is given to deal with the exponential number of variables and constraints. Günneç et al. [9] establish the computational complexity for LCIM based on the reduction from the independent set problem. In particular, when 100% penetration rate is not required, they show that LCIM is NP-hard on arbitrary graphs and bipartite graphs for both equal and unequal influence. For the 100% penetration rate, the optimization of LCIM with unequal influence on a tree remains NP-hard. On the other hand, LCIM with equal influence on a tree with the 100% penetration rate is shown to be polynomially solvable. They give a greedy algorithm and a total unimodular formulation for this special case. In the subsequent paper, Günneç et al. [8] extend their total unimodular formulation for LCIM on a tree to an arbitrary graph. To ensure the solution is acyclic, they give several pre-processing steps and separation for cycle elimination constraints in the branch-and-cut algorithm.

1.1 Notation and Problem Definition

For convenience, we use the notation $[n] = \{1, \cdots, n\}$ and subscripts to indicate the elements of a vector. The n-dimensional jth unit vector is denoted as e_j. For a set $Q \subseteq \mathbb{R}^n$, we use conv (Q) to denote its convex hull of solutions.

Formally, a given network (e.g., a social network) is represented by a directed graph $G = (V, A)$, where the set of nodes V with cardinality n may correspond to the set of people and set of arcs A with cardinality m indicates the connection and influence direction between the people in the network. Each node $i \in V$ has threshold h_i and each arc $(i, j) \in A$ is associated with an influence weight d_{ij}. The coverage (penetration) rate is denoted by τ, where $0 < \tau \leq 1$, and the neighborhood of node i is denoted by $N_i := \{j \in V : (j, i) \in A\}$. We assume that d_{ij} and h_i are positive integers such that $\max\{d_{ji} : j \in N_i\} < h_i$ for all $i \in V$ to omit trivial cases. All nodes are assumed inactive initially and nodes remain active once influences from neighbors and incentives reach the threshold. For each node $i \in V$, let continuous variables x_i be the amount of partial incentives given to user i, binary variables y_{ij} indicate whether influence is exerted from node i to j, and binary variables z_i indicate whether node i is activated. The arc-based formulation of LCIM is given by

$$\min_{x,y,z} \sum_{i \in V} x_i$$

$$x_i + \sum_{j \in N_i} d_{ji} y_{ji} \geq h_i z_i \quad \forall i \in V \tag{1}$$

$$z_i \geq y_{ij} \quad \forall (i,j) \in A \text{ s.t. } (j,i) \notin A \tag{2}$$

$$\sum_{i \in V} z_i \geq \lceil \tau n \rceil \tag{3}$$

$$\sum_{(i,j) \in C} y_{ij} \leq \sum_{i \in V(C) \setminus \{k\}} z_i \quad \forall k \in V(C), \forall \text{ cycles } C \subseteq A \tag{4}$$

$$x \in \mathbb{R}^n_+$$

$$y \in \mathbb{B}^m, z \in \mathbb{B}^n.$$

Node propagation constraints (1) evaluate the total incoming influence from neighbor plus the incentives given to a node. Constraints (2) ensure that arc (i, j) exerts influence if node i is activated. The minimum coverage constraints (3) describe the number of nodes that need to be activated given a predetermined penetration rate τ. The generalized cycle elimination constraints (4) where $V(C) = \{i \in V : (i,j) \in C\}$ cut off solutions that form a cycle as the induced optimal influence propagation graph is supposed to be acyclic. Note that the arc-based formulation proposed by [2] is different from this paper as the influence weights are coming solely from their neighbors without incentives. Günneç et al. [8] and Günneç et al. [9] on the other hand, consider the arc-based formulation with time index. Finally, Fischetti et al. [6]. adopt this arc-based formulation for computational performance comparison but the possible values of incentives are represented by a set of binary variables.

1.2 Main Contribution

Our main contribution can be summarized as follows: We give a class of valid inequalities derived from the substructure of the model that describes the propagation via deterministic linear threshold model. The substructure can be transformed to the mixed 0-1 knapsack polyhedron with additional binary restriction on partial knapsack size. Hence, it is a relaxation containing known valid inequalities from mixed 0-1 knapsack set studied by Marchand and Wolsey [13]. We introduce a new class of valid inequalities and give an exact polynomial separation algorithm for them. We also show that by exploiting the result of our separation algorithm, the inequalities proposed in [13] with heuristic separation only, can now be separated exactly as well.

2 Valid Inequalities in LCIM Based on Mixed 0-1 Knapsack Polyhedron

To develop a strong formulation for LCIM, we study the polyhedral structure of constraints (1). Assume N_i is nonempty with cardinality t_i and $\sum_{i \in V} t_i = m$. For $i \in [n]$, let

$$\mathcal{X}_i = \left\{ (x_i, y, z_i) \in \mathbb{R}_+ \times \mathbb{B}^{t_i} \times \mathbb{B} : x_i + \sum_{j \in N_i} d_{ji} y_{ji} \geq h z_i \right\}.$$

The set $\mathcal{X}_i$ describes the node propagation in LCIM, which can be regarded as a mixing set with a binary variable on the right-hand side value. Any inequality that is facet-defining for $\operatorname{conv}(\mathcal{X}_i)$ is facet-defining for $\operatorname{conv}(\cap_{i \in [n]} \mathcal{X}_i)$ as well. Therefore, we now consider a single node propagation by dropping the subscript i and obtain the following set

$$\mathcal{X} = \left\{ (x, y, z) \in \mathbb{R}_+ \times \mathbb{B}^t \times \mathbb{B} : x + \sum_{j \in N} d_j y_j \geq h z \right\}.$$

Observe that the set $\mathcal{X}$ contains a mixed 0-1 knapsack structure. Let set $\overline{\mathcal{X}}$ be obtained from $\mathcal{X}$ by setting $\overline{y}_j = 1 - y_j$, $j \in N$ and $z = 1$. Then we obtain the mixed 0-1 knapsack set $\overline{\mathcal{X}}$ with weight d_j for each item $j \in N$ and the capacity of knapsack $\left(\sum_{j \in N} d_j - h\right)$ plus an unbounded continuous variable x in the following

$$\overline{\mathcal{X}} = \left\{ (x, \overline{y}, z) \in \mathbb{R}_+ \times \mathbb{B}^t \times \{1\} : \sum_{j \in N} d_j \overline{y}_j \leq \left(\sum_{j \in N} d_j - h \right) + x \right\}.$$

Such set can be interpreted as a special case of traditional 0-1 knapsack problem where the knapsack size is expanded with additional capacity. Marchand and Wolsey [13] propose two classes of valid inequalities for $\overline{\mathcal{X}}$ based on mixed-integer rounding and lifting function, namely, the continuous cover inequalities and continuous reverse cover inequalities, and they can immediately be used to strengthen the formulation of LCIM as $\overline{\mathcal{X}} \subset \mathcal{X}$.

Proposition 1 [13]. *Let index k, set $S \subseteq N$ and set $T \subseteq N$ be a (k, S, T) cover pair that satisfies (i) $S \cap T = \{k\}$, $S \cup T = N$, (ii) $\pi = h + \sum_{j \in S} d_j - \sum_{j \in N} d_j > 0$, and $h + \sum_{j \in S \setminus \{k\}} d_j - \sum_{j \in N} d_j < 0$, (iii)$\rho = \sum_{j \in T} d_j - h > 0$, and $\sum_{j \in T \setminus \{k\}} d_j - h < 0$. Note that these conditions also imply $\pi + \rho = d_k > 0$. Let $r_S = \min\{j \in S : d_j > \pi\}$ where $d_j \in S$ are in non-decreasing order such that $d_1 \geq d_2 \geq \cdots \geq d_{r_S}$. Similarly, let $r_T = \min\{j \in T : d_j > \rho\}$ where $d_j \in T$ are in non-decreasing order such that $d_1 \geq d_2 \geq \cdots \geq d_{r_T}$. In addition, let $D_0^S = D_0^T = 0$, $D_j^S = \sum_{\ell=1}^{j} d_\ell, j \in [r_S]$, $D_j^T = \sum_{\ell=1}^{j} d_\ell, j \in [r_T]$. Then the* *following continuous cover and continuous reverse cover inequalities are valid for $\mathcal{X}$.*

$$x + \sum_{j \in S} \min\{\pi, d_j\} y_j + \sum_{j \in T \setminus \{k\}} \phi_S(d_j) y_j \geq \left(\min\{\pi, d_k\} + \sum_{j \in T \setminus \{k\}} \phi_S(d_j) \right) z \tag{5}$$

and
$$x + \sum_{j \in T} \max\{0, d_j - \rho\} y_j + \sum_{j \in S \setminus \{k\}} \psi_T(d_j) y_j \geq \left(\sum_{j \in T} \max\{0, d_j - \rho\} \right) z \tag{6}$$

where

$$\phi_S(g) = \begin{cases} (j-1)\pi & D_{j-1}^S \leq g \leq D_j^S - \pi, \quad j \in [r_S] \\ (j-1)\pi + g - D_j^S + \pi & D_j^S - \pi \leq g \leq D_j^S, \quad j \in [r_S - 1] \\ (r_S - 1)\pi + g - D_{r_S}^S + \pi & D_{r_S}^S - \pi \leq g, \end{cases} \tag{7}$$

and

$$\psi_T(g) = \begin{cases} g - j\rho & D_j^T \leq g \leq D_{j+1}^T - \rho, \quad j \in [r_T - 1] \cup \{0\} \\ D_j^T - j\rho & D_j^T - \rho \leq g \leq D_j^T, \quad j \in [r_T - 1] \\ D_{r_T}^T - \rho r_T & D_{r_T}^T - \rho \leq g. \end{cases} \tag{8}$$

Proof. If $z = 0$, both inequalities (5) and (6) are trivially satisfied. Otherwise, the validity and facet proof of both inequalities directly follows from [13].

Example 1. Let $d = (7, 6, 5, 4)$ and $h = 8$, we list the facet-defining inequalities from each (k, S, T) pair of inequality (5) and (6) in Table 1. For example, for $k = 1$, $S = \{1, 2, 4\}$ and $T = \{1, 3\}$, we have $\pi = 3$, $\rho = 4$, $r_S = 3$, and $r_T = 2$. Then the lifting function ϕ_S is given by

$$\phi_S(g) = \begin{cases} 0 & 0 \leq g \leq 4 \\ g - 4 & 4 \leq g \leq 7 \\ 3 & 7 \leq g \leq 10 \\ g - 7 & 10 \leq g \leq 13 \\ 6 & 13 \leq g \leq 14 \\ g - 8 & 14 \leq g \end{cases}$$

Hence the coefficient of y_3 is $\phi_S(d_3) = \phi_S(5) = 5 - 4 = 1$.

Essentially, the continuous cover inequalities (5) and continuous reverse cover inequalities (6) are not sufficient to describe conv $(\mathcal{X})$, as the additional binary variable z creates new extreme points. Furthermore, no exact separation algorithm for inequalities (5) and (6) has been proposed yet. Next we introduce a new class of valid inequalities for $\mathcal{X}$ that utilizes the concept of minimal influencing set. We use the similar definition of minimal influencing set from [6], which we include here for the reader's convenience:

Table 1. Continuous cover and continuous reverse cover inequalities of Example 1

$x + 7y_1 + 6y_2 + 5y_3 + 4y_4 \geq 8z$		
Index k	Set	Facet-defining inequality
2	$S = \{2,3,4\}$, $T = \{1,2\}$	$x + y_1 + y_2 + y_3 + y_4 \geq 2z$
1	$S = \{1,3,4\}$, $T = \{1,2\}$	$x + 2y_1 + y_2 + 2y_3 + 2y_4 \geq 3z$
1	$S = \{1,2,4\}$, $T = \{1,3\}$	$x + 3y_1 + 3y_2 + y_3 + 3y_4 \geq 4z$
1	$S = \{1,2,3\}$, $T = \{1,4\}$	$x + 4y_1 + 4y_2 + 4y_3 + y_4 \geq 5z$
2	$S = \{1,2,4\}$, $T = \{2,3\}$	$x + 4y_1 + 3y_2 + 2y_3 + 3y_4 \geq 5z$
2	$S = \{1,2,3\}$, $T = \{2,4\}$	$x + 5y_1 + 4y_2 + 4y_3 + 2y_4 \geq 6z$
3	$S = \{1,2,3\}$, $T = \{3,4\}$	$x + 6y_1 + 5y_2 + 4y_3 + 3y_4 \geq 7z$

Definition 1 [6]. *Let $p_i \in [h_i - 1] \cup \{0\}$ be an incentive payment to node $i \in V$ and $M \subseteq N_i$ be a set of active neighbors of node $i \in V$, such that $p_i + \sum_{j \in M} d_{ji} = h_i$. We say M is a minimal influencing set for node $i \in V$ if and only if for a fixed incentive payment $\overline{p}_i$, it satisfies $\overline{p}_i + \sum_{j \in M} d_{ji} = h_i$ and $\overline{p}_i + \sum_{j \in M \setminus \{k\}} d_{ji} < h_i$ for any $k \in M$. In other words, a strict subset of M with the same incentive payment are not sufficient to activate node i. For each node $i \in V$, let $\Omega_i \subseteq N_i$ be the superset of all minimal influencing sets.*

Theorem 1. *Let $M \subseteq N$ be a minimum influencing subset with an incentive payment $p > 0$. The minimal influencing subset inequality*

$$x + \sum_{j \in N \setminus M} \min\{d_j, p\} y_j \geq pz \tag{9}$$

is valid for $\mathcal{X}$.

Proof. If $z = 0$ then inequality (9) is trivially satisfied. If $y_j = 0$ for all $j \in N \setminus M$, then either $x = 0$ for $z = 0$ or $x = p$ for $z = 1$. Assume that none of these cases hold, given a $p > 0$, rewrite the left term of the inequality in $\mathcal{X}$ in the following form

$$\begin{aligned} & x + \sum_{j \in N} d_j y_j \\ = \; & x + \sum_{j \in N \setminus M : d_j \leq p} d_j y_j + p \sum_{j \in N \setminus M : d_j > p} y_j + \sum_{j \in M} d_j y_j \geq h, \end{aligned}$$

which implies

$$x + \sum_{j \in N \setminus M : d_j \leq p} d_j y_j + p \sum_{j \in N \setminus M : d_j > p} y_j \geq h - \sum_{j \in M} d_j y_j \geq h - \sum_{j \in M} d_j = p.$$

Theorem 2. *Inequality* (9) *is facet-defining for* conv ($\mathcal{X}$) *if and only if* $p > 0$. *Moreover, for a given* $i \in V$ *and a set* N_i, *for each* $M \subseteq N_i$ *such that* $h_i - \sum_{j \in M} d_{ji} = p_i > 0$, *the minimal influencing subset inequality*

$$x_i + \sum_{j \in N_i \setminus M} \min\{d_{ji}, p_i\} y_{ji} \geq p_i z_i \tag{10}$$

is facet-defining for conv ($\cap_{i \in [n]} \mathcal{X}_i$).

Proof. Note that $\mathcal{X}$ is full-dimensional and contains the origin. If $p = 0$, the inequality (9) reduces to $x \geq 0$, therefore $p > 0$ is a necessary and sufficient facet condition. To show that inequalities (9) is facet-defining for $\mathcal{X}$, we exhibit $t + 1$ linearly independent points on the face defined by inequality (9). Consider the two feasible points where $x^0 = z^0 = 0$, $x^1 = h - d_j$, $z^1 = 1$, $y_j^0 = y_j^1 = 1$ if $j \in M$ and $y_j^0 = y_j^1 = 0$ otherwise. Next, for a fixed $j \in M$ and for each $k \in N \setminus M$, consider the feasible points $(x^k, y_j^k, z^k) = (0, y_j^0 + e_k, 1)$. It is straightforward to verify that these $t + 1$ points are linearly independent and satisfy inequality (9) at equality. The second part of this theorem directly follows the above by considering $(x_i^0, y_{ji}^0, z_i^0) = (0, e_j, 0)$ and $(x_i^1, y_{ji}^1, z_i^1) = (h_i - d_{ji}, 1, 1)$ if $j \in M$, $y_{ji}^0 = y_{ji}^1 = 0$ otherwise, there are $2n$ points in this form for $i \in V$. Also, consider the $m - 1$ points $(x_i^k, y_{ji}^k, z_i^k) = (0, y_{ji}^0 + e_k, 1)$ for $i \in V$, a fixed $j \in M$ and for each $k \in N_i \setminus M$. These $2n + m - 1$ points on the face defined by inequality (10) are linearly independent, therefore inequality (10) is facet-defining for conv ($\cap_{i \in [n]} \mathcal{X}_i$).

Example 1 (Continued). The facet-defining inequalities of (9) for Example 1 are listed in Table 2

Table 2. Minimal influencing subset inequalities of Example 1

$x + 7y_1 + 6y_2 + 5y_3 + 4y_4 \geq 8z$	
Set	Facet-defining inequality
$M = \{1\}$	$x + y_2 + y_3 + y_4 \geq z$
$M = \{2\}$	$x + 2y_1 + 2y_3 + 2y_4 \geq 2z$
$M = \{3\}$	$x + 3y_1 + 3y_2 + 3y_4 \geq 3z$
$M = \{4\}$	$x + 4y_1 + 4y_2 + 4y_3 \geq 4z$

Although inequalities (5), (6) and (9) define a large number of facets for conv ($\mathcal{X}$), they are not sufficient to completely describe conv ($\mathcal{X}$) in its original space of variables. Particularly, the following inequality is valid and facet-defining for this example but cannot be obtained through inequalities (5), (6) or (9):

$$x + 3y_1 + 2y_2 + 2y_3 + 2y_4 \geq 4z.$$

2.1 Separation of Minimal Influencing Subset Inequalities

In this section, we give an exact polynomial time separation algorithm for finding the most violated minimal influencing subset inequality. From inequality (10), we observe that finding the most violated inequality for a given fractional solution $(x^*, y^*, z^*) \in \mathbb{R}_+^{2n+m}$ consists of choosing a set $M \subseteq N_i$ such that $p_i z_i - \sum_{j \in N_i \setminus M} \min\{d_{ji}, p_i\} y_{ji}$ is maximized. Let $t := \max\{|N_i| : i \in V\}$.

Theorem 3. *Given a fractional solution* $(x^*, y^*, z^*) \in \mathbb{R}_+^{2n+m}$ *from solving LCIM, there exists an* $O(nt \log t)$ *separation algorithm for inequality* (10).

Proof. Recall that a violated cut can be found if

$$p_i \left(z_i^* - \sum_{j \in N_i \setminus M : d_{ji} > p_i} y_{ji}^* \right) - \sum_{j \in N_i \setminus M : d_{ji} \le p_i} d_{ji} y_{ji}^* > x_i^*,$$

which implies that it suffices to consider y_{ji}^* for some $j \in N_i$ such that $z_i^* - \sum_{j \in N_i} y_{ji}^* > 0$ and $p_i > 0$. To do so, we sort y_{ji}^* in a non-decreasing order for $j \in N_i$ with indices $j_1, j_2, \cdots, j_t$ such that $y_{j_1 i}^* \le y_{j_2 i}^* \le \cdots \le y_{j_t i}^*$. For $j_1 \le j_r \le j_t$, we sum up first r elements, then we check if $z_i^* - \sum_{\ell=1}^{r} y_{j_\ell i}^* > 0$ and $p_i' = h_i - \sum_{\ell=r+1}^{t} d_{j_\ell i} > 0$, until $z_i^* - \sum_{\ell=1}^{r+1} y_{j_\ell i}^* < 0$. These r elements constitute the subset M and $N_i \setminus M$ simultaneously and ensure $z_i^* - \sum_{j \in N_i \setminus M} y_{ji}^* > 0$ and $p_i > 0$ in order to generate a violated cut. The set M that corresponds to the most violated cut can be determined by evaluating $\max\left\{0, p_i'(z_i^* - \sum_{\ell=1}^{r} y_{j_\ell i}^*) : r \in [1, t]\right\}$. If $\max\left\{0, p_i'(z_i^* - \sum_{\ell=1}^{r} y_{j_\ell i}^*) : r \in [1, t]\right\} = 0$, then there are no violated cuts. The sorting process runs in $O(t \log t)$ time and the evaluation takes $O(t)$ time, since we have to check for every node $i \in V$; thus, overall the separation algorithm runs in $O(nt \log t)$ time.

Example 2. Consider a directed tree graph where $V = \{1, 2, 3, 4, 5\}$ and $A = \{(1,5), (2,5), (3,5), (4,5)\}$. Assume the influence weight vector $\mathbf{d} = \langle 7, 6, 5, 4 \rangle$ and $h_5 = 8$. Let $\tau = 0.2$, the linear programming relaxation solution is $\mathbf{x}^* = \langle 0.53, 0, 0, 0, 0 \rangle$, $\mathbf{z}^* = \langle 0.53, 0, 0, 0, 0.47 \rangle$ and $\mathbf{y}^* = \langle 0.53, 0, 0, 0 \rangle$. To generate inequality (10) for node 5, we sort $\mathbf{y}^*$ in a non-decreasing order and compute $z_5^* - \sum_{\ell=1}^{r} y_{j_\ell 5}^*$ for $r \in [4]$. In this example, when $r = 3$, we have $M = \{2, 3, 4\}$ and $p_5 = 8 - 7 = 1$, therefore

$$x_5 + y_{25} + y_{35} + y_{45} \ge z_5$$

cut off this fractional solution.

2.2 Separation for Continuous Cover and Continuous Reverse Cover Inequalities

Until now we give an exact polynomial separation algorithm for inequalities (10). Next, we show that a violated continuous cover inequality for $\operatorname{conv}(\cap_{i \in [n]} \mathcal{X}_i)$ can be identified by the result of Theorem 3. First, we establish the relationship between sets S and M formally.

Lemma 1. *Given $p = h - \sum_{j\in M} d_j > 0$, if there exists $k \in N\backslash M$ such that $\sum_{j\in M\cup\{k\}} d_j > h$, then $p = \pi$, $S = N\backslash M$, $\sum_{j\in M\cup\{k\}} d_j - h = \rho$ and $T = M \cup \{k\}$.*

Proof. First we arrange the term in the definition of p, let

$$p = h - \sum_{j\in M} d_j = h + \sum_{j\in N\backslash M} d_j - \sum_{j\in N} d_j.$$

Now, suppose there exists an element $k \in N\backslash M$ such that $\sum_{j\in M\cup\{k\}} d_j > h$. Since we have $\{M \cup \{k\}\} \cap N\backslash M = \{k\}$ and $\{M \cup \{k\}\} \cup N\backslash M = N$, it is clear that $S = N\backslash M$ and $T = M \cup \{k\}$ from Proposition 1. Note that p is not necessary equal to π as the range of p contains 0.

Following Lemma 1, we give a theorem on how to determine a violated continuous cover inequality efficiently by using the information of the set M. Let $\hat{t} = \max\{|S| : S \subset N_i, i \in V\}$.

Theorem 4. *Given a fractional solution $(x^*, y^*, z^*) \in \mathbb{R}_+^{2n+m}$ from solving LCIM and a set M corresponding to a violated inequality (10) for a fixed node $i \in V$, the most violated continuous cover inequality can be separated in $O(n\hat{t})$ time, if there exists any.*

Proof. Note that here we add an index i to inequalities (5) similar to (10) for LCIM. Recall that inequality (10) is violated if

$$p_i \left(z_i^* - \sum_{j\in N_i\backslash M: d_{ji} > p_i} y_{ji}^* \right) - \sum_{j\in N_i\backslash M: d_{ji} \le p_i} d_{ji} y_{ji}^* > x_i^*,$$

or equivalently by Lemma 1,

$$\pi_i z_i^* - \pi_i \sum_{j\in S: d_{ji} > \pi_i} y_{ji}^* - \sum_{j\in S: d_{ji} \le \pi_i} d_{ji} y_{ji}^* > x_i^*.$$

Now, a continuous cover inequality for a fixed node $i \in V$ and $k \in S \cap T$ is violated if

$$\min\{\pi_i, d_{ki}\} z_i^* + \sum_{j\in T\backslash\{k\}} \phi_S(d_{ji})(z_i^* - y_{ji}^*) - \sum_{j\in S} \min\{\pi_i, d_{ji}\} y_{ji}^* > x_i^*.$$

Suppose $d_{ki} \ge \pi_i$, then the left term of the continuous cover inequality can be further written as

$$\pi_i z_i^* + \sum_{j\in N\backslash S} \phi_S(d_{ji})(z_i^* - y_{ji}^*) - \pi_i \sum_{j\in S: d_{ji} > \pi_i} y_{ji}^* - \sum_{j\in S: d_{ji} \le \pi_i} d_{ji} y_{ji}^*.$$

Since $(z_i^* - y_{ji}^*) \ge 0$ holds and the lifting function ϕ_S is nonnegative, the left term of the continuous cover inequality clearly violates the current solution

(x^*, y^*, z^*) when inequality (10) is violated. Otherwise, we need to compute $d_{ki}z_i^* + \sum_{j\in N\setminus S} \phi_S(d_{ji})(z_i^* - y_{ji}^*)$ to determine if it violates the current fractional solution. It takes $O(\hat{t})$ steps to compare d_{ki} and π_i for some $k \in S$ and for a fixed $i \in V$, hence, overall the complexity is $O(n\hat{t})$ to evaluate every node. In addition, the proof also suggests that $\pi_i < d_{ki}$ for $k \in S$ is necessary and sufficient to generate a violated continuous cover inequality.

Corollary 1. *Using the result of Theorem 3, the most violated continuous reverse cover inequality can be separated in $O(n\hat{t})$ time, if there exists any.*

3 Preliminary Computational Results

In this section, we report the preliminary computational results obtained by applying the aforementioned techniques on network instances from Fischetti et al. [6]. In particular, the data instances are generated based on directed small-world (SW) graphs [16], with node set $V \in \{50, 75, 100\}$ and average node degree $k \in \{4, 8, 12, 16\}$. The influence factor d_{ij} for all $(i, j) \in A$ are generated uniformly randomly in $\{1, \cdots, 10\}$. For each node $i \in V$, the threshold $h_i = \max\{1, \min\{\eta_i, \sum_{j\in N_i} d_{ji}\}\}$, where η_i is a random variable follows normal distribution with mean $0.7\sum_{j\in N_i} d_{ji}$ and variance $\frac{\sum_{j\in N_i} d_{ji}}{|N_i|}$. The data instances are available at http://mario.ruthmair.at/wp-content/uploads/2020/04/socnet-instances-v2.zip. Here, we take five SW instances with $n = 50$, $m = 200$, where the average node degree is 4 and the connection probability between nodes is 0.1. We let τ be 0.1. The experiments are performed on a Quad-Core Intel Core i7 machine with 3.1 GHz and the memory limit is 16 GB. The computation time limit is set to 3600 s. The model and branch-and-cut algorithm are implemented in Python 3 with the Python-MIP package [1]. Gurobi 9.0.1 is used as the optimization solver. The minimum subset inequalities are separated and added to the branch-and-bound nodes dynamically, while the generalized cycle elimination constraints are implemented as lazy constraints. In Table 3, we report the final gap, number of user cuts and lazy constraints added, overall computational time, and time spent on the separation routine. Based on these small-scale computations, the results

Table 3. Computational results for SW-50-200 instances from [6].

Instance #	User cuts	Lazy constraints	Overall time (sec)	SEP time (sec)	Gap
1	3	1101	2.44	2.14	0
2	72	5734	29.21	21.31	0
3	29	174	34.65	23.54	0
4	195	6857	26.6	15.78	0
5	192	623	1.59	1.24	0

appear encouraging in the sense that the application of the proposed techniques allows one to find solutions with zero gap in a reasonable time. Thus, we believe that these approaches should be further addressed in larger-scale computational experiments.

4 Conclusion

We study the polyhedral structure of least cost influence maximization problem where the influence propagation is based on deterministic linear threshold model. In the process we exploit existing results on mixed 0-1 knapsack polyhedron and present a new class of valid inequalities for the influence propagation constraint in a single-node relaxation. We show that even for a small instance, these facet-defining inequalities are not sufficient to describe the convex hull. We propose an exact separation for the new valid inequalities and take advantage of the result to separate the inequalities proposed by [13]. The preliminary computations demonstrate the separation routine does not consume too much time in the experiments. Promising future research works include the development of a branch-and-cut algorithm that utilizes our proposed inequalities together with some pre-processing enhancements to reduce the computational burden on large social network instances.

References

1. https://www.python-mip.com/
2. Ackerman, E., Ben-Zwi, O., Wolfovitz, G.: Combinatorial model and bounds for target set selection. Theor. Comput. Sci. **411**(44–46), 4017–4022 (2010)
3. Chen, N.: On the approximability of influence in social networks. SIAM J. Discret. Math. **23**(3), 1400–1415 (2009)
4. Chen, W., Lakshmanan, L.V., Castillo, C.: Information and influence propagation in social networks. Synth. Lect. Data Manag. **5**(4), 1–177 (2013)
5. Demaine, E.D., et al.: How to influence people with partial incentives. In: Proceedings of the 23rd International Conference on World Wide Web, pp. 937–948 (2014)
6. Fischetti, M., Kahr, M., Leitner, M., Monaci, M., Ruthmair, M.: Least cost influence propagation in (social) networks. Math. Program. **170**(1), 293–325 (2018)
7. Granovetter, M.: Threshold models of collective behavior. Am. J. Sociol. **83**(6), 1420–1443 (1978)
8. Günneç, D., Raghavan, S., Zhang, R.: A branch-and-cut approach for the least cost influence problem on social networks. Networks **76**(1), 84–105 (2020)
9. Günneç, D., Raghavan, S., Zhang, R.: Least-cost influence maximization on social networks. INFORMS J. Comput. **32**(2), 289–302 (2020)
10. Gursoy, F., Günneç, D.: Influence maximization in social networks under deterministic linear threshold model. Knowl.-Based Syst. **161**, 111–123 (2018)
11. Kempe, D., Kleinberg, J., Tardos, É.: Maximizing the spread of influence through a social network. In: Proceedings of the Ninth ACM SIGKDD International Conference on Knowledge Discovery and Data Mining, pp. 137–146 (2003)

12. Kempe, D., Kleinberg, J., Tardos, E.: Maximizing the spread of influence through a social network. Theory Comput. **11**(4), 105–147 (2015)
13. Marchand, H., Wolsey, L.A.: The 0–1 knapsack problem with a single continuous variable. Math. Program. **85**(1), 15–33 (1999)
14. Nannicini, G., Sartor, G., Traversi, E., Wolfler Calvo, R.: An exact algorithm for robust influence maximization. Math. Program. **183**(1), 419–453 (2020)
15. Raghavan, S., Zhang, R.: A branch-and-cut approach for the weighted target set selection problem on social networks. Inf. J. Optim. **1**(4), 304–322 (2019)
16. Watts, D.J., Strogatz, S.H.: Collective dynamics of 'small-world' networks. Nature **393**(6684), 440–442 (1998)
17. Wu, H.H., Küçükyavuz, S.: A two-stage stochastic programming approach for influence maximization in social networks. Comput. Optim. Appl. **69**(3), 563–595 (2018)

Double-Threshold Models for Network Influence Propagation

Alexander Semenov[1], Alexander Veremyev[2], Eduardo L. Pasiliao[3], and Vladimir Boginski[2(✉)]

[1] University of Florida, Gainesville, FL, USA
[2] University of Central Florida, Orlando, FL, USA
vladimir.boginski@ucf.edu
[3] Air Force Research Laboratory, Eglin AFB, FL, USA

Abstract. We consider new models of activation/influence propagation in networks based on the concept of *double thresholds*: a node will "activate" if at least a certain minimum fraction of its neighbors are active and no more than a certain maximum fraction of neighbors are active. These models are more flexible than standard threshold models as they allow to incorporate more complex dynamics of diffusion processes when nodes can activate and deactivate, which have possible interpretations, for instance, in the context of communication and social networks. In a social network, consistently with the hypothesis originally mentioned by Granovetter (1978), a person may "activate" (e.g., adopt and/or repost an opinion) if *sufficiently many* but *not too many* of their friends (i.e., neighbors in a network) have adopted this opinion. We study several versions of this problem setup under different assumptions on activation/deactivation mechanisms and initial choices of seed nodes, and compare the results to the well-known "single threshold" (e.g., linear threshold) models.

Keywords: Influence propagation · Double-threshold models · Social networks

1 Introduction

Activation and influence propagation processes are common in certain types of real-world networks, such as social networks (i.e., friends in a social media network influence each other's opinions, beliefs, etc.) and communication networks (i.e., communication devices transmitting information to neighboring nodes). Mathematical modeling of influence propagation in graphs, as well as the identification of the actors that can play an important role in facilitating such activation cascades have recently received significant attention in the research community.

This material is based on work supported by the AFRL Mathematical Modeling and Optimization Institute.

S. Chellappan et al. (Eds.): CSoNet 2020, LNCS 12575, pp. 512–523, 2020.
https://doi.org/10.1007/978-3-030-66046-8_42

The most commonly used influence propagation models considered in the literature are based on activation thresholds [7,18] which include "linear threshold" models [10,20], where a node in a network would "activate" if a certain minimum fraction of its neighbors are active. One can refer to such models as *"single threshold"* models.

In this work, we consider linear threshold models of activation/influence propagation in networks based on the concept of *double thresholds*: a node will "activate" if at least a certain *minimum* fraction of its neighbors are active and no more than a certain *maximum* fraction of neighbors are active. The hypothesis of the existence of both lower and upper activation thresholds in a social network was first mentioned in the seminal work on threshold models by Granovetter [7]: *"Suppose you are in an unfamiliar town and enter an unknown restaurant on Saturday evening at seven o'clock. Whether or not you decide to take a meal there will depend in part on how many others have also decided to do so. If the place is nearly empty, it is probably a bad sign - without some minimum number of diners, one would probably try another place. But the (benefit) curve will cross the x-axis again at a later point - where the restaurant is so crowded that the waiting time would be unbearable. Some cautious individuals might join a riot when 50% of the others have but leave when the total passed 90% for fear that so large a riot would bring official reprisals."* In other contexts, for instance, in online social networks, a person may "activate" (e.g., adopt and/or repost an opinion) if sufficiently many but not too many of their friends (neighbors in a network) have adopted this opinion. In communication networks, a node (device) would transmit information if it has been obtained and deemed reliable by a certain minimum number of neighbors; however, to save power, it might not transmit that information if most of the neighbors already have it. Simply speaking, when activation incurs some cost, the total benefit from activation might be positive only when sufficiently many but not too many neighbors are active.

Another advantage that double threshold models have over their standard single threshold counterparts is in their ability to model more complex dynamics of influence propagation processes when nodes can activate and deactivate. Indeed, one can imagine the situation when an active node may decide to deactivate if the number of its active neighbors becomes too large or too small.

To understand the effect of such ability of nodes to deactivate and compare the corresponding influence propagation processes we consider two baseline models:

1. A node will activate if the number of active neighbors falls between the lower and upper thresholds and will not activate otherwise. If a node activates, it will then stay active (e.g., if one decides to repost something on social media, they would not "un-repost"); *or*
2. A node will activate under the aforementioned conditions, but may later deactivate if the number of active neighbors is no longer between the specified lower and upper thresholds.

Each of the above assumptions can be easily motivated by real-life situations. For instance, for the first case (without deactivation), if a person has "activated" in the context that they have bought a car of a certain make/model, they would be unlikely to switch to a different car in a short-term horizon, even if too many of their peers have got the same car. In the second case (with deactivation), a researcher may decide to work in a certain area if it becomes popular among sufficiently many of their peers, but they may change their mind later (i.e., "deactivate") if too many other researchers start working in that area, making it more competitive and harder to produce new and significant results.

Under either of the above setups, we also assume that the activation cascade starts from a small subset of *"seed nodes"* that are active at the initial time moment and stay active throughout the process.

To our knowledge, there are no previous studies that analyze the double threshold models from a rigorous mathematical modeling and computational perspective. In the sections below, we first introduce formal definitions and notation that will be used in this paper; then we briefly review several well-known techniques for choosing seed nodes for influence maximization in networks. We then present and compare the results of applying double-threshold versus single-threshold models to select network datasets under different assumptions on the selection of seed nodes.

2 Model Definitions and Notation

Consider a finite graph $G = (N, \mathcal{A})$ with a set of n nodes (vertices) $N = \{1, ..., n\}$ and a set of m arcs $\mathcal{A} \subset N \times N$, $|N| = n$ and $|\mathcal{A}| = m$. If $(i, j) \in \mathcal{A}$, then it is assumed that node i has an influence over node j. The neighborhood $\mathcal{N}(i)$ of a node i is a set of all nodes k influencing node i, i.e., $k \in \mathcal{N}(i)$ for all $(k, i) \in \mathcal{A}$.

When a node of a graph adopts certain information, in parlance of [10] it gets "activated". Guille et al. [8] define **activation sequence** as an *ordered set of nodes capturing the order in which the vertices of the network adopted a piece of information.* The first node in the activation sequence is referred to as *seed node.* Then, ***spreading cascade*** *is a directed tree having as a root the first node of the activation sequence. The tree captures the influence between nodes (branches represent who transmitted the information to whom) and unfolds in the same order as the activation sequence. Influence* of a set of nodes S is the expected number of activated nodes at the end of the cascade process, given that nodes in S are *seed nodes* [10]. Then, *influence maximization* is a problem to find such a set S that will result in maximal influence. Further, if node i is activated, we denote it as i_+; if node is not activated, we denote it as i_-. Then, $\mathcal{N}_+(i)$ is the set of active neighbors of node i. In the original linear threshold model, each node $i \in N$ is equipped with a threshold $\theta_i \in [0, 1]$. In each timestep $\{1, ..., T\}$ of the information propagation process each node i receives pieces of information from its active neighbors $\mathcal{N}_+(i)$ and computes $\widehat{\theta}_i = \frac{|\mathcal{N}_+(i)|}{|\mathcal{N}(i)|}$. If $\widehat{\theta}_i \geq \theta_i$, the node i gets activated, otherwise node keeps being inactive.

In the proposed *double threshold model*, each node i is equipped with two thresholds: lower threshold θ_i^ℓ, and upper threshold θ_i^u. As in a single threshold model, each node i receives information from its active neighbors, and computes $\widehat{\theta}_i$, but this time decision to become activated is made only if $\theta_i^\ell \leq \widehat{\theta}_i < \theta_i^u$. This expression models the process of adopting certain opinion if some fraction of the peers, but not too many peers, have adopted it. Note that the double threshold model becomes equivalent to the single threshold model if $\theta_i^u > 1$ for all nodes $i \in N$.

An interesting feature that the double threshold model brings to the cascade propagation process is the possibility of node *deactivations*. Indeed, when a node activates, it is possible that later the fraction of its active neighbors moves outside the upper and lower threshold limits, and one can make a modeling assumption that a node may decide to deactivate in such a situation. One of the models considered in this paper allows nodes, after activation, to deactivate once. Note that the spreading cascade may no longer be directed tree. We demonstrate that this assumption may result in significant differences is cascade propagation. To illustrate the intuition behind it, we provide a simple example for the considered models on the same small network: single threshold (Fig. 1), double thresholds without deactivation (Fig. 2), and double threshold with deactivation (Fig. 3). One can easily observe that the resulting sets of active nodes (after the end of the cascading process) are different for each model, even though the values of lower and upper (where applicable) thresholds are the same for all three cases.

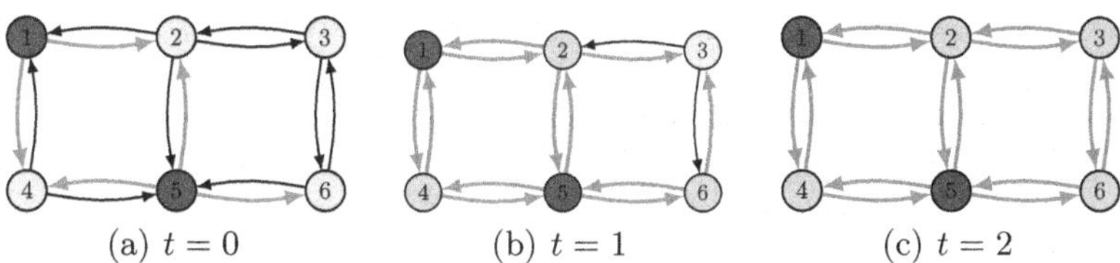

Fig. 1. Activation cascade in single threshold model where each node i has activation threshold $\theta_i = 0.3$ (same for all nodes) and nodes 1 and 5 are active (seed) nodes at time $t = 0$. At time $t = 1$ nodes 2, 4 and 6 become active. At time $t = 2$ node 3 becomes active and all nodes are active.

3 Seed Selection for Influence Maximization

There is large body of research on influence maximization in social networks (see, e.g., recent surveys [1,12,22]). Kempe et al. [10] have shown that influence maximization problem for both linear threshold and independent cascade models is NP-hard. Erkol et al. [6] reported a systematic comparison of heuristic algorithms for influence maximization. In addition to greedy influence maximization methods [4,10] and a random baseline, previous studies have evaluated various criteria of seed nodes selection, including taking nodes with highest degrees,

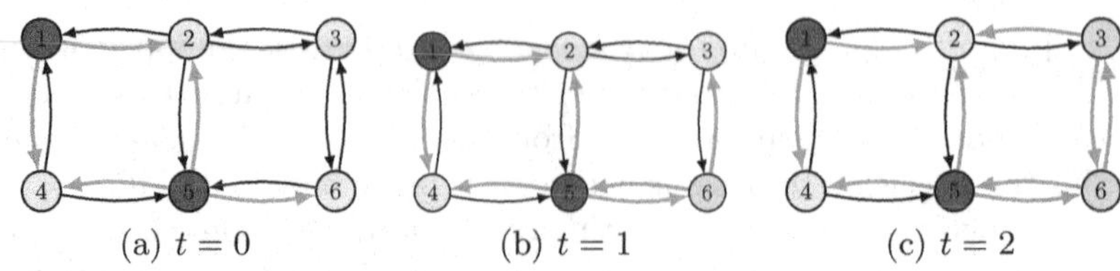

Fig. 2. Activation cascade in double threshold model without deactivation (once node becomes active, it stays active) where each node i has a double activation threshold $\theta_i^\ell = 0.3$ and $\theta_i^u = 0.6$ (node activates only if fraction of its active in-neighbors is in this interval). Nodes 1 and 5 are active (seed) nodes at time $t = 0$. At time $t = 1$ node 6 activates (50% of its neighbors are active), and nodes 2 and 4 do not activate (too many neighbors are active). At time $t = 2$ node 3 activates and nodes 2, 5 remain inactive, cascade stops.

highest adaptive degrees, betweenness, closeness, eigenvector, and Katz centralities, PageRank, non-backtracking, MinSum [2], k-shell [11], LocalRank (measure based on size of neighborhood and neighborhoods of nearest neighbors) [3], h-index, a metric commonly used in scientists' performance measurements [19], CoreHD [21], Collective Influence (CI) [13], and explosive immunization score [5]. According to [6], choosing seeds using simple measures, such as adaptive degree and closeness centrality, is efficient for influence maximization. There are also other comparisons of influence maximization algorithms, for example, collective influence method is compared with belief propagation-based decimation, in the favor of the latter, in [9]. Another comparison of heuristics for social influence maximization [15] concluded that degree- and PageRank-based techniques do not perform well in this task, but the best seeds are located in a k-core of the network. Further in the paper, we will use some of the aforementioned heuristics in the context of double-threshold models.

It should be noted that in addition to finding a set of nodes having maximal influence, there is a related optimization problem: finding such a set of "superblocker" nodes that would block the spread of information [16]. Besides linear threshold and independent cascade models, there are other models proposed for modelling propagation dynamics. They include models with dynamic propagation rate [14] and partial parallel cascade model, where nodes may also have negative influence [17]. Although we do not consider those models in this study, it might be interesting to put them in the context of double threshold models in future work.

4 Results

In this section, we investigate the performance of our proposed double-threshold models (both with and without deactivation of nodes) under various approaches to selecting the initially activated seed nodes. In addition, we compare the results of influence propagation cascades in the settings of double thresholds with the classical "single" (linear) threshold model.

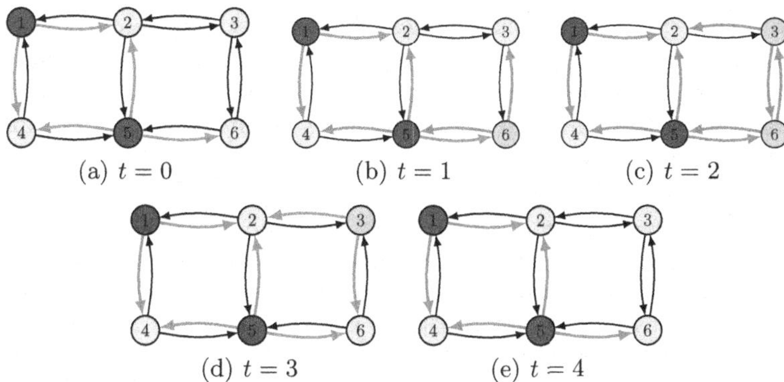

Fig. 3. Activation cascade in double threshold model where each node i has a double activation threshold $\theta_i^\ell = 0.3$ and $\theta_i^u = 0.6$ and nodes can deactivate once if the fraction of active in-neighbors is outside the double threshold limits. Seed nodes 1 and 5 are active at time $t = 0$ and do not deactivate. At time $t = 1$ node 6 activates (50% of its neighbors are active), and nodes 2 and 4 do not activate (too many neighbors are active). At time $t = 2$ node 3 activates and nodes 2, 5 remain inactive. At time $t = 3$ node 6 deactivates (too many active neighbors). At time $t = 4$ node 3 deactivates (no active neighbors) and cascade stops.

For our computations, we consider 11 heuristics from the ones mentioned in the previous section which are commonly used in target (seed) set selection problem in influence maximization models: LocalRank, PageRank, Eigenvector centrality, coreHD, h-index, Collective Influence (with radius 1 and 2), node degree, closeness, betweenness centralities, and randomly chosen nodes. We have simulated cascade propagation dynamics with varying sizes of the seed set. Specifically, we have performed the simulations for each heuristic with seed set sizes ranging from 1% to 10% of all the nodes in a network.

In order to demonstrate the differences in influence propagation processes between different seed set sizes and selection approaches, as well as between single and double threshold models, we have run simulations on multiple real-world and synthetic networks. Due to space limitations, here we report the results on two representative real-world network instances: the largest connected components of the well-known Enron Email and Facebook datasets (Table 1 in [23]). These networks contain 33,696 nodes and 180,811 edges, and 63,392 nodes and 816,886 edges, respectively (we assume that each edge corresponds to two arcs going in both directions).

In the first set of experiments, we consider the performance of the aforementioned 11 seed selection heuristics for various sizes of the seed set: from 1% to 10% of the network size. We let the node activation cascades run until no further nodes change their activation status and evaluated the percentage of network nodes (which is also referred to as "outbreak size") that are active at the end of the cascading process. Figures 4, 5, 6, 7 and 8 show the results of these experiments using two different setups of the double-threshold models (with and without deactivation of nodes). From these figures, one can observe that the results of the "best" heuristics for seed selection vary depending on the considered model and the percentage of initially selected seeds.

Overall, for the double-threshold model without node deactivation, the coreHD heuristic for seed selection appears to perform well in terms of the final percentage of activated nodes. However, it is sometimes outperformed by the highest degree-based heuristic in the cases of smaller percentages of initially active seed nodes, and by closeness/betweenness centrality-based heuristics for larger percentages of seed nodes. Based on these observations, one may hypothesize that for a cascade that starts from a relatively small number of seeds, *"local"* connectivity/centrality of seed nodes (i.e., nodes that are connected to many immediate neighbors) is important, whereas if the number of initially active seed nodes is large, then *"global"* centrality of these nodes (i.e., how well-positioned these nodes are with respect to information transmission paths in the entire network) becomes more important. As for the model with node deactivation, the results suggest that coreHD and PageRank are often the best approaches for seed selection, especially for larger percentages of initially active seed nodes. However, the highest degree-based approach still appears to be the best for the cases of small percentage of initially selected seeds.

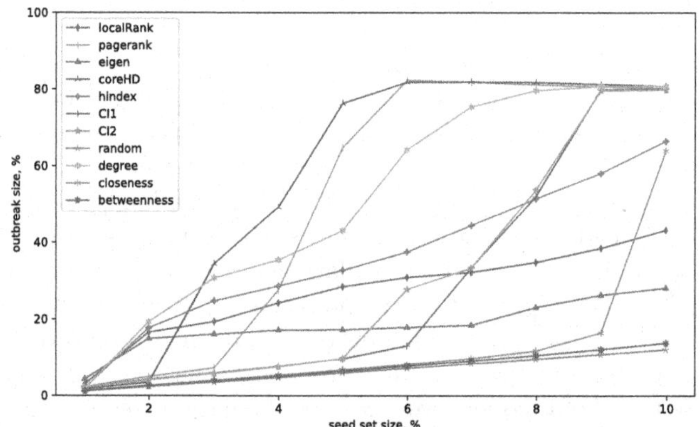

Fig. 4. Dependency of overall outbreak size on the size of the seed set for Facebook dataset (model without node deactivations). Horizontal axis shows seed set size, and vertical axis shows size of the outbreak at the last stage of the cascade. Lower threshold = 0.5, upper threshold = 0.8. It can be observed that coreHD is the best heuristic on average; however, it does not perform well for small sizes of seed set.

In the second set of computational experiments, we compare the percentages of activated nodes for single-threshold (i.e., no upper threshold) versus double-threshold models (with and without deactivation). Figures 9, 10 and 11 show the respective results on the same network datasets as in the first set of experiments. One can observe that for all the presented examples, the percentage of activated nodes in later stages of the cascade is substantially smaller for

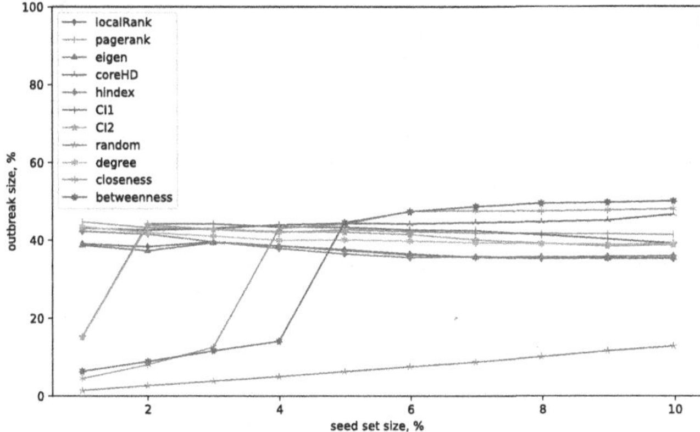

Fig. 5. Dependency of overall outbreak size on the size of the seed set for Enron Email dataset (model without node deactivations). Horizontal axis shows seed set size, and vertical axis shows size of the outbreak at the last stage of the cascade. Lower threshold = 0.5, upper threshold = 0.8. It can be observed that coreHD is outperformed by closeness and betweenness centralities for larger sizes of cascade.

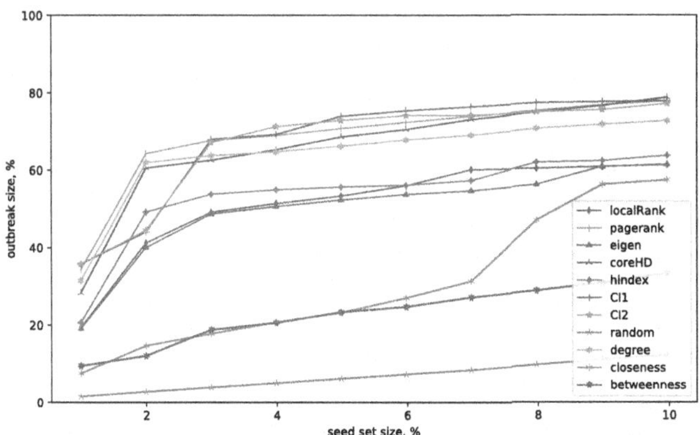

Fig. 6. Dependency of overall outbreak size on the size of the seed set for Enron Email dataset (model without node deactivations). Horizontal axis shows seed set size, and vertical axis shows size of the outbreak at the last stage of the cascade. Lower threshold = 0.6, no upper threshold. It can be observed that coreHD, and collective influences heuristics perform the best. Closeness and betweenness do not perform as well as in the case shown in Fig. 5.

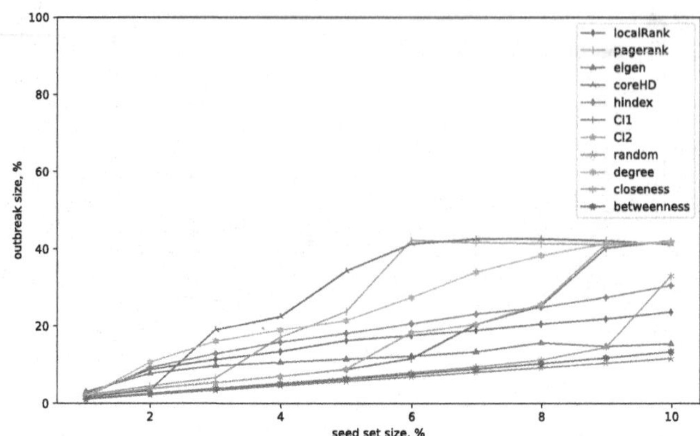

Fig. 7. Dependency of overall outbreak size on the size of the seed set for Facebook dataset (model with one deactivation allowed). Horizontal axis shows seed set size, and vertical axis shows size of the outbreak at the last stage of the cascade. Lower threshold = 0.5, upper threshold = 0.8. It can be observed that degree, coreHD, and Pagerank perform the best.

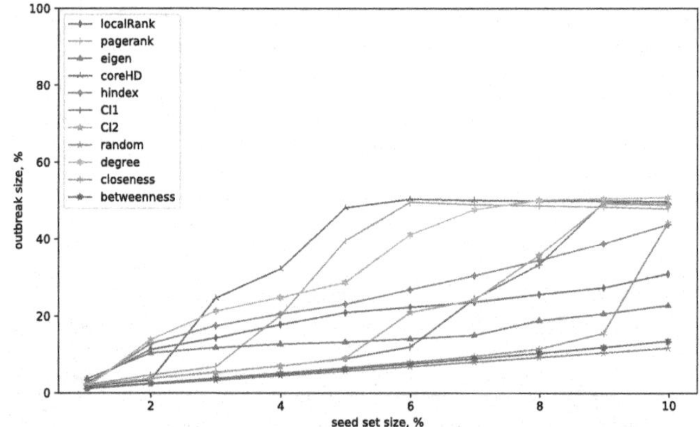

Fig. 8. Dependency of overall outbreak size on the size of the seed set for Facebook dataset (model with one deactivation allowed). Horizontal axis shows seed set size, and vertical axes shows size of the outbreak at the last stage of the cascade. Lower threshold = 0.5, upper threshold = 0.9. It can be observed that degree, coreHD, and Pagerank perform the best.

the double-threshold models compared to the single-threshold model, even if the upper threshold is equal to 1 (i.e., a node will not activate only if *all* of its neighbors are active). The difference between the percentages of activated nodes in the two models also depends on the heuristic for seed selection (e.g., the difference is more pronounced for PageRank-based seed selection). It is also interesting to observe the effect of node deactivation in the respective model (see e.g. Fig. 11 (a)), where the number of active nodes first grows and then drops and stabilizes as the cascading process develops. This observation is consistent with real-world social network behavior where the fraction of "activated" individuals (with respect to certain opinions, preferences, etc.) typically does not get close to 100% (as the single-threshold model would suggest) but rather "saturates" around 50% or lower.

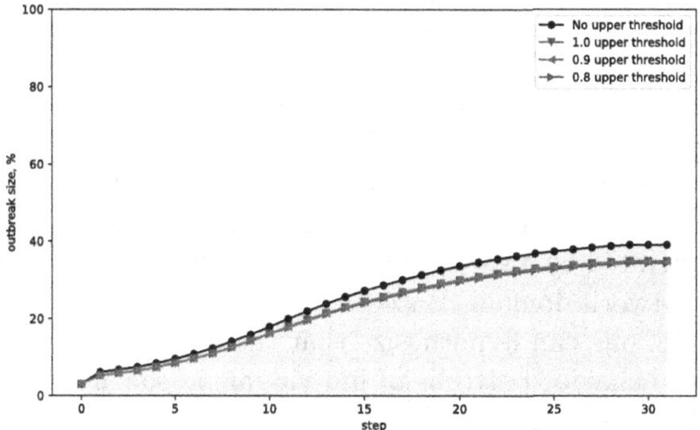

Fig. 9. Outbreak size for each simulation step (no deactivation), Facebook dataset with 3% nodes with the highest coreHD chosen as the seeds. Lower threshold is 0.5.

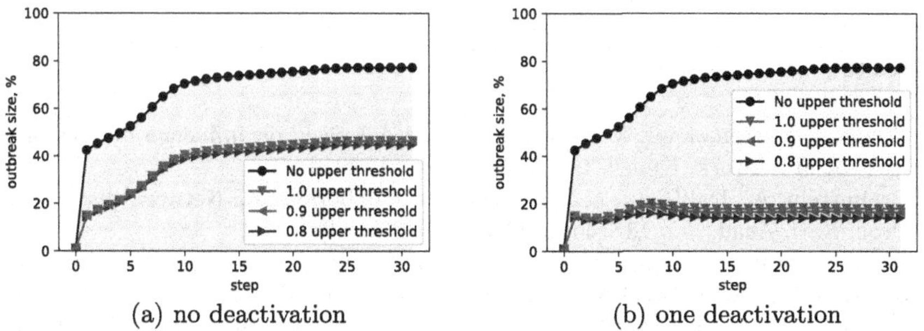

Fig. 10. Outbreak size for each simulation step, Enron Email dataset with 1% nodes with the highest PageRank chosen as the seeds. Lower threshold is 0.5.

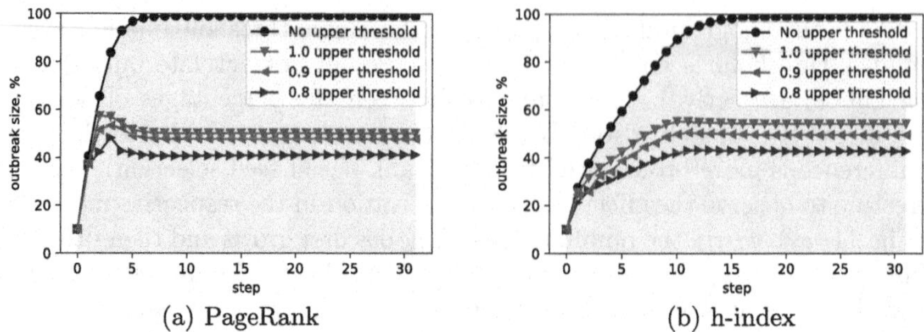

(a) PageRank (b) h-index

Fig. 11. Outbreak size for each simulation step (one deactivation allowed), Facebook dataset with 10% nodes with the highest PageRank and h-index chosen as the seeds. Lower threshold is set to 0.4. In this case effect of deactivations is less pronounced, as compared to the same setup with PageRank activations.

5 Conclusion

In this paper, we have defined and analyzed for the first time the double-threshold model of influence propagation in a network. Possible setups of this model can be motivated by a variety of real-world examples, many of which come from the social network domain. Based on the observations from our computational experiments, one can hypothesize that the double-threshold model might capture collective behavior patterns of individuals in social networks more realistically than the classical linear (single) threshold model. In particular, it can be shown that under double-threshold model assumptions, the cascading process of node activation in a network would "saturate" well before reaching 100%, which is consistent with the fact that typically not all individuals in a social network would share the same opinion, prefer the same product, etc. Overall, the presented results suggest that the proposed models provide interesting insights and should be further studied from theoretical and computational perspectives.

References

1. Banerjee, S., Jenamani, M., Pratihar, D.K.: A survey on influence maximization in a social network. Knowl. Inf. Syst. **62**, 1–39 (2020)
2. Braunstein, A., Dall'Asta, L., Semerjian, G., Zdeborová, L.: Network dismantling. Proc. Natl. Acad. Sci. **113**(44), 12368–12373 (2016)
3. Chen, D., Lü, L., Shang, M.-S., Zhang, Y.-C., Zhou, T.: Identifying influential nodes in complex networks. Phys. A: Stat. Mech. Appl. **391**(4), 1777–1787 (2012)
4. Chen, W., Wang, Y., Yang, S.: Efficient influence maximization in social networks. In: Proceedings of the 15th ACM SIGKDD Conference on Knowledge Discovery and Data Mining (KDD 2009) (June 2009)
5. Clusella, P., Grassberger, P., Pérez-Reche, F., Politi, A.: Immunization and targeted destruction of networks using explosive percolation. Phys. Rev. Lett. **117**(20), 208301 (2016)

6. Erkol, Ş., Castellano, C., Radicchi, F.: Systematic comparison between methods for the detection of influential spreaders in complex networks. Sci. Rep. **9**(1), 1–11 (2019)
7. Granovetter, M.: Threshold models of collective behavior. Am. J. Sociol. **83**(6), 1420–1443 (1978)
8. Guille, A., Hacid, H., Favre, C., Zighed, D.A.: Information diffusion in online social networks: a survey. SIGMOD Rec. **42**(2), 17–28 (2013)
9. Im, Y.S., Kahng, B.: Dismantling efficiency and network fractality. Phys. Rev. E **98**, 012316 (2018)
10. Kempe, D., Kleinberg, J., Tardos, E.: Maximizing the spread of influence through a social network. In Proceedings of the Ninth ACM SIGKDD International Conference on Knowledge Discovery and Data Mining, KDD 2003, pp. 137–146. ACM, New York (2003)
11. Kitsak, M., et al.: Identification of influential spreaders in complex networks. Nat. Phys. **6**(11), 888–893 (2010)
12. Li, Y., Fan, J., Wang, Y., Tan, K.-L.: Influence maximization on social graphs: a survey. IEEE Trans. Knowl. Data Eng. **30**(10), 1852–1872 (2018)
13. Morone, F., Makse, H.A.: Influence maximization in complex networks through optimal percolation. Nature **524**(7563), 65–68 (2015)
14. Pan, T., Li, X., Kuhnle, A., Thai, M.T.: Influence diffusion in online social networks with propagation rate changes. IEEE Trans. Netw. Sci. Eng. 1 (2020)
15. Pei, S., Muchnik, L., Andrade Jr., J.S., Zheng, Z., Makse, H.A.: Searching for superspreaders of information in real-world social media. Sci. Rep. **4**(1), 5547 (2014)
16. Radicchi, F., Castellano, C.: Fundamental difference between superblockers and superspreaders in networks. Phys. Rev. E **95**, 012318 (2017)
17. Samadi, M., Nikolaev, A., Nagi, R.: A subjective evidence model for influence maximization in social networks. Omega **59**, 263–278 (2016)
18. Schelling, T.C.: Micromotives and Macrobehavior. WW Norton & Company, New York (2006)
19. Semenov, A., Veremyev, A., Nikolaev, A., Pasiliao, E.L., Boginski, V.: Network-based indices of individual and collective advising impacts in mathematics. Comput. Soc. Netw. **7**(1), 1–18 (2020). https://doi.org/10.1186/s40649-019-0075-0
20. Shakarian, P., Bhatnagar, A., Aleali, A., Shaabani, E., Guo, R.: The independent cascade and linear threshold models. Diffusion in Social Networks. SCS, pp. 35–48. Springer, Cham (2015). https://doi.org/10.1007/978-3-319-23105-1_4
21. Zdeborová, L., Zhang, P., Zhou, H.-J.: Fast and simple decycling and dismantling of networks. Sci. Rep. **6**(1), 37954 (2016)
22. Zhang, H., Mishra, S., Thai, M.T., Wu, J., Wang, Y.: Recent advances in information diffusion and influence maximization in complex social networks. Oppor. Mob. Soc. Netw. **37**(1.1), 37 (2014)
23. Zhou, F., Lü, L., Mariani, M.S.: Fast influencers in complex networks. Commun. Nonlinear Sci. Numer. Simul. **74**, 69–83 (2019)

Protest Perspective Against COVID-19 Risk Mitigation Strategies on the German Internet

Andrzej Jarynowski[1,2(✉)], Alexander Semenov[3], and Vitaly Belik[2]

[1] Interdisciplinary Research Institute, Wroclaw, Poland
ajarynowski@interdisciplinary-research.eu

[2] System Modeling Group, Institute of Veterinary Epidemiology and Biostatistics, Freie Universität Berlin, Berlin, Germany
vitaly.belik@fu-berlin.de

[3] Herbert Wertheim College of Engineering, University of Florida, Gainesville, FL, USA
asemenov@ufl.edu

Abstract. The aim of this study is to quantitatively assess perception of protests around COVID-19 in Germany from the late July till the end of August 2020 in the Internet media by infodemiological approach. To this end we investigate Google searches, Twitter and Telegram posts, and selection of news articles via EventRegistry. We focus on narratives around Berlin Demonstrations on August 1st and August 29th, 2020. Using media intelligence we spot trends, analyze relevant topics over a longer time span and create sociolinguistic landscapes targeting Querdenken and QAnon movements and other actors such as AfD, SPD, and Green political parties and Antifa. Although the dominant actors of the protest are on the far-right political spectrum, we demonstrate (based on network analysis) that left-wing activists could both sympathize with (e.g. some liberal greens) and oppose (e.g. Antifa) the protest. Although we observe a constant interest in the protest movements in traditional media, their popularity on social media is growing (for Querdenken faster than for QAnon). The revealed insights shed light on social dynamics in the context of such major disruptive events as COVID-19 pandemic and could serve as a basis for optimization of risk awareness campaigns by the authorities.

Keywords: Protest movements · Social network analysis · COVID-19

1 Introduction

Spread of SARS-CoV-2 is mediated by human behavior and it impacts human lives not only in medical, but also in economic or social dimensions [16]. There have been protests and demonstrations around the world [26] against risk mitigation strategies during COVID-19 pandemics such as lockdowns and mandatory

S. Chellappan et al. (Eds.): CSoNet 2020, LNCS 12575, pp. 524–535, 2020.
https://doi.org/10.1007/978-3-030-66046-8_43

mask wearing. German government is longitudinally monitoring public opinion to assess optimal epidemiological effectiveness and acceptance of measures and policies during the COVID-19 pandemic [5]. Every country or even group of protesters has a different perspective and distinct factors are driving the protests. Some protesters questioned the need for a lockdown and were concerned about economical consequences of a disease allegedly "not more dangerous than flu". Some protested against breaking the citizen rights, others claimed the pandemic was planned ("Plandemic"). Such a mosaic in Berlin protests is revealed by our analysis, where representatives of the far right flank of AfD ("Alternative for Germany" political party) as well as far left flanks of liberals and greens could be contextualized around the same idea during 01.08 and 29.08 Berlin demonstrations. In the investigated COVID-19 movements we observe a very rare presence of common interests of right wing of AfD with Green/liberal movements, which must be very carefully monitored due to its potential to reach a big fraction of the population [10].

Social and traditional media can provide information and disinformation about the virus globally and locally causing [20]:

- fear of the disease which increases risk mitigation protective behavior and adherence to measures.
- anger due to the restriction, fueling anti-restriction protests [17] and backflash.

We observe a conflict between minority of population driven by anger against the restrictions with the majority of population, which accepts the measures and are negatively oriented towards anti COVID-19 protesters. Continuous monitoring of the Internet activity, information needs patterns of various groups of interest within COVID-19 discourse and the consequent data analysis is a pillar of the infodemiology [11] and digital epidemiology [24]. We concentrate on two main movements in Germany:

1. Querdenken (in English: latent thinking) – demonstration movement which main goal is to oppose the governmental measures against COVID-19. It originates in the state of Baden-Württenberg and could possibly build on the protest movement against the controversial Stuttgart21 railway renovation project.
2. QAnon - an international conspiracy theory movement popular in Germany, which among others, opposes the governmental measures against COVID-19 [12]. It is worth to mention that majority of supporters of QAnon movement (>95%) are located in English speaking countries [12] and German QAnon movement seems to be more independent and oriented more towards European issues [8,19].

1.1 Data and Methods

As each media has a different audience and reach, we focus on the following platforms:

1. Google (Trends). We have selected search keywords related to protest movements such as QAnon and Querdenken with geographical precision to a federal state, for various time spans. Search keyword intensity is measured in RSV (Relative Search Volume).
2. Twitter. We have collected tweets in German language with hashtags #B0108 (92,474) and #B2908 (345,992) for both main demonstrations on August 1st and August 29th, 2020 in Berlin.
3. News articles. We have collected information on 2,329 articles from 20.07 till 31.08 from German Internet news agencies with a keyword "Querdenken" using EventRegistry representative sample of the articles with the highest reach. QAnon concept is rarely (around 10 times less than Querdenken in September 2020) used in mainstream media (possible auto-censored), so it wasn't included into analysis.
4. Telegram. The data was collected from channels "Querdenken 711", and "QAnon Deutschland".

The passive representativeness of the Internet in Germany is relatively high and constitutes around 80% of adults population [25], but active (own content creation) is biased towards younger age groups and women. Our choice of Internet sources targets a wide share of general population with a relatively high coverage of Internet users with quite a significant audience variability across platforms with active/passive users and traditional/social-content media. We used the following methodological approaches to the analysis of the collected data:

- Statistical analysis of the time series of numbers of posts, tweets and articles in the Internet media. We tested for the change of the trend via the t-test for series and compared the growth slopes with standard error bars to assess statistical significance of the results.
- Natural Language Processing (NLP) methods such as sentiment analysis techniques.
- Social Network Analysis (SNA) of networks of the Internet media users connected via their post or tweets sharing activity.

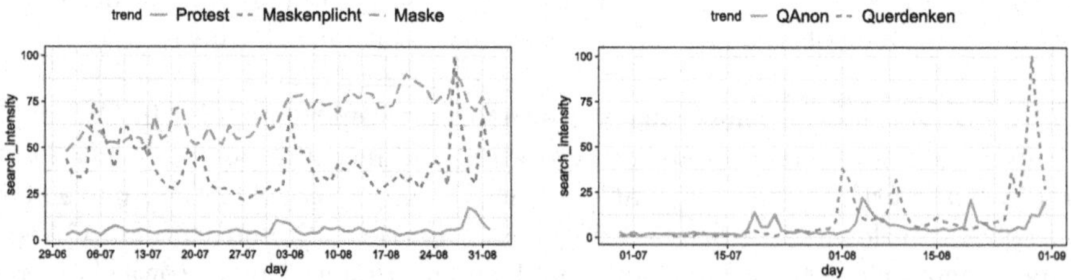

Fig. 1. [Left] The intensity of queries with the phrases "Protest", "Obligation to wear mask", "protective mask" in German Google (01.07–01.09.2020). [Right] The intensity of queries with the phrases "QAnon", "Querdenken" in German Google (15.0–01.09.2020) both generated using the Google Trends tool.

2 Results and Timeline of the Protests

Protests against the lockdown imposed by the government in Germany started already in April with hundreds of people gathering in Berlin and Stuttgart on April 26th, 2020 (Fig. 1). However, the first big event was #B0108 on August 1st, 2020 in Berlin. It gathered around 20 thousands of protesters (however protesters claim the numbers were significantly higher [27]). Even bigger protest against anti-COVID-19 measures happened on August 29, 2020 in Berlin as well (#B2908). However, authorities in the German capital have banned it on August 26, causing an avalanche of interest already before the event (Fig. 1). Eventually the state court allowed demonstrations. According to the authorities, there were around 40,000 protesters on the main demonstration on August 29, 2020 [4]. So media monitoring could be a method for preparing resources and safety cautions before such a protest could take place. In particular, the authorities apparently were not well prepared on August 29, as a group of radical right protesters attempted to enter the Parliament Building yielding very symbolic pictures.

2.1 Google

There are ca. 64,600,000 Google users in Germany with a number of German speaking users being ca. 61,370,000 (according to Google Ads from 05.05.2020). Thus Google is not only the leader on search engine market, but the also the main selector of the digital information to the public during COVID-19 pandemics [6].

Table 1. Descriptive statistics of the trend in RSV of "Querdenken" in Google one month before and one month containing the main demonstrations. Welch's two sample t-test was applied for statistical significance verification.

Querdenken RSV	29.06–30.07	31.07–31.08	t-test (p-value)
Daily RSV	Mean = 2.16	Mean = 18.87	0.00004114
Absolute change	Mean = 0.125	Mean = 0.6875	0.8528
Proportional change	Mean = 14.58	Mean = 24.05	0.5928
Linear regression slope	a = 0.097 ± 0.02	a = 0.70 ± 0.36	NA

Analyzing the trends in RSV of Querdenken and QAnon and by using Welch's two sample t-test we confirmed that popularity of Querdenken increased significantly during the main demonstrations month – August – (Table 1). This increase in popularity sped up as well and significantly if we compare regression slopes with standard errors. QAnon is also gaining popularity, however it is slowing down (Table 2). The protests in August were embedded in a complicated social context of the end of summer holidays and schools starts after holidays (Fig. 2). The interest in masks is linked with interest in anti-COVID-19 measures (Fig. 1). QAnon and Querdenken movements popularity are not

Table 2. Descriptive statistics of the trend in RSV of "QAnon" in Google one month before and one month containing the main demonstrations. Welch's two sample t-test was applied for statistical significance verification.

QAnon RSV	29.06–30.07	31.07–31.08	*t*-test (p-value)
Daily RSV	Mean = 3.3	Mean = 7.8	0.0001
Absolute change	Mean = 0.03	Mean = 0.53	0.64
Proportional change	Mean = 22.77	Mean = 19.79	0.88
Linear regression slope	a = 0.10 ± 0.05	a = 0.055 ± 0.103	NA

equally distributed across Germany (Fig. 2) and there is no significant relationship between the growth in COVID-19 incidence (being at a low level in August) and popularity of the movements which is a proxy for the demonstration attendance all around Germany.

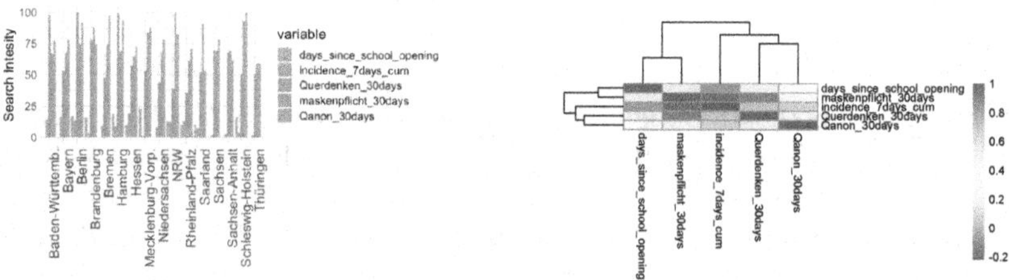

Fig. 2. Potential relationship between the interest (proxy for engagement) in sceptical thinking in terms of 30 days of Google Trends and 7 days of Google Trends, discussing the rules of wearing mask as well as epidemiology (transmission dynamics defined as 7 days incidence), and days since school opening with spatial resolution on the level of Federal States with reference to 24.08. [Left] Interaction between protest intensity, incidence and interest in anti-COVID-19 protest for various German states. [Right] Pearson correlation coefficient between significant events (school starts after holidays) and media activity.

2.2 Twitter

There were numerous attempts to analyze Twitter in the context of COVID-19, e.g. [1,13]. Twitter in Germany has about 11 million users in total and almost 2 million are using Twitter daily [18]. Using Twitter as a sampling tool for the whole society will be most efficient for age groups between 15–40. We choose such keywords or hashtags as #B0108 and #B2908 because others (#Querdenken, #Covidioten, #Deppenparade, #Berlindemo, "BranderburgerTor") are not as prevalent and are often included within the same concept already used for the search which could later come into use as Internet users are changing COVID-19-related hashtags, with selection criteria for a language being German. For these

62% of users who provided their location only less than 15% can be linked to Berlin area. Thus both demonstrations are discussed mainly by non-local populations. The vast majority of the Twitter accounts involved in the discussion were created long before the demonstration. Thus so-called Internet trolls do not seem to play a visible role, but shadowed interventions still need to be further analyzed. Notably, as we observe on Twitter, apparently an unsuccessful attempt to prohibit the #B2908 protests by the local government on August 26th caused significantly more communication volume before the main event #B0108 (Fig. 3). Structure of the retweet network, consisting of vertices being users and edges being retweets, depends on a variety of factors such as temporal dynamics of the protest (Fig. 3) and interactions or communication between and within subpopulations engaged in the protests. We applied unsupervised weighted Louvain algorithm [7] for community detection and revealed those subpopulations. We observe a pattern in the German protests when supporters of AfD party with supporters of liberal or green ideology were highly interconnected between each-others. On the other hand mainstream media with central role of more central SPD party formed a separated structure with a dominant attitude against the protests (concentrated around Saskia Esken account). The dynamics of the #B2908 protest is significantly different from #B0108 due to an attempt of the regional government to cancel the event on August 26th (Fig. 5). The main communities on Fig. 5 are SPD and mainstream (antiprotest) (1); Antifa (antiprotest) (5); AfD (pro protest) (7). Day before the demonstration community of left-wing liberal (antiprotest) (4) appeared, which was taken by mainstream (1) next day. The day after the demonstration the mainstream (1) have divided into more liberal and more acceptable to protest (13) and strictly antiprotest (1). On August 27th (the day after the demonstration ban) a very small community of left-wing users sympathizing with protests appears (13), however they did not agree with all protesters postulate, emphasizing their right to protest and freedom of speech only. As QAnon gather followers of the far-right (Reichsbürger—literally "imperial citizens" – or AfD), Querdenken is entering into German street protest movements with no clear affiliation with a given political option. Thus, it allows for the flow between left-wing communities of anti-protesters to protest sympathizers (Fig. 5) or even the engagement into the protest related activities by some liberals or green party activists (Fig. 4), which could not be probably possible in a political landscape in other countries. The sentiment analysis [23] revealed that the negative sentiment clearly dominated Twitter discourse (Fig. 5) on the ban day – August 26th.

According to the weighted degree centrality (sum of retweets and being retweeted) of retweet networks, the most prominent user during #B0108 was Saskia Esken (@EskenSaskia – SPD leader and trained programmer, centrality 2128), but during #B2908 it was @PolizeiBerlin_E (Berlin Police Department, centrality:10874). During #B0108-event we could observed liberal/Green community was interacting and engaging with the protests (Fig. 4), however during #B2908-event, such a community left-wing community was not directly observed. Some minor left-wing activists formed small cliques, which were too

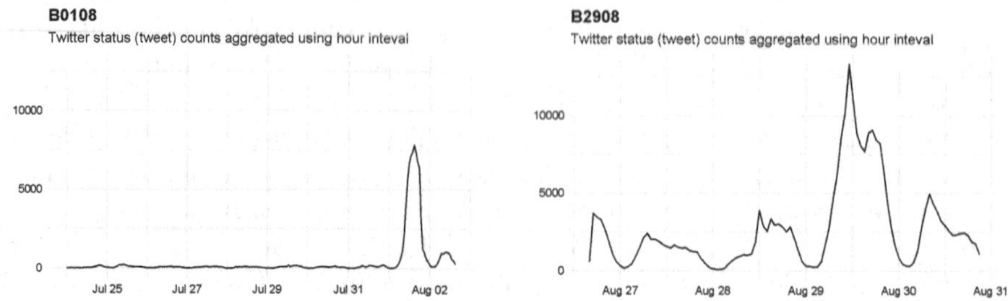

Fig. 3. [Left] Tweet counts aggregated hourly for b0108 [Right] Tweet counts aggregated hourly for b2908.

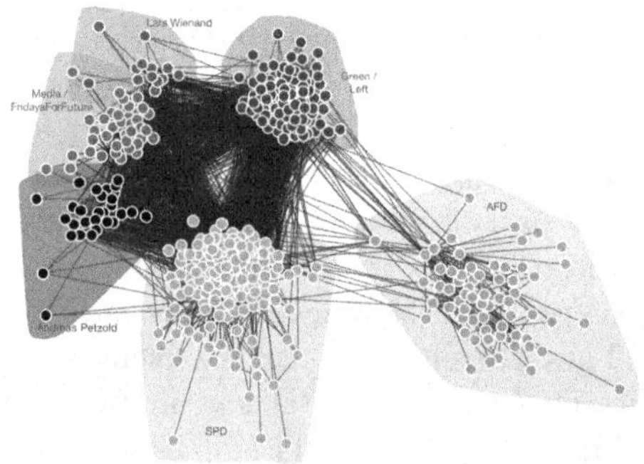

Fig. 4. Polarized communities in retweet network of users constructed from ca. 100,000 tweets (including retweets) with the hashtag #B0108 denoting protests in Berlin mostly against anti-COVID-19 measures (https://bit.ly/30qdNGD). Interesting is the connection of opposite political camps such as AfD far right party and left movements. (Color figure online)

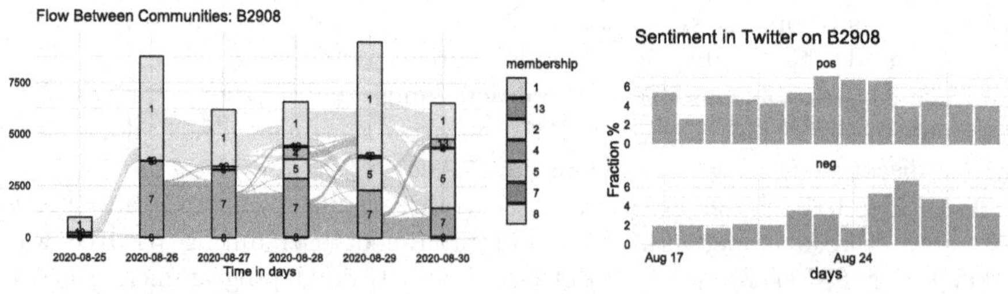

Fig. 5. Daily situation for #B2908 demonstration. [Left] Flow of users between communities with the biggest communities. Codes for the main identified communities: 1 – SPD and mainstream (anti-protest); 5 – Antifa (anti-protest); 7 – AfD (pro-protest); 4 – community of left-wing liberals (anti-protest); 13 – a liberal and more acceptable to protests. [Right] Sentiment analysis

small to be captured by the community detection algorithm. However, some left-wing communities retweeting with protest emerged for a short time only, which was visible mainly on 30.08 day after demonstration (Fig. 5). #B2908-demonstration gathered over 45,000 new users (and lost only 8,000), who were not engaged in #B0108 event. This could indicate that protest movements are getting more and more recognized in the general public.

2.3 News Articles

EventRegistry is a media research service monitoring a few hundred thousand news web pages daily from Germany alone. We choose EventRegistry as a traditional news media search engine because it collects a large range of online magazines and digital versions of other broadcasting channels representing various political sides. Readers of selected articles can be representative for the population of 20–60 age cohort [2]. Mainstream media demonstrated negative attitude towards protests and have been reporting rather rarely (relative small numbers of articles on Fig. 6), linking protests with AfD in general.

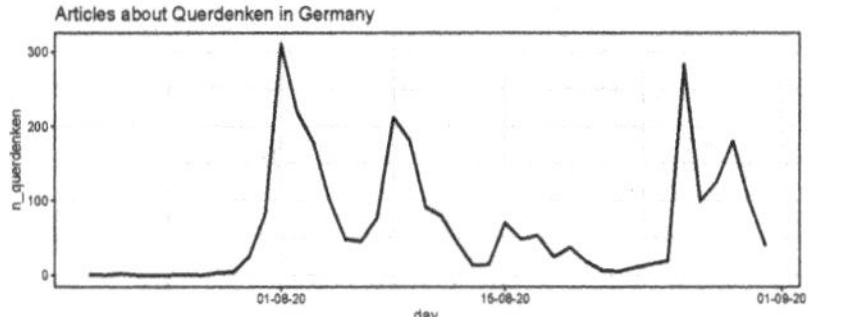

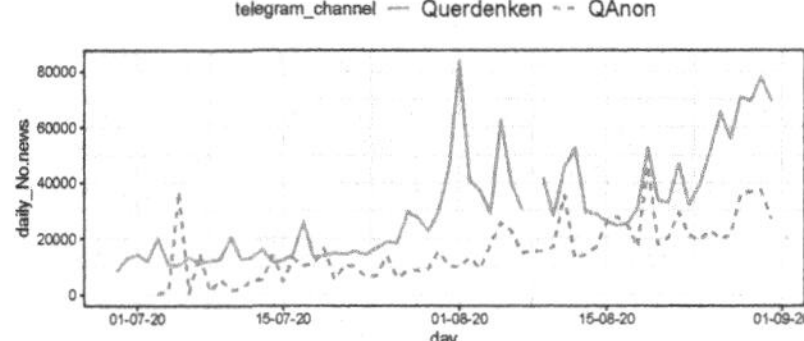

Fig. 6. [Left] Daily no. the articles about Querdenken [Right] Daily no. views on Telegram channels

2.4 Telegram

Telegram is an important communication channel for conspiracy and protest movements against governmental measures. In Germany it has 10% share of users among common messengers [9]. This medium is currently gaining new users very quickly. Moreover, channels involved in the protest such as Querdenken doubled subscribers during investigated period (from less than 30 to over 60 thousands).

The reach of the main QAnon channel content measured by mean daily number of views is increasing (Table 3) during the demonstration period (31.07–31.08) (significantly faster than in the previous month). Querdenken channel is consequently increasing its reach during the demonstration month and it is also speeding up (however insignificantly).

Table 3. Descriptive statistics of trend popularity of "QanonDeutschland" and "Querdenken 711" channels in Telegram during the month before and during the month containing main demonstrations.

Mean daily views (linear regression slope)	29.06–30.07	31.07–31.08	Significance according to coefficients' errors
Qanon	a = 115.4 ± 173.0	a = 560.9 ± 141.3	Yes
Querdenken	a = 390.30 ± 81.94	a = 575.7 ± 316.2	No

2.5 Platform Comparison

The interest in anti-COVID-19 protests in the Internet social-content media (Google, Twitter and Telegram) is growing whereas in the traditional news media it is relatively constant (Fig. 6, Table 4). All these sources complement perception of the COVID-19 pandemics in Germany, while Google has the highest reach, on Twitter there is the most of interactions, Telegram is a platform for conspiracy theorist, and News show how journalists are building narrations. Very fast increase in "Querdenken" queries on Google and number of tweets between demonstrations is related to a growing popularity of the movement in the general population. It is worth to mention than most of tweets were generated by users, who were against the protests. Very high correlation between Google and Twitter series (Fig. 7), suggest that both represent information needs of the general population (mostly not accepting protest). On the other hand, popularity of the protest on Telegram (which is dominated by protesters) is growing much slower. Moreover, the dynamics in the traditional media is substantially different from the rest of media as seen in the correlation pattern as well (Fig. 7) where it forms a separate cluster.

Table 4. Comparison of interest for protest days (01.08 and 29.08) with relative proportion

Interest on a protest day	01.08	29.08	Growth
Google (RSV) - Querdenken	38	100	2.63
Google (RSV) - Protest	11	18	1.64
Google (RSV) - Maskenplicht	27	36	1.33
No. News: Querdenken	310	180	0.58
Telegram (Querdenken 711) Max no. views of a message on a given day	83,436	149,421	1.79
No. of Tweets (B0108 vs B2908)	70,172	136,947	1.95

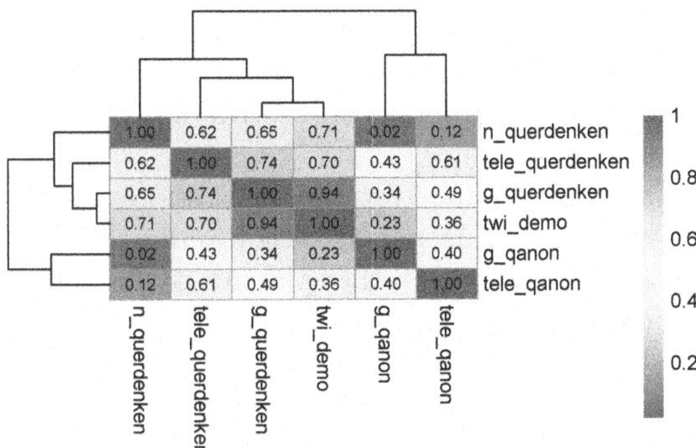

Fig. 7. Pair-wise Pearson correlations between daily series (29.06–01.09.2020). g – for google and its RSV, twi – for number of tweets in with #B0108 and #B0129, n – for number of articles/news collected by Event Registry, tele – for daily average views in a channel on telegram.

3 Conclusions

This study is an attempt to empirically examine the Internet media on the anti-COVID protests in Germany, mainly related to the demonstrations in Berlin on August 1st (#B0109) and August 29th (#B2908). Epidemic containment measures such as face mask wearing, lockdown, physical distancing and potential vaccinations against the disease could suppress infection dynamic. However they also might lead to high socio-economic costs for the German society. QAnon movement is well analyzed [12,21] due its main popularity in the English speaking world, but Querdenken movement needs much more scientific attention. We observe that the majority of general population is sceptical toward protesters (Fig. 4, 7, [22]) and is just observing the movements dominated mainly by far-right organizations. It is important to monitor the anti-COVID movement [26] due to a rare presence of common interests of the right wing of AfD with Green or liberal movements (Fig. 4). It is worth to mention, that still majority of moderate-right, central or left-wing politicians and electorate strongly disagree with protesters. However, protests have a potential to reach a large fraction of the population [10] and could have an effect on the compliance with non-pharmaceutical intervention during the Autumn wave of infections. We proved, that the interest in the main organizer of both events – Querdenken – is growing on each social-content platform from #B0108 to #B2908 (Table 4). Moreover, the growth speed is also increasing (Table 1) in comparison to the baseline before demonstrations. QAnon movement is also increasing popularity, but the growth is slowing down, so it may be close to saturation (Table 2, Fig. 7). However, Internet media are actively censoring QAnon [14] and only Telegram (from presented data sources) probably does not manipulate its reach. On the other side of the society, there are anti-protest movements with SPD party as its core (Fig. 4, 5).

Protesters usually did not apply physical distancing rules and did not use personal protective equipment, but there is no significant effect of the protest on increase of incidence (Fig. 2) probably due to the low viral pressure and open air conditions due to Summer.

This study is a signaling paper for the real-time analysis [15] of protests during COVID-19 pandemic. A deeper investigation of the mutual interrelation of societal reactions (such as protests), the epidemic dynamics [3], its surveillance and measures undertaken is required; it could help for crisis management in Germany and probably other countries as well.

Acknowledgements. AJ was supported with COSTNET (COST Action CA15109) travel grant.

References

1. Alshaabi, T., et al.: How the world's collective attention is being paid to a pandemic: COVID-19 related 1-gram time series for 24 languages on Twitter. arXiv preprint arXiv:2003.12614 (2020)
2. APressInst: Print vs. digital subscribers: demographic differences and paths to subscription (2020). https://www.americanpressinstitute.org/publications/reports/survey-research/print-vs-digital/. Accessed 19 Sep 2020
3. Belik, V., Geisel, T., Brockmann, D.: Natural human mobility patterns and spatial spread of infectious diseases. Phys. Rev. X **1**(1), 011001 (2011)
4. Berlin.de: Rund 38 000 bei corona-demon (2020). https://www.berlin.de/aktuelles/berlin/6277399-958092-rund-38-000-bei-corona-protesten.html. Accessed 04 Sep 2020
5. Betsch, C., et al.: Social and behavioral consequences of mask policies during the COVID-19 pandemic. Proc. Natl. Acad. Sci. **117**(36), 21851–21853 (2020)
6. Beytía, P., Cruz Infante, C.: Digital pathways, pandemic trajectories. Using Google trends to track social responses to COVID-19. HIIG Discussion Paper Series (2020)
7. Blondel, V.D., Guillaume, J.L., Lambiotte, R., Lefebvre, E.: Fast unfolding of communities in large networks. J. Stat. Mech.: Theory Exp. **2008**(10), P10008 (2008)
8. Borsch, A., ter Haar, M., Prohl, I., Schaer, V.: Corona and religion (2020). https://www.zegk.uni-heidelberg.de/religionswissenschaft/veroffentlichungen/veroffentlichungen/Religion%20and%20Coron.pdf. Accessed 20 Sep 2020
9. Bundesnetzagentur: Nutzung von ott-kommunikationsdiensten in deutschland bericht 2020 (2020). https://www.bundesnetzagentur.de/SharedDocs/Mediathek/Berichte/2020/OTT.pdf?__blob=publicationFile. Accessed 04 Sep 2020
10. Cantoni, D., Hagemeister, F., Westcott, M.: Persistence and activation of right-wing political ideology (2019)
11. Eysenbach, G.: How to fight an infodemic: the four pillars of infodemic management. J. Med. Internet Res. **22**(6), e21820 (2020)
12. Gallagher, A., Davey, J., Hart, M.: The genesis of a conspiracy theory: key trends in QAnon activity since 2017. ISD Reports (2020)
13. Gencoglu, O., Gruber, M.: Causal modeling of Twitter activity during COVID-19. arXiv preprint arXiv:2005.07952 (2020)

14. Guardian: 'Quite frankly terrifying': how the QAnon conspiracy theory is taking root in the UK (2020). https://www.theguardian.com/world/2020/sep/20/the-qanon-conspiracy. Accessed 20 Sep 2020
15. Jarynowski, A., Wójta-Kempa, M., Belik, V.: Perception of "coronavirus" on the polish Internet until arrival of SARS-CoV-2 in Poland. Nurs. Public Health **10**(2), 89–106 (2020)
16. Jarynowski, A., Wójta-Kempa, M., Płatek, D., Czopek, K.: Attempt to understand public health relevant social dimensions of COVID-19 outbreak in Poland. Soc. Regist. **4**(3), 7–44 (2020)
17. Katner, A., Brisolara, K., Katner, P., Jacoby, A., Honore, P.: Panic in the streets–pandemic and protests: a manifestation of a failure to achieve democratic ideals. NEW SOLUT. J. Environ. Occup. Health Policy **30**, 161–167 (2020). 1048291120960233
18. Kontor: Social Media 2020: Aktuelle nutzerzahlen (2020). https://www.kontor4.de/beitrag/aktuelle-social-media-nutzerzahlen.html. Accessed 04 Sep 2020
19. Leeb, C.: Narrative "QAnon" (2020). https://cleeb94.github.io/covidinfspreading/portfolio/qanon. Accessed 04 Sep 2020
20. Oh, S.H., Lee, S.Y., Han, C.: The effects of social media use on preventive behaviors during infectious disease outbreaks: the mediating role of self-relevant emotions and public risk perception. Health Commun. 1–10 (2020, ahead-of-print). https://doi.org/10.1080/10410236.2020.1724639
21. Papasavva, A., Blackburn, J., Stringhini, G., Zannettou, S., De Cristofaro, E.: "Is it a qoincidence?": a first step towards understanding and characterizing the QAnon movement on voat. co. arXiv preprint arXiv:2009.04885 (2020)
22. PEW: Most approve of national response to COVID-19 in 14 advanced economies (2020). https://www.pewresearch.org/global/2020/08/27/most-approve-of-national-response-to-covid-19-in-14-advanced-economies/. Accessed 20 Sep 2020
23. Remus, R., Quasthoff, U., Heyer, G.: SentiWS - a publicly available German-language resource for sentiment analysis. In: Proceedings of the 7th International Language Resources and Evaluation (LREC 2010) (2010)
24. Salathé, M.: Digital epidemiology: what is it, and where is it going? Life Sci. Soc. Policy **14**(1), 1–5 (2018). https://doi.org/10.1186/s40504-017-0065-7
25. Statista: Share of Internet users in Germany from 2001 to 2019 (2020). https://www.statista.com/statistics/380514/internet-usage-rate-germany/. Accessed 20 Sep 2020
26. Sternisko, A., Cichocka, A., Van Bavel, J.J.: The dark side of social movements: social identity, non-conformity, and the lure of conspiracy theories. Curr. Opin. Psychol. **35**, 1–6 (2020)
27. Sueddeutsche.Zeitung: 17 000 - oder 1,3 millionen? (2020) https://www.sueddeutsche.de/politik/berlin-corona-demo-teilnehmer-zahlen-1.4987759. Accessed 04 Sep 2020

Author Index

Printed in the United States
By Bookmasters